RECENT REFERENCE BOOKS IN RELIGION

A GUIDE FOR STUDENTS, SCHOLARS, RESEARCHERS, BUYERS, & READERS

REVISED EDITION

WILLIAM M. JOHNSTON

FITZROY DEARBORN PUBLISHERS
CHICAGO AND LONDON

Second edition © 1998 by William M. Johnston
First edition © 1996 by William M. Johnston

For information, write to:

FITZROY DEARBORN PUBLISHERS
70 East Walton Street
Chicago, IL 60611
U.S.A.

or

FITZROY DEARBORN PUBLISHERS
11 Rathbone Place
London W1P 1DE
England

Library of Congress and British Library Cataloging in Publication Data is Available

ISBN 1-57958-035-1

Revised edition first published in the U.S. and U.K. in 1998
Printed by Braun-Brumfield, Ann Arbor, Michigan
Cover Design by Peter Aristedes

To
my beloved wife Claire

Preface

RECENT REFERENCE BOOKS in Religion: A Guide addresses anyone who may have browsed reference shelves yet hesitated to consult more than one or two items. The *Guide* alerts readers to what they can expect in more than three hundred recent reference books concerning the world's religions in general and each of the major traditions and methodologies in particular. A principal aim is to help researchers and students discern which tools they need and why. Where other bibliographic guides laconically describe, this one scrutinizes. By propounding a typology, and indeed by venturing a phenomenology of reference books, the *Guide* advances understanding of their function in postmodern discourse. In so doing it aims to entertain as well as to enlighten.

The Challenge of Oversupply

We live in a golden age of reference books. The *Guide* evaluates more than sixty single-volume works on religion (more than thirty on Christianity) published between 1990 and 1995. Not a few of these rank among the finest ever published in their field, and certain of them pioneer not just new approaches but new fields. In no other six-year period have so many reference works appeared concerning religion, not to mention philosophy or mythology. About a quarter of the *Guide* examines works of the 1990s. Besides calling attention to recent publications, the

Guide canvasses major works published since 1970, emphasizing English-language works but heeding significant ones in French and German as well. About a fifth of the entries assess foreign-language works, and these tend to be magisterial ones with multilingual bibliographies that benefit everyone.

Few indeed will be scholars who have consulted every work featured in this volume that pertains to their field. Overabundance precludes gaining an overview even in one's own field, much less throughout the range of disciplines that comprise religious studies. Amid oversupply, the *Guide* facilitates informed choice. It helps a scholar to decide which works to consult. It helps a librarian to select books for purchase. It helps a student to initiate research.

A Remedy for Overabundance: A Phenomenology of Types

Exposure to hundreds of reference books, ranging from one-hundred-page glossaries to twenty-thousand-page mega-encyclopedias, reveals how many approaches lurk behind labels like "dictionary," "lexicon" or "encyclopedia." Some reference books supply data, while others advance ideas. Some deliver lore, while others venture novelty; a few try to do it all. Some cultivate brevity, others all-inclusiveness. Many are written by one author, others by several hundred. Some address a national or confessional audience, others address a world or ecumenical audience. Most abound in bibliography, while a few eschew it.

In order to map this profusion, the *Guide* articulates the goals (and corresponding limitations) to which reference works may aspire. One reason that too few readers treasure reference books is a lack of understanding about what they accomplish. As introduction one argues, few users have pondered what a reference book can and cannot achieve. To fill this gap the glossary classifies twenty-two types and functions of reference books. This schema compares types with one another and formulates insights about them. Each of 318 numbered entries in the directory of reference books evokes these types and functions. By reconfiguring conventional categories, the typology generates what may be called a phenomenology of reference works and their uses. Such an endeavor is intended to raise consciousness in readers, authors and editors alike. The postmodern revolution in reference works cries out for attention.

Scope of the Field of Religious Studies

This *Guide* construes religious studies as broadly as possible. Five variables define the parameters. First, the *Guide* tackles clusters of disciplines that commonly serve to study the world's religions, namely history of religion, scriptural studies, philosophy of religion, and social sciences. Second, religious studies is taken to encompass the history and present status of major traditions, including Christianity, Judaism, Islam, Hinduism, Buddhism and other South Asian religions,

Chinese religion and Japanese religion. Third, within each tradition religious studies examines the seven "dimensions" that Ninian Smart has isolated: myth, doctrine, ritual, ethics, institutions, spirituality (experience) and art. Reference works in religious studies may focus on one, several or all of these dimensions. Fourth, half of the entries in the *Guide* concern Christianity. Within Christianity the *Guide* differentiates among reference works that address (1) Catholic, Protestant and Eastern traditions, (2) fields like ecumenism, biblical studies, theology, spirituality and liturgy, and (3) principal periods (early church, medieval church, modern church, American church). Since 1980 each of these twelve subfields of Christian studies (including the Eastern tradition) has spawned at least three or four major reference works. Biblical studies has unleashed no fewer than a dozen. Fifth, works on myth, philosophy and the social sciences of religion have proliferated since 1980, and many are analyzed here.

Criteria of Evaluation
In assessing reference books, I have invoked my experience living with them. Most entries deploy five subheads: "Scope," "Strengths," "Weaknesses," "Competitors" and "Summary." The goal is to delineate coverage, highlight outstanding articles and contributors, specify omissions and situate a work in relation to rivals. Within a field entries are arranged in chronological order of publication so as to disclose development. From a given entry a reader can discern how a work will or will not aid research, expand information or stimulate ideas. On lesser (or less available) works, particularly those in French or German, the first four subheads get telescoped into a single critique that is followed by a summary. Many works excel at fostering what may be called self-teaching. The directory calls attention to this potential wherever it flowers, and introduction two explores its varieties.

Personal judgments inevitably figure into assessing works that are so varied. I have a professional interest in history (particularly history of thought), crosscultural comparisons and conceptual breakthroughs, and this interest shines through. Preferring as I do nonconfessional approaches, I identify confessional utterance wherever it obtrudes. I endeavor to be fair, and I find something to praise in nearly every work. Not a few elicit extravagant praise, and certain ones get chided.

At the same time, the *Guide* formulates ways of conceptualizing religious studies. Trends in how fields subdivide and debates unfold get highlighted, particularly in the overview at the head of each section of the directory. Individual entries specify assumptions, schemata and methodologies on hundreds of topics. Designed to be read at one sitting or consulted at random, the book advises readers how to tackle myriad questions large and small. Five indexes facilitate recourse to (1) book titles, (2) editors and authors, (3) topics, (4) persons and (5) places. The index of subjects directs readers to reference books on countless topics. The *Guide* elucidates not just reference books but also the scholarly issues that generate them. It is a guide to scholarly debates, particularly about Christianity, as well as to reference works that map them.

Acknowledgments

At an early stage research was supported by a Healey Endowment Grant from the Faculty Research Council, University of Massachusetts.

Libraries pivotal to research include those at seven seminaries: Harvard Divinity School, Yale Divinity School, Princeton Theological Seminary, Union Theological Seminary, New Brunswick Theological Seminary, Hartford Seminary and the Weston School of Theology. Major research libraries include those at Harvard, Yale, Columbia, Princeton, Dartmouth, Rutgers and New York universities. In my neighborhood, libraries at the University of Massachusetts, Smith College, Amherst College, Mount Holyoke College, Boston College, Williams College and the Clark Institute of Art dispensed diverse riches. In Britain the British Library, the Bodleian Library (through both its Oriental Collection and Indian Institute), and the library at the School of Oriental and African Studies, London (SOAS) proved indispensable. In Paris the library of the Institut du Monde Arabe stood unrivaled for books on Islam. In Parma, Italy, French reference works abound at the Biblioteca Palatina. As a rule of thumb, nearly every American library consulted, whether large or small, boasted at least one or two, and sometimes four or five, reference works all but unknown elsewhere. Looked at another way, some fifty of the works analyzed in this guide appear on reference shelves in only one or two of the American libraries listed above!

It has been a pleasure working with InterVarsity Press. For wise counsel I am grateful to Daniel G. Reid, IVP's editor of reference books.

Introduction 1

The Postmodern Revolution in Reference Books

W E LIVE IN A GOLDEN age of reference books, and yet many scholars disdain them. Never before have so many first-rate reference books appeared as in the last five to ten years, and yet few readers take pride in this achievement. Reference works proliferate, yet no scholar boasts of having digested the best of them. Like icebergs, reference books float nine-tenths submerged, glanced at but largely unused.

To be sure, most researchers own perhaps half a dozen favorite one-volume works, but few endeavor to keep up with new ones, and hardly any journal evaluates which of each year's crop are the best. Never have reference books been so numerous, so comprehensive or so inventive as during the past ten years, and yet few critics have saluted this accomplishment. Nor has anyone investigated its causes or appraised its results. Reference works remain unsung masterpieces of postmodernism.

Toward a Phenomenology of Reference Books and Their Uses

Clearly, postmodernism has pluralized discourse. Older methods, fields, paradigms and taboos have lost their monopoly. Boundaries have collapsed between fields and between approaches. In the humanities and social sciences most researchers now work in several fields as part of interdisciplinary networks. Yet in a climate of pluralism and "blurred genres," reference books have if anything lost prestige, sinking in esteem compared with works of theory or of interdisciplinary discourse. Many postmoderns regard reference works as a necessary evil. They are viewed as storage mechanisms to tap occasionally, not as fuses to ignite thinking. They are valued chiefly because they save time, not because they open frontiers.

Reference books proliferate in a vacuum of theory about them. No one has written a defense of reference works for the postmodern era. Each year thousands of specialists contribute entries and essays to hundreds of reference books, but who has arisen to praise the genre? Editors, planners and teams labor for love of learning, but no one has formulated what reference books can and cannot accomplish, how they function in postmodern discourse, or how attitudes toward them have altered. In a word, no one has generalized about the purposes, history and prospects of reference works. In response, the *Guide* will venture a phenomenology of reference works and their uses. It will amend conventional taxonomy with novel categories, and it will apply such categories to every work described. By asking simple questions again and again, phenomenology weaves a web of analysis.

Compared to monographs, journal articles, translations or even papers at conferences, reference books command low prestige. Few if any scholars in the humanities or the social sciences admit to enjoying reference books. Few boast of owning dozens of them or of having contributed to major ones or of having edited some. More often than not, devotees of reference books hesitate to admit to a passion for these outcasts of the library.

Computer networks, CD-ROM disks and electronic library catalogs seem to have rendered reference books obsolete. Yet they appear in greater numbers, greater sophistication and greater variety than ever before. A phenomenology of types and functions can mediate between flourishing practice and languishing theory concerning reference books. Are they as stultified as many assume? Or do some of them pioneer fresh approaches? Do certain ones respond to a consumer boom in self-help books? Or as befits postmodern discourse, do they undertake new purposes? It is high time to chart the functions of reference books in modern academia and update criteria for evaluating them. That task falls to a phenomenology of reference works and their uses.

Religious Studies as a Test Case

The consortium of disciplines known as "religious studies" supplies a test case for examining use and abuse of reference books for several reasons. One is that the field of religious studies itself emerged during the postmodern era. Conceived during the 1960s and institutionalized during the early 1970s, the approach known as religious studies pluralized the study of religions. Spearheaded in Britain by Ninian Smart at the University of Lancaster and in the United States by Mircea Eliade at the University of Chicago, this approach abandoned the notion that any faith, method, belief or tradition merits privileging. Hegemonies of belief, method, period or region were abandoned in favor of a universal pluralism that some would call pan-relativism. Each religion is taught on a par with others. Faith commitment of teachers and researchers withdraws. It may be discussed in the home or with one's pastor but seldom if ever with fellow researchers, students or readers. Accordingly, reference works in the field divide between those that eschew confessional identity and those that proclaim it. The former attitude this *Guide* calls "confessional neutrality," and the latter it calls "confessional self-definition."

During the past twenty-five years religious studies has prospered in colleges and universities of the United States and Great Britain, transforming traditional departments of religion. Since the early nineteenth century American universities have implemented a Protestant emphasis on biblical studies, church history and Christian ethics. Now hundreds of departments of religious studies proclaim a postmodern approach, and thousands of scholars evoke pluralist assumptions. Previously confessional fields like biblical studies have been deconfessionalized. Protestant evangelicals no less than Roman Catholics now collaborate in nonconfessional enterprises like **60** *The Anchor Bible Dictionary* (1992). Increasingly, postmodern openness pervades books designed even for confessional self-definition.

The explosion of religious studies since 1970 has ignited an explosion in reference books. The sheer quantity of works canvassing individual traditions, social sciences of religion and the panorama of religions defies belief. Because religious studies incorporates so many subfields, disciplines and periods from 4000 B.C.E. to the present, it engenders reflection about reference books.

Religious studies constitutes a consortium of entire fields and disciplines rather that one field or one discipline. Within the humanities come history, literary studies, philosophy and theology, while within the social sciences priority goes to sociology, psychology and anthropology together with their subdisciplines. Because in religious studies reference works serve a consortium of disciplines, the books must address broader needs than might be the case in a narrower field. Thus an inventory of reference books published in religious studies during the past twenty years supplies a fulcrum from which to theorize about reference works in the humanities and social sciences in general. Indeed, the over three hundred works examined in the directory of the *Guide* offer a chance to elaborate a phenomenology of reference works. A vacuum of theory favors the kind of unbiased description that phenomenology promises. As a first step toward phenomenology, introduction one sketches a typology of reference works and applies it to explaining their low prestige.

Two Functions of Reference Works: Recapitulation Versus Revision

Phenomenology of uses begins with typology. A basic distinction separates *past-oriented* or *recapitulatory* works from *future-oriented* or *revisionist* ones. The former summarize what is already known; the latter propose or pursue new approaches. Recapitulatory works deliver what most people associate with "reference books." They are expected to expound acquired knowledge, authenticate data and assert certitudes within a field. In contrast, some (perhaps many) users overlook the fact that not a few reference works either advocate or execute novel approaches. Such revisionist works have proliferated since 1980 and now abound in any reference collection. Not the least of their functions is to elucidate the "blurring of genres" that has engulfed both the humanities and social sciences. Fields, approaches, methods and genres of scholarship have merged since the 1960s. To elucidate such interactions, postmodernism devises revisionist reference works.

Recapitulatory works serve at least four functions. The most basic is to supply information or data ("facts") about easily verified matters like names, dates, definitions, chronology and bibliography. A database of facts that can be "looked up" is the staple of reference books. A second function, one that goes back at least to Diderot's *Encyclopédie* (1752-72), is to expound methods, research problems and obstacles inhabiting a field. Not only do reference books expound the "state of knowledge" concerning a method, subfield or issue, but they explicate approaches needed to advance such knowledge. What gets recapitulated is not just data or facts but methods and research debates that manipulate the data. A recent thirty-volume general work in French, **298** the *Encyclopaedia universalis* (1968, 1990), executes for our time the dissemination of methodology.

A third function is to expound a field for nonspecialists, particularly for experts in other domains who venture into an area unfamiliar to them. Reference books introduce practitioners of one field to data and research issues of another. This third function of teaching a field and its research problems looms large in an era of interdisciplinary research. One reason for proliferation of reference books since 1980 is that researchers crave access to fields in which they received too little training.

A fourth function of recapitulatory works is less often noticed. If used imaginatively, a conspectus of a field can yield a synoptic or even "panoptic" view of it. By browsing through a reference book that canvasses a field, one can survey that field in its entirety. Such sweeps of the horizon proceed most readily through well-chosen reference books. They furnish a mode of self-teaching that interdisciplinary researchers should welcome. Once an individual has absorbed rudiments of a field, no other practice illuminates the thickets so clearly as well-planned reading of reference books. Part two of this introduction recommends ways to make reference works function as self-teachers.

Among revisionist works two types stand out. The first implements innovations of the kind that it advocates, while the second advocates improvements that it urges others to execute. Some, perhaps most, revisionist works do both. Not confining themselves to the already documented, such works stipulate what remains to be achieved. Whether through execution or advocacy, innovation in reference works marks one of the breakthroughs of the past decade. Because revisionist works have gone largely unheralded, the *Guide* proclaims their merits.

Unnoticed among those merits, revisionist works often encapsulate a school of thought whose energy exudes a group personality. Sometimes this spirit coalesces like the charism of a religious community. More than other types, revisionist reference works radiate a shared personality. To immerse oneself in these volumes is to imbibe a group ethos.

Toward Explaining the Low Prestige of Reference Books: The Case of Religious Studies

Reference books occupy a place at or near the bottom of publishing prestige. A phenomenology of contemporary reference books and their uses must formulate reasons for this anomaly. Specifically, an inquiry into the low esteem of reference books needs to address the following issues:

1. Why do otherwise sophisticated scholars continue to view reference books as though they were exclusively recapitulatory?

2. Why do scholars hesitate to acknowledge how reference books facilitate entry into unfamiliar fields?

3. Why have categories for evaluating reference books not undergone revision? Why has the impact of postmodernism on reference works not initiated reappraisal of their functions?

4. Why do reference works continue to be despised by theorists when in fact reference works are being transformed by the same trends as other vehicles of postmodern scholarship? In a word, why do reference works lag in attracting theoretical appraisal?

5. Why have scholars in religious studies not recognized the revolution that has transformed reference books? Everyone acknowledges that the field of religious studies has been transformed not once but several times since the 1960s. Why has the impact of these revolutions on reference books been noticed only sporadically?

6. Why has the ensemble of reference books in religious studies not been assessed as a whole? Why are new reference books evaluated ad hoc and hardly ever as part of a library of postmodernism that has been accumulating since the 1970s?

This is not the place to tackle these questions one by one, except to point out that they pivot around a single phenomenon, namely, a lag in characterizing the changes that have transformed reference works in general. Although a revolution has occurred, accumulating impressive results, hardly anyone has looked at its causes or consequences. No theory and no phenomenology has tackled the postmodern revolution in reference books. An underlying cause of this neglect is preoccupation with those kinds of research that further career advancement. In today's academia scholars get so lavishly rewarded for honing specialized expertise that they hesitate to put forward knowledge that may seem "merely" encyclopedic. Wide-ranging knowledge is undervalued except when it enhances specialization.

Yet a paradox leaps out. Interdisciplinary research requires participants to diversify. A contradiction exists between belittling reference books and expecting scholars continually to enlarge their expertise, for reference works facilitate precisely this task. Scholars can use reference books to prize open fields previously closed to them. In no area is this more easily accomplished than in religious studies, where reference books of every type and level beckon.

Another reason that reference works in religious studies ought to stimulate theorizing is that the field itself attracts several types of inquirers. Because religious studies comprises not a single discipline but rather a consortium of them, practitioners of one or two specialties need access to others. Reference works can help scholars in, say, modern church history to explore the psychology of religion or biblical studies. Such diversifying of expertise by specialists may be called "internal outreach." "External outreach" involves outsiders who seek to learn about religious studies but have received little or no training in it or its components. Such seekers can benefit from some (but not all) the reference books that serve insiders. A third group of inquirers comprises nonacademics who desire acquaintance not so much with methods of study as with individual religions or their leaders. Probably few other fields attract as many nonspecialists as religious studies. Any sort of spiritual quest can impel nonacademics to forage among reference books. A whole library now exists to assist these seekers. Probably no other area of scholarship has courted outsiders so skillfully through reference books as has religious studies.

Genres of Reference Works: The Familiar Three Versus the Two Poles (Mega-encyclopedias and Anatomies)

A hindrance to appreciation of reference books, particularly revisionist ones, is a misunderstanding of what constitutes a reference book. Here too phenomenology can help. Too many scholars limit their conception to the "big three": dictionaries, lexicons and encyclopedias. These stand in ascending order of complexity and comprehensiveness. All of them share alphabetical arrangement, desire to recapitulate the known, and ambition to wield authority. Most users see the big three as tools rather than as spurs to reflection or recreation.

Phenomenology delineates innovative genres of reference books. Among the most versatile are COMPENDIA, which consist of articles commissioned to survey a field in a manner neither alphabetical nor exhaustive. Anyone who acknowledges compendia to be reference works finds a bonanza. Compendia reinvigorate a field by encouraging creative scholars to rethink it.

Another way to outgrow preconceptions is to encounter genres that flourish in other cultures. For 250 years publishers in France and Germany have competed in refining reference books. Germans pioneered the HANDBOOK as a conspectus of methods, tools and problems in a research field. Written by founders and shapers, a HANDBOOK couples recapitulatory with revisionist functions and overflows with bibliography. It both sums up and reshapes a field. An American exemplar is **311** David Wulff's *Psychology of Religion* (1991).

An even more daunting European type is the MEGA-ENCYCLOPEDIA, perfected separately by French Benedictines and Jewish savants. A mega-encyclopedia formulates all that is considered worth recording about a particular swath of history, usually religious. By pressing all-inclusiveness to the limit, MEGA-ENCY-CLOPEDIAS overshadow but do not supplant less ambitious rivals. Taken together, MEGA-ENCYCLOPEDIAS on Roman Catholicism and Judaism constitute a utopian reference library, in which one can imagine an omnivore like Jorge Luis Borges browsing. A phenomenologist will want to inquire why secular historians have essayed MEGA-ENCYCLOPEDIAS less often than have scholars of religion.

A third European genre is the ANATOMY, in which a single author endeavors to encapsulate everything that he or she considers worthwhile about a topic. Idiosyncratic often to the point of being cranky, anatomies multiply lists. Sustained bursts of what Northrop Frye called "maddened pedantry" occupy one pole of comprehensiveness, while MEGA-ENCYCLOPEDIAS occupy the other. ANATOMIES distill a single author's vision, while MEGA-ENCYCLOPEDIAS deploy ever larger teams. Less exhaustive genres extend between them.

Today's reference books draw energy from the fact that postmodern research necessitates access to unfamiliar fields. HANDBOOKS, COMPENDIA and LEXICONS offer the quickest ways to familiarize oneself with a new field or approach. Reference books written to help a specialist enter adjacent fields now abound. One goal of the *Guide* is to help researchers identify which works function best and in what sequence, as one's repertoire extends into the unfamiliar.

Difficulties of Selection Encountered in Reference Collections

The unwary might suppose that the surest way to locate reference works would be to rummage in a good academic library. But frustration awaits any frequenter of reference shelves. So many works of so many types have emerged since the 1970s that no one can reckon which to use first. A browser among reference works confronts the following puzzles:

1. Which books help to introduce a field to a scholar trained in a different field?

2. Which books should be used first, which second and which much later?

3. Which lexicons offer an overview of a field? And in what sequence should they be read?

4. Which compendia digest the mainstream of a field and which advance new approaches?

5. Which books should be avoided and why?

The *Guide* is intended to answer questions such as these. As a user's companion, it assesses which functions a given reference work does and does not perform and contrasts each with competitors.

There is another reason that browsers need the *Guide*. Trawling through library reference shelves leads to an alarming conclusion. No library, not even the most prestigious and best financed, stocks all or even most reference works in a given field. No library in North America or Great Britain displays on its reference shelves even three quarters of the works that the *Guide* discusses. Most academic libraries stock between 40 and 60 percent of them. In other words, no browser can rely on a given library to deliver a definitive selection of reference works in religious studies. No matter how prestigious a library, no matter how generous its budget, no matter how astute its buyers, a number of important works (particularly COMPENDIA) will be absent from its reference shelves. This holds true for seminary libraries as well as for research libraries at great universities, not to mention libraries at medium-sized universities or four-year colleges. It holds true even for the Library of Congress and the British Library. The *Guide* does what no library can, namely, list and evaluate virtually all the better reference publications of the past fifteen to twenty years. Not only has no American or British library assembled them, but most libraries lack pivotal ones, including some of those best suited to introduce a field to nonspecialists.

Conclusion: An Appeal to Students

In order to initiate a phenomenology of reference works and their uses, the *Guide* does four things. First, the glossary formulates criteria for classifying functions of reference works. Second, the directory applies these criteria to over three hundred volumes published since the 1970s. Third, the *Guide* helps users discern what information and insights to expect from newer types of reference books. It calls attention to newer genres like REVISIONIST COMPENDIA and HANDBOOKS OF

BIBLE INTERPRETATION. Fourth, just as practicing a religion stimulates spiritual quest, so studying religion stimulates research to deepen the quest. Reference books now exist to further nearly every sort of quest, and the *Guide* invites resort to a wide range of them.

Still another paradox looms. Computer technology ought to increase recourse to reference books, but it does not always do so. Computer adepts need to learn to exploit analogous features in reference works. Cross-referencing, funneling of bibliographies and contextualizing of issues have long flourished in reference books. Readers who pursue these tasks via CD-ROM or the Internet will discover similar or greater prowess in LEXICONS and ENCYCLOPEDIAS. Computerization has improved indexing and cross-referencing within reference works, and of course photocopying permits excerpting of articles from bulky volumes. All these are reasons why computer buffs should like reference books.

It goes without saying that students in college and graduate school should learn to exploit reference works. No other skill will save so much time or harvest such rich insights as knowing when and how to consult reference books. Seminary students in particular enjoy unparalleled opportunities. In fields like church history, world religions and above all biblical studies, reference tools abound beyond measure. In resurgent fields like ecumenism, spirituality and psychology of religion, reliable works have mushroomed since 1980. The sooner a student starts, the better he or she will navigate. A lifetime of enrichment awaits.

If the past ten years offer a precedent, we can expect reference books to continue to improve. To further this end the *Guide* ventures to counsel editors of future works. It does so in several ways, not least by raising consciousness about boundaries between genres and by recommending improvements like topical indexes. Specifically, the *Guide* highlights a lack of attention that existing works pay to topics such as African Christianity, Zoroastrianism and Islamic folk religion. More broadly, it identifies entire fields that cry out for a reference work. In English, for example, there exists no reference book on sociology of religion or on anthropology of religion, not to mention Eastern Christianity, Shiism or African religions. Appendix 2 itemizes such needs.

Above all, this book encourages researchers to consult masterpieces of the late twentieth century. Any scholar in the humanities or social sciences can discover through the *Guide* works that will have escaped notice, including some that meet needs that he or she had not envisioned. Postmodern reference works are more incisive and more comprehensive, as well as more imaginative and more icono- clastic, than casual users may suppose. By initiating a phenomenology, the *Guide* will help any inquirer to broaden his or her repertoire not only of reference works but of categories for assessing them. In the postmodern era reference books foster sophistication. They deserve a reference book of their own.

Introduction 2

Reference Books
as Self-Teachers

*H*OW MANY READERS realize that we live in a golden age of reference books? More and better self-teachers, aids to study and endlessly diversified encyclopedias now beckon in nearly every field of the humanities. Not only do elementary, intermediate and advanced tools abound, but new ones appear every year and classic ones get updated. What explains this explosion in the market? Again, a phenomenology of the uses of reference works supplies answers.

A Need for Tools of Adult Education in the Humanities
A glance at the cultural situation of the United States and Western Europe in the mid-1990s discloses a number of differences from the climate forty years ago. A comparison between the educational needs of the 1990s and those of the 1950s sheds light on how reference books function today and why so many find buyers. The fundamental difference between now and then is that adults today bring a less rigorous preliminary training to their studies. A decline of general education during high school and elementary school means that fewer adults have acquired even rudimentary knowledge of basic fields. After graduating from college, many adults discover to their chagrin a desire to learn about subjects in which they lack even elementary training, for example, geography, history, philosophy and art history. No area of the humanities suffers so pervasively from a deficit of basic information as does religious studies. In the United States, albeit not in Britain,

study of religion has vanished from secondary schools. Even schools that teach history and art history exclude religion.

Strange to say, humanities have dwindled in secondary schools even as fresh incentives impel adults to tackle these very fields. A gap between deficient secondary education and mounting demand by adults elicits reference works of a new kind. Twenty-five years ago reference works about religion catered primarily to professionals who already possessed expertise and desired tools to deepen it. German HANDBOOKS, French MEGA-ENCYCLOPEDIAS, and even an all-purpose LEXICON like **29** Cross, ed., *The Oxford Dictionary of the Christian Church* (1957, 1974) served mainly professionals.

Successive Revolutions in Scholarship

Since the 1960s, however, a revolution in publishing has devised reference books for beginners in nearly every field. The same revolution has pioneered works for professionals who wish to expand into fields in which they received little or no training. Publishers no longer assume that users of a reference book will have acquired a smattering of that subject in school or university. The reference work itself imparts a grounding in the basics as well as in the subtleties. Absence in high school and even in college of the kind of preparatory training that the French call *propédeutique* and the Germans *Vorschule* creates a vacuum that reference works aspire to fill.

The withering of preparatory training in the humanities comes at a time when adults in the United States and Europe routinely frequent a wider range of communities than ever before. Participants in religious communities enjoy more opportunities to know outsiders than did their parents or grandparents. Within Christian churches ecumenism causes Catholics, Protestants and Orthodox to intersect with one another in ways unheard of forty years ago. Ecumenical contact prompts members of one branch of Christianity to read about another. Increasingly, evangelical Christians seek mainstream formulations, and liberals countenance conservative ones. In response, reference books by and about individual confessions, not to mention denominations and ethnicities, reach wide audiences. The series of Catholic *New Dictionaries* from Michael Glazier/Liturgical Press or tools from Protestant publishers like Abingdon, Eerdmans and InterVarsity Press address such needs. These works serve audiences far beyond denominational ones.

If ecumenism and crosscultural contact incite nonexperts to seek wider information than ever before, even weightier challenges perplex scholars. In the field of religious studies perhaps more than any other, pressure to diversify comes from all quarters. Factors as heterogeneous as ecumenical and crosscultural dialogue, interdisciplinary scholarship, travel abroad and erosion of previous assumptions combine to demand a wider range of expertise than ever before. Above all, interdisciplinary research obliges scholars to read up on fields outside their graduate training so that they can keep abreast of and even contribute to fields new to them and in some cases new to everyone else.

Just as demand for introductory books is surging, major fields have revolutionized themselves in ways that elicit new kinds of reference tools. Perhaps no other endeavor in the humanities has deployed so many innovative tools as has biblical studies. Since the 1960s a field that had long excelled at crafting reference tools has hived off subdisciplines at a dizzying rate. Experts in one or several areas must scour reference works in order to track developments in adjacent areas. The same holds true in the history of the early church and in the history of Christian theology. Thriving fields bristle with new reference works.

The situation is somewhat different in the study of world religions, a field that has mushroomed only since the 1970s. Because adequate English-language reference tools did not exist thirty years ago, an entire library has flowered since then. 5 Eliade, ed., *The Encyclopedia of Religion* (1987) crowns a vast endeavor, which continues apace. Instead of supplanting predecessors, recent DICTIONARIES and COMPENDIA on the world's religions more often rank as the first of their kind. Moreover, demand keeps growing for GLOSSARIES because terminology needed to study the world's religions is both extensive and precise. Although GLOSSARIES cannot by themselves remove differences among European, Middle Eastern and Asian ways of interpreting religion, comparative lexicography helps make interaction effective. No other work exploits this potential so fully as Jonathan Z. Smith, ed., *The HarperCollins Dictionary of Religion* (1995).

Similar revolutions have swept the social sciences of religion. Since the 1960s sociology, anthropology and psychology have generated a vast literature on world religions. Yet of the three fields, only psychology of religion has produced adequate reference tools. Lack of HANDBOOKS and DICTIONARIES in sociology of religion and anthropology of religion highlights an abundance that favors other fields like history of religion, biblical studies and history of Christian thought. Nothing would so benefit sociology of religion as a reliable English-language HANDBOOK comparable to **311** David Wulff's *Psychology of Religion* (1991). The heirs of Marx, Durkheim and Weber deserve no less.

Exemplary Authors

In an era when reference books proliferate, both the marketplace and laws of probability assure that the ablest scholars write for them. The epoch is long since past, if it ever existed, when chiefly hacks wrote encyclopedias. Today the most accomplished scholars contribute to reference books, and not a few compose ones of their own. Single-author masterpieces like **73** John Macquarrie's *Twentieth-*

Century Religious Thought (1963, 1988), **35** Jaroslav Pelikan's *The Melody of Theology* (1988) and **206** Annemarie Schimmel's *Deciphering the Signs of God* (1994) set a standard for comprehensiveness, insight and originality. Multiauthor volumes like **89** Gordon S. Wakefield, ed., *The Westminster Dictionary of Christian Spirituality* (1983) or **21** Stewart Sutherland et al., eds., *The World's Religions* (1988) overflow with virtuosity. Not uncommonly scholars put their very best effort into collective volumes. In works like **76** Musser and Price, eds., *A New Handbook of Christian Theology* (1992) and **63** Brown et al., eds., *The New Jerome Biblical Commentary* (1990) the contributors have done their utmost. Where else do so many authors distill their life's work?

As might be expected, our era has produced not a few reference works that defy precedent. **32** David B. Barrett, ed., *World Christian Encyclopedia* (1982) is a dazzling performance that interweaves statistics, national profiles, chronologies and photographs in a unique blend. Expected in 1997, a new edition in three volumes will be a major event. As rearranged by Wendy Doniger, **259** Yves Bonnefoy's *Mythologies* (1981, 1992) examines world mythologies and religions in unprecedented depth and brilliance. **9** John R. Hinnells, ed., *Who's Who of World Religions* (1991) assembles religious biographies across an unheard range of cultures. By collating everything known about four hundred names, **275** van der Toorn, Becking and van der Horst, eds., *Dictionary of Deities and Demons in the Bible (DDD)* (1995) grants access to ancient Near Eastern religion.

Americans and British naturally prefer reference works written in English. But scholars in religious studies quickly learn that French and German volumes offer unique advantages. Germans excel at HANDBOOKS that digest an entire discipline, while the French excel at what diplomats call sweeps of the horizon *(tours d'horizon)*. A handbook like **7** Cancik et al., eds., *Handbuch der religionswissenschaftlicher Grundbegriffe* (1988-) unleashes the amplest discussion of methodology in religious studies to be found anywhere. French panoramic flair shines in a MEGA-ENCYCLOPEDIA like **137** Jacquemet, ed., *Catholicisme: Hier—aujourd'hui—demain* (1948-) or in a DICTIONARY, **129** Duchet-Suchaux and Duchet-Suchaux, *Les Ordres religieux* (1993). COMPENDIA like **307** Clévenot, ed., *L'État des religions dans le monde* (1987) or **28** Delumeau, ed., *Le Fait religieux* (1993) display French talent for conspectus.

Over the past twenty years American reference books, particularly concerning Christianity, have proven second to none. But no one can hope to match the Germans at composing HANDBOOKS or the French at composing panoramas of contemporaneity. French and German contributors unfailingly commit their best effort to reference works. Because French and particularly German reference works almost always include English-language bibliography, Americans and British should leaf through these resources.

Choosing Reference Works to Be Self-Teachers

No longer do reference works serve mainly to answer well-conceived questions posed by experts. A phenomenology of uses shows rather that reference works run a gamut from teaching the beginner through informing the journeyman and stimulating the expert to astonishing the master. To savor the gamut, a scholar needs to own a personal collection of reference works that concern his or her field of expertise and skirt its fringes as well. Every serious inquirer should own both general and specialized reference works in which to browse and thereby to grow. No possessions so enrich adult education as reference books.

Above all, everyone needs to select personal favorites. No other habit builds scholarly self-confidence so surely as consultation of trusted tomes. Cultural identity gets reinforced as one turns the familiar pages. Everyone involved in religious studies should own at least one BIBLE DICTIONARY, one BIBLE COMMEN-TARY, one LEXICON each on Christianity, Judaism and Islam, and one DICTION-ARY (as well as one GLOSSARY) of the world's religions. In areas of professional expertise a scholar will want to own several one-volume works. Needless to say, the *Guide,* particularly appendix one, "Favorite Reference Books," facilitates choosing. Among likely candidates to become favorite resources on Christianity must be counted **29** F. L. Cross, ed., *The Oxford Dictionary of the Christian Church* (1957, 1974); **169** Reid, ed., *Dictionary of Christianity in America* (1990); **112** Fink, ed., *The New Dictionary of Sacramental Worship* (1990); **68** Coggins and Houlden, eds., *A Dictionary of Biblical Interpretation* (1990) and **131** McBrien, ed., *The HarperCollins Encyclopedia of Catholicism* (1995). Two French masterpieces pioneer novel approaches to vast topics: **150** Levillain, ed., *Dictionnaire historique de la papauté* (1994) and **126** Gisel, ed., *Encyclopédie du protestantisme* (1995). On non-Christian topics likely favorites include **2** Crim, ed., *The Perennial Dictionary of World Religions* (1981, 1989); **9** Hinnells, ed., *Who's Who of World Religions* (1991) and **25** Sharma, ed., *Our Religions* (1993). The French reader will find **4** Poupard, ed., *Dictionnaire des religions* (1984, 1993) indispensable.

Few volumes occasion so much pleasure to browsers as well-chosen reference books. Often shorter ones work best. GLOSSARIES like **1** Parrinder, *A Dictionary of Non-Christian Religions* (1971) or **13** Pye, ed., *The Continuum Dictionary of Religion* (1994) lead the eye from entry to entry without flagging. In the field of Asian religions INTRODUCTORY LEXICONS like **235** Stutley and Stutley, *A Dictionary of Hinduism* (1977) or **216** Schumacher and Woerner, eds., *The Encyclopedia of Eastern Philosophy and Religion* (1986, 1989) explain intricacies with aplomb. MEGA-ENCYCLOPEDIAS, at the other extreme of length, bring their own rewards. A massive BIBLE DICTIONARY like **52** Bromiley, ed., *The International Standard Bible Encyclopedia* (1979-88), dispenses stimulation to anyone who cares about Bible studies. Those who read French will find it bracing to browse in recent volumes of MEGA-ENCYCLOPEDIAS like **49** Pirot, ed., *Dictionnaire de la Bible: Supplément* (1928-) or **88** Viller, ed., *Dictionnaire de spiritualité* (1937-1994). One marvels at how hackneyed issues can sparkle when treated amply.

More often than happens in periodicals or even books, authors pour their finest efforts into reference books. Chances of finding a writer in top form loom higher in a distinguished reference book than almost anywhere else. Readers who want to skim the cream off a scholar's output should consult reference books to which that figure has contributed abundantly. Indeed, reference books often furnish a shortcut into a scholar's lifework. Articles in **181** Cohen and Mendes-Flohr, eds., *Contemporary Jewish Religious Thought* (1987) or **77** McGrath, ed., *The Blackwell Encyclopedia of Modern Christian Thought* (1993) invite such quests. Authors there often outline their own work while appraising another's.

Not surprisingly, assessments of contemporary scholars and schools enliven HANDBOOKS OF BIBLE INTERPRETATION and, less expectedly, French ENCYCLO-PEDIAS. Few works digest scholarly debates so cogently as **70** Green and McKnight, eds., *Dictionary of Jesus and the Gospels* (1992) or **300** Châtelet et al., eds., *Dictionnaire des oeuvres politiques* (1986, 1989). The same holds true of a thirty-volume French general ENCYCLOPEDIA, **298** *Encyclopaedia universalis* (1968, 1990). A REVISIONIST masterpiece, **110** Sartore and Triacca, eds., *Dictionnaire encyclopédique de la liturgie* (1984, 1992-) marshals scholarship in such a way as to transform its field. Happily, another exemplar of a new field has appeared into English: **48** Latourelle and Fisichella, eds., *Dictionary of Fundamental Theology* (1990, 1994). Coming from European Catholics, these pioneering works exhibit a group personality that recalls the charism of a religious community. Vitality shared lifts all participants, and they in turn pass the energy to us.

Armchair travelers will rejoice to discover how many reference works on the world's religions boast color illustrations. Since about 1980 COMPENDIA abounding in color photographs deploy vistas of religious life. Works like **27** Clarke, ed., *The World's Religions* (1993) and a French five-volume series **215** *Mythes et croyances du monde entier* (1985, 1991) lead the field. Older treasures like **241** Berval, ed., *Présence du bouddhisme* (1959, 1987) deploy black-and-white photographs of elegiac beauty. Appendix 1.4, "Illustrated Reference Books," lists such works.

Assisted by computers, scholars linger over bibliographic searches conducted via the Internet in catalogs of libraries worldwide. Such researchers should not overlook bibliographies that fill reference works. Almost always, the best sifted bibliographies on any question, great or small, pop up not in a computer database but rather in an up-to-date reference book. In the field of biblical studies, DICTIONARIES and HANDBOOKS in English have refined bibliographical discernment exquisitely.

In general, however, German and French reference works expend greater effort sorting bibliography than do English-language ones. The German notion of a HANDBOOK requires authors to align bibliography to diverse needs. Skill in sifting bibliography in major languages pervades German multivolume ENCYCLO-PEDIAS as diverse as **31** Müller, ed., *Theologische Realenzyklopädie* (1977-), **257** Ranke, ed., *Enzyklopädie des Märchens* (1977-), or **45** Fahlbusch, ed., *Evangelisches Kirchenlexikon*, 3d ed. (1986-), not to mention **128** Kasper, ed., *Lexikon für Theologie und Kirche*, 3d ed. (1993-). French MEGA-ENCYCLOPEDIAS also excel at compiling bibliography, but their stately pace of publication means that only a few volumes remain up-to-date. Anyone doing research in the history of Christianity or the world's religions should scour major German works and recent volumes of French MEGA-ENCYCLOPEDIAS for bibliography. They have no peer.

Reference books fulfill a wider range of purposes than most users recognize. As a phenomenology of reference books and their uses portends, individual entries in the *Guide* call attention to a diversity of merits. From skimming saints' lives to pondering controversies, from extracting bibliography to pinpointing definitions, from recalling dates to weighing methods, from assaying pivotal figures to appraising current debates, any reader can make reference works serve almost any need.

Those readers who regret that they acquired little information about certain subjects in secondary school can as adults broaden and deepen their grasp through recourse to reference books. Such readers can do so systematically through note-taking or desultorily through browsing. Rigor that has largely disappeared from early instruction can be retrieved by living with reference works. Today's golden age of reference books can become a golden age of adult education.

Glossary

Types & Functions
of Reference Books

OVERVIEW Twenty-two words appear in small capitals throughout the directory of reference books. They serve as technical terms to differentiate types and functions of reference books.

A NOTE ON THE BLURRING OF GENRES A caveat is in order. Postmodern discourse has encouraged what in 1980 Clifford Geertz called "the blurring of genres."[1] Since the 1960s fields, approaches, methods and genres of scholarship have elided into one another. Curiously, interfusing of types has occurred less conspicuously among reference works than in any other sector of publishing. Even REVISIONIST reference works adhere to recognizable genres. Conservatism, which restricts reference works to conventional structures, allows the following classification to claim a certain authority. Even adventurous editors seldom violate these distinctions.

To be sure, certain volumes may map blurring of genres within a given field. In biblical studies, for example, **68** Coggins and Houlden, eds., *A Dictionary of Biblical Interpretation* (1990) tracks the blurring of genres but does not itself adopt a trendy structure. The same applies to works that outline fields which have emerged from the blurring of genres. Examples include LEXICONS on **48** "fundamental theology" and **110** "metaliturgics." In these works content is radical but form is not. At least as regards format, reference books tend to resolve "blurred genres" back into the twenty-two types and functions outlined below. Moreover, perseverance of genres facilitates a phenomenology of reference books and their uses. A theorem of postmodernism declares that while uses of reference books proliferate, genres do not.

1. ANATOMY An exhaustive treatment of a vast subject, propounded by a single author in a single volume. Lists, classifications and quotations convey erudition with an ardor that may tip over into self-parody. In *An Anatomy of Criticism* (1957) Northrop Frye allied such bravura to the MENIPPEAN SATIRE of the ancients, in which spurts of "maddened pedantry" exude a veneer of comprehensiveness. Reference books embody encyclopedic learning, whereas MENIPPEAN SATIRES parody it.

According to Northrop Frye, classic exemplars of the "creative treatment of exhaustive erudition" include Boethius, *The Consolation of Philosophy* (524 C.E.), Robert Burton, *The Anatomy of Melancholy* (1621, 1651) and Izaak Walton, *The Compleat Angler* (1653, 1661). Encyclopedic learning also erupts, sometimes barely under control, in Rabelais, *Pantagruel* (1532-52),

[1]Clifford Geertz, "Blurred Genres: The Refiguration of Social Thought," in *Local Knowledge: Further Essays in Interpretive Anthropology* (New York: Basic Books, 1983), pp. 19-35.

Cervantes, *Don Quixote* (1605-15), Laurence Sterne, *Tristram Shandy* (1760-67) and James Joyce, *Ulysses* (1922). An ANATOMY of "hope," written by a German exiled in the United States, comes in Ernst Bloch, *The Principle of Hope,* 3 vols. [1937-46] (Oxford: Blackwell Reference, 1986). Recently Roberto Calasso wrote an ANATOMY of Greek myths from Homer through Plato to Lucian of Samosata. *The Marriage of Cadmus and Harmony* [1988] (New York: Knopf, 1993) demonstrates the appeal of the ANATOMY to postmoderns, as do the novels of Umberto Eco.

As might be expected, study of religion has elicited more than a few ANATO-MIES, not least because religion, like the ANATOMY, promises within short compass a "comprehensive survey of human life." Moreover, any entry in a reference work may lapse into MENIPPEAN excess if too many names jostle in too narrow a space. Such prodigality mars certain articles in **69** Jeffrey, ed., *A Dictionary of Biblical Tradition in English Literature* (1992) and **260** Walker, *The Woman's Encyclopedia of Myths and Secrets* (1983). Too much heterogeneity squeezed into too little space is what generates MENIPPEAN satire, whether conscious or unconscious. In contrast, MEGA-ENCYCLOPE-DIAS avoid overcrowding by furnishing room to expatiate.

By definition, an ANATOMY has a single author, whose crotchets tend toward self-parody. Overinsistence on a thesis afflicts ANATOMIES as diverse as Robert Graves, *The White Goddess* (1948), Gerardus van der Leeuw, *Sacred and Profane Beauty: The Holy in Art* (1948, 1963), Walter Kaufmann, *Religion in Four Dimensions* (1976) and Anne Baring and Jules Cashford, *The Myth of the Goddess: Evolution of an Image* (1992). By piling mountains of data onto themes too skewed to carry the load, such works begin to cloy.

See MENIPPEAN SATIRE.

2. ATLAS Traditionally, the term denotes a collection of maps together with head-notes and an index of place names (i.e.,

gazetteer). A HISTORICAL ATLAS traces shifts in boundaries of peoples, nations, languages or religions across wide swaths of time. Too few HISTORICAL ATLASES canvass the world's religions. "Geo-religious studies," as it may be termed, is a neglected field.

Recently publishers have enlarged the term *ATLAS* to designate a COMPENDIUM that scans the history and geography of a particular region (e.g., the Near East) or religion (e.g., Islam) or culture (e.g., Judaism). In these cases ATLAS has come to mean an illustrated INTRODUCTION.

☐ *Examples of Historical Atlases*

17 (1974) Isma'il al Faruqi and David Sopher, eds., *Historical Atlas of the Religions of the World*

220 (1978, 1992) Joseph E. Schwartzberg, ed., *A Historical Atlas of South Asia*

200 (1986) Isma'il al Faruqi and Lois al Faruqi, eds., *The Cultural Atlas of Islam*

3. BIBLE COMMENTARY A collection of chapter-by-chapter or verse-by-verse explications of each book of the Bible, arranged in sequence of the biblical canon. Usually a different expert writes on each book, supplying both conspectus and unit-by-unit (sometimes verse-by-verse) explication as well as specialized bibliography. The volume opens with overviews of recent scholarship together with maps and bibliography. There are BIBLE COMMENTARIES to suit every confession, level of understanding and professional need. COMMENTARIES enhance activities as diverse as evangelizing, teaching and researching. Sermon writers devour them. Most BIBLE COMMENTARIES proclaim confessional allegiance, whereas HANDBOOKS OF INTERPRETATION do not.

☐ *Confessionally Neutral Examples*

62 (1988) James L. Mays, ed., *Harper's Bible Commentary*

64 (1992) Carol A. Newsom and Sharon H. Ringe, eds., *The Women's Bible Commentary*

☐ *Confessionally Shaped Examples*

61 (1984) W. Gunther Plaut, ed.,

The Torah: A Modern Commentary [Reform Jewish]

63 (1968, 1990) Raymond E. Brown et al., eds., *The New Jerome Biblical Commentary* [Roman Catholic]

65 ([1953] 1994) D[onald] A. Carson et al., eds., *New Bible Commentary: 21st Century Edition* [evangelical]

See BIBLE DICTIONARY, HANDBOOK.

4. BIBLE DICTIONARY An alphabetically arranged LEXICON of (nearly) all persons, places, practices and events mentioned in the (Christian) Bible. In addition, each book of the Old Testament, Apocrypha and New Testament elicits an introduction that untangles problems of date, authorship, audience, purpose and content. The term "introduction" (German *Einleitung*) has functioned in this way since the late eighteenth century. Entries on individual biblical books may inject abbreviated COMMENTARY as well. Pioneered by German Protestants in the eighteenth century, BIBLE DICTIONARIES exist in every size and for virtually every confession. Some are scholarly and others devotional. Some so emphasize *realia* as to constitute a REALLEXIKON, while others explore theology. A few, such as **60** Freedman, ed., *The Anchor Bible Dictionary*, 6 vols. (1992), swell into BIBLE ENCYCLOPEDIAS. For amplification see the overview to 2.3 "Biblical Studies."

☐ *Examples*

56 ([1975] 1987) Allen C. Myers, ed., *The Eerdmans Bible Dictionary* [scholarly]

(1990) Lawrence O. Richards, ed., *The Revell Bible Dictionary* [devotional]

58 (1990) Watson E. Mills, ed., *Mercer Dictionary of the Bible* [a REALLEXIKON]

See BIBLE COMMENTARY.

5. COMPANION An INTRODUCTION to a field of study, arranged alphabetically and designed for self-teaching. Usually a COMPANION is a DICTIONARY of notable persons and issues, either with or (too often) without brief bibliographies. Aimed at the general reader rather than the specialist, a COMPANION lacks the comprehensiveness of a HANDBOOK. Pioneered by Oxford University Press with Percy A. Scholes, ed., *The Oxford Companion to Music* (1938), the genre remains preeminently British. It flourishes at Oxford University Press and Blackwell Reference.

☐ *Examples*

183 (1989) Glenda Abramson, ed., *The Blackwell Companion to Jewish Culture from the Eighteenth Century to the Present*

293 (1991) John W. Yolton, ed., *The Blackwell Companion to the Enlightenment*

72 (1993) Bruce Metzger and Michael D. Coogan, eds., *Oxford Companion to the Bible* [a BIBLE DICTIONARY interleaved with a HANDBOOK OF INTERPRETATION]

See INTRODUCTION.

6. COMPENDIUM A collection of synoptic articles designed to map a subject, often a large one like religions of the world. The sequence of chapters may be chronological or geographical but seldom alphabetical. The level may be intermediate or advanced but seldom elementary. Articles are almost always signed and equipped with bibliography. The field of religious studies (particularly history of the world's religions) abounds in such works, often written by the ablest scholars. Some COMPENDIA achieve the authority of a HANDBOOK. The grandest example of all, **67** Haase and Temporini, eds., *Aufstieg und Niedergang der römischen Welt* (1972-), is a MEGA-COMPENDIUM exceeding seventy-five thousand pages.

☐ *Examples*

39 (1990) John McManners, ed., *The Oxford Illustrated History of Christianity*

22 (1990) Charles Baladier, ed., *Le Grand Atlas des religions*

25 (1993) Arvind Sharma, ed., *Our Religions*

See HANDBOOK.

7. DICTIONARY (IN ENGLISH OFTEN SYNONYMOUS WITH LEXICON) A collection of definitions, whether of terms or proper names, arranged alphabetically. If the work tends toward a GLOSSARY, entries will be brief, unsigned and devoid of bibliography. If the work tends toward an ENCYCLOPEDIA, entries will be longer, often signed and equipped with bibliography. Entries may encompass not just terminology, but persons, places and practices. In German the term "lexicon" *(Lexikon)* denotes not a DICTIONARY but a specialized ENCYCLOPEDIA, often in one volume. Subtypes include BIBLE DICTIONARY, ENCYCLOPEDIA, GLOSSARY, LEXICON, WHO'S WHO.

□ *Examples*

(1952) Alfred Bertholet, *Wörterbuch der Religionen*

2 (1981, 1989) Keith Crim, ed., *The Perennial Dictionary of World Religions*

80 (1988) Sinclair B. Ferguson et al., eds., *New Dictionary of Theology*

8 (1989, 1991) Geddes MacGregor, *Dictionary of Religion and Philosophy*

8. ENCYCLOPEDIA The most comprehensive of reference works, an ENCYCLOPEDIA attempts exhaustive coverage of a field or even all fields. A classical ENCYCLOPEDIA is a multivolume collection of commissioned articles that are arranged alphabetically to include bibliography and cross-references. Illustrations, maps and an index usually occur. Strictly speaking, one-volume ENCYCLOPEDIAS are enriched DICTIONARIES.

General ENCYCLOPEDIAS, like the *Encyclopedia Britannica* or **298** the French *Encyclopaedia universalis* (1968, 1990), purport to cover all topics of knowledge but inevitably favor the cultural repertoire of the language in which they appear. Thus Larousse ENCYCLOPEDIAS emphasize French-speaking culture, just as Brockhaus ENCYCLOPEDIAS do German-speaking culture. As pioneered by Diderot and d'Alembert's *Encyclopédie*, 18 vols. (1751-72), a general ENCYCLOPEDIA perpetuates values of the French Enlightenment such as rationalism, progressivism, empiricism, cosmopolitanism and anticlericalism. In a word, ENCYCLOPEDIAS incline toward positivism, exalt-

ing fact and eschewing the unascertainable. One expects ENCYCLOPEDIAS to report fact accurately.

In medieval Byzantium the term *encyclopaideia* designated not a book but rather an ethos. A kind of polymathy, it denoted an all-around cultivation *(paideia)* that regurgitated tradition without advancing it. This ideal favored compilations, anthologies and other recapitulations. Inevitably, such an ideal of polymathy without innovation reinforced the notion that reference books reiterate without renewing. Happily, the Enlightenment supplanted Byzantine *encyclopaideia* by devising works that couple precision of information with novelty of thought. A turning point came with Ephraim Chambers's *Cyclopaedia, or An Universal Dictionary of Arts and Sciences,* 2 vols. (London, 1728). Whereas earlier compilations had boasted a single author, Ephraim Chambers (c. 1680-1740), a cleric, recruited a team.

Specialized ENCYCLOPEDIAS concerning religion divide into one-volume DICTIONARIES (in German referred to as LEXICONS) and multivolume MEGA-ENCYCLOPEDIAS. Some of the latter run twenty or more volumes. Catholic and Jewish MEGA-ENCYCLOPEDIAS remain unexcelled. An example in progress, **31** Müller, ed., *Theologische Realenzyklopädie* (1976-), requires eighteen thousand pages to reach *Obrigkeit* in volume 24 (1994).

□ *Examples*

(1930-37) Edwin R. A. Seligman, ed., *Encyclopedia of the Social Sciences,* 15 vols.

(1971) Cecil Roth, ed., *Encyclopaedia Judaica,* 16 vols.

5 (1987) Mircea Eliade, ed., *The Encyclopedia of Religion,* 16 vols.

See LEXICON, MEGA-ENCYCLOPEDIA.

9. GLOSSARY An alphabetical list of terms with definitions. TEXTBOOKS or HANDBOOKS often append such a word list. Introductory DICTIONARIES resemble expanded GLOSSARIES that may encompass persons as well as terms. As a subtype, Jewish INTRODUCTORY works often take the form of a GLOSSARY of Hebrew words.

The French call a GLOSSARY a *vocabulaire*.

□ *Examples*

291 (1990) Etienne Souriau and Anne Souriau, eds., *Vocabulaire d'esthétique*

192 (1992) Lewis Glinert, *The Joys of Hebrew*

13 (1993) Michael Pye, ed., *The Continuum Dictionary of Religion*

10. GUIDEBOOK A description of a region, arranged place by place, intended for travelers. During the nineteenth century GUIDEBOOKS such as the German Baedeker series or the French and English Blue Guides burst with maps but not illustrations. Since the 1960s, however, photographs have become obligatory. A series that nearly always examines religion is the Insight Guides, published in Singapore and distributed in the United States by Houghton Mifflin. GUIDEBOOKS that scrutinize religious sites include the Traveler's Key series published by Knopf, among them John Anthony West, *The Traveler's Key to Ancient Egypt* (1985) and **222** Alistair Shearer, *The Traveler's Key to Northern India* (1985).

The term *GUIDE* functions also as a synonym for an INTRODUCTION or an introductory COMPENDIUM, as in **10** *The Eliade Guide to World Religions* (1991).

□ *Example*

147 (1967) Louis Chaigne, ed., *Guide religieux de la France*

See INTRODUCTION.

11. HAGIOGRAPHY (A BOOK OF SAINTS' LIVES) *Hagiography* means two things: (1) the activity of gathering and studying documents concerning saints and (2) a collection of saints' lives. The *Guide* uses this term in the second sense to denote a book of saints' lives. Such a work may unfold either alphabetically in a WHO'S WHO or by days of a calendar. Known in Western liturgy as a *martyrology*, a calendar inclines to devotion. To counter credulity, which was famously criticized by Erasmus in *Praise of Folly* (1511) and then by Protestants, Belgian Jesuits led by Johann Bolland (1596-1665) pioneered *critical*

hagiography. Publishing a mega-calendar known as the *Acta sanctorum,* 62 vols. (Antwerp, 1643-1925), the Bollandists collected and weighed sources, particularly manuscripts. Their techniques have fostered innumerable DICTIONARIES, ENCYCLOPEDIAS and WHO'S WHOS. In the seventeenth and eighteenth centuries DICTIONARIES of saints helped to inaugurate modern reference works.

Study of the principles that guide critical hagiography is known as hagiology. Since about 1980 a spate of WHO'S WHOS of saints have catered to an ongoing "spirituality revolution." By a peculiar convention, hardly any HAGIOGRAPHIES feature illustrations. Clemens Jöckle broke this spell with his opulent **109** *Encyclopedia of Saints* (1995). For amplification see overviews to 2.6 "Hagiography" and 5.3.4 "Folklore" in the directory.

□ *Examples*

96 ([1756-59] 1926-38, 1956) Herbert Thurston and Donald Attwater, eds., *Butler's Lives of the Saints: Complete Edition,* 4 vols. [a calendar]

97 (1935-59) Jules Baudot and Léon Chaussin, eds., *Vies des saints et des bienheureux selon le calendrier,* 13 vols. [a mega-calendar]

100 (1978, 1992) David Hugh Farmer, *The Oxford Dictionary of Saints* [a WHO'S WHO]

See WHO'S WHO.

12. HANDBOOK (GERMAN *HANDBUCH*) A COMPENDIUM of articles commissioned to expound (rather exhaustively) problems, history and bibliography of a research field. As pioneered by Germans in the nineteenth century, a HANDBOOK enlists the finest scholars to outline a vision of a field, often one that they helped to create or redirect. Multilingual bibliographies are obligatory. A classical HANDBOOK maps a field in its entirety, whereas recent American exemplars tend to outline subspecialties while neglecting the whole. In the field of biblical studies a subtype has emerged since 1980, a HANDBOOK OF INTERPRETATION that delineates methods of biblical scholarship from multiple standpoints and eschews confessional utterance.

□ *Examples*

197 (1957-64) F[elix] M. Pareja, ed., *Islamologie*

(1978-) William C. Sturtevant, ed., *Handbook of North American Indians*, planned in 20 vols. (Washington, D.C.: Smithsonian Institution, 1978-)

154 (1987, 1993) Everett Ferguson, *Backgrounds of Early Christianity*

7 (1988-) Hubert Cancik et al., eds., *Handbuch religionswissenschaftlicher Grundbegriffe*, planned in 5 vols.

68 (1990) R[ichard] J. Coggins and J. L[eslie] Houlden, eds., *A Dictionary of Biblical Interpretation*

311 (1991) David M. Wulff, *Psychology of Religion* [a HANDBOOK disguised as a TEXTBOOK]

See LEXICON.

13. INTRODUCTION (French *propédeutique*, German *Vorschule*). A work in any genre that undertakes to introduce a subject to those not yet acquainted with it. Three levels of beginners need to be differentiated. *Elementary* students at an early stage of their education need an introduction to learning as such (i.e., a primer). *Intermediate* students have acquired facility in at least one field and now seek to grow in another. *Advanced* students seek to acquire the rudiments of a field new to them. Generally, TEXTBOOKS meet the needs of elementary and intermediate students, while reference books address intermediate and advanced ones. A primer is the most elementary of textbooks.

A French term, *propédeutique*, denotes a book or course that provides preliminary knowledge required to approach a field. Reference works (particularly GLOSSARIES) may be said to perform a propedeutic function if they further inquiry rather than curtail it. Thus works that flaunt self-sufficiency (for example, by omitting bibliographies) may be introductory, but they do not perform *propédeutique*. A classic is Philip Schaff, *Theological Propaedeutic: A General Introduction to the Study of Theology* (New York: Scribner's, 1893). Such an

INTRODUCTORY HANDBOOK to an entire discipline hardly exists today.

In biblical studies "introduction" (German *Einleitung*) is a genre pioneered in the eighteenth century. Biblical introduction outlines authorship, audience, purpose and argument of individual books of the Bible.

Not enough reference works function as INTRODUCTIONS and hardly any function as primers. Among intermediate INTRODUCTIONS, COMPANIONS flourish in Britain, just as Jewish GLOSSARIES do in the United States. Both shine as self-teachers.

□ *Examples*

116 (1969, 1983) Alan Richardson, ed., *A Dictionary of Christian Theology*

191 (1991) Rabbi Joseph Telushkin, *Jewish Literacy*

303 (1993) Jennifer Bothamley, ed., *Dictionary of Theories*

See COMPANION, GLOSSARY.

14. LEXICON Used in English as a synonym for DICTIONARY, the term is used in German (and in this glossary) to denote a specialized ENCYCLOPEDIA. A LEXICON aspires to greater thoroughness (*Gründlichkeit*) than a DICTIONARY, just as the latter aspires to greater thoroughness than a GLOSSARY. A monumental work like 159 Joseph Strayer, ed., *Dictionary of the Middle Ages*, 13 vols. (1982-89) would be called a LEXICON (or more precisely a REALLEXIKON) in German.

□ *Examples*

158 (1977-) *Lexikon des Mittelalters*. Volume 7 4/5 had reached the entry "Servatius" in 1995.

6 (1987, 1992) Hans Waldenfels, ed., *Lexikon der Religionen*

See DICTIONARY, ENCYCLOPEDIA, REALLEXIKON.

15. MEGA-ENCYCLOPEDIA A multivolume ENCYCLOPEDIA that aspires to exhaust a specialized subject. Since the 1890s French scholars have edited no fewer than eight Catholic MEGA-ENCYCLOPEDIAS, each in seven to thirty volumes, while teams of scholars in pre-1933 Germany and pre-1939 America produced at least five Jewish MEGA-ENCYCLOPEDIAS, such as culminated

in the Israeli *Encyclopaedia Judaica* (1972). Massive length, overwhelming bibliographies and minute erudition (often quoting at length from original languages) characterize these works, whose length saves them from the self-parody of MENIPPEAN SATIRE. The latter erupts mainly in formats too small to permit genuine exhaustiveness.

MEGA-ENCYCLOPEDIAS betray audacity, not to say megalomania. As André Jacob remarks in the *Avant-Propos* of **289** *Encyclopédie philosophique universelle* (1989-92), such vastness evokes a grandeur that is "theocentric" (1: xx). In other words, MEGA-ENCYCLOPEDIAS inspire an awe rivaling that owed to God. For amplification see the overview to 2.9.2 "Churches and Denominations: Roman Catholicism."

□ *Examples*

134 (1912-) Alfred Baudrillart et al., eds., *Dictionnaire d'histoire et de géographie ecclésiastiques.* Volume 25 reached the entry *INDE* in 1995.

(1928-34) Jakob Klatzkin, ed., *Encyclopaedia Judaica: Das Judentum in Geschichte und Gegenwart.* This unfinished masterpiece reached *LYR* at volume 10.

See ENCYCLOPEDIA, REALLEXIKON.

16. MENIPPEAN SATIRE

A genre of encyclopedic posturing defined by Northrop Frye in *The Anatomy of Criticism* (1957). Menippus, a Greek slave who lived around 280 B.C.E., gave his name to an omniumgatherum written by a boastful polymath, who unfurls "maddened pedantry" in order to advance an idiosyncratic view of a subject. Random collecting of facts fuels "creative use of exhaustive erudition," such as Frye discerns in his favorites: Erasmus, Voltaire and Laurence Sterne. Whereas an ANATOMY is a single volume claiming to survey a subject, MENIPPEAN SATIRE is a *technique* for manipulating a surfeit of erudition, often resulting in parody. Umberto Eco wields a postmodern version of the technique in novels like *Foucault's Pendulum* (1988, 1989) and *The Island of the Day Before* (1994, 1995). Disciplined use of lists

likewise elevates **109** Jöckle, *Encyclopedia of Saints* (1995). Unfortunately, heedless cramming of too much into too little space can degenerate into unconscious MENIPPEAN SATIRE, as happens in certain articles of **286** Joachim Ritter, ed., *Historisches Wörterbuch der Philosophie* (1971-) or **260** Barbara G. Walker, *The Woman's Encyclopedia of Myths and Secrets* (1983). MENIPPEAN SATIRE is a vice of encyclopedists. Overeagerness soon palls.

For examples *see* ANATOMY.

17. PHENOMENOLOGY

The discipline of classifying phenomena, religious or otherwise, collected from a spectrum of cultures and used to enliven a novel taxonomy. Confessionally and culturally neutral, such orchestration of the seemingly incompatible tends to foster HANDBOOKS. From time to time MENIPPEAN SATIRE may creep in. Embodying a novel *tour d'horizon*, phenomenologies of religion can be more comprehensive than anything but a MEGA-ENCYCLOPEDIA. Jacques Waardenburg explains the method in *Reflections on the Study of Religion* (The Hague: Mouton, 1978), and Annemarie Schimmel consummates it in **206** *Deciphering the Signs of God: A Phenomenological Approach to Islam* (Albany: SUNY Press, 1994).

The two introductions to this *Recent Reference Books in Religion* apply the discipline of phenomenology not to religions but to reference books about them.

□ *Examples*

(1918, 1932) Friedrich Heiler, *On Prayer*

(1933, 1948) Gerardus van der Leeuw, *Phenomenology of Religion*

(1954) Winston L. King, *Introduction to Religion*

(1960) W. Brede Kristensen, *The Meaning of Religion*

18. PHILOSOPHICAL DICTIONARY

A collection of essays on basic categories written by a single author in order to unsettle opinion. Intended for a wide public, the essays usually follow alphabetical order and tackle pivotal ideas or persons. There is no bibliography. Pioneered by Pierre Bayle (1647-1706) in his *Dictionnaire historique et critique* (1695-97), the genre was perfected by Voltaire in his *Dictionnaire philosophique* (1764). As befits a vehicle of the French Enlightenment, a PHILOSOPHICAL DICTIONARY stems not from cranks but from masters who deploy common sense and wit in order to preach radicality. Jaroslav Pelikan pushed the genre beyond its secular roots by meditating on the history of Christian thought. Since a REVISIONIST LEXICON likewise fosters radical rethinking, his **35** *Melody of Theology* belongs to that genre too. One wishes that savants like John Macquarrie, Martin Marty and Paul Ricoeur would emulate Pelikan in the way that René Latourelle has in **48** *Dictionary of Fundamental Theology* (1990, 1994). As a bonus, dialogues in **306** Daisaku Ikeda and Bryan Wilson, *Human Values in a Changing World* (1984, 1987) frequently attain this standard.

□ *Examples*
   243 (1976, 1991) Claude Durix, *Cent Clés pour comprendre le zen*
   (1986, 1988) Milan Kundera, "Sixty-three Words," in *The Art of the Novel*, pp. 121-53
   35 (1988) Jaroslav Pelikan, *The Melody of Theology: A Philosophical Dictionary*
   48 (1990, 1994) René Latourelle and Rino Fisichella, eds., *Dictionary of Fundamental Theology*. Thirty-six articles by Latourelle comprise a PHILOSOPHICAL DICTIONARY.
See REVISIONIST LEXICON.

19. REALLEXIKON (REALENZYKLOPÄDIE) A German type of historical

LEXICON that inventories tangibles—persons, places, objects and practices—but omits abstract terms and mythical or theological beings. Vigorously antirevisionist, it delineates entities that have enjoyed tangible existence *(realia)* as distinct from those that humans have imagined (e.g., myths, deities, metaphors, methods). If a REALLEXIKON treats myths, it traces function and reception in preference to origins or

psychology. Paying homage to the ascertainable, a REALLEXIKON canvasses people, places, institutions and customs but shuns ideas, myths, abstract terms and debates about methodology. The latter two crop up in a HANDBOOK. In separating fact from value, a REALLEXIKON ignores postmodernism. In practice a REALLEXIKON favors archeology over theology, biography over methodology, and works of art over iconography. It aspires to exhaustiveness, particularly in bibliography. Oddly enough, there has been only one REALLEXIKON of saints: **109** Jöckle, *Encyclopedia of Saints* (1995). Although no equivalent term exists in English, multivolume REALLEXIKONS flourish among historians, particularly medievalists. An obsession with verifying fact while dispelling rumination exalts the modern above the postmodern.

□ *Examples*
   151 (1950-) Theodor Klauser, ed., ***Reallexikon für Antike und Christentum***, 16 vols. to date *("Jesaja")*. This MEGA-ENCYCLOPEDIA incorporates more speculation than most.
   159 (1982-89) Joseph Strayer, ed., *Dictionary of the Middle Ages*, 13 vols.
   58 (1990) Watson E. Mills, ed., *Mercer Dictionary of the Bible*
   144 (1991) Alexander P. Kashdan, ed., *The Oxford Dictionary of Byzantium*, 3 vols.
See ENCYCLOPEDIA, LEXICON.

20. REVISIONIST LEXICON A spe-

cialized LEXICON whose contributors rethink foundations of a field. Whereas a LEXICON digests received wisdom, a REVISIONIST LEXICON reappraises it. By reshaping knowledge in light of avant-garde scholarship, such a work aims to transform a field or even launch a new one, often on behalf of a new generation. The wit of Judaism favors these endeavors, whereas the sobriety of Islam does not. By definition a REALLEXIKON eschews REVISIONISM, while a COMPENDIUM or HANDBOOK favors it. In kindred fashion, a PHILOSOPHICAL DICTIONARY rouses a single author to rethink basics. Almost invariably, a HANDBOOK OF BIBLICAL INTERPRETATION provokes REVISIONISM. Since the mid-1980s numerous reference books have undertaken to disentangle the "blurring of genres" that has engulfed fields like ecumenism, biblical studies, liturgical studies and Judaic studies. No work in English does this more cogently than **48** Latourelle and Fisichella, eds., *Dictionary of Fundamental Theology* (1990, 1994). Christian history has elicited REVISIONISM in LEXICONS like **125** Gisel, *Encyclopédie du protestantisme* (1995) and COMPENDIA like **166** Lippy and Williams, eds., *Encyclopedia of American Religious Experience* (1988). Provided that accuracy persists, all these genres make radicality a virtue.

□ *Examples*

300 (1986, 1989) François Châtelet et al., eds., *Dictionnaire des oeuvres politiques*

181 (1987) Arthur A. Cohen and Paul Mendes-Flohr, eds., *Contemporary Jewish Religious Thought*

21 (1988) Stewart Sutherland et al., eds., *The World's Religions*

112 (1990) Peter E. Fink, S.J., ed., *The New Dictionary of Sacramental Worship*

(1995) Richard Wightman Fox and James T. Kloppenberg, eds., *A Companion to American Thought*

See LEXICON, PHILOSOPHICAL DICTIONARY.

21. TEXTBOOK An INTRODUCTION to a field intended for classroom use and laid out in ascending order of difficulty. By serving beginners, a TEXTBOOK differs from a HANDBOOK, which addresses advanced scholars, and from a COMPENDIUM, which recruits a team of authors and arranges essays in a sequence other than that of difficulty. A TEXTBOOK for beginners is called a primer. Usually American TEXTBOOKS are more elementary than French or German ones. TEXTBOOKS may append a brief GLOSSARY.

□ *Examples*

(1989) Ninian Smart, *The World's Religions*

311 (1991) David Wulff, *Psychology of Religion.* Achieves the thoroughness of a HANDBOOK within the format of a TEXTBOOK.

See COMPANION, INTRODUCTION.

22. WHO'S WHO A DICTIONARY of capsule biographies, arranged alphabetically. Typically it consists of commissioned articles with bibliography. Such a DICTIONARY of persons may or may not include the living. A beloved genre, a WHO'S WHO may stand independently or be interspersed among entries of a DICTIONARY or ENCYCLOPEDIA. The discipline of HAGIOGRAPHY generates a WHO'S WHO of saints, just as study of mythology elicits a WHO'S WHO of mythical beings.

□ *Examples*

148 (1986, 1988) J[ohn] N[orman] D[avidson] Kelly, *The Oxford Dictionary of Popes*

38 (1990, 1992) John Bowden, *Who's Who in Theology*

9 (1991) John R. Hinnells, ed., *Who's Who of World Religions*

(1992, 1993) Michael Jordan, *Encyclopedia of Gods*

See HAGIOGRAPHY.

DIRECTORY OF REFERENCE BOOKS IN RELIGIOUS STUDIES

HOW TO USE THE DIRECTORY OF REFERENCE BOOKS

OVERVIEW This directory assesses over three hundred reference books that scholars in religious studies find useful. Although emphasis falls on works published since 1980, older classics are included, particularly French MEGA-ENCYCLOPEDIAS and a few pioneering volumes that retain their appeal. Pivotal works are characterized under four headings: "Scope," "Strengths," "Weaknesses" and "Competitors." English-language works of lesser interest are assessed under a single heading, "Critique." All but the most imposing or most accessible French and German works are treated in this briefer fashion. Each entry concludes with a summary. Citations at the head of each entry report on indexes, bibliography and illustrations. Entries are numbered consecutively, and other references to a title carry its entry number. In addition, more than a hundred reference works are cited that do not elicit an entry of their own.

Assessments aim to be at once sober and provocative. Certain reference works loom unforgettably. Others prove their worth over time, while still others blend into the pack. A few are scarcely worth consulting. The criteria that matter most include inclusivity, imaginative planning, ratio of stellar articles to perfunctory ones, frequency and gravity of lacunae, adequacy of bibliographies and overall distinction. At the start of each section an overview sketches particularities of that field and specifies criteria of selection used for it. For example, the abundance of 2.3.1 "Bible Dictionaries" requires more rigorous selection than does the relative paucity of 1.1 "Alphabetical Reference Works" (as distinct from COMPENDIA) on the world's religions. The overview also cites guides to reference literature in that field as well as masterpieces of synthesis within it.

DEFINITIONS FROM THE GLOSSARY

A major task of this directory is to assign reference works to categories defined in the glossary. The names of twenty-two categories differentiated there are printed in capital letters whenever they appear. By deploying definitions rigorously, the directory initiates a phenomenology of reference works and their uses.

DATES OF PUBLICATION Within each section entries occur in chronological order based on initial date of publication. Where revision has been massive, a later date determines placement in the time line. Because so many reference works undergo several editions (or translations), earliest and latest dates are coupled (e.g., **259** [1981, 1991] Yves Bonnefoy and Wendy Doniger, eds., *Mythologies*). Where an earlier date is noted but does not dictate the sequence, the form runs **56** ([1975] 1987) Myers, ed., *The Eerdmans Bible Dictionary*.

CUTOFF DATE The directory analyzes works published through October 1995.

1 THE WORLD'S RELIGIONS

OVERVIEW: A LIBRARY CREATED SINCE THE 1970s
Scholarly study of the world's religions has exploded since the 1960s. Whether in English, French or German, admirable works now canvass the field, some in alphabetical format and others in the guise of COMPENDIA. The task of epitomizing the world's religions lends itself to COMPENDIA, in which specialists evoke a religion or a portion of one that they know best. Although **5** Eliade, ed., *The Encyclopedia of Religion,* 16 vols. (1987) established a benchmark, more than a few one-volume LEXICONS and COMPENDIA surpass it in particular virtues. To be sure, *The Encyclopedia of Religion* remains indispensable, but it is surprisingly uneven.

Given the range of information that reference works on the world's religions must incorporate, it is astonishing how many scholars have written entire volumes singlehandedly. Among the best are GLOSSARIES by **1** Parrinder, **8** MacGregor and **11** Hexham. A German classic in this mold is Alfred Bertholet (1868-1951), *Wörterbuch der Religionen* (1952). No one has digested older German scholarship more adeptly. An idiosyncratic work of popularization on Hinduism, Buddhism, Daoism, Judaism, Christianity, Islam and the New Age is Peter Occhiogrosso, *The Joy of Sects: A Spirited Guide to the World's Religious*

Traditions (New York: Doubleday, 1994). On each religion it devises a GLOSSARY and WHO'S WHO.

A WHO'S WHO of four thousand leaders of religious bodies worldwide is Jon C. Jenkins, *International Biographical Dictionary of Religions* (München: K.G. Saur, 1994). Indexed by country, religion and organization, the volume also supplies mailing addresses.

A major DICTIONARY appeared too late to analyze: Jonathan Z. Smith, ed., *The HarperCollins Dictionary of Religion* (San Francisco: Harper, 1995). Its eleven hundred pages promise thirty-one hundred unsigned entries by over three hundred authorities. Eleven feature articles survey major traditions, but there is no bibliography.

1.1 ALPHABETICAL REFERENCE BOOKS (GLOSSARIES, LEXICONS AND ENCYCLOPEDIAS)

LIST OF WORKS ANALYZED
1 (1971) Geoffrey Parrinder, *A Dictionary of Non-Christian Religions* (Amersham: Hulton Educational Books; Philadelphia: Westminster, 1971).

30 (1976-) Gerhard Müller, ed., *Theologische Realenzyklopädie,* 24 vols. to date (Berlin: de Gruyter, 1976-). Analyzed under 2.1 "Christianity: General."

2 (1981, 1989) Keith Crim, ed., *The Abingdon Dictionary of Living Religions* (Nashville: Abingdon, 1981); reprinted without alteration as *The Perennial Dictionary of World Religions* (San Francisco: Harper & Row, 1989)

3 (1984, 1995) John R. Hinnells, ed., *The Penguin Dictionary of Religions* (New York: Viking Penguin, 1984); 2d ed., *New Dictionary of Religions* (Oxford: Blackwell Reference, 1995)

4 (1984, 1993) Paul Poupard, ed., *Dictionnaire des religions* (Paris: Presses Universitaires de France, 1984; 3d ed. in 2 vols., 1993)

5 (1987) Mircea Eliade, editor in chief, *The Encyclopedia of Religion,* 16 vols. (New York: Macmillan, 1987)

6 (1987, 1992) Hans Waldenfels,

ed., *Lexikon der Religionen: Phäno-mene—Geschichte—Ideen* (Freiburg: Herder, 1987)

7 (1988-) **Hubert Cancik, Burkhard Gladigow and Matthias Laubscher, eds.,** *Handbuch religionswissenschaftlicher Grundbegriffe,* 5 vols. planned (Stuttgart: Kohlhammer, 1988-)

8 (1989, 1991) **Geddes MacGregor,** *Dictionary of Religion and Philosophy* (New York: Paragon House, 1989)

9 (1991) **John R. Hinnells, ed.,** *Who's Who of World Religions* (London: Macmillan, 1991; New York: Simon & Schuster, 1992)

10 (1991) **Mircea Eliade and Ioan P. Couliano with Hillary S. Wiesner,** *The Eliade Guide to World Religions* (San Francisco: Harper, 1991)

11 (1993) **Irving Hexham,** *Concise Dictionary of Religion* (Downers Grove, Ill.: InterVarsity Press, 1993)

12 (1993) **Jan Knappert,** *The Encyclopaedia of Middle Eastern Mythology and Religion* (Shaftesbury, U.K., and Rockport, Mass.: Element, 1993)

13 (1994) **Michael Pye, ed.,** *The Continuum Dictionary of Religion* (New York: Crossroad/Continuum, 1994)

14 (1994) **Ian Harris et al., eds.,** *Longman Guide to Living Religions* (London: Longman Current Affairs, 1994)

ANALYSIS OF WORKS

1 (1971) **Geoffrey Parrinder,** *A Dictionary of Non-Christian Religions* (Amersham: Hulton Educational Books; Philadelphia: Westminster, 1971); reprint, Hulton, 1981; 320 pages; bibliography, pp. 318-20; about one hundred line drawings and black-and-white photographs in the text; out of print in the United States.

□ *Scope* This GLOSSARY furnishes about twenty-five hundred brief articles on deities, myths, leaders, scriptures, practices, art genres and holy places of all non-Christian religions. The WHO'S WHO encompasses founders and major teachers but only a few scholars (e.g., Frazer and Tylor). There is a general bibliography at the end of the book, but there are no bibliographies

attached to entries. No entry is longer than half a column, but all are lucid and authoritative. Cross-references abound, as do comparisons between religions (e.g., "Gnosis" to "Jnana," "Haoma" to "Soma," "Swastika" as used among Jains, ancient Romans and the Bön religion). This INTRODUCTION never fails to illuminate.

□ *Strengths* This is at once the best written and most stimulating GLOSSARY on the world's religions (other than Christianity) yet published. In essence it is a compact REALLEXIKON. Every region, period and major development is referenced. Extinct religions (e.g., Norse, Celtic, Egyptian) win equal coverage with living ones (including Maori, Australian and African). Ancient Greek myths and Jewish practices elicit glowing treatment. The capsule summaries, fashioned in ten to twenty lines, could hardly be bettered. Comparative articles include "Calendar," "Fasting," "Fire," "Flood" and "Relic." Omission of Christianity allows other religions to emerge from under its shadow.

□ *Weaknesses* Although this GLOSSARY boasts encyclopedic range, it is not an ENCYCLOPEDIA. In general, it expounds controversies and technical terms less deeply than 2 Crim, ed., *The Perennial Dictionary of World Religions* (1981, 1989). Withal, Parrinder narrates the history of concepts like animism, magic, mana and taboo, but he omits technical terms like *creed, scripture* and *liturgy.* Lack of individual bibliographies obliges one to turn to 21 Sutherland et al., eds., *The World's Religions* (1988) or 6 Waldenfels, ed., *Lexikon der Religionen* (1987, 1992). A pronunciation guide to foreign terms would have been helpful. For this see 2 Crim, ed., *The Perennial Dictionary of Living Religions* (1981, 1989). Apart from omitting bibliographies and eschewing controversies, this volume has scarcely gone out of date.

□ *Competitors* As a GLOSSARY of non-Christian religions, the *Dictionary of Non-Christian Religions* has no peer. As a first reference on non-Christian religions, it nicely complements 8 MacGregor, *Dictionary of Religion and Philosophy* (1989,

1991), which stresses Christianity. An obvious competitor is **13** Pye, ed., *The Continuum Dictionary of Religion* (1994), which has briefer entries and includes Christianity but lacks a winsome style. **2** Crim, ed., *The Perennial Dictionary of World Religions* (1981, 1989) is a LEXICON, not a GLOSSARY, and probes controversies in some depth. **6** Waldenfels, ed., *Lexikon der Religionen* (1987, 1989) compares religions even more systematically and includes Christianity. An older classic, Alfred Bertholet, *Wörterbuch der Religionen* (Stuttgart: Kröner, 1952) digests older German scholarship (on all religions) with acumen worthy of Parrinder. None of these works, however, match Parrinder in deftness. He untangles complexity effortlessly.

□ *Summary* No other INTRODUCTORY GLOSSARY offers such piquant comparisons across continents and centuries. A master epitomizer scintillates.

30 (1976-) Gerhard Müller, ed., *Theologische Realenzyklopädie,* 24 vols. to date (Berlin: de Gruyter, 1976-). Analyzed under 2.1 "Christianity: General." This MEGA-ENCYCLOPEDIA encompasses the world's religions (including new religious movements like Cao Dai) in lengthy articles with multilingual bibliographies that are the fullest anywhere.

2 (1981, 1989) Keith Crim, ed., *The Abingdon Dictionary of Living Religions* (Nashville: Abingdon, 1981); reprinted without alteration in paperback as *The Perennial Dictionary of World Religions* (San Francisco: Harper & Row, 1989); xviii & 830 pp.; no index; colored maps between pp. 814 and 815; many diagrams, charts and black-and-white photographs in the text.

□ *Scope* This splendid LEXICON of all living religions contains over sixteen hundred signed articles by 161 contributors. Three functions may be distinguished: (1) a WHO'S WHO of founders, leaders, rulers and scholars is combined with (2) a GLOSSARY of doctrines (from both Asian and European languages), practices, and events and with (3) a REALLEXIKON of scriptures, movements and art forms. Places are omit-

ted (except within articles that survey the spread of major religions). Entries vary in length from a few lines to eighteen pages on "Hinduism," twenty on "Islam" and twenty-five on "Buddhism." Longer articles append brief English-language bibliographies, and cross-references abound. Foreign words and names carry a pronunciation guide. The writing flows and sometimes sparkles, as in Robert Ellwood on "Demons, Demonology," Winston King on "Meditation, Buddhist" and Gordon Newby on "Muhammad."

□ *Strengths* This remains the most detailed single-volume LEXICON in English on living religions. During the late 1970s scholars (chiefly from North America) were recruited to expound their fields. Overviews like those of Agehanada Bharati on "Tantrism," Khushwant Singh on "Sikhism" and Miriam Levering on "Taoism, Religious" stand out. Certain authorities like Evan Zuesse on "African Traditional Religions," David Kinsley on "Goddess (India)," David Knipe on "Sacrifice" and Sam Gill on "Shamanism" and "Time" penned fresh syntheses. Major scriptures like the "Bhagavad Gita," "Tao-te Ching" and "Lotus Sutra" are not merely introduced but expounded. Crosscultural articles on "Ancestor Veneration," "Dance, Sacred," "Life Cycle Rites," "Pilgrimage" and "Soul, Spirit" synthesize the history of scholarship.

□ *Weaknesses* The abiding irritant is that scholarship has moved on since the late 1970s. Except in very long articles, the bibliographies are skeletal, and even these are rapidly going out of date. They cry out to be updated from **5** Eliade, ed., *Encyclopedia of Religion* (1987), **10** Eliade and Couliano, *The Eliade Guide* (1991) or **9** Hinnells, ed., *Who's Who of World Religions* (1991). Foreign-language bibliography can be gleaned from **6** Waldenfels, ed., *Lexikon der Religionen* (1987, 1992) and **4** Poupard, ed., *Dictionnaire des religions* (1984, 1993). The decision to omit extinct religions necessitates recourse to **3** Hinnells, ed., *The Penguin Dictionary of Religions* (1984, 1995) and **10** *The Eliade Guide.* The omission of cities (except in

"Jerusalem" and "Hindu Sacred Cities") makes this fall short as a REALLEXIKON.

□ *Competitors* As a LEXICON presenting North American scholarship dating from the late 1970s, *The Perennial Dictionary* stands tall. Many of the authors wrote on similar topics in **5** Eliade, ed., *The Encyclopedia of Religion* (1987). No other single-volume work in English recounts scholarly debates in such variety or depth. Six times longer than the largely British **3** Hinnells, ed., *The Penguin Dictionary of Religions* (1984, 1995), the earlier work is incomparably fuller and unmistakably American in style. In the former, however, an excellent index facilitates access, whereas in the latter one must grope. **9** Hinnells, ed., *Who's Who of World Religions* (1991) canvasses hundreds of individuals (as well as recent bibliography) not referenced here. Jonathan Z. Smith, ed., *The HarperCollins Dictionary of Religion* (1995) will no doubt tend to supplant *The Perennial*.

□ *Summary* This is the fullest one-volume LEXICON in English of living religions. Intermediate students will relish its scope, while experts will savor the reflections on methodology.

3 (1984, 1995) John R. Hinnells, ed., *The Penguin Dictionary of Religions* (New York: Viking Penguin, 1984); hardcover as *The Facts on File Dictionary of Religions* (New York and London: Facts on File, 1984); 550 pages; maps, pp. 365-80; bibliography (arranged by religions), pp. 381-446; general index, pp. 465-550; a few illustrations (of emblems). A second enlarged edition with fourteen hundred entries appeared as *New Dictionary of Religions* (Oxford and Cambridge, Mass.: Blackwell Reference, 1995); 760 pages. Analyzed on the basis of the 1984 edition.

□ *Scope* This REALLEXIKON surveys all the world's religions, past and present. Although the approximately twelve hundred articles are unsigned, a list (pp. 9-10) identifies authors by subject. Bibliographies for each article are coded to a master bibliography (pp. 381-446). An enormous range covers movements, founders, doctrines, scriptures, myths, religious orders, countries (but not cities) and cross-religious categories. Apart from religious founders, few individuals are featured (no writers or scholars). The writing is concise and laced with cross-references. An index of eighty-five pages boasts about seven thousand catchwords.

□ *Strengths* As a first reference to all religions, this volume is remarkably complete. Twentieth-century developments within traditional religions as well as new religions are featured (e.g., "Anthroposophy," "Unification Church," "Kimbanguist Church"). The editor excels at elucidating his own specialty, Zoroastrianism. Classified by topic, the bibliography includes imaginative sections on "Magic and the Occult," "New Religious Movements," "Secular Alternatives to Religion" and "Study of Religion." History of the study of religion emerges in articles like "Phenomenology of Religion," "Religion" and "Sciences of Religion." The bibliography on "Study of Religion" is splendid.

□ *Weaknesses* This is not a WHO'S WHO but rather a REALLEXIKON of unusual comprehensiveness. Beginners will find many articles too condensed and too heavily cross-referenced. Four pages of articles on "Christianity," "Christology" and the "Church" are telegraphic. Bibliographies are almost entirely in English.

□ *Competitors* As an inexpensive DICTIONARY of the world's religions, *The Penguin Dictionary of Religions* holds its own. **2** Crim, ed., *The Perennial Dictionary of World Religions* (1981, 1989) is about six times longer and correspondingly deeper. **6** Waldenfels, ed., *Lexikon der Religionen* (1987, 1992) offers fewer but longer entries that deploy virtuosic comparisons and multilingual bibliographies. **4** Poupard, ed., *Dictionnaire des religions* (1984, 1993) stresses history of scholarship on persons, places, methods and religions (both living and extinct). As a GLOSSARY for beginners, **1** Parrinder, *A Dictionary of Non-Christian Religions* (1971) remains unexcelled. The omission of individuals in *The Penguin Dictionary* is compensated in the editor's own **9** *Who's Who of World Religions* (1991), which offers greater sophistication and originality as well as a larger bibliography.

□ *Summary* As a pendant to the COMPEN-DIUM **18** Hinnells, *A Handbook of Living Religions* (1984), *The Penguin Dictionary* furnishes basic information about everything except persons.

4 (1984, 1993) Paul Poupard, ed., *Dictionnaire des religions* (Paris: Presses Universitaires de France, 1984); xiv & 1838 pages; 3d ed. in 2 vols. (Paris: Presses Universitaires de France, 1993); 2218 pages; two indexes (analytic and thematic but not persons), pp. 2191-2218; general bibliography, pp. 2167-78.

□ *Critique* This magisterial LEXICON originated at the Institut Catholique during the early 1980s. Its editor, now a cardinal, pinpoints the range by listing omissions: "A *Dictionary* of religions is not a dictionary of irreligion or atheism, nor of esotericism or sects; neither is it a dictionary of mythology or philosophy, nor a dictionary of the Bible or of Catholic theology" (p. vi). Long articles signed by 187 (mostly French) contributors canvass the history of the world's religions and include massive bibliographies. Regional coverage is unrivaled, offering, for example, no less than seven pages each on "Madagascar" and "Magyars." A WHO'S WHO encompasses scholars of religion (particularly French ones), and articles on methodology cut deep. Jacques Vidal, for example, offers a unique two pages on "Tillich et Eliade." The writing is often brilliant, and the bibliographies are superb. French talent for scanning the horizon complements **3** Crim, ed., *The Perennial Dictionary of World Religions* (1981, 1989) and **5** Eliade, ed., *The Encyclopedia of Religion* (1987). More American libraries should obtain this work.

□ *Summary* This is the fullest LEXICON (as distinct from a MEGA-ENCYCLOPEDIA) of the world's religions. No more insightful overview of persons, methods, regions and religions exists. The WHO'S WHO of scholars will thrill anyone interested in the history of the field.

5 (1987) Mircea Eliade, editor in chief, *The Encyclopedia of Religion*, 16 vols. (New York: Macmillan, 1987; smaller format edition, 1993); about 500 pages per vol., 9112 pages overall; vol. 16 lists the 300 contributors and provides a "Synoptic Outline of Contents" and detailed index. Maps, diagrams and a very few illustrations throughout. A less expensive reprint appeared in 1993.

□ *Scope* This grandest MEGA-ENCYCLOPE-DIA of religions and methods in religious studies surpasses all others in range of coverage (whether geographical, historical or methodological), incisiveness of many (if not all) articles, and attention to methodology. Virtually any issue within any of the world's religions is mentioned somewhere in the 2,734 articles and in the index. History of the study of religion elicits articles on 150 individual scholars as well as on topics like "Study of Religion," "Religion and Psychology Movement," "Dynamism" and "Animism." Eighteen different religious traditions command articles surveying the history of the study of that field crowned by Jacques Waardenburg on "Islamic Studies." Authorities of the early to mid-1980s do not mirror the standpoint of Mircea Eliade to the same degree as do those in **23** Ries, ed., *Traité d'anthropologie du sacré* (1992-). Multilingual bibliographies are ample and often provocative but overlook reference works.

□ *Strengths* Exhaustive coverage is the great asset. One can turn to the index in the assurance that *The Encyclopedia of Religion* will say something (with bibliography) on almost any topic, great or small. Information about scholars and history of separate fields is seldom duplicated elsewhere, except perhaps in **4** Poupard, ed., *Dictionnaire des religions* (1984, 1993). Many articles on the religious significance of natural and humanly made items are highly original. These entries include parts of the body ("Feet," "Knees"), animals ("Elephants," "Foxes," "Pigs"), places ("Crossroads, "Gardens," "Lakes") and implements ("Drums," "Horn," "Jade," "Masks" and "Webs and Nets"). Scholarly terms get expounded in historical depth (e.g., "Axis Mundi," "Fetishism," "Tricksters"). Nearly every article surpasses everything except articles found in the most specialized or gigantic reference works like the Catholic MEGA-ENCYCLOPE-DIAS or **198** Gibb, ed., *Encyclopaedia of Islam* (1960-). In subfields where few if any reference works exist (e.g., Pacific religions, African religions or South American religions), *The Encyclopedia of Religion* remains indispensable. A few articles like Paul Ricoeur's on "Historiography," Raimundo Panikkar's on "Deity" and Richard Schechner's on "Drama" loom as masterpieces.

□ *Weaknesses* In such a monumental enterprise certain articles must disappoint. In "Religion," for example, Winston King fails to provide a working definition of the key terms used by the *Encyclopedia*. Moreover, a reader loses time learning to identify the most helpful articles. For instance, Robert Nisbet writes perfunctorily on "Civil Religion," whereas Charles H. Long deploys seven ideal types in "Popular Religion" and appends more than a page of bibliography. Douglas A. Boon on "Anthropology, Ethnology, and Religion" does not delineate that field coherently, whereas that very task is performed incisively in Alan L. Miller on "Power." Articles on Islam skirt the challenge of coordinating secular views with those of Muslims. An abiding demerit is that in surveying major religions, *The Encyclopedia of Religion* too seldom achieves the highest quality. In contrast to COMPENDIA, the *Encyclopedia* offers surprisingly few magisterial articles to rank with, for example, Henri-Charles Puech's on "Manichéisme" or Jean Doresse's on "La Gnose" in **16** Puech, ed., *Histoire des religions* (1970-76). To be sure, many articles on cruxes of methodology sparkle, such as Ugo Bianchi's on "History of Religions," Carsten Colpe's on "Sacred and Profane" and "Syncretism," Evan Zuesse's on "Ritual" and Paul Vallière's on "Tradition." Bibliographies excel at citing monographs but too often neglect COMPENDIA. A searching critique of *The Encyclopedia of Religion* by seven British scholars appeared in *Religious Studies* 24 (1988): 3-64.

□ *Competitors* The only English-language rival is a venerable MEGA-ENCYCLOPEDIA, James Hastings, ed., *Encyclopaedia of Religion and Ethics* (Edinburgh: T & T Clark, 1908-22). Although the latter is more copious on perhaps most topics, on very few does it remain superior. On too many issues it is simply outdated. Alfonso di Nola, ed., *Enciclopedia delle religioni*, 6 vols. (Florence: Vallecchi, 1970-76) offers more detail on many matters (particularly in anthropology) but predates the revolutions in methodology of the 1970s. Issues of Christian ecumenism that are emphasized by **46** Lossky et al., eds., *Dictionary of the Ecumenical Movement* (1991) receive scant attention in *The Encyclopedia of Religion*. **31** Müller, ed., *Theologische Realenzyklopädie* (1976-) offers lengthier articles and fuller bibliographies while covering fewer figures and movements (particularly from non-Christian religions). Weightier introductions to major religions may be found in **21** Sutherland et al., eds., *The World's Religions* (1988) and **16** Puech, ed., *Histoire des religions* (1970-76). Regarding the history of the study of the world's religions, the chief rival is **7** Cancik et al., eds., *Handbuch religionswissenschaftlicher Grundbegriffe*, 5 vols. (1988-). It is more comprehensive and often more penetrating. A specialist who wishes to gauge how *The Encyclopedia of Religion* has aged should consult works like **9** Hinnells, ed., *Who's Who of World Religions* (1991), **62** Freedman, ed., *The Anchor Bible Dictionary* (1992) and **4** Poupard, ed., *Dictionnaire des religions* (1984, 1993). Clusters of articles from *The Encyclopedia of Religion* have appeared separately in paperback. Examples include Robert M. Seltzer, ed., *Judaism: A People and Its History* (New York: Macmillan, 1989) and **247** Kitagawa and Cummings, eds., *Buddhism and Asian History* (1989).

□ *Summary* This landmark MEGA-ENCYCLOPEDIA triumphs on history of scholarship as well as basic categories but not always on individual religions or controversies. The bibliographies need to be updated.

6 (1987, 1992) Hans Waldenfels, ed., *Lexikon der Religionen: Phänomene—Geschichte—Ideen* (Freiburg: Herder, 1987; paperback, 1992); xiv &

737 pages; index, pp. 730-37; no general bibliography. Analyzed on the basis of the paperback edition, 1992.

□ *Scope* This LEXICON of world religions supplies signed articles by 126 (mostly German) contributors. They canvass religions, movements, basic categories and cross-religious comparisons but not persons. More than any other single volume, this one compares religions. Edited by a Catholic theologian of world religions who is an authority on Buddhism, the *Lexikon der Religionen* restructures a *Religionswissenschaftliches Wörterbuch* edited in 1956 by (Cardinal) Franz König (b. 1905). The latter's surveys of Zoroastrianism and Christianity survive. The writing achieves marvels of compression, and the bibliographies (mostly in German) are up-to-date but not always comprehensive.

□ *Strengths* This work boasts the meatiest comparisons of world religions to be found in any single volume. In about fifty articles, the views of six to eight world religions on a given topic are juxtaposed in subentries written by experts on each. Entries on "Man" *[Mensch]*, "Marriage/Family," "Salvation" *[Heil]*, "Cult," "Sacrifice," "Ethics" and "Guilt/Sin" run ten pages each and include six to nine subentries. A twenty-one page entry on "God" packs ten subentries on the following religions: indigenous religions, extinct religions (including Egyptian, Babylonian, Greek, Roman and Ugaritic), Judaism, Christianity, Islam, Hinduism and Buddhism. Nothing similar exists anywhere else.

Five-page comparisons address such topics as "Underworld," "Image," "Belief," "Grace," "Priest" and "Soul." Each of the world's major religions commands an entry, usually of five to ten pages. Wilhelm K. Müller's eight pages excel on fundamentals of Buddhism, as do Michael von Brück's eleven pages on its spread. There are four pages on "Shinto" and two on "Chinese Religiosity." Franz König's eleven pages on Christianity (revised by Jacob Kremer) treat origin, history and self-understanding in a tour de force of epitomizing. Even more stimulating are articles on "Magic," "Eros and Religion,"

"Matriarchy/Patriarchy" and "Syncretism." An article on "New Religious Movements" (in the West) interprets them as guru-movements that derive ultimately from India. Cargo cults are treated as "Crisis-Cults" *[Krisenkulte]*, and Cao Dai elicits a full entry. Methodology unleashes a sequence on nine disciplines: geography, history, criticism, phenomenology, philosophy, psychology, sociology, statistics and theology of religion (pp. 539-59). Bibliographies cite mainly German works, often specifying entries in Galling, ed., *Die Religion in Geschichte und Gegenwart*, 3d ed. (1956-63) and **31** Müller, ed., *Theologische Realenzyklopädie* (1976-).

□ *Weaknesses* As befits a German LEXICON, this is a specialized ENCYCLOPEDIA that stipulates what it does and does not cover. This one encompasses religious movements and ideas but not persons or scriptures. There is no WHO'S WHO of persons (except founders like the Buddha, Jesus and Moses) or deities (except one or two like Vishnu). Art and literature receive no mention. Moreover, the editor excluded three areas that concern primarily Christians: liturgics, dogmatics and ecumenism. A synoptic table of contents would have listed entries on a given religion, as is done in **9** Hinnells, ed., *Who's Who of World Religions* (1991). A high degree of compression makes this LEXICON unsuitable for beginners.

□ *Competitors* The *Lexikon der Religionen* excels at elucidating categories and comparing their manifestations in East and West. It has no rival for articles that align six or eight religions under a single heading. To a certain extent, it miniaturizes **5** Eliade, ed., *The Encyclopedia of Religion* (1987) but lacks the latter's WHO'S WHO, histories of disciplines and international contributors. In Waldenfels's *Lexikon* German scholarship nicely complements American scholarship in **2** Crim, ed., *The Perennial Dictionary of World Religions* (1981, 1989). Almost twice as long, the latter dispenses much more data on Asian religions (and art) but fewer comparisons. **4** Poupard, ed., *Dictionnaire des religions* (1984, 1993) encompasses persons as well as methods and expatiates on the history of scholarship. In contrast to American works, Waldenfels's deemphasizes myth and recruits few Jewish contributors (chiefly Johann Maier and R. J. Zwi Werblowsky). Another American competitor is **34** Gentz, ed., *The Dictionary of Bible and Religion* (1986), which runs more than twice as long. Its articles on religions of the world (particularly China and India) hit home but lack cross-religious comparisons. Those who seek more intensive scholarship on methodology and history of categories should consult 7 Cancik et al., eds., *Handbuch religionswissenschaftlicher Grundbegriffe* (1988-).

□ *Summary* As the premier LEXICON of comparisons among religions, the *Lexikon der Religionen* conceptualizes ingeniously. It digests German scholarship on the world's religions.

7 (1988-) Hubert Cancik, Burkhard Gladigow and Matthias Laubscher, eds., *Handbuch religionswissenschaftlicher Grundbegriffe,* planned in 5 vols. (Stuttgart: Kohlhammer, 1988-); vol. 1 (1988), 504 pages; vol. 2 (1990), 500 pages; vol. 3 (1993), 488 pages (through *Kult*); no index; no general bibliography.

□ *Scope* This magisterial HANDBOOK originated in the early 1970s. Scrupulously planned, it recruits mostly German scholars to explicate several hundred key terms in religious studies. In addition to four and a quarter volumes of a LEXICON, volume 1 opens with a COMPENDIUM of eleven articles on the history of the field as a whole as well as nine component disciplines. Attached are two brief WHO'S WHOS, one on scholars of religion (1:272-301) and another on philosophers (1:333-83). As explained in the introduction (1:19), alphabetical entries come in three sizes: (1) brief explanations of technical terms like "Agon" or "Charisma" as well as outdated ones like "Animism" and "Fetishism"; (2) intermediate articles on terms touching specific religions like "Anti-Semitism" or "Demon" and (3) major articles on generic concepts like "Asceticism" or "Family" as well as on methodological cruxes like "Historicism" or "Homo religiosus." All entries

recount the history of the term, expound theoretical debates and include massive multilingual bibliography. The writing is clear, if occasionally telegraphic, and the bibliographies nonpareil. No other work explores the tool kit of religious studies so painstakingly.

□ *Strengths* This HANDBOOK coordinates insights from three disparate approaches: the social sciences, philosophy and history of religion. By sifting nearly every concept through this triple grid, the book gratifies social scientists, philosophers and historians alike. To this end, the COMPENDIUM in volume 1 supplies magisterial surveys, notably Karl-Heinz Kohl's forty-five-page "History of *Religionswissenschaft.*" Likewise Gerhard Schlatter's forty-page history of "Ethnology of Religion" covers all schools. Writing on "Culture and Religion," Dario Sabbatucci argues that to dissolve religion into culture succeeds for ethnic and tribal religions but not for prophetic ones (1:57-58). Hubert Cancik and Hubert Mohr delineate a field that remains all but unknown among English speakers, "Aesthetics of Religion." It embraces semiotics, symbolism, study of gestures and theory of the beautiful. Under the rubric "Didactics of *Religionswissenschaft*" an innovative essay plots strategies for teaching. Four articles on philosophy, however, are cursory.

The heart of the enterprise is four and a quarter volumes of LEXICON. Entries on major concepts like "Communication," "Identity" and "Anthropogony/Cosmogony" divide into subsections on history of the concept, typology and case studies. The entry on "Anxiety," for example, examines medical symptoms, theory in Kierkegaard and Freud, and examples from tribes, Greek antiquity, the Bible and existentialism. Comparisons shuttle along this spectrum. The article on "Aggression" suggests medical applications and then expounds theory in Alfred Adler, Nietzsche, Freud, Lacan and Norbert Elias before sifting examples from ancient Greece as viewed by Walter Burkert and René Girard. Carsten Colpe's dissection of "the Holy" (3:80-99) ranks as perhaps the most imaginative on this debate in any reference book. Although scheduled to appear eight years apart, the earliest volume deploys cross-references to the final one. This HAND-BOOK comprises the ne plus ultra on history and theory of methodology in religious studies.

□ *Weaknesses* The German notion of *Religionswissenschaft* as a cluster of intertwined disciplines motivates this HANDBOOK. Its sheer ambition may unsettle those who do not welcome interdisciplinary cross-over. Some may object to tying disciplines into unfamiliar bundles like "Aesthetics of Religion" or "Geography of Religion," while others may prefer to ignore the history of terminology altogether. Still others may dismiss categories like "Conflict," "Crisis," "Law" or "War" as banal. Although clearly written, longer entries make no effort to help beginners. This becomes a serious drawback because everyone remains a beginner vis-à-vis some or even many of the categories. By introducing basics, Eric J. Sharpe's *Comparative Religion: A History* (London: Duckworth, 1975; 2d ed., La Salle, Ill.: Open Court, 1986) and more recently Walter H. Capps, *Religious Studies: The Making of a Discipline* (Minneapolis: Fortress, 1995) help remedy this defect, as does Jan de Vries (1890-1964), *Perspectives in the History of Religions* [1961] (Berkeley: University of California Press, 1967). This HANDBOOK has to be absorbed slowly, over years. The field may require decades to catch up with it. As regards format, volumes 2, 3 and 4 lack a table of contents.

□ *Competitors* This HANDBOOK is a classic in the German manner. Its thoroughness, originality and depth will daunt newcomers. In elucidating concepts, dissecting methods and narrating the history of individual categories and disciplines, it all but eclipses 5 Eliade, ed., *The Encyclopedia of Religion* (1987). But it ignores individual religions (apart from their relevance to cruxes of methodology). Meritoriously, the *Handbuch* probes certain concepts like "Apotropaic," "Age Groups" and "Images of Innocence," which *The Encyclopedia of Religion* ignores. For sheer intellectual

power, the *Handbuch* recalls **151** Klauser, ed., *Reallexikon für Antike und Christentum* (1950-). Another magnificent German enterprise, **31** Müller, ed., *Theologische Realenzykopädie* (1976-), covers a few of the same concepts (e.g., "Anti-Semitism") in far greater depth but generally avoids overlap. Readers of German are fortunate to have these three masterworks. The more the *Handbuch* is consulted, the more it will stimulate reflection. But upon first encounter even experts may well fall speechless. Everyone, however, will relish the bibliographies.

□ *Summary* This magisterial HANDBOOK supplants English and French works on the history of concepts in religious studies. It appraises the tool kit in utmost detail.

8 (1989, 1991) Geddes MacGregor, *Dictionary of Religion and Philosophy* (New York: Paragon House, 1989; paperback, 1991); published in Britain as *The Everyman Dictionary of Religion and Philosophy* (London: Dent, 1990); 696 pages; no index; classified English-language bibliography, pp. 679-96. Analyzed on the basis of the paperback edition of 1991.

□ *Scope* In a riveting WHO'S WHO and GLOSSARY a wry polymath explicates about five thousand persons and terms, chiefly from the Western tradition. Philosophy of religion, patristics, books of the Bible and church history win exemplary coverage. English, German, Italian and particularly French thinkers of all periods are expounded. The key concepts and persons associated with non-Christian religions are explained but in less depth than their Western counterparts. Articles range in length from five lines to almost two pages (on Plato). No bibliography accompanies entries, but a master list harvests a lifetime's reading (pp. 679-96).

□ *Strengths* A Scottish-American savant has fashioned an INTRODUCTION to Christian thought and religion together with Asian parallels. A WHO'S WHO encompasses theologians, founders, some scholars and many philosophers. The latter include twentieth-century analysts of language like John Austin and Nelson Goodman but not Paul Ricoeur or John Hick. Entries on the author's favorites could hardly be bettered (e.g., "Plato," "Origen," "Pascal," "Hegel," "Tolstoy"). New religious movements of Christian origin evoke pungent analysis (e.g., "Swedenborg," "Mormons," "Christian Science," "Jehovah's Witnesses"). Entries on conundrums like "Mind-Body Problem," "Immortality" and "Reason" excel. While surveys of "Philosophy of Religion" and "Psychology of Religion" sparkle, articles on recent fields like "Hermeneutics" and "Structuralism" do not. Christian religious orders, rites, heresies and major sites (e.g., "Montserrat," "Port-Royal," "Notre Dame de Paris") spark witty delineation, but corresponding Jewish entries disappoint (e.g., "Torah," "Cabbala," "Maimonides"). Contemporary comparisons abound, as in a suggestion that ancient Greeks "would have thought of a film star or golf champion as a god or goddess, a *theos* or *thea,* although less permanent than, say, the gods of love and war" (p. 609). MacGregor scintillates as a teacher. Annotated bibliographies (to works in English) cover each of the major world religions as well as such matters as "Afterlife," "Bioethics," "Modern Religious Movements" and "Philosophy of Religion." These are some of the most imaginative, not to say idiosyncratic, bibliographies in any reference book.

□ *Weaknesses* As an INTRODUCTION to the world's religions, the *Dictionary of Religion and Philosophy* declines to give non-Christian topics equal coverage, all but ignoring myth. Essential figures, scriptures, concepts and rites (but few secondary ones) are explained. "Buddha," "Confucius" and "Zen" elicit a column each, "Brahma" and "Mani" half a column and "Nagarjuna" six lines. South Asian topics get covered more fully than Chinese or Japanese ones, while primal religions drop out altogether. Jewish and Muslim topics receive derisorily short shrift. Ancient myths are scanted: "Thor" and "Dyaus" receive six lines, "Athena" and "Ahura Mazda" none, yet "Mystery Religions" and "Gnosticism" thrive. Some postmoderns (and most Jews) may object to a Christian emphasis, but the author warns,

"Many of us in the West do not know our own tradition as well as do others looking at it from the outside." No one redresses cultural illiteracy better than Geddes MacGregor.

□ *Competitors* Devotees of reference works will marvel at MacGregor's epitomizing. No other volume strikes so ingenious a balance between Western philosophy, Christian tradition and Eastern religions. As a miniaturizer, MacGregor ranks with Hans Waldenfels and Geoffrey Parrinder. A younger rival is Peter A. Angeles in **74** *Dictionary of Christian Theology* (1985) and **295** *The HarperCollins Dictionary of Philosophy,* 2d ed. (1992). Those works enumerate definitions even more precociously but lack historical meat. **1** Parrinder's *Dictionary of Non-Christian Religions* (1971) and **3** Hinnells, ed., *The Penguin Dictionary of Religions* (1984, 1995) complement the *Dictionary of Religion and Philosophy* on Eastern and primal religions but play down philosophy. Except for John Macquarrie's entries, **34** Gentz, ed., *The Dictionary of Bible and Religion* (1986) is ponderous by comparison. **29** Cross, ed., *The Oxford Dictionary of the Christian Church* (1957, 1974) covers more individuals but lacks MacGregor's philosophical acumen. The latter's versatility recalls that of another Scottish encyclopedist, James Hastings (1852-1922). MacGregor's ebullience makes the Westminster/SCM dictionaries seem almost labored.

□ *Summary* A consummate teacher has distilled a lifetime of explaining into a pocket history of Western thought and religion. The Jewish entries aside, no one has done the job better.

9 (1991) John R. Hinnells, ed., *Who's Who of World Religions* (London: Macmillan, 1991; New York: Simon & Schuster, 1992); xvi & 560 pages; synoptic index (by religion), pp. 537-46; general index, pp. 547-60; bibliography, pp. 457-519; 12 maps, pp. 521-36.

□ *Scope* This diligent WHO'S WHO enlisted sixty-eight (mostly British) scholars to write thirteen hundred entries on religious leaders spread across twenty-six cultures.

In order to pinpoint religious accomplishments but not general ones, articles average between one-fourth and one-half page, and a few run a full page (e.g., on Maimonides, Jesus, Paul and Aristotle). Representatives from the less studied religions of India (Jains, Parsees, Sikhs) win disproportionate attention, while the Chinese do not. Bibliography for each entry is numbered to twenty-five hundred (English-language) items in the general bibliography. The writing compresses consummately.

□ *Strengths* The merit of this WHO'S WHO lies in its insistence on religious accomplishments. No other work focuses so steadfastly on the religious relevance of biographees. Types of figures encompass founders, teachers, visionaries, miracle workers, ascetics and rulers. Both entries and bibliography are subdivided into twenty-six headings (listed on p. xv). Thirteen hundred entries are apportioned as follows: 403 Christians, 138 Buddhists, 114 Muslims, 90 Jews (including 22 biblical figures), 72 Hindus, 38 Zoroastrians, 31 Sikhs and 21 Jains. "Magic and the Occult" numbers 34 (including Eliphas Levi, Carlos Castaneda and Starhawk), ancient Egyptian religion 28 and ancient Greek religion 21 (including Heraclitus, Epicurus and Plotinus). Among Christians appear painters (Giotto, Leonardo, Michelangelo, Dürer), musicians (Dufay, Lassus, Bach, Mozart) and writers (Bunyan, Emerson, Yeats, C. S. Lewis). There are also philosophers (Kant, Hegel, Kierkegaard, Maritain), theologians (Ritschl, Bultmann, Rahner and Panikkar) and scholars (Ernest Renan, James Hastings, W. Robertson Smith and Nathan Söderblom). Social scientists are excluded.

Some articles deliver fresh research, as Simon Weightman does on John Bennett and John Hinnells and Mary Boyce do on recent Zoroastrians. A page on "Mani" boasts half a column of recent bibliography (mostly in German). The two longest articles occasion surprise: two pages each on "Mahavira" and "Herodotus." In the latter John P. Kane summarizes Herodotus's reports on religion in Greece, Egypt and Persia. Kane contributes brilliant entries on "Homer" and "Hesiod" as well. His rank among the meatiest digests of ancient Greek religion anywhere. Articles on elusive figures like Pythagoras, Prester John and a Jain scholar, Haribhadra (or on legendary ones like Diotima and Hermes Trismegistus) disentangle what little can be documented. Steven Collins's page on the Buddha tackles the controversy concerning his dates (c. 586-486 vs. c. 448-368). Although almost entirely in English, the bibliography of twenty-five hundred items is no less remarkable. Nearly two-fifths concern Christianity (1,000 titles), while Buddhism receives 267, Islam 144, Hinduism 118, Judaism 87, Sikhism 75, new religious movements in the West 71, and Zoroastrianism 57 titles. This constitutes the richest English-language bibliography on the world's religions available in a single volume. If for no other reason, every historian of religion should own this book. It combines the depth of a LEXICON with the clarity of an INTRODUCTION.

□ *Weaknesses* Users should frequent the synoptic index so as to master the twenty-six divisions that structure selection of biographees and sequence of bibliography. This is not a HAGIOGRAPHY; only a few dozen Christian saints get their lives narrated with utmost sobriety, distributed equally among ancient and modern, Eastern and Western. Only a dozen (mostly recent) popes figure. Foreign-language bibliography needs to be supplemented from 4 Poupard, ed., *Dictionnaire des religions* (1984, 1993) or 6 Waldenfels, ed., *Lexikon der Religionen* (1987, 1992). John Hinnells's editing is so skillful that certain cavils hardly matter: the bibliography cries out for running subheads; Christians in the synoptic index ought to have been listed by denominations; the twelve black-and-white maps (pp. 521-36) should have come at the back where they would be noticed.

□ *Competitors* This WHO'S WHO compiles the fullest roster of religious figures in a single volume. It describes individuals scattered across countless works devoted to particular traditions and includes luminaries found nowhere else. 2 Crim, ed., _The Perennial Dictionary of World Religions_ (1981, 1989) omits persons other than religious founders, while reference works like 217 Embree, ed., _Encyclopedia of Asian History_ (1988) or 159 Strayer, ed., _Dictionary of the Middle Ages_ (1981-89) do not isolate religious achievements. The WHO'S WHO included in LEXICONS like 34 Gentz, ed., _The Dictionary of Bible and Religion_ (1986) or 163 J. D. Douglas, ed., _New 20th-Century Encyclopedia of Religious Knowledge_ (1991) cover mainly Judaism and Christianity. None of these works report religious doings of individuals so singlemindedly. As a crowning virtue, the _Who's Who of World Religions_ juxtaposes piquant neighbors on a page. It is bracing to browse among such odd couples as Pelagius and William Penn, Rabia and Rachel, Simon Magus and Menno Simons, Johann Eck and Mary Baker Eddy.

□ _Summary_ This impeccable WHO'S WHO overflows with choice information, subtle appraisals and up-to-date bibliography. Few recent reference books repay so richly both consulting and browsing.

10 (1991) Mircea Eliade and Ioan P. Couliano with Hillary S. Wiesner, _The Eliade Guide to World Religions_ (San Francisco: Harper, 1991); xii & 301 pages; annotated index, pp. 259-301; no general bibliography.

□ _Scope_ Planned by Mircea Eliade (1907-86) and executed by a Romanian colleague, Ioan Couliano (1950-91), _The Eliade Guide_ delivers thirty-three historical chapters, alphabetically arranged, on major religions past and present. Subdivided into titled and numbered sections, each chapter climaxes with bibliography (some brief, some massive) in all Western languages. Eliade's global sweep and gift for synthesis found a worthy successor in Ioan Couliano, a scholar of Gnosticism. The style is austere: proper names and technical terms proliferate, historical sketches abound, theological epitomes daunt. In 250 pages the entire religious heritage of humankind unfolds.

□ _Strengths_ Intended by Eliade as an epitome first of his _History of Religious Ideas_,

3 vols. (1978-86) and then of _The Encyclopedia of Religion_ (1987), this tour de force provides an authorized conspectus of Eliade's mature views. The dizzying breadth that characterized Eliade guarantees chapters on seldom studied religions such as "Central American Religions," "Hittite Religion," "Oceanic Religions," "Prehistoric Religions," "Slavic and Baltic Religions" and "Thracian Religion." These chapters are not easily duplicated. The _Guide_ is unmatched on subjects of Couliano's own expertise, for example "Dualistic Religions," "Hellenistic Religions" and "Mystery Religions." The longest chapter, "Christian Religion" (pp. 58-89), boasts twenty-nine subdivisions, among them a scintillating exposition of christological debates (pp. 78-81). This must be one of the most penetrating brief histories of Christian thought ever written. Similarly, the chapter on Islam (particularly as regards Sufism) stands comparison with 202 Glassé, _The Concise Encyclopedia of Islam_ (1989) at its best.

□ _Weaknesses_ Where two of the most powerful minds in the field have pooled their learning, the density of synthesis will defeat beginners. Apart from chapters like "Dualistic Religions" and "Hellenistic Religion," which summarize Couliano's _The Tree of Gnosis_ (San Francisco: Harper, 1992), any attempt to disentangle Eliade's from Couliano's contributions will falter. One can only wish that Eliade had lived to place his stamp more firmly on chapters that interested Couliano less. Unfortunately, shorter ones such as "Canaanite Religion," "Jainism" and "Tibetan Religion" do little but summarize articles in 5 _The Encyclopedia of Religion_. An annotated index (pp. 259-301) dispenses five- to ten-line definitions of about one-tenth of the entries in 5 _The Encyclopedia_, selected arbitrarily from mythical and historical figures. Located in the index, a page-long entry on "Mormonism" obtrudes. As a source of bibliography in Western languages, the _Guide_ is uneven. Superb on Africa, Buddhism, Christianity, Islam and Judaism, it cites chiefly articles in _The Encyclopedia of Religion_ on "Celtic Religion," "Hinduism" and "Zoroastrianism."

□ *Competitors* As a historical epitome of all the world's religions filtered by two dynamic minds, *The Eliade Guide* stands alone. Joseph M. Kitagawa's article on Eliade in *The Encyclopedia of Religion* (5:85-90) outlines the life's work that culminated in this *Guide*. Yet not everyone will welcome the chutzpah of attempting to compress all the world's religions into 250 pages. **21** Sutherland et al., eds., *The World's Religions* (1988) offers vastly more material (limited to living religions) subtly rethought by the ablest scholars. It reports contemporary scholarship more representatively, as does **2** Crim, ed., *The Perennial Dictionary of World Religions* (1981, 1989). As a GLOSSARY, *The Eliade Guide* includes an annotated index that is too arbitrary to stand comparison with **1** Parrinder, *A Dictionary of Non-Christian Religions* (1971) or **13** Pye, ed., *The Continuum Dictionary of Religion* (1994). Many readers will prefer a COMPENDIUM like **18** Hinnells, ed., *A Handbook of Living Religions* (1984). Others will choose a LEXICON of living and extinct religions like **4** Poupard, ed., *Dictionnaire des religions* (1984, 1993) or **6** Waldenfels, ed., *Lexikon der Religionen* (1987, 1991). The latter, however, scants indigenous religions.

□ *Summary* No other brief volume synthesizes so much history across the entirety of the world's religions. *The Eliade Guide* never fails to stimulate but sometimes induces dizziness.

11 (1993) Irving Hexham, *Concise Dictionary of Religion* (Downers Grove, Ill.: InterVarsity Press, 1993); 245 pages; no index; general bibliography, pp. 241-45; also in paperback.

□ *Scope* Written by an evangelical authority on South Africa, this GLOSSARY and WHO'S WHO is one of a kind. More than two thousand entries elucidate terms and names current in the academic study of world religions. Persons, places, concepts and movements divide attention. The longest entries include "Judaism," "Islam," "Qur'an" and "Buddhism." A WHO'S WHO emphasizes Christian theologians, philosophers, scholars and sect-founders, as well as initiators and thinkers from major traditions. Distilled from hand-outs used in twenty years of teaching, entries tend to exacerbate controversy. New religious movements elicit extensive and often hostile coverage. Although individual bibliographies are few, a "Reading List for Religious Studies" (pp. 241-45) delivers choice titles and wry annotations.

□ *Strengths* Few GLOSSARIES specify the nub of an issue so deftly, sometimes to the point of making mischief. Trained by Ninian Smart (University of Lancaster) and Fred Welbourn (Bristol University), Hexham wants religious studies to highlight "dissenting views." He dissects problem-laden categories like "Animism," "Dualism," "High Gods" and "Myth" by sketching scholarly debates for and against. He weighs methodologies with equal candor in "Biblical Criticism," "Liberation Theology" and "Religion and Modernity," while omitting other tangles such as "Messianism" or "Fetishism." Comparative entries on "God," "Divorce," "Death," "Suicide" and "Metempsycholsis" juxtapose clashing views from ten major religions. A skilled taxonomist, Hexham emphasizes differences where others may exalt similarities. He builds, for example, a distinction between "Abramic" religions (Judaism, Christianity, Islam) and "Yogic" ones (Hinduism, Buddhism, Jainism) into analysis of all these (e.g., in "History"). Somewhat glibly, he views New Age as an attempt to merge the two types. Although he tends to scant social sciences, entries on "Alienation," "Utilitarianism" and "Traditions, Great and Little" incorporate those innovations of social science into religious studies.

Hexham assesses philosophers, sympathizing with René Descartes and Karl Popper while criticizing Hegel and Heidegger. Likewise, he evaluates twentieth-century scholars of religion, deprecating Claude Lévi-Strauss while revering Buddhologist Edward Conze. With impish delight Hexham injects anecdotes, suggesting, for example, under "Qur'an" that Abu Bakr's destruction of alternative texts spared Islam the synoptic problem that has dogged biblical studies. Never one to shirk a verdict, he dubs Arianism "Christianity's most troublesome schism," classifying Unitarians, Christadelphians and Jehovah's Witnesses as revivers of it. As an authority on Zulu religion, Hexham excels on "African Independent Churches" and on leaders like the three Shembes and Simon Kimbangu. The "Reading List for Religious Studies" favors authors who express "contrary views" (e.g., Walter Kaufmann, V. S. Naipaul and Arthur Koestler). Ever the contrarian, Hexham argues that "the old liberal approach" of cultivating "sympathetic insight" was "commendable in situations of religious intolerance and dogmatism" but has degenerated into an "anachronism" among American and British academics. The latter need to proclaim differences, not elide them (p. 241).

□ *Weaknesses* More than most reference book writers, Hexham fans controversy. He flaunts hostility to New Age in entries such as "Occult," "Spiritualism," "Neopaganism" and "Transchanneling." He denounces "Marxism" as "in many ways . . . the great lie of the twentieth century." What may seem acumen to some will seem acrimony to others. Hexham belittles Jung, who is said to "verge on pseudo-science." and Joseph Campbell, who is dismissed as an "occultist" with "confused ideas about mythology." Articles on Hinduism overrate possible Christian influences on it (e.g., "Bhagavad-Gita," "Madhva"). Sheer cussedness leads Hexham to include allegations that George Orwell wrote *1984* against Christianity as well as Marxism and that the Vedantist philosopher Ramanuja accused Shankara of having his intellect "warped through sexual perversions." An aversion to "Mysticism" and "Spirituality" leads to weak coverage of them. The format occasions some cavils: a synoptic index to the WHO'S WHO would have helped the reader locate representatives of Africa, South Asia and new religious movements. A few errors creep into the dating of individuals: Karl Jaspers died in 1969, not 1973; Victor Turner died in 1983, not 1986; Mircea Eliade (whom Hexham distrusts) died in 1986, not 1988. The name of Pierre-Joseph Proudhon is misspelled.

□ *Competitors* For all its argumentativeness, this INTRODUCTION to persons and concepts sparkles, particularly in classroom use. No other GLOSSARY combines range, incisiveness and outspokenness so dexterously. 13 Pye, ed., *The Continuum Dictionary of Religion* (1994) is at once more austere and more reliable but omits persons and plays down the twentieth century. 1 Parrinder, *A Dictionary of Non-Christian Religions* (1971) is more judicious but omits Christianity and is out of print. 8 MacGregor, *Dictionary of Religion and Philosophy* (1989, 1991) is splendid on Christianity but deemphasizes other religions. 10 *The Eliade Guide to World Religions* (1991) is too recondite and has no WHO'S WHO. 3 Hinnells, *The Penguin Dictionary of Religions* (1984, 1995) will discourage most students and tends to scant Christianity. Three times longer, 2 Crim, ed., *The Perennial Dictionary of World Religions* (1981, 1989) is too detailed to be an INTRODUCTION and offers no WHO'S WHO. A Christian evangelical, Hexham lets an academic ethos prevail. Those who fear that combativeness may spoil the *Concise Dictionary of Religion* should consult 79 Elwell, ed., *Evangelical Dictionary of Theology* (1988). Hexham's entry on "Cults" exudes sobriety. He contributes meaty entries on "Sects and Cults" and "Southern Africa" also to 163 Douglas, ed., *New 20th-Century Encyclopedia of Religious Knowledge* (1991). Hexham pays so little heed to "Spirituality" that 89 Wakefield, ed., *The Westminster Dictionary of Christian Spirituality* (1983) is needed to round out the coverage. None of these works matches Hexham at dramatizing controversies.

□ *Summary* This GLOSSARY shows how a reference work can voice dissent without sacrificing rigor. As a primer for students, it dispenses fundamentals. As a refresher for experts, it incites debate. A hard edge may offend the tenderhearted.

12 (1993) Jan Knappert, *The Encyclopaedia of Middle Eastern Mythology and Religion* (Shaftesbury, U.K., and Rockport, Mass.: Element, 1993); 309 pages; no index; bibliography, pp. 303-9; six maps between pp. 9 and 10. Analyzed further under 3.2.1 "Islam: Religion and Culture."

□ *Critique* An imaginative British-Belgian historian compiled this GLOSSARY and WHO'S WHO on all religions of the ancient Near East, including Islam and Baha'i but excluding Christianity and Manichaeism. With REVISIONIST flair about a thousand entries on deities, practices, myths, Old Testament persons and archeological sites synthesize research of the past 150 years. Eschewing the detail of a BIBLE DICTIONARY, the author retells stories concerning deities and persons from Sumerian, Babylonian, Canaanite, Israelite, Egyptian, Persian and Islamic religions. Issues and figures that span two or more religions shine. An entry on "Paradise," for example, traces the concept (with quotations) from Zoroastrian origins to biblical and Qur'anic elaborations. Thus the work complements **275** van der Toorn, Becking and van der Horst, eds., *Dictionary of Deities and Demons in the Bible (DDD)* (1995). Knappert's introduction (pp. 1-38) traces the history of research and sketches interactions among the religions. Entries vary in length from four lines to four pages. Although individual bibliographies are lacking, a general bibliography lists 150 English-language monographs. Apart from a few idiosyncratic sallies (e.g., on "Jihad"), anyone embarking on study of the ancient Near East or Islam can rely on Knappert. No other reference book traces comparisons among these religions so astutely.

□ *Summary* This GLOSSARY and WHO'S WHO scans the spectrum of Near Eastern religions from Sumerian and Canaanite to Islam and Baha'i while bypassing Christianity. Comparisons flower.

13 (1994) Michael Pye, ed., *The Continuum Dictionary of Religion* (New York: Crossroad/Continuum, 1994); published in Britain as *The Macmillan Dictionary of Religion* (London: Macmillan, 1994); xiii & 319 pages; no index; general bibliography, pp. 303-19.

□ *Scope* A distinguished British comparatist has edited a compact GLOSSARY of over five thousand terms. Unsigned brief entries define movements, deities, a few places and above all concepts. Certain longer articles specify bibliography. There is no WHO'S WHO, and new religious movements in the twentieth-century West hardly figure. Forty-three mostly British scholars serve as contributors. Entries on non-English concepts specify language of origin, and cross-references abound.

□ *Strengths* Averaging five to fifteen lines, definitions are formulated with utmost care. Translations of Asian terms are painstaking. The perspective is worldwide, encompassing Africa, the Pacific and Latin America as well as Europe and Asia. Overview articles cross-reference numerous others (e.g., on "African Religion," "Egyptian Religion," "High Gods"). A few issues of methodology elicit essays, as on "Comparative Religion" and "Psychology of Religion" but not on "History of Religions" or "Sociology of Religion." Although the tone is austere, information is, as the editor promises, "clearly and shrewdly presented" (p. xii). No other GLOSSARY commands greater authority.

□ *Weaknesses* This up-to-date reconceptualization of technical terms is marred by lack of signed entries and individual bibliographies. Only a few entries (e.g., "Confucianism," "Logocentrism" and "Shinto") pinpoint items in the general bibliography. Sixteen pages of English-language bibliography would have gained from being subdivided by religion. Sobriety of tone discourages browsing. All of these disadvantages would quickly be forgotten, however, if only non-English-language terms had carried a key to pronunciation.

□ *Competitors* The major competitor remains **1** Parrinder, *A Dictionary of Non-Christian Religions* (1971), whose entries are longer, meatier and illustrated but rather dated. **11** Hexham, *Concise Dictionary of Religion* (1992) is more provocative, at times needlessly so, and occasionally slipshod. On Christianity **8** MacGregor, *Dictionary of Religion and Philosophy* (1989, 1991) remains far livelier. Professionals will find *The Continuum Dictionary* refreshingly up-to-date apart from omission of new religious movements in the West. No doubt shorter articles in Jonathan Z. Smith, ed., *The HarperCollins Dictionary of Religion* (1995) will compete with it. Happily, the latter also indicates pronunciation of foreign terms.

□ *Summary* This GLOSSARY of the world's religions is the most painstaking currently available but not the most enticing.

14 ([1992] 1994) Ian Harris et al., eds., *Longman Guide to Living Religions* (London: Longman Current Affairs, 1994); paperback; xvi & 278 pages; no index; no bibliography. Reprinted from pp. 69-386 of Harris et al., eds., *Contemporary Religions: A World Guide* (London: Longman Current Affairs, 1992); xii & 511 pages.

□ *Critique* Forty-five British scholars collaborated in this DICTIONARY of contemporary religious movements worldwide. About six hundred entries identify religions and their splinterings. The "Introductory Classification" (pp. x-xvi) clusters entries under ten major religions, including no less than seventy-seven movements for Buddhism and ninety for Islam. The full edition of 1992 includes a country-by-country summary (pp. 387-488). The writing is crisp throughout. Although entries go unsigned, authorship is attributed on pages v-ix. John J. Shepherd writes provocatively on both Islamic and New Age groups, while Ninian Smart surveys geo-religious anomalies (pp. 1-10). No other work so painstakingly differentiates contemporary subgroups within major religions.

□ *Summary* This DICTIONARY maps about six hundred subgroups of the world's religions. It furnishes a reliable starting point, particularly for social scientists.

1.2 COMPENDIA

OVERVIEW: A GENRE THAT EN-COURAGES REVISIONISM Study of the world's religions lends itself to COMPENDIA. Topnotch scholars put their best efforts into summarizing a tradition, often delivering original insights and choice bibliography. COMPENDIA invite REVISIONISM. Compilers of reference bibliographies too often ignore these volumes, many of which rank among the meatiest anywhere. Among English-language works **21** Sutherland et al., eds., *The World's Religions* (1988) stands out.

LIST OF WORKS ANALYZED

15 (1969-71) C. Jouco Bleeker and Geo Widengren, eds., *Historia Religionum: Handbook for the History of Religions*, 2 vols. (Leiden: Brill, 1969-71)

16 (1970-76) Henri-Charles Puech, ed., *Histoire des religions*, 3 vols. (Paris: Gallimard, 1970-76); published as vols. 29, 34 and 40 in the series "Encyclopédie de la pléiade."

17 (1974) Isma'il Ragi al Faruqi and David Sopher, eds., *Historical Atlas of the Religions of the World* (New York: Macmillan, 1974)

18 (1984) John R. Hinnells, ed., *A Handbook of Living Religions* (London and New York: Viking, 1984; London: Penguin Books, 1991)

19 (1982) *Eerdmans' Handbook to the World's Religions* (Grand Rapids, Mich.: Eerdmans, 1982); published in Britain as *The Lion Handbook to the World's Religions* (Tring: Lion Publishing, 1982)

20 (1987) Peter Bishop and Michael Darton, eds., *The Encyclopedia of World Faiths: An Illustrated Survey of the World's Living Religions* (New York: Facts on File, 1987)

21 (1988) Stewart Sutherland, Leslie Houlden, Peter Clarke and Friedhelm Hardy, eds., *The World's Religions* (London: Routledge; Boston: G. K. Hall, 1988)

22 (1990) Charles Baladier, ed., *Le Grand Atlas des religions* (Paris: Encyclopaedia Universalis, 1990)

23 (1992-) Julien Ries, ed., *Traité d'anthropologie du sacré*, planned in 7 vols. (Paris: Desclée, 1992-)

24 (1993) Joanne O'Brien and Martin Palmer, *The State of Religion Atlas* (New York and London: Simon & Schuster, 1993)

25 (1993) Arvind Sharma, ed., *Our*

Religions (San Francisco: Harper, 1993)

26 (1993) H. Byron Earhart, ed., *Religious Traditions of the World: A Journey Through Africa, Mesoamerica, North America, Judaism, Christianity, Islam, Hinduism, Buddhism, China, and Japan* (San Francisco: Harper, 1993)

27 (1993) Peter B. Clarke, ed., *The World's Religions: Understanding the Living Faiths* (Pleasantville, N.Y.: Reader's Digest; London: Marshall Editions, 1993)

28 (1993) Jean Delumeau, ed., *Le Fait religieux* (Paris: Fayard, 1993)

ANALYSIS OF WORKS

15 (1969-71) C. Jouco Bleeker [1898-1973] and Geo Widengren, eds., *Historia Religionum: Handbook for the History of Religions,* 2 vols. (Leiden: Brill, 1969-71); viii & 691; vi & 715 pages; two indexes (authors and subjects), 2:652-715; no general bibliography.

□ *Scope* This COMPENDIUM of thirty-two signed chapters examines ancient religions in volume 1 and living religions in volume 2. It imposes on each author a schema of seven rubrics: "Essence," "History," "Conception of Deity," "Worship," "Conception of Man," "Influence or Present Situation," "History of the Study." Sections on "Essence" propound striking characterizations and comparisons. Only rarely has the section on history of (Western) study of a religion been superseded. The first half of volume 1 canvasses the Near East with separate chapters on Egypt, Mesopotamia, Syria, the Hittites, Iran and Israel (1:40-376). Thereafter Greek, Roman, Hellenistic, Gnostic and Manichaean religions receive full chapters (1:377-610). Religions of the ancient Germans, Celts and Slavs are paired briefly with those of ancient Mexico and ancient Peru (1:611-91). Volume 2 devotes separate chapters to Judaism, Christianity, Islam, Zoroastrianism, Hinduism, Jainism and Buddhism while grouping "Religions of China" and "Religions of Japan" into single chapters. Ninety pages on "Religions of Illiterate People" (2:550-641) culminate with Geoffrey Parrinder's survey of the history

of the field (2:629-41). Indexes of names and subjects are comprehensive.

□ *Strengths* To varying degrees thirty-two contributors from fifteen countries acquiesced in the seven-part schema. R. J. Zwi Werblowsky surveys Judaism with his accustomed acumen (2:1-48), expanding on S. R. Hirsch's aphorism, "The catechism of the Jew is his calendar." Annemarie Schimmel's eighty-five pages on Islam (2:125-210) exhilarate, culminating in eight pages on the history of Western study of Islam. Carlo dell Casa's twenty-five pages on Jainism (2:346-71) likewise excel at compression. Jean Doresse's chapter on "Gnosticism" (1:533-79) manages to avoid overlap with his longer treatment in 16 Puech, ed., *Histoire des religions.* Duchesne-Guillemin on "The Religion of Ancient Iran" (1:323-76) climaxes with a discussion of its later influence (1:369-74). The longest chapter is R. N. Dandekar's history of Hinduism (2:237-345), which emphasizes conceptions of deity and man but ignores the history of the study of Indian religion. Alex Wayman's survey of Buddhism (2:372-464) in India, Sri Lanka and Southeast Asia (excluding Tibet) contains spectacular bibliography. A unique contribution is Geo Widengren's "Prolegomena," which compares source-criticism concerning dates of great founders (1:1-22). Multilingual bibliographies are ample but not as copious as in 16 Puech, ed., *Histoire des religions* (1970-76).

□ *Weaknesses* Arguably this HANDBOOK emerged at just the wrong time. It sums up research from the late 1960s without, however, anticipating future directions, particularly in the social sciences. History of religion devoid of sociology and anthropology now seems naive. Some contributors went on to do major work (e.g., Werblowsky, Schimmel, Boyce, Parrinder), while others soon handed off to the next generation. Of only a few chapters can it be said that they rank among the best ever on their topic (e.g., Werblowsky on Judaism, Schimmel on Islam and Dell Casa on Jainism). Some chapters are too brief: Carmen Blacker's thirty-five pages on all the religions of Japan performs a tour de force but ought to have been at least twice as long. Coverage of indigenous religions is spotty and out of date. Polynesia, Indonesia and Tibet scarcely get mentioned. Sikhism is ignored. This HANDBOOK looks backward rather than forward. It lacks a GLOSSARY and makes no attempt to characterize the history of religion as a whole.

□ *Competitors* Published almost simultaneously with **16** Puech, ed., *Histoire des religions* (1970-76), *Historia Religionum* has aged less well. Brilliant writing and unequaled depth of primary sources keeps *Histoire des religions* useful, whereas *Historia religionum* seems a monument to a bygone era. Even so, its recapitulations of the history of the study of each field remain unsurpassed. **5** Eliade, ed., *The Encyclopedia of Religion* (1987) has supplanted most chapters but does not always match the initial characterization of a religion. **7** Cancik et al., eds., *Handbuch religionswissenschaflicher Grundbegriffe* (1988-) probes concepts and methodologies in greater depth and with up-to-date bibliographies but does not tackle individual religions.

□ *Summary* On the cusp between historicism and pluralism, the year 1970 marked a turning point in religious studies. By neglecting sociology and anthropology, no HANDBOOK from that year can hope to survive. Nonetheless, in this one preliminary characterizations of each religion, histories of each field and certain chapters deserve sampling.

16 (1970-76) Henri-Charles Puech [1902-1986], ed., *Histoire des religions*, 3 vols. (Paris: Gallimard, 1970-76); published as vols. 29, 34 and 40 in the series "Encyclopédie de la pléiade"; xxxii & 1488; x & 1596; viii & 1460 pages; maps and analytical table of contents in each volume; four indexes (names, places, deities and book titles) in each volume; no general bibliography.

□ *Scope* This magisterial COMPENDIUM examines religions of the world in ninety-six chapters by sixty authorities, each with lengthy multilingual bibliography. Although the authors are mostly French, the approach is anything but Eurocentric. Volume 1 covers ancient religions of the Slavs,

Balts, Celts and Japanese in twenty chapters. The final six chapters in volume 1 cover Hinduism, Jainism (in forty pages by Colette Caillat), Taoism and Buddhism (in three chapters totaling 170 pages). Volume 2 opens with ten chapters on Mazdaism, mystery religions, postcaptivity Judaism, Christianity, Gnosticism, Hermeticism, Mandeism, Manichaeism and Islam. There follow seven chapters on Christianity and four on various of its offshoots (e.g., esotericism, spiritualism and freemasonry). These 650 pages on Christianity and its progeny constitute a book in themselves. Volume 3 opens with eleven chapters on Tibet, Sri Lanka, China, Vietnam (with ten pages on Cao Dai), Korea and Japan (including twenty pages on new religions). Eight chapters on "Peoples without Written Tradition" furnish 130 pages by Ake Hultkrantz on pre-Columbian and Native American religions as well as chapters on North Africa, Oceania, Siberia and Arctic peoples (the latter with six pages of bibliography). André Leroi-Gourhan contributes twenty-five pages of "Hypotheses on Pre-history." The final seven chapters examine "Religious Movements Born of Acculturation [i.e., Encounter]" in North and South America, Indonesia, Melanesia, Polynesia and Africa. Multilingual bibliographies average two to three pages and cite, where appropriate, items in Asian and native languages.

□ *Strengths* This masterwork is the fullest and in many ways the subtlest COMPENDIUM on the world's religions. With the possible exception of **259** Bonnefoy/Doniger, eds., *Mythologies* (1981, 1991) no other reference work juggles so many primary sources or explores such an array of cultures. No other stimulates so consistently on ancient and modern, Eastern and Western, universal and tribal religions.

Many chapters deserve the label REVISIONIST. Among the most exhilarating are Toufic Fahd's 250 pages on "The Birth of Islam" (2:646-96) and "Islam and Islamic Sects" (3:3-179). He emphasizes how closely pre-Islamic Arabia resembled pre-Israelite Canaan. Henri-Charles Puech's

120 pages on Manichaeism (2:523-645) harvest a lifetime of research and reflection. Jean Doresse's chapter on Gnosticism (2:364-429) abounds in quotations from the sources and climaxes in six pages of bibliography. His chapter on "Egyptianizing Hermeticism" (2:430-97) is even more original and boasts five pages of bibliography. Jules Leroy on "Non-Orthodox Eastern Churches" (2:869-910) traces seven churches from the fourth century to the present and includes bibliography for each. Olivier Clément on "The Orthodox Church" (2:1014-48) illuminates the *filioque* controversy by criticizing the West for subordinating the Holy Spirit (i.e., spontaneity) to the Son (i.e., the church). As a pupil of Vladimir Lossky (1903-58), Clément has become a leading lay theologian of Eastern Christianity. Jean Séguy puts on parade Western nonconformists from Marcion to today's Pentecostalists (2:1229-303). Antoine Faivre's sixty pages on Christian esotericism from Paracelsus to the 1950s (2:1304-62) encompass almost two hundred figures mentioned hardly anywhere else except in his updated *Access to Western Esotericism* (Buffalo, N.Y.: SUNY Press, 1994).

Filling nine hundred pages, twenty chapters on ancient religions offer the fullest tableau of extinct religions to be found in a single volume. Seven chapters in volume 3 on religions born of encounter ("acculturation") are more intimately researched than in any other reference book. Roger Bastide on Afro-American cults (with bibliography on twelve different regions, 3:1027-50) and Georges Balandier on North Africa (3:1243-76) rank as seminal. K. O. L. Burridge's eighty pages on Melanesia and Polynesia weigh ethnographic, Marxist and Hegelian interpretations of cargo cults against evidence from a dozen islands (3:1142-219). A major attraction is lucidity of style. The writing displays a sobriety and polish that make English COMPENDIA like **21** Sutherland (1988) seem breezy and Germanic ones like **15** Bleeker (1969-71) seem ponderous. Jargon and presentism are avoided. Each volume outlines its articles through

at least fifty pages of the "Analytical Table of Contents." Bibliographies are richer than in almost any other reference work, including **5** Eliade, ed., *The Encyclopedia of Religion* (1987). Four indexes in each volume stand unrivaled, and an index of book titles (all in French) is unique. An index of names furnishes dates and brief description, comprising a 110-page WHO'S WHO.

□ *Weaknesses* Allocation of topics among the volumes does not leap out, and no table of contents embraces all three. A decision to place ancient religions in volume 1 and contemporary religions in volume 3 means that material on major regions extends through the three. Although chapters on new religious movements in volume 3 (1976) need updating, they have not been superseded (particularly on Polynesia and Indonesia). The emphasis on history of religion means that social sciences get scanted. Living up to its title, *Histoire des religions* delivers humanists' accounts of the world's religions, not social scientists' reinterpretations of them. Prolegomena on "What Is Religion?" by Angelo Brelich (1:3-59) and an overview of "The History of Religions" by Michel Meslin (3:1279-1328) yield to articles in **5** Eliade, ed., *The Encyclopedia of Religion* (1987) and offer either no bibliography or a francocentric one. The volumes lack a GLOSSARY.

□ *Competitors* With sixty authors writing ninety-six chapters in forty-six hundred pages, this comprises the grandest and deepest COMPENDIUM of the world's religions. Source material sprinkled throughout three hundred pages of bibliography raises synthesis to new heights. *Histoire des religions* outdoes **5** Eliade, ed., *The Encyclopedia of Religion* (1987) at expounding history of individual religions and supplying bibliography but does not match it in (1) untangling technical terms, (2) tracing the history of the study of religion or (3) expounding recent methodologies. Devotees of *The Encyclopedia of Religion* will find *Histoire des religions* often better informed and more searching but devoid of North American perspective. The fourteen hundred pages of **15** Bleeker and Widengren's *Historia Religionum* (1969-71) contain about two-fifths of the bulk and share only three of the same contributors (Vyncke on the Slavs, Doresse on Gnosticism, Duchesne-Guillemin on Iran). Although more logically arranged, its thirty-two chapters do not cover the Third World in depth, ignore new religious movements and supply briefer bibliographies.

Volume 1 of *Historia religionum* on extinct religions does not tackle either the Minoans or the Etruscans, each of whom receive thirty-five pages in *Histoire des religions*. Far less ambitious (at only one-fourth the length), 21 Sutherland et al., eds., *The World's Religions* (1988) omits ancient religions, tends toward presentism and condenses bibliographies. REVISIONIST in methodology, it is thin on new religious movements. *Histoire des religions* formulated the richest account of the world's religions before postmodernism revolutionized discourse. 22 Baladier, ed., *Le Grand atlas des religions* (1990) invited a new generation of French scholars to update research in briefer compass. It is rewarding to compare both works with an ongoing COMPENDIUM, 23 Julien Ries, ed., *Traité d'anthropologie du sacré*, planned in 7 vols. (Paris: Desclée, 1992-). The latter upholds Mircea Eliade's methodology monotonously.

□ *Summary Histoire des religions* remains unexcelled as a COMPENDIUM of the history of religions. Sober yet luminous, it boasts more than its share of the best chapters ever written on major and minor religions.

17 (1974) Isma'il Ragi al Faruqi and David Sopher, eds., *Historical Atlas of the Religions of the World* (New York: Macmillan, 1974); xviii & 346 pages; 65 maps; black-and-white photographs in the text; chronologies, pp. 283-322; two indexes (subjects and proper names), pp. 323-46; no general bibliography.

□ *Critique* This COMPENDIUM of twenty signed articles on past and present religions deploys an ATLAS of sixty-five maps that trace their spread. Fifteen authorities, six of them Asian, narrate the history of their own traditions, each with English-language bibliography. Major authorities

number C. Wei-hsun Fu on China, Joseph Kitagawa on Japan, John Mbiti on Africa and Weston La Barre on North American Indians. Four scholars from South Asia canvass the subcontinent. Isma'il al Faruqi writes on ancient Mesopotamia and Egypt as well as Zoroastrianism and Islam. These articles comprise the germ of what later became his **200** *Cultural Atlas of Islam* (1986). Writing as a committed Muslim, he asserts that Islamic faith underwent no evolution because "Islam was whole and complete at birth" (p. 258). What evolved was "Muslimness," understood as adherents' response to the call of the divine. Al Faruqi takes seriously Zoroastrian theology, viewing that religion as a transmitter of South Asian ideas into Iran. Throughout, articles are clearly subdivided and unusually comprehensive. Edited by David Sopher, the maps attach detailed captions to cover such matters as "The Jewish Diaspora in Roman Times c. 100-400 C.E.," "Buddhism in China," "Japan: Places of Religious Importance" and "Islamic Schools of Law, Sects, and Reform Movements." While later COMPENDIA like **21** Sutherland et al., eds., *The World's Religions* (1988) have supplanted the articles, the maps remain unexcelled. Their usefulness makes one wonder why no one has undertaken a full-scale HISTORICAL ATLAS of the world's religions.

□ *Summary* Overviews by scholars from the world's major religions seem dated, but the maps have no peer. A more ambitious HISTORICAL ATLAS of the world's religions is badly needed.

18 (1984) John R. Hinnells, ed., *A Handbook of Living Religions* (London and New York: Viking, 1984; London: Penguin Books, 1991); 528 pages; general bibliography, p. 499; index, pp. 501-28; more than one hundred maps and diagrams in the text.

□ *Scope* This COMPENDIUM enlisted seventeen mostly British specialists to write sixteen chapters on living religions today. Emphasis falls not on history but on twentieth-century beliefs and practices. Alan Unterman on Judaism, Andrew Walls on Christianity, Mary Boyce on Zoroastrianism, Owen Cole on Sikhism and J. Gordon Melton on alternative religions rank among the best known contributors. Each chapter surveys history before outlining contemporary worship, doctrine and sects. Every chapter furnishes extensive English-language bibliography. Maps, charts and diagrams abound, including flow charts of sects and floor plans of places of worship.

□ *Strengths* This COMPENDIUM delivers skillful syntheses. In sixty-five pages on Christianity Andrew Walls integrates a vast sweep, unfurling cunning diagrams on Eastern Christianity (p. 99), Protestant Christianity (p. 108) and theology (derived from William Perkins of the sixteenth century, pp. 76-77). Walls differentiates seven blocs of traditions: Eastern, Oriental, Latin, Northern, African, other Southern and Marginal. Alford T. Welch's fifty pages on Islam recount beginnings, classify sects, unravel the calendar and climax with chronology and massive bibliography. Denis MacEoin's twenty-five pages on Baha'i are among the meatiest to be found anywhere, enhanced by a diagram of the "Baha'i View of History" (p. 480). As regards Hinduism, Simon Weightman outlines Western approaches, differentiates urban and village practices and narrates the Hindu renaissance. He captions seven pages of drawings of Hindu cult images (pp. 198-99, 201-5). Kendall W. Folkert's twenty pages on Jainism illuminate sources, history of study, history of the religion and twentieth-century practices. With too little space to tackle all regions in depth, in sixty-five pages on Buddhism L. S. Cousins classifies the schools adeptly. Michael Saso on Chinese religions summarizes basics of the "Chinese Religious System" with splendid bibliography (pp. 349-55). David Reid's chapter on Japan climaxes with five pages of bibliography, particularly on new religions. Within a chapter on "Religions in Primal Societies" Joseph Epes Brown synthesizes North American Indian religions, furnishing a four-page chart of tribes and languages, while others survey the Pacific and Africa. Compressing his various DICTIONARIES (pp. 165, 173, 174), J. Gordon Melton sketches a taxonomy of seven

"families" of "Modern Alternative Religions in the West." Diagrams in each chapter are unsurpassed.

□ *Weaknesses* This is not quite the HANDBOOK that the title promises. Foreign-language bibliography is missing, and synopses of the history of study of each field are either too brief or lacking altogether. Ingenious though classifications may be, there is hardly any REVISIONISM. Rather, this COMPENDIUM dispenses information about how religions function for believers today. History is abbreviated, but festivals, liturgies and architecture attain surprising depth. Designed to complement a GLOSSARY (**3** Hinnells's *The Penguin Dictionary of Religions* [1984, 1995]), this work eschews defining terms.

□ *Competitors* Intended for specialists more than generalists, this COMPENDIUM overflows with information on present-day functioning of the world's religions. No other English-language reference work focuses so intently on twentieth-century beliefs, practices and demography worldwide. In contrast to the sobriety of Hinnells's *Handbook*, **21** Sutherland et al., eds., *The World's Religions* (1988) overflows with new hypotheses. Two illustrated COMPENDIA, **20** Bishop and Darton, eds., *The Encyclopedia of World Faiths* (1987) and **27** Clarke, ed., *The World's Religions* (1993) are more INTRODUCTORY. *A Handbook of Living Religions* excels at diagrams that illuminate fuller treatments found in **5** Eliade, ed., *The Encyclopedia of Religion* (1987). The latter does not always supply superior bibliographies.

□ *Summary* This fact-crammed volume arrays information in novel patterns but eschews REVISIONISM. Diagrams of places of worship, genealogies of sects and world-views will instruct everyone.

19 (1982) *Eerdmans' Handbook to the World's Religions* (Grand Rapids, Mich.: Eerdmans, 1982); published in Britain as *The Lion Handbook to the World's Religions* (Tring: Lion Publishing, 1982); 448 pages; index, pp. 438-47; glossary, pp. 389-436; over 200 color and black-and-white photographs; no bibliography.

□ *Scope* This INTRODUCTORY COMPEN-

DIUM canvasses world religions past and present in articles written by fifty-two mostly British contributors. Some essays are confessionally neutral (e.g., on Sikhs, Parsis, Jains, China, Japan), while others lapse into Christian apologetics (e.g., on Hinduism, Judaism, Christianity). Some articles run twenty pages, while many offer one- or two-page summaries like Harold Turner's "Holy Places, Sacred Calendars" or Eric Sharpe's "Six Major Figures in Religious Studies." Such miniarticles excel at popularization.

Six divisions allocate the material as follows: (1) the "Development of Religion" furnishes a virtuosic overview of methodology by Douglas Davies and a masterful survey of "Religion Before History" by Ake Hultkrantz; (2) "Ancient Religions" delivers articles on ten cultures, including pre-Columbian, Mesopotamian, Egyptian, Zoroastrian (by John Hinnells), Greek and Roman, Norse (by Andrew Walls) and Central Asian (by Ake Hultkrantz); (3) the "Primal Religions" features twelve case studies of two pages each, ranging from Orissa, the Philippines, Korea and Papua New Guinea through the Maoris, Australia's aborigines, and Madagascar to Africa, North America and the Andes; (4) "Living Religions of the East" examines Hinduism, the Sikhs (by Douglas Davies), the Jains, the Parsis (by John Hinnells), Buddhism (by Wulf Merz), Chinese religion and Japanese religion (by Michael Pye); (5) "People of a Book" covers Judaism (pp. 272-306) and Islam (pp. 307-34) in fourteen articles each; (6) "Religion: or the Fulfillment of Religion?" pleads the uniqueness of Christianity in sixteen articles (pp. 335-88). A "Rapid Fact-Finder" (pp. 390-436) comprises a GLOSSARY and WHO'S WHO with twelve hundred entries of three to ten lines each. There are no bibliographies. Two hundred illustrations, half of them in color, feature maps, emblems and scenes of worship that are deftly integrated into the text.
□ *Strengths* This COMPENDIUM introduces many of the world's religions. Major scholars contribute articles that are first-rate. John Hinnells writes with his accustomed finesse about Zoroastrianism and the Par-

sis; Andrew Walls contributes incisively on "Religions of Northern Europe"; Ake Hultkrantz writes magisterially on prehistory and Central Asia; Michael Pye's ten pages on Japan are unusually comprehensive. On Islam Montgomery Watt lucidly discusses "The Way of the Prophet," and David Kerr expounds Islamic worship with sympathy. But Lothar Schmalfuss offers just one page on "Islamic Science, Art, and Culture." Religions of smaller groups win exemplary coverage. Twelve case studies of primal religion span the globe. The Mandeans are mentioned as surviving Gnostics (p. 110), and there is an essay on two Vietnamese religious movements: Cao Dai and Hoa Hao (pp. 243-44). Whether discussing the past or the present, nearly all chapters portray religion as part of daily life. Catchy phrases like the "cosmic battle" in Zoroastrianism or the question "Is Hinduism one faith or many?" will intrigue beginners. No other INTRODUCTION except 27 Clarke, ed., *The World's Religions: Understanding the Living Faiths* (1993) offers so many photographs (particularly of worship) or integrates them so tidily into the text. A chart on "The Historical Development of the World's Religions and Civilizations" (pp. 40-41) and another on "Branches of the Church" (pp. 354-55) are gems. A "Basic Fact-Finder" supplies succinct definitions and cross-references. It would be useful in pamphlet form.
□ *Weaknesses* About half of the articles lack confessional neutrality. No representative of any religion but Christianity writes on his own tradition. Essays on Judaism too obviously come from Christians. The weakest sections, the ones that discuss Christianity, are spoiled by proselytizing zeal. Evangelical thrust also surfaces in Wulf Metz's rebuttal to the "Appeal of Buddhism in the West" (p. 242). Raymond Hammer's essays on Hinduism emphasize diversity without adducing the unity of the "eternal tradition." A besetting weakness is utter lack of bibliography. The title notwithstanding, this is anything but a HANDBOOK in the German sense because it cites no secondary works. Non-Christians will want to use *Eerdmans' Handbook* selec-

tively, if at all. This is an INTRODUCTORY COMPENDIUM, in which certain articles excel and others exude evangelical zeal.

□ *Competitors* This is an INTRODUCTION written for believing Christians. Although at least half the authors display confessional neutrality, rival volumes feature nothing else. **20** Bishop and Darton, eds., *The Encyclopedia of World Faiths* (1987) covers only living religions and on a more advanced level while distilling more cross-religious comparisons. **27** Peter B. Clarke, ed., *The World's Religions* (1993) is more lavishly illustrated but more cursory. Both of these provide excellent bibliographies. **21** Sutherland et al., eds., *The World's Religions* (1988) is a gold mine of sophistication, far more searching than any other recent COMPENDIUM on world religions. The *Eerdmans' Handbook* originated in Britain at the evangelical publishing house Lion. Another Lion handbook, *The History of Christianity* (1977, 1990), cuts rather more deeply but likewise omits bibliography. At bottom, the *Eerdmans' Handbook* is designed to help believing Christians "encounter" twenty-five other religions, but too few entries encourage inquiring further.

□ *Summary* Excelling in chapters written by major authorities, elsewhere this COMPENDIUM indulges in Christian apologetics. Superb photographs scarcely compensate for lack of bibliography.

20 (1987) Peter Bishop and Michael Darton, eds., *The Encyclopedia of World Faiths: An Illustrated Survey of the World's Living Religions* (New York: Facts on File, 1987); 352 pages; index, pp. 346-52; general bibliography, pp. 324-26; glossary, pp. 327-45; 64 pages of color photographs; black-and-white photographs and maps throughout.

□ *Scope* This lavish COMPENDIUM enlisted thirty-five British authorities to write unsigned articles on the history of twelve major religions as well as new religious movements. Eight portfolios of colored photographs carry ample captions such as "Faith and Life," "Religious Leaders, Prophets, and Teachers," "Death and the Afterlife," "Gods and Gurus," "Festivals,"

"Myths and Legends," "Worship" and "The Life Cycle." Articles go unsigned, but a list of contributors links authors to chapters.

□ *Strengths* Although illustrated COMPENDIA on the world's religions have proliferated, this stands as one of the most scholarly. Noted authorities recount the history of the major religions. Peter Bishop writes an illuminating introduction on "The Nature of Religion" that invokes Ninian Smart's six dimensions (myth, doctrine, ritual, institutions, ethics, experience). Bishop's conclusion, "Religion in the Modern World," traces interaction between India and the West as well as other interfaith encounters. At the heart of the book lie fourteen chapters on major religions written by leading scholars: Mary Boyce on Zoroastrianism, Owen Cole on Sikhism, Montgomery Watt on Islam, Ursula King on Hinduism and Jainism, and Eileen Barker on "New Religious Movements in Western Society." Seventy pages on Christianity deploy no fewer than twenty experts to describe twenty different traditions. Quakers, Unitarians, Seventh-day Adventists, Jehovah's Witnesses, Christian Scientists and Mormons each receive a page or two on doctrine, worship and organization. Eight color portfolios are a model of their kind. The images startle, the captions burst with information, and the juxtapositions exhilarate. These are among the finest photo-essays in any reference work.

□ *Weaknesses* Although most articles trace history, no extinct religions figure. Allocation of space may displease some. Mahinda Palihawanda's five pages on "Theravada Buddhism" skim over regional variations, while Andrew Rawlinson's twenty-five pages on "Mahayana Buddhism" emphasize China and Tibet at the expense of Japan. Jack Thompson's five pages on "New Religious Movements among Primal Peoples" broach a neglected topic, however briefly.

□ *Competitors* This COMPENDIUM by British academics holds it own among recent surveys of world religions. **27** Peter B. Clarke's *The World's Religions* (1993) is more INTRODUCTORY, not to say cursory, but contains illustrations, particularly cutaway diagrams of buildings that are even more graphic. In **21** *The World's Religions* (1988) Stewart Sutherland and company recruited an entirely different roster of forty-three mostly British authorities to write a work three times longer that favors REVISIONISM. **10** Eliade and Couliano, *The Eliade Guide to World Religions* (1991) includes extinct religions and massive bibliographies but lacks illustrations and can daunt the unwary.

□ *Summary* This expertly edited INTRODUCTION to the world's religions stimulates through luminous chapters and cunning illustrations. No other English-language reference work on world religions assembles color photographs so tellingly.

21 (1988) Stewart Sutherland, Leslie Houlden, Peter Clarke and Friedhelm Hardy, eds., *The World's Religions* (London: Routledge; Boston: G. K. Hall, 1988); xiv & 995 pages; index, pp. 967-95; no general bibliography.

□ *Scope* This REVISIONIST COMPENDIUM of fifty-eight chapters by forty-three (mostly British) scholars delivers up-to-date, often combative scholarship on living religions. Four editors divided the material into six headings. Sutherland edited four chapters on "Religion and the Study of Religions." Houlden edited fourteen chapters on "Judaism and Christianity." Peter Clarke edited three sections: thirteen chapters on "Islam," eight on "Traditional Religions" and six on "New Religious Movements." Friedhelm Hardy edited thirteen chapters on "The Religions of Asia." There are 170 pages on Christianity, 225 on Islam, 150 on Hinduism and 90 on Buddhism. Many of the chapters venture novel, even electrifying, interpretations that include English-language bibliography.

□ *Strengths* This is the most methodologically alert COMPENDIUM on the history of the world's religions. It consistently purveys REVISIONIST radicality. Writing for those who seek knowledge rather than faith (p. ix), the authors, who are mostly academics, adopt adventurous positions on historical questions great and small. Four

introductory chapters allow Peter Byrne to weigh definitions of religion, Stewart Sutherland to survey methods of study, and Anders Jeffner to reflect on "Religion and Ideology" and "Atheism and Agnosticism." He defines atheism as "an eternal companion to religion," which involves "a deliberate rejection of all the religious alternatives available at the time" (p. 52). Judaism wins only two chapters, the principal one by Rabbi Friedlander of the Westminster Synagogue, London, who offers a glowing conspectus of the past three centuries. William Frend writes on the first five centuries of Christianity, and Hugh Wybrew of the Anglican Cathedral, Jerusalem, on "Eastern Christianity since 451."

Five chapters on Christianity since 1500 canvass five regions: Africa, North America, Latin America, India and China. Notably provocative is Simon Barrington-Ward's chapter on "Christianity Today," which weighs possibilities for "reintegration" between "privately held traditional interpretations of life" and "the publicly accepted modern, secular atmosphere of a commercial city" (p. 288). Articles on Islam unfurl a tour d'horizon of North Africa, Iran, India, the Turks, China, Indonesia, the Middle East, Africa, Europe and North America. E. U. Kratz's thirty pages on Indonesia cut deep. Among the most original chapters is Friedhelm Hardy's account of "The Classical Religions of India." In ninety pages he characterizes an "eco-system of religions" that includes Vedic worship, "renouncer" traditions of Jainism and Buddhism, epic and Puranic religion and esoteric traditions. This bravura performance concludes with a splendid bibliography and leads into separate chapters on Shaivism, modern Hinduism and Sikhism. Alexis Sanderson's forty-five pages on Saivism and Tantrism explore how power centers (chakras) function in six different traditions, whose lineage he traces chiefly in Kashmir from the ninth century. Ten line drawings of statues and mandalas enhance vividness. Six chapters on Buddhism examine Nepal, China, Japan, Mongolia and Tibet (in thirty pages), but not Korea.

Each regional survey propounds both history and contemporary reportage. Chapters on "Traditional Religions" pull no punches. I. M. Lewis defines a shaman as one who must undergo three phases of "affliction, cure and control" (pp. 829-30) before tracing metaphors of equestrian and sexual origin in mystical possession. Six regional chapters encompass Australia, New Zealand, Africa, North America and Latin America. T. O. Ranger explains how African religions have adapted to Western ones, and Gordon Brotherstone probes Mesoamerican and Inca liturgies at the time of the conquest. Chapters on new religious movements trace filiations among them in North America (p. 918) and explore "Self-Religions" in Western Europe. Harold Turner's chapter on Africa differentiates four types of new religious movement: Neo-primal, Synthetist, Deviationist and Africanized. The book culminates with Bryan Wilson characterizing (for the umpteenth time) secularization. No other English-language COMPENDIUM proposes so many novel typologies and hypotheses. As befits what may be called a meta-handbook, this work bursts with imaginative interpretations.

□ *Weaknesses* Although many chapters recount history, none investigates extinct religions. A major omission involves China: Confucianism and popular religion are missing. Focus on religions that have survived into the modern world results in odd allocations. Zoroastrianism crops up among Asian religions, Mandeans are not mentioned, and Gnosticism gets short shrift. Withal, in "Mazdaism ('Zoroastrianism')" Julian Baldick sorts out controversies concerning history of Iranian religion. This provocative chapter relies on French scholars in preference to Mary Boyce's "highly romanticised picture of Mazdaism in contemporary Iran" (p. 567). Contentious interpretations mean that this REVISIONIST COMPENDIUM should be read with some understanding of standard views. The book will delight anyone who relishes controversies, even if it omits their history.

□ *Competitors* This REVISIONIST COMPEN-DIUM abandons the convention that a reference book must favor mainstream views. As a COMPENDIUM of recent scholarship on religions today, the work has no rival in reshaping whatever it discusses. It equals or surpasses **25** Sharma, ed., *Our Religions* (1993) in originality of formulations while encompassing many more religions. **18** John Hinnells, ed., *A Handbook of Living Religions* (1984) recruits an entirely different team of seventeen (mostly British) scholars to write a much soberer COMPEN-DIUM of living religions, albeit with longer bibliographies and more diagrams. Sutherland's contributors prove even more venturesome than most in **16** Puech, ed., *Histoire des religions* (1970-76). The latter is, to be sure, three times longer and includes extinct religions. Only **4** Poupard, ed., *Dictionnaire des religions* (1984, 1993) shows flashes of REVISIONISM. In contrast, **5** Eliade, ed., *The Encyclopedia of Religion* (1987) seldom dares exhilarating hypotheses. Moreover, *The World's Religions* is richer on topics like the Maoris, Shaivism, Christianity in India and China, and Islam in Indonesia. On almost every subject *The World's Religions* is more provocative. Almost invariably articles on world religions in LEXICONS like **2** Crim, ed., *The Perennial Dictionary of World Religions* (1981, 1989) are briefer and less penetrating. Even **6** Waldenfels, ed., *Lexikon der Religionen* (1987, 1992) seems pallid by comparison. Sutherland's volume boasts a less adventurous companion in the same format: **288** G. H. R. Parkinson, ed., *The Handbook of Western Philosophy* (1988).

□ *Summary* This exhilarating COMPEN-DIUM pioneers syntheses and appraisals across many fields. Boldness will stimulate and occasionally infuriate even the most jaded.

22 (1990) Charles Baladier, ed., *Le Grand Atlas des religions* (Paris: Encyclopaedia Universalis, 1990); 413 pages; glossary-index, pp. 395-411; classified bibliography, pp. 384-93; more than 500 color photographs.

□ *Critique* This REVISIONIST COMPEN-DIUM recruited 140 (mostly French) authorities, many of them social scientists, to analyze the world's religions under eight headings. The work scatters major religions across all headings: (1) "Contemporary Religion," (2) "Methodology," (3) "Comparisons Among the Major Religions," (4) "Gods," (5) "Scriptures," (6) "Organization," (7) "Practices" and (8) "Religious Experience." Islam and Christianity command far more attention than do Judaism or Zoroastrianism *(Mazdéisme)*, while Baha'i is missing. Hinduism and Buddhism blossom, but mythology is scanted. Focus on social science enhances topics like "Syncretisms" (pp. 130-45), "Religions and Sciences" (pp. 326-39) and history of scholarship within and about various religions (pp. 34-63). Five articles on how major religions interpret one another stand out (pp. 146-61). Each of 173 articles carries multilingual bibliography, much of it rare, adding up to almost three thousand titles (pp. 384-93). More than five hundred (mostly color) illustrations of religious practices are among the finest anywhere. Of all illustrated COMPENDIA, this one boasts the most subtle prose. A briefer and sometimes more original competitor (devoid of photographs) is **307** Clévenot, ed., *L'État des religions dans le monde* (Paris: La Découverte/Le Cerf, 1987). Both are highly intelligent.

□ *Summary* Coupling superb illustrations, REVISIONIST texts and incomparable bibliographies, this COMPENDIUM focuses the social sciences on religions worldwide. Few other works analyze religious practice so astutely.

23 ([1989] 1992-) Julien Ries, ed., *Traité d'anthropologie du sacré,* planned in 7 vols. (Paris: Desclée, 1992-); vol. 1, 358 pages; index to follow in vol. 7; general bibliography, 1:347-52. Translated from the Italian *Trattato di antropologia del sacro* (Milan: Jaca Book, 1989-), of which vols. 1-5 appeared 1989-92. Analyzed on the basis of vol. 1 in French and vols. 2-5 in Italian.

□ *Critique* This ambitious COMPENDIUM synthesizes French and Italian approaches to "study of the sacred" in all the world's religions. A priest at the University at Louvain-la-Neuve, Julien Ries (1920-)

founded there the Center for the History of Religions, which was intended to amplify the lifework of Mircea Eliade (1:27-54). The introduction (1:15-24) announces seven volumes of articles from fifty (mostly European) experts. Volume 1 delivers articles on methodology by Régis Boyer (the sacred), Gilbert Durand (symbolism) and Michel Delahoutre (art). Part 2 of volume 1 delivers overviews of paleolithic religion, ritual and "The Sacred and Death." Part 3 furnishes three weighty articles on religion in Africa. Volume 2 concerns India (by Jean Varenne) and ancient Iran (by Gherardo Gnoli) as well as Celtic, Germanic and Baltic Europe. Volume 3 spans the Mediterranean, and volume 4 East Asia, Australia and American Indians. Volume 5 recruits Pierre Lenhardt on Judaism and Roger Arnaldez on Islam. Contributors write with supreme self-confidence, largely ignoring American and British methodologies. Since the tone discourages debate, it is difficult to know how useful this enterprise will prove to any but Eliadeans.

□ *Summary* This COMPENDIUM brings French and Italian verve to an elaboration of Mircea Eliade's standpoint. Multilingual bibliographies excel.

24 (1993) Joanne O'Brien and Martin Palmer, *The State of Religion Atlas* (New York and London: Simon & Schuster, 1993); 128 pages; 34 full color maps; no index; no general bibliography.

□ *Scope* Deploying thirty-four maps (usually of the entire world), this ATLAS delineates the impact and outreach of seven major religions. Buddhism, Christianity, Hinduism, Sikhism, Judaism, Islam and Taoism (equated with Chinese popular religion) are profiled through maps (pp. 15-87) and detailed captions (pp. 96-126), each with up-to-date bibliography. A leading demographer, David B. Barrett of **32** *World Christian Encyclopedia* (1982), served as consultant. The writing is lucid, the cartography vivid. Even the best informed will find fresh pickings.

□ *Strengths* A unique feature, eight pages on "Fundamentals of Faith," compares (in three to five lines) the position of the seven religions concerning eight variables: the nature of God, the creation, time, life after death, sacred literature, prophets and founders, rites of birth and death, and festivals. Any observer of world religions will find this checklist provocative. Maps fall under six headings: "Past and Present," "Beliefs," "Reaching Out," "The State," "Challenges" and "Foundations." Maps 4-8 trace distribution of the seven religions; map 9 presents indigenous religions, map 10 new religious movements, map 12 "Faith in the Feminine" and map 13 agnostics and avowed atheists. Maps 14-16 chart Christian missions and radio broadcasting, while maps 17-19 identify sources of funding in Christianity and Islam. Maps 20-21 differentiate state involvement in religion, while map 25 depicts religion-generated wars. Maps 27-28 pinpoint interfaith and ecumenical contacts, and map 31 specifies regions of growth and decline worldwide. Maps 32-34 locate founders, holy cities and holy landscapes. Captions that range from a half to a full page supply sources.

□ *Weaknesses* This is not a HISTORICAL ATLAS. However much the maps vary, almost all describe the present. Although readers may deem entries comparing "Fundamentals of Faith" too telegraphic, no one has done such drastic epitomizing better. Shinto, Zoroastrianism and Baha'i receive no coverage. An index as well as a general bibliography would have helped.

□ *Competitors* This array of demographic information for a popular audience has no competitors. 17 Al Faruqi and Sopher, eds., *Historical Atlas of the Religions of the World* (1974) ignores the present, just as this work largely ignores the past. A book translated from the French covers some of the ground: Gerard Chaliand and Jean-Pierre Rageau, *The Penguin Atlas of Diasporas* (New York: Penguin Books, 1995). So-called ATLASES of individual traditions (Christianity, Judaism, Islam) do not adduce the contemporary data elaborated here. 307 Clévenot, ed., *L'État des religions dans le monde* (1987) amplifies statistics on about one hundred individual countries.

□ *Summary* This packaging of current geo-religious information will instruct beginners and masters alike. The maps delight the eye.

25 (1993) Arvind Sharma, ed., *Our Religions* (San Francisco: Harper, 1993); xi & 536 pages; no index; no general bibliography; also in paperback.

□ *Scope* The editor of this REVISIONIST COMPENDIUM invited seven luminaries to rethink how to teach their own tradition. They unfurl history and beliefs in sixty-five to seventy pages (except for one hundred pages on Islam) with annotated bibliography and notes. World-class scholars expound their own faith, balancing past and present, history and doctrine, affirmation and reinterpretation. Innovativeness lifts five of the seven articles, four of which concern Asian religions (Hinduism, Buddhism, Confucianism and Taoism) and three Abrahamic (Judaism, Christianity and Islam). By synthesizing previous scholarship, not least their own, the authors achieve marvels of acuity. Beginners and experts alike will feast. The seven articles need to be evaluated individually.

1. Hinduism. Wittiness enlivens Arvind Sharma's overview of Hinduism (pp. 1-68). Parading typologies, he distinguishes first two kinds of definition (ethnic versus universal) and then specifies three contemporary forms of Hinduism: absolute (e.g., Ramana Maharshi), theistic (e.g., Ramakrishna), and activistic (e.g., Gandhi). Spiritual superstructure is distinguished from "underlying social structure," and eight types of sacred literature get differentiated (pp. 26-33). An outline of history (pp. 35-44) precedes discussion of political issues and Hindu assimilation of non-Hindu practices (p. 59). Elucidating doctrine, history and contemporaneity alike, this may be the best intermediate-level introduction to Hinduism in English. It does not, however, appraise previous scholarship.

2. Buddhism. Arguably, Masao Abe faced the hardest task: to outline schools of Buddhism in sixty-five pages. He does so by substituting taxonomy for history. After expounding the triad of the Buddha, the Dharma and the Sangha (pp. 101-14), he dissects "Emptiness" imaginatively (pp. 114-24). Since his is the least original of the essays, it might have been better to allow someone else to write on Theravada to complement Japanese emphasis on Mahayana.

3. Confucianism. Tu Wei-ming achieves greater success in narrating twenty-five hundred years of Confucian thought (pp. 146-83). Having stipulated that Confucians possess no sacred history distinct from general history (p. 147), he lists "salient features" of Confucianism as (1) "Learning to Be Human," (2) "This-Worldliness," (3) "Transcendence in Immanence" and (4) "Human-Relatedness." Most cunningly, he expounds "Dynamics of the Family" as a springboard from which to appraise the "Confucian Hypothesis" concerning East Asian economic prowess (pp. 218-20). The hypothesis runs as follows: Confucian-derived values promote "superior self-knowledge and knowledge of others." A resulting "communalism based on an ever-expanding network of relationships" proves "highly compatible" with modernity (p. 219). No other reference work juxtaposes ancient and contemporary Confucian views so persuasively.

4. Taoism. Liu Xiaogan's sixty pages on Taoism demonstrate that "the more we know about Taoism, the more difficult it is to define it" (pp. 231-32). He scrutinizes Taoism as philosophy (pp. 240-54) and as religion (pp. 254-80), citing little known thinkers and comparing these two minority movements to Confucian and Buddhist majorities. This virtuosic chapter abounds in surprises.

5. Judaism. Three essays on Abrahamic religions are exceedingly diverse. Jacob Neusner synthesizes his own writing from the past twenty years on tension between the ethnic and the religious in Judaism. Insisting that one identify which questions a given people wants religion to answer, he argues that Judaism emerged after the return from Babylon (538 B.C.E.) as a vehicle to account for the "death and resurrection of Israel" (p. 319). After the temple in Jerusalem was destroyed by the Romans (70 C.E.), the Mishnah with its concept of

dual Torah reenvisioned Judaism without a temple, in which sanctification pertained above all to food and procreating. The Jerusalem Talmud (c. 400 C.E.) confronted a new situation in which a monopoly enjoyed by Christianity after 390 C.E. was making Judaism illicit. Jews now had to choose once and for all between God in heaven and an earthly ruler who was non-Jewish. In order to adjust to Christian society, the Jerusalem Talmud shifted concern from sanctifying activities to sanctifying the holy people itself.

In interpreting the epoch since 1789, Neusner traces how what he calls "Continuator Judaisms" (Orthodox, Reform and Conservative) began to posit a secular realm beyond themselves, thereby implying that traditional Judaism had comprised not a total way of life but merely a religion. Even more electrifying is Neusner's notion of three twentieth-century types of "Political Judaism": (1) Zionism, (2) Jewish Socialism cum Yiddish culture and (3) "Judaism of Holocaust and Redemption" (pp. 336-38). The latter, he avers, overarches all divisions within American Jewry by supplying "generative symbols of mythic proportions" centered in the destruction of European Jewry and the birth of the state of Israel. This pattern recapitulates the frame of exile and return that rabbinic Judaism had fashioned from the Babylonian captivity. As most American Jews retreat into desultory private celebrations, only the Orthodox give serious consideration to the sanctification of daily life. Neusner connects "private" or family Judaism (weddings, the Days of Awe and particularly Passover) with a Jew's self-image as "a post-Nazi member of a minority" who knows, as Moses did in Egypt, what Gentiles can do to Jews (p. 348). In a brilliant peroration Neusner argues that all Judaisms "precipitate and then assuage resentment" at being different. As the Torah teaches, "the Jews' difference is destiny: Holiness is in the here and now, salvation comes at the end of time. . . . Things have deep meaning now, and we will matter even more in time to come" (p. 351). Few summations of a major religion propound so many mind-opening syntheses.

6. *Christianity.* Of necessity, Harvey Cox prunes ruthlessly in order to squeeze Christianity into sixty-five pages. He traces history from Jesus to Nicaea (pp. 361-79), while scarcely mentioning heresies ("rifts"), and then sketches six exemplary lives. Mary, St. Francis and St. Joan of Arc rank as classics, and Dietrich Bonhoeffer, Simone Weil and Dorothy Day as contemporaries (pp. 379-93). Diversity notwithstanding, they all exemplify adherence to three constants: core ideas, community and the person of Jesus Christ. A section on the liturgical year and sacraments ("ordinances") precedes a brilliant conspectus of contemporary issues (pp. 406-19). Writing best about the twentieth century, Cox profiles Pentecostalism, liberation theologies, the new role of women and interactions with other religions. While downplaying history more than the other contributors, Cox injects originality through starkness of selection and shrewdness of cultural criticism.

7. *Islam.* In by far the longest contribution, Seyyed Hossein Nasr deviates from the others by denouncing prevailing assumptions about how to study religion (pp. 427-30, 519, 527-30). Construing Islam as a final revelation that claims to restore humankind's "Primordial Religion," Nasr insists that one accept the authenticity of revelation before expounding it. He scolds secularists and relativists for rejecting the very basis of Islam. True to his Iranian origins, on nearly every topic Nasr balances Sunni and Shi'ite perspectives, allowing the latter's "inwardness" to unfurl (pp. 454-55; 475-76; 506-8). Unmatched are accounts of the foundations of Islam (pp. 445-56), "Doctrines and Beliefs" (pp. 456-64) and particularly of seven civilizations in which Islam took root (pp. 484-503). In addressing "Islam and Other Religions" Nasr reaffirms the Qur'anic notion of the universality of revelation and lauds Frithjof Schuon for rephrasing this precept as "the transcendental unity of religion" (p. 522). While favoring "traditional Islam" over any form of modernism (pp. 518-19), Nasr chides

"revolutionary Fundamentalism" (of the Iranian sort) for manipulating European ideas and techniques in order to implement (an imperfect) return to Islamic norms and practices. Peerless exposition of both history and doctrine as well as his denunciation of Western relativism makes Nasr's essay reverberate. Some will reject the theology, but all will profit from power of synthesis and sympathy for Shi'ism. The essay climaxes an exhilarating volume.

□ *Weaknesses* In this REVISIONIST COMPENDIUM all the authors except perhaps Cox presuppose previous knowledge. No essay is easy, but all are superbly organized. Although bibliographies are up-to-date (if occasionally idiosyncratic, as in Cox and Nasr), the authors do not debate other scholars. One needs to consult 21 Sutherland et al., eds., *The World's Religions* (1988) for that. While history of Confucian, Taoist, Jewish and Islamic thought emerges clearly, Buddhism and Christianity have their history foreshortened. One wishes that a Zoroastrian like Farhang Mehr had participated. He could have broken new ground as Liu Xiaogan does on Taoism. The gap between Cox's mainstream-ism and Nasr's triumphalism is so enormous as to trivialize Sharma's half-page each of "Introduction" (p. xi) and "Conclusion" (p. 533). More of both are needed. Regarding format, the table of contents should have listed subdivisions of each essay. Some readers may regret the lack of maps and charts.

□ *Competitors* This collection by and for teachers of world religions stands alone among COMPENDIA. By inviting seven grand masters to rethink their traditions, the editor elicited a candor rarely encountered in reference works. All too seldom do believers speak so boldly in reference books. Of course, 21 Sutherland et al., eds., *The World's Religions* covers far more religions and debates alternative views more vigorously. Its ingenuity complements the intimacy and reflectiveness of *Our Religions.* More austere and recondite, 10 Eliade and Couliano, *The Eliade Guide* (1991) achieves even greater virtuosity, above all on Christianity. 26 Earhart, ed., *Religious Traditions of the World* (1985, 1993) focuses on regions (Africa, Mesoamerica, North America, China, Japan) as readily as on individual religions. There ethnographic description excludes believers from authorship (except on Judaism and Christianity). **20** Bishop and Darton, eds., *The Encyclopedia of World Faiths* (1987), like **27** Clarke, ed., *The World's Religions* (1993), is still more detached, even clinical, but compensates through lavish illustrations. *Our Religions* is a must for teachers because no other work expounds believers' insights so cogently or offers such thoughtful bibliographies. These deeply pondered essays propose myriad ways of reconfiguring tradition.

□ *Summary* This work brilliantly rethinks five of seven traditions (excepting Buddhism and Christianity). The originality of Sharma, Neusner and Nasr dazzles.

26 (1993) H. Byron Earhart, ed., *Religious Traditions of the World: A Journey Through Africa, Mesoamerica, North America, Judaism, Christianity, Islam, Hinduism, Buddhism, China and Japan* (San Francisco: Harper, 1993); xx & 1204 pages; index, pp. 1189-1204; no general bibliography; maps, charts and black-and-white photographs throughout.

□ *Scope* This TEXTBOOK/COMPENDIUM gathers ten monographs written by American teachers between 1984 and 1991. Intended above all for classroom use in the United States, the chapters balance history, structure ("overall unity") and present-day practices ("dynamics") in lucid if bland prose. Ethnographic description blossoms. Most of the authors highlight their own fieldwork among diverse tribes, such as Zulus, Yoruba, Shoshoni and Zuni, and in rural regions of Indonesia, India, Thailand, Taiwan and Japan. Study aids fill at least one hundred pages: each chapter furnishes maps, charts, chronology, glossary, English-language bibliography and in the case of Hinduism a list of "Deities, Powers, and Deified Heroes." Handsome layout enhances well-chosen black-and-white photographs.

□ *Strengths* Devised for American classrooms, ten monographs report field research in loving detail. The authors plead for acceptance of otherness by recounting their own attempts as outsiders to get to know insiders. Site-specific practices dominate E. Thomas Lawson's account of the Zulu and Yoruba, Ake Hultkrantz's narrative of his initiation into the Shoshoni and Zuni, and David Knipe's description of Hindu devotions and lives. David Carrasco's analysis of "History and Cosmovision" in Mexico among Aztec and Maya deepens evocation of today's practices surrounding the Virgin of Guadeloupe, the peyote cult and the Day of the Dead. The ethnography proves unforgettable. Daniel Overmyer emphasizes systematic interactions among religions in China, as H. Byron Earhart does among seven traditions in Japan. Frederick Denny's account of Islam in Indonesia, like Robert Lester's of Buddhism in rural Thailand and Byron Earhart's of Shinto in rural Japan, counteracts bookish recitals found elsewhere. This work evokes the local with an immediacy that will gratify field researchers and may unsettle students.

□ *Weaknesses* A certain asymmetry unbalances the whole. Eight of ten authors learned as adults the traditions they describe, whereas Michael Fishbane on Judaism and Sandra Sizer Frankiel on Christianity grew up in theirs. Frankiel's section on Christianity is ludicrously selective, concentrating on medieval pilgrimages (particularly to Campostella) and on the lives of Lyman Beecher and his daughter Harriet Beecher Stowe. The twentieth century is hardly mentioned. Michael Fishbane avoids such arbitrariness even though at the end he highlights just two cities: nineteenth-century Vilna, featuring Rabbi Elijah the Gaon and Rabbi Hayyim ben Isaac, and early twentieth-century Frankfurt, featuring Franz Rosenzweig and Martin Buber. The chapter on China covers the period before 1900 in far more detail than the years following it. Certain topics get short shrift: Tibet wins only one page and Zoroastrianism less than a page. Although totaling some twenty-five pages, bibliographies omit both foreign-language works and reference books.

□ *Competitors* Few other COMPENDIA deliver field studies. By elevating six tribes— two African, two ancient Mesoamerican and two Native American—to parity with universal religions, this TEXTBOOK/COMPENDIUM stands alone. The approach seems American in contrast to a British preference for sacred texts and colonial history as in **21** Sutherland et al., eds., *The World's Religions* (1988). The latter surveys whole continents and dissects previous scholarship but fails to personalize peoples or individuals. **20** Bishop and Darton., eds., *The Encyclopedia of World Faiths* (1987) is more succinct and omits primal religions. In contrast, **25** Sharma, ed., *Our Religions* (1993) serves teachers better than students and lacks instructional aids. Written from inside each tradition, it penetrates deeper than any of Earhart's essays except perhaps those of Carrasco on Mesoamerica, Hultkrantz on Native Americans and David Knipe on Hinduism. They combine history and ethnography superbly.

□ *Summary* Startlingly up-to-date, this TEXTBOOK/COMPENDIUM balances history with field investigations while spicing teaching aids with personal insight. The first three chapters on tribal religions have no parallel.

27 (1993) Peter B. Clarke, ed., *The World's Religions: Understanding the Living Faiths* (Pleasantville, N.Y.: Reader's Digest; London: Marshall Editions, 1993); 220 pages; index, pp. 214-19; general bibliography, pp. 212-13; glossary (micropaedia), pp. 202-11.

□ *Critique* This gorgeous COMPENDIUM integrates four hundred color photographs, forty-three maps and numerous charts into chapters introducing ten living religions. Eleven British authorities characterize Judaism, Christianity, Islam, Hinduism, Buddhism and Chinese religion in ten to forty-four pages. Shorter chapters discuss Zoroastrianism, Jainism, Sikhism and Shinto. Historical coverage narrates expansion throughout the world, profiling Christianity in Africa and India, Islam and Hinduism in Indonesia, and Buddhism in North America. A survey of Islam differentiates local traits in fifteen countries ranging from Morocco and Mali through Central Asia to Pakistan and Indonesia. Twenty pages on "China's Religious Tradition" show how Confucianism, Taoism, Buddhism and popular religion interpenetrate. Photographs adorn every page, depicting religious sites, art, practices and personalities. Although Christian, Islamic, Hindu and Buddhist art predominates, the photographs are largely unfamiliar and make all religions seem photogenic. Cutaway drawings dissect the temple in ancient Jerusalem, Chartres cathedral, the great mosque in Kairouan, Tunisia, and the Lakshmana temple in northern India. Bibliography is choice, particularly on Asian religions, and a "micropaedia" documents more than fifty new religious movements. By juxtaposing color photographs with maps, captions and narrative, this work sets a standard for integrating picture and text. Beginners and experts alike will revel.

□ *Summary* No other reference works evokes living religions so vividly. This visual feast functions superbly as a self-teacher.

28 (1993) Jean Delumeau, ed., *Le Fait religieux* (Paris: Fayard, 1993); 781 pages; no index; no general bibliography.

□ *Critique* Addressed to nonbelievers, this REVISIONIST COMPENDIUM enlists sixteen French authorities to write chapters (varying from ten to one hundred pages) on major religions today, including Jainism and Sikhism but not Zoroastrianism. Emphasis falls on continuities between origins and the past fifty years, buttressed with multilingual bibliographies. Four chapters on Christianity include two gems on beliefs and on Eastern Orthodoxy by Olivier Clément as well as Jean Rogues's brooding on the past thousand years of Catholicism. Maurice-Ruben Hayoun's fifty pages on Judaism and Azzedine Guellouz's eighty-five on Islam overflow with fresh facts and aperçus. These introductions rank among the best anywhere. In recounting Hindu practices (notably festivals and the role of women), Lakshmi Kapani keeps preconceptions of Westerners in view, while her chapter on Sikhism rebuts twin misconceptions that that religion is either a syncretism or a Hindu sect. Essays on Taoism by

Kristofer Schipper and on Confucianism by Léon Vandermeersch examine what Americans prefer to call "Chinese folk religion" and delineate revivals of it in Taiwan, Hong Kong and mainland China.

Issiaka-Prosper Laleye of Senegal scrutinizes myths and practices of traditional religions in West Africa (Yoruba, Dogon, Fali), emphasizing "ancestralization" and the role of women. He interprets independent churches like Kimbangism as halfway houses between traditional religion and Christianity. Henri Tincq compares "Integralisms" (a term he prefers to "fundamentalisms") in Christianity, Islam, Judaism and Hinduism, emphasizing diversity of political maneuver while lamenting lack of flexibility in ethics. Françoise Champion characterizes "eclecticism," "syncretism" and "do-it-yourself" (i.e., "bricolage") religions in western Europe. Imagination, lucidity and up-to-the-minute research make this COMPENDIUM a gold mine. Few other works address nonbelievers so explicitly or state continuities across millennia so succinctly. □ *Summary* Precocious Europeans assess religions worldwide in this REVISIONIST COMPENDIUM. No scholar of recent history can afford to neglect it.

2 CHRISTIANITY

OVERVIEW: CRITERIA OF CLASSIFICATION The abundance of reference works on the various denominations, periods and fields of Christianity necessitates care in classifying them. This directory generally respects the designations of editors who place terms like *history, theology, Bible, saints, ecumenism* or *spirituality* in titles. Under 2.4 "Christianity: Theology" and 2.9 "Christianity: Churches and Denominations" Protestant and Catholic works are separated, but nowhere else. Two series stand out. The 2.8 Westminster/SCM series of DICTIONARIES comprises ten volumes on various aspects of Christianity, and the 2.9.2.2 French Catholic MEGA-ENCYCLOPEDIAS comprise eight mammoth works, three of them still only half complete, totaling more than 130 volumes.

Each series is treated as a unit. Because Christianity as a whole has inspired fewer COMPENDIA than has study of the world's religions, this section intermingles COMPENDIA with ENCYCLOPEDIAS and LEXICONS.

For more than three centuries three fields within Christian studies have multiplied DICTIONARIES, ENCYCLOPEDIAS and WHO'S WHOS. Biblical studies, hagiography and history of the early church (patristics) boast some of the finest of reference books. Recently theology and study of spirituality have begun to catch up.

2.1 GENERAL

OVERVIEW: SOME MODELS OF THE ART Reference works that treat Christianity as a whole include summits of lexicon-making. British and German enterprises predominate, while French ones are surprisingly absent. Among single-volume works **29** Cross, ed., *The Oxford Dictionary of the Christian Church* (1957, 1974) and **32** Barrett, ed., *World Christian Encyclopedia* (1982) stand in a class by themselves, while **37** Bautz, ed., *Biographisches Kirchenlexikon* (1975, 1990-) and **31** Müller, ed., *Theologische Realenzyklopädie* (1976-) are the grandest of recent MEGA-ENCYCLOPEDIAS. One can only wish that other religions would sponsor similar masterpieces about their traditions.

LIST OF WORKS ANALYZED
29 (1957, 1974, 1983) F[rank] L[eslie] Cross and E[lizabeth] A. Livingstone, eds., *The Oxford Dictionary of the Christian Church* (London: Oxford University Press, 1957; 2d ed., rev., 1974)

30 (1977) Elizabeth A. Livingstone, ed., *The Concise Oxford Dictionary of the Christian Church* (Oxford and New York: Oxford University Press, 1977)

31 (1976-) Gerhard Müller, ed., *Theologische Realenzyklopädie*, 24 volumes to date (Berlin: de Gruyter, 1976-)

32 (1982) David B. Barrett, ed., *World Christian Encyclopedia: A Comparative Study of Churches and Religions in the Modern World, A.D. 1900-2000*

(Nairobi, Oxford and New York: Oxford University Press, 1982)

33 (1983) J[ohn] C[allan] J[ames] Metford, *Dictionary of Christian Lore and Legend* (London: Thames & Hudson, 1983)

34 (1986) William H. Gentz, ed., *The Dictionary of Bible and Religion* (Nashville: Abingdon, 1986)

35 (1988) Jaroslav Pelikan, *The Melody of Theology: A Philosophical Dictionary* (Cambridge: Harvard University Press, 1988)

36 (1988) Volker Drehsen et al., eds., *Wörterbuch des Christentums* (Gütersloh: Gerd Mohn, 1988)

37 (1975, 1990-) Friedrich Wilhelm Bautz [d. 1979], then Traugott Bautz, eds., *Biographisch-Bibliographisches Kirchenlexikon,* planned in 10 vols. (Hamm: Verlag Bautz, 1975-)

38 (1990, 1992) John Bowden, *Who's Who in Theology: From the First Century to the Present* (London: SCM, 1990; New York: Crossroad, 1992)

39 (1991) John McManners, ed., *The Oxford Illustrated History of Christianity* (Oxford and New York: Oxford University Press, 1991)

40 (1992) J[ames] D[ixon] Douglas and Philip W. Comfort, eds., *Who's Who in Christian History* (Wheaton, Ill.: Tyndale House, 1992)

128 (1993-) Walter Kasper, ed., *Lexikon für Theologie und Kirche,* 3d ed., planned in 10 vols. (Freiburg: Herder, 1993-). Analyzed under 2.9.2.1 "Roman Catholicism: Dictionaries."

ANALYSIS OF WORKS

29 (1957, 1974, 1983) F[rank] L[eslie] Cross and E[lizabeth] A. Livingstone, eds., *The Oxford Dictionary of the Christian Church* (London: Oxford University Press, 1957; 2d ed., rev., 1974); reprinted with corrections and addenda, 1983; xxxii & 1520 pages; no index; general bibliography (i.e., list of abbreviations), pp. xix-xxv.

□ *Scope* This classic LEXICON is the finest one-volume reference work in any language on a single religion. Conceived in 1939 in the format of an Oxford Companion, it appeared in 1957, having been researched by many but written by Frank Leslie Cross (1900-1968). Elizabeth Livingstone completed a revision in 1974, adding a note on her mentor (pp. xxvii-xxxi). More than six thousand entries perform at least six functions. There is (1) a WHO'S WHO of popes, founders, theologians, writers, artists, musicians and scholars, chiefly European; (2) a HAGIOGRAPHY of major saints of East and West; (3) a REALLEXIKON of church history canvassing councils, doctrines, heresies, sacraments, liturgy and practices of all denominations in Europe and North America but less fully in other continents; (4) a gazetteer of Christianity in every European country and British dependency as well as in significant cities like Edessa, Clairvaux, Wittenberg and above all Rome; (5) a brief BIBLE DICTIONARY on every book of the Bible, the pseudepigrapha and matters like "Bible (English Versions)," "Textual Criticism" and "Hermeneutics"; (6) a GLOSSARY of foreign terms from French *(abbé),* Latin *(odium theologicum)* and Greek *(homoousion).* All entries except brief ones dispense multilingual bibliography through 1972. About a third of the bibliographies cite a dozen or more works, and some cite thirty or more (e.g., "Gnostics," "Jesuits"). Cross-references abound, marked by an asterisk. The style enchants. What other LEXICON sustains such winsomeness through so many pages?

□ *Strengths* An almost unprecedented feat of epitomizing enabled an Anglican savant to produce the most impressive one-volume LEXICON of Christianity, or indeed of any other religion. Containing perhaps twenty-five hundred entries, the WHO'S WHO alone comprises a sizable volume. Every pope, every major saint and every significant theologian, founder or heretic receives at least a quarter of a column. Some receive a full page (e.g., John of Damascus, Abelard, Jean Gerson). Theological and historical issues get pinpointed. Theological entries recount the history of debates on even the big issues (e.g., "God," "Church," "Moral Theology"). As regards Europe, albeit not always North America, religious orders, church councils and denominations flourish. There are three pages on "Hymns" and "Luther," two on "Mary, the Blessed Virgin" and "India, Christianity in" and one on "Crusades" and "John Milton." A few books like Calvin's *Institutes,* the *Little Labyrinth* and the *Cloud of Unknowing* command entries.

Not surprisingly, English church history wins more attention than American. British saints, prelates, thinkers, writers, scholars and controversies emerge at length. A substantial volume could be excerpted consisting solely of entries on British church and culture that would be indispensable to Anglicans and Catholics alike. The second edition increased coverage of Eastern Orthodox churches. F. L. Cross eschewed confessionality so habitually that one would never guess him to be High Anglican. In contrast to more trendy writers, he made no attempt to examine the twentieth century more fully than the fourth or the fifteenth. The writing is pellucid throughout, making difficulties plain and complexities transparent.

□ *Weaknesses* This is not a LEXICON of the world's religions. "Islam" receives only half a column and "Buddhism" none. "Missions" are narrated in just two pages, and individual regions and missionaries (other than British) recede. Nor is it a LEXICON of Christian art. Although certain artists feature (e.g., "Fra Angelico" and "Michelangelo" but not Rubens or Delacroix), genres of art and music do not. Conceived and executed in the 1940s and 1950s, this work scants methodology, social history and ethics. Debates pertaining to women, the Third World or bioethics find no place. Consequently, Americanists will prefer **169** Reid, ed., *Dictionary of Christianity in America* (1990). Quite baffling is the function of 250 mostly British contributors listed on pages xiii-xvii. No article is signed (all were rewritten by F. L. Cross or Elizabeth Livingstone), and the collaborators' role is never specified. One imagines that drafts were solicited on thousands of topics and then recast without attribution. Given

the stature of the "contributors," one would like to know who contributed to each entry.

□ *Competitors* The *Oxford Dictionary of the Christian Church* remains the standard by which one-volume LEXICONS of a religion may be judged. **131** McBrien, ed., *The HarperCollins Encyclopedia of Catholicism* (1995) now rivals it in comprehensiveness but not in subtlety, depth or bibliography. The bibliography in Cross is best updated from more specialized works like **152** Di Berardino, ed., *The Encyclopedia of the Early Church* (1991), **89** Wakefield, ed., *The Westminster Dictionary of Christian Spirituality* (1983) or **9** Hinnells, ed., *Who's Who of World Religions* (1991). Although more discursive, particularly on ethics and liturgy, the Westminster/SCM dictionaries are seldom more trenchant. By emphasizing the past hundred years, **163** Douglas, ed., *New 20th-Century Encyclopedia of Religious Knowledge* (1991) complements the *Oxford Dictionary* well. So does **115** Childress and Macquarrie, eds., *The Westminster Dictionary of Christian Ethics* (1983) and **44** Krüger et al., eds., *Ökumene Lexikon* (1983). F. L. Cross belongs to a lineage of master epitomizers among Anglican clergy. A predecessor is John Henry Blunt, ed., *Dictionary of Sects, Heresies, Ecclesiastical Parties and Schools of Religious Thought* (London, 1874). That volume displays a gift for synthesis similar to Cross's and even more wit. (On F. L. Cross see Owen Chadwick, *Times Literary Supplement,* November 22, 1974, pp. 1319-20.)

□ *Summary* Unrivaled in range and depth no less than in evenhandedness and accuracy, *The Oxford Dictionary of the Christian Church* belongs in every library. It should be the work of first resort on any question of Christian history in Europe up to 1960.

30 (1977) **Elizabeth A. Livingstone, ed.,** *The Concise Oxford Dictionary of the Christian Church* (Oxford and New York: Oxford University Press, 1977); vi & 570 pages; no index; no bibliographies; also in paperback.

□ *Critique* This abridgment compresses *The Oxford Dictionary of the Christian*

Church, 2d ed. (1974) into a GLOSSARY. Rather than delete too many entries, more than five thousand have been shortened to as little as three to six lines. Omissions pertain above all to British divines (e.g., Joseph Milner) and writers (e.g., S. T. Coleridge). All bibliographies have been dropped, but cross-references remain. A delightful allusion illumines the purpose: the parent work "provides, as Gregory the Great said of Scripture, water in which lambs may walk and elephants may swim. The aim of the present work is to offer basic information for the lambs who do not need, and perhaps cannot afford, the elephants' swimming pools" (p. iii). There exists no safer pond than this in which lambs may learn to paddle among the basics of Christian history.

□ *Summary* This authoritative GLOSSARY whets the appetite for more lavish fare.

31 (1976-) Gerhard Müller, ed., *Theologische Realenzyklopädie,* 24 vols. through *Obrigkeit* to 1994 (Berlin: de Gruyter, 1976-); vols. 1-17 published in paperback (1993); about 800 pages per volume; about 20,000 pages to date; index of persons, places and themes in each volume; cumulative index to vols. 1-17 (1992), 229 pages; a few black-and-white plates.

□ *Critique* This MEGA-ENCYCLOPEDIA is singular in breadth and depth of coverage. More than one thousand international authorities write lengthy articles (about 175 per volume) on persons, places, movements and concepts in the history of Christianity and other religions (particularly Judaism). It differs from other works in eschewing entries shorter than four or five pages. Bibliographies extend up to six pages. The WHO'S WHO encompasses major figures, including not only principal saints, popes and theologians, but philosophers (e.g., Moses Mendelssohn) and supreme artists (e.g., Michelangelo). Countries and major cities worldwide elicit entries, as do religious orders and all branches of Christianity. Even more remarkable is the coverage of non-Christian religions. All major Asian religions command massive articles, Baha'i receiving seventeen pages, "New

Religions" sixteen, and Cao Dai eight. Certain topics win overwhelming, perhaps even excessive coverage: "Calendar" elicits eighty pages and "Human" (i.e., *Mensch*) 120 (divided into ten parts). There is even an entry on "Futurology." As a rule, one should never assume that a given person, place, movement or concept will be missing from the *Theologische Realenzyklopädie.* Its multilingual bibliographies are the most complete of any recent reference work except **37** Bautz, ed. *Biographisch-Biblio-graphisches Kirchenlexikon* (1975-), and its articles are often at once the most searching and the most up-to-date anywhere.

□ *Summary* Every researcher should consult this MEGA-ENCYCLOPEDIA for incomparable bibliographies. Articles are up-to-date and unsurpassed in comprehensiveness and incisiveness.

32 (1982) David B. Barrett, ed., *World Christian Encyclopedia: A Comparative Study of Churches and Religions in the Modern World, A.D. 1900-2000* (Nairobi, Oxford and New York: Oxford University Press, 1982); xvi & 1010 pages; eight indexes, pp. 979-1009; bibliography, pp. 857-61; charts, maps, black-and-white photographs in the text; color maps, pp. 865-84; a second edition in three volumes is announced for early 1997.

□ *Scope* Thirteen years in preparation, this exhaustive ENCYCLOPEDIA of Christian demography fascinates as often as it daunts. It claims to treat 156 ecclesiastical traditions and twenty thousand denominations. The volume pivots around part 7, "A Survey of Christianity and Religions in 223 Countries," (pp. 131-769). Unsigned alphabetical entries on each country examine the legal and demographic status of Christianity and other religions, delineate membership in all Christian denominations and other religions, and sketch multilingual bibliography. Entries on European and Latin American countries are particularly detailed and constitute the best source anywhere on church-state relations. Anomalies of every sort, including thousands of pockets of minuscule membership, are elucidated. Part 3, "Methodology: Enumerating Christianity and Religions:

Methodology, Sources, Classifications and Codes" (pp. 37-104), explains techniques of gathering and classifying demographic statistics. Part 4, "Culture: Peoples of the World: an Ethnolinguistic Classification" (pp. 105-15), is highly sophisticated. Part 8, "Statistics: Global, Continental and Confessional Tables" (pp. 773-812), collates statistics, using its own codebook (pp. 123-30) and its own index (pp. 1005-9). Part 9, "Dictionary: Survey Dictionary of World Christianity" (pp. 813-48), supplies a GLOSSARY of contemporary usage. Part 12, "Directory: Topical Directory of World Christianity" (pp. 893-977), collates addresses of thousands of organizations arranged country by country under seventy-six headings (including universities and non-Christian religions).

Hundreds of black-and-white photographs evoke religious practice more variously than in perhaps any other source, particularly on pages 39-111. Eight indexes include "Names for God in 900 Languages" (pp. 984-87), "Peoples and Languages" (2,200 entries), "Christian Abbreviations, Acronyms and Initials" and "Locations of Statistical Data" (pp. 1005-9). Twenty pages of maps deploy splendid cartography (pp. 865-84), and thirty-one global tables are a statistician's delight (pp. 3-18, 776-812). David B. Barrett, who cut his teeth authoring *Schism and Renewal in Africa: An Analysis of Six Thousand Contemporary Religious Movements* (Nairobi: Oxford University Press, 1968), supervised all these aids as well as the hundreds of photographs. No editor ever performed a Herculean task better.

□ *Strengths* This austere (not to say mind-boggling) compilation conceals within it more features than can be enumerated. The preface divulges stunning totals: the ENCYCLOPEDIA examines 20,800 denominations among 8,990 peoples who use 7,010 languages (p. v). The languages include the world's smallest, consisting of 150 speakers (p. 13). Part 3 on "Methodology" explicates categories and techniques for collecting and classifying data. Several thousand local informants, together with 370 named experts, helped to document twenty thousand Christian denominations as well as all other religions, including new indigenous ones. No other book sorts categories of religious identity so subtly. Particularly helpful are coinages like "double affiliation" (for members listed by two bodies), "Third World indigenous churches" (for Christian bodies initiated by nonwhites), "minuscule bodies" (for those too small to quantify), "conciliarism" (for membership in any kind of interdenominational movement, as listed on pp. 85-90) and "marginal Protestants" (for derivative bodies like Mormons, Christian Scientists and Unitarians).

A basic organizing concept is "ecclesiastico-cultural bloc," which denotes religious streams defined by a combination of history, belief and ethnicity. Seven are differentiated (on pp. 56-65): Roman Catholicism, Orthodoxy, Anglicanism, Protestantism, marginal Protestantism, non-Roman Catholicism and non-white indigenous Christianity. Part 7, the 640-page "Survey," answers questions about demography, church-state relations and spread of Christianity in individual countries, including some fifty, most of them islands, which do not belong to the United Nations. Eighteen pages on the United States (with 2,050 Christian denominations), twelve on the United Kingdom of Great Britain (530 denominations), twelve on India (330 denominations), nine on Brazil (500 denominations), eight on the Holy See, seven on South Africa (3,500 denominations) and four on Israel (67 denominations) achieve marvels of compression. The 223 national entries scrutinize anomalies of Christian organization. Tracing the status of churches in Alsace (still under the Napoleonic Concordat of 1801, p. 298), intricacies of the hundred indigenous churches in South Korea (including the Unification Church, p. 442) and differences among the seven rites used by Catholics in Egypt (p. 275), this ENCYCLOPEDIA will probably never be surpassed except by its own next edition. By inventorying tens of thousands of bodies and practices and by photographing several hundred of them, it particularizes religious diversity more concretely than any other volume. Statistics and pictures together convey an immediacy beyond imagining. All future research in geo-religious studies will depart from here.

□ *Weaknesses* The chief drawback concerns format. The forbidding size and tiny print of this ENCYCLOPEDIA discourage browsing. Researchers who use this tome fleetingly will not know the astonishment that comes from browsing in it. All scholars of world religions should digest Part 1, "Status: The Expansion and Status of Christianity in the 20th Century" (pp. 1-19). One hundred fifty-six Christian traditions are classified into seven blocs and presented in an eye-catching diagram on page 35. Browsers will enjoy the photographs and their meaty captions. They provide the most intimate, albeit not the most colorful, album of religious practice anywhere. Non-Christian religions get fully illustrated, including a full page on Cao Dai (p. 743). The statistics, based on censuses between 1970 and 1980, have gone out of date, but their extent revolutionizes one's conception of diversity. As the preface warns, "The number of denominations was found to be four times as numerous as the estimates made in 1968" (p. v). No preconception emerges unscathed from contact with this volume. The impact is not just REVISIONIST; it is revelatory.

□ *Competitors* No other work digests so much data on every nook and cranny of peoples, religions and Christian denominations. No other delineates anomalies, novelties and minuscule bodies as scrupulously. All other works, including **163** Douglas, ed., *New 20th-Century Encyclopedia of Religious Knowledge* (1991) and **45** Fahlbusch et al., eds., *Evangelisches Kirchenlexikon* (1986-), merely summarize demographic data that is here anatomized. To be sure, a French COMPENDIUM, **307** Clévenot, *L'État des religions dans le monde* (1987) digests religious demography country by country but at one-twentieth the length. The otherwise estimable **170** Mead and Hill, *Handbook of Denominations in the United States* (1951, 1990) covers just 220 of the thousand-odd

American denominations mentioned on pages 711-28. As the world's premier religious demographer, David B. Barrett updates statistics on "Global Adherents of Major Religions" every year in the *Britannica Book of the Year*. His *World Christian Encyclopedia* stands without peer or rival. Every educated person should ponder its composite picture of human diversity. A second edition in three volumes (1997) is eagerly awaited.

□ *Summary* Indispensable to social scientists, this masterpiece of geo-religious studies may seem ungainly to humanists. Yet all scholars of religion should scrutinize the first hundred pages, and everyone will feast on the photographs. The *World Christian Encyclopedia* constitutes a pinnacle.

33 (1983) J[ohn] C[allan] J[ames] Metford, *Dictionary of Christian Lore and Legend* (London: Thames & Hudson, 1983); 272 pages; no index; no general bibliography; more than 250 black-and-white photographs inset on every second page.

□ *Critique* In more than seventeen hundred brief entries, this DICTIONARY of iconography sketches both biblical figures and Christian saints and practices. An emeritus of Spanish and Latin America studies at Bristol, England, Metford expounds for students of art and literature the lore behind Christian imagery. There are no bibliographies. The work combines a WHO'S WHO of saints and biblical figures with a REALLEXIKON of Christian worship and symbolism. Entries on persons retell that individual's story, while emphasizing those incidents and attributes that attracted artists. An entry on "Jesus," for example, cross-references more than sixty others concerning events of his life. Art historians will want to pursue iconography further in works like **108** Jöckle, *Encyclopedia of Saints* (1995) or the more copious Louis Réau, *Iconographie de l'art chrétien*, 6 vols. in 3 (Paris: Presses Universitaires de France, 1955-59). Metford's limpidity charms.

□ *Summary* This DICTIONARY of Christian stories digests saints' lives, biblical lore and Christian practices for scholars of literature and art.

34 (1986) William H. Gentz, ed., *The Dictionary of Bible and Religion* (Nashville: Abingdon, 1986); 1147 pages; no index; general bibliography, pp. 1144-47; maps and black-and-white photographs throughout.

□ *Scope* This versatile DICTIONARY of Christianity and world religions fulfills four functions. It combines (1) an ample BIBLE DICTIONARY, (2) a DICTIONARY of church history and theology that emphasizes the past hundred years, (3) a WHO'S WHO of theology and (4) a brief DICTIONARY of world religions. Twenty-eight (mostly American) contributors write twenty-eight hundred signed articles without bibliographies. Several authors express colorful views that lend piquancy: John Macquarrie on theology and philosophy, Howard Clark Kee on the ancient Near East, and James Livingston on recent theology. Although the editor describes the work as "lay-oriented" and "ecumenically Christian in origin and outlook" (p. 9), he should have called it "ecumenically Protestant." Black-and-white maps excel on "The Spread of Islam," "Buddhism in China" and "Japanese Religion." Sixteen pages of colored Bible maps (between pp. 1120 and 1121) are lucid but lack a gazetteer. A general bibliography lists English-language surveys and reference works but without evaluation (pp. 1144-47).

□ *Strengths* Each of the four functions needs to be assessed separately. While concise and accurate, the BIBLE DICTIONARY is least original in handling books of the Bible, major persons and places, and methodology. Howard Clark Kee's essays on "Mesopotamia," "Jesus Christ, Life of" and "Miracle," like Bruce Vawter's on "Prophet," shine at synthesis. The DICTIONARY of church history and theology abounds in luminous articles, not least those by John Macquarrie and John Cooper. The WHO'S WHO of Christianity emphasizes Americans and recent theologians such as Moltmann, Pannenberg, Küng, Ricoeur and Henry but limits popes and saints. Written by Robert Ellwood and Keith Crim, the DICTIONARY of world religions stands out. Ellwood's articles on Hindu-

ism, Jainism, Taoism and Japanese religion as well as Crim's on Buddhism, Confucianism and Islam count among the best in any reference book. Although Lionel Koppman handles the Jewish entries adroitly, there are too few of them.

A distinguishing feature is a cluster of more than sixty articles on theology and philosophy by John Macquarrie. They constitute a primer of theology, elucidating issues as general as "Faith," "Fate," "Human Nature," "Incarnation," "Trinity" and "Predestination." His articles on "God" and "Eschatology" are models of pungency. Among his best on philosophy are "Essence/Existence," "Natural Religion and Theology," "Time," "Personalism," "Scholasticism" and "Paradox." Macquarrie's articles comprise an INTRODUCTION to philosophical theology, which he calls "a believing form of academic theology." They complement his **73** *Twentieth-Century Religious Thought,* 4th ed. (1988). With slightly less flair, James Livingston has written several dozen articles on major theologians (e.g., Schleiermacher, Ritschl, Tillich) and historical topics (e.g., "Neo-Orthodoxy," "Rationalism," "Romanticism"). They round out Macquarrie's primer to make this a compelling INTRODUCTION to Christian thought. Apart from the BIBLE DICTIONARY, nearly all the longer entries impel one to read widely. Any beginner should acquire this book.

□ *Weaknesses* This most comprehensive of INTRODUCTORY DICTIONARIES invites criticism for attempting too much. Except for omitting countries and scholars, it succeeds in canvassing the Bible, Christian history and world religions in considerable depth. To be sure, hagiography and liturgics get short shrift as do Eastern Christianity and rabbinic Judaism. The BIBLE DICTIONARY analyzes methodology more thoroughly than does the DICTIONARY of church history. Entries on books of the Bible dispense too much biblical theology and not enough literary analysis. They are too tidy. Otherwise, the ecumenically Protestant outlook hardly obtrudes. Because certain contributors propound dis-

tinctive views, it would have helped to list each author's entries so as to inventory, among others, John Macquarrie's minibook.
□ *Competitors* No other single volume on Christianity in English covers so much ground. 8 MacGregor, *Dictionary of Religion and Philosophy* (1989, 1991) is more incisive but contains no BIBLE DICTIONARY. The nearest rival is 29 Cross, ed., *The Oxford Dictionary of the Christian Church* (1957, 1974), which boasts far more entries and provides bibliographies but lacks pedagogical guile. The Westminster/SCM volumes on 117 the Bible (1970), 118 church history (1971) and 116 theology (1969, 1983) purvey more detail and abound in bibliography but presuppose greater knowledge. The BIBLE DICTIONARY offers a first-rate INTRODUCTION and prepares a beginner for larger tomes. The WHO'S WHO encompasses more theologians of the past 150 years than any other nonspecialized work except 163 Douglas, ed., *New 20th-Century Encyclopedia of Religious Knowledge* (1991). The DICTIONARY of world religions provides splendid overviews but lacks the range of 2 Crim, ed., *The Perennial Dictionary of World Religions* (1981, 1989). Taken together, these primers dispense unrivaled pedagogy.
□ *Summary* Any novice in any field of Christian studies will prize this DICTIONARY. Any teacher of Christian thought will esteem essays by Livingston, Kee and Macquarrie.

35 (1988) Jaroslav Pelikan, *The Melody of Theology: A Philosophical Dictionary* (Cambridge: Harvard University Press, 1988); x & 274 pages; index, pp. 271-74; no general bibliography; also in paperback.
□ *Scope* This beguiling PHILOSOPHICAL DICTIONARY reassesses sixty-eight concepts and fifteen persons crucial to the history of Christianity. Essays of two to four pages by the dean of American historians of Christian thought reappraise issues across all periods, denominations and disciplines. There are no bibliographies. Throughout, the author prods the reader to revise assumptions. He does so by alternating "highly personal judgment, rather techni-

cal scholarly analysis, and audacious historical-theological generalization" (p. x). Several issues stand out. The "Development of Doctrine" surfaces under that title as well as under "Authority," "Continuity," "Historiography" and "Newman, John Henry." Eastern Christianity is examined lovingly in twelve essays such as "Apophatic," "Byzantium," "Cappadocians," "Filioque," "Icons," "Patristics," "Slavs" and "Sobornost." These articles demonstrate how study of the East enriches understanding of the West (p. 27). A scholarly ethos crystallizes in "Dictionary," "Hermeneutics," "Languages," "Libraries," "Melody," "Renaissance," "Scholarship" and "Solitude." Although the collection promises an "intellectual autobiography" (p. ix), more accurately it could be said to subject pivotal questions to a lifetime's reflection.
□ *Strengths* To inspire humanists, Pelikan invokes Goethe on the challenge "of turning heritage into task and thereby of vindicating tradition" (p. 102). Among moderns Pelikan's two favorites are Schleiermacher and Newman. The former devised the metaphor of vocation as a "melody," to which religious tradition supplies accompaniments (p. 167). The latter elucidated the notion of development of doctrine, a calling to which Pelikan has devoted a career (pp. 53-54, 180-81). Origen and Augustine loom as the two great voices of East and West respectively, while Dante is praised for Mariology and Erasmus for ecumenism. Pelikan hails Augustine as "arguably, the only figure from all of late antiquity—whom we can still read with understanding and empathy" (p. 18). A moving essay on Nathan Söderblom concludes by saluting "the effect that even one hour with him could have on an entire lifetime" (p. 241). Pelikan assesses reputations of figures as diverse as Gibbon, Goethe, Emerson and Dostoyevsky, seeing in each the best of a national tradition. A dab hand at maneuvering names, Pelikan lists nearly one hundred "Creeds of Christendom" (pp. 46-48) and rephrases controversies about old chestnuts like "Grace," "Justification" and "Trinity."

An article on "Atheist/Agnostic" contends that T. H. Huxley's definition of "agnostic" does not adequately differentiate the term from "atheist." Essays on "Reformation" and "Renaissance" classify a host of twentieth-century scholars. Although Pelikan calls this "an intellectual autobiography" (p. ix), only a few entries give vent to passion. Entries on "Byzantium," "Cappadocians," "Patristics" and "Slavs" rebuke Western neglect of Eastern Christianity and render moving homage to a mentor, George Florovsky (p. 27). While Pelikan is no radical, he enjoys twitting received opinions. In defending "Hellenization," he lauds "static forms" that transmit the gospel across generations in a "kind of theological cryonics" (p. 116). An entry on "Melody" asserts that music is the only art that Christianity has never at any time or place despised (p. 166). A brief note on "Friendship" laments how Christians have neglected this theme. The essay on "Languages" deplores American neglect of foreign languages and then extols two words unique to English: "worship" and "gospel" (p. 151). Entries rarely repeat one another, and the the tone throughout is gentle rather than barbed.

□ *Weaknesses* As befits a PHILOSOPHICAL DICTIONARY, this one flaunts omissions, neglecting such warhorses as ecumenism, feminism and postmodernism. Avoiding crankiness, Pelikan chooses to whisper critique rather than shout it. Although some readers may desire more polemic, his preference for "both-and" (p. 57) rids the book of invective. Regrettably, in the entry on "Dictionary" Pelikan missed a chance to encapsulate his experience coediting and contributing to reference works. In an editing lapse, the phrase *lex orandi, lex credendi* pervades half a dozen entries but is defined only under "Worship" and is missing from the index. It should have elicited an entry of its own.

□ *Competitors* No other contemporary historian of religion has written a PHILOSOPHICAL DICTIONARY. The incisiveness of this one makes one wish that masters like Geoffrey Parrinder, John Macquarrie, Ninian Smart and R. J. Zwi Werblowsky

had done so. To be sure, whims erupt here and there in a few single-author DICTIONARIES like **313** Guiley, *Harper's Encyclopedia of Mystical and Paranormal Experience* (1991) or **11** Hexham, *Concise Dictionary of Religion* (1993), but these works lack the grandeur of Pelikan's. Although his volume is briefer, it belongs in the company of REVISIONIST LEXICONS such as **181** Cohen and Mendes-Flohr, eds., *Contemporary Jewish Religious Thought* (1987) or **112** Fink, ed., *The New Dictionary of Sacramental Worship* (1990). Authors there reappraise received views with a calm that reminds one of Pelikan. They too radiate a commitment to celebrating continuity by "turning heritage into task." Pelikan's gentle REVISIONISM never lets thought stand still.

□ *Summary* This collection of reappraisals harvests the insights of a lifetime. Wisdom glows.

36 (1988) Volker Drehsen et al., eds., *Wörterbuch des Christentums* (Gütersloh: Gerd Mohn, 1988); 1439 pages; index, pp. 1391-437; no general bibliography.

□ *Critique* This REVISIONIST DICTIONARY recruits 414 mostly German scholars to survey recent Christianity and the world it confronts. Fifteen hundred entries (with superb bibliographies) cover countries, world religions, books of the Bible and controversies (with emphasis on the arts and literature). This is less a DICTIONARY of church history or theology than of "Christianity and culture." Although the WHO'S WHO promises brevity, it incorporates writers ("Brecht," "Döblin"), moviemakers ("Bunuel"), artists ("Barlach"), musicians ("Brahms," "Verdi") and theologians ("Tillich"). An entry on "Barock" surveys the arts. The article on "Jesus" boasts seven subentries, including one on literary depictions. Among world religions Zoroastrianism features under "Parsism." "Candomblé" elicits an entry, but Cao Dai does not. Purporting to be "interconfessional, interdisciplinary and intercultural," this work downplays methodology. Articles on countries and issues can be amplified in **45** Fahlbusch, ed., *Evangelisches Kirchenlexikon* (1986-). Conceived to facilitate rethinking of Christianity, this work will delight the browser. Anyone interested in twentieth-century Europe will benefit.

□ *Summary* This REVISIONIST DICTIONARY incorporates artistic figures and issues not often discussed in reference books on religion.

37 (1975, 1990-) Friedrich Wilhelm Bautz [d. 1979] then Traugott Bautz, eds., *Biographisch-Bibliographisches Kirchenlexikon,* planned in 10 vols. (Hamm: Verlag Bautz, 1975-); 8 vols. through *Schneute* to 1994; about 5600 pages to date.

□ *Critique* This MEGA-WHO'S WHO spans the entirety of Christian history. Volume 1 (1975) was written solely by the founder and completed the letter *F.* His son Traugott then recruited five hundred collaborators for the remaining nine volumes, which resumed with volume 2 in 1990. This most comprehensive WHO'S WHO of Christianity handles not a few non-Christians (e.g., Kambyses I, Karpocrates and Georg Lukács). It favors Germans (particularly writers, rulers and leaders of the Reformation), scholars of religion (e.g., Hubert Jedin, K. S. Latourette and Gerardus van der Leeuw) and musicians (e.g., Josquin Desprez). Many biblical figures and all popes elicit entries. The bibliographies dazzle, dwarfing all others in exhaustiveness. Even a sample proves daunting: Kant elicits thirty-five pages of bibliography; Copernicus, Lactantius and Lamennais five pages each; C. G. Jung four pages; C. S. Lewis, Benjamin Jowett and Frédéric LePlay one page each. Although this WHO'S WHO is rarely found in American libraries, it embraces lesser figures referenced nowhere else, and the bibliographies have no rival. More American academic libraries should obtain this masterwork.

□ *Summary* This ultimate WHO'S WHO of Christianity assembles overwhelming bibliographies in an up-to-date format that everyone can exploit. Scholars of German history will marvel.

38 (1990, 1992) John Bowden, *Who's Who in Theology: From the First Century to the Present* (London: SCM, 1990; New York: Crossroad, 1992); viii & 152 pages; index of popes of Rome, p. 152; general bibliography, p. vi.

□ *Critique* Into this INTRODUCTORY WHO'S WHO the managing director of the SCM Press compressed about a thousand lives significant in Christian, Jewish and Muslim theology and philosophy. Entries average eight to twenty lines, while a few giants like Augustine, Calvin and Luther receive fifty. There are no bibliographies. Thinkers and writers of the past three centuries abound, but artists and musicians are omitted. Theologians of the twentieth century receive the richest coverage. Eschewing "verdicts," the author dubs Arius, for example, a "teacher" rather than a "heretic" and simply omits Donatus. A chronological WHO'S WHO of the popes, however, summarizes papal history with more vinegar than honey (pp. 133-51). These thumbnail sketches burst with unfavorable verdicts. For further study, the author recommends above all **29** Cross, ed., *The Oxford Dictionary of the Christian Church* (1957, 1974). He fails to mention more recent resources like **89** Wakefield, ed., *The Westminster Dictionary of Christian Spirituality* (1983) and **8** MacGregor, *Dictionary of Religion and Philosophy* (1989, 1991). **9** Hinnells, ed., *Who's Who in World Religions* (1991) is far more ambitious and penetrating.

□ *Summary* This briefest of WHO'S WHOS tantalizes more often than it satisfies, but any beginner will appreciate its breadth.

39 (1991) John McManners, ed., *The Oxford Illustrated History of Christianity* (Oxford and New York: Oxford University Press, 1991; paperback, 1993); xii and 724 pages; index, pp. 707-24; classified bibliography, pp. 667-85; chronology, pp. 686-704;18 color plates and about 200 black-and-white illustrations.

□ *Scope* This REVISIONIST COMPENDIUM of nineteen chapters by seventeen mostly British authorities explores the history of Christianity worldwide. Not a few of the articles rank among the very best on a topic. Nine chapters go to the years 1800, six cover the continents since then, and four synopses examine "What Christians Believe" (by Maurice Wiles), "New Images of Christian Community" (by Bryan Wilson) and "The Future of Christianity" (by John Taylor). Grouped on pages 667-85, bibliographies cite only English-language works. Illustrations are lovingly selected and cunningly inserted. The volume exemplifies Oxbridge at its best.

□ **Strengths** The caliber of contributors guarantees distinction. Among uniformly excellent chapters, certain ones loom as strikingly original, not to say REVISIONIST. Jeremy Johns on "Christianity and Islam" and Frederick Pike on "Latin America" propound syntheses found nowhere else. In the latter Pike sketches the fusing of Iberian and Native American motifs. Peter Hinchliff's critique of missionaries in Africa bites deep. In "Eastern Orthodoxy" Kallistos Ware digests his many books into forty glowing pages. Sergei Hackel on "The Orthodox Churches of Eastern Europe" deploys rare material and exotic illustrations. The editor compresses "The Enlightenment: Secular and Christian (1600-1800)" into a rousing narrative. His two chapters are among the most artful. Deploying choice bibliography, John Taylor's meditation on "The Future of Christianity" pricks complacency. As narrative flows from chapter to chapter, REVISIONISM emerges discreetly. The illustrations, particularly from regions outside Western Europe, are little known and sometimes shocking.

□ **Weaknesses** Because this is a COMPENDIUM and not a LEXICON, access requires use of the index. It cites persons and places but not doctrines, heresies or councils. Overall, theology is deemphasized in favor of social history, liturgy and imagery. Surprisingly, Judaism commands far less attention than Islam and hardly more than Hinduism. Women scarcely feature, and visual art elicits vastly more coverage than music.

□ **Competitors** As a REVISIONIST COMPENDIUM of narrative, *The Oxford Illustrated History* is never banal and often exhilarating. Power of synthesis sometimes rivals that exercised on Christianity in **16** Puech, ed., *Histoire des religions* (vols. 2-3, 1972-76). Missions in Africa, Asia and Latin America elicit sharper critique than occurs in **42** Neill, ed., *Concise Dictionary of the*

Christian World Mission (1971). A less subtle competitor is a Lion handbook, *History of Christianity* (1977, 1990), whose articles are jauntier but less reflective.

□ **Summary** This most readable COMPENDIUM on the history of Christianity ranks as a classic. It belongs in any library.

40 1992 J[ames] D[ixon] Douglas and Philip W. Comfort, eds., *Who's Who in Christian History* (Wheaton, Ill.: Tyndale House, 1992); 747 pages; no index; no general bibliography.

□ **Critique** This INTRODUCTORY WHO'S WHO compiles signed articles (devoid of bibliography) on about a thousand persons, many of them Protestant. Only a few saints get included along with some scholars, such as Roland de Vaux. J. Newton's five pages on "Augustine" stand out, but no entry proves indispensable. Beginners will enjoy this primer, but they should soon move on to **29** Cross, ed., *The Oxford Dictionary of the Christian Church* (1957, 1974). A briefer volume treats eight hundred women: Mary L. Hammack, *A Dictionary of Women in Church History* (Chicago: Moody Press, 1984).

□ **Summary** This unambitious WHO'S WHO introduces essential figures.

2.2 ECUMENISM

OVERVIEW: PROCEDURAL ECUMENISM VERSUS UNITIVE ECUMENISM Since Vatican II (1962-65) reference works on ecumenism have proliferated. Ecumenism may be understood as a movement of negotiation and reflection that explores commonalities and differences among Christian bodies. George Lindbeck identifies two types of ecumenism. "Procedural and interdenominational" ecumenism, favored by Protestants (particularly evangelicals), explicates differences that it continues to affirm. "Thematic and unitive" ecumenism, favored by Catholics and Eastern Orthodox, postulates a higher "ecumenicist" unity that it aspires to foster.[1] In either guise ecumen-

---

[1]*See* **75** Ford, ed., *The Modern Theologians*, 2 (1989): 256-58.

ism now furnishes a backdrop against which Christian self-definition proceeds. This directory will treat "confession" as a bridging tendency (i.e., Lindbeck's "unitive" type) and "denomination" as a commitment to a specific organization (i.e., Lindbeck's "procedural" type). Thus an influential Protestant LEXICON, 45 *Evangelisches Kirchenlexikon* (1956-59), surveys in its third edition (1986-) Christian history and thought from an "interdenominational" standpoint. Upholding individual organizations, its procedural approach contrasts with the one found in a volume that advocates alternately the unitive and the procedural: 46 Lossky et al., eds., *Dictionary of the Ecumenical Movement* (1991).

By highlighting ecumenical activities, all these works contrast with two other types: (1) works of self-definition that strive to delineate Christianity at large (like 112 Fink, ed., *The New Dictionary of Sacramental Worship* [1990]) and (2) works of self-definition that isolate their own tradition from others' (like 83 Komonchak et al., eds., *The New Dictionary of Theology* [1987]). Both types discuss ecumenism, whether procedural or unitive, without promoting either. In response to ecumenism a Catholic discipline known as "fundamental theology" evolved out of apologetics (i.e., discourse directed to nonbelievers). The new approach has inspired a masterpiece: 48 Latourelle and Fisichella, eds., *Dictionary of Fundamental Theology* (1990, 1995). Fundamental theology may be said to encapsulate the ecumenical movement in the way that "metaliturgics" encapsulates the liturgical movement. *See* 2.7 "Liturgy."

Because in some measure ecumenism grew out of collaboration among missionaries, two older works on missiology belong here. Study of the history of missions will be transformed as soon as a new volume appears: Gerald H. Anderson, *Biographical Dictionary of Christian Missions* (New York: Simon & Schuster). Michael A. Fahey, *Ecumenism: A Bibliographical Overview* (Westport, Conn. and London: Greenwood, 1992) assesses 1,345 titles,

including fifty reference works listed as #42-90. Practitioners of dialogue will appreciate a guide to etiquette across denominations: Andrea Holberg, ed., *Forms of Address for Business and Social Use* (Houston: Rice University Press, 1994; esp. pp. 139-70 on religious leaders).

LIST OF WORKS ANALYZED

41 (1970) T[homas] C. O'Brien, ed., *Corpus Dictionary of Western Churches* (Washington and Cleveland: Corpus Publications, 1970)

42 (1971) Stephen Neill, Gerald H. Anderson and John Goodwin, eds., *Concise Dictionary of the Christian World Mission* (London: Lutterworth; Nashville and New York: Abingdon, 1971)

43 (1973-82) George Menachery, ed., *The St. Thomas Christian Encyclopaedia of India,* 3 vols. announced (Trichur: St. Thomas Christian Encyclopaedia of India, 1973-82)

44 (1983) Hanfried Krüger, Werner Löser and Walter Müller-Römheld, eds., *Ökumene Lexikon: Kirchen, Religionen, Bewegungen* (Frankfurt am Main: Verlag Otto Lembeck and Verlag Josef Knecht, 1983)

45 (1986-) Erwin Fahlbusch et al., eds., *Evangelisches Kirchenlexikon: Internationale theologische Enzyklopädie,* 3d ed., planned in 4 vols. (Göttingen: Vandenhoeck & Ruprecht, 1986-)

46 (1991) Nicholas Lossky et al., eds., *Dictionary of the Ecumenical Movement* (Geneva: WCC Publications; Grand Rapids, Mich.: Eerdmans, 1991)

47 (1994) Ans Joachim van der Bent, *Historical Dictionary of Ecumenical Christianity* (Metuchen, N.J.: Scarecrow, 1994)

48 ([1990] 1994) René Latourelle and Rino Fisichella, eds., *Dictionary of Fundamental Theology* [1990] (New York: Crossroad, 1994)

ANALYSIS OF WORKS

41 (1970) T[homas] C. O'Brien, ed., *Corpus Dictionary of Western Churches* (Washington and Cleveland: Corpus Publications, 1970); xx & 820 pages; no index; no general bibliography.

□ *Critique* This DICTIONARY of churches and denominations sought to inform Roman Catholics soon after Vatican II about Western Christianity, recruiting over one hundred contributors to write on their own traditions. Every Western denomination (particularly in the United States) is covered, along with founders, missionaries, issues and movements. Articles go unsigned, and most include skeletal bibliography. Ambitious historical overviews number seventeen pages on "Church (General History)" and "Church (U.S. History)," six on "Church and State," five on "Reformation" and three on "Augustinianism." The WHO'S WHO stresses (1) American activists such as Henry Ward Beecher, Phillips Brooks and Dwight Moody, (2) modernizing Catholics such as Ignaz Döllinger and George Tyrrell and (3) European ecumenists such as Lord Halifax, Nathan Söderblom and Étienne Portal but not Cardinal Mercier. Entries all but ignore biblical studies and Protestant theology. Inaugurated as a response to Vatican II, the *Corpus Dictionary* marked an early attempt to acquaint Catholics with other denominations. It introduces essentials of the ecumenical movement among Western churches but omits Eastern Christianity, including church fathers like Origen and Athanasius. Both **44** Krüger et al., eds., *Ökumene Lexikon* (1983) and **46** Lossky et al., eds., *Dictionary of the Ecumenical Movement* (1991) are more comprehensive, while **48** Latourelle and Fisichella, eds., *Dictionary of Fundamental Theology* (1990, 1994) revolutionizes Catholic ecumenism.

□ *Summary* Now dated, this DICTIONARY of Christian denominations and their leaders retains interest chiefly as a document of the aftermath of Vatican II. On no topic does it remain essential.

42 (1971) Stephen Neill, Gerald H. Anderson and John Goodwin, eds., *Concise Dictionary of the Christian World Mission* (London: Lutterworth; Nashville and New York: Abingdon, 1971); xxii & 682 pages; no index; no general bibliography.

□ *Critique* This intelligent LEXICON expounds the expansion of Christianity from 1492 to the late 1960s. More than 230 authorities, many of them active or retired missionaries, contribute about a thousand signed articles on countries, practitioners and concepts of missiology (with English-language bibliography). Articles of six pages each on "China," "India" and "Pacific Islands" and shorter ones concerning some fifty countries abound with information gracefully presented. A master epitomizer, Stephen Neill, analyzes major world religions as well as concepts like "history of religions" and "indigenization." Positions pro and con get expounded on controversial issues like "Cults, Post-Christian and Quasi-Christian," "Latent Church Concept" and "Failure in Mission." A WHO'S WHO canvasses evangelists and missionaries since 1492, focusing on those who were British. It is sobering to contrast the poise of this work with the tentativeness that pervades **46** Lossky et al., eds., *Dictionary of the Ecumenical Movement* (1991). The *Concise Dictionary of Christian World Mission* reaped a harvest of worldwide missionizing just when confidence in that endeavor was about to crumble. Looking back from lifetimes of experience, contributors wax forthright, self-assured and insightful. Their work is a delight to browse in. No doubt the *Biographical Dictionary of Christian Missions* (New York: Simon & Schuster, forthcoming) authored by one of the editors, Gerald H. Anderson, will supplant the WHO'S WHO.

□ *Summary* This LEXICON analyzes Christian missions between 1492 and 1965 with wit and concision.

43 (1973-82) George Menachery, ed., *The St. Thomas Christian Encyclopaedia of India*, 3 vols. announced, 2 published (Trichur: St. Thomas Christian Encyclopaedia of India, 1973-82); 273 & 218 pages; no index; no general bibliography; about one hundred black-and-white and color plates; maps, 1:145-60.

□ *Critique* This COMPENDIUM on Christian interactions in India shows unusual features. Volume 2 on "Apostle Thomas, Kerala, Malabar Christianity" appeared first (in 1973), while volume 1 on Protestant and Catholic Missions appeared only in 1982. Although both volumes announce volume 3, no library seems to own it. Signed articles by Indian Christians of every persuasion expound history and culture in depth with multilingual bibliographies and lavish photographs. Volume 2 recounts the history of the St. Thomas Christians as well as Latin Christians who date from the arrival of St. Francis Xavier at Portuguese Goa in 1542. Hinduism and Jainism are sketched (2:177-79, 181-83), as are the Cochin Jews (2:183-85). Although most articles endorse the story of St. Thomas's sojourn in India, H. Comes in "Did St. Thomas Really Come to India?" (2:23-24) argues convincingly that those Christians emigrated to the Malabar Coast centuries later from the port of Rewardshir in Persia. A series of eighteen articles examines their liturgy, ethos, architecture, sculpture and literature (2:112-70). Placid Podipara's article, "Hindu in Culture, Christian in Religion, Oriental in Worship," vividly evokes Hindu customs of these Christians (2:107-12). A WHO'S WHO and GLOSSARY unfold in "Minor Articles" (2:193-218).

Volume 1 is even more vigorously ecumenical in recounting Protestant and Roman Catholic missions all over India, culminating in a long section on "Catholic Eccelesiastical Divisions of India" that are grouped into nineteen dioceses (1:216-73). Black-and-white maps sketch Indian history (1:145-60). Any scholar of Christian missions, Indian culture or ecumenical contacts will find much to ponder in this COMPENDIUM. Few English-language reference works evoke India so pungently. To be sure, greater judiciousness pervades Stephen Neill, *A History of Christianity in India*, 2 vols. (Cambridge: Cambridge University Press, 1984-85). Neill's assessment of the legend of St. Thomas's visit concludes, "We can only regret the absence of any sure historical evidence to support this view" (1:49).

□ *Summary* This COMPENDIUM is a gold mine of information, reflection and photographs about Christianity in India. It traces ecumenical interactions across four centuries.

44 (1983) Hanfried Krüger, Werner Löser and Walter Müller-Römheld, eds., *Ökumene Lexikon: Kirchen, Religionen, Bewegungen* (Frankfurt am Main: Verlag Otto Lembeck and Verlag Josef Knecht, 1983); x & 663 pages (1326 columns); two indexes (concepts and persons), cols. 1297-326; no general bibliography; a few black-and-white photographs and maps.

□ *Scope* This LEXICON offers signed articles by more than three hundred (mostly German) authorities on countries, ecumenists and concepts. It juxtaposes Protestant, Roman Catholic and often Eastern Orthodox views on the sacraments and theological concepts like "Church," "Catholicity," "Church Unity," "Mary" and "Mysticism." Articles on major religions specify readiness for dialogue, although Zoroastrianism, Jainism and Taoism are omitted. Living denominations of Christianity elicit individual articles (as on Mennonites and Nestorians), but most past movements and heresies do not. Bibliographies to the articles are heavily German.

□ *Strengths* Theological acumen sharpens dual and triple articles on major concepts. An Eastern Orthodox standpoint emerges more fully here than in perhaps any other general reference work. A WHO'S WHO of twentieth-century ecumenists is the most complete anywhere, embracing all denominations and regions. Skillful epitomizing characterizes syntheses on "Modern Religious Movements," "Peace Movements" and "Economic Development." Unusual articles include "Cultural Context," "Migration of Workers" and "Revolution." The entry on "Ökumene" recounts history and theory of the ecumenical movement. An article on "Judaism" inserts twenty lines on the Samaritans and the Karaites, and there is a nuanced entry on "Jewish-Christian Dialogue" but none on Muslim-Christian dialogue.

□ *Weaknesses* Articles on Third World countries often run only ten or twenty lines. They need to be amplified from **32** Barrett, ed., *World Christian Encyclopedia* (1982) or from **45** Fahlbusch et al., eds., *Evangelisches Kirchenlexikon* (1986-).

There is very little on biblical scholarship and no entry on "Hermeneutics." Non-Germans will wish for more English and French bibliography.

□ *Competitors* This is the fullest one-volume LEXICON on contemporary ecumenism and the issues it raises. Nearly all topics except doctrine and ecumenists, however, are covered more fully in **45** Fahlbusch et al., eds., *Evangelisches Kirchenlexikon* (1986-). Somewhat longer than **46** Lossky et al., eds., *Dictionary of the Ecumenical Movement* (1991), the *Ökumene Lexikon* delivers more information, particularly about Europe, and articulates in more detail differences between Protestant, Catholic and Orthodox views. While Islam receives only three pages, parallel articles by Protestants and Catholics recall those in **201** Khoury, ed., *Lexikon religiöser Grundbegriffe* (1987).

□ *Summary* Written by expert epitomizers, this LEXICON summarizes vast material on persons, events and doctrines. It is among the best edited volumes on contemporary Christianity.

45 (1986-) Erwin Fahlbusch et al., eds., *Evangelisches Kirchenlexikon: Internationale theologische Enzyklopädie*, 3d ed., planned in 4 vols. (Göttingen: Vandenhoeck & Ruprecht, 1986-); vol. 1 (1986), xii & 706; vol. 2 (1989), xi & 767; vol. 3 (1992), x & 769 pages; no index; no general bibliography.

□ *Scope* This meticulous ENCYCLOPEDIA of contemporary Christianity improves upon a distinguished predecessor. Published in 3 volumes (1956-59), a second edition canvassed world Christianity from a Protestant perspective. Coming thirty years later, the third edition is unfailingly ecumenical in its choice of 360 (mostly German) contributors and in its ambition to explore both the Third World and major world religions. In contrast to other ecumenical enterprises, this one encompasses history from the first century. It incorporates a gazetteer of countries and a short BIBLE DICTIONARY, not to mention DICTIONARIES of church history, art history and the world's religions. There is no WHO'S WHO. Multilingual bibliographies are among the best any-where, and cross-references abound, sometimes to excess.

□ *Strengths* The fusion of history and contemporaneity with global sweep makes this ENCYCLOPEDIA unique. To an unusual degree authors address one another explicitly. For example, the editor's article on "European Theology" debates issues about Eurocentrism raised in a nine-page article on "Third World" as well as a five-page one on "Pluralism." This comes in addition to entries on more than one hundred countries. Totaling sixteen pages, six articles on the "Ecumenical Movement" take up themes of eight articles and twenty pages concerning "Missions." These two units amplify fifteen pages on "Recent Church History" (since 1648) as well as entries on "Africa," "Asia" and "Latin America." Four pages on "Christian-Jewish Dialogue" address issues raised in "Antijudaism, Antisemitism" and include half a page of bibliography. The topics "Judaism," "Jewish Philosophy" and "Jewish Theology" run fifteen pages. Three pages on "Civil Religion" enlarge American debate beyond one's wildest imaginings. Two pages on "Feminism" and four on "Feminist Theology" connect thorny issues like the gender of God to "Mariology." Blending historical depth with contemporaneity, "Eschatology" gets analyzed separately in the Old Testament, New Testament, Reformation, Roman Catholic Church and Eastern Churches. Eighteen pages on "Luther's Theology" and "Lutheran Churches" outline "Research on Luther." All this amplifies fifteen pages on "Reformation" and "Reformers."

Major world religions win copious entries, and so do many new religious movements. "Psychology," "Psychoanalysis" and "Psychotherapy" elicit synoptic articles with cross-references to "Anxiety," "Counseling" and "Narcissism." The *Evangelisches Kirchenlexikon* paints a variegated picture of Christianity, past and present. Showing how Christianity touches every aspect of life, the authors criticize inherited categories. This ENCYCLOPEDIA dazzles not only by its comprehensiveness but by its vigor.

□ *Weaknesses* Amid such profusion the chief omission is a WHO'S WHO. Major theologians like Augustine, Calvin, Luther and Origen as well as philosophers like Aristotle, Hegel, Kant and Plato command entries, but other individuals do not. Although artists surface under movements like "Expressionism" and "Impressionism," too often these entries degenerate into lists. Although more than one hundred countries receive entries of one to four pages, only a handful of cities do (e.g., Alexandria, Jerusalem, Rome). Oddly, three pages on "Byzantium" narrate imperial history without characterizing the city. The style is succinct, sometimes telegraphic. Some may find all-inclusiveness oppressive, preferring to consult multiple works rather than a single compilation. Nevertheless, this work stands unrivaled for its richly nuanced portrayal of Christian multiplicity.

□ *Competitors* This is the most complete ENCYCLOPEDIA on the history and present status of Chistian churches and thought worldwide. The title notwithstanding, it is not primarily a Protestant work, but an ecumenical one by and for scholars who demand a global perspective. Except as regards persons and the World Council of Churches, nearly every entry in **46** Lossky et al., eds., *Dictionary of the Ecumenical Movement* (1991) finds a counterpart here, often with richer bibliography and a wider horizon. **44** Krüger et al., eds., *Ökumene Lexikon* (1983) presents the theology of ecumenism more fully but otherwise needs to be enriched from the *Evangelisches Kirchenlexikon*. **163** Douglas, ed., *New 20th-Century Encyclopedia of Religious Knowledge* (1991) synthesizes, albeit briefly, much of the same material. It incorporates a WHO'S WHO but offers only skeletal bibliographies. Pending a 1997 new edition of **32** Barrett, ed., *World Christian Encyclopedia* (1982), its statistics can be updated from here. A historian of Christianity who wishes to own only one German-language reference work might well choose the *Evangelisches Kirchenlexikon*. Any scholar of twentieth-century religion should consult its bibliographies.

□ *Summary* This ENCYCLOPEDIA of Christianity covers more topics, presents fuller bibliographes, and integrates history and contemporaneity better than any other. It is a library in itself.

46 (1991) Nicholas Lossky et al., eds., *Dictionary of the Ecumenical Movement* (Geneva: WCC Publications; Grand Rapids, Mich.: Eerdmans, 1991); xvi & 1196 pages; two indexes (subjects and names), pp. 1121-71; no general bibliography; black-and-white photographs throughout.

□ *Scope* This LEXICON of ecumenical endeavors and issues propounds the standpoint of the World Council of Churches (W.C.C.), which sponsored it. More than three hundred contributors write more than six hundred entries (with English-language bibliography) on leaders, denominations, movements, issues and regions involved in Christian ecumenism during the twentieth century. Church history before 1900 recedes. Distilling insights from thousands of discussions sponsored by the W.C.C., the *Dictionary of the Ecumenical Movement* caters above all to participants in ecumenical dialogue. The WHO'S WHO embraces ecumenical leaders of the twentieth century but no one else. Contributors cull theology, church history and social science for material pertinent to interconfessional understanding. Ecumenical Conferences, W.C.C. Assemblies and ecumenical forums like the Groupe des Dombes (but not the Malines Conversations of the early 1920s) are treated in full. Although dialogue with each of the major religions elicits separate entries, the religions themselves do not.

□ *Strengths* This DICTIONARY is written by, for and about ecumenists. Trenchant articles concern points of contention, such as Geoffrey Wainwright expounds in "Church," Avery Dulles in "Communion," Johannes Brosseder in "Grace" and Robert Holtz in "Sacraments." Methodology gets dissected in M. M. Thomas (of Malabar) on "Syncretism," Geiko Müller-Fahrenholz on "History," John Habgood on "Nature," Kallistos Ware on "Tradition and Traditions" and John S. Mbiti on "Indigenous Religions." Slogans like Common Witness, Confessing Church, Life and Work and Sobornost undergo appraisal. In "Hermeneutics," Michael Cartwright canvasses four denominations, and Geoffrey Parrinder delineates "Scripture" in ten world religions. The rubric "Theology" elicits fifteen articles on regional and ideological variants. Social sciences of religion evoke analysis in articles like "Growth, Limits to," "Decolonization," "Transnational Corporations" and "Technology." Choan-Seng Song ruminates on niceties of "Culture." A few articles assess obstacles to consensus: Kern Robert Trembath on "Revelation," Douglas John Hall on "Creation," Marc Spindler on "Diaspora" and Charles C. West on "Secularization." Disarmingly candid is Tom Stransky's inventory of "Criticism of the Ecumenical Movement and of the W.C.C." Composing about one-third of the whole, these analytical entries complement factual ones on organizations, persons and regions (but not countries). The indexes facilitate every sort of search.

□ *Weaknesses Engagé* and presentist, this DICTIONARY disappoints as often as it satisfies. To use George Lindbeck's distinction, its ecumenism fails to choose between the "unitive" and the "procedural." As a work of self-definition by the World Council of Churches, the volume advances that organization's agenda, which is described on pages 1083-1100. To be sure, certain articles propose changes of emphasis within ecumenism, as Owen Cashmore and Joan Puls do on "Spirituality Within the Ecumenical Movement" or Béla Harmati on "Civil Religion." With "unitive" zeal, the estimable Geoffrey Wainwright tends to gloss over confessional differences in "Canon," "Church" and *"Lex orandi, lex credendi."* Inexplicably, there are no entries on media of communication, not even radio or film. Too often the tone is earnest, even portentous. One wishes for the sallies of a John Macquarrie or Irving Hexham. Heterogeneity makes browsing choppy. This is not a book for recreation.

□ *Competitors* As a cheerleader for the World Council of Churches and the twen-

tieth century, the *Dictionary of the Ecumenical Movement* curtails its own usefulness. By a strange twist, a retired officer of the World Council of Churches produced a more cohesive DICTIONARY of history: **47** van der Bent, *Historical Dictionary of Ecumenical Christianity* (1994). **44** Krüger et al., eds., *Ökumene-Lexikon* (1983) is also more comprehensive, sober and reliable. Its approach extends to the even more vigorously historical **45** Fahlbusch et al., eds., *Evangelisches Kirchenlexikon* (1986-). **163** Douglas, ed., *New 20th-Century Encyclopedia of Religious Knowledge* (1991) is more balanced and wide-ranging but scants ecumenism. The Westminster/SCM series likewise downplays ecumenism. Unfortunately, only a few articles in the *Dictionary of the Ecumenical Movement* are as enjoyable as many in **34** Gentz, ed., *The Dictionary of Bible and Religion* (1986). The tendency of the W.C.C. to homogenize differences gets corrected in a REVISIONIST work like **112** Fink, ed., *The New Dictionary of Sacramental Worship* (1990), not to mention a hard-edged one like **79** Elwell, ed., *Evangelical Dictionary of Theology* (1984). By exploring ecumenical thought as a strand within contemporary Christianity, the *Dictionary of the Ecumenical Movement* embodies dilemmas of our time but resolves few if any of them.

□ *Summary* The volume supplies a WHO'S WHO of twentieth-century Christian leaders and a status report on the World Council of Churches. Historians of ecumenism will relish the reportage.

47 (1994) Ans Joachim van der Bent, *Historical Dictionary of Ecumenical Christianity* (Metuchen, N.J.: Scarecrow, 1994); xiii & 600 pages; no index; general bibliography, pp. 527-95; chronology, pp. xiii-xxiii.

□ *Critique* In this DICTIONARY a researcher formerly at the World Council of Churches expounds persons and concepts pivotal to ecumenism. A WHO'S WHO depicts fellow ecumenists. REVISIONIST entries on concepts dissect the routine ("Social Ethics," "Social Gospel") and the challenging ("Ecclesiology," "Theology, Late 20th-century Trends in"). A classified bibliography is magnificent, and cross-references abound. Having edited *Handbook Member Churches: World Council of Churches* (Geneva, 1982), the Dutch author achieves a coherence lacking in **46** Lossky et al., eds., *Dictionary of the Ecumenical Movement* (1991).

□ *Summary* This DICTIONARY of leaders, concepts and events dissects controversies authoritatively.

48 ([1990] 1994) René Latourelle, S.J., and Rino Fisichella, eds., *Dictionary of Fundamental Theology* (New York: Crossroad, 1994); xxxvii & 1222 pages; analytic index (i.e., synopsis of individual articles), pp. 1171-222; no bibliography (except list of abbreviations, pp. xxxix-xxxviii); almost no cross-references. Translated from the Italian *Dizionario di teologia fondamentale* (Assisi: Cittadella, 1990).

□ *Scope* Supremely intelligent, this LEXICON was crafted during the 1980s by a team at the Gregorian University in Rome and adapted into English by an accomplished writer, René Latourelle (p.xi). Two hundred twenty-three articles show how Catholic ecumenism, in response to Vatican II, launched a new discipline, "fundamental theology." Restructuring apologetics, it strives to make Christian revelation credible, a task that Catholic seminaries reportedly neglected during the 1970s (p. 319). Thirty-six articles by Latourelle and twenty-four by Fisichella constitute something like a PHILOSOPHICAL DICTIONARY. Fusing erudition with profundity, the volume reconsiders how to present Christianity to (1) nonbelievers and exbelievers, (2) other Christians and (3) members of other religions. Ninety-three authorities investigate issues, apologists and encyclicals as well as major branches of Christianity and of certain other religions. Thirty-seven of the authors teach at the Pontifical Gregorian University in Rome, and another twenty-one reside in North America, most of them in Canada. Ten women contribute, including Anne Carr on "Feminism" and Pheme Perkins on "Gnosis." Other luminaries from the United States include Avery Dulles on "Apologetics I: History" and

"Conversion," Michael J. Buckley on "Atheism I: Origins" and George Lindbeck on "Lutheranism I: A Lutheran Perspective."

Treating twenty-two "apologists" as precursors, a WHO'S WHO singles out Anselm, Aquinas, Augustine, Irenaeus and Origen among classics and among moderns Blondel, de Lubac, Guardini, Newman, Rahner and Tillich (but not Maritain or Scheler). On five others, Drey, Gardeil, Rosmini, Scheeben and Zubiri, the LEXICON supplies the only recent accounts in English. Portrayals of most are laudatory (e.g., Hegel) or even ecstatic (e.g., Gregory of Nyssa), but at least one is censorious (Bultmann). Subordinating biography to history of thought, these essays rank among the canniest that the biographees have inspired.

□ *Strengths* Few LEXICONS match this one in acumen. Scholars like Marc Maesschalck on "Idealism: German," Solange Lefebvre on "Secularity" and Mariasusai Dhavamony on definition, history and theology of "religions" operate at the highest level. Coining novel conceptualizations, clusters of up to ten subentries tackle "Church," "Christology," "History," "Religion" and "Theologies." Many readers will welcome definitions of notions like "Deposit of Faith," "Dogma" and "Magisterium" as well as of formulas like "Sensus fidei" and "Universale Concretum." With equal clarity the more assertive of the two editors, Rino Fisichella, dissects "Credibility," "Martyrdom," "Prophecy" and "Semeiology," while the more essayistic René Latourelle muses on "Solitude" and "Vatican II" as well as on thinkers like Pascal and Teilhard de Chardin. Controversy enlivens articles on "Hierarchy of Truths," "Fideism and Traditionalism" and above all "Early Catholicism." With MENIPPEAN salvoes Salvatore Spera scans the history of "Humanism," "Ideology" and "Philosophy of History." Imaginatively, Ghislain Lafont reassesses uses in theology of "Time and Temporality," while Julian Naud ruminates on "Symbolism," and Édouard Hamel rethinks both "Justice in the Vision of the Magnificat" and "Election/Covenant/Law." The latter envisions Mary at the neck of an hourglass between the narrowing of the old covenant and the widening of the new (pp. 271-72).

Rabbi Howard Joseph expounds Judaism, while a Canadian Catholic, Ian J. Kagedan, explores Jewish-Christian relations (pp. 538-60). Other religions elicit fact-centered accounts of "Islam," "Hinduism" and "Buddhism" but not of Chinese or Japanese religions. Uncompromisingly, Jacques Dupuis declares "belief in reincarnation" to be irreconcilable with faith in resurrection (p. 818). No other reference book explores underpinnings of ecumenical and interreligious dialogue so searchingly. For transplanting such virtuosity into English, René Latourelle deserves applause.

□ *Weaknesses* Freshly minted since the 1970s, the discipline of fundamental theology exemplifies postmodern "blurring of genres." Unstintingly historical, the field incorporates ecumenism, biblical studies, theology and world religions but excludes liturgy, hagiography, canon law and much of spirituality. Few disciplines aerate the history of thought so inventively. A LEXICON of such intelligence exacts commitment. This is not a work to skim. Certain entries are inexplicably short (e.g., "Analogy," "Hellenism and Christianity"), and there is no entry on "Foundations" or "Hope." Apart from articles on encyclicals and Vatican I and II, popes feature surprisingly little. As regards format, misspellings mar some of the bibliographies, and convoluted structure means that a subject index is badly needed because cross-references are spotty.

□ *Competitors* This REVISIONIST LEXICON is one of the most subtle ever published in English. Its coupling of theology and cultural criticism matches another Italian-French masterpiece, **91** De Fiores and Goffi, eds., *Dictionnaire de la vie spirituelle* (1983, 1987). A more disparate gem, **76** Musser and Price, eds., *A New Handbook of Christian Theology* (1992) unlooses similar creativity onto North American preoccupations. Of four *New Dictionaries* issued for Catholics since 1987 by Michael Gla-

zier/Liturgical Press, only **112** Fink, ed., *The New Dictionary of Sacramental Worship* (1990) approaches the vigor of the Latourelle masterpiece. No other LEXICON captures so well in English the innovativeness of recent Catholic works from France and Italy. To be sure, the original has a rival, Giuseppe Ruggieri, ed., *Enciclopedia di teologia fondamentale: Storia progetto autori categori* (Genoa: Marietti, 1987). It narrates history of the discipline more fully but lacks incandescence. The *Dictionary of Fundamental Theology* knows no equal at dissecting and redirecting contemporary Catholic thought.

□ *Summary* While daring to diagnose culture, this REVISIONIST LEXICON reassesses both ecumenism and interreligious dialogue. Few reference books balance novelty of interpretation and firmness of judgment so adeptly.

2.3 BIBLICAL STUDIES
Because reference books in biblical studies abound, the directory analyzes only works in English (apart from a French MEGA-ENCYCLOPEDIA and a German MEGA-COMPENDIUM). Concordances, as well as tools for exegeting Hebrew and Greek texts, are likewise omitted.

OVERVIEW: THREE OLD GENRES, ONE NEW No field of religious studies has transformed itself more dramatically in the past thirty years than biblical studies. External and internal developments have revolutionized one of the oldest and most meticulous of academic endeavors. From outside the field have come literary theory, liberation theology, women's studies and pluralist appreciation of non-Christian religions. From inside have come discovery of ancient texts at Qumran (since 1947) and Nag Hammadi (since 1945), not to mention ongoing excavations in Israel and elsewhere in the Near East. Further changes stem from developments in biblical theology, a field whose ups and downs Brevard S. Childs delineates magisterially if controversially in *Biblical Theology of the Old and New Testaments* (Minneapolis: Fortress, 1992). Access to that field will be transformed by Walter A. Elwell, ed., *Evangelical Dictionary of Biblical Theology* (Grand Rapids, Mich.: Baker Book House, 1996).

All this ferment has elicited ever deepening collaboration between Protestant and Catholic, not to mention between Jew and Christian, on nearly every topic of investigation. The cumulative impact has been to deconfessionalize the field, and all but a few conservatives have joined this trend. To be sure, reservations crystallize in two evangelical classics: **53** Douglas, ed., *New Bible Dictionary,* 2d ed. (1982) and **65** Carson et al., eds., *New Bible Commentary: 21st Century Edition,* 4th ed. (1994), both of which maximize historicity and minimize methodology while ignoring extracanonical books. Many evangelicals welcome postmodern pluralism, notably in a series of HANDBOOKS that began with **70** Green and McKnight, eds., *Dictionary of Jesus and the Gospels* (1992). Outspoken assessment of these developments unfolds in Ben Witherington III, *The Jesus Quest: The Third Search for the Jew of Nazareth* (Downers Grove, Ill.: InterVarsity Press, 1995).

No other branch of religious studies boasts as many reference works as biblical studies. Although Protestant works held sway for several centuries, Roman Catholic works now abound even if Eastern Orthodox ones do not. In some academic libraries, as well as in the libraries of most Protestant seminaries, reference works on the Bible fill as many shelves as nearly all others in Christian studies combined. By convention, reference tools of biblical research divide into three categories: DICTIONARIES, COMMENTARIES and concordances. A BIBLE DICTIONARY performs at least two functions: (1) it serves as a REAL-LEXIKON to identify (nearly) every person, place, object and concept in the Hebrew Bible, the Apocrypha and the New Testament, and (2) it introduces each book of those canons, often including theology. Complementing a DICTIONARY, a BIBLE COMMENTARY likewise "introduces" each biblical book and then "explicates," unit-by-unit, even verse-by-verse, the argument

of that book. Sometimes based on a particular translation, a COMMENTARY tends to display confessional commitment more openly than a BIBLE DICTIONARY. A multivolume version of the latter may be called a BIBLE ENCYCLOPEDIA.

In biblical studies the term *introduction* functions in a technical way. As pioneered by Johann Gottfried Eichhorn in the 1780s, to "introduce" a book of the Bible means to outline major controversies concerning authorship, historical context and textual transmission. Such an INTRODUCTION (German *Einleitung*) outlines information deemed prerequisite to explication, which expounds the argument unit-by-unit and then assesses possible alternative meanings of each verse or cluster of verses. A subdiscipline of explication is exegesis, which seeks to weigh in each verse alternative meanings inherent in the original vocabulary. Exegesis in Hebrew and Greek has generated a library of specialized tools (notably in German) that draw on ancient languages. No such exegetical dictionary is analyzed here. The fullest COMMENTARY in single volume remains **63** Brown et al., eds., *The New Jerome Biblical Commentary* (1968, 1990).

A Bible concordance lists every mention of a word or proper name, keyed either to the original Hebrew or Greek or to a particular translation. A BIBLE DICTIONARY may incorporate a concordance by listing within each article all locations of that word or name, as is done in **55** Wigoder, ed., *Illustrated Dictionary and Concordance of the Bible* (1986).

A fourth type of biblical reference work has emerged recently. It may be called a HANDBOOK OF INTERPRETATION. It represents perhaps the first genuinely new genre of reference book to have developed in religious studies since MEGA-ENCYCLOPEDIAS debuted in the 1890s. HANDBOOKS OF INTERPRETATION compare methodologies, delineate history of criticism and expound the helping (ancillary) sciences. No other volumes convey the deconfessionalization of biblical studies so vividly. **68** Coggins and Houlden, eds., *A Dictionary of Biblical Interpretation* (1990) is a model of the genre, while at an introductory level. **72** Metzger and Coogan, eds., *The Oxford Companion to the Bible* (1993) combines a HANDBOOK OF INTERPRETATION with a BIBLE DICTIONARY. Although it serves beginners well, they soon outgrow it.

A witty consumer's guide to the tools appears in Erasmus Hort, *The Bible Book: Resources for Reading the New Testament* (New York: Crossroad, 1983). Coining catchy criteria, Hort sorts the "best" from the "rest." But at least half the works he recommends have been supplanted since 1983. A guide for experts is Frederick W. Danker, *Multipurpose Tools for Bible Study,* 4th ed. (Minneapolis: Fortress, 1993). Presupposing knowledge of Hebrew and Greek, Danker situates several hundred works in their scholarly lineage. Chapter 9, "Bible Dictionaries," and chapter 15, "Commentaries and Their Uses," are outstanding. A cunningly annotated bibliography of 524 English-language items appears in Bernhard W. Anderson, *Understanding the Old Testament,* 4th ed. (Englewood Cliffs, N.J.: Prentice-Hall, 1986), pages 652-76.

Although there is no English-language DICTIONARY of the Hebrew Bible written by and for Jews, their needs are met in part by **60** Freedman, ed., *The Anchor Bible Dictionary* (1992). A Reform Jewish COMMENTARY on the Pentateuch is **61** W. Gunther Plaut, ed., *The Torah: A Modern Commentary* (1981). Jewish scholars will relish crosscultural parallels in **275** van der Toorn, Becking and van der Horst, eds., *Dictionary of Deities and Demons in the Bible (DDD)* (1995).

Only major works in English published since 1980 are discussed here (except for **49** Pirot, ed., *Dictionnaire de la Bible* and **67** Haase and Temporini, eds., *Aufstieg und Niedergang der römischen Welt).* There is no attempt to evaluate concordances or specialized tools for exegeting Hebrew and Greek texts. Scholars working in ancient languages should consult the guides by Hort (1983) and Danker, 4th ed. (1993) mentioned above. The aim here is to direct nonspecialists to the most useful recent DICTIONARIES, COMMENTARIES and HANDBOOKS OF INTERPRETATION. Com-

parisons refer only to other works evaluated in these pages. In this field more than most, one needs to identify personal favorites and then live with them. To juggle too many BIBLE DICTIONARIES induces dizziness.

2.3.1 BIBLE DICTIONARIES

OVERVIEW: NONCONFESSIONAL APPROACHES BIBLE DICTIONARIES continue to multiply, and a number of recent ones rank as masterpieces. Although the genre originated to assist believers, deconfessionalization has diminished and sometimes removed such impetus. All but one of these works (**53** Douglas) deploy nonconfessional methodologies, and only a few address theology (**49** Pirot, **52** Bromiley, **56** Myers). Confessional affirmation rebounds in BIBLE COMMENTARIES.

Among illustrated DICTIONARIES John Bimson, ed., *Baker Encyclopedia of Bible Places* (Grand Rapids, Mich.: Baker Book House, 1995) appeared too late to analyze.

LIST OF WORKS ANALYZED
49 (1928-) Louis Pirot, ed., *Dictionnaire de la Bible: Supplément* (Paris: Letouzey et Ané, 1928-); volume 12 (1994) goes through "Sexualité"

50 (1971, 1993) Joan Comay, *Who's Who in the Old Testament Together with Apocrypha* (London: Weidenfeld & Nicolson, 1971); reprinted in paperback (New York: Oxford University Press, 1993)

51 (1971, 1993) Ronald Brownrigg, *Who's Who in the New Testament* (London: Weidenfeld & Nicolson, 1971); reprinted in paperback (New York: Oxford University Press, 1993)

52 ([1915] 1979-88) Geoffrey W. Bromiley, ed., *The International Standard Bible Encyclopedia,* 3d ed., rev., 4 vols. (Grand Rapids, Mich.: Eerdmans, 1979-88)

53 ([1962] 1982) J[ames] D[ixon] Douglas, ed., *New Bible Dictionary,* 2d ed. (Leicester, U.K., and Downers Grove, Ill.: InterVarsity Press, 1982)

54 (1985) Paul J. Achtemeier, ed.,

Harper's Bible Dictionary (San Francisco: Harper & Row, 1985)

55 (1986) Geoffrey Wigoder, ed., *Illustrated Dictionary and Concordance of the Bible* (Jerusalem: Jerusalem Publishing House; New York: Macmillan, 1986)

56 ([1975] 1987) Allen C. Myers, ed., *The Eerdmans Bible Dictionary* (Grand Rapids, Mich.: Eerdmans, 1987)

57 (1989) Bernhard W. Anderson, ed., *The Books of the Bible*, 2 vols. (New York: Scribner's, 1989)

58 (1990) Watson E. Mills, ed., *Mercer Dictionary of the Bible* (Macon, Ga.: Mercer University Press, 1990)

59 (1991) Geoffrey Wigoder, Shalom M. Paul and Benedict T. Viviano, eds., *Almanac of the Bible* (Jerusalem: Jerusalem Publishing House; New York: Henry Holt, 1991)

60 (1992) David Noel Freedman, ed., *The Anchor Bible Dictionary*, 6 vols. (New York: Doubleday, 1992)

275 (1995) Karel van der Toorn, Bob Becking and Pieter W. van der Horst, eds., *Dictionary of Deities and Demons in the Bible* (DDD) (Leiden: Brill, 1995). Analyzed under 5.1.2 "Mythology: WHO'S WHOS."

ANALYSIS OF WORKS

49 (1928-) Louis Pirot, ed., *Dictionnaire de la Bible: Supplément* (Paris: Letouzey et Ané, 1928-); vol. 12 (1994) reaches "Sexualité"; 650 pages per vol.; about 7000 pages to date. Analyzed further under 2.9.2.2 "Roman Catholicism: French Mega-encyclopedias."

□ *Critique* Never did the term *supplement* so mislead as in the title of this MEGA-EN-CYCLOPEDIA. This magnificent work couples a BIBLE DICTIONARY and a history of biblical interpretation at the length familiar in the publisher's **132-137** *Encyclopédie des sciences ecclésiastiques.* The volumes that follow volume 8 (1972) are admirably up-to-date. A WHO'S WHO of scholars delivers articles as long as thirty-five pages on Ernest Renan, with a more modest four pages on Rashi (1040-1105) and two on Pierre Sabatier (1682-1742). Coverage of archeology is unmatched; there are seventy-

seven pages on "Semitic Sanctuaries" (10:1104-1258), eighty-five on "Rome and the Bible" (10:863-1008) and a staggering 175 on "Ras Shamra" (i.e., Ugarit) (9:1124-1466). An unexpected article concerns "Psychoanalysis and Biblical Interpretation" (9:252-60). Even **60** Freedman, ed., *The Anchor Bible Dictionary* (1992) seems spotty by comparison. One could wish, however, for cross-references.

□ *Summary* This most exhaustive of BIBLE DICTIONARIES is a must for specialists. Its dissection of archeology and scholars is without equal. Everyone will relish the bibliographies.

50 (1971, 1993) Joan Comay, *Who's Who in the Old Testament Together with Apocrypha* (London: Weidenfeld & Nicolson, 1971); 448 pages; no index; black-and-white photographs and some color plates. Reprinted in paperback (New York: Oxford University Press, 1993) without illustrations. Analyzed on the basis of the 1971 edition.

□ *Critique* This unusual WHO'S WHO retells stories from the Old Testament and Apocrypha in a confessionally neutral manner. The author recounts narratives of major and minor figures, for major ones assessing archeological and other evidence. Giants like Joshua, Moses and Solomon elicit ten pages, while less prominent figures may receive only five lines. This supple retelling eschews scholarly difficulties, and there are no bibliographies. In avoiding both doctrines and dubieties, Comay's *Who's Who* recalls works that retell classical myths such as *Crowell's Handbook of Classical Mythology* (1970). The writing is graceful, the illustrations lavish and integrated gracefully into the text. A sequel by Comay, *Who's Who in Jewish History* (New York: Oxford University Press, 1974), reappeared as *Routledge Who's Who in Jewish History after the Period of the Old Testament*, 2d ed., rev. Lavinia Cohn-Sherbok (London and New York: Routledge, 1995).

□ *Summary* This unpretentious recounting of biblical stories makes a fine self-teacher. For anyone versed in neither Judaism nor Christianity, it provides a place to begin.

51 (1971, 1993) Ronald Brownrigg, *Who's Who in the New Testament* (London: Weidenfeld & Nicolson, 1971); 448 pages; no index; black-and-white photographs and some color plates. Reprinted in paperback without alteration (New York: Oxford University Press, 1993) but with no illustrations. Analyzed on the basis of the 1971 edition.

□ *Critique* This companion to **50** Comay, *Who's Who in the Old Testament* (1971, 1993) adopts an identical format and purpose. Entries on every person in the New Testament recount stories straightforwardly. The author sidesteps questions of authorship, doctrine and historicity. This book offers neophytes an uncluttered starting point. It is suitable for courses in the Bible as literature. The 1993 reprint lacks the integration of text and illustrations that distinguished the original edition.

□ *Summary* This readable WHO'S WHO retells New Testament stories in an engagingly neutral way.

52 ([1915] 1979-88) Geoffrey W. Bromiley, ed., *The International Standard Bible Encyclopedia,* 3d ed., rev., 4 vols. (Grand Rapids, Mich.: Eerdmans, 1979-88); 4466 pages; no index; general bibliography (list of abbreviations), pp. xiv-xviii in each volume; about 1400 small black-and-white photographs; 56 color plates; 342 maps.

□ *Critique* This largest of illustrated English-language BIBLE DICTIONARIES restructures an earlier work in an evenhanded evangelical manner. The very opposite of a HANDBOOK OF INTERPRETATION, this REALLEXIKON recruits 240 mostly American scholars to write signed articles (most with bibliography) on every topic (except methodology) desired in such a work, but at a length three to four times greater than almost anywhere else. Stress falls on Hebrew and Greek vocabulary. Shades of meaning in Hebrew and Greek are discussed on every page; no other BIBLE DICTIONARY so painstakingly differentiates Hebrew and Greek terminology for every conceivable issue.

Places and objects elicit archeological explication, but most entries on theology are distinctly conservative (e.g., "Biblical Theology, Nature of," "Salvation," "Science and Christianity"). A few entries are REVISIONIST (e.g., George A. F. Knight on "Theophany"), and others are notably deft (e.g., Russell P. Spittler on "Spiritual Gifts"). Jacob Neusner contributes a classic on "Talmud." Seven articles on religions of antiquity (4:79-129) overflow with nuance but discourage hypotheses about Christian borrowings from non-Christian cultures. An even bulkier competitor, **60** Freedman, ed., *The Anchor Bible Dictionary* (1992), is confessionally neutral and treats methodology (but not theology) in far greater depth. Although not so up-to-date as that magnum opus, this one enlarges on DICTIONARIES like **58** Mills, ed., *Mercer Dictionary of the Bible* (1990). Attractive layout and unhurried pace make *The International Standard Bible Encyclopedia* a joy to traverse. This work satisfies the greediest appetite for information, particularly about Hebrew and Greek usage.

□ *Summary* This most spacious of illustrated BIBLE DICTIONARIES will delight devotees of REALLEXIKONS but will disappoint adepts of hermeneutics.

53 ([1962] 1982) J[ames] D[ixon] Douglas, ed., *New Bible Dictionary,* 2d ed. (Leicester, U.K., and Downers Grove, Ill.: InterVarsity Press, 1982); xviii & 1326 pages; index, pp. 1285-1324; no general bibliography; over 200 maps and genealogies throughout. Derek Williams shortened each entry in *New Concise Bible Dictionary* (Downers Grove, Ill.: InterVarsity Press, 1994; paperback, 1995).

□ *Scope* This conservative BIBLE DICTIONARY was executed by the Tyndale Fellowship for Biblical Research in Britain. As the preface explains, "The belief that loyalty to Holy Scripture involves treating as true and trustworthy all its statements of fact, theological, physical, and historical, is an assumption basic to the whole Dictionary" (p. vii). Twenty-one hundred signed entries by 165 mostly British and Australian contributors treat the standard topics while confining "Apocrypha" and "Pseudepigrapha" to two surveys. Most articles align Hebrew and Greek terms with equivalents in both the Authorized and Revised Standard Versions. Because the hermeneutical revolution goes unnoticed, historical topics win all the more space. About half the entries carry English-language bibliography. The writing condenses data effortlessly, and genealogical diagrams outshine all others.

□ *Strengths* This BIBLE DICTIONARY maximizes historicity and minimizes hermeneutics, delivering superb synopses. Forthright articles tackle "Chronology of the Old Testament" and "Chronology of the New Testament." There are eight pages (with time lines) on biblical languages and eight on "English Versions of the Bible." Syntheses wrap up topics like "Health, Disease, and Healing," "Magic and Sorcery," "Priests and Levites," and "Weights and Measures." Without becoming MENIPPEAN, inventories identify "Plants" and "Animals of the Bible" as well as "Music and Musical Instruments" and "Arts and Crafts." Ralph P. Martin's article on "Idols, Meats Offered to" has no parallel elsewhere. Archeology gets highlighted under "Archaeology" and "Wilderness of Wandering." Except as regards Deuteronomy, Job, Proverbs, Habakkuk and Isaiah, entries on individual books defend unity of authorship while rebutting contrary theories, often vigorously, as in Daniel, Zechariah and Epistles of John. E. M. B. Green's weighing of debates over 2 Peter is splendidly judicious. This premier resource for evangelicals deploys historical information straightforwardly.

□ *Weaknesses* This confessional BIBLE DICTIONARY all but ignores the Apocrypha and omits trendy topics like women and myth. Few entries discuss methodology (except as regards philology and archeology), and none treats hermeneutics. Oddly, Henry Leopold Ellison's praise of "Judaism" kindles no entry on Midrash and only a short one on "Targums." Dated bibliographies should be remedied in a 3d edition in 1996.

□ *Competitors* This British-Australian BIBLE DICTIONARY serves evangelicals. Resolutely historical, it dovetails with **65** Carson et al., eds., *New Bible Commentary,* 4th ed. (1994), which asserts unity of

authorship in contested books even more relentlessly. Those seeking still deeper history can turn to **52** Bromiley, ed., *The International Standard Bible Encyclopedia,* 4 vols. (1979-88), whose open-mindedness seems distinctly American. **56** Myers, ed., *The Eerdmans Bible Dictionary* (1975, 1987) dissects theories of authorship more acutely and treats extracanonical books in full. For deconfessionalized debate on the New Testament, evangelicals should consult **70** Green and McKnight, eds., *Dictionary of Jesus and the Gospels* (1992) and its sequels.

□ *Summary* This conservative evangelical BIBLE DICTIONARY downplays theories of multiple authorship and eschews the new hermeneutics but excels at historical synthesis. Nowhere else do fervor and compactness blend so well.

54 (1985) Paul J. Achtemeier, ed., *Harper's Bible Dictionary* (San Francisco: Harper & Row, 1985); xxii & 1176 pages; no index (except to the maps); many black-and-white photographs and diagrams; 16 color plates between pp. 362 and 363, 778 and 779.

□ *Critique* Designed as a companion to **62** Mays, ed., *Harper's Bible Commentary* (1988), this nonconfessional BIBLE DICTIONARY dispenses signed articles by 170 mostly American contributors on the usual topics (persons, places, paraphernalia, books of the Bible) as well as longer essays on matters like "The Bible and Western Art," "Music," and "Texts, Versions, Manuscripts, Editions." Articles on archeological sites are unusually detailed with superb maps. The writing is unadorned and eschews theology. Commentary is relegated to a companion volume, **62** Mays, ed., *Harper's Bible Commentary* (1988). Cross-references to the latter integrate the two works but can distract the unequipped. Devoting more attention to theology, **56** Myers, ed., *The Eerdmans Bible Dictionary* packs in more information and weightier bibliographies but lacks synthetic essays and treats archeology less fully. Articles on methodology are richer in a HANDBOOK OF INTERPRETATION like **68** Coggins and Houlden, eds., *Dictionary of*

Biblical Interpretation (1990).

□ *Summary* Nonspecialists will find this perhaps the best nonconfessional BIBLE DICTIONARY, notable for completeness, directness and lack of theology.

55 (1986) Geoffrey Wigoder, ed., *Illustrated Dictionary and Concordance of the Bible* (Jerusalem: Jerusalem Publishing House; New York: Macmillan, 1986); 1070 pages; no index; color photographs throughout; no bibliography.

□ *Critique* This secular DICTIONARY of the Bible prints concordance references beside each entry. This is an INTRODUCTORY REAL-LEXIKON devoid of bibliography. Unsigned articles offer a confessionally neutral view with little if any attention to methodology. Aiming at non-Christians who seek obligatory information, the work rivals the highly conservative Lawrence O. Richards, ed., *The Revell Bible Dictionary* (New York: Wynwood, 1990) in lavishness of color illustrations. A concordance conveniently accompanies each article.

□ *Summary* This REALLEXIKON combines information about biblical books, figures and places with gorgeous illustrations.

56 ([1975] 1987) Allen C. Myers, ed., *The Eerdmans Bible Dictionary* (Grand Rapids, Mich.: Eerdmans, 1987); translated and expanded from W. H. Gispen, ed., *Bijbelse Encyclopedie* (Kampen: Kok, 1975); x & 1093 pages; no index; eight pages of maps between pp. 630 and 631; black-and-white photographs and line drawings in the text.

□ *Scope* This ingenious BIBLE DICTIONARY interweaves three layers. The core of nearly five thousand unsigned entries derives from a Dutch BIBLE ENCYCLOPEDIA of 1975. Another 286 entries (marked by an asterisk) have been added to this edition, and certain of the Dutch entries (marked by a dagger) have been revised. Appearing only in longer entries, bibliographies have been updated and restricted to English-language works. Most entries conclude with discussion of Protestant biblical theology, a format that allows that excursus to be skipped if desired. Coverage is that of a classical BIBLE DICTIONARY. It encompasses (1) all persons, (2) all places and (3) nearly

all plants, animals and objects mentioned in the Old Testament, the New Testament and extracanonical books of both testaments. In addition, all books of the Old and New Testaments and of the Apocrypha (but not of the Nag Hammadi library) receive copious entries. Ancient civilizations ("Egypt," "Babylonia," "Persia,") and regions ("Ethiopia," "Thessalonica," "Ugarit") elicit entries, as do feasts and customs of the Jewish people. Roman emperors ("Nero," "Vespasian," "Hadrian"), Jewish writers ("Hillel," "Josephus," "Philo") and various sects ("Essenes," "Ebionites") receive lengthy entries. A number of articles explore issues pertinent to a HANDBOOK OF BIBLICAL INTERPRETATION such as "Canon," "Bible, Text of the," "Synoptic Gospels" and "Archaeology, Biblical." The writing is lucid and compact throughout in the fashion of German-language reference works.

□ *Strengths* This is the most versatile one-volume BIBLE DICTIONARY in English. The articles canvass a wide spectrum of interpretations and deploy facts in chronological sequence. Each entry on a person, place or concept summarizes history and states equivalent terms transliterated from Hebrew or Greek. By collating *every* mention of a person, place, object or concept, this DICTIONARY serves also as a concordance. In longer entries bibliographies cite articles as well as books, incorporating items otherwise found only in multivolume works. Entries on "Gnosticism" and on church fathers down to Eusebius carry the coverage into the fourth century. Entries on books of the Bible identify cognate works from ancient literature, including nine analogues to the book of Job.

As in a GLOSSARY, concise articles clarify concepts like "Judaizers," "Miracle," "Millennium," "Prophet" and "Rapture." Entries on objects ("Sandals, Shoes," "Ships and Sailing," "Money," "Tax" and "Water") classify instances, periods, customs and above all symbolism. Jewish practices ("Sacrifices and Offerings") and feasts ("Passover"), as well as Christian sacraments ("Baptism"), command analyses. As befits the Dutch Reformed tradition, fundamentals of theology elicit luminous essays ("Church," "Christology," "Faith," "Sin," "Trinity"), as do basic categories like "Know, Knowledge," "Tradition," "Truth," "Faith" and "Life." Magisterial surveys of "Eschatology," "God," and "Kingdom of God, Kingdom of Heaven" set a high standard. Issues of hermeneutics shine in articles on "Allegory," "Typology" and "Interpretation, Biblical." Entries range in length from a few lines on obscure places through an average of one-half column on objects and persons to a full five pages on "Paul." Nearly all the longer articles conclude by sifting theological implications. Although not in color, the maps are easy to read but have no gazetteer.

□ *Weaknesses* Such an astonishingly comprehensive volume invites certain cavils. Articles are unsigned, and the bibliographies, too often skeletal, are limited to works in English. Although photographs depict ancient art, no generic entries tackle architecture (except "Palace," "Tabernacle" and "Temple") to complement excellent ones on "Music" and "Musical Instruments." The invocation of Protestant biblical theology at the end of articles may deter readers who seek neutrality. Many will regret a relative absence of Jewish scholarship and a total absence of feminist discourse. As regards format, there are too few cross-references, and the print is small.

□ *Competitors* This hypothesis-weighing BIBLE DICTIONARY was written by and for professional scholars, particularly theologians. This work squeezes in more information and more alternative interpretations (particularly of theology) than any other single-volume BIBLE DICTIONARY. An infusion of theology may discourage the secular. **54** Achtemeier, *Harper's Bible Dictionary* (1985) packs less detail into generally shorter entries but deploys both archeological specificity and synoptic essays that have no parallel here. Its lack of theology will appeal to many. **58** Mills, ed., *Mercer Dictionary of the Bible* (1990) excels at synopses of customs, regions and methodology, and discusses even more extracanonical texts. Its longer bibliographies,

like its avoidance of theology, will please historians. Shorter by one-fourth, **72** Metzger and Coogan, eds., *The Oxford Companion to the Bible* (1993) addresses a wider and trendier audience, eschews theology and combines the roles of BIBLE DICTIONARY and HANDBOOK OF BIBLE INTERPRETATION. Amid such competition, *The Eerdmans Bible Dictionary* more than holds its own. Interweaving a concordance, a REALLEXIKON and a DICTIONARY of Protestant biblical theology, it remains the most versatile single-volume BIBLE DICTIONARY available in English.

□ *Summary* This gold mine of information summarizes data pithily and assesses hypotheses shrewdly. Devotees of Protestant theology who wish to own only one BIBLE DICTIONARY will treasure this one.

57 (1989) Bernhard W. Anderson, ed., *The Books of the Bible*, 2 vols. (New York: Scribner's, 1989); xix & 435; xiii & 412 pages; index, 2:385-412; no maps or illustrations.

□ *Scope* This author of a well-known TEXTBOOK, *Understanding the Old Testament* (Englewood Cliffs, N.J.: Prentice Hall, 1957; 4th ed. 1986), has edited an INTRODUCTION to the Bible for students of literature. Signed articles by fifty-eight authorities treat each book "in its final literary form" and ignore "how a biblical book has been read confessionally by religious communities." An entry of five to twenty pages on each book presents background information in the manner of classical German INTRODUCTIONS. The longest article devotes thirty pages to "Isaiah." Contributors represent a wide spectrum of approaches (including Raymond Brown writing "Introduction to the New Testament"). Eschewing methodology and the history of scholarship, this work achieves neither the density of a BIBLE DICTIONARY nor the intricacy of a BIBLE COMMENTARY. Novices will find pointers here but should move on to works like **58** Mills, ed., *Mercer Dictionary of the Bible* (1990) and **62** Mays ed., *Harper's Bible Commentary* (1988).

□ *Summary* This nonconfessional INTRODUCTION to Bible as literature will help beginners and non-Christians. The more advanced can safely ignore it.

58 (1990) Watson E. Mills, ed., *Mercer Dictionary of the Bible* (Macon, Ga.: Mercer University Press, 1990); published in Britain as *The Lutterworth Dictionary of the Bible* (Cambridge: Lutterworth, 1990); xxx & 993 pages; no index; no general bibliography; 62 colored plates (including 25 maps) between pages 482 and 483; also in paperback.

□ *Scope* This down-to-earth BIBLE DICTIONARY is better called a REALLEXIKON of the Bible. It dethrones theology in favor of places, persons and objects, often retracing history of their interpretation. Nearly fifteen hundred signed articles by two hundred (mostly) American Baptists excel at synthesizing material on a wide range of topics: (1) languages ("Greek Language," "Semitic Languages," "Writing Systems"), (2) technology (e.g., "Building Materials," "Water Systems," "Papyrus"), (3) customs ("Hospitality," "Hunting," "Occupations"), (4) religious practices ("Clean/ Unclean," "Sacrifice," "Synagogue"), and above all (5) texts. A special merit is coverage of extracanonical literature, including the apostolic fathers and every item in the Nag Hammadi library. Lexical nicety prevails. Entries differentiate competing Hebrew and Greek terms for concepts (e.g., "Blood," "Law," "Righteousness," "Saint," "Wisdom") besides specifying when postbiblical words like "Shekinah" or "Semitic" originated. The writing is sober and factual, rejoicing in the limits of the knowable. Color plates are vivid, and cross-references abound.

□ *Strengths* As a REALLEXIKON, the *Mercer Dictionary of the Bible* treats objects, persons, places and texts straightforwardly. It eschews theology in favor of history. Languages, cities and regions (e.g., "Assyria," "Canaan," "Persian Empire") elicit narratives that evoke all available sources, including archeology. Superb entries on "Temple/ Temples," "Tomb of Jesus" and "Samaritans" sort out complexities. Taken together, these entries supply an archeologist's GUIDEBOOK to the ancient Near East. Social history emerges in paired entries like

"Economics in the New/Old Testament" and "Sociology of the New/Old Testament." History of methodology is discussed in "Hermeneutics," "Gospels, Critical Study of," "Interpretation, History of" and "New Testament Use of the Old Testament." Most entries on individual biblical and extracanonical books also tackle methodology, notably in "Pastoral Epistles" and "Revelation, Book of." In a tour de force, Russel Gregory's entry on Moses assigns him no fewer than eleven roles. A forte of this REALLEXIKON is extracanonical literature. Three- and four-page synopses of "Apocryphal Literature," "Gnosticism" and "Patristic Literature" supplement entries on "Marcion," each book of the Nag Hammadi library and each of the apostolic fathers. Comprising a mini-patrology, these entries situate the author(s), outline contents and evaluate influence of each text. The same is done for Old Testament pseudepigrapha and for Hellenistic writers on the Jews, like (Pseudo) Hecateus. The *Mercer Dictionary of the Bible* remains the most convenient single volume to discuss not only extracanonical writings but also Near Eastern and Hellenistic customs and history. Empiricism prevails.

□ *Weaknesses* This REALLEXIKON does not aspire to exhaustiveness. It omits minor figures and places and lacks a concordance. Jewish scholars will be disappointed that the work examines Hellenistic writings more thoroughly than rabbinic ones, and New Testament books more searchingly than Old Testament ones. By way of compensation, the *Mercer Dictionary of the Bible* upholds no theological position or method. It confines discussion of theology to classifying biblical approaches (e.g., in "Creation" and "Christology") or assessing biblical roots of postbiblical debates (e.g., in "Faith" and "Justification"). Six pages on "Theology of the New/Old Testament" narrate the history of that discipline. Preachers and theologians may quail at the insistence on empiricism, but historians and literary scholars will rejoice. Regarding flaws of format, the bibliographies omit place and date of publication, and in early printings some of the photographs are blurred. A BIBLE COMMENTARY designed chiefly for use in adult education supplies a companion: Watson E. Mills and Richard F. Wilson, eds., *Mercer Commentary on the Bible* (Macon, Ga.: 1995). Elegantly cross-referenced to the *Mercer Dictionary of the Bible*, it is less sophisticated than either **62** Mays, *Harper's Bible Commentary* (1988) or **63** Brown et al., eds., *The New Jerome Biblical Commentary* (1968, 1990).

◻ *Competitors* This REALLEXIKON does not duplicate other BIBLE DICTIONARIES. Emphasis on tangibles—customs, languages, texts and places (particularly their archeology)—is unique. **54** Achtemeier, ed., *Harper's Bible Dictionary* (1985) is exhaustive on proper names but less thorough on customs and languages. It serves exegetes and literary scholars, while the *Mercer Dictionary of the Bible* serves historians. **56** Myers, ed., *The Eerdmans Bible Dictionary* (1975, 1987) expounds recent scholarship as well as Protestant theology on every conceivable topic but scants customs and later extracanonical texts. Being ten times bulkier, **60** Freedman, ed., *The Anchor Bible Dictionary* (1992) tackles all topics (except theology and hermeneutics) but often at excessive length. The estimable **52** Bromiley, ed., *The International Standard Bible Encyclopedia* (1979-88) likewise supplies similar information more copiously. **72** Coogan and Metzger, eds., *The Oxford Companion to the Bible* (1993) downplays extracanonical texts and daily customs, while canvassing nonconfessional approaches more fully. By expounding social and cultural history, the *Mercer Dictionary of the Bible* prepares one to tackle a MEGA-ENCYCLOPEDIA like **151** Klauser, ed., *Reallexikon für Antike und Christentum* (1950-) or its minirival **275** van der Toorn, Becking and van der Horst, eds., *Dictionary of Deities and Demons in the Bible (DDD)* (1995). The Mercer volume brings to biblical studies the assets of a REALLEXIKON, delineating tangibles while sidestepping speculation. More modern in scope than postmodern, it celebrates the knowable.

◻ *Summary* Readers who seek historical background and summary of extracanonical texts will delight in the *Mercer Dictionary of the Bible*. As a REALLEXIKON, it fills a gap among BIBLE DICTIONARIES, supplanting theology with factuality and literary criticism with history of scholarship.

59 (1991) Geoffrey Wigoder, Shalom M. Paul and Benedict T. Viviano, eds., *Almanac of the Bible* (Jerusalem: Jerusalem Publishing House; New York: Henry Holt, 1991); 448 pages; no index; no bibliography; eight color plates; black-and-white photographs throughout.

◻ *Critique* This COMPENDIUM arranges biblical lore into several dozen compilations deployed across fifty-six chapters. Neither a BIBLE DICTIONARY nor a BIBLE COMMENTARY, this assemblage of lists collates data on a wide range of matters in unsigned articles, often of considerable depth. Arranged into six chronological headings, entries canvass such matters as "Places in the Bible" (pp. 47-96), "Jerusalem in the Bible" (pp. 96-101) and "Famous Quotations and Phrases" (pp. 328-31). The longest scrutinizes "Everyday Life in Bible Times" (pp. 136-95). Separate WHO'S WHOS cover Old Testament and New Testament. A notable cluster of entries assembles data on the Bible's exploitation in fiction, drama, poetry, motion pictures and music. Other articles list "Prophets" and "United States Towns with Old Testament Names." There is no discussion of methodology or history of interpretation. Although longer entries mobilize clear layout and pithy description to avoid Menippean overdoses, some simply list names (e.g., "Angels," p. 213). Anyone who likes to see familiar data grouped in unfamiliar ways will enjoy this masterwork of classification. It clusters information that BIBLE DICTIONARIES disperse.

◻ *Summary* This COMPENDIUM compiles data into categories that serve mainly novices and non-Christians.

60 (1992) David Noel Freedman, ed., *The Anchor Bible Dictionary,* 6 vols. (New York: Doubleday, 1992); lxxviii & 1232; xxxv & 1100; xxxii & 1135; xxxv & 1162; xxxiv & 1230; xxxv & 1176 pages;

no index as yet; no general bibliography; a few black-and-white photographs and diagrams per volume (particularly in vol. 1 on "Art and Architecture"). An index volume is planned.

□ *Scope* This formidable enterprise bears the dimensions of a MEGA-ENCYCLOPEDIA. Seventy-three hundred pages, sixty-four hundred entries and almost a thousand contributors place it in a class by itself among BIBLE DICTIONARIES. Having labored at the University of Michigan for almost ten years, the editors acknowledge that their endeavor may well be the last before computerized databases take over. As the introduction explains, this MEGA-ENCYCLOPEDIA references every proper name and nearly every object in the Bible. It analyzes every book in the canon and nearly all extracanonical ones. It recounts the history of pertinent regions from 3000 B.C.E. to 200 C.E. It explores archeology in exceptional depth, albeit with too few maps. It examines religious practices ("Embalming") and the cultural milieu ("Folklore in the Ancient Near East") but treats theology (e.g., "Freedom") selectively. Having grown in parallel with the *Anchor Bible,* this mammoth DICTIONARY recruits many of the same expositors. The multilingual bibliographies, sometimes running a page or more, are easily the fullest available in an English-language work. The volumes are printed attractively, but the index has yet to appear.

□ *Strengths* This MEGA-ENCYCLOPEDIA exudes largeness. On historical and archeological, but not theological or literary, topics nearly every entry is more extensive and has longer bibliography than anything else in English. Entries on "Israel," "Mesopotamia" and "Christianity" each run fifty pages and those on Egypt ninety pages. "Eschatology" elicits three articles totaling thirty-five pages. Graydon F. Snyder contributes sixty pages on "Art and Architecture" (with ample black-and-white photographs). Kurt Rudolph adds eight pages on "Gnosticism." Particularly useful are sixteen entries on "Languages," including eight pages on "Greek" and twelve on "Hebrew." Entries on individual books of the Bible (and Apocrypha) set a standard for historical reconstruction of what an author might have intended for the audience he might have envisioned at the time of writing. Jewish scholars of the Hebrew Bible will hail the scrupulosity.

□ *Weaknesses* In many ways this is a gargantuan REALLEXIKON, which underplays both theological and literary analysis. In valuing factuality above interplay of competing perspectives, the discourse seems more modern than postmodern. Theology in all its aspects, not least in prayer, gets scanted. Articles on imagery, narrative and theory of interpretation (e.g., five pages on "Hermeneutics") are minimal and do not replace those in a HANDBOOK OF INTERPRETATION. The sheer bulk of this MEGA-ENCYCLOPEDIA means that it is almost never the best place to start an inquiry. A paucity of illustrations and maps is another reason why it does not supplant one-volume BIBLE DICTIONARIES. In contrast to shorter works like **58** Mills., ed., *Mercer Dictionary of the Bible* (1990) or **63** Brown et al., eds., *The New Jerome Biblical Commentary* (1968, 1990), this behemoth too rarely throws up pithy insights. Lack of sparkle does a disservice to a field that has nurtured brilliant writers.

□ *Competitors* Although fuller and better documented than any other English-language BIBLE DICTIONARY, *The Anchor Bible Dictionary* seldom offers the keenest insights except regarding historicity of individual biblical texts. **58** Mills, ed., *Mercer Dictionary of the Bible* (1990) excels at pithy synopses of culture. **56** Myers, ed., *The Eerdmans Bible Dictionary* (1975, 1987) probes theology searchingly and displays a European knack for compression. **54** Achtemeier, ed., *Harper's Bible Dictionary* (1985) summarizes standard topics concisely with superb illustrations. The same can be said even more forcibly of **52** Bromiley, ed., *The International Standard Bible Encyclopedia* (1979-88). **70** Green and McKnight, eds., *Dictionary of Jesus and the Gospels* (1992) and its sequel are pleasanter to read, and they weigh crucial questions more pungently. Any of these is a wiser place to begin than is *The Anchor*

Bible Dictionary. Its chief rival as a MEGA-ENCYCLOPEDIA remains **49** Pirot, ed., *Dictionnaire de la Bible: Supplément* (1928-), now in its twelfth volume. The latter provides often vaster coverage, besides recounting careers of scholars incomparably. The advantage of *The Anchor Bible Dictionary* is that it delivers up-to-date reportage on historical research together with bibliographies unmatched in other English-language works. Its strengths are archeology, political and social history, textual controversies and historicity of individual books. Both theological and literary analyses, however, falter. While advanced researchers would be foolish to neglect this magnum opus, beginners risk suffocation by consulting it prematurely.

□ *Summary* This American MEGA-ENCYCLOPEDIA delivers authoritative monographs and bibliographies on historical research but does not scintillate as frequently as one-volume competitors. A gold mine for specialists, it will likely remain a monument, not a tool, for the less committed.

2.3.2 BIBLE COMMENTARIES

OVERVIEW: CONFESSIONAL DISCOURSE
More than in BIBLE DICTIONARIES, confessional utterance thrives in BIBLE COMMENTARIES. Most such works, even the ones that are pluralist in approach, resist, or at least slow down, the process of deconfessionalization. A conservative Protestant classic (**65** Carson), an eclectic Catholic one (**63** Brown) and a pioneering Reform Jewish work (**61** Plaut) span the options, together with a nonconfessional masterpiece (**62** Mays) and a REVISIONIST one (**64** Newsom and Ringe). Only **61** Plaut and **65** Carson target a particular translation. It goes without saying that a COMMENTARY impels resort to a BIBLE DICTIONARY.

LIST OF WORKS ANALYZED
61 (1981) W. Gunther Plaut, ed., *The Torah: A Modern Commentary* (New York: Union of American Hebrew Congregations, 1981)

62 (1988) James L. Mays, ed., *Harper's Bible Commentary* (San Francisco: Harper, 1988)

63 ([1968] 1990) Raymond E. Brown, S.S., Joseph A. Fitzmyer, S.J. and Roland E. Murphy, O.Carm., eds., *The New Jerome Biblical Commentary* (Englewood Cliffs, N.J.: Prentice-Hall, 1990)

64 (1992) Carol A. Newsom and Sharon H. Ringe, eds., *The Women's Bible Commentary* (Louisville: Westminster/John Knox; London: SPCK, 1992)

65 ([1953] 1994) D[onald] A. Carson et al., eds., *New Bible Commentary: 21st Century Edition* (Downers Grove, Ill., and Leicester, U.K.: InterVarsity Press, 1994)

ANALYSIS OF WORKS
61 (1981) W. Gunther Plaut, ed., *The Torah: A Modern Commentary* (New York: Union of American Hebrew Congregations, 1981; reprinted with corrections, 1985); xxxvii & 1787 pages; no index; no bibliographies.

□ *Critique* Seventeen years in preparation, this Reform Jewish COMMENTARY scrutinizes the first five books of the Hebrew Bible. History and Halakah command equal attention. William W. Hallo writes segments on "Ancient Near Eastern Literature," while a Reform rabbi, Bernard J. Bamberger, handles the book of Leviticus; everything else comes from the editor. Printed in parallel with the Jewish Publication Society of America Bible translation, the Hebrew text is examined section by section at four levels: headnotes, footnotes, expository essays and "Gleanings" from previous interpreters. After each book appear haftarot (traditional synagogue readings allied to it) without interpretation.

Echoing Reform views, Plaut stipulates that this COMMENTARY presupposes "human not divine authorship" (p. xviii) and treats the documentary hypothesis where needed (e.g., pp. 1289-307). A distinguishing feature is 150 bundles of "Gleanings," which attach quotations from previous interpreters, ancient and modern, to every group of verses. No other COMMENTARY comes close to gathering so many meaty quotations or targeting them so precisely. The table of contents is a model of clarity. Jews of all persuasions will mine vast lore (particularly about Halakah) from this volume, while non-Jews will discover three or four diverse and often unfamiliar interpretations of nearly every passage. *The Torah: A Modern Commentary* complements Christian reference works superbly, and its "Gleanings" have no parallel, except as regards persons in **179** Chasidah, *Encyclopedia of Biblical Personalities* (1964, 1994). A rival COMMENTARY runs longer: Nahum M. Sarna, ed., *The JPS Torah Commentary,* planned in 5 vols. (Philadelphia: Jewish Publication Society of America, 1989-96). In four volumes to date it is Conservative rather than Reform, lacking "Gleanings" but including some bibliography.

□ *Summary* No other reference work evokes Jewish understanding of the Pentateuch so conveniently or marshals quotations about it so memorably.

62 (1988) James L. Mays, ed., *Harper's Bible Commentary* (San Francisco: Harper, 1988); xviii & 1326 pages; no index (except to the 16 colored maps); bibliographies at end of chapters; a very few black-and-white photographs.

□ *Scope* Planned as a companion to **54** Achtemeier, ed., *Harper's Bible Dictionary* (1985), this masterpiece encapsulates recent scholarship on every book of the Bible. Seventy-seven chiefly North American experts write on topics they know best. Seven sections, each with introduction, adopt a topical arrangement: (1) "The Biblical Story: Genesis to Esther," (2) "Psalms and Wisdom," (3) "The Prophetic Books," (4) "The Apocrypha," (5) "The Gospels and Acts," (6) "The Pauline Letters" and (7) "The General Letters to the Churches." Each biblical book evokes an introduction and unit-by-unit, occasionally verse-by-verse commentary with brief bibliography (in English). Fifteen books inspire one-page essays (five in Genesis and eight in Jeremiah) interspersed within the commentary. Cross-references to **54** Achtemeier, ed., *Harper's Bible Dictionary* (1985) abound. Whether Jewish, Protes-

tant or Catholic, the seventy-seven authors lay out difficulties tirelessly. Rigorously nonconfessional, this volume eschews nitpicking and unction alike.

□ *Strengths* The caliber of its contributors places this work among the most trenchant of BIBLE COMMENTARIES. Eight chapters of introduction encompass vast amounts of material with minimal repetition. Each of seven principal sections opens with a brilliant overview; among these, Norman R. Peterson's "Introduction to the Gospels and Acts" is a model of how to outline intractable problems. The heart of a BIBLE COMMENTARY is of course chapters on books of the Old and New Testaments and the Apocrypha. These are uniformly candid, learned, and versatile. Each chapter recounts circumstances of composition and canonization, so that a reader can imagine how each book, indeed each passage, has functioned for a succession of readerships from inception to about 200 C.E. On hundreds of unresolved questions, three or four theories get recited with arguments pro and con, so that a reader emerges fully apprised of difficulties, large or small. Such forthrightnees fosters respect for scholars who spend their professional lives navigating among uncertainties. Patience becomes contagious.

□ *Weaknesses* Frequent cross-references to **54** Achtemeier, ed., *Harper's Bible Dictionary* will irritate anyone who lacks it. Bibliographies are skeletal and restricted to English. They need to be amplified from **60** Freedman, ed., *The Anchor Bible Dictionary* (1992). Marring an otherwise perspicuous format is lack of a table of contents, causing one easily to overlook the introductory articles. Although this is a nonconfessional tool, some readers may desire devotional spurts or interconfessional debate; there is none of either.

□ *Competitors* The meatiness of individual commentaries combines with the penetration of the overviews to make this perhaps the best nonconfessional COMMENTARY in print. **63** Brown et al., eds., *The New Jerome Biblical Commentary* (1968, 1990) supplies many more theories about editorial history and far richer bibliographies, but it favors Catholic issues and is more densely printed. Because *Harper's Bible Commentary* cuts to the heart of whatever it discusses, its precision makes **72** Metzger and Coogan, eds., *The Oxford Companion to the Bible* (1990) seem bland. Although the latter dispenses almost no commentary, and its methodological articles cite few biblical texts, it accords more space to a Jewish standpoint. **60** Freedman, ed., *The Anchor Bible Dictionary* (1992) amplifies every question of fact but not of theology and offers only sporadic commentary.

□ *Summary* This most balanced of one-volume BIBLE COMMENTARIES makes one admire the legions of scholars whose lifework it encapsulates. If one were to possess a single COMMENTARY, this one would win the theologically uncommitted.

63 ([1968] 1990) Raymond E. Brown, S.S., Joseph A. Fitzmyer, S.J., and Roland E. Murphy, O.Carm., eds., *The New Jerome Biblical Commentary* (Englewood Cliffs, N.J.: Prentice-Hall, 1990 and London: Geoffrey Chapman, 1989; paperback 1993); thoroughly revised from first edition of 1968; xlviii & 1175 pages; index (keyed to numbered paragraphs), pp. 1433-75; general bibliography, pp. 1427-30. A reduction to one-tenth of the original appeared as *The New Jerome Bible Handbook* (Collegeville, Minn.: Liturgical, 1992).

□ *Critique* This most fastidious of one-volume COMMENTARIES recruited seventy-four Catholic scholars to write eighty-three articles, each with multilingual bibliography. Of twenty-seven general articles, Raymond Brown coauthored eight. Certain entries like "Modern Old Testament Criticism," "Modern New Testament Criticism," "Biblical Archaeology" and "Hermeneutics" constitute a small HANDBOOK OF INTERPRETATION. Overview chapters provide the acutest histories of the field outside **68** Coggins and Houlden, eds., *A Dictionary of Biblical Interpretation* (1990). Frans Neirynck expounds the "Synoptic Problem" dazzlingly, while John P. Meier delineates the historical Jesus in anticipation of his own virtuosic *Jesus: A Marginal Jew,* 2 vols. to date (Garden City,

N.Y.: Doubleday, 1992-). Chapters on individual books include introductions that vary in structure, while the commentaries proceed verse by verse. The depth of analysis is without parallel in a single volume, and the variety of approaches is refreshing, occasionally even REVISIONIST (e.g., Guy P. Couturier on Jeremiah).

Old Testament books get reconfigured into four clusters: Pentateuch (and History), Prophets, Apocalypse (and Eschatology) and Wisdom. Sensible pairing yokes Chronicles with Ezra and Nehemiah. The page layout crams in a maximum of information, and the bibliographies are phenomenal. The index and cross-references save time by citing numbered paragraphs. The first edition of 1968 demonstrated the riches and nonpartisanship of American Catholic biblical scholarship, and this revision ("in a form about two-thirds new") builds on those strengths. Surprisingly, on certain books (e.g., Psalms) the 1968 edition runs longer. More than half the 1990 chapters are by fresh authors, and in retained chapters a footnote explains who added what. No other reference work demonstrates the collaborativeness of biblical research so compellingly. Insights from deconfessionalized research abound, as no difficulty is shirked, no obstacle ignored.

□ *Summary* No one should begin with this masterpiece, but all can work up to it. This unparalleled COMMENTARY provides a capstone.

64 (1992) Carol A. Newsom and Sharon H. Ringe, eds., *The Women's Bible Commentary* (Louisville: Westminster/John Knox Press; London: SPCK, 1992); xix & 396 pages; no index; general bibliography, pp. xix, 9; also in paperback.

□ *Critique* This REVISIONIST BIBLE COMMENTARY commissioned forty-one women scholars to write on every book of the Old and New Testaments. Just nine pages are accorded to the Apocrypha. Chapters range in length from one page on minor epistles and two on minor prophets to eighteen pages on Luke. Each chapter divides into three sections: "Introduction," "Comment" and "Bibliography." Each introduction canvasses general issues, while each comment tackles gender. Four chapters perform synthesis: Sharon H. Ringe on "When Women Interpret the Bible," Eileen M. Schuller on "The Apocrypha," Carol L. Meyers on "Everyday Life: Women in the Period of the Hebrew Bible" and Amy L. Wordelman on "Everyday Life: Women in the Period of the New Testament." While all the authors display gender sensitivity, some are more outspoken than others about the "oppressive dynamics" of androcentrism (notably Jane Schaberg on "Luke"). A few espouse extreme views, as when Joanna Dewey interprets the pastoral epistles as late works (c. 125 C.E.) that exhort women to submit to male authority. Others, such as Judith Romney Wegner on "Leviticus," take pains to contextualize, if not justify, women's exclusion from public worship. Refreshing perspectives concisely formulated make this REVISIONIST COMMENTARY a tonic for the browser and a boon for beginners.

□ *Summary* Few BIBLE COMMENTARIES offer so much lucidity or novel insight as this one, and almost no other so effectively addresses beginner and expert alike.

65 ([1953] 1994) D[onald] A. Carson et al., eds., *New Bible Commentary: 21st Century Edition*, 4th ed. (Leicester, U.K., and Downers Grove, Ill.: InterVarsity Press, 1994); xiii & 1455 pages; no index; no general bibliography; chronology, pp. 22-24; 50 maps and diagrams.

□ *Scope* This conservative COMMENTARY reshapes an evangelical classic of British origin: Donald Guthrie and J. A. Motyer, eds., *The New Bible Commentary*, 3d ed. (Leicester: InterVarsity Press, 1970), which itself refashioned a pioneering work of 1953. The fourth edition supplies fifty-one entirely new commentaries while retaining fifteen, most of them substantially rewritten (except for light retouching of the late Donald Guthrie's articles on both John and the pastoral letters). Seven introductory articles are entirely fresh. The New Testament commands more than a third of the total (550 pages), and J. A. Motyer's reworked treatment of Psalms remains by far the longest chapter, as well as the most subtle. "Apocrypha and Apocalyptic" get

relegated to a synopsis (pp. 890-95). Each chapter furnishes introduction, outline of contents, verse-by-verse commentary (highlighted by two layers of subheadings) and brief English-language bibliography. Unlike other recent BIBLE COMMENTARIES this one stipulates a translation: the New International Version (1973-78). Clear writing and attractive layout make reading a pleasure.

□ *Strengths* This BIBLE COMMENTARY will become standard for evangelicals. Writing on the Pentateuch, Gordon J. Wenham announces the motivation: "If we make the divine purpose of Scripture . . . our paramount concern, we may keep critical debates in their proper perspective." (p. 53). This COMMENTARY expounds biblical teachings while disregarding the new hermeneutics. Relying upon both biblical and church traditions, contributors posit unity of authorship virtually wherever it has been disputed, including in Job, Isaiah and Zechariah as well as between 1 and 2 Peter and among all three letters of John. What Sinclair B. Ferguson says against multiple authorship of Daniel pertains throughout: "The approach adopted in this commentary follows the long-held view of the Christian church that the book of Daniel has its origin [solely] in the sixth century B.C. and in Babylon" (p. 747). The chief exception is Lamentations. And in 2 Corinthians Colin G. Kruse acknowledges two letters divided between chapters 9 and 10.

The *New Bible Commentary* affirms historicity no less resolutely. Barry G. Webb inserts historical "Notes" throughout commentary on Judges. Emphasizing continuity of narrative, 1 and 2 Samuel, like 1 and 2 Kings, get treated as a block. In contrast, Philip Jenson's insightfulness on "Poetry in the Bible" vindicates greater diversity (pp. 453-58). David J. A. Clines writes cunningly on Job, John Goldingay expatiates on Proverbs, and Michael A. Eaton construes Ecclesiastes as an example of "pessimism literature." Most preachers will rejoice that the New Testament elicits greater length and depth than does the Old. Anyone seeking evangelical understanding, whether of a passage, a book or an entire Testament, will treasure the *New Bible Commentary*. Scholarship glows with fervor.

□ *Weaknesses* This COMMENTARY stands at the opposite pole from a HANDBOOK OF INTERPRETATION. Debates about sources and redactors fade into the background so much that controversialists seldom get named. Happy exceptions to such omission include Douglas J. Moo on both Romans and 1 Corinthians and Max Turner on Ephesians as well as a sole woman contributor, Joyce Baldwin, on Esther. In a tour-de-force, after dismissing nearly all preceding commentators (p. 1421), George R. Beasley-Murray eloquently particularizes historical backgrounds of Revelation. Both adepts and opponents of newer methods will esteem the *New Bible Commentary* for asserting so intelligently views that innovators seek to supplant. All camps will applaud the acumen applied to Judges, the Wisdom Literature, Paul's letters and above all Psalms.

□ *Competitors* This tightly argued COMMENTARY serves conservative evangelicals. It complements **53** Douglas, ed., *New Bible Dictionary*, 2d ed. (1982), which likewise favors historicity and shuns hermeneutics, albeit more flexibly. The same readers will find **52** Bromiley, ed., *The International Standard Bible Encyclopedia* (1979-88) both more adventurous and more thorough. Evangelicals pondering controversies in the New Testament should resort to **70** Green and McKnight, eds., *Dictionary of Jesus and the Gospels* (1992) and its sequels. On theology **56** Myers, ed., *The Eerdmans Bible Dictionary* (1975, 1987) dissects debates acutely. Covering every verse of the New Testament, Craig S. Keener, *The IVP Bible Background Commentary: New Testament* (Downers Grove, Ill.: InterVarsity, 1993) marshals often inaccessible historical information. All these volumes equip evangelicals better than ever before.

□ *Summary* This conservative COMMENTARY upholds historicity and unity of authorship with finesse and fervor. It treats Wisdom literature, Paul's letters and Psalms with profundity, exalts gospel

teachings and reads compellingly.

2.3.3 HANDBOOKS OF INTERPRETATION

OVERVIEW: A NEW GENRE FOR NEW APPROACHES HANDBOOKS OF INTERPRETATION are among the most stimulating of recent reference books. The explosion of secular approaches to the Bible since the 1970s has necessitated nonconfessional works that expound divergent methodologies and sort out the "blurring of genres." In explaining innovations, such volumes sometimes undertake cultural history as well. Apart from a German MEGA-COMPENDIUM (**67**), the most satisfactory is **68** Coggins and Houlden, eds., *A Dictionary of Biblical Interpretation* (1990), while **69** Jeffrey, ed., *A Dictionary of Biblical Tradition in English Literature* (1992) is the most daunting. All these works, including even the ostensibly evangelical **70** Green and McKnight, eds., *Dictionary of Jesus and the Gospels* (1992) and its sequel, foster deconfessionalization of the field.

LIST OF WORKS ANALYZED

66 (1976, 1981) Richard N. Soulen, *Handbook of Biblical Criticism* (Atlanta: John Knox, 1976; 2d ed., rev., 1981)

67 (1982-88) Wolfgang Haase and Hildegard Temporini, eds., *Aufstieg und Niedergang der römischen Welt: Geschichte Roms im Spiegel der neueren Forschung. II. Principat,* vols. 25.1—25.6 (Berlin and New York: de Gruyter, 1982-88)

68 (1990) R[ichard] J. Coggins and J. L[eslie] Houlden, eds., *A Dictionary of Biblical Interpretation* (London: SCM; New York: Trinity Press International, 1990)

69 (1992) David Lyle Jeffrey, ed., *A Dictionary of Biblical Tradition in English Literature* (Grand Rapids, Mich.: Eerdmans, 1992)

70 (1992) Joel B. Green and Scot McKnight, eds., *Dictionary of Jesus and the Gospels* (Downers Grove, Ill., and Leicester, U.K.: InterVarsity Press, 1992)

71 (1993) Gerald Hawthorne and Ralph P. Martin, eds., *Dictionary of Paul and His Letters* (Downers Grove, Ill., and Leicester, U.K.: InterVarsity Press, 1993)

72 (1993) Bruce M. Metzger and Michael D. Coogan, eds., *The Oxford Companion to the Bible* (New York and Oxford: Oxford University Press, 1993)

ANALYSIS OF WORKS

66 (1976) Richard N. Soulen, *Handbook of Biblical Criticism* (Atlanta: John Knox, 1976; 2d ed., rev., 1981); 239 pages; no index; general bibliography, pp. 33-34, 233; two lists of abbreviations, pp. 215-33.

□ *Critique* This GLOSSARY of methodology expounds over six hundred terms, principally for seminary students. It combines a GLOSSARY of technical terms (including German and Greek) with a brief WHO'S WHO of (mostly German) scholars. Theology is largely ignored. Longer articles explore the history of such methods as form criticism, literary criticism and hermeneutics (with cross-references and skeletal bibliography). Rich in dates and citations, the writing is often telegraphic. A five-page appendix outlines how to prepare an exegetical paper on the Synoptic Gospels. Ideal as a companion to **68** Coggins and Houlden, eds., *A Dictionary of Biblical Interpretation* (1990), this INTRODUCTION lacks the profundity and range of that masterpiece. Students will find this volume helpful but should plunge at once into BIBLE DICTIONARIES and COMMENTARIES. This book offers a gate, not a path.

□ *Summary* By clarifying technical terms, this GLOSSARY whets the appetite for controversy.

67 (1982-88) Wolfgang Haase and Hildegard Temporini, eds., *Aufstieg und Niedergang der römischen Welt: Geschichte Roms im Spiegel der neueren Forschung. II. Principat.* vol. 25.1—25.6 (Berlin and New York: de Gruyter, 1982-88); 4794 pages. Analyzed further under 2.10.2 "Periods of Church History: Early Church."

□ *Critique* Launched in 1972, this MEGA-COMPENDIUM now totals more than eighty volumes examining the period from Augustus through Constantine. Each volume offers articles commissioned alternately in German, French, English and Italian, not to mention bibliographies running up to fifty pages. About a fifth of the articles are in English. Volumes 25.1—25.6 constitute a HANDBOOK OF INTERPRETATION of the New Testament, the largest ever undertaken. Written by and for specialists, these volumes expound in overwhelming detail the history of research on each biblical and extracanonical book as well as generic problems. The Pauline corpus alone commands almost two thousand pages, including E. P. Sanders on "Jews, Paul and Judaism" (25.1:390-450). Equally stimulating are Max Wilcox on "Jesus in the Light of His Jewish Environment" (25.1:131-95) and J. Duncan M. Derrett on "Law and Society in Jesus's World" (25.1:477-564). J. W. Voelz on "The Language of the New Testament" will thrill scholars of Greek (25.2:893-977). Boasting fifty pages of bibliography, Klaus Berger's "Hellenistische Gattungen im Neuen Testament" constitutes a book in itself (25.2:1031-1432). Equal rigor pervades volume 26.1 (1992) and volume 27.1 (1993), which inaugurate a monumental Patrology. Volumes 36.1—36.7 treat philosophy in comparable depth. No other work, not even **151** Klauser, ed., *Reallexikon für Antike und Christentum* (1950-), blends thoroughness, sophistication and up-to-dateness so compellingly. One gapes in admiration.

□ *Summary* This MEGA-COMPENDIUM explicates history of research in unequaled richness. Six volumes on the New Testament constitute the grandest HANDBOOK OF INTERPRETATION yet attempted.

68 (1990) R[ichard] J. Coggins and J. L[eslie] Houlden, eds., *A Dictionary of Biblical Interpretation* (London: SCM; New York: Trinity Press International, 1990); xiv & 751 pages; index, pp. 745-48; no general bibliography.

□ *Scope* This magisterial LEXICON of methodology in biblical studies recruited 146 mostly British authorities to write some three hundred entries, each with English-language bibliography. Intended "as an aid to those who wish to enter a territory which may appear something of a maze" (p. v), the articles expound history of methodology, history of interpretation of books of the Bible and current trends. Having spent a lifetime in the field, the editors nevertheless confess astonishment at discovering "the ever-widening range of methods and techniques" and report that "to have edited this volume has been an education in itself" (p. v). The level of discourse is unusually high; the writing is pointed and succinct throughout. Entries on major books of the Bible highlight "use and abuse" of that book by interpreters through the ages. The core of the work is fifty-odd surveys of methods. Older ones are weighed in "Allegory," "Introduction" and "Typology," and newer ones in "Form Criticism," "Redaction Criticism" and "Ideology." The WHO'S WHO includes obligatory figures like Origen, Augustine, Luther, Calvin, Schweitzer, Barth and Bultmann as well as less expected ones like James Hastings, Joel Cadbury and C. C. Torrey. The career of each as biblical interpreter is summarized and evaluated. Combining rigor and imagination, this HANDBOOK inserts its subject into the mainstream of Western cultural history.

□ *Strengths* This HANDBOOK of biblical criticism interweaves analysis and synthesis so brilliantly that it qualifies as REVISIONIST on those grounds alone. It surveys classical schools like "Alexandrian," "Antiochene," "Patristic" and "Mediaeval." It disentangles Jewish approaches in articles on "Jewish Exegesis," "Midrash," "Talmud," "Rabbi, Rabbinism" and "Merkabah Mysticism" (but not on Hassidism or Cabalah). There is just one article on "Muslim Interpretation" as well as one on the "Samaritans." Other world religions scarcely get mentioned except by Peter Clarke writing on "New Religious Movements" and Alastair G. Hunter on "Other Faiths." Modern schools are dissected in "German Old Testament Scholarship," "Scandinavian Old Testament Scholarship" and "Tübingen School." It is piquant to compare an entry

on "American Interpretation" with that on "English Interpretation," both eminently fair. No other work elucidates so many disparate schools so deftly. Other syntheses encompass biblical interpretation during the "Reformation" and the "Enlightenment," not to mention that found in "Poetry, English" and "Metaphysical Poets."

Many readers will find the exposition of contemporary methods supremely helpful. Analyses explicate "Structuralism," "Semiotics," "Narrative Criticism" and "Reader-Response Criticism." Methods from the social sciences are canvassed in "Anthropology," "Folklore," "Sociology and Social Anthropology" and "Psychological Interpretaton." Articles on "Archaeology," "Dead Sea Scrolls" and "Epigraphy" sort out technical issues. Insurgent approaches get appraised under "Materialist Interpretation," "Marxist Interpretation" and "Feminist Interpretation." The entry on "Intratextuality" expounds George Lindbeck's thought ingeniously. Among the most unfailingly original entries are fourteen by Robert P. Carroll, among them "Cognitive Dissonance," "Ideology" and "Irony." "Egypt," "Jerusalem," "Babylon" and "Ugarit" are singled out but not Iran or Greece. Theological issues get canvassed in "Fundamentalism," "Liberalism," "Ethics (Old Testament)" and "Theology (New Testament)." A hard-hitting article by Hyam Maccoby pinpoints the "Antisemitism" that pervaded biblical interpretation from Origen, Tertullian and Eusebius through Chrysostom and Augustine to Isidore of Seville. Often less incisive than other portions of the volume, the WHO'S WHO alternates between obligatory masters and underestimated secondary figures, treating solely their biblical interpretation. An itinerary from "Josephus" and "Philo" through "Origen" and "Augustine" to "Calvin" and "Luther" offers no incongruity, but "Dante," "Erasmus" and "Herder" come as a surprise. Schleiermacher gets discussed under "Hermeneutics," but not on his own. Taken together with the historical surveys, the entries on persons constitute something like a cultural history of biblical interpretation (with some omissions). No other reference book does the job better.

□ *Weaknesses* One can only wish that such an authoritative HANDBOOK had addressed even more topics. The WHO'S WHO is so unpredictable that one looks in vain for Milton, Vico and Renan, only to find William Blake, E. C. Hoskyns and Ernst Lohmeyer. French scholars are neglected, and Eastern Christianity gets short shrift. An opportunity was missed to assess the influence of Iranian religion on the Bible. Almost nothing treats reception of the Bible in the Third World, apart from an article on "Materialist Interpretation" and a few paragraphs in entries on "Black Christian Interpretation" and "Liberation Theology." This HANDBOOK badly needs a "Topical Outline" to classify the articles. The "Select Index" omits too many names that pop up in the text.

□ *Competitors* The editors declare that "a dictionary is a point of entry into a world, in this case one that is full of riches, some wildly exotic, others more workaday" (p. vi). The riches in this volume encompass methods and their history, digested in such a way as to encapsulate cultural history. Overviews that sketch the "blurring" of scholarly genres abound, building upon insights formulated in Robert Morgan with John Barton, *Biblical Interpretation* (New York: Oxford University Press, 1988). Entries on individual scholars are unmatched except in a MEGA-ENCYCLOPEDIA, **49** Pirot, ed., *Dictionnaire de la Bible: Supplément* (1928-). Some readers will prefer an INTRODUCTORY HANDBOOK like **66** Soulen, ed., *Handbook of Biblical Criticism* (1976, 1981) with its pedagogical focus. Articles in **34** Gentz, ed., *The Dictionary of Bible and Religion* (1986) likewise prepare one for the complexities of Coggins and Houlden. The nearest rival is **72** Metzger and Coogan, eds., *The Oxford Companion to the Bible* (1993), which summarizes major methods more succinctly but omits nuances. An evangelical HANDBOOK assesses literary approaches and assembles English-language bibliographies: Leland Ryken and Tremper Longman III,

eds., *A Complete Literary Guide to the Bible* (Grand Rapids: Zondervan, 1993). The extravagance of **69** Jeffrey, ed., *A Dictionary of Biblical Tradition in English Literature* (1992) contrasts with the discipline and restraint of this HANDBOOK. The former hardly ever furnishes cultural context. *A Dictionary of Biblical Interpretation* integrates the history of biblical studies into the mainstream of Western culture better than any other reference work.

□ *Summary* This HANDBOOK of methodology in biblical studies situates old and new approaches in countless contexts. No other work expounds the intellectual history of biblical interpretation so fastidiously or unravels centuries of controversy so cunningly.

69 (1992) David Lyle Jeffrey, ed., *A Dictionary of Biblical Tradition in English Literature* (Grand Rapids, Mich.: Eerdmans, 1992); xxxii & 960 pages; no index; eight bibliographies, pp. 857-960.

□ *Scope* This ambitious LEXICON examines how biblical references have percolated through Greek and Latin commentaries and thence throughout English-speaking literature. More than 160 international contributors write nine hundred signed entries (each with bibliography) on an astonishing array of topics. In aspiring to encompass "biblical tradition," the editor traces it through three literary streams: (1) the Bible itself, (2) exegetical traditions both Jewish and Christian and (3) English-speaking literature from Anglo-Saxon to 1990. Heterogeneity prevails, for the entries embody no fewer than fifteen types: (1) persons (e.g., Ananias and Sapphira, Sennacherib, Nicodemus); (2) places (Baca Valley, Tyre, Mesopotamia, Eden); (3) biblical phrases ("Hewers of Wood," "Adam's Ale," "No Respecter of Persons"); (4) parables ("Sower," "Prodigal Son," "Unprofitable Servant"); (5) objects ("Apple," "Balm of Gilead," "Mountain," "Phoenix," "Glass, Mirror"); (6) events ("Annunciation," "Naming of the Animals," "Passion, Cross"); (7) religious practices ("Prayer," "Dreams, Visions," "Conversion"); (8) virtues and vices ("Charity," "Virginity, Chastity," "Mercy, Justice,"

"Adultery," "Madness"); (9) doctrines ("Covenant," "Trinity," "Transubstantiation," "Resurrection," "Predestination"); (10) angels and demons ("Seraph," "Gabriel," "Beelzebub," "Devil"); (11) genres ("Apocalypse," "Hebrew Poetry," but not psalm); (12) interpretive techniques ("Allegory," "Hermeneutics," "Typology," "Numerology"); (13) church seasons ("Advent," "Epiphany," "Pentecost"); (14) nonbiblical beliefs ("Adonis," "Golem," "Unicorn," "Purgatory"); and (15) liturgical practices ("Sacrament," "Eucharist," "Kyrie Eleison," "Corpus Christi," "Tenebrae").

Each entry states a biblical context (or else specifies its absence), recapitulates exegetical tradition and recounts references in English-speaking and sometimes continental European literature, often ad nauseam. Entries vary in length from five lines ("Key of David," "Gershom") to seven pages ("Bride, Bridegroom") and one of ten pages ("Old and New"). A few major figures like David, Peter, Paul and Jesus command four to five pages, but most entries run just two to three. Although bibliographies cite almost entirely English-language sources, the articles range far more widely.

☐ **Strengths** Individual entries excel at bringing together material never before assembled. Certain synopses stand out. Martin Marty's three pages on "Heresy" survey Arianism, Nestorianism, Montanism, Donatism, Docetism, Gnosticism, Manichaeism and Pelagianism (as well as their progeny in several dozen post-1800 writers) in a tour de force of cultural history. Bryan Gooch's five pages on "Music and Musical Instruments" collate musical imagery in forty different writers since Augustine's *De musica*. The editor performs a similar feat for concepts like "Faith," "Grace, Works" and "Holy Spirit."

The core of the book comes in hundreds of entries of two to three pages on biblical persons, phrases and concepts as they filter through fifteen centuries of Greek and Latin commentary and twelve centuries of English-speaking literature.

About fifty figures like "Ishmael," "David," "Jacob," "the Magi" and "Elijah" are made to frequent a coherent stream of utterance from antiquity to the 1980s. Women elicit ample coverage ("Lilith," "Judith," "Bathsheba," Ruth," "Mary Magdalene"). About two hundred phrases get traced in detail, including such Latin ones as "Felix Culpa," "Fiat Lux" and "Hortus Conclusus." Striking entries evoke "Giants in the Earth," "Last Trump," "Lilies of the Field" and "Wheels within Wheels." Another series of entries traces general concepts like "Light," "Wisdom," "Perfection," "Preaching" and "Exile and Pilgrimage." Still other topics are more specifically biblical, such as "Sword of the Spirit," "New Jerusalem," "Millennialism" and "Second Coming." A similar profusion characterizes the eight bibliographies. Their hundred pages cover ground canvassed hardly anywhere else, ranging from "Historical Studies in Biblical Hermeneutics" (covering twenty centuries, pp. 889-900) through "A Checklist of Biblical Commentaries Available to English Authors" (pp. 901-11) to "Use of the Bible by a Single Author or Group of Authors" (pp. 937-60). If nothing else does, the bibliographies require resort to this LEXICON.

☐ **Weaknesses** For all its riches, this LEXICON excites misgivings. A key phrase in the title, "Biblical Tradition," would have been more accurately stated as "Biblical Lore." A decision to use the King James Version of the Bible may disconcert some readers. Focus on English-speaking writers does not exclude major continental ones like Dostoyevsky ("Fool, Folly"), Albert Camus ("Heresy") and Thomas Mann ("Joseph"). Yet profusion generates strange omissions. Saints, theologians and biblical scholars command no entries. Likewise, individual books of the Bible get none unless named for persons (i.e., individual prophets, Job, Esther). To this rule an entry on "Song of Songs" marks a splendid exception. Oddly, the gospelists win entries, but their writings (apart from key phrases and parables) do not. Although no articles treat non-Christian religions, not even "Judaism," brief entries pop up on "Halakah" and "Midrash." Those on "Cabala" and "Pharisees" trace reception chiefly by Christians.

The abiding weakness, if it is that, is a tendency to overdo references, so that at times this LEXICON becomes an ANATOMY about Bible-fancying writers. Unconsciously indulging MENIPPEAN SATIRE, perhaps half the articles engage in citation-gathering for its own sake. Entries like "Fullness of Time," "Giants in the Earth" or "Handwriting on the Wall" juxtapose authors who bear nothing in common except fondness for a given phrase. A typical entry is "Jephthah and his Daughters," which in one and one-half pages invokes, among others, the Talmud, Augustine, Chaucer, Shakespeare, Erasmus, Handel, Lord Byron, Tennyson, Sholem Asch, Lion Feuchtwanger and Naomi Ragen's *Jepthe's Daughter* (1989). Too often one feels that an unruly enumerator like Rabelais or Lawrence Sterne has run amuck. Given such zeal, it is a pity that no index discloses which authors occur most frequently. Even without help, a browser will spot time and again the names of John Dryden, William Cowper, William Blake and Lord Byron.

□ *Competitors* Twelve years in preparation, this work inhabits a category of its own. Although neither a BIBLE DICTIONARY nor a BIBLE COMMENTARY, it traces many of the persons, places and concepts treated in those works. Probably no other reference work on the Bible incorporates so much nonbiblical material. Biblical scholars will find here a gold mine of information (particularly about phrases), public speakers will uncover a treasure trove of quotations, while theologians will discover how meagerly they had grasped subsequent usage of biblical names and phrases. **68** Coggins and Houlden, eds., *A Dictionary of Biblical Interpretation* (1990) complements this work by explicating methodology. Ultimately, one's reaction to *A Dictionary of Biblical Tradition in English Literature* depends upon one's attitude toward having too much of a good thing. One may conjecture that in a schol-

ars' heaven, devotees of excess like Samuel Butler, John Ruskin, James Joyce and Anthony Burgess (not to mention Dr. Casaubon in *Middlemarch*) would adore this cornucopia, while fans of concision like Samuel Johnson, William Hazlitt, Robert Frost and Walker Percy would not. Like any other ANATOMY, this one requires a gargantuan appetite.

□ *Summary* This LEXICON, alias ANATOMY of citations and explanations, inspires both awe and anxiety. Synopses of concepts and phrases will gratify curiosity for decades to come, but overstuffed entries will disconcert even the most willing.

70 (1992) Joel B. Green and Scot McKnight, eds., *Dictionary of Jesus and the Gospels* (Downers Grove, Ill., and Leicester, U.K: InterVarsity Press, 1992); xxv & 934 pages; three indexes (gospel references, subject, articles), pp. 897-934; no general bibliography.

□ *Scope* This hybrid between a BIBLE DICTIONARY and a HANDBOOK OF INTERPRETATION presents 185 signed essays on problems in the four Gospels. Tackling the thorniest difficulties, ninety-three contributors analyze methodology, history and theology, supplying multilingual bibliographies of rare merit. About half the articles run a page or two; the other half average six to ten pages. Billed as "critically responsible and theologically evangelical," (p.ix), the essays deploy up-to-date methodologies and play down theology (except in a few entries like "Preaching from the Gospels"). Even when assessing fraught questions, argumentation is searching, and the writing is clear. A sequel from the same publisher brings equal virtuosity to Pauline materials: **71** Hawthorne and Martin, eds., *Dictionary of Paul and His Letters* (1993). As the intractable yields to finesse, both works harness nonconfessional scholarship to evangelical ends without subverting either.

□ *Strengths* This LEXICON of gospel interpretation does not merely raise difficult issues; it debates and where possible resolves them. Michael O. Wise on "Languages of Palestine" examines myriad hypotheses before concluding "that Jesus certainly spoke a dialect of Aramaic" (p. 442). He argues further that a Semitic source for the Gospels may never have existed: "The earliest traditions may have been in Greek all along" (p. 444). The article on "Midrash" inventories seven rules for its conduct and illustrates their use by Jesus. A fascinating article on "Demon, Devil, Satan" differentiates seven terms used in the Gospels. Customs shine forth in "Bread," "Dreams," "Fasting," "Taxes" and "Wine." Standard entries from a BIBLE DICTIONARY include ones on each of the Gospels as well as on "Parables," "Chronology" and "Miracles and Miracle Stories." Distinctive entries concern "Blindness and Deafness," "Leprosy" and "Mountain and Wilderness." Jewish background looms in "Josephus," "Pharisees," "Synagogue," "Temple," "Samaritans" and "Herodian Dynasty," as well as in ten pages on "Rabbinic Traditions and Writings." Standard entries from a HANDBOOK OF INTERPRETATION include fifteen pages on "Historical Jesus, Quest of," ten on "Dead Sea Scrolls" and surveys of "Form Criticism," "Rhetorical Criticism" and "Liberation Hermeneutics." Unusual entries include "Jesus in Non-Christian Sources" (including the Qur'an), "Old Testament in the Gospels" and "Chreia/Aphorism." Devoting nearly a thousand pages to the Gospels and their puzzles ensures being able to discern innumerable dimensions to any question. Few other reference works unlock debates with such nicety.

□ *Weaknesses* As the first of a series, this volume incurs omissions. Thus although Judaism elicits an array of articles, there is only one each on "Hellenism" and on "Rome." In general, adepts of continuity between ancient Greece and Christianity will have to wait for a sequel, *Dictionary of New Testament Background* (1999). Similarly, except in "Canon," few matters later than 150 C.E. get mentioned because early church history has been assigned to *Dictionary of the Later New Testament and Its Developments* (1997). Catholics will wish for articles on "Mary," "Peter" and "Sacraments." The preface ought to have an-

nounced that sequels were forthcoming.

□ *Competitors* This up-to-date LEXICON raises and answers nagging questions that BIBLE DICTIONARIES seldom address. One of the contributors, Ben Witherington III, shows the urgency of the issues in *The Jesus Quest: The Third Search for the Jew of Nazareth* (Downers Grove, Ill.: InterVarsity Press, 1995). On many matters, both secular and theological, *Dictionary of Jesus and the Gospels* offers keener argumentation than **60** Freedman, ed., *The Anchor Bible Dictionary* (1992), and entries are easier to locate here. To be sure, for synopses of history and texts, one still needs **53** Douglas, ed., *New Bible Dictionary*, 2d ed. (1982) or **58** Mills., ed., *Mercer Dictionary of the Bible* (1990). **68** Coggins and Houlden, eds., *A Dictionary of Biblical Interpretation* (1990) expounds history of interpretation more comprehensively and canvasses a wider range of methods but does not investigate the Gospels in remotely comparable detail. The two works complement each other. **72** Metzger and Coogan, eds., *The Oxford Companion to the Bible* (1993) seems introductory, almost cursory by comparison with either. Together with its sequel, **71** *Dictionary of Paul and His Letters* (1993), this pioneering work belongs in the library of every New Testament scholar.

□ *Summary* This happy blend of BIBLE DICTIONARY and HANDBOOK OF INTERPRETATION attains astonishing depth of argument while using plain language. It masters the intractable.

71 (1993) Gerald Hawthorne and Ralph P. Martin, eds., *Dictionary of Paul and His Letters* (Downers Grove, Ill., and Leicester, U.K.: InterVarsity Press, 1993); xxix & 1038 pages; three indexes (Pauline letters, subject, articles); no general bibliography.

□ *Critique* This sequel to **70** Green and McKnight, eds., *Dictionary of Jesus and the Gospels* (1992) extends that work's excellence to the Pauline letters. One hundred nine evangelical scholars contribute 220 articles (with magnificent bibliographies) on all aspects of scholarship concerning Paul. The preface construes the enterprise as building on the "new look" in Pauline studies that stems from E. P. Sanders, *Paul and Palestinian Judaism* (Philadelphia: Fortress, 1977), page ix. Frank Thielmann on "Law" and William R. Stegner on "Paul the Jew" appraise the "new look" most directly. Remarkable historical syntheses include Mark Reasoner on "Political Systems," David E. Aune on "Religions, Greco-Roman," Stephen F. Noll on "Qumran and Paul" and Edwin M. Yamauchi on both "Gnosis, Gnosticism" and "Hellenism." Surveys of scholarship include Grant R. Osborne on "Hermeneutics/Interpreting Paul," Scott J. Hafemann on "Paul and His Interpreters" and Stephen C. Barton on "Social-Scientific Approaches to Paul." Terence Paige writes arrestingly on "Demons and Exorcism," "Holy Spirit" and "Philosophy." Exhaustive analysis of Paul's quotations distinguishes Moisés Silva on "Old Testament in Paul" and Seeyoon Kim on "Jesus, Sayings of." Five cities elicit separate articles: Antioch, Athens, Ephesus, Jerusalem and Rome (but not Corinth). Everyone in New Testament studies will benefit from this volume.

□ *Summary* This felicitous blend of BIBLE DICTIONARY and HANDBOOK OF INTERPRETATION digests scholarship on Paul with the same authority and ease that its predecessor brings to the Gospels. These works set a new standard for unknotting intricacies.

72 (1993) Bruce M. Metzger and Michael D. Coogan, eds., *The Oxford Companion to the Bible* (New York and Oxford: Oxford University Press, 1993); xxi & 912 pages; index, pp. 834-74; general bibliography, pp. 831-35; fourteen maps with index, pp. 875-912.

□ *Scope* This COMPANION combines a BIBLE DICTIONARY with a HANDBOOK OF BIBLE INTERPRETATION. The first is conventional, referencing persons, places, objects and all books of the Bible in signed entries devoid of bibliography. The second is more original, synthesizing recent scholarship on a wide array of issues. Two hundred fifty scholars contribute about seven hundred articles in lucid prose designed for beginning and intermediate readers. The editors isolate six areas to be covered: (1) the formation of the Bible, (2) the transmission, diffusion and circulation of the Bible, (3) the biblical world, (4) biblical concepts, (5) the interpretation of the Bible, (6) the uses and influence of the Bible (pp. vii-viii). Although each area has elicited other more authoritative reference works, on nearly all of them *The Oxford Companion* suffices as an INTRODUCTION.

□ *Strengths* This COMPANION incorporates the emphases of contemporary North American scholarship. Jewish scholars and topics receive plentiful attention. Krister Stendahl's exposure of anti-Semitism as "the most persistent heresy of Christian theology and practice" (p. 34) rings clear. Sarah J. Tanzer's synthesis of "Judaisms of the First century C.E." is a model. Separate articles introduce Near Eastern religion in Sumer, Egypt, Phoenicia, Ugarit and (too briefly) Persia. Edwin M. Yamauchi contributes eight pages on "Archaeology and the Bible." Contemporary methods are splendidly explicated, particularly in the fourth of four articles on "Interpretation, History of" and in "Social Sciences and the Bible." Four articles on "Women" run twelve pages. Entries on certain books deploy literary criticism, as in "Job" and "Jonah." The abiding merit of the *Companion* lies in surveys such as four entries (two of them by David Lyle Jeffrey) on "Literature and the Bible," five articles on "Printing and Publishing" and ten entries running thirty pages on "Translations." Imaginative entries include Barbara Geller Nathanson's four pages on "Jerusalem: Symbolism," William W. Meissner's three pages on "Jung and the Bible" and Sidnie Ann White's two pages on biblical terms for "Human Person." Useful short articles correct misunderstandings about biblical status of matters like "Christmas," "Magi," "Hell," "Red Sea" and "Brothers and Sisters of Jesus" as well as of words like "Angels," "Conversion," "Paradise," "Peace" and "Sacrament." This COMPANION summarizes methods and issues as lucidly as any of its rivals, but too often the summaries lack nuance.

□ *Weaknesses* As a hybrid between a BIBLE DICTIONARY and a HANDBOOK OF BIBLE INTERPRETATION, *The Oxford Companion to the Bible* all too frequently falls between two stools. It lacks the photographs, inset maps and charts that adorn most BIBLE DICTIONARIES. Entries on books of the Bible follow no fixed format, ranging from literary analysis (on "Ruth") to classical INTRODUCTION (on "Deuteronomy" or "Zechariah"). *The Oxford Companion's* synopses of methodology address nonspecialists in contrast to those in a full-fledged HANDBOOK OF INTERPRETATION like **68** Coggins and Houlden, eds., *A Dictionary of Biblical Interpretation* (1990). By investigating many more issues and scholars, and furnishing individual bibliographies, the latter provides altogether more substance. Moreover, in its function as a HANDBOOK, *The Oxford Companion* incurs astonishing omissions: literary and philosophical peculiarities of Hebrew and Greek elicit no entry (except in "Time, Units of"). Islam is mentioned only in "Qur'an and the Bible," and no one discusses how to compare scriptures among religions. Iranian influence is ignored, as are Asian religions. More inexplicably, terms as diverse as "Hellenism," "Midrash," "Cabala" and "Ritual" elicit no articles. There should have been an entry as well on "Reference Works and Study Tools." Lack of individual bibliographies irks all the more because the general bibliography lacks evaluative comments.

□ *Competitors* This COMPANION functions as an all-in-one INTRODUCTION to biblical studies, chiefly for readers from outside religious studies. Adepts of the latter will prefer BIBLE DICTIONARIES such as **54** Achtemeier, ed., *Harper's Bible Dictionary* (1985) or **58** Mills, ed., *Mercer Dictionary of the Bible* (1990), both of which digest more particulars and provide visual aids. Aiming to transcend confession, all three works shun theology. For theologians **56** Myers, ed., *The Eerdmans Bible Dictionary* (1975, 1987) is unsurpassed unless one wishes to tackle **52** Bromiley, ed., *The International Standard Bible Encyclopedia* (1979-88). Evangelicals may prefer **53**

Douglas, ed., *New Bible Dictionary*, 2d ed. (1982). **68** Coggins and Houlden, eds., *A Dictionary of Biblical Interpretation* (1990) excels at expounding intricacies of method and fitting them into cultural context. It addresses a more demanding readership. Introductory to a fault, *The Oxford Companion* prods readers into seeking greater finesse.

□ *Summary* This multipurpose DICTIONARY cum HANDBOOK suits nonspecialists, but even they will crave something subtler. Primerlike synopses do a disservice to a field that thrives on nuance.

2.4 THEOLOGY

2.4.1. NONCONFESSIONAL

OVERVIEW: THE TRIUMPH OF REVISIONISM Theology deploys reason, argument and systematic reflection to articulate Christian faith. As John Macquarrie puts it, theology is "the attempt to present the entire body of Christian belief as a system of truth in which every doctrine is related to every other doctrine" (**34** Gentz, ed., *The Dictionary of Bible and Religion,* p. 1014). Until recently reference works on theology have tended to speak from a confession even when they survey the field. Six postmodern works stand out for breaking that mold. The two most recent of those analyzed below stand at the pinnacle of recent reference books in English. A shrewd if argumentative overview of major twentieth-century theologians is Clark H. Pinnock, *Tracking the Maze: Finding Our Way Through Modern Theology from an Evangelical Perspective* (San Francisco: Harper & Row, 1990).

A COMPENDIUM of forty-eight essays on academic theology chiefly in Britain appeared too late to analyze: Leslie Houlden and Peter Byrne, eds., *Companion Encyclopedia of Theology* (London and New York: Routledge, 1995), with extensive English-language bibliographies.

LIST OF WORKS ANALYZED
 73 (1963, 1988) John Macquarrie, *Twentieth-Century Religious Thought,*

4th ed. (London: SCM; Philadelphia: Trinity Press International, 1988)

116 (1969, 1983) Alan Richardson, ed., *A Dictionary of Christian Theology* (London: SCM; Philadelphia: Westminster, 1969); second edition published as *The Westminster Dictionary of Christian Theology* (Philadelphia: Westminster, 1983). Analyzed under 2.8 "The Westminster/SCM Dictionaries."

74 (1985) Peter A. Angeles, *Dictionary of Christian Theology* (San Francisco: Harper & Row, 1985)

75 (1989) David F. Ford, ed., *The Modern Theologians: An Introduction to Christian Theology in the Twentieth Century,* 2 vols. (Oxford: Blackwell Reference, 1989)

76 (1992) Donald W. Musser and Joseph L. Price, eds., *A New Handbook of Christian Theology* (Nashville: Abingdon, 1992)

77 (1993) Alister E. McGrath, ed., *The Blackwell Encyclopedia of Modern Christian Thought* (Oxford and Cambridge, Mass.:Blackwell Reference, 1993; paperback, 1995)

ANALYSIS OF WORKS

73 (1963, 1988) John Macquarrie, *Twentieth-Century Religious Thought,* 4th ed. (London: SCM; Philadelphia: Trinity Press International, 1988); 486 pages; index (of names and subjects), pp. 453-68; also in paperback.

□ *Critique* Divided into twenty-four chapters and 121 numbered sections, this virtuosic TEXTBOOK would qualify as a HANDBOOK if only it included secondary bibliography. A distinguished philosophical theologian dissects no fewer than 203 European and American (but not Asian) philosophers, theologians and social scientists, ranging through a hundred years from Edward Caird to Mary Douglas. He discusses seventy British, sixty-two German-speaking, twenty-one French and eighteen American thinkers as well as two or three each of Italian, Dutch, Swedish, Russian and Latin American origin. The chapters range in length from thirteen pages on "Personal Idealism" to seventy-

five on "The Fourth Phase" (since 1965). Each chapter culminates with "Critical Remarks" that combine evenhandedness with panoramas. Four chapters (1, 7, 16 and 24) debate periodization, dividing the material into four phases: (1) nineteenth-century systems, (2) outdated early twentieth-century systems, (3) the period from 1940 to 1965 and (4) the years since 1965. Ten chapters deal with philosophy (idealism, pragmatism, realism, neo-Thomism, logical empiricism), while five handle approaches to religious studies (anthropology, history, sociology, phenomenology) and another five theology.

Labels sprout. "Post-liberal" denotes the Niebuhrs in chapter 21, and "post-existentialist" denotes Heschel, Moltmann and Pannenberg in chapter 23. Major omissions include upholders of the perennial philosophy like René Guénon and of New Age like Fritjof Capra as well as Asians like Keiji Nishitani. The writing is pithy and lucid, never quirky or partisan. One can only bewail the lack of secondary bibliography. For that one must turn to **289** Jacob, ed., *Encyclopédie philosophique universelle,* 5 vols. (1989-92). Macquarrie's articles on philosophical theology in **34** Gentz, ed., *The Dictionary of Bible and Religion* (1986) complement the book exactly.

□ *Summary* This HANDBOOK without bibliography maps twentieth-century systematic thinking on religion. Advanced students will relish the succinctness.

74 (1985) Peter A. Angeles, *Dictionary of Christian Theology* (San Francisco: Harper & Row, 1985); x & 211 pages; no index; no bibliography; many cross-references; also in paperback.

□ *Critique* A professor of philosophy has written that *rara avis,* a nonconfessional GLOSSARY of Christian terminology. It functions as a mate to his **295** *Harper-Collins Dictionary of Philosophy,* 2d ed. (1992). More than a thousand concepts, heresies, sacraments and practices are defined in numbered points (with etymologies but without bibliographies). A singularity is the author's habit of enumerating not only denotations but tenets of theologies. Thus under "Calvinism" come no fewer than seventeen doctrines and under "Lutheranism" five. The entry on "Christology" defines eleven roles that have been assigned to Christ: (1) Culminator, (2) New Adam, (3) Servant, (4) High Priest, (5) Reconciliator, (6) Sufferer and Forgiver, (7) the perfect, single, ideal Redeemer, (8) the Sacrifice, (9) the Satisfier, (10) the Ransom and (11) Conqueror of Satan. Under "Baptism" fourteen numbered points explain how the sacrament may be valid or invalid. A master enumerator gratifies teachers and students alike.

□ *Summary* Any teacher of Christian history will find hints here for repackaging the material. No other epitomizer states niceties so succinctly.

75 (1989) David F. Ford, ed., *The Modern Theologians: An Introduction to Christian Theology in the Twentieth Century,* 2 vols. (Oxford and New York: Blackwell Reference, 1989); xv & 342; xii & 330 pages; indexes, 1:330-43, 2:319-30; glossaries, 1:312-29, 2:300-318; no general bibliography; also in paperback.

□ *Scope* This COMPENDIUM on academic theology since 1914 emerged from instruction at the University of Birmingham. In volume 1 the editor recruited fourteen mostly British scholars to summarize the career, writings, controversies and legacy of fourteen major figures (ten of them German-speaking). In volume 2 a different thirteen authors survey various topics, while deploying subsections on another forty-eight thinkers. Besides chapters on evangelical theology and Eastern Orthodoxy, two on British theology and four on American provide national coverage. Four chapters examine "new challenges" (liberation theology, black theology, Asian theology, feminist theology), while one explores ecumenical theology and another "Theology of Religions." The chapters on individuals range from twelve pages each on Lonergan and Schillebeeckx to thirty-five on Pannenberg. Twin criteria for including a thinker are (1) intensity of engagement with modernity and (2) frequency of appearance on university syllabi in Britain. Coverage is lacking on biblical

theology, Scandinavian thinkers and French theologians (other than Yves Congar). The glossaries address British university students, and each chapter furnishes extensive English-language bibliography.

□ *Strengths* The editor's introduction and epilogue, as well as ten headnotes, attempt not quite successfully to integrate twenty-eight contributions. The introduction adapts from Hans Frei a schema that aligns five types of theology along a continuuum (1:2-4). At one pole stands traditional theology, which construes "all reality in its own terms" and is "hardly modern." At the other pole comes theology that "gives complete priority to some modern secular philosophy or worldview" and is "hardly Christian." Closer to the first pole, type two "gives priority to the self-description of the Christian community" and construes "all other reality" in relation to Christian identity (e.g., Barth, Torrance, Jüngel, Congar and Balthasar). Type three falls exactly in the middle and "tries to correlate" Christian faith with modernity (e.g., Tillich, Schillebeeckx, Küng, Tracy). Closer to the second pole, type four offers a "consistent reinterpretation of Christianity in terms of some contemporary idiom or concern," to which it accords centrality (e.g., Bultmann, Lonergan, Pannenberg, process theology and the "new challenges"). Equally illuminating is an epilogue in which the editor differentiates postmoderns (Barth, Hick, Cupitt, Lindbeck) from late moderns, who tend to be not theologians but philosophers (Habermas, Gadamer, Ricoeur, MacIntyre). Ford argues that a distinction between postmodern *secession* from modernity and late modern *continuation* of it cuts across all five types sketched above.

Unfortunately, these guidelines motivate only a few of the contributors. Among them, William C. Placher situates "Postliberal Theology" in the ambience of Yale University, and Daniel W. Hardy discerns an "English vision" in both Thomas F. Torrance and British "Theology Through Philosophy" (2:30-71). Hardy's delineation of an "English vision" of theology as striving to improve inherited "common practice" guides his assessment of Donald M. MacKinnon, John Macquarrie, John Hick and Don Cupitt. This chapter, together with S. W. Sykes's entry on British "Theology Through History," makes volume 2 essential for historians of Christian thinking in Britain. Other incisive contributions include Patrick A. Kalilombe's on "Black Theology" (in North America and Africa) and George Lindbeck's on "Ecumenical Theology." Lindbeck ranks as the only contributor to be discussed in the volume (under both "Postliberal Theology" and "Theology of Religions"). Among articles on individuals, Robert Morgan on Bultmann, J. A. DiNoia on Rahner and Aidan Nichols on Congar stand out, while the most original may be John Riches's piece on Balthasar. Christoph Schwöbel's thirty-five pages on Pannenberg are detailed but turgid. Although four chapters on "Theologies in the United States" juggle too many names, their bibliographies excel. By cross-weaving among the chapters, a beginner can start to map the field and an expert can fashion a historical tapestry.

□ *Weaknesses* However lucid the chapters, their authors do not converse with one another, and the editor's headnotes do not quite unify the whole. Moreover, the two volumes function independently. Emphasis on "academic theology" focuses on German-speaking thinkers to the exclusion of French ones and induces Ray S. Anderson to declare the achievements of American evangelical theology to be "modest" (2:147). Certain chapters seem confined. Writing on "Asian Theology," Kosuke Koyama examines just one thinker each from India, China, Korea and Japan. Although ample and up-to-date, the bibliographies ignore foreign-language works.

□ *Competitors* This teaching COMPENDIUM schematizes the development of Protestant and Catholic theology in Europe, North America, Latin America and Asia since 1914. The obvious rival is 77 Alister McGrath, ed., *The Blackwell Encyclopedia of Modern Christian Thought* (1993), which not only sweeps vastly more ground but characterizes national schools

decisively. Writing in both on "Eastern Orthodox Theology," for example, Rowan Williams displays greater virtuosity in the later one. Similarly, Gavin D'Costa canvasses many more thinkers in a piece on "Other Faiths and Christianity" in the later volume than he does on "Theology of Religions" in the earlier. In contrast to 78 Marty and Peerman, eds., *A Handbook of Christian Theologians* (1965, 1984), the Ford work is more up-to-date, but the earlier *Handbook* covers more individuals, often with greater rigor. A vigorously REVISIONIST LEXICON, such as 76 Musser and Price, eds., *A New Handbook of Christian Theology* (1992), makes this COMPENDIUM seem tied to the classroom. Ideally all four books would be used together.

□ *Summary* This historical COMPENDIUM introduces major theologians, schools and issues lucidly but not always incisively. It needs to be accompanied by works that venture more boldly.

76 (1992) Donald W. Musser and Joseph L. Price, eds., *A New Handbook of Christian Theology* (Nashville: Abingdon, 1992); 525 pages; no index; no general bibliography; "Routes for Reading," pp. 13-14; also in paperback.

□ *Scope* This REVISIONIST LEXICON of contemporary theology recruited 137 American authorities to write 148 signed articles on major concepts (each with brief bibliography). The preface announces an emphasis on "subjects of current interest" and goes on to list twelve kinds of theology that have emerged in North America since 1950 (pp. 9-10). The preface further differentiates four ways of coping with the "absence of an established method . . . amid cascading streams of thought": (1) to plunge into one of the new methodologies, (2) to reform and refine an established paradigm, (3) to await the arise of new, normative approaches and (4) to retreat from the "cacophony of dissident voices" (p. 10).

This LEXICON facilitates intelligent choice among the options. It replaces an earlier work, Martin Halverson and Arthur A. Cohen, eds., *A Handbook of Christian Theology* (Cleveland: World, 1958), which enlisted seventy-one Protestants to write

101 articles (including Reinhold Niebuhr on "Freedom" and "Self"). Emphatically nonconfessional, the new volume retains only four of the original contributors (Jerald Brauer, Robert MacAfee Brown, Langdon Gilkey and Claude Welch), all writing on fresh topics. A number of authors have helped to shape the debates they describe: William Hamilton on "Death of God Theology," David Ray Griffin on "Process Theology," Dan O. Via on "Structuralism" (in Matthew's Gospel) and Charles Curran on "Moral Theology." Certain others lobby for the approach they exposit: David Polk on "Practical Theology," James H. Evans Jr. on "Black Theology" and Thomas A. Idinopulos in a luminous essay on "Eastern Orthodox Christianity." Three articles evoke events: Lawrence S. Cunningham on "Vatican II" [1962-65], Philip Berryman on "CELAM II" [1968] and Richard John Neuhaus on "The Hartford Appeal" [1975]. In the absence of a WHO'S WHO, certain entries highlight particular individuals: "Insight" features Bernard Lonergan, "Liminality" Victor Turner, "Confessional Theology" H. Richard Niebuhr, "Paradigm" Thomas Kuhn, and both "Correlation" and "Ultimate Concern" Paul Tillich. As an innovation, "Routes of Reading" (pp. 13-14) aligns entries under seventeen headings like "Churches," "Conservative Protestantism," "Theological Method" and "Theology and the Arts." The writing is lucid, sometimes breezy, and the English-language bibliographies pithy.

□ *Strengths* This LEXICON highlights recent debates. Most contributors have absorbed from narrative theology the notion that "we live out of narratives" (p. 327). In order to map profusion, nearly all recount how their movement unfolded in North America, as Nathan A. Scott Jr. does with "Humanism," James A. Mathison with "Civil Religion" and William C. Placher with "Postmodern Theology." A number of articles furnish typologies of contemporary options, as Donald Bloesch does for "Evangelicalism," Frederick Ferré for "Atheism," E. Glenn Hinson for "Tradition" and Carl E. Braaten for "Revela-

tion." William A. Beardslee distinguishes eight approaches to "Biblical Criticism," while John McCarthy identifies six points of agreement and three of dissent concerning "Hermeneutics." The longest entry is Langdon Gilkey's virtuosic nine pages on "God." A useful series clarifies concepts that compare religions. Thus Peter Williams explicates "Popular Religion" as "an ill-digested but intuitively useful category" (p. 370), James B. Wiggins classifies conceptions of "Religion," and Ninian Smart deploys a brilliant typology of "Pluralism." He distinguishes (1) absolute exclusivism (Karl Barth and Hendrik Kraemer), (2) absolute relativism (Jainism, D. Z. Phillips), (3) hegemonic inclusivism (Nicholas of Cusa, Karl Rahner), (4) realistic pluralism (Vivekenanda, John Hick) and (5) regulative pluralism (R. C. Zaehner, Ninian Smart). The latter position argues that "the differing religions . . . are . . . growing toward a common truth. . . . But that common truth is as yet undefined" (p. 364).

A number of articles explore technical intricacies: John Macquarrie on "Systematic Theology," Frank Anthony Spina on "Canon," Eugene Teselle on "Atonement" and most relentlessly Werner Jeanrond on "Theological Method." Entries on philosophy tend to emphasize innovations in technique, as Edward Farley does on "Phenomenology," David B. Burrell on "Metaphysics," Jerry H. Gill on "Language-Religious" and Marjorie Hewitt Suchocki on "Panentheism." Certain authors call for "reconstruction" or "radical reformulation" of classical topics. This is the stance that Leonard J. Biallas takes toward "Dogmatic Theology," Mary Potter Engel toward "Election," Thomas D. Parker toward "Covenant," Jeffery Hopper toward "Soteriology" and James Wm. McLendon toward "Sin." Stephen Happel raises searching questions about "Priesthood," as does Kosuke Koyama about "Missiology." Some of the most exhilarating articles concern unexpected topics: Conrad Hyers expounds the need for "Comedy" as a means to avert tragedy; James P. Wind sifts definitions of "Health";

Joseph L. Price enumerates five functions of "Silence"; and David McKenzie asserts concerning "Miracles" that disbelief in them "is no longer inherently more rational than belief" (p. 312).

Two articles stand out for retrieving historical context. Langdon Gilkey interprets "Neo-orthodoxy" as a response to breakdown of values during the 1920s. Having synthesized the Reformation with nineteenth-century liberalism, neo-orthodoxy itself has yielded since the 1960s to "new political and eschatological theologies with their emphases on human action" (p. 337). George W. Stroup construes "Narrative Theology" as a response to "deep confusion about Christian identity" (p. 324). When all else fails, human beings tell stories, and no stories are richer than those in the Bible. The authors' notion that theology responds to culture by telling stories, rather than dictates to it by reciting creeds, mirrors the pervasive influence of Paul Tillich. As a conspectus of innovation in American theology since 1960, this LEXICON has no rival.

□ *Weaknesses* Contemporary to a fault, this LEXICON favors North America. Europe and Asia get short shrift. The only article on a non-Christian religion is James H. Charlesworth's on "Judaism." A number of articles disappoint: David L. Bartlett avoids debate on "Worship" (in contrast to Geoffrey Wainwright's dialectics on "Sacraments") and Don E. Saliers evades definitions in "Spirituality" (in contrast to James R. Price III's virtuosity in defining "Mysticism"). A few others dodge analysis by reciting history, as does James F. White on "Liturgical Movement" and Douglas F. Ottati on "Social Gospel." At least one neglected topic cries out for an essay: identity. The bibliographies omit place and date of publication. An index of names would have documented frequency of mention. Anyone can see that Paul Tillich looms large and that Teilhard de Chardin has all but disappeared.

□ *Competitors* This REVISIONIST LEXICON delivers outspoken essays on the gamut of contemporary Christian theology in North America. It ponders novel issues and reconstructs classical ones. In candor and contemporaneity it rivals 77 Alister McGrath, ed., *The Blackwell Encyclopedia of Modern Christian Thought* (1993). Written mostly by British scholars, the latter scans a wider swath of history, integrates articles more intricately and adopts a global perspective. Both works demonstrate the vigor of contemporary Christian thought. While affirming a conservative Protestant stance, 80 Ferguson et al., eds., *New Dictionary of Theology* (1988) lucidly introduces persons and concepts. It complements both works. Articles on method in the *New Handbook* update certain ones in 5 Eliade, ed., *The Encyclopedia of Religion* (1987). Ronald Grimes contributed on "Ritual" to both works, and articles on "Civil Religion" and "Pluralism" are superior in the *New Handbook*. In REVISIONIST acumen *A New Handbook of Christian Theology* matches 48 Latourelle and Fisichella, eds., *Dictionary of Fundamental Theology* (1990, 1994). No scholar of contemporary culture should neglect either of these LEXICONS, the one American, the other European. Together they map preoccupations of the 1990s.

□ *Summary* Vigorously up-to-date, this cornucopia rejuvenates contemporary theology. Few American reference books address their era so creatively.

77 (1993) Alister E. McGrath, ed., *The Blackwell Encyclopedia of Modern Christian Thought* (Oxford and Cambridge, Mass.: Blackwell Reference, 1993; paperback, 1995); xiii & 701 pages; index (of persons and themes), pp. 669-701; glossary, pp. 665-68; no general bibliography.

□ *Scope* This REVISIONIST LEXICON canvasses the response of Christian thinkers to culture worldwide since 1700. Ninety-two authorities, fifty-three of them British, write 220 articles on issues, denominations and persons but not places or technical terms (except in the glossary). Choice English-language bibliographies accompany each entry. A WHO'S WHO comprises ninety short entries as well as ten longer signed ones on the likes of Balthasar, Bultmann, Edwards, Pannenberg, Rahner and Tillich.

There are articles as well on "Cartesianism," "Hegelianism," "Kantianism" and "Marxism." The only pope referenced is Leo XIII. A singular feature is the compressing of natural and social sciences into just four articles: "Biological Science," "Physical Science," "Psychological Science" and "Social Science," each considered in relation to "Christian Thought." The entry "Christ, Jesus" pinpoints ten articles that debate issues about him. Nearly all entries deliver what the introduction promises, namely, "a non-advocational stance, avoiding the precommitment to conservative or liberal attitudes which so seriously reduces the value of existing publications of this kind" (p. xi). The editor's "Glossary" defines forty-nine terms with care, venturing to recommend certain usages and to discourage others. The index is a model of its kind. Exceptional intelligence animates this volume.

□ *Strengths* Such a wellspring of originality owes much to its editor. McGrath scintillates on "Doctrine and Dogma," "Enlightenment," "Pannenberg, Wolfhart" and "Soteriology." The latter article, based on his book *Iustitia Dei* (1986), pairs well with Bruce D. Marshall's twelve pages on "Christology." Sweeping the spectrum of theology, this LEXICON classifies arguments by which theologians have assessed achievements of the culture at large. A cluster of eight articles canvasses "Protestant Theology" in Australia, Britain, Canada, Germany (twenty-two pages), the Netherlands, Scandanavia, South Africa and the United States. Each explores responses to diverse milieus and issues.

Articles on the Third World include innovative ones like Jung Young Lee's on "Korean Christian Thought," Kenneth Cragg's on "Arab Christian Thought" and McGrath's on "Indian Christian Thought." Boldly Gavin D'Costa tackles "Other Faiths and Christianity," while in "Culture and Theology" Lesslie Newbigin calls for unleashing insights from Third World missiology onto contemporary Europe. David McClellan notes ironically that the followers of Marxism "have proved better at interpreting the world

than at changing it" (p. 365).

Certain cruxes get illuminated. W. S. F. Pickering differentiates three dimensions of "secularization"—political, intellectual (cognitive) and personal—concluding, "In a simplistic way Protestantism is seen to be its own gravedigger, as indeed is Christianity" (p. 595). Paul S. Fiddes tackles "Suffering, Divine" with the observation that God's willingness to suffer radiates outward into the world but not inward into the godhead. In "Doctrine and Dogma," McGrath expounds George Lindbeck's three types of doctrine ("cognitive-propositional," "experiential-expressivist" and "cultural-linguistic") in order to affirm the latter: "Doctrine . . . describes the regulatory language of the Christian idiom" (p. 118). In "Liturgy and Doctrine" Geoffrey Wainwright highlights instances in which "liturgical practice and doctrinal authority are perceived to be theologically discordant" (p. 340). The prize for wittiness goes jointly to Stewart Sutherland for a typology of "Atheism" and Leslie Houlden for his portrait of "Liberalism: Britain." A scholar of American literature, Robert Detweiler, contributes one of the finest essays anyone has written on "Postmodernism," comparing its quest for self-mirroring to a technique which André Gide called *"mise-en-abîme"*: thus postmodernism replicates a text or picture that "interiorizes a model of itself and sets off a chain of infinite embodiment, since that model has to contain *its* model and so on" (p. 460). Detweiler's exhortation fits this volume as a whole: like the postmodern humanities from which it springs, *The Blackwell Encyclopedia* urges one to regard "the universe as a field of infinite interplay in which humans, never in control, can nonetheless learn how to join in some of its games" (p. 461). This LEXICON invites readers to join in games of culture and theology both—until the games merge.

□ *Weaknesses* This most penetrating of historical LEXICONS in English betrays certain preferences. It devotes more attention to ethics, whether medical, sexual or political, than to spirituality and scants world religions. Judaism elicits just one entry ("Judaism and Christianity") and one biography ("Buber, Martin"), and other religions none. Surveys of Protestant theology require fifty-five pages against ten for Roman Catholic and seven for Eastern Orthodox. Germany and Britain elicit deeper coverage than does the United States. A few entries disappoint. David Jasper waxes pessimistic concerning the interaction of "Literature and Theology" in an era "which has lost its certainty about the nature of time, its myths and narratives" (p. 339). Bernard M. G. Reardon incorporates too many thinkers into his piece on "Romanticism," a failing that Alister McGrath avoids in a pendant on "Enlightenment." The bibliographies cite hardly any foreign-language works and no reference books. Writing on "Spirituality, Christian," Gordon Wakefield does not cite even his own **88** *Westminster Dictionary of Christian Spirituality* (1983). A reference work which ignores others of its kind shirks the kind of self-mirroring that Detweiler's piece on "Postmodernism" would lead one to expect.

□ *Competitors* This magisterial LEXICON carries synthesis to new heights. The authors align innumerable thinkers into movements more convincingly than in any other English-language work. A rival at wringing cultural diagnosis from Christian history is **125** Gisel, ed., *Encyclopédie du protestantisme* (1995), which runs more than twice as long. For at least a generation, Germany, the homeland of theological reference works, has produced none on Christian thought to match either of these. Another REVISIONIST masterpiece, **48** Latourelle and Fisichella, eds., *Dictionary of Fundamental Theology* (1990, 1994), breaks new ground with equal intelligence. Worldwide sweep contrasts with the American focus and occasional trendiness of **76** Musser and Price, eds., *A New Dictionary of Christian Theology* (1992). **80** Ferguson and Wright, eds., *New Dictionary of Theology* (1988) spans nineteen hundred years instead of three hundred and upholds conservative positions. Ten articles in McGrath on seminal theologians compare favorably with those in **78** Marty and Peerman, eds., *A Handbook of Christian Theologians* (1965, 1984). Finally, certain entries

in *The Blackwell Encyclopedia* attain the status of instant classics, including "Doctrine and Dogma," "Eastern Orthodox Theology" and "Secularization" as well as the fifty-five pages on "Protestant Theology." This cornucopia of subtlety belongs in every scholar's library.

□ *Summary* Intelligent in conception and execution, this REVISIONIST LEXICON renews nearly every question it touches. It is a must for scholars of modernity as well as Christianity.

2.4.2 PROTESTANT

OVERVIEW: PROTESTANT PREDILECTION FOR REFERENCE BOOKS Protestant theology has inspired magnificent reference books, particularly in German. Galling, ed., *Die Religion in Geschichte und Gegenwart*, 3d ed., 7 vols. (Tübingen: J. B. C. Mohr, 1956-63) penetrates thinkers and issues superbly. Spread across six thousand pages, its WHO'S WHO is second to none. Since the 1980s American theologians and church historians have edited splendid volumes, the best of which are analyzed here. **125** Gisel, ed., *Encyclopédie du protestantisme* (1995) belongs in their company.

LIST OF WORKS ANALYZED
78 (1965, 1984) Martin E. Marty and Dean G. Peerman, eds., *A Handbook of Christian Theologians* (Nashville: Abingdon, 1965; 2d ed., enl., 1984)
79 (1984) Walter A. Elwell, ed., *Evangelical Dictionary of Theology* (Grand Rapids, Mich.: Baker Book House, 1984)
80 (1988) Sinclair B. Ferguson and David F. Wright, eds., *New Dictionary of Theology* (Downers Grove, Ill., and Leicester, U.K.: InterVarsity Press, 1988)
81 (1995) David J. Atkinson and David H. Field, eds., *New Dictionary of Christian Ethics and Pastoral Theology* (Downers Grove, Ill., and Leicester, U.K.: InterVarsity Press, 1995)

ANALYSIS OF WORKS
78 (1965, 1984) Martin E. Marty

and Dean G. Peerman, eds., *A Handbook of Christian Theologians* (Nashville: Abingdon, 1965; 2d ed., enl., 1984); 735 pages; no index; no general bibliography. Analyzed on the basis of the 1984 edition.

☐ *Scope* Assessing chiefly Protestant theologians who lived between 1800 and 1980, this classic COMPENDIUM divides into two halves of uneven length. Parts 1-3 (pp. 1-500) appraise twenty-six thinkers in contributions written in the early 1960s. Part 4 (pp. 501-726) presents twelve "prime developers and initiators of change in our half-century" in essays written twenty years later. Ranging in length from eleven pages on Anders Nygren and Gustaf Aulén to twenty-five on Adolf von Harnack and Karl Rahner, entries burst with footnotes. But bibliographies cite just one work on and one about each thinker. Eighteen figures are German or Swiss, nine are American, four are British, three Scandinavian, two French, one Dutch (Schillebeeckx) and one Russian (Berdyaev). Contrasts among national schools emerge clearly. The writing ranges from lucid to brilliant.

☐ *Strengths* Skill in matching writer to subject results in more than a few masterpieces. In Parts 1 and 2 (1965) Wilhelm Pauck on Adolf von Harnack, Fritz Buri on Albert Schweitzer, Bernard E. Meland on Rudolf Otto, Robert T. Handy on Walter Rauschenbusch, and Joseph Fletcher on William Temple scintillate. They combine biography, exposition, critique and historical evaluation. In Part 3 (1965) S. C. Guthrie on Oscar Cullmann elucidates *Heilsgeschichte* superbly. Gustaf Wingren relates Gustaf Aulén to Swedish cultural history. George B. Caird on C. H. Dodd writes one of the better essays anywhere on twentieth-century biblical interpretation. Less happily, Walter Leibrecht's piece on Paul Tillich eschews biography for apologia, while Daniel Jenkins lacks distance on Karl Barth. Part 4 (1984) fills one-third of the whole. Many will find its exploration of seminal contemporaries invaluable. Five Roman Catholics (Teilhard de Chardin, Rahner, Schillebeeckx, Tracy and Küng) redress the omission of Catholics from Parts 1-3. Leonard Swidler's personal ac-

quaintance with Hans Küng deepens this essay uncommonly, but Matthew Lamb's interpretation of David Tracy drowns in intricacy. Two French Protestants (Ellul and Ricoeur) win luminous exposition, while the German Lutherans Thielicke and Pannenberg as well as the Reformed Moltmann elicit sparkling critique to boot. Carl Braaten's piece on Pannenberg ranks among the acutest in the volume. Of Americans, Carl F. H. Henry does not appear quite to hold his own with David Tracy and John B. Cobb.

☐ *Weaknesses* Essays from 1984 seem immeasurably closer to us than those from 1965. This discrepancy weighs most heavily on Part 3, whose contributors lacked distance on Gogarten, the Niebuhrs, Barth and Tillich. The format would have gained if each essay had included a half-page summary of career and publications (as is done for Oscar Cullmann on p. 338 and H. Richard Niebuhr on p. 375). The title *Handbook* notwithstanding, this American work does not fulfill German criteria for the genre, which require canvassing methodology and problematics in depth. All the same, this is the finest COMPENDIUM on individual theologians since 1800. It sustains a remarkably high level.

☐ *Competitors* This COMPENDIUM probes its thirty-eight thinkers more deeply than almost any other reference work, including German ones like Galling, ed., *Die Religion in Geschichte und Gegenwart,* 3d ed. (1956-63). The entries go beyond the usual summaries, sketches and overviews, furnishing expert dissections that silhouette contributions against far horizons. The depth makes James Livingston's essays in **34** Gentz, *The Dictionary of Bible and Religion* (1986) seem prefatory. Likewise, conceptual articles in the Westminster/SCM series appear sketchy by comparison, while its volumes on **115** ethics (1967, 1986), **116** theology (1969, 1983) and **118** church history (1971) omit persons. **79** Elwell, ed., *Evangelical Dictionary of Theology* (1984) delivers sharp analysis but scants individuals (omitting Carl Henry altogether). Regrettably, no comparable work examines Roman Catholic or Jewish religious thinkers. Conceived as a companion to Halverson and Cohen, eds., *A Handbook of Christian Theology* (1958), this work transcends its origins. Anyone studying Christian thought since 1800 should use it.

□ *Summary* This COMPENDIUM celebrates theological creativity. No other analyzes seminal post-1800 theologians so incisively.

79 (1984) Walter A. Elwell, ed., *Evangelical Dictionary of Theology* (Grand Rapids, Mich.: Baker Book House, 1984; Basingstoke: Marshall-Pickering, 1985); xxii & 1204 pages; no index; no general bibliography. An abbreviated version appeared as *Concise Evangelical Dictionary of Theology* (1991).

□ *Scope* This meticulous LEXICON abounds in both information and argumentation. Twelve hundred fifty entries by two hundred contributors scrutinize the history of Christianity from an American evangelical perspective. This work formulates self-definition not of a denomination but rather of transdenominational commitment to the Bible. Evangelical positions get differentiated alike from those of fundamentalists, liberals, Catholics and Orthodox. This volume serves as: (1) a GLOSSARY of theology, (2) a WHO'S WHO of theologians of all traditions and periods (with emphasis on Protestants of the past 250 years) and (3) a LEXICON of issues in Christian theology of all periods. Bibliographies range from one or two items to twenty or thirty, almost entirely in English. Nontechnical language makes the volume accessible to all. As a bonus, the WHO'S WHO gets enlarged by thirty-three portraits in a companion volume, Elwell, ed., *Handbook of Evangelical Theologians* (Grand Rapids, Mich.: Baker, 1993), whose entries include Helmut Thielicke, Carl Henry and Alister McGrath.

□ *Strengths* The *Evangelical Dictionary of Theology* pinpoints debates that underlie evangelical self-definition. It formulates positions that intelligent evangelicals can hold on questions great and small. Although this is not a LEXICON of biblical theology, discussion pivots on the author-

ity of the Bible. Addressing systematic theologians, Paul D. Feinberg argues the case for upholding the Princeton theologians' defense of "Bible, Inerrancy and Infallibility of." He presents four arguments in favor and rebuts objections to each (biblical, historical, epistemological, the "slippery slope"). In "Bible, Inspiration of," Carl Henry weighs pros and cons of historical criticism, while Gerhard F. Hasel labels the biblical theology movement of the 1940s and 1950s as "a major attempt . . . to correct liberal theology from within itself" (p. 152). Writing on "Evolution," Pattle P. T. Pun defends "progressive creationism" while rejecting a spectrum from pre-Adamite theories through fiat creationism to theistic evolutionism. Regarding "Relativism," Gordon R. Lewis heatedly defends absolutes of the Bible against both "totalistic" and "limited" relativisms. Contentious entries like these do not mar historical synopses elsewhere. R. Larry Shelton on "Perfection, Perfectionism" anatomizes options stretching from the Gospels to Quakers and Methodists. Thomas Scott Caulley performs a similar feat on the "Holy Spirit," as does Robert G. Clouse on "Millennium, Views of." Sympathy radiates from F. Stuart Piggin on "Roman Catholicism" and Stephen M. Smith on "Kenosis, Kenotic Theology." Judicious discussions probe "Peter, Primacy of" and "Virgin Birth."

Perhaps most useful are articles on twentieth-century theology. Discussions of "Process Theology," "Death of God Theology," "Liberalism, Theological" and "Hope, Theology of" (Moltmann and Pannenberg) sift innumerable points. An article on "Situation Ethics" balances pros and cons. Articles on "Time" and "Eternity" cut deep. Exotic topics include "Asian Theology," "Indian Theology" and "Pain of God Theology." An entry on "Unification Church" is superb, as is Irving Hexham's on "Mormonism." Unexpected topics include "Christians, Names of," "Aesthetics, Christian Views of" and "Aging, Christian Views of." The WHO'S WHO canvasses Christian thinkers and heretics of all periods, ranging from church fathers like Athanasius and Basil through Francis of Assisi and Gregory Palamas to seminal Germans like Adolf von Harnack and Rudolf Otto. Among moderns whose inclusion excites surprise are British writers like G. K. Chesterton, George Macdonald and C. S. Lewis, not to mention Evelyn Underhill, Baron von Hügel and Nikolai Berdyaev. Exceptionally full, this WHO'S WHO of Christian thinkers spells out doctrines and proclaims antitheses.

□ *Weaknesses* One could wish philosophy to be expounded more thoroughly in a LEXICON of systematic theology. Aversion expressed in the entry "Homosexuality" will offend some, and there is no entry on feminism. Although it includes Karl Rahner and Hans Küng, the WHO'S WHO omits surprising names of (then) living figures: Jacques Ellul, Helmut Thielicke, Carl Henry and Jürgen Moltmann, not to mention the deceased Herman Dooyeweerd. Coverage of world religions extends to "Judaism," "Cabbala" and "Manichaeism" but not to Islam, Buddhism or most new religious movements. The argumentativeness that animates this book may repel some. Its notion of doctrine needs to be confronted with George Lindbeck's critique of "propositional" theology in *The Nature of Doctrine* (Philadelphia: Fortress, 1984).

□ *Competitors* For anyone desiring hard-edged formulations, the *Evangelical Dictionary of Theology* comes as a blessing. Articles on doctrine challenge dissent, and entries on thinkers propose novel juxtapositions. Such vigor makes volumes in the Westminster/SCM series recede. However sophisticated, John Macquarrie's many entries there (on theology and ethics) seem elegant but noncommittal. **125** Donald K. McKim, ed., *Encyclopedia of the Reformed Faith* (1992) pursues confessional self-definition less contentiously but no less intelligently. The same can be said of **87** Beinert and Fiorenza, eds., *Handbook of Catholic Theology* (1987, 1995). **163** J. D. Douglas, *New 20th-Century Encyclopedia of Religious Knowledge* (1991) canvasses many of the same persons and issues as Elwell, but more gently. **34** Gentz, ed., *The*

Dictionary of Bible and Religion (1986) discusses certain twentieth-century figures omitted here (e.g., Moltmann, Pannenberg) but covers so much else (the Bible, church history, world religions) that it achieves less depth. Somewhat less conservative, **80** Ferguson and Wright, eds., *New Dictionary of Theology* (1988) expounds a wider range of views for a wider audience. On American topics, **169** Reid, ed., *Dictionary of Christianity in America* (1990) delivers a broader range of views. More than any of these, the *Evangelical Dictionary of Theology* invites theologians to argue a case and impels a reader to choose sides. A sequel of equal length will, one hopes, cultivate the same virtues: Elwell, ed., *Evangelical Dictionary of Biblical Theology* (Grand Rapids, Mich.: Baker Book House, 1996).

□ *Summary* This hard-edged LEXICON subjects theology to some of the keenest analysis in any reference work. Vigor incites debate, and historical grasp generates insight.

80 (1988) Sinclair B. Ferguson and David F. Wright, eds., *New Dictionary of Theology* (Downers Grove, Ill., and Leicester, U.K.: InterVarsity Press, 1988); xix & 738 pages; no index; general bibliography, pp. x-xii ("Abbreviations").

□ *Scope* This historical DICTIONARY of theology recruited 215 mostly American evangelicals to write 630 signed articles of INTRODUCTION. Designed for "biblically centered Christians," the DICTIONARY undertakes nothing less than to "introduce the world of theology—its themes, both majestic and minor, its famous formulations and its important historical moments, its distinguished—and notorious—exponents, and its interaction with other currents of thought and religion" (p. vii). Surveys articulate "reasoned disagreement" (p. 596) on a wide range of issues. The WHO'S WHO tackles a larger number of theologians than does perhaps any other single volume except **29** Cross, ed., *The Oxford Dictionary of the Christian Church* (1957, 1974). The format is alluring, the writing straightforward, and individual bibliographies discriminating. This is the closest thing to a primer in the field.

□ *Strengths* Conservative in name more than in practice, this DICTIONARY largely eschews onesidedness. Articles of two to four pages on classical topics like "Atonement," "Sanctification" and "Trinity" trace positions through nineteen centuries and all camps. Geoffrey W. Bromiley does so for "History of Theology." Overviews excel at constructing typologies, whether of denominations or doctrines. An entry on "Millennium" differentiates five attitudes, while that on "Hermeneutics" sorts out more than a dozen positions. Historical surveys map "Scholasticism," "Puritan Theology," "Jesuit Theology" and "Anglo-Catholic Theology." In a perspicuous three pages Harold O. J. Brown retraces "Russian Orthodox Theology" to 1800, while in two pages Edwin M. Yamauchi untangles "Gnosticism." Methodology evokes typologies of "Myth," "Phenomenology" and "History-of-Religions School."

The work specializes in entries that dissect complexity in a single page, as on "Hypostasis," "Kenoticism" and "History." A GLOSSARY culled from these micromasterpieces would run seventy-five to a hundred pages. Adventurous contributors advocate wider use of "Depth Psychology," "Psychology of Religion," "Sociology of Religion" and "Political Theology." H. M. Conn's four pages on "Liberation Theology" exude judiciousness, as do overviews of "African Christian Theology," "Asian Christian Theology" and "Indian Christian Theology." Wittily, K. Bediako of Ghana refers to "African Independent Churches" as "Africa's Anabaptists" (p. 11). Unexpected entries include an admiring one on the "Frankfurt School."

The WHO'S WHO astonishes by comprehensiveness. Its articles recount career and analyze major publications before assessing impact. Besides dozens of obligatory theologians like Irenaeus, Schleiermacher and Rahner as well as philosophers like Descartes, Kant and Wittgenstein, the *Dictionary* references a galaxy of figures found in few if any other single-volume works:

Drozdov Filaret, Michael Polanyi, Charles Raven and Alvin Plantinga. Particularly welcome is an entry on Herman Dooyeweerd (1894-1977), who like his teacher Abraham Kuyper gets omitted from too many reference works. A few oversights stand out: Martin Heidegger, Paul Ricoeur and Gerardus van der Leeuw. Zeal to dissect complexities disarms suspicion throughout. For all its bibliocentric credentials, a work so temperate in pursuing self-definition cannot be divisive. Catholics and Eastern Christians will enjoy the *New Dictionary of Theology*.

□ *Weaknesses* A conservative stance mars certain articles and excludes others. Insistence on a biblical basis bars entries on new religious movements and addresses world religions only in order to distance them (Buddhism, Confucianism, Hinduism, Islam and Judaism). David Wright's article on "Christianity and Other Religions" does not venture beyond St. Paul. Niceties of biblical interpretation get glossed over. There is no hint of what comes in a HANDBOOK OF BIBLE INTERPRETATION. A few articles celebrate outdated positions, e.g. "Princeton Theology," while inveighing against others like "Hyper-Calvinism." Certain contemporary topics like "Animal Rights" and "Theology of Revolution" excite reservations. In the name of "restoring covenant mutuality" (p. 258), an entry on "Feminist Theology" rebuts more positions than it endorses. Some of the bibliographies are spotty after 1980, but on the whole, this work is far more middle of the road than nonconservatives may expect. It offers something for everyone.

□ *Competitors* This beguiling DICTIONARY delivers an attractive INTRODUCTION to history of Christian theology. Although directed primarily at evangelicals, its historical surveys serve everyone. In contrast, **116** Richardson and Bowden, eds., *The Westminster Dictionary of Christian Theology* (1969, 1983) is ecumenical in an Anglican fashion but seems more convoluted and has no WHO'S WHO. **79** Elwell, ed., *Evangelical Dictionary of Theology* (1984) is more argumentative and requires prior knowledge, as does **87** Beinert and

Fiorenza, eds., *Handbook of Catholic Theology* (1987, 1995). 34 Gentz, ed., *The Dictionary of Bible and Religion* (1986) incorporates John Macquarrie's virtuosic primer of theology, which has no equivalent here. 29 Cross, ed., *The Oxford Dictionary of the Christian Church* (1957, 1974) canvasses many more persons and topics but is dated on twentieth-century matters. The *New Dictionary*'s balance between old and new complements the contemporaneity of 76 Musser and Price., eds., *A New Handbook of Christian Theology* (1992), and it presents theology with more bite than does 169 Reid, ed., *Dictionary of Christianity in America* (1990). All readers, not just Protestants, will benefit from this INTRODUCTION. Whether as a WHO'S WHO or a historical primer, it belongs in every library.

□ *Summary* This winsome DICTIONARY excels as a self-teacher of Protestant thinking concerning Christian thought. Historical overviews and a WHO'S WHO help beginners of every camp.

81 (1995) David J. Atkinson and David H. Field, eds., *New Dictionary of Christian Ethics and Pastoral Theology* (Downers Grove, Ill., and Leicester, U.K.: InterVarsity Press, 1995); xxiii & 918 pages; index of names, pp. 911-18; no general bibliography.

□ *Scope* Emphasizing the timely, this British-edited COMPENDIUM cum DICTIONARY interprets contemporary issues in ethics and counseling from a conservative evangelical standpoint. It opens with a COMPENDIUM of eighteen articles on issues (pp. 3-127) that is followed by a DICTIONARY of over seven hundred entries on ethics, theology and psychology by 240 (mostly British) contributors. Favoring British concerns, the DICTIONARY extends from virtues (e.g., "Benevolence," "Gratitude") and movements (e.g., "Humanism," "Liberation Theology") to practices (e.g., "Battery Farming," "Espionage") and controversies (e.g., "Devlin-Hart Debate," "Free Will and Determinism"). On contemporary practices it formulates ethical judgments. A WHO'S WHO treats ethicists (e.g., Joseph Fletcher, Helmut

Thielicke), theologians (e.g., Ambrose, Ignatius of Loyola), economists (e.g., Malthus, Marx), psychologists (e.g., Viktor Frankl, Rollo May) and British counselors (Frank Lake, Robert Lambourne). Business ethics, health care, and death and dying win notable attention. English-language bibliographies are superb.

□ *Strengths* This bibliocentric COMPENDIUM cum DICTIONARY of ethics highlights pastoral concerns. Both medical ethics and business ethics elicit firm judgments. Although the standpoint is evangelical, ethics in traditions as diverse as Islamic, Buddhist, Confucian and Hindu get sketched. Christian ethics inspires separate articles on "Roman Catholic," "Orthodox," "Calvinistic," "Lutheran," "Pietist," "Anglican" and "Mennonite" (but not Methodist). Eighteen "keynote articles" synthesize swaths of material. Thus R. F. Hurding surveys three thousand years of "Pastoral Care, Counselling, and Psychotherapy," J. E. Hare does the same for "History of Christian Ethics," and as usual Alister McGrath shines on "Sin and Salvation." Within the DICTIONARY N. L. Geisler formulates a stunning typology of "Norms," while David H. Field appraises "Homosexuality" with finesse. Alternative models get weighed concerning "Censorship," "Cross-Cultural Counselling" and "Incest." Timely entries propose "incarnational" positions on "Espionage," "Behaviourism" and "Embryology" and compare Christian approaches to challenges like "Industrial Relations" and "Investment." A few articles qualify as REVISIONIST: G. L. Bray inveighs against "Indoctrination" in religion; G. O. Stone takes a fresh look at "Folk Religion" (with superb bibliography); I. R. Davis on "Architecture" propounds Christian arguments against utopian planning. Lyricism colors meditations by V. M. Sinton on "Singleness" and David Field on "Speech and the Tongue." No other recent theological work in English tackles so many practical issues or proffers such bracing advice.

□ *Weaknesses* This volume works best for topics that lie outside one's professional expertise. In no area is it the most advanced tool available. Moreover, British concerns predominate and may surprise Americans. A few entries debate British legislation and little else (e.g., "Data Protection"). Exhorters like Frank Lake and Robert Lambourne scarcely matter outside Britain, and Eurocentrism excludes voices of Asian and African Christians. American priorities recede. Women's issues get discussed chiefly under "Feminism" and "Sexual Harassment," while questions of race are largely ignored. Americans will regret that church-state relations scarcely rate a mention, that "Identity" gets subsumed under "Adolescence" and that there is no entry on the Holocaust.

□ *Competitors* This British-centered volume digests economics, sociology, psychology and above all ethics for pastors of every sort. Models taken from social science alternate with Bible-centered counseling. The channeling of ethics and social sciences onto current dilemmas recalls a German LEXICON, Ulrich Ruh, David Seeber and Rudolf Walter, eds., *Handwörterbuch religiöser Gegenwartsfragen* (Freiburg, Basel and Vienna: Herder, 1986). Focused on Germany, its hundred-odd essays tackle obstacles even more constructively. The closest rival in English remains Rodney J. Hunter, ed., *Dictionary of Pastoral Care and Counselling* (Nashville: Abingdon, 1990), which likewise addresses clergy but construes theology in a manner less bibliocentric. 115 Childress and Macquarrie, eds., *The Westminster Dictionary of Christian Ethics* (1967, 1986) is vastly more learned but disdains counseling and disregards medicine. A work of simplistic conservatism is R. K. Harrison, ed., *Encyclopedia of Biblical and Christian Ethics* (Nashville: Nelson, 1987; 2d ed. 1992). Catholic reflection plays over some of the same issues in 86 Dwyer, ed., *The New Dictionary of Catholic Social Thought* (1994). Deeper reflection and broader panoramas distinguish 77 McGrath, ed., *The Blackwell Encyclopedia of Modern Christian Thought* (1993). Similarly nonconfessional, 294 Becker and Becker, eds., *Encyclopedia of Ethics* (1992) canvasses history of ethics more thoroughly but scarcely addresses counselors. Among volumes offering guidance, 310 Benner, ed., *Baker Encyclopedia of Psychology* (1984) probes its field in greater depth while largely eschewing theology. Like it, the *New Dictionary* aids self-help while offering blunter advice.

□ *Summary* In rethinking dilemmas in ethics, this Bible-centered COMPENDIUM cum DICTIONARY reflects British rather than American preoccupations. The advice startles, and the bibliographies excel.

2.4.3 ROMAN CATHOLIC

OVERVIEW: UPS AND DOWNS SINCE VATICAN II The Second Vatican Council (1962-65) revolutionized reference works by and for Roman Catholics. Of works dating from before 1960, few besides the French MEGA-ENCYCLOPEDIAS retain their luster. Unwittingly, the Council orphaned a magnificent production, 82 Davis, ed., *A Catholic Dictionary of Theology* (1962-71) and obliged another masterpiece, 137 Jacquemet, ed., *Catholicisme: hier—aujourd'hui—demain* (1948-) to change course. Since 1972 volumes 7-13 of the latter dazzle. No recent book builds on Vatican II more astutely or explains its consequences more vividly than a translation from the Italian, 48 Latourelle and Fisichella, eds., *Dictionary of Fundamental Theology* (1990, 1994). Recent Catholic works originating in English seldom match any of these in sophistication partly because American Catholics scant social sciences. Elsewhere in the directory Catholic contributions appear under 2.5 "Spirituality," 2.6 "Hagiography," 2.7 "Liturgy" and 2.9.2 "Churches and Denominations."

LIST OF WORKS ANALYZED
82 (1962-71) H. Francis Davis et al., eds., *A Catholic Dictionary of Theology*, 3 vols. (London: Thomas Nelson, 1962-1971); vol. 4 never published
83 (1987) Joseph A. Komonchak, Mary Collins and Dermot A. Lane, eds., *The New Dictionary of Theology* (Wilmington, Del.: Michael Glazier, 1987; later Collegeville, Minn.: Michael Gla-

zier/Liturgical)

84 (1987) Michael O'Carroll, *Trinitas: A Theological Encyclopedia of the Holy Trinity* (Wilmington, Del.: Michael Glazier, 1987; later Collegeville, Minn.: Michael Glazier/Liturgical)

85 (1987-90) Emerich Coreth, Walter M. Neidl and Georg Pfligersdorfer, eds., *Christliche Philosophie im katholischen Denken des 19. und 20. Jahrhunderts,* 3 vols. (Graz, Vienna and Cologne: Styria Verlag, 1987-90)

111 (1990) Peter E. Fink, S.J., ed., *The New Dictionary of Sacramental Worship* (Collegeville, Minn.: Michael Glazier/Liturgical, 1990). Analyzed under 2.7 "Liturgy."

48 ([1990] 1994) René Latourelle and Rino Fisichella, eds., *Dictionary of Fundamental Theology* [1990] (New York: Crossroad, 1994). Analyzed under 2.2 "Ecumenism."

86 (1994) Judith Dwyer, ed., *The New Dictionary of Catholic Social Thought* (Collegeville, Minn.: Michael Glazier/Liturgical, 1994)

87 (1987, 1995) Wolfgang Beinert and Francis Schüssler Fiorenza, eds., *Handbook of Catholic Theology* (New York: Crossroad, 1995)

ANALYSIS OF WORKS

82 (1962-1971) H. Francis Davis et al., eds., *A Catholic Dictionary of Theology,* 3 vols. (London: Thomas Nelson, 1962-71); xvi & 32; xii & 360; xii & 399 pages; vol. 4 (from *PAS* to end) was never published; no index; no general bibliography.

□ *Scope* This winsome ENCYCLOPEDIA of the history of Catholic theology began before Vatican II and fizzled out after it. Volume 1 (A-B) boasts almost three times the density of volume 2 (1967) and four times that of volume 3 (1971). As momentum faded, Joseph Crehan, S.J. wrote almost three-fourths of volume 3. Written almost entirely by British and Irish Catholics, most of them clerics, the articles sparkle. Doctrines, concepts, controversies and persons (both church fathers and heretics) get aired. Each entry traces the history and

subsequent influence of its topic, subdividing material lucidly into subheads and providing multilingual bibliography, sometimes at length. Perhaps no other religious reference work in English since 1960 delivers so many stylish articles.

□ *Strengths* Imaginative planning makes *A Catholic Dictionary of Theology* a self-teacher beyond compare. In the hands of master expounders (led by Joseph Crehan), the abstruse becomes obvious and the elusive concrete. Sacraments, doctrines, heresies, major thinkers and heretics, councils and some concepts ("Mystical Body," "Eros," "Light, Metaphysic of") elicit 360 entries. The history of major doctrines is expounded magisterially, notably by Joseph Crehan ("Free Will," "Immortality," "Miracles," "Original Sin") and Edward Sillem ("Attributes of God"). The editor, Francis Davis, contributes a luminous article on "Doctrine, Development of." Every church council and every sacrament (except "Penance" and "Unction" in the unpublished volume 4) commands a lengthy article. A handful of ethical issues like "Abortion," "Apostasy" and "Christian Ethics" creep in. Historical surveys canvass "Bible, Use of," "Church and State," "Feasts," "Indulgences," "Limbo" and "Mysticism." Heresies stimulate articles like "Arianism," "Donatism," "Gnosticism" and "Manichaeism." Lesser heretics like Bardesanes, Basilides, Cerinthus and Eutyches command attention.

Controversies surrounding "Gallicanism," "Jansenism" and "Origenism" are unraveled with aplomb. Upheavals between 1800 and 1960 inspire entries like "Brownson," "Hegelianism," "Kant," "Lamennais," "Liberal Catholicism," "Marxism" and "Modernism." Entries on non-Catholic Christian topics include "Calvinism," "Luther" and a choice ten-page conspectus of "Anglicanism" (by Humphrey Johnson). An article on "Islam and Theology" (by W. Montgomery Watt) lacks, however, a pendant on Judaism. Innovative entries tackle issues in science, as in "Astrology and Theology," "Biology, Impact upon Theology," "Cosmogony,"

"Evolution" and "Magic." E. E. Evans-Pritchard contributes a page on "Animism." The arts elicit "Art and the Church," "Baroque," "Byzantine Art," "Gothic" and "Music and Theology."

A unique feature is a series (chiefly in volume 1) that outlines not the lives but rather the subsequent influence of figures like Cardinal Bellarmine, St. Benedict, Pierre de Bérulle, Duns Scotus and Johannes Eck. Unexpected entries include "Egyptian Liturgy" (on Nag Hammadi papyri), "Elias, Theology of" (on Elijah as a prototype of John the Baptist and the religious life), and "Feudalism and Theology" on five ethical issues of feudal times. "Animals in Theology" examines the Bible, Pythagoras and papal teaching on bullfighting. Among English-language Catholic works, volume 1 purveys the fullest coverage of topics alphabetized through *B*. Even as density diminished, *A Catholic Dictionary of Theology* upheld a high standard. Joseph Crehan's nearly single-handed authorship of volume 3 yielded eighty articles out of 110, totaling about three hundred pages. They soar like any in volume 1.

□ *Weaknesses* Even at its most supple, this monument to pre-Vatican II thought could not evade omissions that startle us today. Judaism is scanted except for articles on "Ebionism" and "Jewish Christianity." Women's issues, Asian religions (except "Buddhism") and missions (apart from an article on "America, Theological Significance of") receive no mention. Inexplicably, Eastern Orthodoxy recedes, and certain church fathers are omitted (e.g., Athanasius, Cassian, Jerome). Only two popes get referenced: Honorius I (625-638) for his attempt to halt the development of doctrine (an action that influenced Vatican I) and Hormisdas (514-523) for his reconciliation with Constantinople. As space dwindled, one suspects that certain entries survived because Joseph Crehan itched to write them (e.g., "Lollards," "Masonry," "Memory and God," "Mithraism"). In none of the volumes does the one-page editor's preface adequately explain the genesis or evolution of the project. The toll that Vatican II wreaked on

this enterprise emerges from the following data. Of sixty contributors to volume 1, only eleven continued among the thirty-five in volume 2, and of these only the editor and Joseph Crehan persevered among the twenty in volume 3. Later the editor left both the priesthood and the church. Yet apart from a decline in density of entries per letter of the alphabet, no decline in quality marks Joseph Crehan's entries in volume 3.

□ *Competitors* As possibly the best written religious reference work of the past fifty years in English, *A Catholic Dictionary of Theology* retains both usefulness and charm. It expounds history of doctrines, controversies and heresies more lucidly than perhaps any other except **84** O'Carroll, *Trinitas* (1987) and **137** Jacquemet, ed., *Catholicisme: Hier—aujourd'hui—demain* (1948-). **112** Fink, ed., *The New Dictionary of Sacramental Worship* (1990) sustains a similar spirit of openmindedness and erudition. So does **48** Latourelle and Fisichella, eds., *Dictionary of Fundamental Theology* (1990, 1994). Karl Rahner et al., eds., *Sacramentum Mundi*, 6 vols. (New York: Herder and Herder, 1968-70) tackles more issues while rethinking everything from the vantage of Vatican II. It is, however, less elegantly written and lacks specificity, especially on the early church. A work of the same era, McDonald, ed., *The New Catholic Encyclopedia*, 15 vols. (1967), is too packed to reward browsing and cries out to be updated from **128** Kasper, ed., *Lexikon für Theologie und Kirche*, 3d ed. (1993-). As a one-volume LEXICON, **83** Komonchak et al., eds., *The New Dictionary of Theology* (1987) is too cautious to be mentioned in the same breath.

Not surprisingly, French MEGA-ENCYCLOPEDIAS gain in accessibility if first one peruses pertinent entries in *A Catholic Dictionary of Theology*. Even after one has consulted *magna opera* like **152** Di Berardino, ed., *Encyclopedia of the Early Church* (1982, 1992) or the Westminster/SCM Dictionaries, it is a pleasure to return to *A Catholic Dictionary of Theology*. One can imagine giants of English Catholicism like Lord Acton or Baron von Hügel, not to mention polymath priests like Ronald Knox or even Cardinal Newman, relishing these pages. Here is the nearest thing to a reference book that they themselves might have written. No reference work concerning religion is more readable, and few are so imaginatively planned. Not least among the casualties of Vatican II must rank volume 4 of this enterprise.

□ *Summary* A browser's paradise, *A Catholic Encyclopedia of Theology* remains unsurpassed at elucidating the history of Catholic thought in resonant English. Few reference works in any field tackle so many daunting topics with such freshness.

83 (1987) Joseph A. Komonchak, Mary Collins and Dermot A. Lane, eds., *The New Dictionary of Theology* (Wilmington, Del.: Michael Glazier, 1987; later, Collegeville, Minn.: Michael Glazier/Liturgical; Dublin: Gill & Macmillan, 1990); viii & 1112 pages; subject index, pp. ii-iv; no general bibliography.

□ *Scope* This LEXICON of Catholic self-definition places post-Vatican II developments in historical context. Its 165 contributors are nearly all American clerics, and most of the 435 entries recapitulate teaching of the magisterium. Articles delineate issues rather than persons or places. A GLOSSARY of ten-line definitions alternates with articles averaging one to two pages, most of which provide skeletal bibliography. Caution borders on timidity.

□ *Strengths* In order to highlight a "hierarchy of truths" (p. v), twenty-four "focal articles" explore topics like "Anthropology, Christian," "Creation," "Holy Spirit," "Ministry," "Reign of God" and "Trinity." A very few examine historical movements like "Church Fathers," "Enlightenment," "Modernism" and "Protestantism." Forty pages address the Bible. To be sure, certain articles venture into boldness. George Tavard sparkles on "Tradition," as do John H. Wright, S.J. on "Providence," William J. Hill, O.P. on "Theology" and Mark D. Jordan on "Theology, History of." A few REVISIONIST articles creep in, as in Rosemary Radford Ruether's on "Feminist Theology" and Dermot A. Lane's on "Eschatology." On

the whole, however, anyone seeking breakthroughs on ethics, the sacraments or church history should look elsewhere.

□ *Weaknesses* Emphasis on the magisterium colors too many entries. Art and literature hardly get mentioned except in Stephen Happel's glowing conspectus of "Imagination, Religious." Definitions in short articles purvey Roman Catholic rather than ecumenical usage. Most grievously, a LEXICON that lacks a WHO'S WHO cries out for indexes both of names and of topics. Their absence makes it impossible to trace thinkers or correlations.

□ *Competitors* This inward-looking LEXICON lacks the energy that lifts a companion volume, **112** Fink, ed., *The New Dictionary of Sacramental Worship* (1990). The latter shows that liturgics inspires American Catholics to greater finesse than does theology overall. Albeit more up-to-date, the writing here does not begin to rival that in **82** Davis, ed., *A Catholic Dictionary of Theology* (1962-71). That work makes this one seem straitjacketed. Sadly, *The New Dictionary of Theology* quite lacks the sophistication of **77** McGrath, ed., *The Blackwell Encyclopedia of Modern Christian Thought* (1993). The sprightliest DICTIONARY of normative Catholic theology in English remains **87** Beinert and Schüssler Fiorenza, eds., *Handbook of Catholic Theology* (1995).

□ *Summary* This LEXICON pursues Catholic self-definition without furthering either historical insight or theological renewal.

84 (1987) Michael O'Carroll, *Trinitas: A Theological Encyclopedia of the Holy Trinity* (Wilmington, Del.: Michael Glazier, 1987; later Collegeville, Minn.: Michael Glazier/Liturgical); vols. 1-17 published in paperback (1993); x & 220 pages; no index; no general bibliography.

□ *Critique* This lively LEXICON expounds persons, councils, concepts and doctrines connected with the doctrine of the Trinity. Having rethought a swath of Christian history, an independent mind recounts it with wit and wisdom. Limpid articles on theologians of the early church, as well as on heresies and church councils, rank among the clearest anywhere. "Arius" and

"Arianism" elicit fifteen pages, "Athanasius" eight and "Augustine" four. Concepts like "Consubstantial," "Creation" and "Filioque" stimulate energy and insight. Twentieth-century theologians like Barth, Lonergan and Rahner win judicious treatment. Defining "Mysticism" as "immediate awareness of the Trinity," that entry reviews Catholic contemplatives astutely. Well-chosen quotations enliven many entries, each with bibliographical footnotes. Articles are longer and wittier than in the author's earlier *Theotokos* (Wilmington, Del.: Michael Glazier, 1982). In like format came three more volumes: *Corpus Christi* (1989), *Veni Creator Spiritus* (1990) and *Verbum Caro* (1992). In the manner of Ronald Knox, this Irish priest has written some of the best self-teachers on doctrinal roots of Christianity. Non-Catholic Christians will find much to ponder.

□ *Summary* This LEXICON makes fourth- and fifth-century controversies come alive.

85 (1987-89) Emerich Coreth, Walter M. Neidl and Georg Pfligersdorfer, eds., *Christliche Philosophie im katholischen Denken des 19. und 20. Jahrhunderts*, vol. 1, *Neue Ansätze im 19. Jahrhundert* (Graz, Vienna and Cologne: Styria Verlag, 1987); 799 pages; vol. 2, *Rückgriff auf scholastisches Erbe* (1988), 872 pages; vol. 3, *Moderne Strömungen im 20. Jahrhundert* (1989), 920 pages; also available in Italian translation (Rome: Città Nuova, 1992-95); index and general bibliography in each volume.

□ *Critique* This magisterial HANDBOOK recruited over a hundred authorities (about two-thirds of them German) to compose chapters on major and minor Catholic philosophers and theologians of Europe and the Americas from 1800 to 1985. Whereas volume 1 appeared entirely in German, volumes 2 and 3 offer chapters in English, French and Spanish as well. Volume 1 handles the earlier nineteenth century (particularly in Germany and France), volume 2 dissects Neo-Scholasticism in all its ramifications (including in Latin America), and volume 3 explores twentieth-century figures in unheard-of diversity. Scrupulous periodizations, subtle comparisons and multilingual bibliographies reconfigure each thinker, while overviews propound diverse, often clashing syntheses. Although Rosino Gibellini, *Panorama de la théologie au XXe siècle,* translated from the Italian (Paris: Cerf, 1994) synthesizes some of this material, no other reference work interprets so coherently the history of German, French and Italian Catholic thought since 1800. It makes **73** John Macquarrie's *Twentieth-Century Religious Thought* (1965, 1990) seem something of a primer. If made available in English, this German masterwork could revolutionize how Americans and British construe Catholic intellectual history.

□ *Summary* This model HANDBOOK unlocks access to more than one hundred often neglected philosophers and theologians. It opens countless doors on European thought.

86 (1994) Judith Dwyer, ed., *The New Dictionary of Catholic Social Thought* (Collegeville, Minn.: Michael Glazier/Liturgical, 1994); xxxi & 1019 pages; no index (except a synopsis of each article, pp. 1005-19); no general bibliography.

□ *Scope* This path-breaking LEXICON places Catholic social thought since 1800 into historical context. Of 170 contributors, eighty are clerics and only twenty-one women. Nearly all 282 entries supply English-language bibliography. American-Catholic self-definition imposes two foci: (1) papal pronouncements and (2) North American debates (including the ones concerning Québec). A majority of entries require one to three pages to delineate concepts, conferences and practices, but not places (except Medellín in 1968 and Puebla in 1979). Although social sciences scarcely figure, ideologies range from neo-conservative through pluralist to feminist and liberationist. A WHO'S WHO treats only seventeen persons, embracing five popes as well as militants like John Lafarge, Wilhelm von Ketteler and Marc Sangnier. Disappointingly, the writing ranges from plain to vapid.

□ *Strengths* This LEXICON exalts analysis of

the past above diagnosis of the present. Summaries of up to twenty pages outline "Modern Catholic Social Thought," "Church, Social Mission of," "Human Rights" and "Scripture, Use of in Catholic Social Ethics." Battles over "Americanism," "Associationism" and "Modernism" (but not liberalism) get retold. In a major undertaking, ten papal encyclicals and exhortations elicit eight to twelve pages each. Recounting historical context while skirting today's impasses, these articles comprise a book in themselves. A few REVISIONIST essays come from the likes of John T. Pawlikowski, O.S.M. on "Holocaust, The," M. Shawn Copeland on "Black Theology" and Walter J. Burghardt, S.J. on "Preaching, Role of." Refreshingly, June O'Connor celebrates "The Catholic Worker" and John A. Coleman, S.J. the "British Distributists." An elegy commemorates Collegeville's own Virgil Michel (1890-1938). Unexpected articles include "Computerization," "Aborigines, Australian," "Animal Rights" and "Knights of Labor." Historians of thought will applaud, but militants will yearn for something feistier.

□ *Weaknesses* Historical expertise languishes when it ignores the social sciences. This LEXICON explores ethical principles but not sources of resistance to them, except in articles like "Affirmative Action" and "Base Communities." Unsurprisingly, no one mentions the church's failure to apply its principles to its own employees by paying them a just wage. Not even Gustavo Gutiérrez writing on "Liberation Theology" raises this specter. In an editing lapse, the index merely outlines each article, and in bibliographies French and German titles surface too rarely. However useful as history, this volume will alarm enthusiasts. Its complacency serves scholars, not militants.

□ *Competitors* Albeit tepidly, this historical LEXICON fills a gap, for no other reference book in English sifts Catholic social teachings. Italians, to be sure, can resort to a thousand pages of Raimondo Spiazzi, ed., *Enciclopedia del pensiero sociale cristiano* (Bologna: Edizioni Studio Domenicano, 1992). In contrast to both, a German

competitor bursts with originality: Ulrich Ruh, David Seeber and Rudolf Walter, eds., *Handwörterbuch religiöser Gegenwartsfragen* (Freiburg, Basel and Vienna: Herder, 1986). Rich in German-language bibliography, its 107 articles exalt social sciences. Editors at Collegeville seem to fear such bluntness. Yet a masterpiece like **110** Sartore and Triacca, eds., *Dictionnaire encyclopédique de la liturgie* (1984, 1992-) shows how European Catholics are wedding social science to theology. Americans need to join that endeavor.

□ *Summary* This historical LEXICON cautiously retraces Catholic social thought and its historical settings, above all in Italy and North America since 1800. English-language bibliographies excel, but the social sciences are missing.

87 (1987, 1995) Wolfgang Beinert and Francis Schüssler Fiorenza, eds., *Handbook of Catholic Theology* (New York: Crossroad, 1995); translated from Beinert, ed., *Lexikon der katholischen Dogmatik* (Freiburg: Herder, 1987); xiv & 783 pages; index of subjects, pp. 761-83; no general bibliography other than list of abbreviations, pp. 753-58; 59 tables.

□ *Critique* In one to eight pages, this methodical GLOSSARY subjects more than three hundred concepts to normative appraisal. About half the entries run two pages or less. The American edition enriches a German predecessor with English-language bibliographies and at least ten articles on "Contemporary Issues." Nearly all other entries follow a schema: (1) biblical background, (2) history of theology, (3) church teaching, (4) ecumenical perspectives and (5) systematic reflections. Almost invariably, the fifth section is the most provocative. A major aim is to chart affinities among eleven branches of dogmatic theology: method, God, creation, anthropology, Christ, Mary, ecclesiology, pneumatology, grace, sacraments and eschatology. Furthering this goal, nearly sixty tables assemble information that has seldom if ever been grouped so cogently. A chart of sixteen of "God's Attributes," for example, astonishes by its compactness (pp. 273-74). Listing more than 150 thinkers, a table of four pages compresses twenty-six "Epochs of the History of Theology and Dogma" (pp. 704-7). Although German authorities predominate, eight Americans dissect "Contemporary Issues," including Peter Fink on "Sacraments," Elizabeth A. Johnson on "Mary" and Anne M. Clifford on "Anthropology" and "Creation." As a singularity among works of this caliber, there is no list of contributors. No other volume enumerates options in theology or norms in Catholic teaching so graphically. Utterly up-to-date, this masterpiece of condensation injects into the contemporary a note of *gravitas*. A larger rival, **48** Latourelle and Fisichella, eds., *Dictionary of Fundamental Theology* (1990, 1994) is less systematic but more adventurous. Although both benefit students of all camps, Fiorenza's formulates Catholic self-definition, while Latourelle's undertakes cultural diagnosis.

□ *Summary* Deploying remarkable charts, this rigorous GLOSSARY elucidates three hundred categories of dogmatic theology. It compares conceptualizations meticulously, and its charts have no peer.

2.5 SPIRITUALITY

OVERVIEW: A "SPIRITUALITY REVOLUTION" AND POSTMODERNISM Fascination with spirituality has surged since the 1960s, yet few reference works single it out. The ones that do differ in delimiting the concept. To the surprise of many, the term *spirituality* has become democratized since monastics in seventeenth-century France first disseminated it. Then the notion denoted "ascetical and mystical theology" as a spur to sanctity. Whereas contemplatives then aspired to sanctity, today they cultivate spirituality. Having become accessible, ideals that for centuries an elite viewed as virtually unattainable now prompt spiritual growth in everyone. In a word, a "spirituality revolution" during the past thirty years has democratized pursuit of holiness. In consequence of that transition, the term *spirituality* is more easily described than defined.[1]

Why has spirituality blossomed since the 1960s? Scholars now take as axiomatic the realization that every worshiper, like every religious body, cultivates a distinctive way of assimilating worship and doctrine. Whether as regards doctrine, discipline, liturgy or fellowship, a unique style of incorporating inwardly what is shared outwardly constitutes a "spirituality." The latter accumulates through acts of reception, which taken together embody a "slant" or "take" on core phenomena. Insofar as spirituality favors "reception" of tradition by individuals or groups, it parallels endeavors by literary scholars to trace "reception" of texts as practiced by generations of readers. Postmoderns relish spirituality not least because study of it connects academic specialties both with one another and with experience. Promoting the "blurring of genres," spirituality bridges life and thought, devotion and work, denomination and universality. Postmodernism and the study of spirituality go together. Both recombine predecessors without aiming to supplant them. What modernism in homage to rationality discards, postmodernism in homage to spirituality revives.

Study of spirituality lends itself to COMPENDIA and LEXICONS, for spiritual aspiration yearns to sweep horizons. Toward that goal, for example, Ewert Cousins has commissioned twenty-five volumes of COMPENDIA in a series, *World Spirituality: An Encyclopedic History of the Religious Quest* (New York: Crossroad, 1985-). Although too specialized to evaluate here, this American behemoth rivals European MEGA-ENCYCLOPEDIAS by exploring history in ravishing depth. **89** Wakefield, ed., *The Westminster Dictionary of Christian Spirituality* (1983) supplies an unequaled WHO'S WHO, and on innumerable topics a Catholic MEGA-ENCYCLOPEDIA, **88** Viller, ed., *Dictionnaire de spiritualité* (1937-94) remains unexcelled. We must wait, however, for Ewert Cousins, ed., *Dictionary of World Spirituality* to canvass spirituality

---

[1] Thus concludes Aimé Solignac in a learned article, "Spiritualité: Le mot et l'histoire," in **88** Viller, ed., *Dictionnaire de spiritualité*, 14 (1990): 1142-60.

worldwide as thoroughly as **45** Fahlbusch et al., eds., *Evangelisches Kirchenlexikon* (1986-) handles almost every other topic. Regrettably, no reference book canvasses spiritual autobiography.[2] To be sure, a REVISIONIST COMPENDIUM, Vincent L. Wimbaugh and Richard Valantasis, eds., *Asceticism* (New York: Oxford University Press, 1995) reexamines that one dimension worldwide. One grows in appreciation of what the spirituality revolution has wrought by consulting a REAL-LEXIKON like Pelliccia and Rocca, eds., *Dizionario degli istituti di perfezione,* 8 vols. to date (Rome, 1974-). It documents Christian religious institutions without invoking spirituality. Today such fact-gathering begins to pall.

LIST OF WORKS ANALYZED
   88 ([1932] 1937-94) **Marcel Viller, S.J., ed.** [founding editor; many successors], *Dictionnaire de spiritualité, ascétique et mystique,* 20 vols. in 16 (Paris: Beauchesne, [1932] 1937-94)
   89 (1983) **Gordon S. Wakefield, ed.,** *The Westminster Dictionary of Christian Spirituality* (Philadelphia: Westminster, 1983)
   90 (1983) **Ernesto Caroli, ed.,** *Dizionario francescano: Spiritualità* (Padua: Edizioni Messagero, 1983)
   91 (1983, 1987) **Stefano de Fiores and Tullo Goffi, eds.,** *Dictionnaire de la vie spirituelle* (Paris: Le Cerf, 1987); French version edited by François Vial
   92 (1988) **Frank N. Magill** (1907-) and **Ian P. McGreal, eds.,** *Christian Spirituality: The Essential Guide to the Most Influential Spiritual Writings of the Christian Tradition* (San Francisco: Harper & Row, 1988)
   93 (1992-) **Bernard McGinn,** *The Presence of God: A History of Western Christian Mysticism,* planned in 4 vols. (New York: Crossroad, 1992-)
   94 (1993) **Michael Downey, ed.,** *The New Dictionary of Catholic Spirituality*

---

[2]A starting point is Gustav Adolf Benrath, "Autobiographie," in **31** Müller, ed., *Theologische Realenzyklopädie,* 4 (1979): 772-89.

(Collegeville, Minn.: Michael Glazier/Liturgical, 1993)
   95 (1993) **Michael Walsh,** *Dictionary of Catholic Devotions* (San Francisco: Harper, 1993)

ANALYSIS OF WORKS
   88 ([1932] 1937-94) **Marcel Viller, S.J. [founding editor; many successors],** *Dictionnaire de spiritualité, ascétique et mystique,* 20 vols. in 16 (Paris: Beauchesne, 1937-94). The first fascicules appeared in 1932, but vol. 1 is dated 1937. About 16,000 pages; no index; no general bibliography.
   □ *Scope* This MEGA-ENCYCLOPEDIA contrived to interpret spirituality ever more broadly as it proceeded. Since the first fascicule appeared in 1932, this increasingly REVISIONIST work helped to legitimate the term *spirituality,* and its final six volumes (1982-94) rank among the shrewdest anywhere. Articles characterizing the spirituality of saints, theologians, mystics and religious orders make the *Dictionnaire de spiritualité* (together with **137** Jacquemet, ed., *Catholicisme*) the most alluring of French MEGA-ENCYCLOPEDIAS.
   Major synthetic articles include "Spiritual Biographies" (1:1624-1719), which cites hundreds of titles from all periods, and "Psychism and Spiritual Life," which (without endorsing any) examines dozens of schools of psychology (12.2:2569-2605). Naturally, French protagonists shine. Pierre de Bérulle gets twenty-one pages (1:1539-81) and Madame Guyon fifteen (6:1306-36), but Prosper Guéranger only five (6:1097-1106). An article on "Quietism" in Italy, Spain and France runs forty-three pages (12.2:2756-2842). Articles on countries as diverse as Poland, Portugal and Greece cover all branches of Christianity, not just Roman Catholicism. An early article on "German Spirituality" (1:314-51) encompasses all denominations, as does one written fifty years later on "Pietism" (12.2:1743-58). Under the founder of a religious order comes discussion of that order's spirituality, so that, for example, under Robert de

Molesmes come forty pages on "Cistercian Spirituality" (13:736-814). An article on the "Virgin Mary in Catholic Spirituality" runs thirty-five pages (10:409-82). Later volumes are astonishingly up-to-date. Volume 12.2 (1986) includes twelve pages on Qumran (12:2858-82). Eastern Christian thinkers evoke copious coverage. Both Gregory Nazianzen and Gregory of Nyssa get twenty pages each plus more than a page of bibliography (6:932-71 and 6:972-1011). An article on "Russia" (13:1140-90) explores Orthodox spirituality in depth, as does François Rouleau on "Slavophilism."

□ **Strengths** Through volume 10 (1980), articles on concepts, religious orders, countries (e.g., "Mexico," 10:1132-47) and images (e.g., "Mirror," 10:1290-303) alternate with those on persons. After volume 11 (1982), however, the work becomes more and more a REVISIONIST WHO'S WHO of contemplatives, theologians and founders of religious orders. There are fewer (but meaty) articles on concepts (e.g., "Search for God" *[Recueillement]*) and practices (e.g., "Spiritual Retreats"). Thinkers of all periods undergo the conceptual rigor that is to be expected from a patrology (e.g., Thomas More, George Tyrell, Edith Stein, Paul Tillich, Simone Weil). Equally stimulating are articles on non-Christian topics. The article on "Monasticism" (10:1524-617), for example, climaxes with six pages on Islamic, Hindu and Buddhist practices (10:1525-36). Yves Raguin expounds "Taoism" with verve. Among highly creative entries are "Theater and Spirituality" (15 [1991]: 328-80), Antoine Faivre on "Theosophy" (15 [1991]: 548-62) and René Marlé, "Religion and Faith," (13 [1988]: 321-35). Indeed, articles from the final six volumes could be culled to comprise a PHILOSOPHICAL DICTIONARY. Few works would be more riveting.

□ **Weaknesses** Through volume 10, this is almost never a work of first or even second resort. Not every seeker needs or wants such coverage. The social sciences do not figure, even in the later volumes. Indeed, one wishes that criteria of inclusion had been spelled out afresh for volumes 11-16

(1982-94). Why are Seneca, Shankara and Tagore included, but not Virgil, Ramakrishna and Frithjof Schuon? One wishes too that having issued the final six volumes with dispatch, the editors had assessed their accomplishment in a "postface."

□ **Competitors** Together with **137** Jacquemet, ed., *Catholicisme,* the *Dictionnaire de spiritualité* is, in its post-1980 volumes, the most appealing of French MEGA-ENCYCLO-PEDIAS. Both have become increasingly RE-VISIONIST. Numerous shorter works help prepare one to ascend these pinnacles. **29** Cross, ed., *The Oxford Dictionary of the Christian Church* (1957, 1974) holds its own as a universal self-teacher. **91** Magill and McGreal, eds., *Christian Spirituality* (1988) expounds 125 pivotal texts with verve. **94** Downey, ed., *The New Dictionary of Catholic Spirituality* (1993) discusses concepts but not persons in workmanlike, if somewhat perfunctory, fashion while **89** Wakefield, ed., *The Westminster Dictionary of Christian Spirituality* (1983) analyzes major and minor figures. When complete, **93** Bernard McGinn's *The Presence of God* (1992-) will offer an ideal companion to this extravaganza. An early MEGA-ENCYCLOPEDIA from the same publisher, Adhémar d'Alès (1861-1938), ed., *Dictionnaire apologétique de la foi catholique,* 4th ed., 4 vols. (Paris: Beauchesne, 1925-28) was as combative as this one is irenic. Few MEGA-ENCYCLOPEDIAS are so consistently readable.

□ **Summary** Anyone interested in the inner life will find this work irresistible. It is without rival in interpreting discourse about Christian (and to some extent Asian) interiority in all periods, places and traditions. Its post-1980 volumes deliver some of the most persuasive rethinking in any MEGA-ENCYCLOPEDIA.

89 (1983) Gordon S. Wakefield, ed., *The Westminster Dictionary of Christian Spirituality* (Philadelphia: Westminster, 1983); published in Britain as *A Dictionary of Christian Spirituality* (London: SCM, 1983; paperback, 1988); xvi & 400 pages; no index; no general bibliography. Analyzed further under 2.8 "The Westminster/SCM Dictionaries."

□ *Critique* Coming from 150 mostly British contributors, this LEXICON has no peer as a one-volume conspectus of mystical and spiritual movements worldwide. Syntheses on world religions, as well as on French, German, English, Irish, Greek, Syrian and Coptic spirituality, balance appreciation and critique. None other than John Macquarrie depicts Celtic spirituality. Post-1945 movements figure prominently, as in "Focolare" and "Radical Spirituality." One hundred twenty-seven entries on persons embrace saints, laypersons like Charles Péguy and Simone Weil, and contemporaries like Bede Griffiths (1906-93). Some biographees like Jean-Pierre de Caussade crop up only in French MEGA-ENCYCLOPEDIAS or in **92** Magill and McGreal, eds., *Christian Spirituality* (1988). Geoffrey Parrinder's synopses of Buddhism, Hinduism, Islam and Sufism show a master epitomizer at his finest. Unusual articles address "Nature Mysticism," "Rastafarianism" and "Second Journey." Wakefield's definitional articles on topics like "The English Mystics," "Love" and "Spirituality" exude a spirit of, Why not try this? Benedicta Ward's entries on monastic spirituality are pungent, as are eight articles on "Prayer." Of all Westminster/SCM volumes, this one interprets the familiar in the most refreshing way. Many of the same authors contributed 103 articles to a HANDBOOK: Cheslyn Jones, Geoffrey Wainwright and Edward Yarnold, S.J., eds., *The Study of Spirituality* (New York and Oxford: Oxford University Press, 1986).

□ *Summary* This volume scintillates. It offers an ideal gateway into the endless paths of **88** Viller, ed., *Dictionnaire de spiritualité* (1937-94).

90 (1983) Ernesto Caroli, ed., *Dizionario francescano: Spiritualità* (Padua: Edizioni Messagero, 1983); xxii and 2375 columns; analytic-thematic index, cols. 2041-362; no general bibliography.

□ *Critique* This historical LEXICON performs a feat so unique as to merit making an exception for an Italian-language volume. Articles by fifty-five mostly Italian contributors digest the teaching of St. Francis and St. Claire on about fifty topics

of spirituality. Through painstaking use of the *Fonti francescane* (1977), contributors disentangle the teachings of the founders of Franciscan orders from the claims made about them. This LEXICON devotes a thousand pages to St. Francis and St. Claire but ignores subsequent Franciscans. No other single volume so intelligently disengages the thought of an order's founders from later accretions. One wishes for a comparable work about the Jesuits.

□ *Summary* This LEXICON articulates the thought of St. Francis and St. Claire with clarity and singleness of purpose.

91 (1983, 1987) Stefano de Fiores and Tullo Goffi, eds., *Dictionnaire de la vie spirituelle* (Paris: Le Cerf, 1987); François Vial adapted the French version from *Nuovo Dizionario di spiritualità* (Rome: Edizioni Paoline, 1983); xxii & 1246 pages; analytical index, pp. 1215-44; no general bibliography.

□ *Critique* This lively LEXICON of contemporary Christian spirituality was written chiefly by Italians and adapted into French by François Vial. Critique of "sacerdotalism" prevails. One hundred five essays canvass practices ("Asceticism"), symbols ("Desert"), movements ("Charismatics"), psychology ("Spiritual Pathology") and Christian catchphrases ("Evangelical Counsels," "Spiritual Father," "Signs of the Times"). The longest article is Bruno Maggioni's book-by-book appraisal of "Spiritual Experience in the Bible" (pp. 372-411). Synopses of Buddhism, Hinduism, Islam and Judaism expand a Catholic perspective. Although there is no WHO'S WHO or index of persons, multilingual bibliographies are superb. Some essays are REVISIONIST. Giuseppe Mattai writes memorably on four topics, "Popular Religion" (pp. 951-62), "Sociology (and Spirituality)" (pp. 1044-53), "Free Time" (pp. 1101-8) and "Worker" (pp. 1129-43). Gian Carlo Vendrame compares typologies of "Horizontalism/Verticalism" (pp. 513-20), and Giovanni Gennari reexamines "Signs of the Times" (pp. 1030-43). Bernhard Häring (1912-) condenses a lifetime of pastoral advice concerning "Atheist," "Prayer," "Prophet" and "Sense of God."

Such articles cut deeper than any in **94** Downey, ed., *The New Dictionary of Catholic Spirituality* (1993) and expand thematic ones in **89** Wakefield, ed., *The Westminster Dictionary of Christian Spirituality* (1983). Functioning as a miniature of **88** Viller, ed., *Dictionnaire de spiritualité* (1937-94), this LEXICON fuses learning and vigor with an assurance characteristic of French and Italian savants. Discernment shines through.

□ *Summary* This bracing LEXICON dissects classical and contemporary issues in Catholic spirituality, adding astute advice and remarkable bibliographies. Anyone seeking fresh ideas about Christian spirituality should start here.

92 (1988) Frank N. Magill (1907-) and Ian P. McGreal, eds., *Christian Spirituality: The Essential Guide to the Most Influential Spiritual Writings of the Christian Tradition* (San Francisco: Harper & Row, 1988); xix & 694 pages; four indexes (titles, contributors, major themes, authors), pp. 679-94; no general bibliography.

□ *Scope* This unusual COMPENDIUM delivers signed digests of 125 major writings. Twenty-four mostly North American authorities summarize and assess one work each by 124 Christian authors. Exceptionally, Jonathan Edwards gets two entries. Up to 1500 essays follow chronological order of writing, and after 1500 of publication. Treatments begin with Clement of Alexandria (c. 200 C.E.) and end with Gustavo Gutiérrez (1983). Entries follow a uniform format: a sketch of the author, a list of three to six "Major Themes," a digest of the work (in three to six pages), and brief bibliography (in English). Except for poets like William Blake and Gerard Manley Hopkins, essays focus on a single work, rarely situating it in an author's oeuvre. Eighty-two works date after 1500, there being eight from the sixteenth century, sixteen from the seventeenth, nine from the eighteenth, ten from the nineteenth and thirty-nine from the twentieth. Of the post-1500 works, twenty-five are by British writers, twenty by Americans, eleven by French, eight by Germans and five by

Spanish. Four authors are unknown.

□ *Strengths* This COMPENDIUM thrives on the adroitness of its contributors. Intimacy with a text and affection for its author draw a reader into each encounter. Although dazzling throughout, the range becomes even more imaginative after 1700. Greek fathers occasion no surprises: Clement of Alexandria, Origen, Cyprian, Athanasius, Basil, Gregory of Nyssa, Evagrius Ponticus, Dionysius, John Climacus, Maximus the Confessor and Symeon the New Theologian. They outnumber Latins: Jerome, Augustine, Cassian, Benedict and Gregory the Great. But the Greeks disappear after the year 1000. From the Middle Ages come six Germans: Mechtild of Magdeburg, Eckart, Suso, the author of the *Theologia germanica*, Tauler and Nicholas of Cusa. Four British follow: Richard Rolle, Walter Hilton, Julian and Margery Kempe. Saint Francis is treated through *The Little Flowers of St. Francis* (c. 1330) and also through G. K. Chesterton, *St. Francis of Assisi* (1924). Otherwise only four figures from Italy are covered: Anselm, Bonaventura, Catherine of Siena and Catherine of Genoa (through Baron von Hügel).

Sixteenth-century giants like Erasmus, Luther, More, Loyola, John of the Cross and Teresa vie predictably with seventeenth-century successors like François de Sales, Boehme, Donne, Browne, Taylor, Pascal, Spener, Bunyan and Guyon. The only author to have two works treated in separate essays is Jonathan Edwards. After 1750 the choices become less predictable, starting with five American Quakers: John Woolman, Rufus Jones, Elton Trueblood, Thomas Kelly and Douglas Steere. Among the French, Louis Lavelle and Jacques Ellul, as well as Thérèse of Lisieux and Simone Weil, inspire luminous essays. Other women since 1800 include Hannah More, Phoebe Palmer, Hannah Whitall Smith, Evelyn Underhill, Amy Carmichael, Olive Wyon, Elisabeth Elliot and Agnes Sanford. Among the most memorable essays is Dallas Willard's on Frank Laubach's letters from the Philippines (1930-32), in which Laubach avowed, "Concentration is merely the continuous return to the same problem from a million angles. . . . So my problem is this: Can I bring God back in my mind-flow every few seconds? I choose to make the rest of my life an experiment in answering this question" (p. 518).

The volume recruits major authorities, who in most cases know the works inside out. The most frequent contributor is Jean Faurot, who composes twenty-two sparkling essays ranging from the church fathers through Tauler, Cusa and Lancelot Andrewes to Kierkegaard and Baron von Hügel. His essay on Thomas More's *A Dialogue of Comfort against Tribulation* (1534-35) is a masterpiece. Nancy Hardesty contributes twelve lively pieces, many on women as well as two on Eastern Orthodox texts: the Russian *The Way of a Pilgrim* (1884) and Anthony Bloom's *Beginning to Pray* (1970). In a unique feature, two of the most frequent authors, E. Glenn Hinson on ten texts and M. Basil Pennington on twelve, have one of their own writings featured. Pennington writes superbly on the Greek fathers, on the *Cloud of Unknowing* and on Thomas Merton. Throughout, the level is astoundingly high. On even the most daunting texts, trenchancy seldom flags.

□ *Weaknesses* The essays omit historical context. Except for poets like John of the Cross, John Donne and William Blake, entries tackle just one work, seldom relating it to an author's career. Unaccountably, criteria of selection are not stated in the two-page preface, nor is "spirituality" defined. A very few entries seem arid (Pascal, Bushnell) or prolix (Spener, Zinzendorf). Only a minority of essays, notably those by Ian McGreal, quote original passages often. Certain omissions surprise: Erigena, Dante, Gregory Palamas, Schleiermacher and Solovyov. These oversights are compensated by inclusion of at least a dozen post-1750 writers treated in no other reference work, not even in **37** Bautz, ed., *Biographisches Kirchenlexikon* (1975-) or in **169** Reid, ed., *Dictionary of Christianity in America* (1990). Post-1500 works unfold in sequence of publication, which means that a posthumous text like Caussade's *Self-Abandonment* (1851, 1861) crops up a hundred years after

he died (1751).

□ *Competitors* By virtue of including rare writers and of expounding individual works, this COMPENDIUM stands alone. It enlarges an earlier enterprise by one of the editors, Frank N. Magill, ed., *Masterpieces of Catholic Literature in Summary Form,* 2 vols. (New York: Salem, 1965), which in a similar format summarizes three hundred works, including one hundred from the twentieth century. The successor volume is far more ecumenical and diverse. Considered merely as a WHO'S WHO, *Christian Spirituality* fills a gap. Although **89** Wakefield, ed., *The Westminster Dictionary of Christian Spirituality* (1983) omits many of these names, it places the others in context. **88** Viller, ed., *Dictionnaire de spiritualité* (1937-94) supplies magnificent depth on classic figures but omits most of the post-1700 writers and does not evoke individual texts so fully. Because few of the texts are autobiographies, a need remains for a *Dictionary of Spiritual Autobiography*. Everyone interested in the subject of spirituality should own *Christian Spirituality*. One imagines that nearly all the authors analyzed in it would have devoured it.

□ *Summary* Acute, often brilliant summaries plunge the reader into the heart of 125 pivotal works—works that are more often praised than read. No other reference work in English digests so many masterpieces so compellingly.

93 (1992-) Bernard McGinn, *The Presence of God: A History of Western Christian Mysticism,* planned in 4 vols. (New York: Crossroad, 1992-); vol. 1: xxii & 494 pages; three indexes (name, biblical, subject), pp. 484-94; general bibliography, pp. 442-83; vol. 2: xvii & 630 pages; three indexes, pp. 623-30; general bibliography, pp. 601-22. Also in paperback. Analyzed on the basis of vol. 1, *The Foundations of Mysticism* (1992) and vol. 2, *The Growth of Mysticism: Gregory the Great through the Twelfth Century* (1994).

□ *Critique* This magisterial HANDBOOK expounds the history of Western Christian mysticism with rigor and insight. McGinn construes "mysticism" as a "process or way of life" involving "an attempt to express a direct consciousness of the presence of God" (p. xvi). Volume 1 surveys Greek Christian thinkers, particularly Origen and Evagrius Ponticus, as a background to Ambrose, Cassian and Augustine. Volume 2 reaches through the twelfth century, emphasizing Gregory the Great and Bernard of Clairvaux. Volume 3, *The Flowering of Mysticism,* will treat the period from the thirteenth through the sixteenth centuries, and volume 4, *The Crisis of Mysticism,* will carry the story into the present. The work complements another HANDBOOK, Tomáš Špidlík, S.J., *The Spirituality of the Christian East: A Systematic Handbook* [1978] (Kalamazoo, Mich.: Cistercian Publications, 1986). McGinn makes the most abstruse questions plain, and his methodological acumen is second to none. The footnotes and bibliographies recall those in a MEGA-ENCYCLOPEDIA. Enriching volume 1 is an eighty-page appendix, "Theoretical Foundations: The Modern Study of Mysticism," which dissects secondary works by at least fifty theologians, philosophers and psychologists. It offers the astutest assessment anyone has written of English, French and German authorities since 1900. No one expounds the history of mysticism or scholarship about it better than Bernard McGinn.

□ *Summary* This meticulous HANDBOOK places Western Christian mysticism in multiple contexts, both historical and methodological. It is a must for all concerned.

94 (1993) Michael Downey, ed., *The New Dictionary of Catholic Spirituality* (Collegeville, Minn.: Michael Glazier/Liturgical, 1993); xxxvi & 1084 pages; two indexes (of articles and names), pp. 1065-83; no general bibliography (other than "Abbreviations," pp. xxxiii-xxxvi).

□ *Critique* Planned as a companion to **83** Komonchak et al., eds., *The New Dictionary of Theology* (1987), this LEXICON recruited 160 Catholics (mostly American clerics) to expound about three hundred concepts and schools (but not persons) important in contemporary Catholic spirituality. The latter is construed as being "concerned with the human person in relation to God" (p. viii). Each entry offers choice English-language bibliography. In contrast to a second companion volume, **112** Fink, ed., *The New Dictionary of Sacramental Worship* (1990), this work makes no breakthroughs. Methodology seldom gets aired. A topical index differentiates ten foci: (1) Christian mysteries, (2) the human person, (3) the moral life, (4) the person in relation to the world, (5) growth and development in the spiritual life, (6) prayer, (7) liturgy and devotion, (8) discipline(s), (9) history, (10) types and schools of spirituality. The latter elicits thirty-nine articles such as "Carmelite," "Celtic," "Ignatian," "Jewish," "Opus Dei," "Eastern Christian" and "Eastern (Asian)," but most entries deemphasize history. Many of them stipulate guidelines for practice by Catholics. Among the more imaginative entries are "Journey," "Canon Law, Spirituality in" and "Nuclear Age, Impact on Spirituality." Lack of a WHO'S WHO disappoints, and the social sciences get little attention. **89** Wakefield, ed., *The Westminster Dictionary of Christian Spirtuality* (1983) is both more adventurous and more historical, while masterpieces like **91** De Fiores and Goffi, eds., *Dictionnaire de la vie spirituelle* (1983, 1987) or **88** Viller, ed., *Dictionnaire de la spiritualité* (1937-94) make this work seem perfunctory. Study of spirituality demands audacity.

□ *Summary* Written by and for Catholics, this LEXICON of the spiritual life is too timid to hold its own in a field of dazzling competitors.

95 (1993) Michael Walsh, *Dictionary of Catholic Devotions* (London: Burns & Oates; San Francisco: Harper, 1993); 366 pages; index, pp. 323-66; general bibliography, pp. 317-21; calendar, pp. 289-315; also in paperback.

□ *Critique* This historical GLOSSARY delineates over twelve hundred "objects, saints, titles, and practices" that constitute the "private pieties of individuals." Major topics like "Confraternities," "Indulgences," "Litanies" and "Saints" alternate with arcane ones, some of them colorful and not a few bizarre. More than one hundred entries evoke apparitions of the

Virgin Mary, who commands the longest individual entry as well. Although there are no individual bibliographies, a list of eighty-five mostly English-language titles fills a gap. Adepts of Christian folklore will rejoice to find elusive information gathered so deftly.

□ *Summary* This pioneering GLOSSARY pinpoints persons, objects, places and organizations which channel Catholic devotion.

2.6 HAGIOGRAPHY (LIVES OF SAINTS)

OVERVIEW: TYPES OF COMPILATIONS IN EAST AND WEST

The study of the lives of Christian saints is a discipline unto itself, known as hagiography. Whether construed devotionally or critically or both, lives of saints lend themselves to reference books. In the early seventeenth century a group of Belgian Jesuits known as Bollandists initiated critical reference works in the *Acta sanctorum*, 64 vols. (Antwerp, 1643-1925), which having been interrupted between 1794 and 1837 reached November 10 before suspending publication in 1925.[3] Two types of WHO'S WHO emerge: (1) devotional works (also called martyrologies), usually arranged by days of the calendar, and (2) critical works, which may be either alphabetical or calendrical. Beginners should note that DICTIONARIES alphabetize saints according to Christian name, not family name or place of origin. It is not uncommon to find, for example, between ten and one hundred individuals alphabetized under the name "John." In works arranged by the liturgical calendar, as in martyrologies and Eastern menologies, a saint's feast falls on his or her day of death or burial *(dies natalis)*, not of birth.

In the West a fundamental distinction differentiates between the Roman *martyrology*, which lists in brief notices by days of death all saints with their cult sites, and the Roman liturgical *calendar*, which since

1969 has designated about 150 saints to be venerated on certain days by all Catholics. Works published after 1969 reflect Paul VI's reorganization of the Roman calendar to delete legendary figures like Ursula and Catherine of Alexandria. The Bollandists are preparing a new Roman martyrology to incorporate about ten thousand saints and blesseds, including at least eight hundred from the pontificate of John Paul II (1978-). A martyrology of 1956, adapted from that of 1922-24, appeared in English as J. B. O'Connell, ed., *The Roman Martyrology* (Westminster, Md.: Newman, 1962). Prepared by an Oratorian Cardinal Baronius (1538-1607), the first *Roman Martyrology* was published in 1584. Current procedures for canonization are explained in Kenneth L. Woodward, *Making Saints* (New York: Simon & Schuster, 1990).

Eastern Orthodox churches call a calendar a menology, featuring entire lives *(vitae)*, while a greater *synaxarion* delivers briefer notices to be read on feast days. A *menaion* collects liturgical poems and prayers pertaining to saints of each month. Earnestly liturgical, Eastern churches lack the investigative procedures known in Rome as (1) beatification, which confers the status of *beatus* or "blessed," and (2) canonization, which confers the status of *sanctus* or "saint." Having been initiated on St. Ulrich in 993, the latter procedure was gradually tightened until its present form became obligatory under Urban VIII (1623-44). Lists of beatifications and canonizations since 1585 appear in **150** Levillain, ed., *Dictionnaire historique de la papauté* (1994), pages 192-98, 270-75, and 307-12, as does a history (to the year 600) of the "Cult of Saints," pages 492-97. Whereas the Fourth Lateran Council of 1215 formalized papal procedures, Eastern churches perpetuate to this day an older reliance on canonization by tradition, generally as approved by local bishops. A roster of twelve types of Eastern saints appears in Tomáš Špidlík, S.J., "Saint: I. Dans les églises byzantine et russe," **88** *Dictionnaire de spiritualité*, 14 (1990): 197-202.

Herbert Thurston's and Donald Attwa-

---

[3]See Hippolyte Delehaye, S.J., *L'Oeuvre des Bollandistes à travers trois siècles (1615-1915)* (Brussels, 1959).

ter's revisions in 1926-38 and again in 1956 of **96** *Butler's Lives of the Saints* (1756-59) popularized the practice of inserting critical assessment into quasi-devotional narrative. In contrast, Eastern Orthodox calendars (menologies) express liturgical impetus by shunning critical comment. French scholars excel at delineating saints, notably in a mega-calendar: **97** Baudot and Chaussin, eds., *Vies des saints et des bienheureux selon l'ordre du calendrier,* 13 vols. (Paris, 1935-59), as well as in a MEGA-ENCYCLOPEDIA: **134** Baudrillart, ed., *Dictionnaire d'histoire et de géographie ecclésiastiques,* 24 1/2 vols. to date through *INDE* (1912-). A recent illustrated work, Francesco Chiovaro et al., eds., *Histoire des saints et de la sainteté chrétienne,* 11 vols. (Paris: Hachette, 1986-88) continues this tradition but arranges saints by historical periods. Written in four languages, an ambitious HANDBOOK will inventory editions of saints' lives and their authors up to 1550: Guy Philippart, *Hagiographies,* planned in 4 vols. (Turnhout: Brepols, 1994-). Most European Catholic ENCYCLOPEDIAS incorporate a WHO'S WHO of saints, notably **128** Kasper, ed., *Lexikon für Theologie und Kirche,* 3d ed. (1993-), and so does **29** Cross, ed., *The Oxford Dictionary of the Christian Church* (1957, 1974). Although the latter eschews devotionality, non-Catholics may prefer the utter impartiality of **100** Farmer, *The Oxford Dictionary of Saints* (1978, 1992). A monumental non-confessional WHO'S WHO is **37** Bautz, ed., *Biographisch-Bibliographisches Kirchenlexikon* (1975-), which boasts unrivaled bibliographies. Hundreds of medieval saints appear also in the **158** *Lexikon des Mittelalters,* 7 and 4/5 volumes to date through "Servatius" (1977-), likewise with splendid bibliographies.

Since about 1980 HAGIOGRAPHIES have flooded the market, including a number of shorter WHO'S WHOS. Among the best brief ones is Alison Jones, *Saints* (Edinburgh and New York: Chambers, 1992), which supplies some illustrations. An eighty-page HAGIOGRAPHY in **127** Dubost, ed., *Théo* (1989, 1993) sketches about a thousand chiefly French saints (pp. 45-124). For rollicking narrative **108** Kelly and Rogers, *Saints Preserve Us!* (1993) has no peer. An illustrated REALLEXIKON of three hundred major saints, **109** Jöckle, *Encyclopedia of Saints* (1995) itemizes with MENIPPEAN verve legends, cult sites and representations in European art. Joseph N. Tylenda, S.J., treats 160 Jesuits in *Jesuit Saints and Martyrs* (Chicago: Loyola University Press, 1984). One hundred saints since 1800 get recounted minutely and devoutly (with photographs) in Ann Ball, *Modern Saints: Their Lives and Faces,* 2 vols. (Rockford, Ill.: Tan, 1983-90). Similar zeal pervades two hundred portraits in Ronda De Sola Chervin, *Treasury of Women Saints* (New York and London: HarperCollins, 1991). In a pioneering enterprise, cultural anthropologist Alfredo Cattabiani in *Santi d'Italia* (Milan: Rizzoli, 1993) compares cults that have emerged in Italy regarding 250 saints. He emphasizes pre-Christian roots. Indeed, one wishes that folklorists would supply for saints crosscultural parallels such as Alison Jones does in **318** *Larousse Dictionary of World Folklore* (1995). A superb annotated bibliography appears in Stephen Wilson, ed., *Saints and Their Cults* (Cambridge: Cambridge University Press, 1983), pp. 309-417. It can be updated from Werner Williams-Krapp, "Hagiographie," in **257** Ranke, ed., *Enzyklopädie des Märchens,* 6 (1990):355-80.

See also the overview to 5.3.4 "Social Sciences of Religion: Folklore."

LIST OF WORKS ANALYZED

96 ([1756-59] 1926-38, 1956) Herbert Thurston [1856-1939] and Donald Attwater [1892-1977], eds., *Butler's Lives of the Saints: Complete Edition,* 4 vols. (London: Burnes & Oates; Westminster, Md.: Christian Classics, 1956); reprinted with revisions, 1966

97 (1935-59) Jules Baudot [1857-1929] and Léon Chaussin [1891-1945], eds. [through vol. 3], thereafter Bénédictins de Paris, eds., *Vies des saints et des bienheureux selon l'ordre du calendrier, avec l'historique des fêtes,* 13 vols. (Paris: Letouzey et Ané, 1935-59)

98 (1965, 1983) Donald Attwater

[1892-1977], *The Penguin Dictionary of Saints* (Baltimore: Penguin, 1965; 2d ed., rev., 1983)

99 (1975, 1983) Augustine Kalberer, O.S.B., *Lives of the Saints: Daily Readings* (Chicago: Franciscan Herald, 1975; 2d ed., enl., 1983)

100 (1978, 1992) David Hugh Farmer, *The Oxford Dictionary of Saints* (Oxford and New York: Oxford University Press, 1978; 3d ed., 1992)

101 (1980) John J. Delaney, *Dictionary of Saints* (Garden City, N.Y.: Doubleday, 1980)

102 (1987) Michael Walsh, ed., *Butler's Lives of Patron Saints* (San Francisco: Harper & Row, 1987)

103 ([1921] 1989) St. Augustine's Abbey, Ramsgate, *The Book of Saints: A Dictionary of Servants of God,* 6th ed. (London: A. & C. Black, 1989); also in paperback (Wilton, Conn.: Morehouse, 1993)

104 (1990-92) George Poulos, *Orthodox Saints: Spiritual Profiles for Modern Man,* 2d ed., rev., 4 vols. (Brookline, Mass.: Holy Cross Orthodox Press, 1990-92)

105 (1990, 1994) Gaston Duchet-Suchaux and Michel Pastoureau, *The Bible and the Saints* (Paris and New York: Flammarion, 1994); translated from *La Bible et les saints: Guide iconographique* (Paris: Flammarion, 1990)

106 (1992) Enzo Lodi, *Saints of the Roman Calendar Including Feasts Proper to the English-Speaking World,* trans. and ed. Jordan Aumann, O.P. (New York: Alba House, 1992)

107 ([1938, 1958] 1993) Donald Attwater and John Cumming, *A New Dictionary of Saints* (Collegeville, Minn.: Liturgical, 1993)

108 (1993) Sean Kelly and Rosemary Rogers, *Saints Preserve Us!* (New York: Random House, 1993; London: Robson Books, 1995)

109 (1995) Clemens Jöckle, *Encyclopedia of Saints* (London: Alpine Fine Arts Collection, 1995)

ANALYSIS OF WORKS
96 ([1756-59] 1926-38, 1956) Her-

bert Thurston, S.J. [1856-1939] and Donald Attwater [1892-1977], eds., *Butler's Lives of the Saints: Complete Edition,* 4 vols. (London: Burnes & Oates; Westminster, Md.: Christian Classics, 1956); reprinted with revisions, 1966; 2900 pages; general index, 4:681-707; general bibliography, 1:xxxi-xxxii. A new edition is in preparation.

□ *Critique* Alban Butler (1710-1773), an English Catholic priest active both in France and in Norwich, England, compiled almost fifteen hundred saints' lives in a calendar published as *The Lives of the Fathers, Martyrs and Other Principal Saints* (London, 1756-59), reprinted in four volumes (London, Dublin and Belfast: Virtue, 1926).[4] During the 1920s Herbert Thurston revised volumes for January through June, pruning the "Gibbonesque" prose while adding recent saints as well as critical comments and up-to-date bibliography.[5] Upon taking charge in 1934, Donald Attwater retained in volumes for July to December more of Butler's digressiveness. Often Menippean loquacity breaks into these pages, as does pious exhortation. Executing a second revision in 1956, Attwater pruned about a tenth of the prose and added a thousand saints to reach a total of twenty-five hundred. Pending a new edition now in preparation, the 1966 reprinting remains the fullest source of saints' lives available in English. 107 Attwater and Cumming, *A New Dictionary of Saints* (1938, 1993) supplies a one-volume index to the 1956 edition together with abstracts of more than four thousand saints and blesseds. It omits saints who disappeared from the Roman calendar since 1969 and includes many added since. An epitome, Walsh, ed., *Butler's Lives of the Saints: Concise Edition* (London: Burns & Oates; San Francisco: Harper, 1985), selects one saint per day, many of them obscure, and provides a useful editor's introduction. Each successive

---

[4]On Butler see the 1956 edition, 4:651-66.
[5]On Thurston see Michael J. Walsh, "Thurston, Herbert," in **87** Viller, ed., *Dictionnaire de spiritualité,* 15 (1991): 911-13.

edition of Butler's *Lives* injects more scholarship and less exhortation. A new edition is eagerly awaited.

□ *Summary* The 1956 revised edition of this calendar combines elevated diction, critical acumen and extraordinary comprehensiveness. It constitutes the bedrock of English-language hagiography.

97 (1935-59) Jules Baudot [1857-1929] and Léon Chaussin [1891-1945], eds. [through vol. 3], thereafter Bénédictins de Paris, eds., *Vies des saints et des bienheureux selon l'ordre du calendrier, avec l'historique des fêtes,* 13 vols. (Paris: Letouzey et Ané, 1935-59); about 7500 pages; index in each volume; general index, 13:245-593.

□ *Critique* This massive WHO'S WHO offers the fullest calendar of the saints available outside of Latin or Italian. Conceived by Baudot, who wrote the first five volumes (which Chaussin then edited), the series was completed by fellow Benedictines of Paris. Later spurts inserted more and more historical criticism, as in volumes 6-9 (1948-50) and volumes 10-12 (1952-56). Volumes for each month contain about 350 longer notices and three to four hundred shorter ones. Critical analysis sifts "the least controverted facts" (1:5) concerning almost ten thousand saints and blesseds. Notices after November 10 suffer from lack of the Bollandist *Acta sanctorum* for those dates. Lucid style, ample bibliographies and unmatched coverage make this a treasure trove. Jacques Dubois's "En guise de conclusion" (13:7-15) provides a model editor's farewell to a giant enterprise. Although smaller in format than seven MEGA-ENCYCLOPEDIAS from the same publisher, this work claims similar authority. Arranged chronologically and amply illustrated, Chiovoro, ed., *Histoire des saints et de la sainteté,* 11 vols. (1986-88) supplies coverage almost as wide.

□ *Summary* Arranged as a mega-calendar, this WHO'S WHO furnishes scrupulous scholarship, penetrating asides and unequaled range.

98 (1965, 1983) Donald Attwater [1892-1977], *The Penguin Dictionary of Saints* (Baltimore: Penguin, 1965); 2d ed., rev., Catherine Rachel John (New York: Penguin, 1983); 352 pages; no index; general bibliography, pp. 17-18; glossary, pp. 19-26; list of feast days, pp. 341-52.

□ *Critique* Written for a wide public, this DICTIONARY sketches more than 750 saints. It omits devotional overlay. Ranging in length from one-third to a full page, narratives identify emblems and differentiate the better known from the lesser known of the same name. A very few entries carry bibliography. **100** Farmer, ed., *The Oxford Dictionary of Saints* (1978, 1992) is both more up-to-date and more complete.

□ *Summary* Bald narratives digest the learning that went into the 1956 revision of **96** *Butler's Lives.*

99 (1975, 1983) Augustine Kalberer, O.S.B., *Lives of the Saints: Daily Readings* (Chicago: Franciscan Herald, 1975; 2d ed., enl., 1983); xviii & 495 pages; index, pp. 481-95; no general bibliography.

□ *Critique* This calendar tersely narrates about a thousand lives. The work supplies a martyrology to be read each day, summarizing devotional motifs soberly. The author warns, "In hagiography it is difficult to avoid the fanciful and legendary. One needs to become cautious without becoming hypercritical" (p. vii). He carries out this precept admirably.

□ *Summary* This devotional HAGIOGRAPHY cultivates pith and excludes hyperbole.

100 (1978, 1992) David Hugh Farmer, *The Oxford Dictionary of Saints* (Oxford and New York: Oxford University Press, 1978; 3d ed., 1992); xxviii & 530 pages; index of places in Great Britain, pp. 519-25; no general bibliography (except list of abbreviations, pp. xxv-xxviii); calendar, pp. 526-30; also in paperback.

□ *Scope* This nonconfessional WHO'S WHO of almost fifteen hundred saints focuses on those venerated in Britain and Ireland, as well as on major figures elsewhere. Farmer treats a few who never lived, such as Catherine of Alexandria, as well as the archangels Gabriel and Raphael and certain blesseds like Fra Angelico. Ranging in length from five lines to five columns on

Francis of Assisi, entries recount the life, assess legends, sketch influence, pinpoint the cult and assemble choice bibliography. All English saints, all saints with a notable cult in England, and representative Scottish, Welsh and Irish saints win an entry. European saints and those recently canonized also figure.

☐ *Strengths* Written by a master epitomizer, this WHO'S WHO eschews devotional language, spicing compression with good sense. Lives are retold vividly, and legends are explored in depth (e.g., on "George"). Each article concludes by tracing the cult. Mighty doers get their lives assessed, prompting, for example, endorsement of Christopher Dawson's judgment that Boniface "had a deeper influence on Europe than any other Englishman" (p. 61). Besides weighing sources on British saints, the introduction sketches a history of the cult of saints (pp. ix-xxiv). Farmer expatiates on methods of hagiography in **31** Müller, ed., *Theologische Realenzyklopädie,* 14 (1985): 360-80.

☐ *Weaknesses* Focus on British and Irish saints makes one wish that other Celtic saints, particularly in Brittany, had won equal coverage. Saints from the Third World are scanted. Modern rather than postmodern, Farmer chronicles legends without adducing crosscultural comparisons familiar in study of folklore. Indeed, fuller analysis of techniques of critical hagiography and of its relation to folklore would have been welcome. One could wish for an "Index of Places in Continental Europe Associated with Particular Saints" to match the one on Britain (pp. 519-25).

☐ *Competitors* This is the soundest nonconfessional WHO'S WHO of saints available in English. Critical evaluations and bibliographies are second to none, and the "Calendar" is unusually full (pp. 526-30). To be sure, three hundred entries in **109** Jöckle, *Encyclopedia of Saints* (1995) inventory more thoroughly legends, cult sites and artistic representations, but without bibliography. **107** Attwater and Cumming, *A New Dictionary of Saints* (1938, 1993) canvasses succinctly almost three times more saints, with candid critique.

103 *The Book of Saints* (1921, 1989) from Ramsgate handles six times more individuals but in disconcerting brevity. Many of Farmer's British saints crop up in **29** Cross, ed., *The Oxford Dictionary of the Christian Church* (1957, 1974). Unfortunately, all of these works fall short of Alfredo Cattabiani, *Santi d'Italia* (Milan: Rizzoli, 1993) in focusing anthropology onto cults.

☐ *Summary* Dissecting life, legend and cult, this rigorous WHO'S WHO favors saints of the British Isles and those revered there. It is the fullest nonconfessional HAGIOGRAPHY available in English.

101 (1980) **John J. Delaney,** *Dictionary of Saints* (Garden City, N.Y.: Doubleday, 1980); 647 pages; no index; no bibliography.

☐ *Critique* This DICTIONARY narrates for nonscholars the lives of over three thousand saints. Averaging one-half column in length, entries are arranged alphabetically but lack either critique or bibliography. Scholar-saints rarely get their writings mentioned. The prose is plain in contrast to the roundness of Butler. Appendices include "The Roman Calendar" (pp. 622-38) and most usefully "The Byzantine Calendar" (pp. 638-47). Scholars will prefer **100** Farmer's *The Oxford Dictionary of Saints* (1978, 1992) or **96** Thurston and Attwater, eds., *Butler's Lives of the Saints* (1956).

☐ *Summary* This DICTIONARY dispenses devotional narrative in plain language.

102 (1987) **Michael Walsh, ed.,** *Butler's Lives of Patron Saints* (San Francisco: Harper & Row, 1987); xvi & 476 pages; three indexes (devotions, saints, dates), pp. 3-22, 443-76; general bibliography, p. xvi.

☐ *Critique* This DICTIONARY reshapes Alban Butler's accounts of 222 saints so as to elucidate their patronage of a wide range of activities. An "Index of Devotions to Patron Saints" (pp. 3-22) is among the most complete anywhere. A unique entry sorts out fifty titles of the Virgin Mary according to links with professions, places and persons (pp. 311-38). An "Editor's Introduction" (pp. ix-xvi) brings wit and wisdom to issues of choosing and ratifying patrons. A companion volume, **95** *Dic-*

tionary of Catholic Devotions (1993), enlarges the material to encompass practices as well as saints. Few works evoke the oddity of saints so tellingly as these two volumes. A jaunty INTRODUCTION to patronage is Enid Broderick Fisher, *Saints Alive!* (London: Fount, 1995), and a rollicking account of patron saints comes in **108** Kelly and Rogers, *Saints Preserve Us!* (1993).

□ *Summary* This comprehensive DICTIONARY of patron saints makes splendid browsing.

103 ([1921] 1989) St. Augustine's Abbey, Ramsgate, *The Book of Saints: A Dictionary of Servants of God,* 6th ed. (London: A. & C. Black, 1989); also in paperback (Wilton, Conn.: Morehouse, 1993); xii & 606 pages; bibliography, pp. 593-95; emblems, pp. 596-603; patron saints of professions, pp. 604-5; about 140 black-and-white illustrations. Also available in French, German and Italian translation.

□ *Critique* This condensed martyrology identifies almost ten thousand saints in three- to fifteen-line entries devoid of bibliography. Inaugurated in 1921 by Thomas Bergh, Abbot of Ramsgate, *The Book of Saints* couples succinctness of phrase with completeness of coverage. Even more telegraphic than previous editions, the 1989 one averages fifteen entries per page. This winnowing embraces more than twice as many saints as does **107** Attwater and Cumming, *A New Dictionary of Saints* (1938, 1993), but the latter is more readable.

□ *Summary* More a GLOSSARY than a LEXICON, this austere WHO'S WHO offers comprehensiveness without effusiveness.

104 (1990-92) George Poulos, *Orthodox Saints: Spiritual Profiles for Modern Man,* 2d ed., rev., 4 vols. (Brookline, Mass.: Holy Cross Orthodox Press, 1990-92); 1050 pages; index in each volume; general index, 4:235-43; no bibliography; a line drawing accompanies each entry.

□ *Critique* Written for the faithful, this calendar (menology) narrates the lives of about 470 Eastern Christian saints, each in two pages devoid alike of critique and bibliography. Greek, Russian, Serbian, Egyptian, Syrian, Armenian, Ethiopian and biblical saints figure, but no Westerners. Since at least half the saints are missing from the 1956 edition of Butler, these volumes abound in little known lore, much of it unverified. About twenty feasts such as the "Chains of St. Peter" (January 16), "Discoveries of the Head of St. John the Baptist" (February 24) and the "Recovery of the Relics of St. Stephen" (August 2) also elicit entries. Lucid and compact, the narratives read like an Eastern counterpart to the 1920s volumes of Butler. Indeed, a tone of uncritical admiration reflects the liturgical bent of a menology, and at times edification cloys. Legends now discounted in the West (e.g., "Seven Saints [Sleepers] of Ephesos" on August 4 or St. Joasaph and Barlaam on August 26) are recounted without demur. At times credibility collapses, as when Menas of Egypt (November 11) is credited with assisting the Allied victory in 1942 fought near his tomb at El Alamein. As regards gender of saints, the ratio of women to men (about 1:4) appears to be lower than in the West. An essay on how the Eastern churches elevate saints without resort to formal canonization would have been helpful, since the East's lack of juridical procedure perpetuates hearsay. A more stringent view of Eastern saints may be gleaned from articles such as "Menologion," "Synaxarion," "Menaion," "Hagiography," "Vita" and "Canonization" in **144** Kashdan, ed., *Oxford Dictionary of Byzantium* (1991).

□ *Summary* This calendar (menology) recounts with fervor but without critique the lives of over 450 Eastern Christian saints. Much of the material crops up nowhere else.

105 (1990, 1994) Gaston Duchet-Suchaux and Michel Pastoureau, *The Bible and the Saints: Flammarion Iconographic Guides* (Paris and New York, Flammarion, 1994); translated from *La Bible et les saints: Guide iconographique* (Paris: Flammarion, 1990); French edition: 319 pages; no index; 32 color plates and about 250 black-and-white photographs; general bibliography, p. 318. Analyzed on the basis of the French edition.

□ *Critique* This DICTIONARY of European iconography examines ninety postbiblical saints as well as more than one hundred biblical figures and themes. Averaging one page in length, each entry digests "Life and Legend," "Representations" and "Attributes" (usually with bibliography). Critical hagiography, art history and scrutiny of sources interact throughout. The writing is terse, the tone guarded. Although more than two-thirds of entries concern biblical persons and symbols, this volume supplied the handiest INTRODUCTION to iconography of major saints in European art until a MENIPPEAN masterpiece, **109** Jöckle, *Encyclopedia of Saints* (1995), swept the field. A bibliography lists twenty-five English, French and German reference works concerning Christian iconography.

□ *Summary* This DICTIONARY offers a sober introduction to one of the most daunting of humanistic endeavors: Christian iconography.

106 (1992) Enzo Lodi, *Saints of the Roman Calendar Including Feasts Proper to the English-Speaking World,* trans. and ed. Jordan Aumann, O.P. (New York: Alba House, 1992); xxv & 419 pages; index, pp. 414-19; no bibliography; also in paperback.

□ *Critique* Written by and for Catholic liturgists, this calendar of 204 feasts in current Roman usage bursts with lore. In each entry a "Historical-Liturgical Note" recounts known facts about the saint of the day (or the origin of the feast), while a longer section on "Message and Relevance" connects the facts to prayers for the day. The latter passage often conveys choice information. An American editor deleted some material from the Italian edition and added entries on American saints. Whether used for study or devotion, this book makes the Roman calendar resonate. No other volume explains so concisely why particular saints remain in the liturgy.

□ *Summary* This astute Roman calendar recites facts and outlines devotions with authority.

107 ([1938, 1958] 1993) Donald Attwater [1892-1977] and John Cum- ming, *A New Dictionary of Saints* (Collegeville, Minn.: Liturgical, 1993); 332 pages; no index; no bibliography; also in paperback.

□ *Critique* In 1938 Donald Attwater launched this DICTIONARY as an abstract of the 1926-38 edition of **96** *Butler's Lives of the Saints.* The 1958 edition of *A New Dictionary* miniaturized the 2,550 entries in the 1956 revision of Butler. John Cumming's revision of 1993 drops saints who have disappeared from the Roman calendar (e.g., Barbara, Ursula, Catherine of Alexandria) while culling a couple of thousand persons canonized or beatified since the 1960s. An asterisk identifies those appearing in the Roman martyrology (p. 6). In a "catalogue with brief particulars of the principal saints" entries range in length from three lines to almost a column (on the Virgin Mary). Individual bibliographies are lacking, but critical asides abound. Twenty-six place names appear individually as sites of martyrs, many of whom were canonized only recently. Cumming specifies the persons' names if known, and an entry "Martyrs" itemizes the places (pp. 212-13). More than half the entries state corresponding pages in the 1956 edition of **96** *Butler's Lives.*

□ *Summary* This up-to-date DICTIONARY delineates over four thousand saints and blesseds cannily. It is the most convenient Catholic work of its kind.

108 (1993) Sean Kelly and Rosemary Rogers, *Saints Preserve Us!* (New York: Random House, 1993; London: Robson Books, 1995); vii & 343 pages; no index; general bibliography, pp. 342-43; calendar of saints, pp. 297-313; two appendices (name saints, patron saints), pp. 313-41; some black-and-white illustrations; also in paperback. Analyzed on the basis of the British edition of 1995.

□ *Critique* This WHO'S WHO is that unheard-of thing, a droll book of saints. About six hundred accounts wittily assess lives, legends and reasons for popularity. Although dates sometimes are missing, rare saints emerge colorfully (e.g., Dymphna, Peter Mary Chanel, Sithney). Where else can one learn that the Grand Guignol is named for Guignolé (Gwenno), who functioned as "the French equivalent of Punch" (p. 131), or that the English word "pants" derives from San Pantaleone, whom the Venetians venerated solely because his name recalled their battle cry "Piante Leone" (p. 220)? This winsome volume exhumes bizarre lore and classifies patron saints almost as skillfully as **102** Walsh, *Butler's Lives of Patron Saints* (1987). A bibliography cites thirty-eight choice items. A few errors creep in, as when Clement VIII is called Clement VII (p. 243). By highlighting Christian folklore, this volume will awaken enthusiasm for saints' lives. Its rollicking narratives have no rival.

□ *Summary* Infectious but not irreverent, this WHO'S WHO deserves a wide audience. It makes saint-watching a joy.

109 (1995) Clemens Jöckle, *Encyclopedia of Saints* (London: Fine Arts Collection, 1995); translated from the German; 480 pages; no index, no bibliography; 82 color plates and about 150 black-and-white illustrations.

□ *Scope* Compiled by a private scholar in Speyer, Germany, this MENIPPEAN REALLEXIKON inventories three hundred saints, above all as regards iconography. Biblical figures like Gabriel and the three kings (but not Jesus) also figure, along with one or two beatifieds like Charlemagne. Each entry deploys a schema of up to seven headings: (1) "Feast Day," (2) "Life," (3) "Legends," (4) "Patronage," (5) "Veneration and Cult Sites," (6) "Superstition" and (7) "Representation in Art," i.e., iconography. The latter section differentiates portrayals of (1) apparel, (2) attributes, (3) personifications, (4) special scenes and (5) martyrdom. With MENIPPEAN momentum the author itemizes images in all genres throughout Europe (particularly in Poland and Hungary), while downplaying Britain. Unfortunately, these lists follow no fixed pattern, either alphabetical or chronological. Length of entry varies from one-half column on Bede to four pages on Francis and ten on the Virgin Mary. The writing can be telegraphic when narrating a life and becomes MENIPPEAN when listing legends and representations. With some excep-

tions, however, the lists keep MENIPPEAN extravagance at bay. Color plates or black-and-white illustrations (without captions) accompany most entries.

□ *Strengths* This labor of love (not to say "labor of lists") breaks new ground in several ways, first of all by functioning as a REALLEXIKON. Nearly all other hagiographies inject devotional touches, but this one does not. Second, no other WHO'S WHO of saints so methodically disentangles life from legend. Several like Anne, Ursula and Christopher have no life to record apart from legend. Where legends have proliferated (e.g., around Andrew, James the Great or Mary Magdalene), the author revels in the bizarre but does not not scant saints who generated no legends (e.g., Thomas More, Teresa of Ávila, Vincent de Paul). Third, no other WHO'S WHO lists cult sites so reliably. Fourth, no other HAGIOGRAPHY enumerates artistic representations, much less sorts them by apparel, attributes, special scenes, personifications and martyrdom. Although lacking discernible sequence, these enumerations know no rival except in a MEGA-ENCYCLOPEDIA, Wolfgang Braunfels, ed., *Lexikon der christlichen Ikonographie*, vols. 5-8 (Rome: Herder, 1973-76). Jöckle shows that recent saints tend to inspire a narrower range of iconography; at least one, Edmund Campion, inspired none. Fifth, the illustrations stand in a class by themselves, both in rarity and splendor. Eighty-two color plates deliver spectacular images, including some from Eastern Europe, but black-and-white ones (often from prints) lack captions. Art historians will wallow.

□ *Weaknesses* Imposing a schema on each entry entails drawbacks. Telegraphic style makes the narratives clumsy and sometimes MENIPPEAN. However useful, lists of legends or images, running as many as a hundred, follow no fixed sequence and sometimes overwhelm (as on Christopher, the Virgin Mary, Mary Magdalene). Although in the foreword Jöckle evinces Catholic attitudes (p. 5), everywhere else he writes nonconfessionally (except when he titles Mary "the Blessed Virgin," p. 299). More surprisingly, Jöckle omits both methodology and bibliography. Many will wish that he had situated his book in relation to rivals. Seldom if ever has a master compilation, verging on a HANDBOOK, so disdained scholarly apparatus.

□ *Competitors* This MENIPPEAN REALLEXIKON unmasks how previous WHO'S WHOS spurn iconography. No other major HAGIOGRAPHY in English furnishes illustrations! A devotional calendar, Vincent Cronin, *A Calendar of Saints* (Westminster, Md.: Newman, 1963) deploys for each of 365 days a black-and-white image and condensed information on a single saint, often an unusual one. **105** Duchet-Suchaux and Pastoureau, *The Bible and Saints* (1990, 1994) tackles only ninety postbiblical saints and serves chiefly art historians. An uncritical grab bag devoid of dates, Tom Morgan's *Saints* (San Francisco: Chronicle Books, 1994) illustrates legends of 110 saints. Likewise a selection from **96** *Butler's Lives* published as *One Hundred Saints* (Boston: Bulfinch Press, 1993) provides color plates. Images of 140 saints in British churches adorn Edward G. Tasker, *Encyclopedia of Medieval Church Art*, ed. John Beaumont (London: Batsford, 1993), pp. 99-170. To supply bibliographies lacking in Jöckle, **100** Farmer, *The Oxford Dictionary of Saints* (1978, 1992) probably works best. Although Jöckle eschews any concept of "Christian folklore," his weighing of legends fuels that endeavor. Anyone wishing to possess only one WHO'S WHO of saints cannot do better than this. Never did MENIPPEAN technique reap finer rewards.

□ *Summary* This REALLEXIKON inventories three hundred saints and their iconography, while supplying choice illustrations. Only lack of bibliography and MENIPPEAN flurries keep this WHO'S WHO from eclipsing its predecessors.

2.7 LITURGY

OVERVIEW: CATHOLIC, ORTHODOX AND ANGLICAN LEADERSHIP If theology, hagiography and above all biblical studies favor reference works, the study of liturgy does not. To compensate for a dearth of specialized volumes, liturgy blossoms in general ones like **29** Cross, ed., *The Oxford Dictionary of the Christian Church* (1957, 1974) as well as in confessional ones like **142** Patrinacos, *A Dictionary of Greek Orthodoxy* (1982). Nearly all the works analyzed under 2.9.3 "Eastern Christianity" emphasize liturgy. Perhaps the richest synthesis in English of twentieth-century thinking about liturgy remains a HANDBOOK: Geoffrey Wainwright, *Doxology: The Praise of God in Worship, Doctrine and Life: A Systematic Theology* (New York: Oxford University Press, 1980). Sixty-five articles in another HANDBOOK enlarge upon it: Cheslyn Jones, Geoffrey Wainwright, Edward Yarnold, S.J., and Paul Bradshaw, eds., *The Study of Liturgy* [1978], 2d ed. (London: SPCK; New York: Oxford University Press, 1992). Both of them pale beside the creativity that pours from **110** Sartore and Triacca, eds., *Dictionnaire encylopédique de la liturgie* (1984, 1992-). Promoting "blurring of genres" among the social sciences, this work pioneers a new field that it calls "meta-liturgics." Americans ought to join its pursuit of cultural diagnosis.

LIST OF WORKS ANALYZED
132 (1907-53) Fernand Cabrol and Henri Leclercq, eds., *Dictionnaire d'archéologie chrétienne et de liturgie,* 30 vols. in 15 (Paris: Letouzey & Ané, 1903-53). Analyzed under 2.9.2.2 "French Megaencyclopedias."

119 (1972, 1986) J[ohn] G[ordon] Davies, *The New Westminster Dictionary of Liturgy and Worship* (Philadelphia: Westminster, 1986). Analyzed under 2.8 "The Westminster/SCM Dictionaries."

110 (1984, 1992-) Domenico Sartore and Achille M. Triacca, eds., *Dictionnaire encyclopédique de la liturgie,* planned in 2 vols. (Turnhout: Brepols, 1992-)

111 (1989) Edward N. West, *Outward Signs: The Language of Christian Symbolism* (New York: Walker, 1989)

112 (1990) Peter E. Fink, S.J., ed., *The New Dictionary of Sacramental Worship* (Collegeville, Minn.: Michael Glazier/Liturgical, 1990)

113 (1991) Philip H. Pfatteicher, *A Dictionary of Liturgical Terms* (Philadelphia: Trinity Press International, 1991)

ANALYSIS OF WORKS

110 (1984, 1992-) Domenico Sartore and Achille M. Triacca, eds., *Dictionnaire encyclopédique de la liturgie,* planned in 2 vols. (Turnhout: Brepols, 1992-); adapted by Henri Delhougne, O.S.B. from *Nuovo Dizionario di liturgia* (Roma: Edizioni Paoline, 1984); vol. 1: xxxiii & 678 pages; index planned in vol. 2; "Proposals for Systematic Reading," 1:xvi-xxiii; no general bibliography. Analyzed on the basis of vol. 1.

□ *Scope* Conceived and edited by Benedictines in Italy and Luxembourg, this REVISIONIST LEXICON astonishes by its originality. In Italy it appeared in the same series as **91** De Fiores and Goffi, eds., *Dictionnaire de la vie spirituelle* (1983, 1987). Sixty-one mostly Italian contributors rethink contemporary Roman Catholic liturgy from innumerable standpoints, not least from the social sciences. Exemplifying recent "blurring of genres," in volume 1 sixty-two essays propound novel views, buttressed by massive footnotes and multilingual bibliographies. The French edition inserts articles on "France (Liturgy in)" (1:462-500) as well as addenda elsewhere. Italian commitment to cultural anthropology invigorates this most exhilarating of reference books.

□ *Strengths* By invoking cultural anthropology, this LEXICON may be said to climax the Roman Catholic liturgical movement, which it both scrutinizes and transcends. Aldo Natale Terrin sets the tone in a magisterial survey of "Cultural Anthropology," which expounds American and British approaches to primal societies. He assigns rites to three types: those of (1) crisis, (2) passage (life-stages) and (3) seasons. Writing in a similar vein on "Culture and Liturgy," Carmine Di Sante invokes Clifford Geertz and Ludwig Wittgenstein in order to differentiate the enactment of "liturgy" from the theory (meta-liturgics) that interprets it. Indeed, the entire book serves to legitimate the enterprise of meta-liturgics. In a masterful diagnosis Silvano Maggiani

expounds a dozen cultural anthropologists in order to explain why "Festival" has recently fallen into crisis, but for some reason he overlooks Victor Turner. In treating "Language," Gianfranco Venturi suggests that liturgical terminology constitutes an "interlanguage" (i.e., jargon) such as all professions cultivate. Franco Lever construes "coding" and "decoding" as undergirding "Communication in the Assembly." Luca Brandolini examines "Animation" as a cluster of procedures and attitudes for "enlivening" liturgies and then implements some of them to enliven an essay on "Sunday." Cervera Jesús Castellano waxes visionary on how liturgies mirror "Eschatology."

The ebullition peaks in a trio of articles by Alessandro Pistoia on "Commitment" [Engagement], "History of Salvation" and above all "Creativity." Other articles trace history from the Old Testament onward, as Carlo Cibien does on "Gestures," Luigi Della Torre on "Homily" and Manlio Sodi on "Blessing" *[Bénédiction]*. Effortlessly Burkhard Neunhauser of Maria Laach summarizes the "History of Liturgy" in twenty pages. Achille Triacca's overview of "Bible and Liturgy" averages eight weighty footnotes per page, while his twenty-five pages on the "Ambrosian Liturgy" explode with erudition. More conventionally Ildobrando Scicolone surveys "Liturgical Books," while Jordi Pinell tracks "Local Liturgies in Antiquity." Naturally, each of the sacraments gets dissected. Pedagogy surfaces in articles on "Family" and on "Liturgical Training" as regards both laity and priests (1:446-62). No less original are separate essays on religiosity in "Children" and in "Young People." Perhaps no other reference work in Christian studies delivers so many radical essays. It makes theory of liturgy (meta-liturgics) seem indispensable, for no other field so encourages cultural diagnosis.

□ *Weaknesses* If such a thing is possible, this Italo-French LEXICON manifests too high a degree of creativity. Where so many fresh ideas bubble, one can no longer speak of confessional self-definition. Indeed, if a single author had penned this volume, one would hail it as a PHILOSOPHICAL DICTION-ARY. Unfortunately, there is no WHO'S WHO or GLOSSARY to anchor rethinking in the mundane. Certain omissions spark surprise. The focus on Western liturgies precludes even passing mention of parallels in Eastern Christianity. One wonders too why the long delayed volume 2 announces no entries on "pilgrimage" or "relics." The delay of volume 2 irks all the more because so many entries, not least those on "Psychology," "Secularization" and "Sociology," promise to tighten the notion of meta-liturgics.

□ *Competitors* This REVISIONIST masterpiece confirms that liturgy incites Roman Catholic creativity like no other topic. Here the ferment outdoes that even in later volumes of **87** Viller, *Dictionnaire de spiritualité* (1937-94) or of **137** Jacquemet, ed., *Catholicisme* (1948-). One is reminded of anthropologists doing cultural diagnosis in **215** Akoun, ed., *Mythes et croyances du monde entier* (1985). An obvious rival is **112** Fink, *The New Dictionary of Sacramental Worship* (1990), whose essays soar less but supply a WHO'S WHO and GLOSSARY. **119** Davies, ed., *The New Westminster Dictionary of Liturgy* (1986) excels as a REALLEXIKON but only occasionally achieves incandescence. None of these volumes tackles meta-liturgics head-on.

□ *Summary* This REVISIONIST ENCYCLO-PEDIA unleashes a torrent of rethinking about Roman Catholic liturgy. Social scientists will revel, and everyone will prize the bibliographies, even if some conservatives quail at the notion of meta-liturgics.

111 (1989) Edward N. West, *Outward Signs: The Language of Christian Symbolism* (New York: Walker, 1989); xvii & 237 pages; index, pp. 229-37; general bibliography, pp. 224-27; glossary, pp. 173-223; 455 line drawings.

□ *Critique* This historical INTRODUCTION and GLOSSARY deploys 455 drawings to scan thousands of variations in liturgy and architecture. Writing with a touch of whimsy, an Episcopalian priest expounds in fourteen chapters such matters as "3. Primary Christian Symbols," "11. Symbolism in Liturgy" and "12. Symbolism in Vest-

ments." A GLOSSARY defines about five hundred terms. A spectacular chapter describes and illustrates no fewer than 166 varieties of cross. Chapter "9. Symbolism Representative of the Saints" brings to life sixty saints from East and West. No other reference work highlights visual symbolism so vividly or learnedly. The quotations are juicy, the anecdotes irresistible and the bibliography superb.

□ *Summary* This lively INTRODUCTION expounds and illustrates visual symbols in delectable profusion.

112 (1990) Peter E. Fink, S.J., ed., *The New Dictionary of Sacramental Worship* (Collegeville, Minn.: Michael Glazier/Liturgical, 1990); 1352 pages; topical index, pp. 1339-45; no general bibliography.

□ *Scope* This REVISIONIST LEXICON of liturgics and sacraments reformulates Roman Catholic identity with aplomb. In 320 articles by 165 contributors, it delivers the best of contemporary Catholic thinking on history, theology, social sciences and pastoral wisdom concerning worship. Each entry carries headings and subheadings, and almost all include English-language bibliography. A topical index (pp. 1339-45) divides the material into seven sections: (1) "The Worshipping Church," (2) "The Heritage of the Church," (3) "The Sacramental Life of the Church," (4) "The Church at Prayer," (5) "The Church and the Arts," (6) "The Reflecting Church" and (7) "The Pastoral Mission of the Church." Sections three and four are by far the longest. It goes without saying that the sacraments, church seasons and feasts, and every sort of prayer are explored historically and pastorally. Pastoral advice abounds on preaching, counseling, conducting marriages and funerals, and serving the marginalized. Four articles on music and liturgy, as well as two on art and liturgy, deepen the perspective. The writing is lucid, sometimes almost jaunty, and authors sound realistic about resistance to certain Catholic teachings. In some cases a scholar suggests ever so gently that teachings need to change (e.g., in "Ordination of Women"). This book never hectors or wheedles.

□ *Strengths* This REVISIONIST LEXICON shows that liturgics is the liveliest area of Roman Catholic thought today. Shrewdly, the editor invited contributors to follow their own judgment in framing issues. The result is REVISIONIST thinking of a high order. Historical articles on liturgy in general and on individual sacraments are among the best in English. Major surveys include three on the "History of the Eucharist," six on liturgical traditions and six on "Liturgical Renewal" or "Liturgical Reform," in which Benedictines have played a preponderant role. A few liturgical reformers like Maurice de la Taille and Prosper Guéranger (but not Odo Casel or Lambert Beaudoin) receive short entries. Patristic and medieval sources undergird some fifty different articles. The editor sets a high standard in surveying "Eucharist, Theology of" and "Traditions, Liturgical in the East," not to mention a pioneering discussion of "Imagination and Worship." Other innovative entries include John M. Staudenmaier on "Liturgy in a Technological Age," which weighs how advertising affects responses to ritual (pp. 765-66), and George Goethals on "Secular Rituals" as rivals to religious ones. Karl Rahner's book *Man at Play* (1972) looms large in Goethals.

In "Human Sciences, Sacraments and the," Joseph Martos scans five academic disciplines for insights into contemporary attitudes. Following Mary Douglas, he emphasizes that ritual is "easier to enter into" in socially stratified cultures than in socially mobile ones like America's (p. 585). Teresa Berger's piece on "Ecumenism and the Liturgy" affirms that prayer is "the soul of the whole ecumenical movement" (p. 388). In a candid assessment of "Devotions, Popular" Carl Dehne declares their great days finished and deduces from their repetitiveness that "variety . . . is not the spice of liturgical prayer" (p. 340). George Tavard tackles "Ordination of Women," tracing resistance back to Aquinas, who assigned to women "a position in humanity and society that is incompatible with the duties and responsibilities of priests" (p.

914). In striving to renew "theological anthropology," Tavard exemplifies REVISIONIST thinking at its best. Pastoral articles deal with human realities forthrightly, as in "Divorced, Ministry to" or "Death, Theology of." No one offers namby-pamby advice.

□ *Weaknesses* In an imaginative way this REVISIONIST LEXICON formulates Roman Catholic self-definition. Rigorists may find some contributors too fond of change. And a Roman focus inevitably entails certain omissions. For all its attention to history, the work does not delineate the practice of Anglican or nonliturgical Protestant churches. Although two articles survey "Jewish Worship" and "Jewish Roots of Christian Worship," no other religion wins notice. At the very least, mention should have gone to attempts at syncretism between Catholic and Hindu worship (e.g., by Bede Griffiths) or between Catholic and Buddhist meditation (e.g., by William M. Johnston, S.J.). Coverage of Africa and Latin America is sorely missed. Running heads on each page would improve format. An index of persons would have helped to assemble references to church fathers and to liturgical reformers.

□ *Competitors* This is the liveliest and most openminded LEXICON of American Catholic thought. It demonstrates that liturgy inspires Catholics to more realistic reflection than perhaps any other topic. In contrast to two companion volumes, **83** Komonchak et al., eds., *The New Dictionary of Theology* (1987) and **94** Downey, ed., *The New Dictionary of Catholic Spirituality* (1993), this one confronts human needs and social realities. As in **86** Dwyer, ed., *The New Dictionary of Catholic Social Thought* (1994), contemporary endeavors elicit historical grounding. All four works make **119** Davies, ed., *The New Westminster Dictionary of Liturgy and Worship* (1986) seem unmistakably Anglican, but to its credit the latter encompasses major world religions. Considered as a REVISIONIST LEXICON of self-definition, *The New Dictionary of Sacramental Worship* takes its place with another American masterpiece, **181** Cohen and Mendes-Flohr, eds., *Con-*

temporary Jewish Religious Thought
(1987). The latter is more original and
wide-ranging, but the former tackles bedrock difficulties just as shrewdly and expounds history more thoroughly. Both
books dissect causes of contemporary resistance to religion. Among older works,
82 Davis, ed., *A Catholic Dictionary of
Theology* (1962-71) is more limpid and
probes history more searchingly, while
often exuding a kindred REVISIONISM.
Among contemporary Catholic reference
books in English, *The New Dictionary of
Sacramental Worship* comes closest to
matching that masterpiece of the 1960s in
vigor of thought and sweep of vision.
Fink's achievement seems circumspect,
however, when compared with the ferment
that pervades **110** Sartore and Triacca,
eds., *Dictionnaire encyclopédique de la liturgie* (1984, 1992-). The two works function well in tandem, the American one
seeming discreet and the Italo-French one
electrifying.

□ *Summary* Every educated Christian
should ponder this book. No other recent
Catholic reference work in English blends
history, theology and pastoral advice so
profoundly. The best of American Catholic
thinking blossoms here.

**113 (1991) Philip H. Pfatteicher, *A
Dictionary of Liturgical Terms*** (Philadelphia: Trinity Press International, 1991); x
& 133 pages; no index; general bibliography, pp. viii-ix.

□ *Critique* This GLOSSARY of terms in Lutheran, Anglican and Roman Catholic liturgical practice overflows with wit.
Derivation, history and current applications are deliciously sketched. Latin and
Hebrew phrases jostle with plain English
words as well as terms of utmost rarity. The
Lutheran author takes precedent from Dr.
Johnson's "tradition of singularity" for featuring oddities such as "heortology," i.e.,
"the study of days and seasons of the Christian year." Even the most well-versed will
find subtleties to savor. This companion to
119 Davies, ed., *The New Westminster Dictionary of Liturgy and Worship* (1986)
makes self-teaching a pleasure.

□ *Summary* This GLOSSARY is one of the

most enjoyable on any religious topic.

2.8 THE WESTMINSTER/SCM DICTIONARIES

**OVERVIEW: CLASSICS OF SELF-
TEACHING** The ten volumes analyzed
here appeared between 1963 and 1992 in
nearly uniform format. Half of them originated with the Student Christian Movement (SCM) Press in London, and all but
one (**120** *A Dictionary of Religious Education* [1983]) have been published in the
United States by Westminster/John Knox
Press (originally of Philadelphia, now of
Knoxville). The earliest one, **114** Cully,
ed., *The Westminster Dictionary of Christian Education* (1963), saw a second edition published by Harper and Row in 1990
and in that sense no longer belongs to the
series. Because the Westminster/SCM dictionaries implement a consistent style of
self-teaching, they function as a unit. Many
readers will prefer certain of these volumes
to any others on a given subject.

Articles are signed except in **118** *The
Westminster Dictionary of Church History*,
each with English-language bibliography.
Usually there is no index or general bibliography. No illustrations appear except in
119 *A Dictionary of Liturgy and Worship*
and **116** *The New Westminster Dictionary
of the Bible*. Volumes published since 1980
feature cross-references.

LIST OF WORKS ANALYZED (IN CHRONOLOGICAL ORDER OF FIRST EDITION)

**114 (1963) Kendig Brubaker Cully,
ed., *The Westminster Dictionary of Christian Education*** (Philadelphia: Westminster, 1963); 812 pages; general
bibliography (of 1277 items), pp. 756-97;
table of subject headings, pp. 749-55.

A second edition was published as Iris
V. Cully and Kendig Brubaker Cully,
eds., *Harper's Encyclopedia of Religious
Education* (San Francisco: Harper,
1990); xxiii & 716 pages. This work is
not to be confused with **120** John M.
Sutcliffe, ed., *A Dictionary of Religious
Education* (London: SCM, 1984).

115 (1967, 1986) **John Macquarrie, ed.,** *Dictionary of Christian Ethics* (London: SCM; Philadelphia: Westminster, 1967); x & 366 pages; no index; 75 contributors. A second edition appeared as James F. Childress and John Macquarrie, eds., *The Westminster Dictionary of Christian Ethics* (Philadelphia: Westminster, 1986); published in Britain as *A New Dictionary of Christian Ethics* (London: SCM, 1986; paperback, 1993); xvii & 670 pages; index of names, pp. 671-78; 167 contributors; 620 entries (entirely on concepts; no persons or places). Forty percent of the entries are retained from the 1967 version (p. vii).

116 (1969, 1983) **Alan Richardson [1905-75], ed.,** *A Dictionary of Christian Theology* (London: SCM; Philadelphia: Westminster, 1969); xii & 364 pages; 36 almost entirely British contributors; second edition published as Alan Richardson and John Bowden, eds., *The Westminster Dictionary of Christian Theology* (Philadelphia: Westminster, 1983); published in Britain as *A New Dictionary of Theology* (London: SCM, 1983; paperback, 1989); xvii & 614 pages; index of names, pp. 611-14; 170 contributors; entries entirely on concepts (no persons or places). The second edition has been totally rewritten except for 45 entries by Richardson.

117 (1970) **Henry Snyder Gehman, ed.,** *The New Westminster Dictionary of the Bible* (Philadelphia: Westminster, 1970); xi & 1064 pages; 450 photos; 60 maps. This BIBLE DICTIONARY has been eclipsed by numerous successors and will not be analyzed in detail.

118 (1971) **Jerald C. Brauer, ed.,** *The Westminster Dictionary of Church History* (Philadelphia: Westminster, 1971); xii & 887 pages; 140 contributors; unsigned entries on persons, events, practices and concepts with emphasis on post-1700 North America. No revised edition has appeared.

1 (1971) **Geoffrey Parrinder,** *A Dictionary of Non-Christian Religions* (Amersham: Hulton Educational Books; Philadelphia: Westminster, 1971); 320 pages. This is the only volume in the series currently out of print in the United States. Analyzed under 1.1 "The World's Religions: Alphabetical Reference Books."

119 (1972, 1986) **J[ohn] G[ordon] Davies, ed.,** *A Dictionary of Liturgy and Worship* (London: SCM; New York: Macmillan, 1972; reprinted as *The Westminster Dictionary of Worship*, 1974); xiv & 385 pages; 64 (mostly Anglican) contributors; a few diagrams and black-and-white photographs.

A second edition appeared as J[ohn] G[ordon] Davies, ed., *The New Westminster Dictionary of Liturgy and Worship* (Philadelphia: Westminster, 1986); published in Britain as *A New Dictionary of Liturgy and Worship* (London: SCM, 1986; paperback, 1989); xvi & 544 pages; 100 (mostly British) contributors. Entries on practices, sacraments, liturgies, architecture and music but not persons or places. The 1986 revision emphasizes Anglican liturgical changes since 1972. Analyzed under 2.7 "Liturgy."

89 (1983) **Gordon S. Wakefield, ed.,** *The Westminster Dictionary of Christian Spirituality* (Philadelphia: Westminster, 1983); published in Britain as *A Dictionary of Christian Spirituality* (London: SCM, 1983; paperback, 1988); xvi & 400 pages; 150 (mostly British) contributors; entries on 127 persons as well as concepts, national traditions and practices. The bibliographies are unusually rich. Analyzed under 2.5 "Spirituality."

120 (1984) **John M. Sutcliffe, ed.,** *A Dictionary of Religious Education* (London: SCM, 1984); xvii & 376 pages; mostly British contributors; entries on nations, concepts and a few persons (e.g., Rousseau). This British publication does not appear in the Westminster series but bears an identical format. It addresses teachers in Britain.

68 (1990) **R[ichard] J. Coggins and J. L[eslie] Houlden, eds.,** *A Dictionary of Biblical Interpretation* (London: SCM, 1990; paperback, 1993; New York: Trinity Press International, 1990); xvi & 751 pages; index, pp. 745-48. Although published by SCM in the format of the series, this magisterial work does not feature in it.

Arguably the book would be better known if it had. Analyzed under 2.3.3 "Biblical Studies: Handbooks of Interpretation."

124 (1992) Donald F. McKim with David F. Wright, eds., *Encyclopedia of the Reformed Faith* (Louisville: Westminster/John Knox; Edinburgh: Saint Andrew, 1992); xxiv & 414 pages; 200 (nearly all Reformed) contributors; entries on concepts, certain countries, a few persons and issues of concern to the Reformed tradition. Analyzed under 2.9.1 "Churches and Denominations: Protestantism."

EVALUATION OF THE SERIES AS A WHOLE

□ *Scope (of the series)* Launched as a series in Britain by John Macquarrie and Alan Richardson in the late 1960s, these ten DICTIONARIES are masterpieces of popularization. Total length of over four thousand pages affords ample coverage and deft syntheses, notably in volumes on **115** ethics and on **89** spirituality. Overlapping between volumes is rare. Taken together, six new editions since 1983 package Christian lore in a fashion that nonexperts will savor. At least three, on **119** liturgy (1972, 1986), **89** spirituality (1983) and **125** the Reformed tradition (1992), are indispensable for specialists, while **115** on ethics (1967, 1986) abounds in elegant, often profound synopses. All four achieve REVISIONISM without fanfare.

□ *Strengths (of one new volume and three new editions since 1983)* In **115** Alan Richardson's *A Dictionary of Christian Theology* (1967) fifteen articles by the editor pioneered a style of rethinking abstractions. Virtuosic syntheses in the second edition (1983) include articles (of at least eight pages) on "God," "Trinity, Doctrine of," "Christology" and "Holy Spirit." Historical synopses excel, among them William H. C. Frend on "Augustinianism," Frances Young on "Patristics" and R. Mcl. Wilson on "Gnosticism." Summaries of the social sciences unfold in Robin Gill on "Sociology of Religion," Adrian Cunningham on "Psychology of Religion" and Bryan Wilson on "Secularization" and "Secularism." Particularly in Richardson's

articles, this most readable of nonconfessional DICTIONARIES of theology reads almost as winsomely as **82** Davis, ed., *A Catholic Dictionary of Theology* (1962-71).

With REVISIONIST flair, **114** James F. Childress and John Macquarrie's *Dictionary of Christian Ethics* (1967, 1986) encompasses world religions, social sciences, philosophy, contemporary issues, biblical ethics and denominational ethics. Dating from 1967, John Macquarrie's seventy-five articles differentiate denotations but do not always shine as brightly as his entries in **34** Gentz, ed., *The Dictionary of Bible and Religion* (1986). Another polymath, Donald MacKinnon, writes concisely on "Intuition," "Socratic Ethics" and "Sophists." Innovative entries include David Little, "Comparative Religious Ethics," Margaret Fairley, "Feminist Ethics" and E. J. Tinsley, "Mysticism and Ethics." Charles C. West's "Ecumenical Movement, Ethics in" is a major synthesis, as are articles on "Anglican Ethics," "Eastern Orthodox Christian Ethics" and "Platonic Ethics." Six hundred twenty entries offer refreshing, often REVISIONIST reflection on contemporary issues. This volume matches **181** Cohen and Mendes-Flohr, eds., *Contemporary Jewish Religious Thought* (1987) in reappraising fundamentals.

119 J[ohn] G[ordon] Davies, *A Dictionary of Liturgy and Worship* (1972, 1986) has no rival in presenting the history and norms of liturgies East and West. Written mainly by Anglican clergy, articles take a layperson into the sacristy and behind the altar to explain theory and practice. In sparkling prose, synopses rich in detail cover all branches of Christianity and supply multilingual bibliographies. Major syntheses running twenty pages or more include "Architectural Setting," "Books, Liturgical" and "Liturgies," but there is no entry on "Church Year." Each of the sacraments gets explored in depth. **112** Fink, ed., *The New Dictionary of Sacramental Worship* (1990) is more comprehensive and up-to-date but lacks hands-on directness. Davies's WHO'S WHO and GLOSSARY help to stabilize the creativity that pervades **110** Sartore and Triacca, eds., *Dictionnaire* *encyclopédieque de la liturgie* (1984, 1992-). Of all the Westminster/SCM volumes, Davies addresses the highest percentage of topics not readily duplicated elsewhere, except at overwhelming length in **132** Cabrol and Leclercq, eds., *Dictionnaire d'archéologie chrétienne et de liturgie* (1903-53).

89 Gordon S. Wakefield, *The Westminster Dictionary of Christian Spirituality* (1983) is analyzed under 2.5 "Spirituality."

120 John M. Sutcliffe's *A Dictionary of Religious Education* (1983) serves British teachers of education in church, school and university. It summarizes issues, curriculum and national schemes of religious education in ways that will aid teachers in Britain. The WHO'S WHO is minimal.

□ *Weaknesses (of the series)* The Westminster/SCM dictionaries omit foreign-language bibliography except in **119** Davies's first edition (1972) on liturgy. Individual bibliographies in the volumes on **118** church history (1971) and on **116** theology (1969, 1983) tend to be skeletal, and all volumes would gain from a general bibliography. Emphasis on concepts and persons excludes cities and countries, although surveys of African, Asian and American spirituality enrich **89** Wakefield's volume (1983). World religions feature only in volumes on **115** ethics (1986) and **89** spirituality (1983) as well as **1** Parrinder's *Dictionary of Non-Christian Religions* (1971). Except **125** McKim, most of the volumes emphasize Britain above North America. **117** *The Westminster Dictionary of Church History* (1971) is the least original, covering much the same ground in slightly pedestrian fashion as **29** Cross, ed., *Oxford Dictionary of the Christian Church* (1957, 1974) or **34** Gentz, ed., *The Dictionary of Bible and Religion* (1986). It lacks the sparkle of later volumes in the series, and too few of its articles have bibliographies.

□ *Competitors* These ten volumes constitute a series that is unique. Careful prioritizing minimizes overlapping. On concepts, the nearest rival is **45** Fahlbusch, ed., *Evangelisches Kirchenlexikon* (1986-), which covers countries but neglects spirituality and liturgy. On persons the predes-

tined rival will soon be the ten volumes of **128** Kasper, ed., *Lexikon für Thelogie und Kirche* (1993-), which is admirably ecumenical and offers multilingual bibliographies. **46** Lossky et al., eds., *Dictionary of the Ecumenical Movement* (1991) discusses theology and contemporary issues with a forthrightness reminiscent of the Westminster/SCM volumes on **115** ethics and **116** theology. Westminster/SCM articles tend to be more spacious and sprightly than those in **163** Douglas, ed., *New 20th-Century Encyclopedia of Religious Knowledge* (1991) but less virtuosic than ones in **77** McGrath, ed., *The Blackwell Encyclopedia of Modern Christian Thought* (1993).

□ *Summary* If one disregards **116** *The New Westminster Dictionary of the Bible* (1970), **117** *The Westminster Dictionary of Church History* (1971) and **120** *A Dictionary of Religious Education* (1984), the other seven volumes fuse British elegance and erudition with American openmindedness and vigor to forge superb tools. Their dexterity will delight anyone who wishes to explore or rethink liturgy, spirituality, ethics, theology, education or the Reformed tradition. No other *series* of reference works advances self-teaching so astutely or purveys REVISIONISM so tactfully.

2.9 CHURCHES AND DENOMINATIONS

2.9.1 PROTESTANTISM

OVERVIEW: A CLASH BETWEEN SELF-DEFINITION AND REVISIONISM A vigorous REVISIONIST LEXICON, **125** Gisel, ed., *Encyclopédie du protestantisme* (1995), edited in Switzerland, reassesses the role of Protestantism in Europe. In a different vein, since the 1950s a number of Protestant denominations in the United States have edited ENCYCLOPEDIAS of history and doctrine. Written by and for their communities, these works of self-definition trace roots in Europe but emphasize American persons and places. They help social historians who seek exhaustive WHO'S WHOS and gazetteers. Except for **121** Bodensieck and **125** Gisel, theology emerges more adroitly in works listed under 2.4.2 "Theology." A number of volumes concerning Protestantism in the United States appear under 2.10.6 "Periods of Church History." All scholars of Protestantism will want to frequent Hans J. Hillerbrand, ed., *The Oxford Encyclopedia of the Reformation,* 4 vols. (New York and Oxford: Oxford University Press, 1996), which appeared too late to analyze. So did a magisterial WHO'S WHO of the English-speaking world: Donald M. Lewis, ed., *The Blackwell Dictionary of Evangelical Biography 1730-1860,* 2 vols. (Oxford and Cambridge, Mass.: Blackwell Reference, 1995).

LIST OF WORKS ANALYZED

121 (1965) Julius Bodensieck, ed., *The Encyclopedia of the Lutheran Church,* 3 vols. (Minneapolis: Augsburg, 1965)

122 (1974) Nolan B. Harmon, ed., *The Encyclopedia of World Methodism,* 2 vols. (Nashville: United Methodist Publishing House, 1974)

123 (1983) *The Brethren Encyclopedia,* 3 vols. (Philadelphia and Oak Brook, Ill.: The Brethren Encyclopedia, 1983)

124 (1992) Donald K. McKim, ed., *Encyclopedia of the Reformed Faith* (Louisville: Westminster, 1992). Analyzed also under 2.8 "The Westminster/SCM Dictionaries."

125 (1995) Pierre Gisel, ed., *Encyclopédie du protestantisme* (Paris: Cerf and Geneva: Labor et Fides, 1995)

ANALYSIS OF WORKS

121 (1965) Julius Bodensieck, ed., *The Encyclopedia of the Lutheran Church,* 3 vols. (Minneapolis: Augsburg, 1965); 2575 pages; no index; no general bibliography; some photographs in the text.

□ *Scope* This ENCYCLOPEDIA provides a model of denominational self-definition. More than seven hundred contributors write signed articles on the "Lutheran concept" of nearly every topic in church history. Countries (but not cities) with Lutheran communities, persons (including musicians), concepts, practices and issues

in church history elicit entries (usually with multilingual bibliography). Every conceivable aspect of Martin Luther is probed backward and forward. The writing is dignified, the pace stately.

□ *Strengths* This ENCYCLOPEDIA of self-definition overflows with reflectiveness. Its mostly American authors propound a Lutheran view of the entire gamut of Christian discourse. Unusual articles include "The Eastern Orthodox Church and Lutheranism" and "Enthusiasm" *(Schwärmerei).* Twenty pages on "Bible Use" canvass all periods and denominations. Marginally Lutheran figures like Zinzendorf get reinterpreted. Germanic formality frames entries into subdivisions such as "Terminological Observations" and "Lutheran Applications." The reflectiveness has aged well, making this a font of wisdom on Christian history.

□ *Weaknesses* Although averaging two pages in length, biographical entries too often lack bibliography. This monument from the early 1960s highlights German theologians from the past (1930-60), many of whom now seem dated. In contrast to Jewish ENCYCLOPEDIAS, individual cities lack entries.

□ *Competitors* The tone is reminiscent of a German MEGA-ENCYCLOPEDIA, Galling, ed., *Die Religion in Geschichte und Gegenwart,* 3d ed. (1956-63), whose entries are more concise but not always superior in synthesis. Davis, ed., *A Catholic Dictionary of Theology* (1962-71) is more meditative and felicitous but not always so original in allocating articles. This exemplar of denominational self-definition is more sprightly than the four-volume *Mennonite Encyclopedia* (1956-59) but more ponderous than the one-volume **124** McKim, ed., *Encyclopedia of the Reformed Faith* (1992). The latter's briskness and originality suggest that a one-volume reworking of *The Encyclopedia of the Lutheran Church* would reap dividends. Pending that outcome, Hans J. Hillerbrand, ed., *The Oxford Encyclopedia of the Reformation,* 4 vols. (New York and Oxford: Oxford University Press, 1996) promises to become standard.

□ *Summary* Although the bibliographies

are dated, this ENCYCLOPEDIA exudes dignity and reflectiveness. Large-mindedness triumphs.

122 (1974) Nolan B. Harmon, ed., *The Encyclopedia of World Methodism,* 2 vols. (Nashville: United Methodist Publishing House, 1974); 2814 pages; index, pp. 2767-2814; general bibliography, pp. 2721-66; chronology, pp. 2634-2720; black-and-white photographs throughout.

□ *Critique* This massive DICTIONARY of Methodists worldwide offers chiefly a WHO'S WHO and gazetteer. Signed articles (with bibliography) canvass thousands of personalities as well as cities and some events. Entries favor the United States. Historians will find the compilation exhaustive, but articles do not elucidate social context so graphically as those in **124** *The Brethren Encyclopedia* (1983).

□ *Summary* A detailed WHO'S WHO and forty-page bibliography may overwhelm any but the most dedicated researcher.

123 (1983) *The Brethren Encyclopedia,* 3 vols. (Philadelphia and Oak Brook, Ill.: The Brethren Encyclopedia, 1983); 2126 pages; no index; general bibliography, pp. 1857-2111; many black-and-white photographs.

□ *Critique* This ENCYCLOPEDIA chronicles the spread and splintering of the "Dunkers," or Church of the Brethren, from their founding in Schwarzenau, Hesse, in 1708. From 1719 these pietistic Baptists multiplied in North America. This lovingly prepared ENCYCLOPEDIA encompasses persons, places, sects and practices worldwide, but above all in North America. A "List of Ordained Ministers and Elders" fills nearly three hundred pages (3:1539-823), and the general bibliography runs half that long (3:1857-2111). By dint of modesty and thoroughness, this ENCYCLOPEDIA of self-definition conveys denominational identity. Few reference works are so authentic to their communities.

□ *Summary* Local and family history fill this ENCYCLOPEDIA of self-presentation. Social historians will esteem a plethora of Americana.

124 (1992) Donald F. McKim with

David F. Wright, eds., *Encyclopedia of the Reformed Faith* (Louisville: Westminster/John Knox; Edinburgh: Saint Andrew, 1992); xxiv & 414 pages; no index; no general bibliography.

□ *Critique* This historical LEXICON rethinks the Reformed tradition worldwide. Careful planning makes this a model of REVISIONIST self-definition. Historical synopses of topics like "Calvinism," "Presbyterianism in America" and "Orthodoxy, Reformed" integrate swaths of information. Peter Toon's article on "Christology" is among the most trenchant on this topic in any DICTIONARY. Synopses of "Creeds and Confessions," "Dialectical Theology" and "Preaching, History of" situate the Reformed tradition within two thousand years of Christianity, but biblical scholarship is ignored. Articles on concepts like "Atonement," "Humanity," "Justification" and "Lord's Supper" tackle issues that sometimes disquiet the liturgically inclined. Surprisingly, however, world religions, social sciences and fundamentalism are largely overlooked. Regional surveys encompass "Africa" and "Australasia" but not "Asia." Whereas other volumes in the Westminster/SCM format recruit contributors ecumenically, this one draws two hundred authorities overwhelmingly from one confession. Vigor and originality make this a model of how a denomination can define itself through a reference work. Nowhere does analysis succumb to apologetics. An obvious companion is **149** Cameron, ed., *Dictionary of Scottish Church History and Theology* (1993), which supplies more detail but less eloquence. Four times longer, **125** Gisel, ed., *Encyclopédie du protestantisme* (1995) favors culture and Europe above theology and North America.

□ *Summary* By rethinking history, this fastidious LEXICON reshapes a denomination's self-understanding.

125 (1995) Pierre Gisel, ed., *Encyclopédie du protestantisme* (Paris: Cerf and Geneva: Labor et Fides, 1995); 1700 pages; no index; no general bibliography; 1500 black-and-white illustrations.

□ *Critique* This boldly REVISIONIST LEXI-

CON reconfigures European Protestantism from innumerable perspectives. Edited at the University of Lausanne, it recruited three hundred (mostly French and Swiss) authorities to write more than fourteen hundred signed articles, each with multilingual bibliography (particularly in German). Apart from forty-four "Dossiers," the articles constitute a GLOSSARY of Protestant history (above all in Europe) and a WHO'S WHO of Protestant luminaries in art, literature, science, film and politics. This is one of the sprightliest WHO'S WHOS anywhere. Without being presentist, this historical LEXICON ponders contemporary issues. REVISIONISM pervades forty-four "Dossiers" on concepts like "Bioethics," "Culture," "Ecology," "Europe," "Modernity," "Religion and Religions" and "Utopia" but not secularization or death of God. No other LEXICON on a sprawling tradition so provokes rethinking, not even 77 McGrath, ed., *The Blackwell Encyclopedia of Modern Christian Thought* (1993). A French and Swiss masterpiece revolutionizes Protestant self-definition.

□ *Summary* This REVISIONIST LEXICON reappraises European Protestantism with vigor and candor. Forty-four dossiers challenge assumptions from the past five hundred years.

2.9.2 ROMAN CATHOLICISM

2.9.2.1 LEXICONS AND COMPENDIA

OVERVIEW: THE TRIUMPH OF FRENCH ERUDITION Reference works by and for Catholics come in all formats and on virtually all topics. Ranging from a MEGA-ENCYCLOPEDIA like 137 Jacquemet, ed., *Catholicisme: hier—aujourd'hui—demain* (1948-) to specialized works on theology, liturgy and hagiography, Catholic reference works crop up throughout the directory. This section features general works on Roman Catholicism, its history and present outlook. Although written by and primarily for Catholics, these works go far beyond confessional self-definition. In contrast to pre-

Vatican II works, postmodern Catholic discourse tends to straddle a divide between the normative and the descriptive, as becomes evident in a new standard work, 131 McBrien, ed., The HarperCollins Encyclopedia of Catholicism (1995). Even more imaginatively than Americans, European Catholics welcome postmodernism. This predilection is apparent in REVISIONIST LEXICONS analyzed under 2.2 "Ecumenism," 2.5 "Spirituality" and 2.7 "Liturgy." In France and Italy the "blurring of genres" has inaugurated among Catholics new disciplines like 48 "fundamental theology," 110 "meta-liturgics" and 91 spirituality as a basis for cultural diagnosis. Each of these disciplines has inspired its LEXICON. Interestingly, an older general encyclopedia, William J. McDonald, ed., The New Catholic Encyclopedia, 15 vols. (New York: McGraw-Hill, 1967) has found no successor in a Western language. On pre-1988 works see James Patrick McCabe, O.S.F.S., Critical Guide to Catholic Reference Books, 3d ed. (Littleton, Colo.: Libraries Unlimited, 1989).

See 2.4.3 "Theology: Roman Catholic," 2.5 "Spirituality," 2.6 "Hagiography," 2.7 "Liturgy."

LIST OF WORKS ANALYZED

137 ([1941] 1948-) G. Jacquemet, ed., *Catholicisme: Hier—aujourd'hui—demain* (Paris: Letouzey et Ané, 1948-). Analyzed under 2.9.2.2 "Churches and Denominations: French Mega-Encyclopedias."

126 (1979-80) Gabriel Le Bras, ed., *Les Ordres religieux: La Vie et l'art*, 2 vols. (Paris: Flammarion, 1979)

127 (1989, 1993) Michel Dubost, ed., *Théo: Nouvelle encyclopédie catholique* (Paris: Droguet-Ardant/Fayard, 1989; 2d ed., rev., 1993)

128 (1993-) Walter Kasper, ed., *Lexikon für Theologie und Kirche*, 3d ed. (Freiburg: Herder, 1993-)

129 (1993) Gaston Duchet-Suchaux and Monique Duchet-Suchaux, *Les Ordres religieux: Guide historique* (Paris: Flammarion, 1993)

130 (1994) Michael Glazier and

Monika Hellwig, eds., The Modern Catholic Encyclopedia (Collegeville, Minn.: Michael Glazier/ Liturgical, 1994)

150 (1994) Philippe Levillain, ed., *Dictionnaire historique de la papauté* (Paris: Fayard, 1994). Analyzed under 2.10.1 "Periods of Church History: Surveys of the Papacy and National Churches."

131 (1995) Richard P. McBrien, ed., *The HarperCollins Encyclopedia of Catholicism* (San Francisco: Harper; London: HarperCollins, 1995)

ANALYSIS OF WORKS

126 (1979-80) Gabriel Le Bras, ed., *Les Ordres religieux: La Vie et l'art: 1. Les Ordres contemplatifs* (Paris: Flammarion, 1979); ***2. Les Ordres actifs*** (Paris: Flammarion, 1980); 736 and 789 pages; no index; no bibliography; 1427 photographs in vol. 1, about 1500 in vol. 2, half of them in color; "Dictionnaire des instituts religieux," 2:737-82; indexes of illustrations (by persons and places), 1:728-35, 2:783-89.

□ *Critique* This sumptuous COMPENDIUM assembles a historical and visual record of eleven contemplative orders in volume 1 and of seven active ones in volume 2. A member of the order recounts its history in nearly every case. In volume 1 Dom Jacques Hourlier narrates the history of the Benedictines with 536 illustrations, Dom Maur Cocheril treats the Cistercians with 404, Gabriel Le Bras the Carthusians with 200 and Dom Cocheril eight military orders with 150, including Templars, Teutonic Knights, Knights of Saint John and five others. In volume 2 Augustinian canons, Carmelites, Franciscans, Dominicans and Jesuits fill nine-tenths of the text. A "Dictionary of Male and Female Religious Institutes" (2:737-82) itemizes over two thousand religious bodies. The writing ranges from workmanlike to vivacious. Thanks to picture editing by Paul and Madeleine Hartmann, no other work matches carefully captioned photographs of buildings, frescoes and manuscript illuminations. Averaging two photographs per page, European Catholic orders blossom in visual profusion beyond compare. **130**

Duchet-Suchaux and Duchet-Suchaux, *Les Ordres religieux: Guide historique* (1993) covers the same ground at one-eighth the length and supplies bibliographies, but it shimmers less.

□ *Summary* This spacious COMPENDIUM illustrates more than 3,000 buildings and art objects belonging to eighteen Catholic orders worldwide. It flatters the eye.

127 (1989, 1993) Michel Dubost, ed., *Théo: Nouvelle encyclopédie catholique* (Paris: Droguet-Ardant/Fayard, 1989); 1235 pages; index, pp. 1161-1235; general bibliography, pp. 1138-40; hundreds of black-and-white photos and diagrams in the text. Second edition published as *Théo: L'Encyclopédie catholique pour tous* (Paris: Droguet & Ardant/Fayard, 1993); 1327 pages. Analyzed on the basis of the 1989 edition.

□ *Scope* This sprightly REALLEXIKON and anthology delivers thousands of unsigned articles on all aspects of Catholic faith and tradition. Although apologetics intrudes now and then, factuality predominates. Bundling several reference books into one, *Théo* purveys no fewer than three WHO'S WHOS: of saints (pp. 45-124) and contemporary witnesses (pp. 125-33), of major thinkers (pp. 627-34), and of French Catholic writers (pp. 647-56). In addition, the volume delivers a history of Christianity (pp. 207-515); it outlines Catholic teaching on ethics (pp. 773-831), society (pp. 843-86) and liturgy (pp. 906-86); and it explicates church institutions (pp. 987-1137). Interspersed come prayers, poems and sermon extracts, while charts, chronologies and maps illustrate more than a hundred topics. Bibliographies are few (pp. 133, 513, 684-85, 1138-40), but their paucity is compensated by listing addresses in France of parishes, pilgrimages and retreat houses (pp. 1111-37). An index of seventy-five pages cites every mention of every topic.

□ *Strengths* This ingenious INTRODUCTION in the guise of a REALLEXIKON interweaves apologetics with history. Named in abbreviation of "Théophile" (i.e., "Lover of God"), *Théo* situates French Catholicism within the universal church. A three-hundred page history of Christianity comprises a book in itself, bursting with profiles, chronologies, maps and quotations (pp. 207-515). Coverage from 1789 to 1985 is stunning (pp. 420-513). A WHO'S WHO of saints favors French ones (pp. 45-124), reporting, for example, that Bernadette of Lourdes is the earliest saint of whom a photograph has survived (from 1862). Comparison among Catholic, Protestant and Orthodox beliefs is scrupulous (pp. 152-64). Reportage on demography of religions in the world and in France overflows with data (pp. 165-201). A conspectus of Catholic spiritualities glows (pp. 728-72), and moral theology elicits pastoral advice (pp. 773-832). Eschatology calls forth quotations (pp. 886-97), while Mariology encourages apologetics (pp. 898-904). Presentation of liturgics achieves utmost precision (pp. 905-86). By drawing a reader inside beliefs, practices and operations, this REALLEXIKON renders the church hospitable.

□ *Weaknesses* The "Plan of the Work" (pp. 1147-54) is so convoluted as to leave one bewildered. Moreover, the volume's second half on the church as "people of the Covenant" lacks the lucidity of the first half. Surprisingly, the concept of "fundamental theology" has not supplanted that of traditional apologetics. Oddly, canon law scarcely features. Since only the WHO'S WHOS get alphabetized, too frequently one must turn to the index. A page layout boasting as many as five inserts per page makes *Théo* seem like a deluxe periodical rather than a reference book. The print can be tiny.

□ *Competitors* As a volume of Catholic self-definition, *Théo* addresses a wide public: families as well as libraries, parishes as well as scholars. Standing in a tradition inaugurated by the publishing house of Larousse, such "encylopedism for everyone" affirms that everything worth knowing fits into a REALLEXIKON. Naturally, the approach excludes REVISIONISM. A less learned equivalent in English might be Peter M. J. Stravinskas, ed., *Our Sunday Visitor's Catholic Encyclopedia* (Huntington, Ind., 1991), which purveys perhaps one-fifth as much information in DICTIONARY format and supplies no quotations or chronologies. An American DICTIONARY of denominational self-definition, **124** McKim, ed., *Encyclopedia of the Reformed Faith* (1992), lacks a sprightly format but rethinks its tradition more astutely. Among Jewish works of self-definition, Rabbi Telushkin's *Jewish Literacy* (1991) enlivens an equally wide spectrum of history, doctrine and lore. But what other reference book boasts such a varied page layout as *Théo*?

□ *Summary* Unabashed in Francocentricity and vivacious alike in scope, layout and argument, this REALLEXIKON rewards browsing to an uncommon degree. Three or four books wrapped into one, *Théo* squeezes useful information into a convoluted structure.

128 (1993-) Walter Kasper, ed., *Lexikon für Theologie und Kirche*, 3d ed. (Freiburg: Herder, 1993-); planned in 10 vols., 7000 pages; a very few maps; approximately 700 pages per volume; abundant cross-references. The first edition was published in 10 vols. (1930-38); a second edition in 11 vols. (1957-65); 3 vols. on Vatican II appeared in 1966-68. Analyzed on the basis of vol. 1 (1993) and vol. 2 (1994) through "Damador."

□ *Scope* This large-scale LEXIKON on all matters of interest to Christians has been planned to appeal to readers of every camp. Signed articles, invariably with multilingual bibliography, encompass persons, doctrines, concepts, academic disciplines, artistic styles, nations, peoples and Catholic organizations. Some entries contain as few as four lines, while others run ten pages. Longer articles subdivide in up to ten subsections, each written by a leading authority offering a distinct viewpoint and bibliography. "Apologetics," for example, boasts six subsections: concept, biblical, historical, systematic, Protestant, applied theology. Articles on methods of biblical scholarship total thirty-seven pages. A doctrinal article may cross-reference up to thirty or forty thinkers, most of whom will appear in future volumes. Hundreds of contributors achieve a style that is lucid and succinct. Throughout, discipline in length, acumen and ecumenism dispels MENIPPEAN extravagance.

□ *Strengths* As the most up-to-date LEXICON on Christianity now in progress, the *Lexikon für Theologie und Kirche* never ceases to astonish. Bibliographies are incomparable, accompanying even the minutest entry, and should be consulted by every researcher. Ecumenism predominates: all Christian denominations command detailed articles, including, for example, eight subsections on Anglicanism by four authors. Eastern churches get covered in depth, as does the early church. Heresies are probed at length, as in four pages on "Arianism." Every nation of the world elicits an article on its government and Christian activity. Likewise, every order of the Catholic Church receives meticulous analysis, as does every dogma (e.g., "Assumption of the Virgin"). So do contemporary topics like "Base Community." Every pope and every Catholic diocese wins an entry. Any thinker gets compared with numerous others, and articles on literary genres such as "Apology" list exemplars (with cross-references). Unlike French or Italian competitors, the *Lexikon* eschews confessional assertiveness. Incisiveness, clarity and erudition prevail.

□ *Weaknesses* World religions get scanted. As is common in German theological reference works, there are no illustrations and almost no maps (except four pages of black-and-white maps of Africa in volume 1 and of Brazil in volume 2. Minor saints are ignored. Emulating earlier editions, the *Lexikon* avoids Catholic self-proclamation in favor of ecumenical self-effacement. This stance may disappoint some.

□ *Competitors* Numerous merits make this the most useful of Catholic, indeed of Christian, MEGA-LEXICONS. Bibliographies are beyond praise, choice and length of entries is rigorous, and diversity of voices unique. Among current works, **45** Fahlbusch et al., eds., *Evangelisches Kirchenlexikon* (1986-) deploys a similar format but omits persons in order to stress concepts and places as well as world religions. The two works fit together. **31**

Müller, ed., *Theologische Realenzyklopädie* (1976-) covers fewer topics in a depth that exceeds most needs. Among older works, the unfinished **126** Davis, ed., *Catholic Dictionary of Theology* (1962-71) remains unexcelled for limpidity; its entries can be updated from this *Lexikon*. Unfortunately, the *Lexikon* features fewer English-speaking persons than does McDonald, ed., *The New Catholic Encyclopedia*, 15 vols. (1967), but the latter is a general ENCYCLOPEDIA, not a religious one. A Protestant masterpiece, Galling, ed., *Die Religion in Geschichte und Gegenwart*, 3d ed., 7 vols. (1956-63) delivers similar breadth and depth (notably on world religions), but its theology has aged. No competitor on Christianity matches the *Lexikon für Theologie und Kirche* at combining balance, acuity and thoroughness in both text and bibliographies.

□ *Summary* This finest of contemporary Christian LEXICONS astonishes through rigorous planning, divergent voices and fastidious bibliographies. More information, more cross-references and more citations are dispensed than in perhaps any other religious reference work recently begun. Readers with no German will welcome the bibliographies.

129 (1993) Gaston Duchet-Suchaux and Monique Duchet-Suchaux, *Les Ordres religieux: Guide historique* (Paris: Flammarion, 1993); 320 pages; index, pp. 309-14; general bibliography, pp. 305-8; 290 black-and-white photos; 32 color plates.

□ *Critique* This DICTIONARY of European and especially French religious orders, both active and contemplative, coordinates historical sketches with fundamentals of iconography. Founders (e.g., Bruno, Mother Teresa), scholars (e.g., John of the Cross, Mabillon), orders (e.g., Carmelites, Cluny), customs (e.g., cloister, vows) and European monasteries (e.g., Bobbio, Montserrat) elicit entries, each with bibliography. France is favored, while Eastern Christianity gets scanted except for founders like Pachomius. Most entries reach down to the present. Designed to serve art historians, this DICTIONARY compiles essentials that come together nowhere else. Cross-references abound, and illustrations hit home better than in **126** Le Bras, ed., *Les Ordres religieux: La Vie et l'art* (1979-80). This volume sweeps the horizon in a classic French manner.

□ *Summary* Emphasizing Western Europe and above all France, this DICTION-ARY orients travelers and art historians to basics of religious orders and their iconography.

130 (1994) Michael Glazier and Monika Hellwig, eds., *The Modern Catholic Encyclopedia* (Collegeville, Minn.: Michael Glazier/Liturgical; London: Gill & Macmillan, 1994); xxv & 933 pages; no index; no bibliography; 16 color plates between pp. 454 and 455; almost 200 black-and-white photographs.

□ *Critique* Designed by and for contemporary Catholics, this WHO'S WHO and GLOSSARY assigned 190 contributors (more than half of them clerics) to write on persons, practices, concepts, religious orders and English-speaking countries. A WHO'S WHO of about three hundred persons features attractive narrative. But even for a work of self-definition, most of the thousand other entries remain introductory and on theology downright banal, except for a few like George Tavard's on "Eastern Churches." Overviews treat nineteen "Ecumenical Councils," describe all "Sacraments," and narrate history of the "Reformation" (pp. 722-30). Favoring Americans, liturgical reformers and the twentieth century, articles in the WHO'S WHO are lively. They vary in length from one-fourth column on Josef Jungmann to four pages on John XXIII. Happily, accounts of figures as diverse as Thérèse of Lisieux, Teilhard de Chardin and Hans Urs von Balthasar narrate details omitted elsewhere. The writing, however, is plain, and lack of bibliography frustrates. Except for a winsome WHO'S WHO and convenient overviews, most readers will want to move on to **131** McBrien, ed., *The HarperCollins Encyclopedia of Catholicism* (1995).

□ *Summary* This WHO'S WHO and GLOS-SARY suits the Catholic home, but scholars will desire something more ambitious.

131 (1995) Richard P. McBrien, ed., *The HarperCollins Encyclopedia of Catholicism* (San Francisco: Harper; London: HarperCollins, 1995); xxxviii & 1349 pages; no index; no general bibliography; time line, pp. xxviii-xxxviii; 16 color plates; 300 black-and-white photographs, drawings and maps.

□ *Scope* Six years in preparation, this historical DICTIONARY recruited 280 overwhelmingly American contributors to write no fewer than forty-two hundred entries on all aspects of Roman Catholicism. The seventeen associate editors hail now or formerly from the University of Notre Dame, and twelve still teach theology there. Functioning as a GLOSSARY, more than half the entries vary from just five to twenty-five lines and lack bibliography. Only longer articles are signed, and not many of them carry bibliography. Designed to articulate self-definition, twenty-nine "feature articles" of three to twelve pages tackle major saints (Aquinas, Augustine, Peter), the sacraments and theological issues like "God," "Grace" and "Holy Spirit." Some address general topics like "Catholic Church," "The Papacy" and "Women in the Church." In a WHO'S WHO that canvasses perhaps two thousand names, entries average just five to twenty lines. At least one hundred countries, sites of all councils and a very few cities (e.g., Canterbury, Constantinople, Rome) elicit entries. Amid writing that is factual and succinct, some of the twenty-nine "feature articles" fail to specify how normative is the authority they claim.

□ *Strengths* Crafted for the widest possible scholarly audience, this one-volume DIC-TIONARY will quickly become standard. Historical syntheses number in the dozens: a sequence on "Catholicism and . . ." (pp. 258-78) embraces in succession "Architecture," "Culture," "Education," "Journalism," "Massmedia," "Music," "Psychology" and "the Visual Arts." Synopses of "Catholic Social Teachings," "Canon Law," "Ecumenical Councils" and "Liturgical Calendar" are marvels of precision, as are lists of patron saints, popes and committees of the Roman curia. Statistical tables enrich entries on "Catholic colleges and universities" and "Catholics." Uniate churches get differentiated to a nicety, while Robert F. Taft assesses "Uniatism" tactfully. Totaling about two thousand names, the WHO'S WHO encompasses popes and antipopes, many saints, prelates, authors and scholars (including Nietzsche). It shows only slight predilection for Americans, but the living persons are selected rather arbitrarily. Unfortunately, many biographical entries are too brief, particularly on popes and saints. Liturgy, social issues and theology win comprehensive coverage. In a unique feature, phrases in Latin and Greek carry guides to pronunciation. At last, scholars have an English-language DICTIONARY of Roman Catholicism that they can savor.

□ *Weaknesses* Such all-inclusiveness makes omissions more painful. There is too little on canon law, history of missions and Asia. In all but a few articles lack of bibliography sends one scurrying. Only Judaism and Islam, of other religions, command the degree of attention that goes to half a dozen Protestant churches. A difficulty arises in trying to discern whether the twenty-nine feature articles (almost one-third of them by women) are delivering normative teaching or are airing dissent. Elizabeth A. Johnson on "Blessed Virgin Mary" upholds the nonprescriptive and Michael G. Lawler on "Marriage" the normative, with many gradations in between. In shorter articles, George H. Tavard on "Anglican Ordination" waxes optimistic about convergence of views, while Charles Curran worries about "Academic Freedom" in Catholic higher education. Being on the whole neither REVISIONIST nor normative, this work occupies an uneasy middle ground, thereby mirroring the church it depicts.

□ *Competitors* Long needed, this volume ranks as the meatiest DICTIONARY in English on Roman Catholicism. Only certain of the "feature articles" purvey self-definition. In contrast, while addressing primarily Catholics, **130** Glazier and Hellwig, eds., *The Modern Catholic Encyclopedia* (1994) furnishes fewer but longer entries,

albeit without bibliography. Specialized LEXICONS like **112** Fink, ed., *The New Dictionary of Sacramental Worship* (1990) or **86** Dwyer, ed., *The New Dictionary of Catholic Social Thought* (1994) debate more vigorously. On Catholic topics *The HarperCollins Encyclopedia of Catholicism* rivals and sometimes surpasses **29** Cross, ed., *The Oxford Dictionary of the Christian Church* (1957, 1974), but the latter is one-third longer (particularly on popes and saints), eschews the normative and furnishes vastly more bibliography. A French parallel is **127** *Théo: Nouvelle encyclopédie catholique* (1989, 1993), which stresses self-definition and is confusingly arranged. A French masterpiece, **150** Levillain, ed., *Dictionnaire historique de la papauté* (1994) remains rigorously nonconfessional and more learned than any of these. Nonetheless, *The HarperCollins Encyclopedia of Catholicism* furnishes the best starting point in English for almost any query about the Roman Catholic Church.

□ *Summary* This historical DICTIONARY deftly encompasses Roman Catholicism past and present. Every scholar of Christianity should own it.

2.9.2.2 FRENCH MEGA-ENCYCLOPEDIAS

OVERVIEW: THE ULTIMATE IN DEPTH AND BREADTH These eight MEGA-ENCYCLOPEDIAS stand alone for trenchancy, comprehensiveness and serendipity. Few other publishing ventures unleash so many surprises. Printed two columns to the page, more than 130 volumes of approximately eight hundred quarto pages each furnish signed articles with massive multilingual bibliographies. Five of the eight series stand completed, four of them having required about half a century each; one is about three-quarters complete **49**; another has reached the entry "Inde" after more than ninety years (**134**); and an eighth stands on the verge of completion (**137**). Indexes have appeared for **133** and part of **134**.

Whether viewed singly or collectively, the French MEGA-ENCYCLOPEDIAS inspire

awe. Inaugurated by biblical scholar Fulcran Vigouroux with the *Dictionnaire de
la Bible* (1891-1912), seven of the eight
works have been published by Letouzey et
Ané of Paris to make up what they call an
"Encyclopédie des sciences ecclésiastiques." In addition, Letouzey published
in a smaller format a martyrology, **97**
Baudot and Chaussin, *Vies des saints et des
bienheureux,* 13 vols. (1935-59). Until the
1970s most contributors were priests or
religious, above all Benedictines. A passion
to fashion coherence out of heterogeneity
makes Benedictines avid encyclopedists.
Whether originating before or after Vatican
II, the scholarship is rigorous, often overwhelming, and consistently irenic. Articles
in volumes up to about 1938 boast unprecedented length, many running beyond
one hundred pages. For this reason authors
seldom if ever indulged in the frantic pedantry of MENIPPEAN SATIRE, for even the
most obsessed disposed of space enough to
do justice to any topic. Quotations in
Latin, Greek and Hebrew abound. Persons
are referenced in six of the works (**132,
133, 134, 49, 87,** and **137**) so that on
major and minor figures all six can be
consulted with profit.

Altogether more than 130 volumes (totaling about 105,000 quarto pages) have
been published, building up a veritable wall
of books. On the history of places, persons
and doctrines (particularly concerning
France) they will never be superseded, even
though the pre-1968 volumes ignore social and political issues that Vatican II
raised. Even **31** Müller, ed., *Theologische
Realenzyklopädie* (1976-), with twenty-
four volumes and eighteen thousand medium-sized pages to 1994, is dwarfed by
comparison. The chief rival in brilliance
remains **151** Klauser, ed., *Reallexikon für
Antike und Christentum* (1950-), where
German rigor takes the palm for interweaving classical antiquity with early Christianity. Together with **257** Ranke, ed.,
Enzyklopädie des Märchens (1977-), it is the
only MEGA-ENCYCLOPEDIA that makes
these Catholic ones seem parochial. An
entry "Dictionnaire" delineates them in
137 Jacquemet, ed., *Catholicisme,* 3

(1952): 742-44.

A cross section of the series to date
appeared as **135** J[oseph] Bricout, ed.,
*Dictionnaire pratique des connaissances
religieuses,* 6 vols. (Paris, 1925-28). A
second cross section began as **137** G.
Jacquemet, ed., *Catholicisme: hier—aujourd'hui—demain,* 13 vols. to date
(1948-). Since its restructuring with volume 7 (1975), the latter work has infused
up-to-date scholarship with ecumenism.
Browsers who wish to sample French
MEGA-ENCYCLOPEDIAS should start with
the latter's post-1975 volumes. They
constitute one of the distinguished publishing ventures of our time.

LIST OF WORKS ANALYZED

**132 (1903-53) Fernand Cabrol,
O.S.B. and Henri Leclercq, O.S.B.,
eds.,** *Dictionnaire d'archéologie chrétienne et de liturgie,* 30 vols. in 15 (Paris:
Letouzey & Ané, 1903-53)

**133 (1909-72) A[lfred] Vacant,
E[ugène] Mangenot and É[mile]
Amann, eds.,** *Dictionnaire de théologie
catholique,* 30 vols. in 15 (Paris: Letouzey
& Ané, 1909-50)

**134 (1912-) Alfred Baudrillart and
R[oger] Aubert, ed.,** *Dictionnaire d'his-
toire et de géographie ecclésiastiques* (Paris:
Letouzey & Ané, 1912-)

**135 (1925-28) J[oseph] Bricout,
ed.,** *Dictionnaire pratique des connaissances religieuses,* 6 vols. (Paris: Letouzey
et Ané, 1925-28)

49 (1928-) Louis Pirot, ed., *Dictionnaire de la Bible: Supplément* (Paris: Letouzey et Ané, 1928-). Analyzed further
under 2.3.1 "Biblical Studies: Bible Dictionaries."

**88 ([1932] 1937-94) Marcel Viller,
S.J., ed.,** *Dictionnaire de spiritualité,
ascétique et mystique,* 20 vols. in 16 (Paris:
Beauchesne, [1932] 1937-94). Analyzed
under 2.5 "Spirituality."

136 (1935-65) R[aoul] Naz, ed.,
*Dictionnaire de droit canonique, conten-
ant tous les termes du droit canonique,* 7
vols. (Paris: Letouzey & Ané, 1935-65)

**137 ([1941] 1948-) G. Jacquemet,
G. Mathon and Gérard-Henry Baudry,**

eds., *Catholicisme: Hier—aujourd'hui—demain,* planned in about 15 vols. (Paris: Letouzey et Ané, [1941] 1948-)

ANALYSIS OF WORKS

132 (1903-53) Fernand Cabrol, O.S.B. [1855-1937, founding editor] and Henri Leclercq, O.S.B. [1869-1945], eds., *Dictionnaire d'archéologie chrétienne et de liturgie,* 30 vols. in 15 (Paris: Letouzey & Ané, 1903-53); about 23,000 pages; many plates and drawings. The scope is outlined in F. Cabrol, "Préface," 1 (1903): i-xix.

□ *Critique* This MEGA-ENCYCLOPEDIA of liturgy and Christian antiquities concentrates on places (cities and regions, particularly French and Italian), rites (and their languages), music (especially chant), architecture (building types), artistic genres (e.g., "Graffites"), church fathers (e.g., Gregory Nazianzen, Gregory of Tours) and French antiquarians (e.g., Mabillon). Eastern Christianity elicits full coverage, but most saints do not. Working in the British Museum from 1913 on, Dom Henri Leclercq wrote more than half the entries, including one on "Mahomet" (10.1 [1931]: 1133-94) and one of 150 pages on Mabillon (10.1:427-724). Leclercq's hundred-page survey of "Historians of Christianity" (6 [1925]: 2533-735) is not to be missed. Domiciled in London, this French cleric wrote nearly every entry in the final volumes, including virtually all of volume 15.2 (1953) from "Smyrne" to "Zraia." Fifty-five pages there on the city of Tours show that the master's powers had not failed. Totaling at least ten thousand pages, Dom Leclercq's entries may well constitute the largest outpouring by an encyclopedist in the twentieth century. A one-man team, Dom Leclercq is the Pierre Larousse of Roman Catholicism. His like will not be seen again.

□ *Summary* Students of liturgy and Christian art will relish this treasure trove. It is leisurely beyond compare.

133 (1909-72) A[lfred] Vacant [1852-1901, founding editor], E[ugène] Mangenot [1856-1922], then É[mile] Amann [1880-1948], eds., *Dictionnaire de théologie catholique,* 30 vols. in 15 (Paris: Letouzey & Ané, 1909-50); about 20,000 pages; with maps; index published as *Tables générales,* 3 vols. (1953-72).

□ *Critique* This MEGA-ENCYCLOPEDIA of Catholic thought and history investigates thinkers, concepts, religious orders, councils and countries. Averaging fourteen hundred pages each, its fifteen volumes incorporate (1) a WHO'S WHO of theologians and saints, (2) a DICTIONARY of theological concepts, (3) a REALLEXIKON of church history arranged by country in both Eastern and Western Europe and (4) a history of religious orders. French saints and bishops are described exhaustively. Many articles and their bibliographies are among the most learned ever published. Each section is subdivided into titled subsections that abound in Greek and Latin quotations and examine dozens of thinkers. Twenty-three pages on "Gloire" (6:1386-432), for example, cover (1) "Glory of God," (2) "Glory of the Elect" and (3) "Human Glory." Yves Congar's article "Theology" (volume 15.1 [1939]: 341-502) was translated as *A History of Theology* (Garden City, N.Y.: Doubleday, 1968). Working in Strasbourg, Émile Amann completed many of the later entries. Because Vatican II so enlarged the scope of Catholic theology, this masterwork became dated more quickly than other MEGA-ENCYCLOPEDIAS. It does not treat such contemporary topics as family, women's issues or work. A magnificent index enhances utility.

□ *Summary* Historians of Christian thought still rely on this most detailed of theological reference works.

134 (1912-) Alfred Baudrillart [1859-1942, founding editor] and R[oger] Aubert, ed. [since 1960], *Dictionnaire d'histoire et de géographie ecclésiastiques* (Paris: Letouzey & Ané, 1912-); about 18,000 pages to date; fascicule 147 of volume 25 (1995) goes to "Inde"; index published in 1937.

□ *Critique* This most massive of REALLEXIKONS covers persons and places (i.e., countries, regions and cities) of all periods worldwide. Since Roger Aubert took over as editor with volume 14 (1960), the pace has gradually increased to yield a volume every two years. Volume 17 appeared in 1971, volume 19 in 1981 and volume 24 in 1993. All Catholic dioceses command an entry. Favoring saints and prelates, the WHO'S WHO encompasses Catholic and Eastern Christian leaders of all regions and periods. Volume 15, for example, contains eighty-two entries on "Étienne," volume 20 contains eighty-four on "Georges" and volume 23 includes 208 on "Henri." Religious orders elicit detailed treatment; volume 18, for example, furnishes sixty-nine entries on "Frères." There are none, however, on concepts, councils or history of thought. Volume 18 (1977) unfurls magnificent coverage of France across 544 columns, including an alphabetical WHO'S WHO of 3,207 French bishops (18:161-532). Robert F. McNamara's twenty pages on the United States in volume 15 (1963) climax with four columns of bibliography. Any scholar of urban history, Christian biography or church administration will feast on this REALLEXIKON.

□ *Summary* Not yet half complete, this most imposing of MEGA-ENCYCLOPEDIAS gets better and better. No more thorough coverage of Christian places and persons exists.

135 (1925-28) J[oseph] Bricout [1867-1930], ed., *Dictionnaire pratique des connaissances religieuses,* 6 vols. (Paris: Letouzey et Ané, 1925-28); about 3700 pages; index, 6:985-1242. A supplement of 600 pages (edited by G. Jacquemet) incorporating five annual updatings appeared in 1933.

□ *Critique* This abbreviated MEGA-ENCYCLOPEDIA offers a cross section of the others. Printed in a slightly smaller format, it canvassed Roman Catholic lore, particularly concerning France, during the 1920s. Intended as a kind of "Encyclopédie Larousse" for lay Catholics, it emphasized not only liturgy and church history but also French literature, Christian art and contemporary social questions. Articles on world religions exude attitudes of the 1920s.

□ *Summary* Few other works evoke French Catholicism of the interwar years so compellingly.

49 (1928-) Louis Pirot [1881-1939], ed., *Dictionnaire de la Bible: Supplément* (Paris: Letouzey et Ané, 1928-); 12 vols. published to 1994 (through "Sexualité"); about 7000 pages to date. Analyzed further under 2.3.1 "Biblical Studies: Bible Dictionaries."

□ *Critique* This largest of BIBLE ENCYCLOPEDIAS encompasses far more than that label implies. It examines the history of the early church to about 200 C.E., it scrutinizes scholars of the Bible, and it discusses theology as well as life in biblical times. An article on Ernest Renan runs thirty-five pages (10:277-344), while 150 pages on the "Samaritans" (12:740-1047) remain unmatched. Too few American libraries own this masterpiece, which is not supplanted by **60** Freedman, ed., *The Anchor Bible Dictionary* (1992). The work that this one "supplements" is Fulcran Vigouroux, ed., *Dictionnaire de la Bible,* 5 vols. (Paris, 1891-1912) in 5600 pages; 2d ed. (Paris, 1926-28). It pioneered the French MEGA-ENCYCLOPEDIAS.

□ *Summary* This ultimate in BIBLE ENCYCLOPEDIAS keeps improving.

88 ([1932] 1937-94) Marcel Viller, S.J. [founding editor; many successors], *Dictionnaire de spiritualité, ascétique et mystique,* 20 vols. in 16 (Paris: Beauchesne, [1932] 1937-94). The first fascicules appeared in 1932, but vol. 1 is dated 1937 and vol. 2 1953. About 16,000 pages. Analyzed under 2.5 "Spirituality."

136 (1935-65) R[aoul] Naz, ed., *Dictionnaire de droit canonique, contenant tous les termes du droit canonique,* 7 vols. (Paris: Letouzey & Ané, 1935-65); about 6000 pages; no index; no general bibliography.

□ *Critique* This little known MEGA-ENCYCLOPEDIA transforms understanding of a recondite field: history of canon law. Unfortunately, the enterprise got truncated after volume 4 (1949) (through "Droits") and a revised code of canon law itself appeared in February 1983.[1] Luminous exegesis abounds in *The Canon Law: Letter and Spirit: A Practical Guide to the Code of Canon Law* (London: Geoffrey Chapman, 1995). Nevertheless, articles on rules of religious orders, canon lawyers, basic concepts, and a few places (e.g., "Alexandria") make the early volumes a gold mine. No other work explores "Calendars" so elaborately (2:1195-252) or explains minutiae of Eastern Uniate practice so copiously (e.g., "Chaldéen [Droit]," 3:292-388). Totaling more than one hundred pages, articles on each of the sacraments expound developments in Eastern rites as well as Western. Articles excel on Rules of St. Benedict (2:297-349) and St. Columban (3:1005-24). Beginning with volume 5 (1953), entries become fewer if not always briefer, focusing on major concepts like "Epikie" and "Priest" and on canonists like Innocent III and Guillaume Durand. Despite the condensing, colorful reading abounds on topics such as "Epilepsy," "Heraldry," "Hermits" and "Indulgences." By no means has the historical data gone out of date, and some of the bibliographies cite titles from as early as 1600. By covering from "Pont" to "ZZ," however, volume 7 (1965) omits too much to suit a MEGA-ENCYCLOPEDIA. Written by and for canon lawyers, the *Dictionnaire de droit canonique* speaks with authority concerning matters that are more often gossiped about than explained. Useful overviews of canon law unfold in **150** Levillain, ed., *Dictionnaire historique de la papauté* (1994), pages 398-408, 544-48, 583-93, 1616-20. An up-to-date GLOSSARY of concepts and canonists is Jean Werckmeister, *Petit Dictionnaire de droit canonique* (Paris: Cerf, 1993). Neither of these, however, matches the *Dictionnaire de droit canonique* in fastidiousness.

□ *Summary* The first six volumes make this one of the most beguiling of MEGA-ENCYCLOPEDIAS. Hardly ever overlapping with articles elsewhere, those on canonists,

Eastern rites and ecclesiastical oddities have no peer.

137 ([1941] 1948-) G. Jacquemet and [since 1972] G. Mathon and Gérard-Henry Baudry, eds., *Catholicisme: Hier—aujourd'hui—demain*, planned in about 15 vols. (Paris: Letouzey et Ané, [1941] 1948-); about 8800 pages through vol. 14, fasc. 2 (1995) (up to "Structure").

□ *Critique* Planned in the early 1940s as a seven-volume successor to **136** Bricout, ed., *Dictionnaire pratique des connaissances religieuses* (1925-28), whose annual supplements Jacquemet had edited between 1929 and 1933, this treasury of historical research broadened its scope after volume 6 (1967 through "Latran"). The original conception owed something as well to an imaginative but abortive enterprise, Jacquemet, ed., *Dictionnaire de sociologie familiale, politique, économique, spirituelle, générale* (Paris: Letouzey et Ané, 1933). A team led by G. Mathon and Gérard-Henry Baudry at the Centre Interdisciplinaire des Facultés catholiques de Lille took over with volume 7 (1972-75). Coverage expanded to embrace debates not only on methodology but also on Christian doctrine, practices and French dioceses. Earlier volumes deliver penetrating analysis of Buddhism, Hinduism ("Inde," 1957), Islam and Zoroastrianism ("Iran," 1966). Since 1975 the finest French scholars have brought REVISIONIST acumen to nearly every question, not least regarding methodology, while furnishing phenomenal bibliographies. The WHO'S WHO applies sophistication to European saints, French writers (e.g., Charles Péguy), and twentieth-century scholars (e.g., Louis Massignon). After volume 8 living persons are omitted.

Highly original entries include H. Maurier's thirteen pages on "Paganism" and G. Mathon's twenty pages each on "Prostitution" and "Sexuality and Society," not to mention Mathon's fourteen pages on AIDS ("SIDA"). Articles in volume 12 (1990) on "Psychology" and "Religion and Religions" are among the most trenchant anywhere. Volume 13 (1991-

---

[1]A translation from the Latin appears as *The Code of Canon Law* (London: Collins; Grand Rapids, Mich.: Eerdmans, 1983).

93) offers Julien Ries on "The Sacred" and
L. Debarge on "Secularization" as well as
nearly one hundred pages on place-names
and persons beginning "Saint-." The
"Encyclopédie des sciences ecclésiastiques," which began inconspicuously in
1891 as a Catholic exploration of the Bible,
has flowered since Vatican II into this ecumenical masterpiece. No other work recapitulates recent debates concerning
religious history in Europe, both East and
West, so incisively. Particularly after volume 7, the bibliographies are a must. The
chief rival in up-to-dateness will soon become **128** Kasper, ed., *Lexikon für Theologie und Kirche,* 3d ed. (1993-), which
covers vastly more, albeit less copiously.
□ *Summary* This is the richest reference
work on contemporary European Catholicism. After volume 7 its REVISIONISM excites wonder.

2.9.3 EASTERN CHRISTIANITY

**OVERVIEW: LACK OF INDIGE-
NOUS REFERENCE BOOKS** The paucity of reference works written by Eastern
Christians requires explanation. Up to
1914, whether in Russia, post-Ottoman
Greece or elsewhere in the Ottoman Empire, Eastern Christians did not have to
contend with the European Enlightenment being popularized in their native languages, as did Roman Catholics and
Protestants in Britain, France and Germany from 1700 on. As a result, Eastern
Christians seldom felt challenged by secular thinkers to expound history and theology in ENCYCLOPEDIAS or other vehicles of
popularization. To this day, reference
books on Eastern Christianity remain far
fewer than those on Roman Catholicism or
Protestantism. Apart from 142 Patrinacos,
A Dictionary of Greek Orthodoxy (1982)
and **143** Atiya, ed., *The Coptic Encyclopedia* (1991), Eastern Christians writing in
Western languages have produced nothing
comparable to the Westminster/SCM DIC-
TIONARIES or to Catholic ENCYCLOPE-
DIAS. As in study of Islam, one must rely
on tools executed by Western scholars, in
this case particularly by Germans. Boast-

ing nearly one hundred pages of bibliography is a French classic: Tomáš Špidlík,
S.J., *The Spirituality of the Christian East:
A Systematic Handbook* [1978] (Kalamazoo, Mich.: Cistercian Publications,
1986). No less an authority than Jaroslav
Pelikan laments a shortage of works by
Eastern scholars (other than Russian) in
his magisterial *The Christian Tradition:
2. The Spirit of Eastern Christendom
(600-1700)* (Chicago: University of Chicago Press, 1974), p. viii. No field of
Christian history has generated so little
REVISIONISM as this one.

LIST OF WORKS ANALYZED
**137 ([1941] 1948-) G. Jacquemet,
ed.,** *Catholicisme: Hier—aujourd'hui—
demain,* planned in about 15 vols. (Paris:
Letouzey et Ané, 1948-)
**29 (1957, 1974) F. L. Cross and E.
Livingstone, eds.,** *The Oxford Dictionary
of the Christian Church* (London: Oxford
University Press, 1957; 2d ed., rev., 1974).
Analyzed under 2.1 "Christianity: General."
138 (1962-68) *Threskeutike kai
ethike enkyklopaideia* [Religious and Ethical Encyclopedia], 12 vols. (Athens: Martinos, 1962-68)
**139 (1963-) Klaus Wessel and [later]
Marcell Restle, eds.,** *Reallexikon zur
byzantinischen Kunst* (Stuttgart: Hiersemann, 1963-)
**140 (1971, 1990-93) Endre von
Ivánka, Julius Tyciak and Paul Wiertz,
eds.,** *Handbuch der Ostkirchenkunde*
(Düsseldorf: Patmos, 1971; 2d ed. in 3
vols., 1990-93)
**43 (1973-82) George Menachery,
ed.,** *The St. Thomas Christian Encyclopaedia of India,* 3 vols. announced (Trichur:
St. Thomas Christian Encyclopaedia of India, 1973-82). Analyzed further under 2.2
"Ecumenism."
**141 (1975, 1991) Julius Assfalg and
Paul Krüger,** *Kleines Wörterbuch des
christlichen Orients* (Wiesbaden: Harrassowitz, 1975); French edition available
(Turnhout: Brepols, 1991)
**152 (1983, 1992) Angelo di Ber-
ardino, ed.,** *Encyclopedia of the Early*

Church, 2 vols. (New York: Oxford University Press, 1992). Analyzed under 2.10.2 "Periods of Church History: Early Church."

142 (1984) Nicon D. Patrinacos, *A Dictionary of Greek Orthodoxy* (Pleasantville, N.Y.: Hellenic Heritage Publications, 1984)

162 (1988-) Paul D. Steeves, ed., *The Modern Encyclopedia of Religion in Russia and the Soviet Union,* planned in 25 vols. (Gulf Breeze, Fla.: Academic International, 1988-). Analyzed under 2.10.5 "Periods of Church History: Modernity."

103 (1990-92) George Poulos, *Orthodox Saints: Spiritual Profiles for Modern Man,* 2d ed., rev., 4 vols. (Brookline, Mass.: Holy Cross Orthodox Press, 1990-92). Analyzed under 2.6 "Hagiography."

143 (1991-) Aziz S. Atiya, ed., *The Coptic Encyclopedia,* 8 vols. (New York: Macmillan, 1991)

144 (1991) Alexander P. Kashdan, ed., *The Oxford Dictionary of Byzantium,* 3 vols. (New York and Oxford: Oxford University Press, 1991)

145 (1991) Donald Nicol, *A Biographical Dictionary of the Byzantine Empire* (London: Seaby, 1991)

146 (1993) Peter D. Day, *The Liturgical Dictionary of Eastern Christianity* (Collegeville, Minn.: Michael Glazier/Liturgical, 1993)

ANALYSIS OF WORKS

137 ([1941] 1948-) G. Jacquemet, ed., *Catholicisme: Hier—aujourd'hui—demain,* planned in about 15 vols. (Paris: Letouzey et Ané, [1941] 1948-). Analyzed further under 2.9.2.2 "Churches and Denominations: French Mega-encyclopedias." Trenchant articles concerning Eastern Christianity occur in vol. 3 (1953) under "Églises orientales," in vol. 7 (1975) under "Lossky (Vladimir)," in vol. 10 (1985) under "Orthodoxie" and "Orient catholique," and in vol. 11 under "Pierre le Grand." These are among the acutest treatments of Eastern Christianity in any general work.

138 (1962-68) *Threskeutike kai ethike enkyklopaideia* [Religious and Ethical Encyclopedia], 12 vols. (Athens: Martinos, 1962-68); about 600 pages per volume, 7200 pages overall; black-and-white photographs.

☐ *Critique* This Greek-language ENCYCLOPEDIA of religion recruited 125 collaborators to elucidate the history and doctrine of Eastern Orthodoxy. Signed articles include a comprehensive WHO'S WHO of church leaders. Anyone with a smattering of Greek can use the multilingual bibliographies. Greek Orthodox self-definition shines through.

☐ *Summary* This detailed ENCYCLOPEDIA of religion and ethics expounds the history and teaching of Eastern Christianity exhaustively.

139 (1963-) Klaus Wessel and [later] Marcell Restle, eds., *Reallexikon zur byzantinischen Kunst* (Stuttgart: Hiersemann, 1963-); 4 and 3/4 vols. to 1994 (through "Madaba"); about 2800 pages to date; no general bibliography; index of places in each volume.

☐ *Critique* This MEGA-ENCYCLOPEDIA explores how art and religiosity have interacted in Eastern Christianity. To date almost two hundred articles examine cities, regions, genres and liturgical practices as well as images of biblical figures. Edited at Munich, the format is identical to that of the much longer **151** Klauser, ed., *Reallexikon zur Antike und Christentum* (1950-). Articles by Klaus Wessel in 1965 on "Image" *(Bild)* and "Image of Christ" *(Christusbild),* as well as later ones on "Cross" and on liturgical paraphernalia (1993), expound historical niceties discussed in no other reference work. Almost two hundred pages each on "Konstantinopel" and "Crete," like forty-five on Jerusalem and thirty-two on Korinth, trace the history of religious building. Information about religion pervades shorter entries on cities like Carthage, Damascus and Kiev as well as on regions like Calabria, Cappadocia and Georgia. Multilingual bibliographies and quotations in Greek enrich the articles. Few reference works make religion and art interact so seamlessly, or explain rationales for liturgy so persuasively. An INTRODUCTION to such symbiosis of art and liturgy unfolds in Günter Spitzing, *Lexikon byzantinisch-christlicher Symbole: Die Bilderwelt Griechenlands und Kleinasiens* (Munich: Diederichs, 1989).

□ *Summary* This MEGA-ENCYCLOPEDIA delivers lucid explanations, exhaustive inventories and magnificent bibliographies. Historians of liturgy will revel.

140 (1971, 1990-93) Endre von Ivánka, Julius Tyciak and Paul Wiertz, eds., *Handbuch der Ostkirchenkunde* (Düsseldorf: Patmos, 1971); xxxii & 839 pages; two indexes (persons, topics), pp. 819-37; second edition in 3 vols. (Düsseldorf: Patmos, 1990-93); 392, 276, 320 pages. Analyzed on the basis of the first edition of 1971.

□ *Critique* This historical HANDBOOK furnishes signed articles on all branches of Eastern Christianity. Part 1, "History" (pp. 1-237), and part 2, "Liturgy and Styles of Thought" (pp. 239-664), supply exceptional detail. Chapters on "liturgical families" differentiate three groupings: (1) Byzantine, (2) Antiochene (i.e., Eastern and Western Syrian, Armenian) and (3) Alexandrian (i.e., Coptic and Ethopian). Bibliographies are massive. This remains the most thorough Western reference work on Eastern Christianity. Its second edition (1990-93) sweeps the field. Concurrently, three French HANDBOOKS add their own weight: R. Janin, *Les Églises orientales et les rites orientaux* (Paris: Letouzey et Ané, 1922, 4th ed., rev. 1955) expounds liturgy. Micheline Albert et al., *Christianismes orientaux: Introduction à l'étude des langues et des littératures* (Paris: Cerf, 1993) scrutinizes research materials concerning six Christian cultures: Arabic, Armenian, Coptic, Ethiopian, Georgian and Syriac. Jean-Pierre Valognes, *Vie et mort des chrétiens d'Orient* (Paris: Fayard, 1994) assesses in massive detail the history and present status of these peoples.

□ *Summary* This HANDBOOK investigates history and particularly liturgies of Eastern Christianity. Everyone should use the bibliographies.

43 (1973-78) George Menachery, ed., *The St. Thomas Christian Encyclopaedia of India*, 3 vols. announced, 2 published (Trichur: St. Thomas Christian Encyclopaedia of India, 1973-82). Analyzed further under 2.2 "Ecumenism." Vol. 2 (1973) recounts history, liturgy and art of the Mar Thoma Church (Malabar) in detail. Signed articles by Indian authorities evoke the St. Thomas Christians prior to the Portuguese arrival (2:1-36), describe Syrian Orthodox (i.e., Monophysites) in relation to the Jesuits (2:36-107) and debate whether St. Thomas reached India (2:18-29).

141 (1975, 1991) Julius Assfalg and Paul Krüger, *Kleines Wörterbuch des christlichen Orients* (Wiesbaden: Harrassowitz, 1975); xxxiii & 460 pages; index, pp. 407-60; general bibliography, pp. xxviii-xxxiii; chronologies, pp. 389-406; six foldout maps; 16 black-and-white plates; architectural diagrams throughout. Translated into French as *Petit dictionnaire de l'Orient chrétien* (Turnhout: Brepols, 1991); xxxiii & 551 pages; updated bibliographies.

□ *Critique* This compact REALLEXIKON by nineteen Germans examines all churches of Eastern Christianity in surprising detail (with bibliography in the longer articles). Copious entries treat at least eight branches: Armenian, Byzantine, Copt, Ethiopian, Georgian, Jacobite, Syrian and Syro-Malabar (i.e., South Indian). Gnostics like the Mandeans and Paulicians get discussed as well. Entries on music, liturgy and architecture (with diagrams and photographs) make this an ideal travel companion. A splendid entry on "Liturgical Books" canvasses all denominations. Major cities (Antioch, Cairo, Constantinople, Jerusalem) elicit entries, as do pivotal doctrines (e.g., "Christology"). The WHO'S WHO is meager, and there is no material on Judaism or Islam. The French edition of 1991 updates bibliography but little else. This work takes its place next to the massive **141** Ivánka, ed., *Handbuch der Ostkirchenkunde* (1971, 1990-93). Regrettably, no equivalent volume exists in English, obliging English users to resort to general works like **144** Kashdan, ed., *The Oxford Dictionary of Byzantium* (1990) or specialized ones like **145** Atiya, ed., *The Coptic*

Encyclopedia (1991). This book is a gem.

□ *Summary* This concise REALLEXIKON is ideal for travel or scholarship. It deserves to be widely known.

142 (1984) Nicon D. Patrinacos, *A Dictionary of Greek Orthodoxy* (Pleasantville, N.Y.: Hellenic Heritage Publications, 1984); 391 pages; index, pp. 383-91; no bibliography; a few line drawings throughout.

□ *Scope* This historical LEXICON promotes Greek Orthodox self-definition by expounding history, theology and above all liturgy. It combines a REALLEXIKON of liturgics with a WHO'S WHO of church fathers and saints, explicating Greek terminology throughout. A few places like "Mount Athos" and "Constantinople" as well as ethical issues like "Abortion" and "Lying" elicit entries. A twelve-page appendix briefly identifies six heresies (e.g., "Nestorianism"), nineteen church fathers (e.g., "Eusebios") and eight movements (e.g., "Hesychasm"). The author is an Oxford-trained scholar who expounds subtleties adroitly. Regrettably he supplies no bibliographies.

□ *Strengths* One of the most elegant of recent LEXICONS, this work of self-definition fills a gap. No other reference work in English spells out Greek Orthodox lore from within. Historical essays analyze each of the seven ecumenical councils, including the development of the "Ecumenical Patrarchate." Controversies concerning "Iconoclasm" and the "Filioque" get their due. The majority of articles address liturgy in all its aspects. Dozens of technical terms for prayers, ceremonies, objects, vestments and music are defined, and some inspire line drawings. *A Dictionary of Greek Orthodoxy* makes an ideal companion for a visit to a Greek church. Each of the sacraments is explicated, with emphasis on its distinctiveness for the Greek Orthodox. Anyone interested in comparing Eastern and Western rites will find these entries invaluable for clarifying terminology that Protestants and Catholics tend to take for granted. Entries on "Iconography," "Relics" and "Devil" narrate history of the Eastern position.

Each of the Gospels is examined, as are all epistles of St. Paul (pp. 280-99). Although there is no discussion of the Old Testament, Western scholars will benefit from sampling an Eastern perspective on the New. Similarly, articles on doctrine throw fresh light on topics such as "Holy Tradition," "Sin" and "Grace of God." Entries on "Fall," "Trinity" and "Immortality of the Soul" eschew categories ingrained in Protestants and Catholics such as "Atonement," "Justification" or "Sanctification." Instead of an entry on spirituality, there is one on "Superstition," instead of "Liberation Theology," "Desecration." Even the WHO'S WHO avoids banality because saints and church fathers stand in an Eastern perspective. Like **103** George Poulos in *Orthodox Saints* (1990-92), Patrinacos accords to legends of saints such as St. Demetrios and St. George greater credence than do Western scholars. A labor of love, this LEXICON defamiliarizes practices of Western churches by vindicating Greek counterparts. This LEXICON imparts to Protestants and Roman Catholics the "otherness" of Greek Orthodoxy. Rootedness in the first six centuries, obsession with liturgy and disregard of Western trendiness shine through.

□ *Weaknesses* Focusing on Greek rather than Russian or Syrian Orthodoxy, this LEXICON articulates self-definition for Greek Orthodox in the United States. A broader horizon would have strengthened the endeavor by, for example, specifying contrasts with Roman Catholicism or Coptic Monophysitism. A few entries like "Theology" lapse into platitudes. Surprisingly, the author ignores pre-Christian origins in Hellenistic religions and philosophy, never mentioning Plato or Plotinus. A major flaw is lack of bibliographies. The author missed an opportunity to sift secondary literature from the standpoint of Eastern Orthodoxy. Likewise, it would have been useful to evoke contemporary theologians like John Zizioulas and Christos Yannaras, as Rowan Williams does in introducing "Eastern Orthodox Theology" in 77 McGrath, ed., *The Blackwell Encyclopedia of Modern Christian Thought* (1993). Another drawback is that the volume is owned by few libraries, partly because of the obscurity of its publisher. Every comparatist of church history should consult this book.

□ *Competitors* Until this volume appeared, no branch of Christianity so desperately needed a LEXICON in English as did Eastern Orthodoxy. This work interprets the Greek wing of Orthodoxy with authority. By emphasizing liturgy, it enlarges **112** Fink, ed., *The New Dictionary of Sacramental Worship* (1990) and **119** Davies, ed., *The New Westminster Dictionary of Worship and Liturgy* (1986), both of which explore vastly more topics. By expounding an insider's view, it amplifies German LEXICONS on Eastern Christianity as well as Olivier Clément's chapter, "L'Église orthodoxe," in **16** Puech, ed., *Histoire des religions,* 2 (1972): 1014-48. It also corrects a tendency in Western reference works on the early church to neglect perseverance of Eastern traditions after 1054. **151** Klauser, ed., *Reallexikon für Antike und Christentum* (1950-) upholds a different worldview in articulating continuities between pre-Christian antiquity and early Christianity. Patrinacos ignores, not to say disdains, such matters. His explanations furnish material for cross-denominational comparisons such as Jaroslav Pelikan undertakes in **35** *The Melody of Theology* (1988). Regrettably, Patrinacos did not impart breadth of vision to the sequel that he wrote for members of his church. His *All That A Greek Orthodox Should Know* (New York: Greek Orthodox Archdiocese, 1986) does not help outsiders. Through its singularity, *A Dictionary of Greek Orthodoxy* calls attention to works of self-definition that abound for Roman Catholics and Protestants. As a solitary lexicon-maker from the East, Patrinacos holds his own amid Western oversupply.

□ *Summary* This little-known LEXICON belongs in the library of every seminary and every church historian. No other single-author reference book conveys so pungently a venerable tradition's self-understanding.

142 (1991) Aziz S. Atiya, ed., *The Coptic Encyclopedia,* 8 vols. (New York: Macmillan, 1991); lxxiii & 2372 plus 371 pages; index, 8:229-371; general bibliography, 1:lxix-lxxiii; maps, 8:1-12.

□ *Scope* This historical ENCYCLOPEDIA of Christian Egypt fulfilled a dream of its editor, who conceived the project in Alexandria in the 1950s. In 1975 he began implementation at the University of Utah (1:lxix-lx). Twenty-eight hundred articles by 218 contributors canvass the history of Christianity in Egypt, Nubia and Ethiopia. Certain articles examine the entire early church (to 451 C.E.) from the perspective of Alexandria. Those on heresies, Alexandrian church fathers and the seven ecumenical councils are among the fullest in any reference work. Art (particularly icons), architecture, textiles (twenty pages), music (thirty pages) and literature elicit clusters of miniarticles. Five contributors wrote about a third of the total. An appendix (8:13-227) examines the Coptic language in unprecedented detail.

□ *Strengths* By celebrating a single region within Eastern Christianity, this ENCYCLOPEDIA achieves unique depth. Historical entries are among the best anywhere. Heinz Heinen writes acutely on "Alexandria in Late Antiquity," as does Aziz S. Atiya on "Catechetical School of Alexandria." Whether written in Coptic or not, every tractate in the Nag Hammadi library elicits an entry. Gilles Quispel interprets Christianizing "Gnosticism" as "largely an Alexandrian phenomenon" (p. 1149). Surprisingly, liturgy gets expounded chiefly under "Music." In "Art, Coptic and Irish" Monique Blanche-Ortolan and Pierre du Bourguet, S.J., resolve the question of possible Irish borrowings from Coptic art by tracing interlacings back to pre-Christian Celts, who thus had no need to borrow from Coptic monks. An entry on "Jerusalem" elucidates Coptic participation in the Church of the Holy Sepulchre. The WHO'S WHO encompasses patriarchs, church fathers and heretics active in Egypt, as well as scholars of Coptic culture. An aura of Egypt pervades these pages. No other ENCYCLOPEDIA evokes the ups and downs of a small church so exhaustively.

□ *Weaknesses* Emphasis on self-definition discourages comparisons. One wishes for treatment of ancient Egyptian myth and of Roman reworking of Egyptian themes. Why refuse to explicate the Byzantine orthodoxy that Copts rejected after 451 C.E.? Although a fine article discusses "Greek Language," none addresses Byzantium, Hellenism, orthodoxy or mysticism. Entries on Egypt in the Coptic period (100 C.E. to 641 C.E.) and in the Islamic period in Egypt (after 641 C.E.) cry out for comparisons to regions such as Palestine, Anatolia and Italy.

□ *Competitors* This labor of love is the most searching Western ENCYCLOPEDIA on any aspect of Eastern Christianity. Although a work of self-definition, it boasts articles by scholars from diverse traditions. Oddly, a defense of Monophysitism in the entry on "Council of Chalcedon" overlooks efforts since the 1960s to diminish christological disputes between Monophysites and Orthodox. On this one may consult K. M. George's article "Oriental Orthodox—Orthodox Dialogue" in **46** Lossky at al., eds., *Dictionary of the Ecumenical Movement* (1991). Entries on liturgy need to be enlarged through resort to **142** Patrinacos, *A Dictionary of Greek Orthodoxy* (1984).

□ *Summary* This winning ENCYCLOPEDIA explores Egyptian Christianity in astonishing depth but avoids crosscultural comparisons.

144 (1991) Alexander P. Kashdan, ed., *The Oxford Dictionary of Byzantium,* 3 vols. (New York and Oxford: Oxford University Press, 1991); liv & 728; xxxiv & 729-1473; xxxiv & 1475-2232 pages; no index; general bibliography (i.e., list of abbreviations), 1:xxi-xlv.

□ *Critique* Alexander Kashdan (1922-), who left the Soviet Union in 1978, initiated this REALLEXIKON and then guided it to completion at Dumbarton Oaks. The enterprise recruited 135 contributors to write five thousand highly compressed articles on all aspects of the Byzantine empire from the fourth to the fifteenth century. Cross-references abound, and every entry has multilingual bibliography, whose citations reportedly total more than thirty-five thousand. For better or worse, this REALLEXIKON canvasses Byzantium and only secondarily its church. As is usual among academic medievalists, religion fills a modest niche among rulers, conquests, administration, law, objects *(realia),* customs and art. Place names (e.g., Venice) command detailed coverage, while religious leaders, thinkers, heretics, disputes and practices elicit just a few hundred words each. Although entries on "Hagiography," "Vita" and "Canonization" are notably useful, theological disputes get scanted. In a jarring entry on Judaism, Steven B. Bowman reports that "Byzantium deprecated the observances and practices of Judaism, yet it was necessary to have practicing Jews to demonstrate that God rejected and abandoned them, and because their voluntary conversion was both a proof of the truth of Christianity and a prerequisite for Christ's return" (p. 1077). Many of the topics win fuller coverage in **158** *Lexikon des Mittelalters* (1977-) and to a lesser extent in **159** Strayer, ed., *Dictionary of the Middle Ages* (1982-89).

□ *Summary* A model of how to encapsulate up-to-date research into a REALLEXIKON, this work deemphasizes religious history. It addresses specialists rather than generalists.

145 (1991) Donald Nicol, *A Biographical Dictionary of the Byzantine Empire* (London: Seaby, 1991); xxvii & 156 pages; indexes, pp. 139-47; general bibliography, pp. 149-56; genealogical tables, pp. xvii-xxviii.

□ *Critique* This WHO'S WHO examines all emperors, most saints and many writers in entries averaging one-fourth to one-half a column. Genealogies are superb. Bibliographies favor English-language works from before 1980, reaching back as far as the 1830s. Entries on saints are sober rather than devotional. Concision prevails.

□ *Summary* This WHO'S WHO combines a handy introduction to major figures with choice older bibliography.

146 (1993) Peter D. Day, *The Liturgical Dictionary of Eastern Christianity*

(London: Burns & Oates; Collegeville, Minn.: Michael Glazier/Liturgical, 1993); viii & 334 pages; no index; no general bibliography; a "Quick Reference Guide" to 140 foreign terms, pp. 315-27.

□ *Critique* In this multicultural GLOSSARY a British scholar defines almost two thousand liturgical terms taken from all Eastern churches. Byzantine, Slavonic, Armenian, Coptic, West Syrian, East Syrian (both Nestorian and Chaldean), Maronite and Indian traditions are included. Slavonic churches get differentiated further into Georgian, Russian, Serbian and Ukrainian. Most catchwords come in either English or Greek; a few are in Armenian, Coptic, Slavonic and Syrian. All entries specify the tradition(s) to which they pertain. Definitional articles discriminate among up to eight traditions but lack bibliography. The longest entries deliver six pages each on "Liturgical Books" and "Orders, Holy." Certain entries like "Epiclesis" or "Iconostasis," as well as those on individual traditions, narrate history, whereas definitional articles do not. Sacraments, vestments and liturgical languages are aligned in six tables (pp. 329-34), and "A Quick Reference Guide" specifies for 140 English terms equivalents in up to eight languages (pp. 315-27). A bibliography is sorely missed, for the list of thirty-one authors (p. vii) hardly suffices. Although experts will relish this compilation of the recondite, beginners may prefer **142** Patrinacos, *A Dictionary of Greek Orthodoxy* (1984), even though it ignores all traditions but the Byzantine.

□ *Summary* This GLOSSARY sorts out a dozen Eastern rites. Beginners may find it too intricate.

2.10 PERIODS OF CHURCH HISTORY

OVERVIEW: PROFUSION ONLY ON THE EARLY CHURCH Most reference books about Christianity discuss church history, but different periods invite different genres. The early church fares best. Works not primarily historical are analyzed above under 2.1 "Christianity: Gen-

eral" and throughout other sections on Christianity. French MEGA-ENCYCLOPEDIAS in particular overflow with historical material. A major gap in the literature remains a one-volume reference work that canvasses Christian monasticism through the ages. Perhaps the finest such tool is still a German HANDBOOK: Max Heimbucher, *Die Orden und Kongregationen der katholischen Kirche* [1896, 1933], 2 vols. (reprint; Paderborn: Schöningh, 1980).

2.10.1 SURVEYS OF THE PAPACY AND NATIONAL CHURCHES

OVERVIEW: A MISCELLANY OF POPES, SCOTS AND THE FRENCH This section treats surveys of the papacy and of national churches other than American. A GUIDEBOOK to France stands alone, while **150** Levillain, ed., *Dictionnaire historique de la papauté* (1994) is a supreme masterpiece.

LIST OF WORKS ANALYZED
    147 (1967) Louis Chaigne et al., eds., *Guide religieux de la France* (Paris: Hachette, 1967)
    148 (1986) J[ohn] N[orman] D[avidson] Kelly [1909-], *The Oxford Dictionary of Popes* (New York and Oxford: Oxford University Press, 1986)
    149 (1993) Nigel M. de S. Cameron, ed., *Dictionary of Scottish Church History and Theology* (Edinburgh: T & T Clark, 1993; Downers Grove, Ill.: InterVarsity Press, 1994)
    150 (1994) Philippe Levillain, ed., *Dictionnaire historique de la papauté* (Paris: Fayard, 1994)

ANALYSIS OF WORKS
    147 (1967) Louis Chaigne et al., eds., *Guide religieux de la France* (Paris: Hachette, 1967); 1235 pages; two indexes (of places and persons), pp. 1073-1221; bibliography, pp. 1056-58; glossary, pp. 1059-72; maps throughout.
    □ *Critique* A team of Catholics, Protestants, Jews and Muslims put together a travel guide *(Guide bleu)* to religious sites and persons in every city and town in

France. Religious history of major towns gets recounted; places of worship are inventoried and major ones described; notable persons are traced both to birthplaces and places of residence. Every religious notable (whether saint, monarch, warrior, bishop, artist or writer) who ever sojourned in a town is referenced. Authors like Maurice Barrès, Paul Claudel, Joris-Karl Huysmans and Charles Péguy crop up in dozens of locales, as do priests like St. François de Sales, St. Vincent de Paul and Henri Lacordaire. Musicians, however, are scanted. Paris comes to life in a street-by-street LEXICON (pp. 133-312). Maps reconstruct such matters as Joan of Arc's journeys (pp. 430-31), the Jewish population of Paris in 1967 (pp. 316-17) and the war against Protestants in the Cévennes (pp. 702-3).

Catholicism, Protestantism, Judaism and Islam win equal treatment; synagogues are described as fully as any cathedral. Events of the Holocaust are recounted, notably in Strasbourg (pp. 460-62) and Lyon (pp. 538-39). Four introductions (pp. 1-128) expound at equal length the history of French Catholicism, Protestantism, Judaism and Islam (the latter outlining "Saracen" invasions between 710 and 1406 C.E. (pp. 117-19). Rabbi Josy Eisenberg's survey of Judaism (pp. 75-99) is unusually informative, noting that the oath "more judaico" was abolished only in 1846. A companion volume *Guide littéraire de la France* (Paris: Hachette, 1964) encompasses some of the same figures. Both complement Georges Brunel and Marie-Laure Deschamps-Bourgeon, *Dictionnaire des églises de Paris* (Paris: Hervas, 1995).

□ *Summary* A model of its kind, the *Guide religieux de la France* is the most fact-crammed religious GUIDEBOOK on any European country. Admirers of France will find so much to savor that the volume would repay updating.

148 (1986) J[ohn] N[orman] D[avidson] Kelly [1909-], *The Oxford Dictionary of Popes* (New York and Oxford: Oxford University Press, 1986; paperback, 1988); xiv & 347 pages; index,

pp. 331-47; general bibliography (i.e., list of abbreviations), pp. x-xiii. An Italian translation, *Vite dei papi* (Monferrato: Piemme, 1995) updates the bibliographies. Analyzed on the basis of the paperback edition.

□ *Critique* An Anglican historian of the early church has compiled a WHO'S WHO of 271 popes and thirty-eight antipopes. Arranged in chronological order, entries vary from two pages (on "Gregory I" and nearly all popes since 1750) to one-fourth page on minor figures, each climaxing with select bibliography and a peroration. Antipopes appear in sequence with popes and command equal space. In each pontificate emphasis falls on politics, diplomacy, theological controversies and art patronage so that a narrative of the papacy itself unfolds. Encyclicals are mentioned but seldom expounded. Coverage from the sixth to eleventh centuries (pp. 52-138) illuminates in depth one of the least studied periods of papal and indeed of central Italian history. One hundred pages suffice to cover almost six hundred years since 1400. The longest entry concerns John Paul II. Writing with verve, a master epitomizer entrances the browser. His dexterity will please historians, not to mention curiosity-seekers. A French masterwork, **150** Levillain, ed., *Dictionnaire historique de la papauté* (1994) is eight times longer and investigates institutions, practices and documents as well as pontificates. Donald Attwater penned a graceful WHO'S WHO, *A Dictionary of the Popes: From Peter to Pius XII* (London: Burns, Oates & Washbourne, 1939) that rivals Kelly in fluency but lacks bibliographies. John Bowden compresses the material into nineteen virtuosic pages in **38** *Who's Who in Theology* (1990, 1992). An Italian WHO'S WHO, Battista Mondin, *Dizionario enciclopedico dei Papi* (Rome: Città Nuova, 1995), runs twice as long and emphasizes contributions to the faith.

□ *Summary* This model WHO'S WHO interprets pontificates in sequence. Few brief reference works dissect so much history so adroitly.

149 (1993) Nigel M. de S. Cameron,

ed., *Dictionary of Scottish Church History and Theology* (Edinburgh: T & T Clark, 1993; Downers Grove, Ill.: InterVarsity Press, 1994); 906 pages; no index; no general bibliography.

□ *Scope* Edited in Edinburgh over a period of seven years, this historical DICTIONARY recounts all phases of Christianity in Scotland. Nearly four hundred authorities write over two thousand entries on persons, places, institutions, ideas and controversies. Every branch of Christianity from Celtic saints to the Salvation Army receives its due. Filling perhaps half the volume, a WHO'S WHO instances more than five hundred Scots (nearly all deceased) who shaped or mirrored religious life. Founders, saints, ministers, thinkers and writers have career narrated and contribution assessed, but freethinkers do not. Regrettably, the writing is more often workmanlike than sprightly, but the bibliographies excel.

□ *Strengths* Historical synthesis flourishes. "Missions" inspires Andrew F. Walls to two stellar articles with phenomenal bibliography (pp. 567-94), not to mention entries by others on Australia, Canada, New Zealand and the Dutch Reformed Church in South Africa. Periods such as "Renaissance," "Reformation, Scottish" "Commonwealth" and "Enlightenment" elicit meaty articles, as do denominations like "Calvin, Calvinism," "Methodism" and "Lutheranism." Ian Campbell surveys little-known aspects of "Literature, Religion in Scottish," and Donald E. Meek does the same on "Revivals." David F. Wright shines on "Education, Theological" and Richard B. Sher on "Clubs and Societies, Eighteenth Century." A charming catalog sketches thirty-five "Celtic Saints," and monasticism evokes its share of entries, as in "Benedictines," "Cistercians," "Cluniacs," and "Monasticism." Theologians, and above all Thomas Torrance, get differentiated as regards "Atonement," "Christology" and "Covenant Theology." Art commands rubrics like "Arts and Churches," "Cathedral Churches" and "Crosses, Celtic," not to mention splendid synopses of "Hymnology" and "Music, Church."

The WHO'S WHO is remarkable. Rulers as diverse as Robert the Bruce, Mary of Guise and James VI elicit nuances, while John Knox and Thomas Chalmers win two pages each. In sketching luminaries, the *Dictionary* endeavors to pinpoint religious views, for example of Thomas Carlyle, Walter Scott and James Clerk Maxwell (but not of James Boswell). The editor's elegy on William Robertson Smith resounds and might have incited similar depth on James Hastings and Sir James Fraser. Theologians who spent half a career in England get their due (e.g., Donald MacKinnon), but why is there no entry on Scots at Oxford and Cambridge? Many will welcome entries on "Gifford Lectures," "Liberalism" and "Malthusian Theory," but Robert Owen at New Lanark is passed over. Piquant lore crops up in "Gaelic," "Hymnology," "Jansenism" and "Picts," while an entry on "Traveling People" startles by stretching into the 1990s. Entries on "Millennialism" and "Sandeman, Robert" evoke some of the odder sects to have erupted anywhere since 1800.

□ *Weaknesses* The WHO'S WHO suffers anomalies. Zeal to include all Christians does not extend to freethinkers other than David Hume. There is no entry on Francis Hutcheson or his pupil Adam Smith. Nor do dissident Scots in England like James Boswell, Lord Byron or John Ruskin rate a mention. Dugald Stewart wins a column to himself, yet Thomas Reid crops up only under "Scottish Realism." Likewise, it seems odd to feature John Buchan yet to omit a favorite of his, Robert Louis Stevenson. One could wish as well for entries on Edinburgh and Glasgow to complement excellent ones on "Highlands" and "Clearances." Fortunately, places abound in John Keay and Julia Keay, *Collins Encyclopedia of Scotland* (London: Collins, 1994). Less fortunately, a chance was missed to assess French (as distinct from Genevan) impact on Scottish churches, not to mention Scotland's impact on American ones. Material on the United States lies scattered through articles like "Emigration," "Princeton Theological Seminary" and "Union Theological Seminary, New York." Americans are sure to savor entries on Jonathan Edwards and Dwight Moody, whose prestige in Scotland almost rivaled that of John Wesley.

□ *Competitors* This DICTIONARY of Christianity in a small country has no parallel. It may be said to supplement a classic, S[amuel] L[eslie] Ollard (1875-1949), ed., *A Dictionary of English Church History* (London: Mowbray, 1912; 3d ed., 1948), which disregards Scotland. Anyone seeking REVISIONISM should consult articles concerning Scotland by Michael Lynch, James K. Cameron and Keith Robbins in Sheridan Gilley and W. J. Sheils, eds., *A History of Religion in Britain* (Oxford and Cambridge, Mass.: Blackwell Reference, 1994). The present DICTIONARY is justified above all by the worldwide activities of Scottish missions and organizations after 1700. Thus American Protestants will find much to ponder. A similar volume on Ireland would be welcome, but dare one hope for a touch of drollery? There is too little of that here.

□ *Summary* This DICTIONARY of Christian history and thought among Scots addresses all pertinent topics except nonbelief. Unfortunately, it lacks an index to facilitate research, particularly on Scots abroad.

150 (1994) Philippe Levillain, ed., *Dictionnaire historique de la papauté* (Paris: Fayard, 1994); 1776 pages; no index; no general bibliography; 32 color plates between pp. 336-37 and 1344-45; four maps of the papal states on pp. 600-601; 46 black-and-white illustrations at the start and end of letters of the alphabet; a flow chart of the Holy See (p. 1540) and a map of Vatican City (p. 623).

□ *Scope* This spectacular REALLEXIKON examines every aspect of papal history in 912 signed entries with superb multilingual bibliographies. Two hundred eight contributors are mostly French and mostly academics, while only a handful are clerics. Although a few hail from the Vatican Library, the volume does not speak for the Vatican. With just four exceptions, the WHO'S WHO encompasses solely popes and antipopes. These entries vary from half a

column to nine pages on John Paul II (plus four more on his trips). At least half the articles address (1) events (e.g., "Crusades," "Sack of Rome," "Roman Republic of 1849"), (2) institutions (e.g., "Curia," "Pontifical Finances," "Holy See") and (3) controversies (e.g., "Great Schism of the West," "Investiture Quarrel," "Reformation"). Papal claims are weighed under "Infallibility," "Magisterium" and "Ultramontanism." The city of Rome is portrayed overall (pp. 1140-43, 1460-81) as well as through individual monuments (e.g., "Coliseum," "Lateran," "Pantheon"), and so is the Vatican. Other papal cities like Avignon, Milan, Ravenna and Viterbo evoke entries, but individual countries do not (except in "Holy Roman Empire" and "Unification of Italy"). Thirty-two color plates deploy seventy images of popes and their splendor. Throughout the tone is nonconfessional, even sober, as information flows unquenchably.

□ *Strengths* This resplendent REALLEXIKON scrutinizes how the papacy affected Rome, central Italy and Europe. Exhaustive lists catalog canonizations, concordats, congregations, councils, decretals, encyclicals, prophecies, renunciations, schisms, tombs of popes and Roman colleges (with addresses), but not papal miracles, scandals or saints. Often subdivided chronologically, historical surveys trace institutions as varied as the "Inquisition" and "Curia" (in thirty pages), canon law, church orders ("Dominicans," "Jesuits"), schools ("Seminaries," "Universities") and political parties ("Christian Democracy"). Ceremony, liturgy and heraldry dot the pages, and mass media crop up under "Vatican Radio," "Filmography," "Humor," "Photography" and "Social Communications." A GLOSSARY explicates terms like "Bull," "Nicolaism" and "Simony." Art features in entries on "Architecture," "Mosaics," "Painting," "Saint Peter's" (sixteen pages), "Sistine Chapel," "Vatican Museums" and "Foreign Artists in Rome," while music surfaces under "Castrati," "Hymns" and "Roman Liturgical Chant." Folklore creeps into "Carnival," "Bells" *[Cloches]* and "Pilgrimage." Without trace of

MENIPPEAN excess, two long articles narrate the "Image of Rome in Literature." Pathos haunts Jacques Nobécourt's piece on "'Silence' of Pius XII" (about the Holocaust). Waxing REVISIONIST, an authority on worker priests, Émile Poulat, ironizes about inadequacies of three terms: "Integralism," "Modernism" and "Modernity." In general, any event, institution or practice in Europe that the Papacy initiated, combated or co-opted resounds here.

□ *Weaknesses* With four exceptions—Paul, Catherine of Siena, Dante and Julian the Apostate—the WHO'S WHO excludes everyone but popes and antipopes. No saints, artists or secular rulers win entries. Nor do polemics for or against the papacy command much attention, although "Freemasonry," *"Kulturkampf"* and the Enlightenment *("Lumières")* elicit entries. An article on "Ecumenism" accompanies others on "Anglicanism," "Moscow" and "Byzantium" (in ten pages), but not on individual Protestant traditions. "Judaism" and "Israel" alone, among other religions, win articles, and the Third World is all but ignored. As regards format, to have separated the WHO'S WHO from other articles would have highlighted the latter. As it is, an index and a list of articles are badly needed. More maps, particularly of military campaigns, would also be welcome.

□ *Competitors* Far more than a WHO'S WHO of popes and antipopes, this REALLEXIKON canvasses the history of papal innovation and intervention in Rome and throughout Europe. It has no competitor. Rudolf Fischer-Wollpert, *Lexikon der Päpste* (Regensburg: Pustet, 1985) is an introductory WHO'S WHO and GLOSSARY devoid of bibliography. In contrast, Levillain's masterpiece confronts controversies, elucidates arcana and assembles bibliographies. Historians, art historians and browsers will marvel.

□ *Summary* This nonconfessional REALLEXIKON scrutinizes the highways and byways of papal history. Probably no other institution in Europe, and certainly no other monarchy, has inspired a reference book of comparable rigor or subtlety.

2.10.2 EARLY CHURCH (TO 600/800)

OVERVIEW: ENCYCLOPEDISM TRIUMPHANT History of the early church has generated reference works galore. Since the Middle Ages, the field of patristics (i.e., study of early Christian literature) has investigated works by and about the church fathers. Since the 1650s conspectuses of this literature have been known as "patrologies." Likewise during the seventeenth century Benedictines of St. Maur at Saint-Germain in Paris pioneered techniques for evaluating manuscripts. In their wake several French MEGA-ENCYCLO-PEDIAS, particularly **132** Cabrol and Leclercq, eds., *Dictionnaire d'archéologie chrétienne et de liturgie* (1907-53), concentrate on the early church. So do nearly all works analyzed under 2.9.3 "Eastern Christianity." At least one of the works analyzed here, **151** Klauser, ed., *Reallexikon für Antike und Christentum* (1950-), is a supreme masterpiece, while **152** Di Berardino, ed., *Encyclopedia of the Early Church* (1983, 1992) ranks not far behind. A model bibliography, Thomas A. Robinson, ed., *The Early Church: An Annotated Bibliography of Literature in English* (Metuchen, N.J., and London: Scarecrow, 1993), spans the field.

LIST OF WORKS ANALYZED

151 ([1941] 1950-) Theodor **Klauser [d. 1984] and [since 1984] Ernst Dassmann, eds., *Reallexikon für Antike und Christentum: Sachwörterbuch zur Auseinandersetzung des Christentums mit der antiken Welt* (Stuttgart: Hiersemann, [1941] 1950-)**

67 (1972-) Wolfgang Haase and **Hildegard Temporini, eds., *Aufstieg und Niedergang der römischen Welt: Geschichte Roms im Spiegel der neueren Forschung. II. Principat* (Berlin and New York: de Gruyter, 1972-). Analyzed further under 2.3.3 "Biblical Studies: Handbooks of Interpretation."**

152 (1983, 1992) Angelo di Ber-**ardino, ed., *Encyclopedia of the Early Church*, 2 vols. (New York: Oxford Uni-**

versity Press; London: James Clarke, 1992)

153 (1986-) Cornelius Mayer, ed., *Augustinus-Lexikon,* planned in 7 vols. (Basel: Schwabe, 1986-)

154 (1987, 1993) Everett Ferguson, *Backgrounds of Early Christianity* (Grand Rapids, Mich.: Eerdmans, 1987; 2d ed., 1993)

155 (1988) Michael Grant and Rachel Kitzinger, eds., *Civilization of the Ancient Mediterranean: Greece and Rome,* 3 vols. (New York: Scribner's, 1988)

156 (1990) Everett Ferguson, ed., *Encyclopedia of Early Christianity* (New York and London: Garland Publishing, 1990)

143 (1991) Aziz S. Atiya, ed., *The Coptic Encyclopedia,* 8 vols. (New York: Macmillan, 1991)

157 (1992) Joseph F. Kelly, *The Concise Dictionary of Early Christianity* (Collegeville, Minn.: Michael Glazier/Liturgical, 1992)

ANALYSIS OF WORKS

151 ([1941] 1950-) Theodor Klauser [d. 1984] and [since 1984] Ernst Dassmann, eds., *Reallexikon für Antike und Christentum: Sachwörterbuch zur Auseinandersetzung des Christentums mit der antiken Welt,* planned in 30 to 40 vols. with supplements (Stuttgart: Hiersemann, 1941-); 16 1/2 vols. to 1995 (through *"Jesaja"*); about 625 pages per vol., 10,000 pages to date; index of articles and authors published 1994; no general bibliography; line drawings through vol. 13; black-and-white photographs thereafter. Editorial policies are explained in a supplement: *Das Reallexikon für Antike und Christentum und das F. J. Dölger-Institut in Bonn* (1994), pp. 1-22.

□ *Scope* This magnificent MEGA-ENCYCLO-PEDIA originated at the University of Bonn in the early 1930s. Franz Joseph Dölger (1879-1940) initiated the project and gave his name to an institute (founded there in 1955) whose team has edited the *Reallexikon* since 1935. The first fascicules appeared in 1941, the first volume in 1950. The editors undertook nothing less than to analyze every aspect of Mediterranean culture from Spain to Iran in interaction with Christianity up to about 600 C.E. The result is a MEGA-ENCYCLOPEDIA by and for classical scholars who care about any aspect of Christianity or of late antiquity. To paraphrase the tag, Athens and Alexandria here educate Jerusalem and Rome. Focus falls on reception by Christians of ancient Greek, Roman, Egyptian, Iranian and Jewish culture from the first to the sixth centuries C.E. Most entries cite hundreds of passages in both pagan and Christian sources, filling each volume with tens of thousands of citations of ancient texts. The length of articles changed with volume 8 (1972). Whereas earlier volumes averaged over a hundred articles, later ones count no more than forty, requiring, for example, five volumes (1972-86) for two hundred articles beginning with the letter *G.*

All volumes cast their net widely. They reference not only church fathers, heresies, saints and art forms, but at least ten other major categories: (1) philosophers ("Aristotle," "Epictetus," "Epikurus"), (2) biblical figures ("Abraham," "Ezekiel"), (3) biblical concepts ("Apocalyptic," "Holy Scriptures"), (4) mythic figures (usually in the Greek spelling, e.g., "Athena," "Attis" and "Herakles"), (5) countries ("Egypt," "Hispania"), (6) philosophical concepts ("Aether," "Ataraxia,"), (7) legal practices ("Actio," "Adoptio," "Auctoritas"), (8) diseases ("Epilepsy"), (9) religious practices ("Askesis," "Poverty," "Altar") and (10) animals ("Eel," "Eagle," "Ape"). There are even articles on mental processes like "Learning by Heart," patterns like "Upwards-Downwards" *("Aufwärts-abwärts")* and genres of literature ("Autobiography"). This profusion lasted through volume 7 (1969). It permitted such extravagances as ten articles (totaling 190 pages) on "Angels," including an entry that itemizes 266 names of them. Each entry supplies multilingual bibliography in addition to innumerable citations from ancient sources. The combination of rigor, imagination and absence of confessional bias is unparalleled. One emerges from immersion in ancient authors and attitudes both rejuvenated and disoriented.

□ *Strengths* Few MEGA-ENCYCLOPEDIAS address such a wide range of specialists. Historians of pre-Christian Greece, Rome, Israel and Egypt will find material on concepts, customs, symbols, art, myths and luminaries. Scholars of early Christianity will find thinkers, saints, biblical figures, heresies, places, philosophy, science, images and concepts. This ENCYCLOPEDIA reconstructs trajectories of culture within the Mediterranean world down to 600 C.E. Nearly all entries posit migration of ideas across cultures, eras, languages and religions. A typical article (on "Aether") in four pages (and with at least 250 citations) traces a Greek concept from Homer and Hesiod through the pre-Socratics, tragedians and pagan eschatologists to early church fathers and Christian apocalyptic. Similar treatment of "Aion" traces its trajectory from Iranian Zurvanism through Hellenistic Syria and Phoenicia to the Janus cult in Rome, where it inspired concepts of *aeternitas* and *saeculum,* and thence through the Mithras cult to Sophia and Christian Neo-Platonism. The article climaxes with Justinian's closing of the philosophy schools in Athens in 529 C.E.

Even more virtuosic is a twenty-five-page article on "Baal," which itemizes no fewer than eighty deities who incorporate that name, including Allah (no. 3, said to have begun as Hubal the Moon-god) and Baal-Zebub (no. 26) among the Philistines. There follow four pages on "Baalbek" in its pre-Christian and Christian phases down to 579 C.E. and eight pages on "Babylon" (from 2000 B.C.E.). Following the change of format that began with volume 8 (1972), volume 15 devotes no less than thirteen pages to Ireland ("Hibernia"), fifteen to Hilary of Poitiers, eleven to Jerome and twelve to Hippo Regius. Less expected are fifteen pages on "Shepherd," twelve on "Stag," thirty-eight on the book of Job and eight on Hippocrates. Among the most arresting come articles on "Limping," "Wedding," "Hope" and "Hierodulia" (i.e., sacred prostitution). An innovative piece on "Hearing" compares auditory and visual practices and symbolism through a thousand years (requiring forty-five pages and at least a thousand citations). A panorama on "Heaven" traverses Babylon, Iran, Greece and Israel before explicating Christian views of heaven's three guises: as the seat of God, as realm of the blessed, and as spheres. Thereafter come entries on "Ascent to Heaven," "Queen of Heaven," "Cultic Orientation" *("Himmelsrichtung")* and "Voice of Heaven." A magnificent sequence in volume 13 (1986) requires 150 pages to examine "House" as (1) "Domestic Deity," (2) "Household" and (3) "Metaphor." All these discussions document cultural transfer in mind-boggling depth.

If the present pace of five volumes published per decade is maintained, publication may extend to the year 2060. Not least for this reason the *Reallexikon* is constantly being updated. Since 1958 the Dölger-Institut has published a *Jahrbuch für Antike und Christentum,* which prints supplementary articles to the *Reallexikon.* They are, moreover, being incorporated into "Supplement Volumes," the first of which (covering through "Barbar") appeared between 1986 and 1992. New entries treat "Aaron," "Aeschylus," "Aristophanes" and "Aeneas," while an updated one greatly expands coverage of "Egypt." Thus articles tend not to go out of date.

□ *Weaknesses* Far from being postmodern, the *Reallexikon für Antike und Christentum* is not even modernist. Its ethos derives from a nineteenth-century vision of continuity between pagan antiquity and early Christianity. By encompassing Greek, Roman, Egyptian and "Oriental" (i.e., Near Eastern) thought and mythology, the editors sponsor an extravaganza without equal. Browsing here is like walking through the collections of the Louvre—one shuttles back and forth from Egypt to Assyria to Greece to Rome to early Christianity amid unheard-of riches. Not everyone will relish the profusion. Some might prefer greater selectivity or greater attention to methodology. In particular, adepts of "Reception Theory" will want to see the notion of "reception" get debated and refined. At bottom, this magnum opus addresses devotees of an old-fashioned humanistic education. Knowledge of Latin and Greek is presumed, as is training in philosophy. Christian scholars of antiquity all the way from Erasmus, Scaliger and Mabillon to Schleiermacher, Lord Acton and Werner Jaeger would have savored this MEGA-ENCYCLOPEDIA. So would skeptics like Gibbon, Burckhardt and Renan. But for many, perhaps even most readers today, such a pedigree no longer carries weight. For most of us, Justinian's closing of the philosophy schools at Athens in 529 C.E. no longer incites the pathos that it does for authors of these volumes.

□ *Competitors* This MEGA-ENCYCLOPEDIA inherits from half a dozen generations of German scholarship a vision of how classical antiquity transformed itself into early Christianity. To browse in these volumes is to step back fifty or a hundred years into the German classical culture that educated Friedrich Nietzsche, Wilhelm Dilthey, Albert Schweitzer, Paul Tillich and Hans Urs von Balthasar. One imbibes deeply of Mediterranean cultures stretching across a thousand years, bridging via myriad trajectories a gap between pagan and Christian that many postmoderns deem unbridgeable. It is not just wealth of detail or audacity of vision that distinguishes this enterprise; an entire worldview integrates for purposes of mutual elucidation two successive epochs that many, perhaps most, Christians prefer to sunder. The German theologian Adolf von Harnack (1851-1930) deplored efforts by the "History of Religions School" (led c. 1900 by Richard Reitzenstein and Wilhelm Bousset) to fathom what Harnack denounced as the "Hellenization" of the gospel. This *Reallexikon* reexamines everything that the arch-Lutheran Harnack disapproved about the syncretizing tendencies of early Christianity.

In Great Britain such issues were pursued by Arthur Darby Nock, Donald MacKinnon and David Daube. In Germany one of few ongoing works to perpetuate the endeavor is Hans Martin von Erffa, *Ikonologie der Genesis: Die christ-* *lichen Bildthemas aus dem alten Testament und ihre Quellen,* vol. 1 (Munich: Deutscher Kunstverlag, 1989-). It inventories texts that illuminate depictions of themes from the book of Genesis. Similar sweep across Greece and the Near East sustains **275** van der Toorn, Becking and van der Horst, eds., *Dictionary of Deities and Demons in the Bible (DDD)* (1995).

Imaginativeness, precision and wealth of citations make the *Reallexikon für Antike und Christentum* one of very few works to eclipse French MEGA-ENCYCLOPEDIAS in range and depth of coverage. Closest among them comes **132** Cabrol and Leclercq, eds., *Dictionnaire d'archéologie chrétienne et de liturgie* (1903-53), but it ignores paganism and emphasizes France while omitting Egypt and Iran. It plays up Catholic issues. For all its merits, **152** Di Berardino, ed., *Encyclopedia of the Early Church* (1982, 1992) examines almost nothing before 30 C.E. and addresses exclusively Christian topics. **139** Wessel and Restle, eds., *Reallexikon zur byzantinischen Kunst* (1963-) explores Eastern Christian art and liturgy in an identical format but with less vigor. **5** Eliade, ed., *The Encyclopedia of Religion* (1987) rivals the *Reallexikon für Antike und Christentum* in imaginative articles on animals, attitudes, parts of the body and cosmology as well as ancient religions. But the German work delves deeper and evokes ancient cultures more vividly. Carsten Colpe contributed to both, but his sixty pages on "Gnosticism" in the *Reallexikon* outclasses anything in the American volumes. Indeed, *The Encyclopedia of Religion* ought to have included a salute to its chief rival. An excellent companion is **154** Everett Ferguson's *Backgrounds of Early Christianity* (1987, 1993), which cites Arthur Darby Nock's review of 1948. Reprinted in Nock's *Essays on Religion and the Ancient World* (Oxford and New York: Oxford University Press, 1972), 2:676-81, the review extols the "breadth of vision" demonstrated in the *Reallexikon* as it untangles "the great problems of continuity." The *Reallexikon* is the ne plus ultra of encyclopedias on cultural history. It makes other works seem either partisan or abbreviated or unambitious.

□ *Summary* This incomparable work, a continuation of older traditions as well as a gold mine of contemporary scholarship, sets a standard for MEGA-ENCYCLOPEDIAS. No other work integrates religion and culture so confidently or so meticulously, but appraisal of methodology is lacking.

67 (1972-) Wolfgang Haase and Hildegard Temporini, eds., *Aufstieg und Niedergang der römischen Welt: Geschichte Roms im Spiegel der neueren Forschung. II. Principat* (Berlin and New York: de Gruyter, 1972-). Analyzed further under 2.3.3 "Biblical Studies." This mightiest of COMPENDIA comprises over eighty volumes (totaling about 75,000 pages) on the cultural history of the ancient Mediterranean basin from the reign of Augustus through that of Constantine. Volumes 26.1 (1992) and 27.1 (1993) inaugurate a patrology, while volumes 19.1—19.9 and 20.1—20.2 examine Judaism. Volumes 25.1—25.6 constitute a HANDBOOK OF BIBLICAL INTERPRETATION. About one-half the articles are in German, about one-fifth in English. The bibliographies dazzle.

152 (1983, 1992) Angelo di Berardino, ed., *Encyclopedia of the Early Church*, 2 vols. (New York: Oxford University Press; London: James Clarke, 1992); xxviii & 578; x & 579-1130 pages; general bibliography (i.e., bibliographical abbreviations), 1:xvii-xxv; index, pp. 1095-130; synoptic table (i.e., chronology), pp. 887-917; 44 maps, pp. 919-48; 320 (mostly black-and-white) illustrations, pp. 949-1094; translated (with amendments) by W[illiam] H. C. Frend from *Dizionario patristico e di antichità cristiane*, 3 vols. (Casale Monferrato: Marietti, 1983); 2320 pages. A French translation appeared as *Dictionnaire encyclopédique du christianisme ancien*, 2 vols. (Paris: Cerf, 1990); 2641 pages.

□ *Scope* This monumental ENCYCLOPEDIA enlisted 167 mostly Italian specialists to write signed articles on nearly every aspect of Christianity down to the year 750 C.E. (i.e., to Bede but not Charlemagne). William H. C. Frend updated the multilingual

bibliographies through 1990. The scholarship is mainly Italian and Roman Catholic, incorporating research through 1981. Emphasis falls on regions, cities, institutions, languages, liturgies, arts, doctrines, heretics and leaders of the church in the territory of the Roman Empire. Regions as distant as Britain, Ethiopia, Persia and the Malabar Coast elicit entries spanning the entire period. Articles on Old and New Testament figures and events trace reception among church fathers as well as iconography across seven centuries (e.g., "Joseph," "Job," "Exodus," "Evangelists"). Archeology receives equal coverage with patristics, but world religions do not. This is an Italian work, boasting the density of references and sallies of wit that characterize that nation's reference works. The English edition incorporates from the Italian edition forty-four maps and 320 photographs, the latter arranged alphabetically. The bibliographies have no rival.

□ *Strengths* This magnificent ENCYCLOPEDIA incorporates a REALLEXIKON, a WHO'S WHO and a LEXICON of doctrine. It cuts into the core of whatever it addresses. A few articles elucidate history of methodology, as in "Archaeology, Christian," "Patrology—Patristics," "Palaeography," "Manuscript Tradition" and even the field known as "protology" (i.e., "study of beginnings").

Major clusters deserve enumerating:

1. Places. The art and archeology of more than thirty provinces is surveyed (e.g., "Africa," "Asia Minor," "Britain and Ireland," "Corsica," "Dalmatia," "Gaul," "Pannonia"). More than one hundred cities (e.g., "Antioch," "Carthage," "Marseilles," "Ravenna," "Thessalonica," "Toledo") elicit depictions of history, councils, liturgy, thinkers and archeology. The longest regional articles concern "Italy" (seven pages) and "Rome" (five pages). Invaders like the "Franks," "Goths," "Longobards (Lombards)" and "Vandals" win detailed entries, but peoples such as Scandinavians and Slavs, who were Christianized after 800, do not (except in "Palaeoslavonic, Translations in").

2. *Languages and literature.* Major and minor languages of the early church elicit articles on history, literature and liturgy (e.g., "Greek," "Latin," "Coptic," "Syriac," even "Georgian" and "Sogdian" but not "Aramaic" or "Hebrew"). There is also an overview on "Languages of the Fathers." Philological entries explore translations from Greek to Latin in "Flesh," "Hypostasis," "Lay-Layman-Laity," "Paradise," "Pneuma," "Refrigerium" and "Saeculum." Articles on "Love of God and Neighbour" and on "Mysticism" stand out among these inventories of denotations. Compilations list "Latin Translations of Greek Texts" and "Literary Genres." The notions of "Tragedy" and "Comedy," however, get ignored, as do nearly all non-Christian writers except Pliny the Younger on the topic of Christians.

3. *Art.* The article "Church Buildings" surveys history, types and liturgical uses, while that on "Image" explores the theology of veneration. Entries on "Diptych," "Fibula," "Lamp," "Mosaic," "Portrait," "Sarcophagi" and "Sculpture" delineate types and dissemination. Technical terms receive their due, as in "Etimasia" (i.e., "depiction of the divine throne"). Representative works from throughout the Roman Empire get illustrated in over three hundred superbly captioned photographs including about fifty in color. Art historians will feast.

4. *Liturgy.* The book's longest entry (ten pages) examines practices, languages and texts of "Liturgy" East and West. An article on "Liturgical Furniture" itemizes thirty-four types and that on "Vestments, Liturgical" seventeen. Regional liturgies such as the "Ambrosian," "Byzantine," "Gallican" and "Hispanic" command lengthy articles, but inexplicably church "Calendar" elicits only twenty-five lines. Even more unaccountably, music evokes meager entries under "Chant" and "Hymn-Hymnology," while "Dance" gets just thirty lines.

5. *Customs.* Entries on "Dress," "Entertainments," "Fasting and Abstinence," "Hospitality, Christian," "Letter, Epistle" and "Schools" depict daily life. Another

series examines "Dead, Cult of the," "Resurrection of the Dead," "Martyr-Martyrdom" and "Cemetery" (but not "Catacomb" or "Relics"). The entry "Ministries, Ordained Ministers" is a gem. Although "War" receives one-half column, individual wars are ignored.

6. *Religions.* Judaism gets referenced under "Jews and Christians," "Judaeo-Hellenism," "Judaizers," "Mishnah" and "Antisemitism," but seldom for its own sake, and there seem to be no Jewish contributors. Islam wins only seven passing mentions, Zoroastrianism five, and Buddhism four. Nevertheless, mystery cults like "Mithras and Mithraism" and rival religions like "Mani-Manichees-Manichaeism" and "Mandaeans and Mandaeism" win ample analysis.

7. *Persons.* The WHO'S WHO encompasses popes, bishops (particularly patriarchs), scholars, heretics and saints, not to mention civil rulers of empire, provinces and cities. There are entries on fifty-three "Johns," eighteen "Peters," seventeen "Pauls" and eleven each of "Gregory," "Leontius" and "Maximus." These range in length from three lines to three pages. Major Church fathers elicit copious coverage of life, works and doctrine but not influence. On giants like "Athanasius," "Augustine" and "Origen," bibliography fills a column.

8. *Saints.* The HAGIOGRAPHY dismisses "Catherine of Alexandria," "Lucy of Syracuse" and "Ursula" as entirely legendary and does the same for tales concerning "Cecilia," "Christopher" and "Lawrence." Lives of saints are not retold.

9. *Doctrine.* Comparisons abound between Eastern and Western views concerning "Anthropology," "Christology," "Ecclesiology," "Faith," "God," "Grace," "Sin" and "Trinity." An entry on "Creeds and Confessions of Faith" assembles almost one hundred examples. Each of the sacraments and its components (e.g., "Anaphora" and "Intercession") get scrutinized. Biblical study is examined in "Apocrypha," "Bible," "Exegesis, Patristic" and "Scripture, Holy" as well as in entries on major biblical figures and books.

Major and minor heresies are scrutinized through leaders ("Arius-Arians-Arianism," "Donatism-Donatists," "Pelagius-Pelagians-Pelagianism"), through opponents ("Athanasius," "Augustine") and through overviews ("Gnosis-Gnosticism," "Heresiologists," "Heresy-Heretic").

10. Philosophy. Masterful syntheses include "Hellenism and Christianity," "Stoicism and the Fathers" and "Platonism and the Fathers" [in nine pages], not to mention briefer articles on "Encyclopaedia," "Hermetism" and "Syncretism." An article of eight pages explicates "Neo-Platonism" in Plotinus, Porphyry and Proclus, but no entries handle Cynicism, Epicureanism or Skepticism. A few concepts like "Dualism" and "Pantheism" elicit definitions.

11. Oddities. Few reference books boast so many offbeat articles. A sample includes: "Cryptography" on techniques of dissimulation in writing; "Colour" on the symbolism of black, white, red and green; "Consolatio" on writing for the bereaved; "Kiss" on the multiple meanings and contexts of that gesture; "Members of the Church" on social classes and the role of laity; "Virgin-Virginity-Velatio" on motivation for this form of asceticism; "Vision" on the evolution of depictions of the afterlife both before and after these supposedly originated with Gregory I; "Roman Law and Christianity" on borrowings in theology and institutions from legal terminology. In a word, on almost any topic, the *Encyclopedia of the Early Church* repays a browser beyond all dreams of avarice.

□ *Weaknesses* This ENCYCLOPEDIA confines itself to Christianity and its relations to contemporary antiquity. This is neither a LEXICON of the ancient world nor a BIBLE DICTIONARY. The Bible figures only insofar as church fathers reacted to it. Likewise, the work eschews presentism. Although it traces methods of scholarship into the twentieth century (particularly as regards archeology and manuscript studies), it does not pursue reception of biblical figures, the church fathers or liturgies (except the "Byzantine") beyond the year 800. Nor does the *Encyclopedia* accommodate

twentieth-century assumptions. Prissily, the entry on "Spirituality" proposes to suppress the term because the ancients "preferred to speak of spiritual theology, ascesis, and mysticism, or simply, of Christian and evangelical life" (p. 792). Concepts of modern origin like hermeneutics, idealism, kenosis and salvation history get ignored, as do gender issues and homosexuality. None of these appears in the index. Nor are there any syntheses of non-Christian topics like Mediterranean culture or empire. Indeed, politics and economics are scanted except insofar as they impinged on the church, as in "Church and Empire" or "Slave-Slavery." Even canon law gets short shrift. As regards cross-references, a thematic index would have been a boon, as would a listing of related entries at the end of major ones. Only seldom is this done, as in "Bible" and "Literary Genres." As a rule, in order to pursue a theme, one must scour the index, which contains no subheads.

□ *Competitors* On almost any topic this ENCYCLOPEDIA offers incomparably greater depth than any rival except the French MEGA-ENCYCLOPEDIAS and specialized works like **143** Atiya, ed., *The Coptic Encyclopedia* (1991). No other reference work in church history supplies such copious photographs, maps and chronologies. Standbys like **29** Cross, ed., *The Oxford Dictionary of the Christian Church* (1957, 1974) and **156** Ferguson, ed., *Encyclopedia of Early Christianity* (1990) help prepare the reader to profit from this magnum opus, as do works on Eastern Christianity like **141** Assfalg and Krüger, *Kleines Wörterbuch des christlichen Orients* (1975, 1991). **72** Metzger and Coogan, eds., *The Oxford Companion to the Bible* (1993) helps to update methodology. Among Catholic MEGA-ENCYCLOPEDIAS, the closest overlap occurs with **132** Cabrol and Leclercq, eds., *Dictionnaire d'archéologie chrétienne et de liturgie,* 30 vols. in 15 (1903-53). Although the latter delivers almost unimaginable depth, the *Encyclopedia of the Early Church* is more up-to-date and more imaginative. It lacks, however, articles for beginners such as occur in **34**

Gentz, ed., *The Dictionary of Bible and Religion* (1986). In a word, this is a pinnacle resource that requires decades to exploit. No other work except **151** Klauser, ed., *Reallexikon für Antike und Christentum* (1950-) induces such immersion in the Christian past.

☐ *Summary* This magisterial ENCYCLOPEDIA is a "swimming pool for elephants" rather than a "wading pool for lambs" (to paraphrase Elizabeth Livingstone's reference to Gregory the Great in **30** *The Concise Oxford Dictionary of the Christian Church* [1977], p. iii). Lucky is anyone who starts as a youth to explore these depths. They will require more than a lifetime to exhaust.

153 (1986-) Cornelius Mayer, ed., *Augustinus-Lexikon,* planned in 7 vols. (Basel: Schwabe, 1986-); vol. 1 (through "Conversio") completed in 1994, lxiv & 651 pages; list of Augustine's works, 1:xxvi-xli; a few maps. An index volume is planned.

☐ *Critique* This unprecedented LEXICON promises about twelve hundred signed articles expounding Augustine's life and thought, while ignoring later controversies occasioned by him. Volume 1 contains ninety-five entries in German, sixty-eight in French and twenty in English (including one on Augustine's life). All have multilingual bibliographies that run up to two pages. Titles of articles use Latin terms exclusively, covering regions (Africa, Egypt, Babylon), cities (Caesarea, Carthage), persons (Abraham, Ambrose, Basil), heretics (Apollinaristae, Ariani) and concepts (allegory, angel, animal), not to mention every one of Augustine's 131 works. Neither Augustine's interpreters nor controversies like Jansenism command entries. Latin quotations abound, and citations accumulate beyond number. The longest entry in volume 1 is Goulven Madec's thirty pages on "Christus" (in French). Notable entries in English include crucial ones by Gerald Bonner on "Adam," "Augustinus (vita)" and "Concupiscentia." Gerard J. P. O'Daly expounds "Affectus," "Anima, Animus," and in one of the longest entries "Civitate dei." Gerard Watson scintillates

on "Cogitatio" and "Cognitio." Those who read neither German nor French will feast on these hundred-odd pages in English. No scholar of early Christian thought can afford to neglect this masterpiece. Once it is complete, probably no other single thinker (not even Dante, Luther, Shakespeare or Goethe) will have inspired a reference work of comparable scope or depth.

☐ *Summary* This LEXICON explores Augustine's life and thought with unheard thoroughness. Although articles are nine-tenths in German or French, English ones address central topics. The bibliographies are irreplaceable.

154 (1987, 1993) Everett Ferguson, *Backgrounds of Early Christianity* (Grand Rapids, Mich.: Eerdmans, 1987; 2d ed., 1993); xx & 611 pages; two indexes (subject and scriptural), pp. 585-605; general bibliography, pp. xix-xx; black-and-white photographs throughout.

☐ *Critique* This introductory HANDBOOK embraces far more than its title implies. It is that rarity, an authentic German-style HANDBOOK written by an American. Six chapters divide into fifty-six sections and more than two hundred subsections, offering 109 separate bibliographies (of works in English and German, arranged chronologically). Eight hundred fifty footnotes cite further literature. Ninety pages on "Society and Culture" evoke Roman political, social and economic life. One hundred sixty pages on "Hellenistic-Roman Religions" itemize Greek, Roman, personal and Eastern religions, culminating with Gnosticism. Seventy pages on "Hellenistic Roman Philosophies" summarize all schools from Plato to Plotinus, paying particular attention to the Cynics and Stoics. A perspicuous 175 pages on Judaism introduces writers, parties, beliefs and institutions with outlines of sources, including the Mishnah. Another HANDBOOK enlarges this coverage: Lester L. Grabbe, *Judaism from Cyrus to Hadrian,* 2 vols. (Minneapolis: Fortress, 1992; London: SCM, 1994). After all this, Ferguson requires a mere thirty-eight pages to outline little-known sources on early Christianity, while ignoring biblical studies. As a student of Arthur Darby Nock (1902-1963), Ferguson combines that master's acumen and range with a knack for organization. One wishes for a comparably pithy HANDBOOK on early Islam. Anyone interested in classical antiquity will delight in this panorama.

□ *Summary* This HANDBOOK is a gold mine of bibliography, summaries and analysis. It miniaturizes a library.

155 (1988) Michael Grant and Rachel Kitzinger, eds., *Civilization of the Ancient Mediterranean: Greece and Rome,* 3 vols. (New York: Scribner's, 1988); ·xxvii & 1980 pages; index, pp. 1853-1980; no general bibliography.

□ *Critique* This magnificent COMPENDIUM dispenses signed articles (with multilingual bibliography) on nearly every aspect of history, culture and daily life in ancient Greece and Rome. Sixteen articles on religion (pp. 847-1073) include pairs that examine four topics each for Greece and Rome ("Priesthoods," "Divinations and Oracles," "Sacrifice and Ritual" and "The Afterlife"). John Ferguson excels on "Divinities" and "Magic." Seth Schwartz's eighteen-page essay on "Judaism" from 538 B.C.E. to 324 C.E. is among the best anywhere, and Helmut Koester and Vasiliki Limberis sparkle in their chapter on "Christianity." The index permits use as a REALLEXIKON. Lucid writing, sweeping overviews and superb bibliographies make these volumes a model of their kind. They inspired an equally distinguished companion on the Eastern Mediterranean: Jack M. Sasson, ed., *Civilizations of the Ancient Near East,* 4 vols. (New York: Scribner's, 1995), whose 189 essays scrutinize Egypt, Palestine, Syria, Mesopotamia and Anatolia from 3000 B.C.E. to 300 B.C.E. Four articles analyze religion in Canaan and ancient Israel (3:2031-94).

□ *Summary* This COMPENDIUM on ancient Greece and Rome offers some of the acutest writing on religion in the ancient Mediterranean.

156 (1990) Everett Ferguson, ed., *Encyclopedia of Early Christianity* (New York and London: Garland Publishing, 1990); xx & 983 pages; index, pp. 947-83;

general bibliography, p. viii; black-and-white photos in the text; also in paperback.

□ *Scope* This LEXICON of early Christian history covers "persons, cities, doctrines, practices, art, liturgy, heresies, and schisms" to 600 C.E. Nearly a thousand signed articles by 135 (mostly American) authorities boast multilingual bibliographies. Isidore of Seville (c. 560-636) is declared the last of the church fathers, although on topics like "Filioque" the coverage reaches into the eleventh century. Each entry begins with a definition and expounds history in detail. Syntheses abound, notably Frederick Norris on "Christ, Christology," Everett Ferguson on "Apologetics" and James E. Goehring on "Monasticism." As in a patrology, articles on persons (i.e., martyrs, church fathers, heretics) outline major writings by and about the individual. Bibliographies are exemplary.

□ *Strengths* Everett Ferguson deploys skill as an panoramist to conceive another model reference work. Clarity of writing, skill in selection and a sense of proportion make entries excel at teaching. They recount how rapidly the early church changed in both doctrine and practice. Ancient philosophy gets stressed; an entry on "Sacrifice," for example, expounds Plato, Porphyry and various rabbis as background to Christian views. Articles on cities like Alexandria, Corinth, Constantinople and Ravenna narrate events of local history. "Celtic Christianity" is characterized in some depth. On saints, critique of sources is sometimes extensive, as when the "miracle-working" of Saint Patrick is construed as a creation of the Middle Ages. Attention flows to both recent scholars (e.g., Philip Schaff, Johannes Quasten, Jean Daniélou) and earlier shapers of the field (e.g., the Bollandists). Definitions that open each article are often engagingly simple, as when "Iconography" is called "the reasoning behind Christian art." Articles on visual art carry excellent illustrations (e.g., "Baptistery," "Mosaics," "Sarcophagus"). A few churches elicit individual entries as in "Holy Sepulchre, Church of the," "S. Apollinare Nuovo" and "Sta Maria Maggiore."

□ *Weaknesses* This LEXICON functions as an intermediate INTRODUCTION. It does not pursue methodology or hermeneutics, nor as a rule does it address controversies among recent scholars. Some will wish for overviews of scholarship such as adorn **72** Metzger and Coogan, eds., *The Oxford Companion to the Bible* (1993). Although seldom bland, a nonconfessional tone deprives articles about doctrine and heresies of bite such as enlivens **84** O'Carroll's *Trinitas* (1987) or **143** Atiya, ed., *The Coptic Encyclopedia* (1991).

□ *Competitors* This winsome LEXICON held sway in English for only two years. A larger rival, **152** Di Berardino, ed., *Encyclopedia of the Early Church* (1982, 1992), probes far deeper on nearly every topic. By tackling methodology, the Italian work emulates the mastery of **82** Davis, ed., *A Catholic Dictionary of Theology* (1962-71). The latter remains the most captivating of English-language works on the church fathers. If the Ferguson volume suits students, the Di Berardino one will delight researchers. By sorting out Greek, Roman, Eastern and Jewish materials, **154** Ferguson's HANDBOOK, *Backgrounds of Early Christianity* (1987, 1993) complements both.

□ *Summary* For anyone pursuing the origin of any Christian practice or belief, the *Encyclopedia of Early Christianity* is an ideal place to start. Historians of Mediterranean antiquity and of the early Middle Ages will enjoy browsing.

143 (1991) Aziz S. Atiya, ed., *The Coptic Encyclopedia*, 8 vols. (New York: Macmillan, 1991). Analyzed further under 2.9.3 "Eastern Christianity." This ENCYCLOPEDIA on Christianity in Egypt assesses the early church from the perspective of Alexandria. Heresies and material culture are stressed. Each of the tractates in the Nag Hammadi library elicits an entry.

157 (1992) Joseph F. Kelly, *The Concise Dictionary of Early Christianity* (Collegeville, Minn.: Michael Glazier/Liturgical, 1992); 203 pages; no index; general bibliography, pp. 201-3.

□ *Critique* This primer furnishes about one thousand brief entries on persons,

councils and a few concepts (e.g., "gnostic") down to 600 C.E. It is chiefly a WHO'S WHO of church personalities but without individual bibliographies. There are no entries on places. Beginners will find the succinctness helpful but should move quickly to **156** Ferguson, ed., *Encyclopedia of Early Christianity* (1990) and thence to **152** Di Berardino, ed., *Encyclopedia of the Early Church* (1982, 1992).

□ *Summary* This primer on persons and events will point beginners toward more advanced works.

2.10.3 MEDIEVAL CHURCH (313-1400)

OVERVIEW: A MONOPOLY OF REALLEXIKONS
Postmodern REVISIONISM has not yet reshaped reference books in this field, which continues to be dominated by REALLEXIKONS.

LIST OF WORKS ANALYZED
158 (1977-) *Lexikon der Mittelalters*, planned in 10 vols. (Munich and Zürich: Artemis, 1977-)

159 (1982-89) Joseph R. Strayer, ed., *Dictionary of the Middle Ages*, 13 vols. (New York: Scribner's, 1982-89)

160 (1992) Jeremiah Hackett, ed., *Medieval Philosophers* (Detroit: Gale, 1992)

ANALYSIS OF WORKS
158 (1977-) *Lexikon der Mittelalters*, planned in 10 vols. (Munich and Zürich: Artemis, 1977-); vol. 7, fasc. 4 (1995) goes through "Servatius"; 1100 pages per volume.

□ *Critique* This awe-inspiring MEGA-REALLEXIKON spans the history of Europe and the Mediterranean from about 300 C.E. to about 1500 C.E. Hundreds of contributors write signed articles (each with multilingual bibliography) on persons, places, concepts and practices. Theologians, saints, heretics, religious orders and artists receive detailed entries. Fifty-seven persons named "Hugo" and 192 named "Johannes" (plus fifty-six named "Johann") win numbered entries, exceeding by a factor of four the WHO'S WHO in **159** Strayer, ed., *The Dictionary of the Middle Ages* (1982-89). European knack for compression shines through.

□ *Summary* One of the most comprehensive historical REALLEXIKONS currently in progress, the *Lexikon des Mittelalters* surveys scholarship on every conceivable person and issue between 300 and 1500. The bibliographies are in a class by themselves.

159 (1982-89) **Joseph R. Strayer, ed., *Dictionary of the Middle Ages*,** 13 vols. (New York: Scribner's, 1982-89); volumes vary between 520 and 760 pages, totaling about 8000 pages; index of 565 pages in vol. 13; maps, charts and black-and-white photographs throughout; no general bibliography.

□ *Scope* This comprehensive teaching EN-CYCLOPEDIA is a REALLEXIKON in all but name. Five thousand signed articles by about thirteen hundred contributors include multilingual bibliographies. Coverage stretches from about 500 C.E. to about 1500 C.E., ranging geographically from Spain, Ireland and Scandinavia through North Africa to Russia and Iran (but not India). Discussion of Islam extends similarly from Spain and North Africa to Iran. Several types of entries stand out. There is a WHO'S WHO of thinkers, artists, musicians, saints, heretics and rulers (including Byzantine emperors, caliphs, popes and French and English kings). Entries embrace regions (e.g., "Ireland," "Iraq") and capital cities (e.g., "Isfahan," "Kiev"). Languages and literary traditions inspire lengthy surveys, ranging from Armenian and Hungarian to German, Greek, Italian and Latin. Painting and architecture elicit surveys of both Christian and Islamic production. Music evokes twenty-three articles filling one hundred pages. Numerous entries elucidate economic institutions ("Guilds and Métiers," "Masons and Builders") and practices ("Castles and Fortifications," "Clocks and Reckoning of Time"). A splendid series examines economic techniques (e.g., "Heating," "Hunting and Fowling," "Irrigation"), while shorter articles explain uses of products like "Barrels," "Hemp," "Herbs" and "Honey."

Short articles constitute a GLOSSARY (e.g., "Holyrood," "Hagia Sophia [Kiev]," "Lavra"). The index of 565 pages is beyond praise. It claims to list no fewer than one hundred thousand persons, places and concepts (including Latin titles of treatises). The level of an intermediate INTRO-DUCTION is maintained throughout. The style is plain, and cross-references abound.

□ *Strengths* The editor, Joseph Strayer (1904-87), announced an intention to "render the field surveyable to scholars, offering them a singular means of coordinating the various branches of medieval scholarship into an accessible and coherent whole" (1:x). As this forewarns, range exceeds depth. The WHO'S WHO may be the most consistently satisfactory component, for many entries, particularly on writers (e.g., "Hrotswitha of Gandersheim"), achieve a specificity often missing in the surveys. There are ten entries for "Hugh" (or "Hugo"), fourteen for "Henry" and fifty-four for "John." England, France, Germany and Italy stand at the core of the work, but coverage of Byzantium as well as of Russia is excellent.

Articles on methodology vary. Five articles on "Historiography" inventory medieval chroniclers without discussing modern historians. In contrast, an entry on "Hagiography, Western" evaluates not only medieval sources but critical works since the seventeenth century. On religious matters, surveys abound. The term *liturgy* evokes eight entries filling twenty-five pages, including Celtic, Islamic and Jewish practices. The topic "Law" unleashes two dozen articles in 150 pages, including overviews of Jewish and Islamic law. An entry on the "Latin Church" recapitulates one thousand years in thirty-five pages. Christian doctrine ("Christology") and Islamic sects ("Isma'iliya") are expounded, while "Heresy" elicits surveys of "Armenian," "Byzantine," "Western European" and "Islamic" varieties. Four articles under "Islam" explore "Conquests," "Religion," "Administration" and "Art and Architecture." The latter piece by Priscilla Soucek deploys eighteen black-and-white photographs in twenty-two pages. Judaism elicits similar surveys (e.g., "Hebrew Belles Lettres," "Hebrew Poetry") as well as four incisive pages by Moshe Idel on "Cabala." Individual entries describe eight "Judeo-" languages ranging from "Judeo-Arabic" and "Judeo-Persian" to "Judeo-Provençal" and "Yiddish." However conducive to teaching, the writing seldom attains integrative power.

□ *Weaknesses* An "international" team of thirteen hundred mostly American contributors wrote primarily for students, both beginning and advanced. They produced a work to consult rather than to treasure. It lacks both the grandeur of a MEGA-ENCY-CLOPEDIA and the penetration of LEXICONS on early church history, Judaism or Islam. Scholars of religion will discover that specialized works cover nearly all topics more searchingly. For them the *Dictionary of the Middle Ages* helps above all to expound nonreligious topics, particularly political, economic and literary ones. On matters like "Chronology," "Heraldry" and "Mongol Empire" it offers a fine introduction. Absence of confessional commitment will please the secular but may disappoint devotees of the Catholic MEGA-ENCYCLOPEDIAS. For all its comprehensiveness, this work lacks flair.

□ *Competitors* This REALLEXIKON seeks primarily to teach and only secondarily to further research. Having differentiated three levels of readers (high school students, college students and specialists), the editor warns that "the deeper one digs [here], the wider the gaps." While coverage is admirably broad, it does not delve nearly as deeply as German works like the **158** *Lexikon des Mittelalters* (1986-), which is also more up-to-date and cites vastly more bibliography. Users of that MEGA-ENCYCLOPEDIA will scarcely need this one. Another German masterpiece, **151** Klauser, ed., *Reallexikon für Antike und Christentum* (1950-) seems to come from a different world, upholding an altogether higher standard of penetration and documentation. Another REALLEXIKON on the Middle Ages, **144** Kashdan, ed., *The Oxford Dictionary of Byzantium* (1990) covers more persons and events from Byzantium and probes with greater astute-

ness relations between East and West as well as between Orthodoxy and Islam. Recently, a thousand-page REALLEXIKON of persons, places and institutions updated bibliography on France: William W. Kibler and Grover A. Zinn, eds., *Medieval France: An Encyclopedia* (New York and London: Garland Publishing, 1995). A companion volume treats Scandinavia: Phillip Pulsiano, ed., *Medieval Scandinavia: An Encyclopedia* (1993). The *Dictionary of the Middle Ages* will help specialists to become generalists, and students at any level to map a field. It excels at overviews, while seldom probing depths.

□ *Summary* This intermediate REAL-LEXIKON serves students admirably but will disappoint researchers, particularly those who frequent the German masterworks. An overdose of surveys begins to pall.

160 (1992) Jeremiah Hackett, ed., *Medieval Philosophers* (Detroit: Gale, 1992); xiv & 465 pages; published as vol. 115 in "Dictionary of Literary Biography"; general bibliography, pp. 381-90; cumulative index (to the series, vol. 1-115), pp. 381-90.

□ *Critique* Published toward the end of an ambitious series dedicated to European and American writers, this WHO'S WHO analyzes forty-one philosophers from about 400 to about 1490. Six are Muslim, two are Jewish (Maimonides and Crescas) and the remainder Christian. Averaging ten to fifteen pages in length, the entries address college students, supplying copious primary and secondary bibliographies. Biographies recount careers and expound doctrines but do not sketch social context. Anyone embarking upon study of a medieval philosopher will find this an ideal starting point.

□ *Summary* This introductory WHO'S WHO summarizes careers and thought with superb bibliographies.

2.10.4 EARLY MODERN CHURCH (1400-1700)

OVERVIEW: AMAZING GAPS The era of the Reformation has inspired few reference works apart from a WHO'S WHO of Germans: Robert Stupperich, *Reforma-*

torenlexikon (Gütersloh: Gerd Mohn, 1984). The topic tends to be subsumed either in general works on Christianity or in works of confessional self-definition (for which see 2.9.1 "Churches and Denominations: Protestantism"). The shortage was eased, however, with publication of Hans J. Hillerbrand, ed., *The Oxford Encyclopedia of the Reformation*, 4 vols. (New York and London: Oxford University Press, 1996). Twelve hundred articles with multilingual bibliographies canvass political, social, cultural and religious history of the sixteenth century. It appeared too late to be analyzed in this directory.

LIST OF WORKS ANALYZED

161 (1934) Ludwig Koch, S.J., ed., *Jesuiten-Lexikon: Die Gesellschaft Jesu einst und jetzt*, 2 vols. (Paderborn, 1934; reprint, Löwen: Bibliothek SJ, 1962)

37 ([1975] 1990-) Friedrich Wilhelm Bautz [d. 1979], then Traugott Bautz, eds., *Biographisch-Bibliographisches Kirchen-lexikon*, planned in 10 vols. (Hamm: Verlag Bautz, 1975-). Analyzed under 2.1 "Christianity: General."

ANALYSIS OF WORKS

161 (1934) Ludwig Koch, S.J., ed., *Jesuiten-Lexikon: Die Gesellschaft Jesu einst und jetzt*, 2 vols. (Paderborn, 1934; reprint, Löwen: Bibliothek SJ, 1962); 939 pages; no index; no general bibliography.

□ *Critique* This historical LEXICON of Jesuits and Jesuit activities worldwide was written by a dozen contributors. Only a few of the unsigned articles have bibliography. More than half the entries compose a WHO'S WHO of Jesuits. Entries on cities (Köln, Coimbra, Shanghai), countries (Argentina, Germany) and continents (Africa) recount the order's activities in each location. The order's history is narrated (cols. 665-84) and each of its generals characterized. Entries on major thinkers (e.g., Aristotle) and individual sciences (e.g., mathematics, liturgics) recount Jesuit contributions to their study. Latin terms are defined and their history sketched (e.g., "monita secreta"). The writing is crisp and candid.

□ *Summary* A unique view of world history between 1534 and 1934 unfolds in this forthright LEXICON.

2.10.5 MODERNITY (SINCE 1700)

OVERVIEW: OVERLAP WITH OTHER CATEGORIES Works on Christianity in the modern era overlap with works in at least five other categories. Those on 2.10.6 "North America" are treated separately below, while works on 2.2 "Ecumenism," 2.3 "Biblical Studies," 2.4 "Theology" and 2.5 "Spirituality" have been treated earlier. Besides a work on Russia, this section features a LEXICON that confines itself to Christianity in the twentieth century. A REVISIONIST classic, 125 Gisel, ed., *Encyclopédie du protestantisme* (1995), reinterprets innumerable aspects of modernity. So does **215** Akoun, ed., *Mythes et croyances du monde entier*, esp. vol. 5 (1985).

LIST OF WORKS ANALYZED

162 (1988-) Paul D. Steeves, ed., *The Modern Encyclopedia of Religion in Russia and the Soviet Union*, planned in 25 vols. (Gulf Breeze, Fla.: Academic International, 1988-)

163 ([1955] 1991) J[ames] D[ixon] Douglas, ed., *New 20th-Century Encyclopedia of Religious Knowledge*, 2d ed. (Grand Rapids, Mich.: Baker Book House, 1991)

125 (1995) Pierre Gisel, ed., *Encyclopédie du protestantisme* (Paris: Cerf and Geneva: Labor et Fides, 1995). Analyzed under 2.9.1 "Churches and Denominations: Protestantism."

ANALYSIS OF WORKS

162 (1988-) Paul D. Steeves, ed., *The Modern Encyclopedia of Religion in Russia and the Soviet Union*, planned in 25 vols. (Gulf Breeze, Fla.: Academic International Press, 1988-); vol. 5 (1993) goes through "Council"; 242 pages per volume; no index; no general bibliography.

□ *Critique* This historical LEXICON investigates all religions in Russia and the former Soviet Union, starting with Kievan Rus.

The format matches that of a companion, Joseph L. Wiecynski, ed., *The Modern Encyclopedia of Russian and Soviet History*, 58 vols. (Gulf Breeze, Fla.: Academic International, 1976-94), whose thirteen thousand pages scant religion. All branches of Christianity elicit entries, but Orthodoxy (particularly its liturgy, leaders and councils) predominates. The WHO'S WHO instances rulers, writers and theologians. A few places ("Mount Athos," "California") figure, but no cities. In a unique feature, about one-third of the entries come from Russian reference works on Orthodoxy and Judaism, many carrying lengthy bibliographies. Articles on the Bible, "Baptists" and "Catholics" run up to fifteen pages. Every historian of Russia will make discoveries galore. A REALLEXIKON on the Ukraine, Volodymyr Kubijovyc, ed., *Encyclopedia of Ukraine*, 5 vols. (Toronto: University of Toronto Press, 1984-93) discusses chiefly "Church" (1:468-93) and "Icons" (2: 294-99), while generally minimizing religion.

□ *Summary* This ambitious LEXICON probes the history of all religions in the former Soviet Union. The depth surprises.

163 ([1955] 1991) J[ames] D[ixon] Douglas, ed., *New 20th-Century Encyclopedia of Religious Knowledge*, 2d ed. (Grand Rapids, Mich.: Baker Book House, 1991); xvi & 896 pages; no index; no general bibliography.

□ *Scope* Artfully this LEXICON recapitulates Christianity and its interactions with world religions since about 1880. Reworked by evangelicals from a landmark, Lefferts A. Loetscher, ed., *Twentieth Century Encyclopedia of Religious Knowledge* (1955), this amounts to a new work. Twenty-one hundred mostly signed articles by 350 authors trace developments in Christianity worldwide, together with biblical roots. A WHO'S WHO on more than a thousand theologians, scholars, popes, missionaries and evangelists lists writings *by* but hardly ever *about* each individual. A REALLEXIKON treats denominations, ecumenism, missions, theology, ethics, trends in scholarship and at least a hundred nations. Bibliography accompanies only grand overviews such as

"Hermeneutics, Biblical," "Reformation Studies in the 20th Century" and "Student Organizations, Religious." Tight editing assures succinctness.

□ *Strengths* This LEXICON digests the past 120 years of Christian history consummately. Surveys (ranging from two to five pages) of twentieth-century scholarship on topics like "Christology," "Patristics" and "Church History Studies" are outstanding. Five pages on "Paul, The Apostle," three on "Jesus Christ" and three on "Myth in the NT" outline a century of research. The sweep of church history unfolds in "Calendar, Christian," "Calvinism" and "Protestantism." Philosophy of religion surfaces in "Existentialism, Christian," "Ego and Egoism," "Irrationalism" and "Proofs of God's Existence." An entry on "Science and Religion" appraises the Gifford Lectures. Nearly every Protestant denomination, large or small (at least in Europe and the United States), elicits an entry and usually bibliography, but new churches in Africa do not. Controversies surrounding "Charismatic Movement" and "Divine Healing" get aired. Missions worldwide are highlighted, including twenty pages listing "Bible Translations, Modern Versions" in fifty-nine languages. Social sciences crop up in "Peace Movements," "Psychology of Religion" and "Revolution and Religion." Of particular note are articles on each of about one hundred countries (including the Seychelles and Singapore) as well as regions such as "East Africa," "West Africa" and "South Pacific, Islands of." No other single volume in English except **32** Barrett, ed., *World Christian Encyclopedia* (1982) reports demography of individual nations so thoroughly. Moreover, the WHO'S WHO embraces more twentieth-century Christians, particularly from Europe and the United States, than does any other single volume in English. Some biographical sketches survive from 1955, while entries like "Theology, 20th-Century Trends in" and "Liberalism" conjoin an earlier article with a new one that covers developments since 1950. Thus survives William Foxwell Albright's classic on "Archeology, Biblical."

□ *Weaknesses* Although the 350 contributors are nearly all Protestant, theological articles achieve impartiality except for a few like "Biblical Theology (NT)," "Conscience" and "Man, Doctrine of." While entries on persons and events uphold neutrality, selection of topics favors Protestantism. Indeed, many more Protestants than Catholics win biographies. To be sure, John Lynch shines on Catholic matters like "Breviary," "Canon Law" and "Cardinals, College of." Synopses of "Congregations, Roman" and of "Legates and Nuncios" stand out, as well as synopses of particular religious orders. But no articles treat hagiography or individual saints, and only fifteen lines go to "Patron Saints." Inexplicably, an article on "Eastern Orthodox Churches" that is cross-referenced under both "Byzantine Rite" and "Orthodox Churches" was omitted. Whereas "Contemplation" and "Meditation" merit a page each, "Sufism" gets two. Oddly, neither mysticism nor spirituality inspired an entry. Coverage of non-Christian religions is spotty and tends to recapitulate history from long before the twentieth century, as in "Shi'ism," "Shinto" and "Sikhism." Articles on "Phenomenology of Religion" and "Worship in Non-Christian Religions," however, betray unease alike with dialogue, new religious movements and pluralism. Although essays scold "New Age Movement," "Occultism" and "Spiritualism, Spiritism," Irving Hexham exudes good sense on "Comparative Religion" and "Sects and Cults."

□ *Competitors* As a single-volume LEXICON delineating persons, countries, scholarship and movements connected with Christianity since 1880, the *New 20th-Century Dictionary* has no peer in English. The range and reliability perpetuate virtues of Loetscher, ed., *Twentieth Century Encyclopedia of Religious Knowledge* (1955), albeit in a more attractive format and largely shorn of pre-1850 issues. Surveys of twentieth-century scholarship are scarcely equaled even in **45** Fahlbusch et al., eds., *Evangelisches Kirchenlexikon* (1986-) or in **36** Drehsen et al., eds.,

Wörterbuch des Christentums (1988). **46** Lossky et al., *Dictionary of the Ecumenical Movement* (1991) tackles more theological questions (and in greater depth) but lacks entries on individual nations or a wide-ranging WHO'S WHO. Among Westminster/SCM dictionaries, that on **116** Christian theology (1969, 1983) is more open-minded but scants detail from our century. **115** Childress and Macquarrie, eds., *The New Westminster Dictionary of Christian Ethics* (1986) probes issues more deeply but lacks a WHO'S WHO. Sober where the Westminster/SCM volumes tend to be jaunty, the *New 20th-Century Encyclopedia* boasts a steadier focus and summarizes trends in scholarship more authoritatively. **125** McKim, ed., *Encyclopedia of the Reformed Faith* (1992) underplays the twentieth century. Naturally **29** Cross, ed., *The Oxford Dictionary of the Christian Church* (1957, 1974) holds its own concerning the first half of the century but falls out of date on post-1950 topics. The *New 20th-Century Encyclopedia* is one of few English-language works to rival it in power of historical synthesis.

□ *Summary* A master editor has refashioned a classic, allowing sobriety to dispel trendiness. Anyone seeking comprehensiveness, fairness and synthesis concerning recent Christianity should sample this book.

2.10.6 NORTH AMERICA

OVERVIEW: AN INVITATION TO REVISIONISM American church history has generated a library of reference works, both general and specialized. The directory analyzes denominational ones under 2.9.1 "Churches and Denominations: Protestantism," while American theologians appear also under 2.4 "Theology." This section treats general works on Christianity in North America. Most of them encompass Canada as well as the United States, but hardly ever Mexico. General historians and social scientists, not just scholars of religion, will benefit from these volumes. Two REVISIONIST volumes stand out. Up-to-date reappraisal of American culture and theologians pervades the several hundred essays in Richard Wightman Fox and James T. Kloppenberg, eds., *A Companion to American Thought* (Oxford and Cambridge, Mass.: Blackwell Reference, 1995). In eight hundred pages it retraces reception of thinkers and assesses the latest methodologies. Vigorous rethinking of recent history of American Christianity unfolds in the twenty chapters of David W. Lotz, ed., *Altered Landscapes: Christianity in America, 1935-1985* (Grand Rapids, Mich.: Eerdmans, 1989). A trenchant overview comes in Martin Marty's "Introduction" in Robert deV. Brunkow, ed., *Religion and Society in North America: An Annotated Bibliography* (Santa Barbara, Calif.: ABC-CLIO, 1983), pp. ix-xi.

Michael Glazier and Thomas Shelley, eds., *The Encyclopedia of American Catholic History* (Collegeville, Minn.: Michael Glazier/Liturgical, 1996) will fill a gap. Another REVISIONIST LEXICON, Edward L. Queen II, Stephen R. Prothero and Gardiner H. Shattuck, eds. *Encyclopedia of American Religious History*, 2 vols. (New York and Oxford: Facts on File, 1996), appeared too late to analyze.

LIST OF WORKS ANALYZED

164 (1972) Sydney E. Ahlstrom, *A Religious History of the American People* (New Haven: Yale University Press, 1972)

165 (1986, 1992) J. Gordon Melton, ed., *Encyclopedic Handbook of Cults in America* (New York and London: Garland Publishing, 1986)

166 (1988) Charles H. Lippy and Peter N. Williams, eds., *Encyclopedia of American Religious Experience*, 3 vols. (New York: Scribner's, 1988)

167 (1988) Stanley M. Burgess and Gary B. McGee, eds., *Dictionary of Pentecostal and Charismatic Movements* (Grand Rapids, Mich.: Zondervan, 1988)

168 (1989) Charles H. Lippy, ed., *Twentieth-Century Shapers of American Popular Religion* (New York: Greenwood, 1989)

169 (1990) Daniel G. Reid, ed., *Dictionary of Christianity in America* (Downers Grove, Ill.: InterVarsity Press, 1990)

170 ([1951] 1990) Frank S. Mead (1898-1982), *Handbook of Denominations in the United States*, rev. Samuel S. Hill, 9th ed. (Nashville: Abingdon, 1990)

171 (1992) Arlene Hirschfelder and Paulette Molin, eds., *The Encyclopedia of Native American Religion: An Introduction* (New York and Oxford: Facts on File, 1992)

172 (1992) Daniel H. Ludlow, ed., *Encyclopedia of Mormonism*, 5 vols. (New York: Macmillan, 1992)

173 ([1978/1987/1989] 1993) J. Gordon Melton, *The Encyclopedia of American Religions*, 4th ed. (Detroit: Gale, 1993)

174 (1993) Larry G. Murphy, J. Gordon Melton and Gary L. Ward, eds., *Encyclopedia of African American Religions* (New York: Garland Publishing, 1993)

175 (1993) George A. Mather and Larry A. Nichols, *Dictionary of Cults, Sects, Religions and the Occult* (Grand Rapids, Mich.: Zondervan, 1993)

176 ([1977] 1993) Henry Warner Bowden, *Dictionary of American Religious Biography* (Westport, Conn.: Greenwood, 1977; 2d ed., rev., 1993)

177 (1994) Jacob Neusner, ed., *World Religions in America: An Introduction* (Louisville: Westminster/John Knox, 1994)

ANALYSIS OF WORKS

164 (1972) Sydney E. Ahlstrom, *A Religious History of the American People* (New Haven: Yale University Press, 1972); also in paperback (Garden City, N.Y.: Doubleday, 1975); xvi & 1158 pages; index, pp. 1129-58; general bibliography, pp. 1097-1128.

□ *Critique* This magnificent "synoptic history" is a HANDBOOK in all but name. Arranged into nine sections, its sixty-three chapters expose all aspects of "American religious experience" to a rich contextualism. Portraits of several hundred individuals constitute a WHO'S WHO. The writing is unusually quotable, even aphoristic. A historiographer's wit evaluates hundreds of historians and classifies thirty pages of bibliography under thirty-three subheadings. Few fields of study can boast a single-author synthesis of such range, acumen and lucidity.

□ *Summary* This magisterial HANDBOOK supplies social and intellectual context for virtually every topic in American religious history. Nuance abounds.

165 (1986, 1992) J. Gordon Melton, ed., *Encyclopedic Handbook of Cults in America* (New York and London: Garland Publishing, 1986; 2d ed., rev., 1992); xv & 407 pages; index, pp. 385-407; no general bibliography.

□ *Critique* This directory in the guise of a LEXICON assigns cults to three categories: (1) "Established Cults," (2) "The New Age Movement" and (3) "The Newer Cults." The volume functions in conjunction with a separate WHO'S WHO: Melton, ed., *Biographical Dictionary of American Cult and Sect Leaders* (New York and London: Garland Publishing, 1986), which probes 220 figures. Together the two works canvass the field, not overlooking "Counter-Cult Groups."

□ *Summary* This authoritative LEXICON documents cults old and new.

166 (1988) Charles H. Lippy and Peter N. Williams, eds., *Encyclopedia of American Religious Experience*, 3 vols. (New York: Scribner's, 1988); xvi & 1872 pages; index, pp. 1759-1872; no general bibliography.

□ *Scope* This magnificent COMPENDIUM revitalizes study of the history of religion in the United States through 105 essays of fifteen to twenty pages each. Three articles on Canada and three on Mexico enhance the coverage. Power of synthesis lifts the essays, over one-half of which defy conventional categories. Part three delivers twenty articles on Christian denominations and three on Judaism, while part four includes three on Asian religions, one on Islam and four on movements like "Occult" and "Free Thought." Part five's thirteen essays on "Movements in American Religion" abound in historical syntheses (notably by Charles H. Lippy on both "Communitarianism" and "Social Christianity), while

part six examines seventeen movements in "Religious Thought and Literature." Imagination bubbles, anchored in massive bibliographies.

□ *Strengths* Few COMPENDIA boast so many gems. Jacob Neusner on "Judaism in Contemporary America," Jaroslav Pelikan on "Lutheran Heritage" and Martin E. Marty on "Free Thought and Ethical Movements" scintillate predictably. Many articles purvey REVISIONISM. Examining "The Impact of Puritanism on American Culture," Daniel Walker Howe concludes that "postindustrial America is largely post-Puritan" (p. 1074)." Grant Wacker characterizes the first two generations of "Pentecostalism" as a "burst of radical perfection" that "was by any reasonable measure, socially dysfunctional" (p. 944). Stuart C. Henry dubs "Revivalism" a "distinctively American phenomenon" (p. 777). Robert Emmett Curran weaves back and forth across three centuries of "American Catholic Thought." Leo P. Ribuffo assembles dozens of case studies of "Religious Prejudice and Nativism." Paul D. Garrett's survey of "Eastern Christianity" sketches European heritage, narrates vicissitudes in North America, and expounds innumerable splits along ethnic lines. He calls Eastern liturgy "verbally and ritually florid yet theologically sober" (p. 329).

A superb trio of essays comes from John Corrigan, George H. Shriver and Catherine L. Albanese analyzing in turn "The Enlightenment," "Romantic Religion" and "Transcendentalism." Aspects of "Social Reform" evoke a kindred trio. Beyond Christianity, Sam Gill shines on "Native American Religions," as do Charles S. Prebish on "Buddhism," John Y. Fenton on "Hinduism" and C. Carlyle Haaland on "Shinto and Indigenous Chinese Religion." These authors elaborate how foreign heritages were modified in the United States. Essays on method explore "Historiography," "Institutional Forms," "Sociological Study" and "Geography and Demography." James H. Moorhead bursts with originality concerning "Theological Interpretations and Critiques of American Society and Culture." Donald E. Byrne Jr.

neatly defines "Folk Religion" as the "folk dimensions of religion and the religious dimensions of folklore" (p. 7). He concludes that "whereas Western religion tends to demythologize, folk religion remythologizes" (p. 99). Donald G. Jones sorts out debate on "Civil and Public Religion," dubbing it "primarily an academic venture of a select group of American scholars" (p. 1408). Cross-references and a superb index permit correlating disparate essays on a given issue. Boldness prevails.

□ *Weaknesses* However brilliant the essays, this is a COMPENDIUM of syntheses, not a HANDBOOK. There is no WHO'S WHO, and the only regions to evoke essays are "The South" and "California and the Southwest." Despite protestations to the contrary, Canada and Mexico get short shrift. Recourse to the index is essential if one is to exploit the whole. A general bibliography, particularly of reference books, would have been helpful.

□ *Competitors* This COMPENDIUM of historical essays matches 77 McGrath, ed., *The Blackwell Encyclopedia of Modern Christian Thought* (1993) in daring and comprehensiveness, while running three times longer. Similar depth distinguishes Timothy Miller, ed., *America's Alternative Religions* (Albany: SUNY Press, 1995). For a WHO'S WHO, **169** Reid, ed., *Dictionary of Christianity in America* (1990) remains irreplaceable. Since the *Encyclopedia of American Religious Experience* mentions almost any conceivable topic, its index should be consulted during any research project. It makes other reference works on religion in the United States (except **164** Ahlstrom 1972) seem cursory. Recently a REVISIONIST COMPENDIUM has treated religion in Great Britain in similar (if much briefer) fashion: Sheridan Gilley and W. J. Sheils, ed., *A History of Religion in Britain: Practice and Belief from Pre-Roman Times to the Present* (Oxford and Cambridge, Mass.: Blackwell, 1994). One wishes for something similar on Latin America.

□ *Summary* This COMPENDIUM sets a standard for historical syntheses imaginatively conceived. It persuades scholars of American history to rethink.

167 (1988) Stanley M. Burgess and Gary B. McGee, eds., *Dictionary of Pentecostal and Charismatic Movements* (Grand Rapids, Mich.: Zondervan, 1988); xiii & 914 pages; no index; general bibliography, pp. 5-6; black-and-white photographs throughout.

□ *Scope* This historical LEXICON examines Pentecostal and charismatic movements worldwide but above all in North America. Sixty-four (mostly American) contributors furnish a WHO'S WHO as well as synopses of concepts, doctrines and happenings since 1900 (with massive bibliographies). Europe elicits surveys like "European Pentecostalism" and "European Pietist Roots of Pentecostalism." The volume opens with an overview, "The Pentecostal and Charismatic Movements" (pp. 1-6). There is no mention of non-Christian religions and hardly any of the Third World. Emphasizing history and doctrine, this work of confessional self-definition eschews self-congratulation.

□ *Strengths* Long narratives make this a major resource for historians, who will relish "Bibliography and Historiography of Pentecostalism (USA)." Surveys canvass "Charismatic Movement," "Charismatic Renewal," "Healing Movements," "Hispanic Pentecostalism" and "Black Holiness-Pentecostalism." Demographer David Barrett contributes a virtuosic twenty pages on "Statistics, Global," differentiating the "Three Waves" (p. 820). Statistics likewise embellish entries on "Church Growth," "Women, Role of" and "Missions, Overseas (North American)." Doctrine gets articulated in depth. Writing thirty-five pages on "The Holy Spirit, Doctrine of," Stanley Burgess scours Eastern and Western church fathers, while more briefly P. D. Hocken explores "Church, Theology of" and D. J. Wilson probes "Eschatology, Pentecostal Perspectives on." Books of the Bible are clustered, as in "Pentateuch," "Pauline Literature," "Petrine Literature" and "Letters of John." Each of the Gospels elicits an entry, as do other major utterances on the role of the Holy Spirit (e.g., in Ezekiel, Joel, James and the Apocalypse). A twelve-page essay by French Arrington on "Hermeneutics" tackles Pentecostal interpretation of Scripture. Notably useful are entries on phrases peculiar to the movement, such as "Fruit of the Spirit," "Slain in the Spirit," "Jesus People," "Initial Evidence" and "Positive Confession Theology." Movements like "Shepherding Movement," "Latter Rain Movement" and "Women's Aglow Fellowship" get expounded, while founding events like the "Azusa Street Revival" and "Oneness Pentecostalism" elicit five pages each. Candid articles explain practices like "Exorcism," "Gift of Prophecy" and "Serpent Handling." Throughout the tone is sober, even documentary, and largely devoid of self-serving rhetoric. This volume exemplifies the range and dignity of Pentecostal self-expression.

□ *Weaknesses* In furthering self-definition for Pentecostals and charismatics, this historical LEXICON omits broader Christian trends, not to mention secular developments. Non-Christian religions never surface. Particularly regrettable is a decision to ignore parallels to independent churches in Africa. Social sciences crop up in only a few entries like David Barrett's "Statistics, Global" and J. W. Sheppard's "Sociology of Pentecostalism." There is no entry on psychology of religion or secularization. All this makes the evocation of Pentecostals intense but claustrophobic.

□ *Competitors* This historical LEXICON focuses relentlessly on one proclivity within Christianity. Sound but parochial, the scholarship needs to be supplemented from **169** Reid, ed., *Dictionary of Christianity in America* (1990) or **166** Lippy and Williams, eds., *Encyclopedia of American Religious Experience* (1988). No other volume comes close to supplying comparable detail on Pentecostal and charismatic leaders and activities.

□ *Summary* Historians of North America will applaud the synopses and bibliographies but will crave cannier interpretations.

168 (1989) Charles H. Lippy, ed., *Twentieth-Century Shapers of American Popular Religion* (New York: Greenwood, 1989); xxv & 494 pages; index, pp.

463-87; general bibliography, pp. xxiv-xxv.

□ *Scope* This imaginative WHO'S WHO supplies signed analyses of sixty-two figures pivotal to popular religion in twentieth-century North America. Invoking Robert Redfield, the "Introduction" distinguishes the "great tradition" or "established religion" of professionals from the "little tradition" or "invisible religion" of the people. In featuring individuals who have shaped the latter, this volume could easily have embraced twice as many figures as it does. Each six-to-eight-page article carries four parts: biography, appraisal, survey of criticism and bibliography. Choice of biographees is discriminating, level of scholarship demanding and handling of controversy forthright. The mainstream and the bizarre jostle disconcertingly.

□ *Strengths* The range of biographees dazzles. Besides the likes of Billy Sunday, Billy Graham and Norman Vincent Peale come less predictable figures, particularly among writers. Best-selling authors include Fulton Oursler Jr., Sinclair Lewis, Bruce Barton, Harvey Cox and Hal Lindsey. Catholics encompass Daniel and Philip Berrigan, Thomas Merton, Fulton J. Sheen and Morris L. West. Mainstream preachers number Harry Emerson Fosdick, Ralph Sockman and Peter Marshall. African-Americans range from Father Divine and Charles Manuel "Sweet Daddy" Grace through Martin Luther King to Marcus Garvey and Malcolm X. Fundamentalists include Carl McIntire, William Jennings Bryan and the Canadian Thomas Todhunter. A missionary to India, E. Stanley Jones, and a biblical scholar, C. I. Scofield, stand in isolation, as do Mordecai Kaplan, the only Jew, and Wowoka, the sole native American. Amazingly, only seven women figure: Dorothy Day, Kathryn Kuhlman, Aimee Semple McPherson and wives in four couples (Bakker, Gaither, LaHaye and Marshall). Controversy swirls around James Pike, Alan Watts and Jimmy Swaggart. Nearly every entry tackles "Appraisal" and "Survey of criticism" candidly and proposes future research. This is a work of substance.

□ *Weaknesses* The sixty-two case studies

cry out for thematic synthesis. If only the introduction had correlated themes and probed the notion of "popular culture," the volume might have reformulated how to study popular religion. Because contemporaries loom so large, the work has dated. The omission of New Age leaders and Asian gurus should be redressed in a later edition.

❑ *Competitors* This pioneering WHO'S WHO fills a niche. By eschewing theology, the book avoids overlapping with **78** Marty and Peerman, eds., *A Handbook of Christian Theologians* (1965, 1984), and by minimizing spirituality it incorporates no one (except Thomas Merton) referenced in **90** Magill and McGreal, eds., *Christian Spirituality* (1988). Taken together, these three volumes expound a wide spectrum of Christian self-expression. But **169** Reid, ed., *Dictionary of Christianity in America* (1990) remains indispensable for the wider picture. *Twentieth-Century Shapers of American Popular Religion* deserves to be enlarged. It will not soon be replaced, and comparable volumes on Islam, on Latin America and particularly on Africa would be irresistible.

❑ *Summary* Imaginative selection and hard-hitting scholarship make this a gold mine for historians and a feast for browsers. This volume holds surprises for everyone.

169 (1990) Daniel G. Reid, ed., *Dictionary of Christianity in America* (Downers Grove, Ill.: InterVarsity Press, 1990); xxx & 1305 pages; no index; general bibliography, pp. 21-22. An abridgment is available: *Concise Dictionary of Christianity in America* (paperback, 1995); 350 pages.

❑ *Scope* This historical LEXICON recruited over four hundred authorities to write more than twenty-four hundred signed articles on nearly every aspect of Christianity in the United States and Canada except interreligious dialogue. Fifteen hundred entries make up a WHO'S WHO of persons in both countries from 1600. Without exception, each biography identifies the denomination of that individual and supplies select bibliography. All presidents of the United States as well as many Catholic archbishops

are referenced. At least one hundred articles of historical synthesis (e.g., "Publishing, Religious," "Social Ethics" and "Education, Protestant Theological") silhouette movements against the sweep of American (but not world) history. There is a GLOSSARY on concepts and practices (particularly of Roman Catholicism). Flow charts diagram splits in Baptist, Lutheran, Methodist, Mennonite and Presbyterian churches (not to mention the United Church of Canada). There is also a chart of "Denominational Divisions over Slavery and the Civil War." The volume opens with a twenty-page essay, "Division and Unity: The Paradox of Christianity in America" by R. D. Linder, who contributed also on "Civil Religion." Although cities and states command no entries, most seminaries and many universities do. The writing is lucid, and editorial control is firm. Cross-references abound, both by asterisk within entries and by list at the end.

❑ *Strengths* This LEXICON excels both as a WHO'S WHO and as an anthology of syntheses. Preachers, thinkers, organizers and critics from every camp and period elicit sketches. These articles specify contribution not just to church history but to American life at large. The WHO'S WHO shows its caliber in the variety of terms coined to designate roles: "exhorter," "promoter of separatism" (John Darby), "labor priest" (Francis Haas), "Bible expositor" (Henry Ironside), "religious loner" (Roger Williams), "healing revivalist" (Jack Coe), "agnostic controversialist" (Robert Ingersoll) and "sidewalk philosopher" (Peter Maurin). These sobriquets come in addition to more conventional ones: minister, bishop, missionary, revivalist, theologian and scholar. Twentieth-century scholars ranging from Sydney Ahlstrom and William Foxwell Albright to Williston Walker and Samuel Zwemer receive their due. Articles on European theologians like Barth, Bonhoeffer, Brunner, Bultmann, Küng, C. S. Lewis and Rahner sketch their reception in the United States. Other non-Americans include Alexis de Tocqueville, Jenny Lind and William Booth (founder of the Salvation Army) together with three of his children. Not everyone will expect entries on writers like Emily Dickinson, Flannery O'Connor and Lewis Wallace (of *Ben Hur*), given that Walt Whitman and Sinclair Lewis are omitted. Unfortunately, a survey "Literature, Christianity and" does not furnish criteria for these choices. Artists and musicians are omitted, except in three overviews: "Art and Christianity," "Architecture, Church" and "Music, Christian."

Apart from the WHO'S WHO, a great strength of this LEXICON is commitment to historical synthesis. Major surveys include "Supreme Court Decisions on Religious Issues," "Public Policy and Christianity," "Bible and American Culture" and "Reform Movements." Splendid synopses of "World War 1" and "World War 2" fill eight pages. Mark Noll's article on "Biblical Interpretation" squeezes nearly four centuries of intellectual history into four pages. Three articles across seven pages differentiate "Spirituality" among thirteen denominations. Similar virtuosity allows Donald McKim to distinguish views on "Scripture" in eleven denominations. Adroit taxonomy distinguishes articles on "Evangelicalism," "Fundamentalism," "Free Church Tradition," "Holiness Movements," "Reformed Tradition" and "Orthodox Tradition." Three articles on "Worship" in Orthodox, Protestant and Roman Catholic traditions complement five on "Liturgies." Nuances of "Dispensationalism," "Premillennialism," "Postmillennialism" and "Rapture of the Church" get explicated in full. On "Missions" fifteen articles across twenty pages examine everything from "Missiology, Protestant" through "Missions, Evangelical Foreign" to "Missions to the Slaves." Articles on theology classify up to a dozen positions each on "Atonement, Theories of," "Christology," "Eschatology," "Justification," "Predestination" (six positions), "Sacraments and Ordinances" and "Theism," but not on the Trinity or tradition. Academic fields like "Process Theology," "Philosophy of Religion" and "Psychology and Christianity" elicit entries, but not sociology of religion.

The sophistication of the syntheses makes some of the definitional articles appear almost elementary. The volume incorporates what amounts to a primer on practices of Roman Catholicism (sacraments, doctrines, devotions, bureaucracy) as well as a list of Catholic religious orders (pp. 997-1002). Incisive essays examine "Radical Catholicism" and "Peace Movement, Catholic." Delightful entries explicate phrases like "Manifest Destiny," "Positive Thinking," "Sawdust Trail" and "Burnt-over District." Ethnic groups win broad coverage, from "Armenian Church" and "Asian-American Protestants" through "Greek Orthodox Archdiocese," "Syrian Orthodox Church of Antioch" and "Hispanic Churches of America" to "Black Religion" and "Black Theology." There is even an entry on "Revivalism, German-American." No Christian group (except native Americans) gets slighted. Coverage of Canada is less thorough than that of the United States, embracing legislation ("The Quebec Act"), ecumenism ("Canadian Council of Churches") and a WHO'S WHO of missionaries (Lalemant, La Salle), prelates (Laval, Lartigue) and thinkers (Lonergan but not Northrop Frye). Canadian regions and seminaries are omitted. Articles on individual denominations chronicle Canadian branches, but not Latin American. Protestant, Roman Catholic and Orthodox churches, together with their derivatives, emerge here in full plumage.

□ *Weaknesses* Sometimes this historical LEXICON adopts a conservative evangelical stance. Secular issues, whether in ethics, art or the social sciences, receive minimal attention. World religions are omitted except for four entries on Jewish-Christian interactions. Asian religions are not mentioned, not even in an article on "Asian-American Protestants." There is no entry on dialogue. While flavoring a few entries like "New Age" and "Occultism," evangelical zeal surfaces chiefly in the fulsomeness showered upon biographees like Harold Ockenga and Arno Gaebelein. A plethora of names reduces insight concerning theologies like "Neo-orthodoxy" or "Liberalism/Modernism." **76** Musser and Price, eds., *A New Handbook of Christian Theology* (1992) cuts deeper. Nor is ethics a strong point. Similarly, spirituality and spiritual writers get short shrift. One needs to consult **90** Magill and McGreal, eds., *Christian Spirituality* (1988) to round out the picture. Otherwise Roman Catholics will be delighted by the coverage of practices, issues and persons of their church. Places are omitted entirely (except for "California, Christianity in"), and one sorely misses entries on missions in Alaska and Hawaii. None of these oversights, however, detracts from the vigor of historical synthesis, the range of the WHO'S WHO or the mastery in defining pivotal concepts.

□ *Competitors* This LEXICON on history of Christianity in the United States and Canada fills a gap. It remains the most cogent alphabetical reference book on the subject, not only on persons but also for syntheses. It encompasses American life as a whole and not just church activities. Skill at taxonomy sorts out denominational nuances. It stands with **170** Mead, ed., *Handbook of Denominations in the United States* (1951, 1990) as a clarifier of minute distinctions. General DICTIONARIES like **34** Gentz, ed., *The Dictionary of Bible and Religion* (1986) or **163** Douglas, *New 20th-Century Encyclopedia of Religious Knowledge* (1991) embrace many fewer persons and lack synopses of American phenomena. **176** Bowden, *Dictionary of American Religious Biography* (1993) omits bibliographies and specialized expertise from its 550 entries. A massive COMPENDIUM like **166** Lippy and Williams, eds., *Encyclopedia of American Religious Experience* (1988) encompasses all religions, not just Christianity. It delivers extended narratives but requires use of the index to locate persons and issues. **46** Lossky et al., eds., *Dictionary of the Ecumenical Movement* (1991) expatiates on ecumenism, not to mention interreligious dialogue. The *Dictionary of Christianity in America* delivers more information and more taxonomies more quickly than any other single volume on the subject. Beginning with Bill J. Leonard, ed., *Dictionary of Baptists in America* (Downers Grove, Ill.: InterVarsity

Press, 1994), it inspired a series of guides (with bibliography) to persons and movements within confessions in North America.

□ *Summary* A superlative WHO'S WHO, an incisive GLOSSARY and sophisticated syntheses make this LEXICON indispensable for scholars of American culture. No historian can afford to ignore it.

170 ([1951] 1990) Frank S. Mead (1898-1982), *Handbook of Denominations in the United States,* rev. Samuel S. Hill, 9th ed. (Nashville: Abingdon, 1990); 316 pages; index, pp. 301-16; glossary, pp. 275-82; general bibliography, pp. 283-300.

□ *Critique* This historical DICTIONARY sketches about 220 religious bodies in the United States, arranged alphabetically by their own names. Umbrella labels like "Baptist" shelter twenty-five entries, "Mennonite" thirteen and "Brethren" seven. Besides mapping more than two hundred Christian bodies, the authors supply six pages on Judaism as well as entries on "Baha'i," "Buddhist Churches of America," "Muslim" and "Vedanta Society." New religious movements (since 1950) are omitted, as is any discussion of methodology. Synopses of history and demography play down doctrine. A masterpiece of compression, this DICTIONARY functions as a GLOSSARY introducing various groups and their history. By defining denominational labels, it prepares one for the massiveness of **173** Melton, *The Encyclopedia of American Religions,* 4th ed. (1993), which references eight times more religious bodies. The English-language bibliography deploys thirty groupings (including "Black Churches") in eighteen pages, and the index is superb.

□ *Summary* This DICTIONARY is a handy starting place for research on older (pre-1950) Christian denominations in the United States.

171 (1992) Arlene Hirschfelder and Paulette Molin, eds., *The Encyclopedia of Native American Religion: An Introduction* (New York and Oxford: Facts on File, 1992); xii & 367 pages; index, pp. 359-67; general bibliography, pp. 342-57; black-

and-white photographs throughout.

□ *Critique* This GLOSSARY and WHO'S WHO expounds Native American ceremonies, deities and practitioners with utmost respect. Entries explain activities like "Sand Painting" and "Eagle Dance" with loving care. Retellings of myth protect the sacredness of names, places and actions against idle curiosity. A unique feature is a WHO'S WHO of at least a hundred Catholic and Protestant missionaries of all periods. Individual entries omit bibliography, but a general bibliography excels. Except for accounts of missionaries, this work addresses mainly beginners.

□ *Summary* This introductory DICTIONARY explains practices and sketches careers of both Native American practitioners and Christian missionaries.

172 (1992) Daniel H. Ludlow, ed., *Encyclopedia of Mormonism,* 5 vols. (New York: Macmillan, 1992); 2300 pages; index, pp. 1775-848; 13 appendices, pp. 1631-764; glossary, pp 1764-73; black-and-white photographs.

□ *Critique* This ENCYCLOPEDIA expounds the history and doctrine of Mormonism in exhaustive detail. Seven hundred fifty contributors write thirteen hundred entries on persons, places, practices and beliefs. Volume 5 reprints Joseph Smith's three texts: *The Book of Mormon, The Doctrine and the Covenants* and *The Pearl of Great Price.* In a model of self-definition, the tone is sober and the scholarship meticulous.

□ *Summary* This monumental ENCYCLOPEDIA expounds Mormonism in utmost detail. It is one of the fullest reference works on an American religious body.

173 ([1978/1987/1989] 1993) J. Gordon Melton, *The Encyclopedia of American Religions,* 4th ed. (Detroit: Gale, 1993); xx & 1217 pages; six indexes, pp. 1027-217; no general bibliography.

□ *Critique* This HANDBOOK of religions, denominations and new religious movements has become an institution since it appeared in 1978. Edited at the Institute for the Study of American Religion at Santa Barbara, the fourth edition arranges no fewer than seventeen hundred thirty "churches" into twenty-four "families"

(including two designated as "unclassified"). A first edition of 1978 arranged over twelve hundred bodies into seventeen families. In the "Directory Listings" (pp. 221-1026), each entry furnishes mailing address, synopsis of history and beliefs, and English-language bibliography. "Historical essays" (pp. 39-219, with bibliography) delineate twenty-two of the families. The classification of Christian denominations supplants Ernst Troeltsch's triad of "Church, Sect, Cult" with notions like "Western Liturgical Family," "Pietist-Methodist Family," "European Free-Church Family" and "Adventist Family." New religious movements inspire labels like "Communal Family," "Ancient Wisdom Family" and "Magick Family." Entries recount history and beliefs soberly, while alignment into "families" stimulates rethinking. Native American religions are omitted. This HANDBOOK offers the fullest listing for the United States of schismatic churches, Asian religious bodies and new religious movements (including defunct ones). The writing, however, is too bland to excite browsers.

□ *Summary* This HANDBOOK classifies and describes an ever-growing number of religious bodies in the United States. On schismatic churches and new religious movements it has no rival.

174 (1993) Larry G. Murphy, J. Gordon Melton and Gary L. Ward, eds., *Encyclopedia of African American Religions* (New York: Garland Publishing, 1993); lxxvi & 926 pages; index, pp. 891-926; general bibliography, pp. 865-75.

□ *Critique* This historical LEXICON fills a gap by canvassing persons, concepts and organizations in African-American religion. Unsigned entries by thirty-two contributors average four to five pages with lengthy bibliographies but do not explore African origins. Three introductory essays examine "Religion in the African American Community," "Martin Luther King" and "Womanist Theology." Alphabetical entries (pp. 1-864) deliver no fewer than 777 biographies. Cultural analysis pervades entries like "Colonial Era, African American Christians during the," "Music in the African American Church" and "Islam as an African American Religion." Discussion of "Rastafarianism" and "Voudou" excels, but African topics like "High God" or "Orisha" are missing. No places or tribes in Africa elicit entries. Quotations from African-Americans are included at the head of each letter of the alphabet. An appendix lists 341 African-American churches and religious organizations. Scholars of American religion will relish this DICTIONARY, but Africanists will find it disappointing.

□ *Summary* This LEXICON supplies a wealth of detail compiled nowhere else. Its WHO'S WHO is incomparable.

175 (1993) George A. Mather and Larry A. Nichols, *Dictionary of Cults, Sects, Religions and the Occult* (Grand Rapids, Mich.: Zondervan, 1993); xii & 384 pages; no index; classified bibliography, pp. 343-84; four appendices (on christological heresies and other influences), pp. 331-42; black-and-white photographs throughout.

□ *Critique* This uneven DICTIONARY of alternative religions highlights contemporary North America. The volume was researched by Mather, written by Nichols and vetted by Alvin J. Schmidt. A GLOSSARY defines themes and practices in five to ten lines, while articles of three to thirteen pages characterize import religions ("Rastafarianism," "Vedanta Society," "Witchcraft"), para-Christian movements ("Swedenborgianism," "Christadelphianism," "Unification Church") and New Age phenomena ("Arica," "Eckankar," "Scientology"). A meager WHO'S WHO identifies founders like William Marion Branham and Sun Myung Moon. Throughout, divergences from Christianity are pinpointed. Quasi-Christian movements elicit diagnosis in terms of christological heresies, as defined from the early church. This approach works well for syncretisms like "Macumba," "Santería" and "Christian Science" as well as for Jesus movements of the 1960s ("Alamo Christian Foundation"), but not for Asian religions. Parallels between classical heresies and new movements are codified on pages 333-35. Thirteen pages each on "Jehovah's Witnesses"

and "Mormonism" are surprisingly judicious, while fourteen pages on "Christianity" all but scintillate. Apart from an admiring entry on "Judaism," articles on non-Christian religions ("Hinduism," "Sufism," "Taoism") overstate what Americans have borrowed from them. An English-language bibliography, divided into fifty-nine subheads, is superb. Although misprints abound, the interpretation of new religious movements commands attention, while that of Asian religions does not. A focus on North America makes this a guide not to the world's religions, but solely to their adaptation by Americans. Far more penetrating is a COMPENDIUM: Timothy Miller, ed., *America's Alternative Religions* (Albany: SUNY Press, 1995).

□ *Summary* This outspoken DICTIONARY compares new religious movements in North America to evangelical Christianity. Devotees of the new will be affronted, but evangelicals will applaud, and historians will find much to ponder. The bibliography is one of the fullest anywhere.

176 ([1977] 1993) Henry Warner Bowden, *Dictionary of American Religious Biography*, 2d ed. (Westport, Conn.: Greenwood, 1993); xi & 687 pages; index, pp. 673-86; general bibliography, pp. 667-71.

□ *Critique* This WHO'S WHO recounts the lives of 550 Americans "who played a religiously significant role" in the United States. Only persons who died before July 1, 1992, figure. Averaging one to two pages, accounts are workmanlike, supplying both primary and secondary bibliography. In the second edition just seventy-five of the original 425 entries stand unrevised. The work lacks the flair of **168** Charles Lippy, ed., *Twentieth-Century Shapers of American Popular Religion* (1989), but it will help historians of many camps.

□ *Summary* This solid WHO'S WHO addresses general historians.

177 (1994) Jacob Neusner, ed., *World Religions in America: An Introduction* (Louisville: Westminster/John Knox, 1994); x & 308 pages; index, pp. 303-8; no general bibliography; also in

paperback.

□ *Critique* This introductory COMPEN-
DIUM recruits thirteen top authorities to
write chapters on five branches of Christianity and five other world religions as well
as on women, politics and society. Emphasis falls on how each religion came to
America and on how Americans altered it.
Sam Gill summons his accustomed acumen
on "Native American Religion," while Peter J. Paris excels on "African-American
Religion." Martin Marty devotes thirty-
five pages to "Protestantism," but Andrew
Greeley takes just eighteen to tell "the
slightly different story" of "The Catholics
in the World and in America." Robert S.
Ellwood furnishes a fine conspectus of
"East Asian Religions in Today's America,"
while Gerald James Larson epitomizes
Hinduism deftly. An apparatus of "Study
Questions," "Essay Topics" and "Word
Exploration" accompanies each chapter,
but only Jaroslav Pelikan writing on "Orthodox Christianity" supplies adequate
bibliography.

□ *Summary* This uneven COMPENDIUM
introduces a vast range of religious phenomena in America. Apart from Pelikan's
chapter, bibliographies are meager or non-
existent.

3 OTHER PROPHETIC RELIGIONS

3.1 JUDAISM

**OVERVIEW: THE KINGDOM OF
WIT** Since the mid-nineteenth century
scholars of Judaism and Jewish life have
produced magnificent reference works.
Because Jewish identity straddles religion
and culture, the works divide between a
majority, which embrace religion as part of
culture, and a minority, which separate
religion from all else. The latter omit topics
and persons whose Jewishness is strictly
cultural. Among works that emphasize religion, Jews favor GLOSSARIES of history
and customs. A number of these excel as
INTRODUCTIONS and will delight the non-
Jew. Overall, Jewish reference works evince
an almost religious awe toward knowledge.
    The excellence of reference works on

Judaism stems in part from facility in
Midrash. The practice of interpreting canonical texts in conversation across millennia connects fresh nuances to old. Judaism
thereby generates an enormous body of
discourse that hovers between the normative and the idiosyncratic. In a word, REVI-
SIONISM springs from Midrash. Such
discourse stands in contrast to that of contemporary Islam, which prefers the cut-
and-dried. Wherever nuance thrives,
encyclopedia-making and indeed REVI-
SIONISM is likely to follow. Best of all, since
nuance invites wit, Jewish reference works
more than any others scintillate. Subtlety
thrives.

3.1.1 GENERAL

**OVERVIEW: BRIDGING RELIG-
ION AND CULTURE** Judaic ENCYCLO-
PEDIAS that cover both religion and culture
include a number of MEGA-ENCYCLOPEDIAS
(in both English and German), culminating in Roth, ed., *Encyclopaedia Judaica*, 16
vols. (Jerusalem: Keter, 1972). Since no
comparable work has appeared since then,
their like is not treated here. Contributions
in German and French being too few, the
directory discusses only works in English.
A 750-page French COMPENDIUM (not
analyzed here) stands out: Armand Abécas-
sis and Georges Nataf, eds., *Encyclopédie de
la mystique juive* (Paris: Berg International,
1977). A major event in late 1996 will be
publication after thirty years of a second
edition (under a new title) of **180** Werblowsky and Wigoder, eds., *The Oxford
Dictionary of the Jewish Religion* (New
York and London: Oxford University
Press, 1996). Jacob Neusner, ed., *Dictionary of Judaism in the Biblical Period: 450
B.C.E. to 600 C.E.*, planned in 3 vols. (New
York: Macmillan, 1996) will also have wide
impact. A winsome REVISIONIST LEXICON
appeared too late to analyze: Louis Jacobs,
The Jewish Religion: A Companion (New
York and London: Oxford University
Press, 1995).

    A work of appraisal is Shimeon Bris-
man's *A History and Guide to Judaic Encyclopedias and Lexicons* (Cincinnati:

Hebrew Union College Press, 1987). It evaluates works in all major languages including Hebrew, assessing inclusivity (i.e., lacunae) rather than insight (i.e., conceptual power). Briefer and often innocuous evaluations mark the 888 entries of Charles Cutter and Micha Falk Oppenheim, *Judaic Reference Sources: A Selective, Annotated Bibliographic Guide,* 2d ed. (Juneau, Alaska: Denale, 1993).

LIST OF WORKS ANALYZED
178 (1947-1984, 1969-) Rabbi Meyer Berlin, *Encyclopedia Talmudica: A Digest of Halachic Literature and Jewish Law from the Tannaitic Period to the Present Time Alphabetically Arranged,* ed. Rabbi Shlomo Josef Zevin, 4 vols. to date (Jerusalem: Talmudic Encyclopedia Institute, 1969-)

179 (1964, 1994) Yishai Chasidah, *Encyclopedia of Biblical Personalities* (Brooklyn: Shaar, 1994); Hebrew edition, 1964

180 (1965, 1986, 1996) R. J. Zwi Werblowsky and Geoffrey Wigoder, eds., *The Encyclopedia of the Jewish Religion* (Jerusalem: Massada, 1965; New York: Holt, Rinehart & Winston, 1966); reprinted with very minor revisions (New York: Adama, 1986). A second revised edition will be published as *The Oxford Dictionary of the Jewish Religion* (New York and London: Oxford University Press, 1996).

61 (1981) W. Gunther Plaut, ed., *The Torah: A Modern Commentary* (New York: Union of American Hebrew Congregations, 1981)

181 (1987) Arthur A. Cohen and Paul Mendes-Flohr, eds., *Contemporary Jewish Religious Thought: Original Essays on Critical Concepts, Movements and Beliefs* (New York: Scribner's, 1987)

182 (1988) Pamela S. Nadell, *Conservative Judaism in America: A Biographical Dictionary and Handbook* (Westport, Conn. and London: Greenwood, 1988)

183 (1989) Glenda Abramson, ed., *The Blackwell Companion to Jewish Culture: From the Eighteenth Century to the Present* (Oxford and Cambridge, Mass.: Blackwell Reference, 1989)

184 (1989) Geoffrey Wigoder, ed., *The Encyclopedia of Judaism* (Jerusalem: Jerusalem Publishing House and New York: Macmillan, 1989)

185 (1990) Avraham Yaakov Finkel, *The Great Torah Commentators* (Northvale, N.J., and London: Aronson, 1990)

186 (1991) Geoffrey Wigoder, ed., *Dictionary of Jewish Biography* (Jerusalem: Jerusalem Publishing House; New York: Simon & Schuster, 1991)

187 (1993) Kerry M. Olitzky, Lance J. Sussman and Malcolm H. Stern, eds., *Reform Judaism in America: A Biographical Dictionary and Sourcebook* (Westport, Conn., and London: Greenwood, 1993)

188 (1994) Saul S. Friedman, ed., *Holocaust Literature: A Handbook of Critical, Historical and Literary Writings* (Westport, Conn., and London: Greenwood, 1994)

ANALYSIS OF WORKS
178 (1947-84, 1969-) Rabbi Meyer Berlin [d. 1949], ed., *Encyclopedia Talmudica: A Digest of Halachic Literature and Jewish Law from the Tannaitic Period to the Present Time Alphabetically Arranged,* ed. Rabbi Shlomo Josef Zevin, 4 vols. to date (Jerusalem: Talmudic Encyclopedia Institute, 1969-); translated from the Hebrew edition of 18 vols. (1947-84); vol. 4 appeared in 1992; subject index in each volume; about 2900 pages to date.

□ *Critique* This MEGA-ENCYCLOPEDIA of Talmudic reasoning through twenty centuries arranges Hebrew names of issues and tractates alphabetically. Gradually being translated from the Hebrew, the work facilitates access to topics of Halakah (i.e., Jewish law) as debated down to the present. Quotations, cross-references and commentary clarify issues without imposing solutions. The compilation is descriptive, not normative. It invites Jews and non-Jews alike to savor Talmudic argument, since topical headings make this MEGA-ENCYCLOPEDIA easier to consult than the Talmud itself. The writing is lucid, the tone level-headed, the debates endless.

□ *Summary* This rearrangement of the Talmud by topics invites nonspecialists to browse. Hardly any other tool in English anatomizes the Talmud so winningly.

179 (1964, 1994) Yishai Chasidah, *Encyclopedia of Biblical Personalities Anthologized from the Talmud, Midrash, and Rabbinic Writings* (Brooklyn: Shaar, 1994); Hebrew edition, 1964; 541 pages; index of Anglicized names, pp. 535-41; no general bibliography.

□ *Critique* This WHO'S WHO aligns "Gleanings" from Talmudic and Midrashic sources with nearly six hundred persons mentioned in the Hebrew Bible. Using numerous subheads, entries assemble short passages, usually a single sentence, excerpted from the two Talmuds and from Midrashim. Moses commands sixty pages, David thirty, Abraham and Jacob twenty-five each, and Solomon sixteen. Gleanings on the prophets and on Job stand out. Even the most learned will profit as the "seven seas" of rabbinic literature yield their bounty in the format of a WHO'S WHO.

□ *Summary* This WHO'S WHO scours rabbinic literature for sentences describing nearly six hundred persons in the Hebrew Bible.

180 (1965, 1986, 1996) R. J. Zwi Werblowsky and Geoffrey Wigoder, eds., *The Encyclopedia of the Jewish Religion* (Jerusalem: Massada, 1965; New York: Holt, Rinehart & Winston, 1966); reprinted with very minor revisions (New York: Adama, 1986); xii & 415 pages; no index; no bibliography; 48 black-and-white plates. A second revised edition will be published as *The Oxford Dictionary of the Jewish Religion* (New York and London: Oxford University Press, 1996). Analyzed on the basis of the 1965 edition.

□ *Scope* This LEXICON on religion (as distinct from history, culture or tradition) delivers unsigned articles by twenty-four (mostly Israeli) contributors. Books of the Hebrew Bible, scholars, treatises, places, practices, festivals, images and concepts get expounded in depth, with frequent cross-references. Catchwords come in both English and Hebrew. A WHO'S WHO embraces above all sages and rabbis, particularly those who launched new directions (e.g., Abraham Geiger, Israel Salanter, Raphael Samson Hirsch). Werblowsky's virtuosity guarantees thoroughness, accuracy and objectivity. Alas, there are no bibliographies. The style is dense and sometimes telegraphic.

□ *Strengths* On the eve of being revised, this remains after thirty years the authoritative LEXICON of Jewish religion in English. In more than two thousand entries ranging from one-eighth to two pages, hardly a word goes to waste, and titled subsections abound. Long articles on matters as diverse as "Aggadah," "Benediction," "Bible Exegesis," "God," "Halakhah," "Mysticism" and "Temple" accompany briefer ones on nearly every conceivable topic of liturgy, law and custom. Historical panoramas encapsulate twenty-five hundred years in a page regarding, for example, "Creed," "Ethics," "Exile," "Messiah," "Music," "Philosophy" and "Revelation." Succinct summaries of law on topics like "Burial," "Circumcision," "Confession," "Divorce," "Fast," "Ordination," "Prayer," "Proselytes" and "Women" encompass the sweep of history. Digests of biblical teaching on "Angels," "Death," "Providence," "Sabbath" and "Theodicy" stand out, while the entry "Talmud" achieves a tour de force of selection. Few reference works teach so much so concisely.

□ *Weaknesses* About to be revised for the first time since 1965, this historical LEXICON predates the postmodern era of biblical scholarship. All contributors are Jewish, and they minimize the role of Islam (e.g., "Koran") and Zoroastrianism (e.g., "Dualism"). Meaty articles on "Christianity," "Ebionites," "Karaites" and "Samaritans" state traditional Jewish views. Given the prestige of the contributors, they should have signed their articles. An abiding weakness is absence of bibliographies.

□ *Competitors* Being perhaps forty times longer, Roth, ed., *Encyclopedia Judaica* (1972) supplies greater depth but often less insight. **184** Wigoder, ed., *The Encyclopedia of Judaism* (1989) expounds the same material for the less learned. More anecdotal is 191 Rabbi Joseph Telushkin's *Jewish Literacy* (1991), which emphasizes North America. Articles on Judaism in 5 Eliade, ed., *The Encyclopedia of Religion* (1987) lack concision but are collected conveniently in Robert M. Seltzer, ed., *Judaism: A People and Its History* (New York: Macmillan, 1989). 183 Abramson, ed., *The Blackwell Companion to Jewish Culture* (1989) scants issues of religious law and practice but includes bibliographies. None of these matches *The Encyclopedia of the Jewish Religion* at explicating religious history. Perhaps no other single volume except 29 Cross, ed., *The Oxford Dictionary of the Christian Church* (1957, 1974) so intelligently digests an entire religious tradition. A second edition from Oxford University Press in late 1996 may well transform access to the field.

□ *Summary* On religion as distinct from culture, *The Encyclopedia of the Jewish Religion* remains indispensable. It is one of the ablest historical LEXICONS of a religion ever published.

61 (1981) W. Gunther Plaut, ed., *The Torah: A Modern Commentary* (New York: Union of American Hebrew Congregations, 1981); xxxvii & 1787 pages; no index; no bibliography. Analyzed further under 2.3.2 "Biblical Studies: Bible Commentaries."

This COMMENTARY on the Pentateuch presupposes "human, not divine authorship" and explores each verse in painstaking detail. Composed by Reform Jewish scholars, this masterwork deploys interpretations of history and Halakah from all schools. A more recent and bulkier COMMENTARY, Nahum M. Sarna, ed., *The JPS Torah Commentary*, 5 vols. (Philadelphia: Jewish Publication Society of America, 1989-) is Conservative rather than Reform and lacks "Gleanings."

181 (1987) Arthur A. Cohen and Paul Mendes-Flohr, eds., *Contemporary Jewish Religious Thought: Original Essays on Critical Concepts, Movements and Beliefs* (New York: Scribner's, 1987); xx & 1163 pages; index, pp. 1117-63; no general bibliography; glossary, pp. 1077-96.

□ *Scope* Prepared by over one hundred contributors, this REVISIONIST LEXICON reassesses Jewish theology, philosophy and cultural criticism but not literature, art or social science. One hundred forty signed essays of between four and twenty pages unfold alphabetically, each with brief English-language bibliography. One half of the authors comes from Israel and the other half from the United States, with only six from Europe. More than three-quarters are professors, and only about twenty are rabbis. The editors' introduction promises "conceptual reconstruction collectively engaged in" through recourse to Hebrew texts (p. xvii). As a follow-up, Paul Mendes-Flohr's essays on "Culture" and "History" vindicate the enterprise by addressing Jews and non-Jews alike. Among major authorities who write on their life's work come Adin Steinsalz on "Talmud" and "Sin," Maurice Friedman on "I and Thou" and Jacob Neusner on "Oral Law." R. J. Zwi Werblowsky tackles "Messianism," Moshe Idel "Mysticism" and Natan Rotenstreich "Tradition." There is even an essay from 1974 by Gershom Scholem on "Judaism."

Distinguished Holocaust theologians confront one another in Richard Rubenstein's "Evil," Emil Fackenheim's "Holocaust," Albert H. Friedlander's "Destiny and Fate" and Yossi Klein Heller's "Survival." Essays on Jewish denominations cut deep. Writing on "Orthodox Judaism," Emmanuel Rackman differentiates five attitudes toward non-Orthodox Jews, while on "Reconstructionism," Harold Schulweis construes Mordecai Kaplan's "Copernican Revolution" as a kind of "Social Existentialism." About a third of the articles trace the history among Jews of a pivotal idea like "Exile," "Miracle," "Tolerance" or "Soul." Law, ethics and history intertwine, while ritual, biblical studies and apologetics do not. Although no entries are named for persons (except in the glossary), the index notes every person discussed. A striking number of authors invoke Maimonides. He crops up in more than 50 percent of the articles, whereas Rosenzweig and Buber come up in 18 percent and Rashi in just 4 percent.

□ *Strengths* Inspired choice of contributors makes this one of the most stimulating of REVISIONIST LEXICONS. No entry is boring, and more than a few are exhilarating. Among the most original are essays by David G. Roskies on "Memory," which traces changing archetypes of Jewish group memory; Alan Udoff on "Metaphysics," which contrasts Maimonides and Martin Heidegger; Hyam Maccoby on "Sanctification of the Name," which classifies types of martyrdom; Adin Steinsalz on "Soul Searching," which traces through the Bible and the Talmud a principled willingness to revise assumptions. The longest entry is Geoffrey Hartman's analysis of Jewish "Imagination" as analogical (particularly in cabala). Equally exciting are novel typologies spun around familiar topics. Shalom Rosenberg examines in "Ethics" four ethical theories that flourished across the centuries. Galit Hasan-Rokem uncovers in "Myth" new types that Judaism evolved, while Josef Stern does the same for "Symbol and Gesture." Purely historical surveys come from David Stern on "Midrash," Marc Saperstein on "Sermon," Jacob B. Agus on "Medieval Jewish Philosophy" and Jeffrey Macy on "Natural Law." Whereas most articles remain academic in tone, a few undertake apologetics. Yeshayahu Leibowitz waxes compulsive on "Commandments" and "Idolatry," while Louis Jacobs makes the case more gently for "Faith" and "God." Only rarely is the tone defensive, as in Gerson D. Cohen's "Conservative Judaism."

□ *Weaknesses* Sheer cogency means that the essays must be read through; they cannot be dipped into. Coverage of world religions is uneven. David Flusser writes authoritatively on how "Christianity" emerged from Judaism, but Geoffrey Wigoder sounds noncommital on "Ecumenism." Nissim Rejwan summarizes Islam's attitude toward Judaism but not vice versa (albeit with excellent bibliography). No article tackles Zoroastrianism to complement David Satran's fine "Hellenism." The Bible gets short shrift (except for articles on "Bible-Criticism," "Hermeneutics,"

"Torah" and "Sacred Text and Canon"). Certain omissions, like Arthur Hertzberg, Harold Bloom and Emmanuel Levinas, surprise. Hertzberg and Bloom are not even mentioned. Topics that cry out for an essay include existentialism, identity and sociology of religion. Significant thinkers who are completely overlooked include Emile Durkheim and Georg Simmel. Lack of foreign-language bibliographies irks all the more because no comparable French or German work exists to supply them.

□ *Competitors* Perhaps no other religious tradition could succeed so spectacularly by inviting one hundred intellectuals to rethink fundamentals. To be sure, American Protestants recently recruited a hundred professionals to rethink roots of theology in **76** Donald W. Musser and Joseph L. Price, *A New Handbook of Christian Theology* (1992), but that work is more academic and breaks less fresh ground. Interestingly, the 1958 version of that volume, which Arthur A. Cohen coedited, helped to inspire this Jewish counterpart. No other recent Jewish reference work comes close to matching this REVISIONIST LEXICON in diversity, originality or vigor, although **180** Werblowsky and Wigoder, eds., *The Encyclopedia of the Jewish Religion* (1965) excels at compressing. For sheer originality the nearest competitor is **25** Arvind Sharma, *Our Religions* (1993), in which Jacob Neusner's contribution outshines many of those in *Contemporary Jewish Religious Thought.* Among LEXICONS on other traditions, **77** Alister E. McGrath, ed., *The Blackwell Encyclopedia of Modern Christian Thought* (1993) is comparably exhilarating, as is **202** Cyril Glassé's *The Concise Encyclopedia of Islam* (1989). None of these, however, sustains virtuosity so consistently or unleashes so many novel interpretations. Indeed, no other American LEXICON on religion exemplifies REVISIONISM so splendidly.

□ *Summary* This REVISIONIST LEXICON abounds in syntheses, typologies and rereadings. Few other reference works throw up so many novelties of thought or defend them so persuasively.

182 (1988) Pamela S. Nadell, *Con-*

servative Judaism in America: A Biographical Dictionary and Handbook (Westport, Conn., and London: Greenwood, 1988); xvi & 409 pages; index, pp. 393-409; general bibliography, pp. 393-409. Volume 1 of the series "Jewish Denominations in America," edited by Marc Lee Raphael.

□ *Critique* This WHO'S WHO of Conservative Jewish leaders in the United States appends a portrait of the Jewish Theological Seminary of America (pp. 263-94) and a brief GLOSSARY. The WHO'S WHO (pp. 25-261) recounts careers of more than 150 figures as well as writings by and about them. The coverage is thorough and the bibliography splendid. The series promises to revolutionize study of Judaism in America.

□ *Summary* Historians will profit from this detailed WHO'S WHO.

183 (1989) Glenda Abramson, ed., *The Blackwell Companion to Jewish Culture: From the Eighteenth Century to the Present* (Oxford and Cambridge, Mass.: Blackwell Reference, 1989); xxiv & 853 pages; index, pp. 833-53; no general bibliography; about 120 black-and-white photographs throughout.

□ *Scope* Edited at the Oxford Centre for Postgraduate Hebrew Studies, this COMPANION to Jewish culture all but ignores religion. It compiles a REALLEXIKON of cultural achievement as well as a WHO'S WHO of over a thousand Jewish figures active since 1750 in "Ashkenazi-western culture" (p. xiii). Over two hundred contributors from Britain, Israel and the United States furnish signed articles. Averaging a half to a full page, biographies pinpoint an individual's attitude toward Jewish tradition. Surveys of archeology, publishing, the arts, religious movements, languages and the social sciences stand out, while worship and religious learning get scanted (except in "Jewish Studies"). The writing is prosaic rather than sprightly. Entirely in English, bibliographies too often number just one or two titles. Photographs alternate individual portraits with glimpses of daily life.

□ *Strengths* Avoiding clichés that mar earlier LEXICONS of Jewish life, *The Blackwell*

Companion specifies how renowned Jews viewed religious tradition, but without explicating the latter in any depth. Articles on culture tend to show more verve than the biographies. Overviews recount such obligatory topics as "Ethics, Jewish, in the twentieth century," "Jewish Studies" and "Hebrew Literature," as well as unexpected ones like "Educational culture, Jewish," "Films, European, Jews in" and "Sectarian trends in modern Israel." Twenty-five pages on Jewish music (including in Terezin), as well as eight to ten pages on Jews in art, the press, Marxism and cinema, not to mention brief pieces on costume, dance and cooking, attest to adventurous editing. No country receives undue emphasis, and twelve pages on the Holocaust are a model of restraint.

□ *Weaknesses* This COMPANION lacks the system and comprehensiveness of an ENCYCLOPEDIA. Four pages on "Russian-Jewish culture before 1917" and three pages on "Soviet-Jewish culture" evoke no parallel entries on "German-Jewish culture" or "Italian Jewish culture." Music, whether classical, popular or liturgical, gets treated more deeply than painting, theater or film, while contemporary writers in Western Europe and the United States elicit fuller coverage than do those in Eastern Europe or Israel. Israel and Zionism win less attention than does the United States. While culture commands sophisticated treatment, religion does not. Brevity of bibliography detracts from an otherwise useful WHO'S WHO. Certain entries like the four pages on "Feminism, modern Judaism and" are cursory, while literary theory is scarcely mentioned. A British focus will startle anyone familiar with Israeli and American reference works, for attention lavished on scholars active in Great Britain, like S. S. Prawer and David Daube, should have extended to colleagues in America like Nahum Glatzer and Jacob Neusner.

□ *Competitors* Concerning recent Jewish culture and Jewish creators, Roth, ed., *Encyclopaedia Judaica* (1972) badly needs updating, and *The Blackwell Companion* executes this task with authority. Articles are fewer but deeper than in **184** Wigoder,

The Encyclopedia of Judaism (1989). A more inclusive but even more cursory German work is Julius H. Schoeps, ed., *Neues Lexikon des Judentums* (Frankfurt: Bertelsmann, 1992). On Zionism nothing can match Geoffrey Wigoder, ed., *New Encyclopedia of Zionism and Israel,* 2d ed., 2 vols. (London and Toronto: Associated University Presses, 1994). On matters of Jewish religion, **191** Telushkin's *Jewish Literacy* (1991) is preferable to all of these. As a WHO'S WHO and REALLEXIKON of Jewish creativity, *The Blackwell Companion* lacks the REVISIONIST flair of **181** Cohen and Mendes-Flohr, eds., *Contemporary Jewish Religious Thought* (1987). A work from the same publisher, 77 McGrath, ed., *The Blackwell Encyclopedia of Modern Christian Thought* (1993) casts its net more widely and has incomparably richer bibliographies. It knows no parallel pertaining to Jewish religion.

□ *Summary* As a WHO'S WHO of Jewish creators since 1750, *The Blackwell Companion to Jewish Culture* performs reliably. As a REALLEXIKON of culture, it synthesizes unusual topics.

184 (1989) Geoffrey Wigoder, ed., *The Encyclopedia of Judaism* (Jerusalem: Jerusalem Publishing House; New York: Macmillan, 1989); 786 pages; index, pp. 752-66; no bibliography; 40 color plates; black-and-white photographs throughout.

□ *Critique* This middle-level DICTIONARY expounds Jewish religious practices in unsigned articles by seventy-eight contributors. A WHO'S WHO of rabbis and other teachers alternates with a GLOSSARY of religious practices. Topics in cultural Judaism are omitted. The articles are lucid but less subtle than those in **180** Werblowsky and Wigoder, eds., *The Encyclopedia of the Jewish Religion* (1965). Both works suffer from lack of bibliographies.

□ *Summary* This DICTIONARY explicates Jewish religious practices at an intermediate level.

185 (1990) Avraham Yaakov Finkel, *The Great Torah Commentators* (Northvale, N.J., and London: Aronson, 1990); xi & 256 pages; two indexes (of Bible passages and names), pp. 249-56; no general bibli-

ography; photographs throughout.

□ *Critique* This infectious WHO'S WHO profiles eighty-one rabbis of all periods who wrote COMMENTARIES on the Torah. A life sketch and up to twenty short excerpts from the writings (often with anecdotes) enliven each entry. Finkel's knack for bringing Torah scholars to life sustains two sequels, *The Great Chasidic Masters* (1992), containing fifty profiles, and *Contemporary Sages: The Great Chasidic Masters of the Twentieth Century* (1994), including thirty-seven profiles. Between ten and twenty excerpts per entry place these works among the most vivid of WHO'S WHOS. An even fuller guide to ancient rabbis is Shulamis Frieman, *Who's Who in the Talmud* (Northvale, N.J., and London: Aronson, 1995).

□ *Summary* These WHO'S WHOS elucidate masters of Torah through delectable quotations.

186 (1991) Geoffrey Wigoder, ed., *Dictionary of Jewish Biography* (Jerusalem: Jerusalem Publishing House; New York: Simon & Schuster, 1991); 568 pages; no index; no general bibliography; black-and-white photographs.

□ *Critique* This well-edited WHO'S WHO supplies about eight hundred unsigned entries on significant Jews, of whom an overwhelming majority lived after 1800. No living figures feature. Averaging one-half to one and one-half pages, biographies outline careers, characterize creativity and furnish anecdotes (as well as skeletal bibliography). Sidebars feature quotations by or about major figures like Freud and Einstein. The editor apologizes for including too few women, and some of the reportage needs to be verified. This remains, nonetheless, the richest WHO'S WHO of Jewry available in a single volume.

□ *Summary* This alluring WHO'S WHO offers lively narration and juicy anecdotes.

187 (1993) Kerry M. Olitzky, Lance J. Sussman and Malcolm H. Stern, eds., *Reform Judaism in America: A Biographical Dictionary and Sourcebook* (Westport, Conn., and London: Greenwood, 1993); xxxi & 349 pages; index, pp. 339-43; general bibliography, pp. 295-

337.

□ *Critique* This companion volume to **182** Nadell, ed., *Conservative Judaism* (1988) recruits forty-nine authorities to write a WHO'S WHO on 170 Reform leaders. Signed entries furnish bibliography by and about biographees. A forty-page general bibliography is superb. Historians of Reform Judaism will find this tool indispensable.

□ *Summary* This WHO'S WHO is a must for historians of American Judaism.

188 (1994) Saul S. Friedman, ed., *Holocaust Literature: A Handbook of Critical, Historical and Literary Writings* (Westport, Conn., and London: Greenwood, 1994); xxx & 677 pages; two indexes, pp. 633-71; general bibliography, pp. xxix-xxx.

□ *Critique* This HANDBOOK of literature concerning the Holocaust delivers thirty-two signed chapters with massive multilingual bibliographies. Canvassing all of Europe, regional and thematic chapters supply historical introductions. Coverage is comprehensive and sober. Anyone studying the Holocaust should own this guide to the literature. It is more scholarly than Israel Guttman, ed., *Encyclopedia of the Holocaust,* 4 vols. (New York and London: Macmillan, 1990).

□ *Summary* This HANDBOOK evaluates primary and secondary literature about the Holocaust with utmost thoroughness.

3.1.2 INTRODUCTORY GLOSSARIES

OVERVIEW: SELF-TEACHING AT ITS BEST Jewish scholars excel at the introductory GLOSSARY. Some of them (e.g., **191** Telushkin and **192** Glinert) are highly entertaining, but most suffer from lack of secondary bibliographies. It is worth noting that comparable books on Islam tend to be peremptory rather than discursive, and utterly lacking in humor, e.g., Yusuf Al-Qaradawi, *The Lawful and the Prohibited in Islam,* 20th ed. (Plainfield, Ind.: American Trust, 1994).

LIST OF WORKS ANALYZED
189 (1942, 1967) Abraham Mayer Heller, *The Vocabulary of Jewish Life* (New York: Hebrew Publishing, 1942; 2d ed., rev., 1967)

190 (1964, 1975) Philip Birnbaum, *A Book of Jewish Concepts* (New York: Hebrew Publishing, 1964; 2d ed., rev., 1975)

191 (1991) Rabbi Joseph Telushkin, *Jewish Literacy: The Most Important Things to Know About the Jewish Religion, Its People and Its History* (New York: William Morrow, 1991)

192 (1992) Lewis Glinert, *The Joys of Hebrew* (New York and Oxford: Oxford University Press, 1992)

193 (1992) Kerry M. Olitzky and Ronald H. Isaacs, eds., *A Glossary of Jewish Life* (Northvale, N.J., and London: Aronson, 1992)

194 (1992) Ellen Frankel and Betsy Platkin Teutsch, eds., *The Encyclopedia of Jewish Symbols* (Northvale, N.J., and London: Aronson, 1992)

195 (1992) Dan Cohn-Sherbok, *The Blackwell Dictionary of Judaica* (Oxford and Cambridge, Mass.: Blackwell Reference, 1992)

ANALYSIS OF WORKS
189 (1942, 1967) Abraham Mayer Heller, *The Vocabulary of Jewish Life* (New York: Hebrew Publishing, 1942; 2d ed., rev., 1967); xiv & 353 pages; index, pp. 343-53; no general bibliography.

□ *Critique* This GLOSSARY of over one thousand Hebrew terms aims to be normative for observant Jews. It deploys nineteen headings that range from "The Jewish Home" and "The Synagogue" through "Mourning" and "Theological Terms" to "Jewish Learning" and "Jewish Law and Authority." Catchwords come entirely in Hebrew, with Israeli and Ashkenazi pronunciations specified for each term. Entries, usually of five to fifteen lines, define a word and specify its function in Jewish observance. Sections on "Magic and Superstition" (pp. 161-65) and "The Poor and Underprivileged" (pp. 235-37) are highly original, but there is no section on the Hebrew Bible. Each of nineteen sections opens with a headnote that thunders out what is expected of a religiously observant Jew. In contrast to alphabetical arrangement in **190** Birnbaum, *A Book of Jewish Concepts* (1964, 1975), topical arrangement encourages browsing. Apart from the headnotes, there is hardly any pontificating. In contrast to **192** Glinert, *The Joys of Hebrew* (1992), there are no quotations, anecdotes or witticisms.

□ *Summary* For all its sobriety, this ranks as one of the most bracing of normative GLOSSARIES.

190 (1964, 1975) Philip Birnbaum, *A Book of Jewish Concepts* (New York: Hebrew Publishing, 1964; 2nd ed., rev., 1975; paperback, 1988); x & 722 pages; index, pp. 695-713; topical index, pp. 715-22; no bibliography.

□ *Critique* This GLOSSARY of over five hundred concepts (but not persons) is arranged alphabetically according to Hebrew terms. A topical index enables non-Hebrew speakers to find entries. They cover all books of the Hebrew Bible as well as ethics, law, history, Talmud, Cabala and above all worship (prayer, Sabbath, festivals, fasts, the life cycle). Designed to supply norms for observant Jews, the entries explicate laws, customs and liturgies with sympathy and choice quotations but do not invoke Jewish denominations (except "Hasidism") or other religions. There are no entries on persons, and no bibliographies. Composed in the early 1960s and revised in the mid-1970s, this work retains its usefulness, particularly on liturgy and festivals, but tends to downplay mysticism. Because Birnbaum's sequence of entries follows the Hebrew alphabet, non-Jewish browsers may falter. The tone is more austere than in **191** Rabbi Telushkin's *Jewish Literacy* (1991), which boasts an easier arrangement based on English terms but treats fewer concepts. Of all Jewish GLOSSARIES, this one comes closest in tone to a Muslim book of dos and don'ts.

□ *Summary* Although this work of Jewish self-definition ignores both Jewish denominations and other religions, its explanations of liturgy and festivals purvey splendid detail.

191 (1991) Rabbi Joseph Telushkin, *Jewish Literacy: The Most Important Things to Know About the Jewish Religion, Its People and Its History* (New York: William Morrow, 1991); 688 pages; index, pp. 671-88; no general bibliography.

□ *Scope* This ebullient GLOSSARY arranges 346 entries under fifteen headings intended for the "Jewishly illiterate" Jew. Arranged in roughly chronological order, the first eight headings cover Jewish history with attention to the Bible and the Middle Ages, as well as to the Holocaust, the State of Israel and American Jewish life. The second half explores Jewish texts, ethics, holidays, life cycle and prayers. The author excels at storytelling: some fifty rabbis (e.g., Israel Salanter, Rav Kook), scholars (e.g., Martin Buber, Eliezir Ben-Yehuda) and innovators (e.g., Louis Brandeis, Sigmund Freud) of all periods come to life. Pungent quotations dot the narratives. Most entries supply brief English-language bibliography. Using asterisks, cross-references radiate to items in the index.

□ *Strengths* This INTRODUCTION pioneers a mix of persons, practices, texts and concepts that is unique. The author tested much of the material in lectures to adults. The result is one of the most beguiling works of popularization about any religion. Grouping of entries is astute and makes browsing a pleasure. Telushkin excels at depicting giants of religious thought: portrayals of figures like Saadyah Gaon, Rashi and Maimonides deploy superb quotations and emphasize contemporary pertinence. Nor does this popularizer skirt controversy. He assesses Jesus, Paul, Muhammad and Luther in hard-hitting articles that shun the courtesies of interreligious dialogue. A section on "American Jewish Life" narrates highpoints and life stories with gusto and explicates denominational conflicts with candor. A section on "The Hebrew Calendar and Jewish Holidays" compresses vast information and wry anecdotes into fifty pages. The section on "Jewish Ethics and Basic Beliefs" includes entries on "Hospitality," "Righteous Non-Jews" and "Family Harmony." On nearly every topic the author inserts musings that sound unambiguously American. Yet for all his candor, Rabbi Telushkin conceals his denominational identity. This is one of the best condensed and least impersonal INTRODUCTIONS to any religion.

□ *Weaknesses* As a GLOSSARY introducing Jewish religion, this volume has few equals. Its pursuit of self-definition means that nonprophetic (i.e., Asian) religions are excluded, as are the Samaritans and Zoroastrians. Some will regard its handling of earliest Christianity and Islam as needlessly provocative. Cabala is deemphasized, and there is no material on art or architecture. Unfortunately, bibliographies omit place and date of publication.

□ *Competitors* This canny INTRODUCTION to Jewish history, teaching and present status transcends the genre of GLOSSARY. A wealth of quotations, anecdotes and potted history distinguish it from **190** Birnbaum, *A Book of Jewish Concepts* (1964, 1975) or the much briefer **192** Glinert, *The Joys of Hebrew* (1992). In contrast to these GLOSSARIES of Hebrew words, Telushkin titles entries in English (as regards the calendar, life cycle and synagogue). No comparable INTRODUCTION to Christianity exists, although (at twice the length) **127** *Théo* (1989, 1993) comes close for French Catholics.

□ *Summary* This captivating INTRODUCTION excels at recounting highpoints, untangling controversies and explaining worship. No other GLOSSARY of any religion reads so compellingly.

192 (1992) Lewis Glinert, *The Joys of Hebrew* (New York and Oxford: Oxford University Press, 1992); xii & 292 pages; glossary of Hebrew lettering, pp. 270-90; no index; no bibliography anywhere except in "Acknowledgments," pp. ix-x.

□ *Critique* This GLOSSARY of over six hundred Hebrew terms (arranged alphabetically in transliteration) is a delight. A distinguished British Hebraist has assembled definitions, examples and anecdotes to illustrate nuances of usage and wit. Each entry differentiates Israeli and Ashkenazi pronunciation, as well as variations among European, American and Israeli customs. Glinert has culled the choicest examples to enliven his book. Quotations range from the Hebrew Bible and the Talmud through Saadyah Gaon and Maimonides to Abraham Heschel and Joseph Soloveitchik. Emphasis falls on Jewish life rather than religion. No other reference book deploys more or better wit.

□ *Summary* This drollest of GLOSSARIES illuminates Jewish life by elucidating Hebrew usage.

193 (1992) Kerry M. Olitzky and Ronald H. Isaacs, eds., *A Glossary of Jewish Life* (Northvale, N.J., and London: Aronson, 1992); 254 pages; index, pp. 227-54; no bibliography.

□ *Critique* This GLOSSARY arranges very brief definitions of two thousand four hundred terms under eight headings. The latter range from "Religious Practice" and "Bible and Commentaries" to "Israel," "Philosophy and Theology" and "Daily Jewish Living." Essentially an INTRODUCTION for Jews to vocabulary in which they find themselves immersed, this GLOSSARY lacks scholarly apparatus. Since the definitions average just two to six lines each, researchers will do better to consult **191** Telushkin, *Jewish Literacy* (1991) or else the following entry.

□ *Summary* This GLOSSARY is introductory to a fault.

194 (1992) Ellen Frankel and Betsy Platkin Teutsch, eds., *The Encyclopedia of Jewish Symbols* (Northvale, N.J., and London: Aronson, 1992); xxiii & 235 pages; 2 indexes, pp. 217-21, 229-34; general bibliography, pp. 225-28; glossary, pp. 201-6; line drawings throughout.

□ *Critique* This historical DICTIONARY expounds 266 objects, biblical persons and holidays in articles of one to two pages that overflow with biblical and Talmudic references. Objects like "Golem," "Ladder," "Rose" and "Zodiac" get probed historically. Abounding in cross-references, this DICTIONARY achieves a depth that is lacking in a companion volume, **193** Olitzky and Isaacs, eds., *A Glossary of Jewish Life* (1992).

□ *Summary* Learned entries on objects and holidays fill a gap among introductory GLOSSARIES.

195 (1992) Dan Cohn-Sherbok, *The Blackwell Dictionary of Judaica* (Oxford and Cambridge, Mass.: Blackwell Reference, 1992); xviii & 624 pages; no index; no secondary bibliographies anywhere (except p. ix); two maps; also in paperback.

□ *Critique* This introductory GLOSSARY and WHO'S WHO provides seven thousand brief entries on every aspect of Jewish life. Definitions average five to seven lines and lack bibliography. A WHO'S WHO sketches the career and lists major writings of several thousand figures. Deliberately elementary, this work offers a clue to everything and depth on nothing.

□ *Summary* This GLOSSARY and WHO'S WHO serves beginners.

3.2 ISLAM

3.2.1 GENERAL

OVERVIEW: THE CLASH BETWEEN WESTERN AND ISLAMIC APPROACHES Until the 1990s Islam had elicited fewer reference works in the West than had Christianity, Judaism or Buddhism. While monographs proliferated, ambitious reference works lagged. At least for the period since 1789, a gap was filled by **207** Esposito, ed., *The Oxford Encyclopedia of the Modern Islamic World*, 4 vols. (1995). Annotations in its bibliographies are unique. On doctrines and practices an older HANDBOOK, **197** Pareja, ed., *Islamologie* (1957-64), remains useful, not least for chronology and for Qur'anic references. Of two ongoing MEGA-ENCYCLOPEDIAS an older one, **198** Gibb et al., eds., *The Encyclopaedia of Islam: New Edition* (1960-), reached the letters *SAM* in 1995, while the newer **199** *Encyclopaedia Iranica* (1985-) reached "Deylam" in 1994.

Why do Muslims eschew Western-style reference books? The answer is simple: Western notions of encyclopedia-making distort a religion whose scripture and precepts are held to have issued from God. Whereas Judaism cherishes Midrashim and Christianity hermeneutics, Islam supplies little to fill a zone midway between normative rules (or revelation) and nonnormative

oral traditions (or folklore). In Islam revelation stipulates so much that too little occupies the zone where encyclopedia-makers dwell—halfway between the obligatory and the casual. As a result, contemporary Islam does not favor REVISIONISM or humor.

Apart from three exceptions, **202** Glassé, *The Concise Encyclopedia of Islam* (1989), Nasr's chapter in **25** Sharma, ed., *Our Religions* (1993), and portions of **207** Esposito, ed., *The Oxford Encyclopedia* (1995), Muslims have furnished no equivalent in English to reference works composed by Jews on Judaism or Buddhists on Buddhism. Certain volumes in French fill the void, for example Tahar Gaid, *Dictionnaire élémentaire de l'Islam* (Alger: Office des Publications Universitaires, 1982) and **207** Chebel, *Dictionnaire des symboles musulmans* (1995). But except for these and portions of **207** Esposito, ed., *The Oxford Encyclopedia* (1995), the chief tools outside of Arabic come from scholars in the West, hardly any of whom are Muslim (except Glassé, Nasr and al Faruqi). Inevitably, Muslims will resent many of the works analyzed below, including at times even **202** Glassé, *The Concise Encyclopedia of Islam* (1989). Happily, offensiveness is absent from **206** Annemarie Schimmel's *Deciphering the Signs of God* (1994), which reinterprets Islamic spirituality from within and without.

Although this directory groups Qur'anic DICTIONARIES and COMMENTARIES under 3.2.2 "The Qur'an," general works on Islam also scrutinize the scripture. C. L. Geddes, *Guide to Reference Books for Islamic Studies* (Denver: American Institute of Islamic Studies, 1985) analyzes twelve hundred tools (about half of them in Arabic) that examine Islam from Spain to China, spanning the period from 610 to 1924.

LIST OF WORKS ANALYZED
196 (1953, 1965) Hamilton A. R. Gibb [1895-1971] and J[ohannes] H[endrik] Kramers [1891-1951], eds., *Shorter Encyclopaedia of Islam* (Ithaca, N.Y.: Cornell University Press, 1953;

Leiden: Brill, 1965)

197 (1957-64) F[elix] M. Pareja, ed., *Islamologie* (Beyrouth: Imprimerie Catholique, 1957-64)

198 (1960-) Hamilton A. R. Gibb [1895-1971] et al. and C. E. Bosworth [since 1978] et al., eds., *The Encyclopaedia of Islam: New Edition* (Leiden: Brill, 1960-)

199 (1985-) Ehsan Yarshater, ed., *Encyclopaedia Iranica*, vols. 1-4 (London and New York: Routledge & Kegan Paul, 1985-90); vols. 5- (Costa Mesa, Calif.: Mazda Publishing, 1992-)

200 (1986) Isma'il R. al Faruqi and Lois Lamya al Faruqi, *The Cultural Atlas of Islam* (New York: Macmillan, 1986)

201 (1987) Adel Theodor Khoury [1930-], ed., *Lexikon religiöser Grundbegriffe: Judentum, Christentum, Islam* (Graz: Styria, 1987)

202 (1989) Cyril Glassé, *The Concise Encyclopedia of Islam* (San Francisco: Harper, 1989; paperback, 1991)

289 (1989-92) André Jacob, ed., *Encyclopédie philosophique universelle*, 5 vols. (Paris: Presses Universitaires de France, 1989-92)

203 (1992) Ian Richard Netton, *A Popular Dictionary of Islam* (London: Curzon, 1992)

204 (1992) Farzana Shaikh, ed., *Islam and Islamic Groups: A Worldwide Reference Guide* (Harlow, Essex: Longman, 1992)

12 (1993) Jan Knappert, *The Encyclopaedia of Middle Eastern Mythology and Religion* (Shaftesbury, U.K., and Rockport, Mass.: Element, 1993)

25 (1993) Arvind Sharma, ed., *Our Religions* (San Francisco: Harper, 1993); includes a chapter by Seyyed Hossein Nasr on Islam.

205 (1994) E[meri] van Donzel, ed., *Islamic Desk Reference* (Leiden, New York and Köln: Brill, 1994)

206 (1994) Annemarie Schimmel, *Deciphering the Signs of God: A Phenomenological Approach to Islam* (Albany: SUNY Press, 1994)

207 (1995) John L. Esposito, ed., *The Oxford Encyclopedia of the Modern Islamic World*, 4 vols. (New York: Oxford University Press, 1995)

208 (1995) Malek Chebel, *Dictionnaire de symboles musulmans: Rites, mystique et civilisation* (Paris: Albin Michel, 1995)

ANALYSIS OF WORKS

196 (1953, 1965) Hamilton A. R. Gibb [1895-1971] and J[ohannes] H[endrik] Kramers [1891-1951], eds., *Shorter Encyclopaedia of Islam* (Ithaca, N.Y.: Cornell University Press, 1953; Leiden: Brill, 1965); 671 pages; no index.

□ *Critique* This LEXICON reprints major articles from the first edition of the *Encyclopaedia of Islam*, 4 volumes and supplement (1913-38, repr. 1987). Although multilingual bibliographies were updated, articles were not. Having recapitulated scholarship of the 1920s and 1930s, this volume is superseded by the ongoing second edition of **198** *The Encyclopaedia of Islam* (1960-) as well as by its digest, **205** van Donzel ed., *Islamic Desk Reference* (1994). This volume remains current on very few matters.

□ *Summary* This one-volume LEXICON is now out of date.

197 (1957-64) F[elix] M. Pareja, ed., *Islamologie* (Beyrouth: Imprimerie catholique, 1957-64); 1149 pages; two indexes (authors, general), pp. 1073-143; general bibliography, pp. 4-8, 14.

□ *Critique* A Madrid Islamologist edited this French HANDBOOK of scholarship on Islam, having earlier prepared a shorter Spanish version (Rome: Orbis Catholicus, 1951). Alessandro Bausani of Rome and Ludwig Hertling of Munich assisted. Twenty-two chapters divide into 3-10 on history, 11-17 on institutions, 18-20 on literatures (by Bausani) and 21-22 on sciences and art, each with multilingual bibliography of one to ten pages. Dates abound, keyed to both Western and Islamic calendars. Obligatory topics include technical ones like calendar conversion, transliteration and statistics. This HANDBOOK recapitulates the state of the field as it was in the mid-1950s. A late colonial European perspective obtrudes chiefly in chapter 10, which narrates the history of fifteen regions from 1800 to 1957 (pp. 339-596). Chapter 11 on the Qur'an, chapter 13 on dogmatics and chapter 15 on the tariqas dispense rare information, while chapter 17 on "Sects of Islam" (pp. 814-58) is one of the fullest anywhere. Chapter 12 on the Sharia differentiates sources to a nicety. A general index lists over five thousand persons, places and Arabic terms, while the author index cites over twenty-two hundred individuals. The writing purveys memorable formulations, and the bibliographies are unmatched. Few other HANDBOOKS map complexity so adroitly.

□ *Summary* Lucidity, comprehensiveness and synthesis make this a model HANDBOOK. It badly needs updating.

198 (1960-) Hamilton A. R Gibb [1895-1971] et al. and C. E[dmund] Bosworth [since 1978] et al., eds., *The Encyclopaedia of Islam: New Edition* (Leiden: Brill, 1960-); vol. 8 (through *SAM*, 1995); about 9000 pages to date; drawings, black-and-white photographs and maps throughout; index of subjects in vols. 1-6 (1991), 180 pages; index of proper names in vols. 1-7 (1993), 400 pages. Supplements to earlier volumes have appeared since 1982.

□ *Critique* This MEGA-ENCYCLOPEDIA by Western scholars examines the history, art, beliefs and practices of Islam worldwide in unprecedented depth. This edition supplants an earlier one published in four volumes with supplement (1913-38, repr. 1987), which appeared concurrently in German as the *Enzyklopädie des Islam*. Knowledge of Arabic is presupposed. Pace of publication has increased since volume 4 (1978). Volume 5 appeared in 1986, volume 6 in 1991, volume 7 in 1993 and volume 8 in 1995. Massive multilingual bibliographies make articles on persons, doctrines, places, languages, Arabic terms and art indispensable to specialists, but beginners should look elsewhere. Although Arabic terminology abounds, Western authors pay little heed to Muslim sensitivities. Two indexes (1993) are superb. **205** van Donzel, ed., *An Islamic*

Desk Reference (1994) recapitulates the marrow of this work.

□ *Summary* This MEGA-ENCYCLOPEDIA formulates Western scholarship on all aspects of Islam in daunting detail. As with **199** Yarshater, ed., *Encyclopaedia Iranica* (1985-), only experts can profit to the full.

199 (1985-) Ehsan Yarshater, ed., *Encyclopaedia Iranica,* vols. 1-4 (London and New York: Routledge & Kegan Paul, 1985-90); vols. 5- (Costa Mesa, Calif.: Mazda Publishing, 1992-); vol. 7, fasc. 3 (1994) goes through "Deylam"; approximately 1000 pages per volume; no index; general bibliography (i.e., "Short References and Abbreviations") at the beginning of each volume; charts, maps and black-and-white photographs in the text.

□ *Scope* This MEGA-ENCYCLOPEDIA (or rather MEGA-REALLEXIKON) is one of the grand scholarly enterprises of our time. Conceived in Iran before the 1978 revolution, it was later relaunched from Columbia University. Nearly all contributors reside in Europe, North America or South Asia. History and culture of all regions influenced by Iranian peoples since remote antiquity are expounded in staggering depth. More than three hundred Westerners write signed articles (each with multilingual bibliography) on persons, regions, cultural practices and history. Regions encompass Iran, Baluchistan, the Deccan, Central Asia, Chinese Turkestan and kindred areas. Persian literature, music and art of each region wins exhaustive coverage. Ceramics, for example, commands eighty pages with photographs (5:265-331). Articles and bibliographies overflow with titles in Persian, Turkish, Arabic and Central Asian languages.

□ *Strengths* Most articles in this MEGA-REAL-LEXIKON deploy multiple sections, each written by a pertinent authority. Tracing Iranian culture as it infiltrated adjacent areas, entries expound geography and history region by region. Most Western Orientalists who ever worked on Iranian topics receive notices, as do earlier authors who mentioned Iran (e.g., "Cassiodorus"). Both Shiite and Sunni Islam are treated in depth. Christianity evokes twenty-five pages in eight subentries (5:523-48), while Zoroastrianism and Baha'i elicit unprecedented coverage. The topic of "Cleansing in Zoroastrianism," for example, fills eight pages. Twelve articles on "Baha'i Faith" run nearly forty pages. Volumes yet to appear will explore Manichaeism and Gnosticism. Scholars of Zoroastrianism, Baha'i and Shiism, as well as of Gnosticism, have a cornucopia in the making. One can imagine how founders of Iranian studies like Eugène Burnouf and James Darmesteter would rejoice that their field should sponsor one of the most authoritative of MEGA-ENCYCLOPEDIAS.

□ *Weaknesses* This is a MEGA-REALLEXIKON by and for master scholars. Nonspecialists can admire but seldom quibble, for one needs high expertise just to discern gaps. Emphasis on factuality makes the enterprise modern rather than postmodern. Although it exemplifies the stance that Edward Said calls "Orientalism," early volumes do not analyze that concept. Fact is king.

□ *Competitors* Outsiders will gape in awe at the ambition of this enterprise, which bids fair to exceed twenty thousand pages. When complete in another fifteen to twenty volumes, the *Encyclopaedia Iranica* will constitute a MEGA-ENCYCLOPEDIA without peer. On Iranian and Shiite topics, the ongoing **198** *Encyclopaedia of Islam* (1960-) remains less comprehensive and less detailed (except on theology and law) but more rapid in publication. On art, particularly architecture, the *Encyclopaedia Iranica* is exceptionally searching and up-to-date. One wishes that Western scholars would launch a comparable REALLEXIKON about South Asia.

□ *Summary* This awe-inspiring MEGA-ENCYCLOPEDIA goes forward with zeal. Perhaps no other smallish region of the world currently elicits in a reference work such loving detail or such bibliographical density.

200 (1986) Isma'il R. al Faruqi and Lois Lamya al Faruqi, *The Cultural Atlas of Islam* (New York: Macmillan, 1986); xvi & 512 pages; index, pp. 481-501; map index, pp. 503-12; no general bibliography; 300 black-and-white photographs; 77 maps.

□ *Scope* A husband-and-wife team completed this COMPENDIUM of history, religion and culture just before they were assassinated in 1986. Twenty-three chapters pivot on a distinction used in phenomenology of religion between "essence" and "manifestation." Part 1, "The Origin" (chaps. 1-3), portrays four millennia of the ancient Near East as a seedbed of Islam. Jews and Christians will find the viewpoint unfamiliar, sometimes even off-putting. Part 2 (chap. 4) on "The Essence of Islamic Civilization" squeezes a lifetime of reflection into fourteen pages. Part 3, "The Form" (chaps. 5-8), on the Qur'an, the Sunnah, institutions, and the arts abounds in maps, genealogical tables and narratives that illuminate norms. Two-thirds of the book is comprised by part 4, "The Manifestation" (chaps. 9-23). Superbly researched chapters explore Islam's "manifestation" in the humanities, encompassing sciences of the Qur'an and of the hadith, law, theology *(kalam),* mysticism, philosophy, letters and above all the visual arts. Every chapter overflows with maps and photographs. Bibliographies emerge in footnotes and a few headnotes, such as on music (p. 449).

□ *Strengths* Written by observant Muslims, this COMPENDIUM devotes its finest sections, one-third of the whole, to the arts. Chapter 19 on "The Art of Letters" designates the style of the Qur'an as "the literary sublime" in form, content and effect, and then surveys in ten pages Arabic prose and poetry down to the thirteenth century. Chapter 20 on "Calligraphy" classifies eleven "regionally significant" scripts, culminating in "Pseudo-calligraphy or pure abstraction." Chapter 21, "Ornamentation in the Islamic Arts," interprets "transfiguration" of materials and structures as an emblem of *tawhid* (i.e., remembrance of God's unity). Ten pages of sample ornamentation (pp. 386-95) and thirty photos enhance a bravura performance. Chapter 22, "The Spatial Arts," differentiates five "core characteristics" of the "abstract" in mosque architecture: (1)

overlay, (2) transfiguration of materials, (3) transfiguration of structures, (4) transfiguration of enclosure, (5) ambiguity of function. Chapters 21 and 22 rank among the acutest anywhere on religious dimensions of Islamic art. Chapter 23, "The Art of Sound," compares instruments and chants across the Islamic world, besides listing almost 120 Arab authorities on music theory (pp. 449-54). By interpreting visual arts and music as observant Muslims, the al Faruqis redress neglect of religion among Western art historians. To be sure, the historical chapters (4-10) dispense lore that is readily gleaned elsewhere. The writing is vigorous, the assemblage of charts, maps and photos unequaled. Maps of seven battles fought by the Prophet are unique (pp. 196-200). A general index facilitates reference to persons and concepts.

□ *Weaknesses* This so-called ATLAS fits no category. Indeed, its anomalous character can only confuse the reader. Discussion of methodology is skeletal and does not invoke other scholars (pp. xii-xiv). As a labor of love by observant Muslims, the ATLAS will seem overly committed ("normative") to many, particularly social scientists. Nor will everyone welcome a distinction between "essence" and "manifestation" or the resulting inquiry into how the "essence" of Islam took shape in various civilizations ("manifestations"). Moreover, emphasis on things Arab tends to neglect things Persian. Having pervaded the first half of the volume, material on Christians, Jews and Zoroastrians disappears in the second half on art. Comparisons run within Islamic art, not between it and Christian or Hellenistic examples. Hasty readers must slow down for chapters 19-23, which need to be read through and cannot be dipped into. A glossary of Arabic terms would have been useful.

□ *Competitors* Not a LEXICON nor a GLOSSARY nor a WHO'S WHO, this hybrid work stands in splendid isolation. No other reference book presents Islamic arts so insightfully or compactly, but many others provide easier access to history and religious norms. **202** Glassé, *The Concise Encyclopedia of Islam* (1989) cuts deeper on theology and history, but not on the arts, and has many fewer maps. Articles in **5** Eliade, ed., *The Encyclopedia of Religion* (1987), particularly those by Jacques Waardenburg on history of the study of Islam, show how unbending is the authors' standpoint. **205** van Donzel, ed., *Islamic Desk Reference* (1994) delivers Western positivism in contrast to the al Faruqis' commitment to Islam. Their jarring reconfiguration of the pre-Islamic Near East (chaps. 1-3) surfaced earlier in **17** Isma'il al Faruqi's *Historical Atlas of the Religions of the World* (1974). The latter's forty-five pages on Islam contain the germ of this work, and its bibliography on page 281 should have been reprinted here.

□ *Summary* Breathtaking syntheses of visual arts and music accompany one-sided views of Islamic history in this lovingly illustrated COMPENDIUM. The seventy-seven maps are unrivaled.

201 (1987) Adel Theodor Khoury (1930-), ed., *Lexikon religiöser Grundbegriffe: Judentum, Christentum, Islam* (Graz: Styria, 1987); xlix & 588 pages; no index; no general bibliography; synoptic chronology, pp. xxxix-xlvi.

□ *Scope* This comparative LEXICON compiles 166 substantive entries totaling almost five hundred separate essays. They methodically contrast doctrines and norms of Judaism, Christianity and Islam. Nearly all entries deploy three signed articles, one on each of the faiths, while a few like "Fatima" and "Hidjra" touch only Islam. Whereas four authorities write on Judaism and twenty on Christianity, all but six of the Islamic entries come from S. Balic, who relies heavily on *Handwörterbuch des Islam* (1941), which in turn derived from the first edition of the *Encyclopaedia of Islam* (1913-38). The volume opens with three synoptic essays by Dieter Vetter on Judaism, Ludwig Hagemann on Christianity and Theodor Khoury on Islam. Bibliographies are skeletal.

□ *Strengths* Entries focus on norms. Balic's 160 articles digest major and minor points, emphasizing parallels to and divergences from both Judaism and Christianity. Having differentiated among schools of law, he inserts choice details such as the prohibition within the sacred zones of Mecca, Medina and Jerusalem against killing animals, mowing grass or breaking twigs (p. 528). Among arresting essays are those on "Diaspora," "Hospitality," "Jerusalem," "Martyrdom," "Philosophy," "Sacrifice" and "Symbol." Only five persons elicit entries: Abraham, Ismail, Jesus, Muhammad and Moses. Anyone pursuing nuances of Islamic belief and practice will applaud.

□ *Weaknesses* Exemplifying a German notion of fundamental categories *(Grundbegriffe),* the focus on norms seems schematic concerning Christianity, where philosophy and modern theology demand greater attention. Regrettably, Asian religions are ignored. The WHO'S WHO is derisorily brief.

□ *Competitors* For comparing fundamentals in the three prophetic religions, this LEXICON has no rival. Only 6 Waldenfels, ed., *Lexikon der Religionen* (1987, 1992) schematizes major religions under similar headings, but more tersely. As the only work of its kind, the *Lexikon religiöser Grundbegriffe* deserves to be better known. It gave rise to an even more comprehensive LEXICON of 340 entries, Adel Theodor Khoury et al., eds., *Dictionnaire de l'Islam: Histoire, idées, grandes figures* (Turnhout: Brepols, 1995).

□ *Summary* This LEXICON compares norms of Judaism, Christianity and Islam unforgettably.

202 (1989) Cyril Glassé, *The Concise Encyclopedia of Islam* (San Francisco: Harper, 1989; paperback, 1991); 472 pages; no index; maps, pp. 438-47; genealogies, pp. 450-53; chronology, pp. 454-67; bibliography, pp. 468-72; 24 colored plates.

□ *Scope* By construing Islam as both culture and religion, this REVISIONIST LEXICON filled a vacuum, for there had been no single-author LEXICON of Islam in English since Thomas Patrick Hughes, *Dictionary of Islam* (1885). An American Muslim, Glassé penned twelve hundred entries, ranging from two lines to five pages, to encompass persons, places, peoples, sects, concepts, practices, books and controver-

sies. Persons include rulers, thinkers and biblical personages. Places number Islamic regions ("Iran," "Delhi," "Lebanon," but not Indonesia) and Arab capital cities ("Cairo," "Damascus," "Medina," "Jeddah," but not Cordova). Events of the seventh century C.E. get narrated in detail, including a page on the Byzantine emperor Heraclius (610-641), but the twentieth century gets scanted. Longer articles disclose Glassé's passion for mysticism: six pages on "Isma'ilis," five pages on "Muhammad," "Philosophy," "Manicheism," "Shi'ism" and "Sufism," four pages on "Koran," "Pilgrimage," "Salah" [prayer] and "Five Divine Presences." Mysticism wins more space than law, and al-Hallaj commands the longest treatment of any thinker. Individual bibliographies being absent, a general one assembles works in English, French and German.

□ *Strengths* This LEXICON conveys mastery of the history of Islam, at least in Arabic-speaking countries. It radiates REVISIONIST insurgence. The first article, "Aaron," announces a pivotal distinction between "exoteric" and "esoteric." Discourse on the latter pervades entries on "Philosophy," "Sufism," "Dualism" and "Eschatology," not to mention those on "tawhid" (acknowledging the Oneness of God), "dhikr" (remembrance of God) and "hijab" (the veil that separates humans from God). An essay on "Arabic" extols that language, proclaiming how it allows roots of verbs to "shatter concepts or submerge them and return to a threshold between the world and pure mind" (p. 47). An entry on "Five Divine Presences" declares that this "universal metaphysical doctrine . . . reflects the nature of things, and is no more the creation of human thought than the rings of Saturn are the creation of Galileo" (p. 128). Other entries rebut Western misunderstandings. "Fallacies About Islam" lists five such, while "Bible" affirms that the Qur'an reveres the Pentateuch, Psalms and Gospels as divinely revealed, although most Muslims ignore them. Other entries, like "Creed," "Miracles" and "Saints," specify what Muslims do and do not believe. Entries on world religions ("Christianity," "Nestorians," "Zoroastrianism," "Manicheism," "Yazidis") generate fresh insights. Yet Glassé never parades learning for its own sake. Declining to luxuriate in lists, an entry on "Divine Names" simply prints the ninety-nine adjectives with their location in the Qur'an. Eschewing MENIPPEAN overdoses, Glassé's LEXICON feels as chaste as an arabesque.

□ *Weaknesses* Concerning a religion as conservative as Islam, a REVISIONIST LEXICON cannot fail to exhilarate, but of course it may alarm rigorists who shun the esoteric. Not everyone will fancy a reference book that alternates inner and outer perspectives and affirms the cosmic subsistence of doctrines that it studies. Given a fondness for mysticism, certain omissions astonish, such as mystery, Cabala and light. Moreover, Glassé scants methodology and hermeneutics. Western scholars win no entries, and lack of individual bibliographies conceals Glassé's scholarly debts. One would like to know his opinion of (to name a few) Fritjof Schuon, Henry Corbin, Anne-Marie Schimmel and Seyyed Hossein Nasr. There being no index, cross-references seem too few.

□ *Competitors* The REVISIONISM of this LEXICON makes other reference works on Islam appear staid. In contrast, **196** Gibb, ed., *The Shorter Encyclopaedia of Islam* (1965) and **205** van Donzel, ed., *Islamic Desk Reference* (1994) loom as the least metaphysical of reference books. **200** The al Faruqis' *Cultural Atlas of Islam* (1986) explores a greater swath of art and literature but, except on visual art, lacks philosophical acumen. **203** Netton, *A Popular Dictionary of Islam* (1992) is much briefer and underplays history of thought. S. Balic's articles in **201** Khoury, ed., *Lexikon religiöser Grundbegriffe* (1987) delineate normative Islam and scant the mystical. **208** Chebel, *Dictionnaire des symboles musulmans* (1995) dispenses information on folklore not cited elsewhere. Even more persistently, **12** Knappert, *The Encyclopaedia of Middle Eastern Mythology and Religion* (1993) aligns Islam with earlier religions. Articles in **5** Eliade, ed., *The Encyclopedia of Religion* (1987) redress

Glassé's penchant for mysticism and his neglect of methodology. Towering over other works on mystical Islam, **206** Schimmel, *Deciphering the Signs of God* (1994) makes Glassé seem austere, but his ingenuity helps one to appreciate hers.

□ *Summary* Audacious blending of academic research and mystical disquisition makes this LEXICON unique. No other alphabetical reference work on any religion weds factual accuracy and metaphysical boldness so discerningly.

289 (1989-92) André Jacob, ed., *Encyclopédie philosophique universelle,* 5 vols. in 3 (Paris: Presses Universitaires de France, 1989-92); general bibliography on Islam, 1:1791-94. Analyzed further under 4.1 "Asian Religions," 5.2 "Philosophy of Religion" and 5.3.1 "Social Sciences of Religion."

□ *Critique* Scattered through the historical GLOSSARY (vol. 2) of this MEGA-ENCYCLOPEDIA come articles on fifty-one concepts in medieval Islamic philosophy. Focusing on logic, epistemology and metaphysics, articles are listed in 2:3263-64. Six authors stand out. D. Kouloughli on "Mutazalism" (2:1708-9), A. Hasnawi on "Dahr (éternité, perpétuité)" (2:542-43) and E. M. Kudsi on "Sufism" (2:2432-34) excel at exposition. A. Hilal highlights concepts of possibility and the origin of forms in "Wagib al-Wugud" and "Wahib al-Suwar" (2:2767-70). In a long entry A. Hasnawi explores "Fayd (épanchement, émanation)" (2:966-72), adding a full column of bibliography. Roger Arnaldez, who writes on individual Arabic works in volume 3, scintillates on "Halq (création)" (2:1112-14).

Even more exhilarating are four REVISIONIST articles by A. Elamrani-Jamal on "hikma (sagesse)," "nubuwwa (prophétie)," "saria (loi révélée)" and "Tawil (interprétation)." He recounts how primordial wisdom was held to have passed from Hermes (known as Idriss in the Qur'an) to companions of Solomon as well as from the sage Luqman to the Greek philosopher Empedocles (2:1143-44). Each entry adduces dozens of Arabic terms, explaining how they relate both to

Greek philosophy and to the Qur'an, and dispenses often startling bibliography. Volume 3 expounds major works by fifty-five medieval Islamic authors and thirteen later ones, who are indexed 3:3263-64. In addition, volume 1 delivers Roger Arnaldez's trenchant "Panorama of Islamic Thought" (1:1666-72) and Paul Ottino's remarkable "The Muslim Cultural Imprint Around the Indian Ocean" (1:1497-504). Arnaldez interprets Muslim philosophy as one sect among many that perpetuated Neo-Platonism in the aftermath of Hellenistic syncretism. Finally, a general bibliography on Islam and its philosophy is not to be missed (1:1791-94). No other reference work explicates Islamic philosophy so brilliantly or affirms its importance so persuasively.

□ *Summary* A historical GLOSSARY of Arabic terms embedded in volume 2, as well as exposition of major treatises in volume 3, elucidates medieval Islamic philosophy. Bibliographies overflow with rarities.

203 (1992) Ian Richard Netton, *A Popular Dictionary of Islam* (London: Curzon, 1992); 279 pages; no index; general bibliography, pp. 269-79.

□ *Critique* This GLOSSARY describes concepts, practices, schools of thought and surahs of the Qur'an as well as a few persons. Definitions of five to fifteen lines lack individual bibliographies. This guide to Arabic terms lacks the depth of a LEXICON but will help a beginner to tackle **202** Glassé, *The Concise Encyclopedia of Islam* (1989).

□ *Summary* This GLOSSARY of Arabic terms serves beginners.

204 (1992) Farzana Shaikh, ed., *Islam and Islamic Groups: A Worldwide Reference Guide* (Harlow, Essex: Longman, 1992); ix & 310 pages; index, pp. 293-310; general bibliography, p. 291; glossary, pp. 289-90.

□ *Critique* This DICTIONARY of political Islam canvasses 110 countries in alphabetical entries ranging in length from three lines to seven pages (on Pakistan). Each entry outlines Islamic demography in a country, sketches recent history of Islamic politics there, and lists Islamic organizations but omits bibliography. Entries on

Indonesia, Nigeria, Pakistan and the Russian federation excel. A glossary defines Arabic political terms, but the general bibliography cites only ten items. Social scientists will profit from this roster of political alignments, but humanists may balk at undigested reportage.

□ *Summary* This DICTIONARY by and for political scientists inventories Islamic political groupings in 110 countries.

12 (1993) Jan Knappert, *The Encyclopaedia of Middle Eastern Mythology and Religion* (Shaftesbury, U.K., and Rockport, Mass.: Element, 1993); 309 pages; no index; general bibliography, pp. 303-19. Analyzed further under 1.1 "The World's Religions: Alphabetical Reference Books."

□ *Critique* This GLOSSARY and WHO'S WHO squeezes in a lifetime's research about Islam and its folklore, treating enough unheard-of topics to qualify as REVISIONIST. The recounting of Muslim legends is irreplaceable (e.g., on Burda, Sa'd, Zuleika). In-depth entries probe "Shia," "Sufism," "Iblis" and "Isra" (i.e., Muhammad's night journey), while thematic ones compare Islamic views with those in earlier Near Eastern religions (e.g., "Paradise," "Shaytan," "Death"). The WHO'S WHO sometimes omits dates (e.g., of al-Hallaj) and evokes certain odd fellows (e.g., Bahirah) at uncanny length.

□ *Summary* No other reference work except perhaps **206** Schimmel, *Deciphering the Signs of God* (1994) connects Islam so intimately with predecessors and their legends.

25 (1993) Arvind Sharma, ed., *Our Religions* (San Francisco: Harper, 1993); xi & 536 pages. Analyzed under 1.2 "The World's Religions: Compendia." Seyyed Hossein Nasr's chapter (pp. 427-532) is the finest on "Islam" in any multiauthor work. It recounts the spread, doctrines and divisions of Islam worldwide with insight and conviction. It is not to be missed.

205 (1994) E[meri] van Donzel, ed., *Islamic Desk Reference: Compiled from the Encyclopaedia of Islam* (Leiden, New York and Köln: Brill, 1994); xi & 492 pages; no index; no bibliography; eight color plates at back; 16 black-and-white maps.

□ *Critique* Executed by a master epitomizer, this historical GLOSSARY features succinctness in five thousand entries, each with Arabic spellings but devoid of bibliography. Functioning as a brief REALLEXIKON, it summarizes persons and dynasties, cities and regions, languages and practices, but not methodology. By shortening entries from **198** Gibb., ed., *The Encyclopaedia of Islam* (using the second edition through *RAF* and the first edition thereafter), the editor crystallizes current Western scholarship, albeit without bibliography. The WHO'S WHO sketches about one thousand political figures, often in two or three lines, whereas dynasties command more detail, as in two pages on the Umayyads. Unusual entries like "Falconry, "Library" and "Pythagoras" overflow with oddities from Arabic sources. Historians will delight.

□ *Summary* This REALLEXIKON in the guise of a GLOSSARY condenses mountains of scholarship. It miniaturizes a MEGA-ENCYCLOPEDIA.

206 (1994) Annemarie Schimmel, *Deciphering the Signs of God: A Phenomenological Approach to Islam* (Albany: SUNY Press, 1994); xvii & 302 pages; index, pp. 280-300; general bibliography, pp. 258-79.

□ *Critique* This magisterial PHENOMENOLOGY condenses a lifetime of research by a discerning scholar. Refining categories taken from her mentor, Friedrich Heiler, Schimmel interweaves German, French and English scholarship with a dazzling array of texts from the Islamic world. Dozens of figures ranging from the Prophet and al-Hallaj to Rumi and Iqbal emerge in stark clarity. Spiraling from outer to inner, three chapters on "Sacred Aspects of Nature and Culture," "Sacred Space and Time" and "Sacred Action" lead to three on "The Word and the Script," "Individual and Society" and "God and His Creation: Eschatology." A final chapter, "How to Approach Islam?" sifts methodologies. The index references persons, places and themes. Rare quotations, superb bibliog-

raphy and delicate comparisons set this work in a class by itself. A lifetime of interpreting Islamic spirituality reaps a harvest that Muslims and Westerners alike will treasure.

□ *Summary* This model PHENOMENOLOGY synthesizes vast and intricate material. It repays endless rereading.

207 (1995) John L. Esposito, ed., *The Oxford Encyclopedia of the Modern Islamic World,* 4 vols. (New York: Oxford University Press, 1995); 1920 pages; index, 4:407-60; "Synoptic Outline of Contents," 4:399-406; no general bibliography; 40 photographs and line drawings (on art history); no maps.

□ *Critique* Seldom has an ENCYCLOPEDIA so transformed access to a field as this one does for Islam since 1789. Over 750 articles signed by more than 450 contributors (about one-third of them Muslim and the rest mostly American) delineate "the Islamic dimension of Muslim experience." Nations, practices, movements, concepts, art objects and thinkers worldwide elicit entries. At last we have an ENCYCLOPEDIA that alternates Muslim and non-Muslim points of view on religion, inviting Muslims to expound self-definition to a degree unique in a Western ENCYCLOPEDIA. No other reference work juxtaposes Western and Islamic standpoints so deliberately. To this end, "Popular Religion" inspires six articles (3:336-58) and "Mosque" five (3: 133-51), while the topic "Women" elicits seven articles (4:322-52). Charles D. Smith shines on "Secularism" (4:20-30). History of scholarship unfolds through surveys of it and through a WHO'S WHO of scholars. Evaluative comments enliven nearly all the bibliographies, making one wish that **5** Eliade, ed., *The Encyclopedia of Religion* (1987) had adopted a similar practice. Social scientists will relish these volumes, while historians of pre-1789 Islam must rely on **198** Gibb, ed., *The Encyclopaedia of Islam* (1960-). One could wish for greater sprightliness, however.

□ *Summary* No other ENCYCLOPEDIA of Islam solicits analysis of the past two centuries worldwide from both Muslims and non-Muslims. Social scientists will applaud the contemporaneity, and religionists will welcome the Muslim self-definition.

208 (1995) Malek Chebel, *Dictionnaire des symboles musulmans: Rites, mystique et civilisation* (Paris: Albin Michel, 1995); 501 pages; no index; general bibliography, pp. 455-501.

□ *Scope* Under the label "symbolism," this multifaceted DICTIONARY expounds folklore in the Qur'an and throughout Islamic culture from Morocco to Iran. An Arab anthropologist living in Paris writes sixteen hundred entries on Islamic folklore, each keyed to a multilingual bibliography of 850 items. This DICTIONARY executes four distinct functions: (1) a WHO'S WHO of the Qur'an, (2) a concordance of the Qur'an (affixed to individual entries), (3) a bestiary of animals (including insects) mentioned in the Qur'an and in folklore and (4) a GLOSSARY of terms (about half in Arabic and half in French) for objects, parts of the body, clothing and concepts. Instead of using the term *folklore* to denote non-normative oral traditions, the introduction (pp. 7-12) discriminates four types of symbols: (1) Qur'anic images, (2) emblems (as on flags), (3) significant objects (e.g., "Fingers") and (4) ensembles of meaning, chiefly theological (e.g., "Cosmology"). The visual arts figure as in "Arts of Islam," but iconography less so. Entries vary in length from four lines on "Queen of Saba" to three pages on "Confréries," three and a half on "Allah," and four on "Flags" (in a *tour d'horizon* of flags of thirty-seven countries). Few reference books are more thoroughly cross-referenced.

□ *Strengths* Ten years in preparation, this polymathic LEXICON never ceases to astonish. It propounds a "cultural geography" (p. 8) of oral lore in Islam from Iran westward, albeit stinting on sub-Saharan Africa. Every entry marshals Qur'anic passages, pinpoints other entries and adduces often exotic bibliography. Doctrine concerning matters like "Angelology," "Cosmology" and "Hell" is sketched, albeit sometimes telegraphically. Certain Qur'anic phrases are dissected (e.g., "Fatiha," "Night of Destiny"), as are the so-called Satanic Verses (pp. 291-92). The

conflating of dozens of Islamic practices with pre-Islamic ones is traced. Jewish concepts like "Thora," "Bible" and "Eating Practices" as well as biblical figures elicit Islamic interpretations. Objects like "Iron," "Musk" and "Star" become loci of the exotic. Certain entries have no competitor: "Astrology," "Science of Letters" and "Physiognomy," not to mention "Mythological Birds," "Sacred Geography of Islam" and "Free-Masonry." "Numerology" inspires a main entry as well as others on numerals from one to five, seven, seventeen, nineteen, forty, sixty and ninety-nine. Folklore concerning matters as diverse as "Colors," "Evil Eye," "Henna" and "Horseshoe" proves riveting. No other DICTIONARY explores folk Islam so thoroughly or imaginatively. The bizarre erupts.

□ *Weaknesses* Chebel's labor of love unfortunately lacks rigor. Although he asserts that symbols in Islam (as well as in Arabic) are "polysemic" (p. 8), he does not stipulate usage of the term *symbol,* not even in an entry on "Local Symbolism" (pp. 402-3). Still worse, he never indicates when he is writing descriptively as an anthropologist, and when (if ever) normatively as a Muslim. Moreover, neither introduction nor entries cite Western methodologists, further concealing the author's preferences. Originality so unbuttoned scarcely merits the term REVISIONIST because it does not specify which arguments are being revisited. Everywhere discrepancy in level of difficulty obtrudes: some entries presuppose a beginner, while others (e.g., "Hadith," "Mohamed") envision a MENIPPEAN appetite, and a very few quote the Qur'an without comment (e.g., "Mosquée extrême"). Many readers will wish that Islamic art had won more attention.

□ *Competitors* This precocious LEXICON defies classification. The author wrote it to accompany an even longer and odder DICTIONARY, Chebel, *Encyclopédie de l'amour en Islam: Érotisme, beauté et sexualité dans le monde arabe, en Perse et en Turquie* (Paris: Payot et Rivages, 1995), which explicates Islamic sexual mores in seven hundred pages. That work makes this one seem almost conventional. Among works by other Muslims, **202** Glassé, *The Concise Encyclopedia of Islam* (1989) runs nearly twice as long, digests vastly more history and defends a methodology but lacks individual bibliographies and scants folklore. Entries by Muslim scholars in **207** Esposito, ed., *The Oxford Encyclopedia of the Modern Islamic World* (1995) tend to be normative and cover only since 1789. **12** Knappert, *The Encyclopaedia of Middle Eastern Mythology and Religion* (1993) traces major Islamic folk beliefs to previous cultures. Those seeking a normative compilation of what Islam permits (halal) and prohibits (haram) should consult Yusuf Al-Qaradawi, *The Lawful and the Prohibited in Islam,* 20th ed. (Plainfield, Ind.: American Trust, 1994), translated from the French. A more popular presentation is Abdur Rahman Shad, *Do's and Do Nots in Islam* (Delhi: Adam, 1992). Compared to all these, the *Dictionnaire des symboles musulmans* explores folklore with finesse but badly needs methodological backbone. □ *Summary* This idiosyncratic DICTION-ARY dissects Islamic folklore from Morocco to Iran but garbles methodology. The bibliography knows no rival, and cross-references propel browsing.

3.2.2 THE QUR'AN

OVERVIEW: A CLASH BETWEEN WESTERN AND MUSLIM APPROACHES

Islam precludes subjecting the Qur'an to critical tools such as the Bible has both withstood and instigated. Qualifying as a major difference between Islam and Christianity, this gap frustrates biblical scholars who investigate the Qur'an. Of two critical COMMENTARIES (**210** Paret and **209** Bell), only Bell gratifies biblicists by defying Islamic assumptions about composition of the text. Recent debates pervade G. R. Hawting and Abdul-Kader A. Shareef, eds., *Approaches to the Qur'an* (London and New York: Routledge, 1993). A magnificent compilation of Muslim COMMENTARIES *(tafsir),* arranged surah by surah, is Mahmoud Ayoub, *The Qur'an and Its*

*Interpreters,*planned in 10 vols. (Albany: SUNY Press, 1984-).

LIST OF WORKS ANALYZED

209 (1940s, 1991) Richard Bell [1876-1952], *A Commentary on the Qur'an,* 2 vols. (Manchester: University of Manchester Press, 1991)

210 (1971, 1994) Rudi Paret [1901-1983], *Der Koran: Kommentar und Konkordanz* (Stuttgart: Kohlhammer, 1971; 5th ed., 1994)

211 (1983) Hanna E. Kassis, *A Concordance of the Qur'an* (Berkeley: University of California Press, 1983)

212 (1987) Mustansir Mir, *Dictionary of Qur'anic Terms and Concepts* (New York and London: Garland Publishing, 1987)

213 (1992) Idriss Kharchaf, *Lexicon of Human Rights in Coran/Lexique coranique des droits de l'homme* (Rabat: El Maarif Al Jadida, 1992)

ANALYSIS OF WORKS

209 (1940s, 1991) Richard Bell [1876-1952], *A Commentary on the Qur'an,* ed. C. Edmund Bosworth and M. E. J. Richardson, 2 vols. (Manchester: University of Manchester Press, 1991); xxii & 608; 603 pages; no index; general bibliography, 1:v-xi.

□ *Critique* Drafted by Bell during the 1930s and 1940s as "philological and exegetical notes" to his *The Qur'an Translated* (1937-39), this surah-by-surah REVISION-IST COMMENTARY was rediscovered in the 1970s and deciphered from microfilm by the editors. While translating the Qur'an as Reader in Arabic at the University of Edinburgh, Bell grappled with "grammatical unevennesses," "interruptions of sense" and "displacements." He subdivided surahs into component parts, which he contended had been woven together from texts not posthumously but directly under the Prophet's supervision. Reconstructing a "process of composition" that jettisons Islamic assumptions, Bell illuminates thousands of passages with the kind of virtuosity one expects in a biblical COMMENTARY. His student Montgomery Watt assessed Bell's

REVISIONIST views in *Bell's Introduction to the Qur'an, Completely Revised and Enlarged* (Edinburgh: Edinburgh University Press, 1970), a book that appeared before *A Commentary on the Qur'an* had reemerged. Needless to say, the latter cites no works published after 1950. A number of tools complement this one. **210** Paret, *Der Koran: Kommentar und Konkordanz* (1971, 1994) provides a foil by addressing individual words rather than problems of composition. A French classic, Régis Blachère, *Introduction au Coran* (Paris: Maisonneuve, 1947; 2d ed., rev., 1958) criticizes Bell's willingness to subdivide surahs. For comparatists Johann-Dietrich Thyen, *Bibel und Koran: Eine Synopse der gemeinsamen Überlieferungen* (Köln and Vienna: Böhlau, 1989; 2d ed., rev., 1993) juxtaposes passages from the Bible and the Qur'an on ninety-four topics.

□ *Summary* Contravening Islamic precepts in this REVISIONIST COMMENTARY, a Western Arabist defies Islamicists and gratifies biblical scholars.

210 (1971, 1994) Rudi Paret [1901-83], *Der Koran: Kommentar und Konkordanz* (Stuttgart: Kohlhammer, 1971; 5th ed., 1994); 555 pages; no index; no general bibliography (except list of abbreviations, pp. 9-10).

□ *Critique* Prepared in conjunction with the author's translation, *Der Koran Übersetzt* (Stuttgart: Kohlhammer, 1966; 5th ed., 1989), this COMMENTARY tackles problems in Arabic philology and syntax. Less REVISIONIST than **209** Bell's *Commentary* (1940s, 1991), Paret provides a corrective to that work. Bell is mentioned under Surah 9:1-37. The fifth edition of 1994 is only slightly revised from the third edition of 1979.

□ *Summary* Paling beside the vigor of **209** Bell's *Commentary* (1991), this workmanlike COMMENTARY remains indispensable for philology.

211 (1983) Hanna E. Kassis, *A Concordance of the Qur'an* (Berkeley: University of California Press, 1983); xxxix & 1444 pages; three indexes of English terms (divine names, proper names, general), pp. 1351-444.

□ *Critique* This English-language concordance of Arabic vocabulary in the Qur'an suits Arabists and non-Arabists alike. Each entry quotes in Qur'anic sequence every line that features a given Arabic word as A. J. Arberry rendered it in *The Koran Interpreted* (1964). Thus a non-Arabist can see at a glance all occurrences (in Arberry's translation) of any Arabic term, including proper names. When used as keywords, Arabic terms are both transliterated (i.e., romanized) and translated into English. Because individual lines nearly always make sense even out of context, the semantic range of a word coalesces as one traverses its occurrences. Moreover, subdividing verbs into tenses and participles elucidates functions. A section on Allah ("The Divine Name") fills one hundred pages and boasts more than three hundred catchwords, mostly verbs. These entries explore in unheard-of depth the ninety-nine names of Allah. Otherwise, the longest entries pursue "Amana" (believe) across twenty pages and "Rabb" (master) across eighteen. An introduction outlines Arabic morphology (pp. xvii-xxxiv), while three indexes locate Arabic equivalents for any English term. This labor of love enables scholars innocent of Arabic to confront keywords and to acquire a feel for their interconnections.

□ *Summary* This concordance pioneers a path into the Qur'an, particularly for non-Arabists. It elucidates Arabic words by itemizing in translation passages that contain them.

212 (1987) Mustansir Mir, *Dictionary of Qur'anic Terms and Concepts* (New York and London: Garland Publishing, 1987); 244 pages; list of terms and concepts, pp. 225-44; no bibliography.

□ *Critique* This GLOSSARY of terms in the Qur'an places most catchwords in English. It locates Qur'anic passages and explicates their significance without tackling hermeneutics.

□ *Summary* This INTRODUCTION to Qur'anic vocabulary presupposes little or no sophistication.

213 (1992) Idriss Kharchaf, *Lexicon of Human Rights in Coran/Lexique coranique des droits de l'homme* (Rabat: El

Maarif Al Jadida, 1992); 600 pages; no index; no general bibliography.

□ *Critique* This bilingual anthology aligns quotations from the Qur'an under sixty rubrics concerning human biology and human rights. There is no COMMENTARY, only quotations of thousands of passages skillfully arranged and supplied in both the Hamidullah French version and the Yusuf Ali English version. Social scientists will applaud the rubrics: those on biology include skin, menses, pregnancy, old age and death, while those on human rights include the poor, parents, neighbors, wayfarers and education. Although the English (albeit not the French) can be quaint, this anthology abounds in provocative juxtapositions. A companion volume, Kharchaf, *Lexique des versets coraniques scientifiques/Lexicon of the Coranic Scientific Verses* (Rabat: Datapress, 1989) winnows the Qur'an concerning biology, mathematics, geography and astronomy. Both works repay browsing.

□ *Summary* This novel anthology arrays Qur'anic passages around sixty topics of human biology and human rights. Absence of commentary stimulates pondering.

4 ASIAN RELIGIONS

4.1 GENERAL

OVERVIEW: UNEXPECTED GAPS
Reference works that treat Asian religions collectively are few, although there are many on Indian religions and Buddhism. Unfortunately, no reference volume canvasses new religions in Asia or religion in Japan. On the latter topic Winston Davis, *Japanese Religion and Society: Paradigms of Structure and Change* (Albany: SUNY Press, 1992) formulates up-to-date rethinking. The richest WHO'S WHO of religious leaders remains 9 Hinnells, ed., *Who's Who of World Religions* (1991). Startling disclosures, particularly about the role of Nestorians in Central Asia, enliven Samuel Hugh Moffett, *History of Christianity in Asia,* vol. 1, *Beginnings to 1500* (San Francisco: Harper, 1992-).

This section excludes works that cover all the world's religions (see 1 "The World's Religions"). A masterwork on Zoroastrianism (**199** Yarshater, ed., *Encyclopaedia Iranica)* appears under 3.2.1 "Islam: Religion and Culture." Specialized bibliography comes in a thousand entries of David C. Yu, *Religion in Postwar China: A Critical Analysis and Annotated Bibliography* (Westport, Conn., and London: Greenwood, 1994).

Appearing too late to analyze, Ian P. McGreal, ed., *Great Thinkers of the Eastern World* (New York and London: HarperCollins, 1995) delivers more than a hundred signed articles with English-language bibliography.

LIST OF WORKS ANALYZED
214 (1983) *Kodansha Encyclopedia of Japan,* 9 vols. (Tokyo: Kodansha, 1983)

215 (1985, 1991) André Akoun, ed., *Mythes et croyances du monde entier,* 5 vols. (Paris: Lidis-Brepols, 1985, 1991)

216 (1986, 1989) Stephan Schuhmacher and Gert Woerner, eds., *The Encyclopedia of Eastern Philosophy and Religion: Buddhism, Hinduism, Taoism, Zen* (Boston: Shambhala, 1989)

217 (1988) Ainslee T. Embree, ed., *Encyclopedia of Asian History,* 4 vols. (New York: Scribner's, 1988)

289 (1989-92) André Jacob, ed., *Encyclopédie philosophique universelle,* 5 vols. in 3 (Paris: Presses Universitaires de France, 1989-92)

ANALYSIS OF WORKS
214 (1983) *Kodansha Encyclopedia of Japan,* 9 vols. (Tokyo: Kodansha, 1983); about 3000 pages; index, 9:1-210; maps and black-and-white photographs throughout.

□ *Critique* This English-language ENCYCLOPEDIA of Japan enlisted 680 Japanese and 524 foreigners to write almost ninety-five hundred entries. The longer and middle-sized articles are signed and include English and Japanese bibliography. Buddhism and Shinto receive lavish coverage, while many new religions elicit about a column, with bibliography. H. Byron Earhart surveys "Religion" (6:290-93) and "New Religions" (5:366-68), while Hajime Nakamura characterizes "Buddhism" (2:176-80). Bunsaku Kurata's piece on "Buddhist Sculpture" is unusually detailed. A condensed version, *Japan: An Illustrated Encyclopedia,* 2 vols. (Tokyo; Kodansha, 1993), supplies superb color photographs but omits bibliographies. "The Japanese Year: Cycles of Renewal" (1:1074-75) is a gem. The tone of both ENCYCLOPEDIAS is sober, even laconic. A British competitor, Richard Bowring and Peter Kornicki, eds., *The Cambridge Encyclopedia of Japan* (Cambridge and New York: Cambridge University Press, 1993) excels on "Thought and Religion" (pp. 152-83, 379-80). Its photographs are riveting. Beginners will treasure Kaneyoshi Nakayama, *Pictorial Encyclopedia of Japanese Culture: The Soul and Heritage of Japan* (Tokyo: Gakken, 1987).

□ *Summary* This ENCYCLOPEDIA of history and culture recruits major authorities to expound (amid much else) religions of Japan, with bibliography.

215 (1985, 1991) André Akoun, ed., *Mythes et croyances du monde entier* (Paris: Lidis-Brepols, 1985); volume 4, *Les Mondes asiatiques* republished as *L'Asie: Mythes et traditions* (Turnhout: Brepols, 1991); 492 pages; index, pp. 484-85; vol. 5, *Le Monde occidental moderne* (Paris: Lidis-Brepols, 1985); 524 pages; index, pp. 505-21; about 300 color photographs.

□ *Critique* Volume 4 of this opulent COMPENDIUM enlisted twenty-seven (mostly Parisian) ethnologists to write thirty-four signed articles on religions and folklore of Lapland, North Asia, India, Southeast Asia, China, Korea, Japan, Indonesia and the Philippines. India elicits one hundred pages, China 150 pages, and Japan sixty. Coverage of Burma, Thailand, Cambodia and Vietnam is particularly welcome, while that of Lapps, Mongolians and Siberians is unique. Densely factual, each article (of five to fifteen pages) carries choice French and English bibliography. The series title "Myths and Beliefs" misleads because the essays favor rites, festivals and folk practices over story or doctrine. Enhanced by detailed captions, about three hundred color

photographs rank among the most spectacular anywhere. No other COMPENDIUM delivers such magnificent illustrations or examines so lovingly every region of Asia. Other volumes in this enterprise of 1985 treat monotheism (vol. 2), Africa, the Americas and Oceania (vol. 3).

Having analyzed mythology of the globe in volumes 1-4, this MEGA-COMPENDIUM culminates in reflection on myth and ritual in the contemporary West. Fifty-three chapters of volume 5 range from utopia and "the mythic Jew" (pp. 176-81) through cinema, science fiction and comic strips to a conspectus of methodologies (pp. 347-501). Gilbert Durand explicates "Archetype and Myth" incomparably (pp. 433-52). Glossing a *tour d'horizon,* in volume 5 thirty-nine French anthropologists pull out all stops, not least in assembling French-language bibliography.

□ *Summary* In volume 5 this most gorgeous of COMPENDIA explores regions and rites neglected elsewhere. The likes of Georges Balandier, François Châtelet, Marcel Gauchet and Jean Séguy diagnose culture clairvoyantly. Combining splendor and acumen to a rare degree, the series belongs in more American libraries. Color photographs woo the browser.

216 (1986, 1989) Stephan Schuhmacher and Gert Woerner, eds., *The Encyclopedia of Eastern Philosophy and Religion: Buddhism, Hinduism, Taoism, Zen* (Boston: Shambhala, 1989; paperback, 1994); translated from *Lexikon der östlichen Weisheitslehren* (Bern and Munich: Otto Barth, 1986); xv & 468 pages; no index; general bibliography, pp. 451-68; Ch'an/Zen lineage chart, pp. 445-50; a very few black-and-white photographs and diagrams. Also available in French translation. *The Shambhala Dictionary of Buddhism and Zen* (Boston: Shambhala, 1991) omits entries on Taoism and Hinduism.

□ *Scope* This historical GLOSSARY and WHO'S WHO of Buddhism, Hinduism, Taoism and Zen assigned the four religions to each of four German scholars. Ingrid Fischer-Schreiber writes on Buddhism and Taoism, Franz-Karl Ehrhard on Tibetan

Buddhism, Kurt Friedrichs on Hinduism and Michael S. Diener on Zen. Shinto, folk religions and new religious movements are omitted. About four thousand entries treat persons, terms, texts and schools but not regions or periods. Entries affix an emblem assigning them to one or more of the religions but lack bibliographies. Anecdotes heighten about a third of the articles with Zen-like playfulness. The general bibliography is subdivided among the four religions and then split into primary and secondary sources. The writing is succinct and abounds in cross-references.

□ *Strengths* A WHO'S WHO includes more than five hundred entries, which often insert a life sketch and anecdotes in smaller print. A GLOSSARY defines a couple of thousand terms from religious practice, often in three to ten lines. Synoptic articles on "Hinduism," "Taoism" and "Zen" run a couple of pages each, while a survey of "Buddhism" in eight countries fills four pages. Buddhism emerges more vividly than other religions because it inspires more anecdotes.

□ *Weaknesses* This is a GLOSSARY for adepts who know which Sanskrit, Pali, Chinese or Japanese term to seek. English words command hardly any entries. Articles on Hinduism skim over Sikhism and Jainism. Although there are no articles on pan-Asian topics like Silk Road or martial arts, there is one on "Meditation." History of the field gets omitted. Pronunciation of terms should have been indicated.

□ *Competitors* This single-volume reference book is the handiest on religions of Asia. Works on individual religions cover more, but they execute summaries less incisively. Although less technical, **250** Prebish, *Historical Dictionary of Buddhism* (1993) boasts fuller bibliography. **235** Stutley and Stutley, *A Dictionary of Hinduism* (1977) furnishes greater depth and fuller bibliography on topics to 1500 C.E., while **2** Crim, ed., *The Perennial Dictionary of World Religions* (1981, 1989) functions better as a self-teacher but on fewer topics. **238** Reyna, *Dictionary of Oriental Philosophy* (1984) defines concepts and persons attractively but lacks depth. *The*

Encyclopedia of Eastern Philosophy and Religion makes an excellent companion to COMPENDIA like **25** Sharma, ed., *Our Religions* (1993) or **26** Earhart, ed., *Religious Traditions of the World* (1984, 1993). Anecdotes enliven information.

□ *Summary* This GLOSSARY and WHO'S WHO becomes more helpful the further one advances. Its anecdotes will startle even the jaded.

217 (1988) Ainslee T. Embree, ed., *Encyclopedia of Asian History,* 4 vols. (New York: Scribner's, 1988); 2060 pages; index, 4:413-78; no general bibliography; synoptic outline, 4:387-412; maps and black-and-white photographs throughout.

□ *Scope* This REALLEXIKON presents three thousand signed articles by four hundred authorities on major topics from all periods of Asian history, with bibliographies entirely in English. Asia is held to comprise the landmass stretching from Iran to Indochina and Korea as well as Japan, Indonesia and the Philippines but not Oceania or Australia. Political entries address regions, cities, eras, rulers, dynasties, wars and treaties. Religious topics encompass a dozen religions (including Christianity, Judaism and Manichaeism), scriptures, leaders and (deceased) Western scholars. Cultural topics include languages, major literary texts and music as well as art and architecture but not artists. A WHO'S WHO emphasizes twentieth-century leaders. Writing is straightforward, the English-language bibliographies brief but choice. Cross-references amplify nearly every article.

□ *Strengths* India, China and Japan receive fullest coverage, but Korea and Southeast Asia also fare well, while former Soviet Asia does not. Synopses of "Calendars and Eras," "Economic Development," "Famine," "Imperialism," "Land Tenure," "Law" and "Literacy" integrate material from all or nearly all of Asia. Individual entries on "Language and Literature" extend to Dravidian, Indo-Aryan, Kurdish and Sogdian. Surveys of "Buddhism," "Confucianism," "Hinduism," "Islam," "Shaivism," "Sikhism," "Daoism" and "New Religions in Japan" will satisfy chiefly beginners. John Stratton Hawley's article on "Bhakti," however, shines. Unexpected entries include "Piracy," "Armenians in South Asia" and "Alexander III of Macedon." History of Western study of Asia can be pieced together from biographies of (deceased) Orientalists like "Anquetil-Duperron," "Bentinck" and "Macaulay," but an overview of Indology and Sinology is missing.

□ *Weaknesses* This introductory REALLEXIKON digests recent Western and Asian scholarship for nonspecialists. It functions as a self-teacher in history of countries, regions, leaders and cities, but it does not engage scholarly controversies or living scholars. Similar in format to **159** Strayer, ed., *Dictionary of the Middle Ages* (1981-89), the *Encyclopedia of Asian History* canvasses four times the history and three times the area in one-third the space. Religion inspires hardly any insights additional to those in Richard F. Nyrop, ed., *India: A Country Study,* 4th ed. (Washington, D.C.: Government Printing Office, 1985), pp. 133-75, or in **5** Eliade., ed., *The Encyclopedia of Religion* (1987). Absence of non-English-language bibliography irks.

□ *Competitors* No other reference work expounds Asian history so comprehensively or so lucidly. Geography, politics and languages predominate, while religion features only insofar as general history requires. The same can be said of a sequel, Barbara A. Tenenbaum, ed., *Encyclopedia of Latin American History,* 4 vols. (New York: Scribner's, 1995). Concerning South Asia, various English-language encyclopedias such as **219** Walker, *The Hindu World* (1968) or **230** Garg, *Encyclopedia of the Hindu World* (1992-), offer greater range and depth. As regards Anglo-Indian history, **223** Mehra, *A Dictionary of Modern Indian History, 1707-1947* (Delhi: Oxford University Press, 1985) sparkles. On Islam, **198** Gibb et al., eds., *The Encyclopaedia of Islam* (1960-) and **199** Yarshater, ed., *Encyclopaedia Iranica* (1985-) supply incomparably greater detail. **214** *Kodansha Encyclopedia of Japan,* 9 vols. (1983) carries analysis several steps further.

□ *Summary* This introductory REALLEXIKON equips a reader to use more specialized tools. Entries can be reread with profit.

289 (1989-92) André Jacob, ed., *Encyclopédie philosophique universelle,* 5 vols. in 3 (Paris: Presses Universitaires de France, 1989-92); vol. 2.2, *Les Notions philosophiques: Dictionnaire* (1990), pp. 2781-3044 (on "Pensée asiatique") and vol. 3.2, *Les Oeuvres philosophiques* (1992), pp. 3887-4124 (on India, China, Japan, Korea). General bibliography on Asia, 1:1764-76. Analyzed also under 3.2.1 "Islam: Religion and Culture," 5.2 "Philosophy of Religion and Ethics" and 5.3.1 "Social Sciences of Religion."

□ *Critique* Part 2 of the historical GLOSSARY (vol. 2.2) recruits mostly French specialists to expound over seven hundred Indian, Chinese and Japanese terms in signed articles with bibliography. Divided into 160 pages on India, seventy-five on China and twenty-seven on Japan, the articles canvass religious, philosophical and social concepts, averaging one-fourth column to two pages in length. Entries on India differentiate among seven communities of usage: Brahmanism, ancient Buddhism, Mahayana, Hindu yoga, Vedanta, Jainism and Indian tantrism. Entries by André Bareau and J. May on Buddhism stand out, as do C. Malamoud's on topics like dharma and satya. In addition, volume 3.2 digests more than five hundred texts from all periods and regions of Asia (3:4572-76). Finally, volume 1 deploys sixteen overviews of "Writings and Traditions" in individual Asian countries, covering not only Tibet, China and Japan but also Malaysia, Java and Vietnam (1:1571-637). The more one knows about Asia, the more these volumes resonate.

□ *Summary* The historical GLOSSARY defines terms copiously, while surveys of traditions break fresh ground. The bibliographies dazzle.

4.2 SOUTH ASIA

OVERVIEW: MAPPING THE UNMAPPABLE The ecosystem of religions known as Hinduism challenges and more often than not defeats the chutzpah of encyclopedists. Many have tried, but few have succeeded in compressing South Asia's cultural sprawl into a textual universe. Probably 224 Louis Frédéric, *Dictionnaire de la civilisation indienne* (1987) comes closest to success. An exuberant GLOSSARY, 238 Reyna, *Dictionary of Oriental Philosophy* (1984) awakens zest for the culture. Probably there will never be a MEGA-ENCYCLOPEDIA INDICA to rival ones on Judaism, Christianity, Islam and Iran. Failing that, what is needed is a REVISIONIST LEXICON of South Asian religions to match 202 Glassé, *The Concise Encyclopedia of Islam* (1989). The nearest approximation is 235 Stutley and Stutley, *A Dictionary of Hinduism* (1977). Unfortunately, this self-teacher is becoming out of date.

4.2.1 GENERAL

OVERVIEW: WESTERN VERSUS SOUTH ASIAN MODES OF ENCYCLOPEDISM Works divide between those by Western scholars and those by South Asians. Reference books by Indian scholars exude a charm and loquacity all their own. For example, 230 Garg's *Encyclopaedia of the Hindu World* (1992-), announced in one hundred volumes, may well be the largest single-author enterprise of our time. Those who seek a PHILOSOPHICAL DICTIONARY about South Asia will be interested in Richard Lannoy, *The Speaking Tree: A Study of Indian Culture and Society* (London: Oxford University Press, 1971). Helpful on South Asians in the Americas are nine hundred entries in John Y. Fenton, *South Asian Religions in the Americas: An Annotated Bibliography of Immigrant Religious Traditions* (Westport, Conn., and London: Greenwood, 1995). Certain works on South Asia rank with masterpieces inspired by Christianity and Judaism, including 235 Stutley and Stutley, *A Dictionary of Hinduism* (1977), 256 Haussig, ed., *Wörterbuch der Mythologie*, vol. 5 (1984), 224 Frédéric, *Dictionnaire de la civilisation indienne* (1987) and 220 Schwartzberg, ed., *A Historical Atlas of South Asia* (1978, 1992), not to mention

259 Bonnefoy/Doniger, eds., *Mythologies* (1981, 1991). Too many others are either introductory or quaint.

LIST OF WORKS ANALYZED

218 (1967) Sachchidananda Bhattacharya, *A Dictionary of Indian History* (New York: Braziller, 1967)

219 (1968) Benjamin Walker, *The Hindu World: An Encyclopedic Survey,* 2 vols. (London: Allen & Unwin; New York: Praeger, 1968)

220 (1978, 1992) Joseph E. Schwartzberg, ed., *A Historical Atlas of South Asia* (Chicago: University of Chicago Press, 1978); second impression with additional material (New York: Oxford University Press, 1992)

221 (1983-86) Ashim Kumar Roy and N. N. Gidwani, *A Dictionary of Indology,* 4 vols. (New Delhi: Oxford & Ibh Publishing, 1983-86)

222 (1983) Alistair Shearer, *The Traveler's Key to Northern India* (New York: Knopf, 1983)

223 (1985, 1987) Parshotam Mehra, *A Dictionary of Modern Indian History, 1707-1947* (Delhi: Oxford University Press, 1985; reprinted with corrections, 1987)

224 (1987) Louis Frédéric, *Dictionnaire de la civilisation indienne* (Paris: Laffont, 1987)

225 (1987-94) Amaresh Datta, ed., *Encyclopaedia of Indian Literature,* 6 vols. (New Delhi: Sahitya Akademi, 1987-94)

226 (1990-) V. I. Subramoniam, ed., *Dravidian Encyclopedia,* planned in 3 vols. (Thiruvananthapuram: International School of Dravidian Linguistics, 1990-)

227 (1990) Georg Feuerstein, *Encyclopedic Dictionary of Yoga* (New York: Paragon; London: Unwin Hyman, 1990)

228 (1991) M. L. Varadpande, *A Dictionary of Indian Culture* (New Delhi: Arnold; Edinburgh: Aspect, 1991)

229 (1991) Ivor Lewis, *Sahibs, Nabobs and Boxwallahs: A Dictionary of the Words of Anglo-Indian* (Oxford: Oxford University Press, 1991)

230 (1992-) Ganga Ram Garg, ed., *Encyclopaedia of the Hindu World,* announced in 100 vols. (New Delhi: Concept Publishing, 1992-)

231 (1992-) Harbans Singh, ed., *The Encyclopaedia of Sikhism,* planned in 5 or 6 vols. (Patiala: Punjabi University, 1992-)

232 (1992) Vijaya Ghose, ed., *Tirtha: The Treasury of Indian Expressions* (New Delhi: CMC, 1992)

233 (1994) Karel Werner, *A Popular Dictionary of Hinduism* (Richmond, U.K.: Curzon, 1994)

ANALYSIS OF WORKS

218 (1967) Sachchidananda Bhattacharya, *A Dictionary of Indian History* (New York: Braziller, 1967); xii & 889 pages; no index; no general bibliography; "Important Dates," pp. 867-88.

□ *Critique* This DICTIONARY of Indian political and military history unfurls 2785 entries on persons, dynasties, places, movements and wars to the year 1965. About three quarters of the entries concern British India. Copious articles cover regions ("The Deccan," "Oudh," "Assam"), cities ("Bombay," "Calcutta," "Delhi") and wars ("Carnatic Wars," "Maratha Wars," "Sikh Wars"). The strength of the book is a WHO'S WHO of British officials and Indian leaders. The longest entries concern administration ("British Administration," "Covenanted Civil Service"), administrators ("Warren Hastings," "William Bentinck") and Indian politicians ("Mohandas Gandhi," "Surendranath Banerjee"). On such topics 223 Mehra, *A Dictionary of Modern Indian History, 1707-1947* (1985, 1987) is subtler but less comprehensive. Articles on "Buddhism," "Hinduism" and "Jainism" are perfunctory, and bibliographies are skeletal.

□ *Summary* This workmanlike DICTIONARY of persons, places and institutions narrates events and pinpoints their significance, but religion is scanted. Historians of administration and of British India will find the work indispensable.

219 (1968) Benjamin Walker, *The Hindu World: An Encyclopedic Survey,* 2 vols. (London: Allen & Unwin; New York:

Praeger, 1968); xiv & 609; xii & 696 pages; index (to entry titles, not pages), pp. 625-96; no general bibliography.

□ *Scope* This LEXICON of 723 entries assembles information about Indian culture and religion using exclusively English sources published between 1850 and 1960. This epitome of British Indology addresses an astonishing array of topics in articles averaging one to two pages, each with English-language bibliography. Its REALLEXIKON covers regions and land features, languages and tribes, epics and deities, plants and animals, religious and sexual practices, sciences and arts. Its WHO'S WHO encompasses writers and philosophers, dynasties and rulers, religious founders and reformers. Myths and epics get recounted, regions and tribes delineated. Foreign countries and peoples that interacted with India win full treatment, including not only Greece, Rome and China but also Phoenicia, Mesopotamia and Mongolia. Survey articles on "Travel," "Mountains," "Rivers," "Architecture" and "Music" marshal dozens of examples. Hinduism predominates, while Buddhism, Jainism and Sikhism are construed as reforms of it. Generic entries have catchwords in English, and both Sanskrit and Pali terms are explained in full. The writing carries a personal stamp, and certain articles smack of idiosyncrasy, notably on "Erotics" and foreign influences. This is an individual, not to say an eccentric, synthesis.

□ *Strengths* This LEXICON reaps a harvest of British Indologists from 1860 to 1960. Each of more than seven hundred essays traces a topic from pre-Vedic times to 1960, recounting what British monographs had established by then. Panoramas of standard topics like "Geography," "Indology," "Law" and "Literary Forms" are models of their kind. Chronological surveys excel on science ("Mathematics," "Psychology," "Astronomy," "Ayurveda") and on art ("Dance," "Painting," "Sculpture," "Music"). Technical articles on "Canons of Proportion," "Columns" and "Gems" also stand out. No less convenient are enumerations of Sanskrit terms for types of "Festivals," "Sacrifices," "Purification" and "Hierophants." Most unusual are twenty or so entries on sexual customs. Entries on "Erotics," "Perversions," "Prostitution," "Antinomianism" and "Olisboi" lapse into sensational (and sexist) reportage. Articles on "Human Sacrifice," "Miscegenation" and "Nekrophilia" recite whatever British scholars had gleaned. Further oddities concern "Mango Trick" and "Rope Trick." Trained as a Hellenist, Walker was obsessed by possible influences of other cultures on India. He weighs hypotheses concerning transfer from a dozen cultures ("Iran," "Egypt," "Europeans") as well as from major religions ("Christianity," "Muslims," "Zoroastrians"). On these and other issues Walker's surmises cry out to be tested.

□ *Weaknesses* This tantalizing LEXICON makes one crave verification. Uncertainty is aggravated by recourse to sources that speculate heedlessly. Because entries read seductively, they need to be offset by soberer ones. Walker's obsession with foreign influences leads to speculations found hardly anywhere else, for example, concerning Zoroastrian influences on the Buddha (2:623) and Greek influences on Indian literature (1:406-12). For quaintness and sexism, Walker's evocation of sexual customs remains Victorian. Awkwardly, the index supplies not page numbers but entry titles. Not everyone will relish this synthesis of British monographs, mostly from the colonial era, but its reconfiguring of British Indology remains pungent.

□ *Competitors* This LEXICON needs to be read conjointly with recent ones. Articles in **5** Eliade, ed., *The Encyclopedia of Religion* (1987) discuss some of the elusive topics, while on regions and rulers, **217** Embree, ed., *Encyclopedia of Asian History* (1988) offers a crosscheck. **235** Stutley and Stutley, *A Dictionary of Hinduism* (1977) digests a wider spectrum of sources with greater precision and avoids eccentricity. When completed, the magnum opus of **230** Garg, *Encyclopaedia of the Hindu World* (1992-) will furnish a corrective on recondite topics, but its third volume barely completes the letter *A*. Probably India will never inspire a Western MEGA-

ENCYLOPEDIA to match **199** Yarshater, ed., *Encyclopedia Iranica* (1985-) or **198** Gibb, ed., *Encyclopaedia of Islam* (1960-). Pending such an enterprise, Walker's *The Hindu World* remains wayward but stimulating.

□ *Summary* This digest of British monographs makes up in piquancy what it lacks in reliability.

220 (1978, 1992) Joseph E. Schwartzberg, ed., *A Historical Atlas of South Asia* (Chicago: University of Chicago Press, 1978); second impression with additional material (New York: Oxford University Press, 1992); xxxvi & 376 folio pages; index, pp. 327-76; classified bibliography, pp. 283-326.

□ *Critique* Drawing on material collected by Charles Lesley Ames (1884-1969), this exemplary HISTORICAL ATLAS was produced at the University of Minnesota between 1961 and 1978. A second impression of 1992 adds twenty pages of "Addenda and Corrigenda" and seven of fresh bibliography but hardly any new maps. Nearly 150 plates match 130 pages of captions, each with multilingual bibliography. Captions deliver miniessays on all periods and regions and rank among the most readable summaries of South Asian history. Among other things, maps document religious communities (pp. 91-9), languages (pp. 99-101), and castes and ethnic groups (pp. 106-9) as well as "Fiction in English on Life in South Asia" (p. 144). Ten plates of antique maps and five of notable buildings venture beyond cartography. The classified bibliography, updated through 1990, is beyond praise. Almost five thousand items encompass bibliographies, reference works, documents, periodicals and printed works in all European languages, as well as primary sources in South Asian ones. This is one of the imposing ATLASES of our time.

□ *Summary* Abounding in maps, photographs, essays and bibliography, this HISTORICAL ATLAS combines comprehensiveness, accuracy and imaginativeness to an unheard-of degree.

221 (1983-86) Ashim Kumar Roy and N. N. Gidwani, *A Dictionary of Indology,* 4 vols. (New Delhi: Oxford &

Ibh Publishing, 1983-86); about 1300 pages; no index; no general bibliography.

□ *Critique* This DICTIONARY of Indian history and culture supplies about five thousand entries on persons, places, sects, texts, sciences, deities and more than five hundred jatakas (i.e., accounts of previous lives of the Buddha). Entries in this "'all-in-one' library of essential information" range in length from three lines through an average of fifteen lines to two pages (on some of the jatakas). In a unique feature a WHO'S WHO sketches the careers of about two hundred Western Indologists such as Paul Hacker, Monier Monier-Williams and Louis Renou. These are the only entries to carry bibliography. Hinduism, Buddhism and Sikhism are covered in detail, Parsism in outline, and Islam not at all. These unpretentious volumes pack an enormous amount of information, eschewing the floweriness and overcrowding that mar certain Indian reference works. Nothing is probed in depth, but everything is summarized adroitly.

□ *Summary* This INTRODUCTORY DICTIONARY to Indian culture is one of the finest of its kind. Every scholar of South Asia should consult it.

222 (1983) Alistair Shearer, *The Traveler's Key to Northern India* (New York: Knopf, 1983); ix & 547 pages; index, pp. 533-47; general bibliography, pp. 507-9; glossary, pp. 510-15; black-and-white photos and diagrams throughout.

□ *Critique* This meticulous GUIDEBOOK delineates nineteen sites ranging from the caves of Elephanta, Ellora and Ajanta and the Jain shrine of Mount Abu to Muslim locations in Delhi and Agra as well as Buddhist ones at Sanchi, Sarnath and Bodh Gaya. The Golden Temple of the Sikhs at Amritsar balances Hindu temples at Khajuraho, Bubaneshwar and Konarak, not to mention Banaras. Diagrams, maps and itineraries are second to none. A background chapter of over fifty pages introduces Hinduism, Buddhism and Islam astutely. This masterpiece of popularization will enlighten travelers and art historians alike. Only experts need consult Prasanna K. Acharya, *A Dictionary of Indian Architec-*

ture (Oxford: Oxford University Press, 1927; reprint, Bhopal: J.K. Publishing House, 1978).

□ *Summary* Lavish descriptions and ingenious illustrations make this GUIDEBOOK a boon for browser or traveler.

223 (1985, 1987) Parshotam Mehra, *A Dictionary of Modern Indian History, 1707-1947* (Delhi: Oxford University Press, 1985; reprinted with corrections, 1987); xv & 823 pages; index, pp. 809-23; selected chronology, pp. 769-803.

□ *Critique* This REVISIONIST DICTIONARY ponders political, military and diplomatic history in four hundred essays, each with bibliography. About half the entries concern British and Indian statesmen or military leaders but not scholars or religious figures. Regions are covered chiefly in connection with battles or treaties. Besides recounting careers, entries on persons weigh alternative interpretations, often with surprising results. Sparkling prose, apt quotations and startling judgments make this one of the most readable of reference books. One wishes for something as pungent on African history.

□ *Summary* This sprightly DICTIONARY ruminates on persons, events and movements. The effect resembles that of a good curry.

224 (1987) Louis Frédéric (1923-), *Dictionnaire de la civilisation indienne* (Paris: Laffont, 1987); xv & 1277 pages; index (keyed to entries), pp. 1233-76; general bibliography, pp. 1195-1229; chronology, pp. 1169-92; a few black-and-white drawings and maps; also in paperback.

□ *Critique* Within this DICTIONARY a French savant has compressed South Asian civilization into ten thousand entries. Length varies from four lines to sixteen pages on "Art and Architecture" and twenty-five on "India." Three functions interact with each other: (1) a GLOSSARY expounds religious terms and literary titles; (2) a REALLEXIKON explores places and practices, not to mention issues in politics, economics and history; (3) a WHO'S WHO ranges through dynasties, deities, authors and scholars. A meaty article canvasses

"Religions and Philosophies" (pp. 915-26, with bibliography, pp. 1215-21). About a tenth of the entries carry bibliography, and a general one is classified under fourteen heads. Frédéric's tour de force remains the closest thing to a one-volume library on South Asia. His **249** *Buddhism* (1992, 1995) is equally precocious. Both are easier to swallow than the telegraphic WHO'S WHO and GLOSSARY in his *Encyclopaedia of Asian Civilization,* 10 vols. (Villecresnes and Paris: Jean-Michel Place, 1977-84). The latter's vol. 11 (1987), however, deploys a stupendous bibliography.

□ *Summary* This cornucopia of South Asian lore quickly becomes addictive. An English version would fill a gap.

225 (1987-94) Amaresh Datta, ed., *Encyclopaedia of Indian Literature,* 6 vols. (New Delhi: Sahitya Akademi, 1987-94); 5160 pages; index, 6:4901-5160; no general bibliography.

□ *Critique* Written entirely by Indian authorities, this ENCYCLOPEDIA of literary culture excludes deities and myths in order to characterize authors, texts and genres in twenty-five languages. Typical articles survey "Mysticism" or "Drama" that has unfolded in up to eight languages. Synopses delineate regional literatures, but bibliographies are minimal or absent. Postcolonial authors such as Nirad Chaudhuri are greeted with acerbity. Such disdain contrasts with the judiciousness of a Canadian LEXICON, Eugene Benson and L. W. Conolly, eds., *Encyclopedia of Post-colonial Literatures in English,* 2 vols. (London and New York: Routledge, 1994).

□ *Summary* This ENCYCLOPEDIA formulates a pan-Indian perspective on authors and genres in major languages of South Asia.

226 (1990-) V. I. Subramoniam, ed., *Dravidian Encyclopedia,* planned in 3 vols. (Thiruvananthapuram: International School of Dravidian Linguistics, 1990-); 2 vols. to date: 656 & lii; 840 & lx pages; index in each volume.

□ *Critique* Begun in 1981, this ENCYCLO-PEDIA of South Indian culture devotes volume 1 (1990) to history and volume 2 (1993) to "Contemporary Peoples and Cultures." It is more disciplined and less quaint than many other South Asian reference works. Signed articles with bibliography canvass an astonishing array of topics in religion, art, folklore and ethnology. Tribal peoples win detailed attention, and Northern India commands overviews. An article on Jainism (1:355-65) excels.

□ *Summary* This authoritative ENCYCLO-PEDIA digests history and culture extending southward from the Deccan. Unusual depth of coverage repays browsing.

227 (1990) Georg Feuerstein, *Encyclopedic Dictionary of Yoga* (New York: Paragon; London: Unwin Hyman, 1990); xxix & 430 pages; no index; no bibliography; black-and-white photographs throughout; also in paperback.

□ *Critique* Written for practitioners, this GLOSSARY of almost one thousand Sanskrit terms explains techniques, concepts and schools of yoga. Key concepts like "dhyana," "samadhi," "siddhi" and "tapas" elicit long entries, steeped in Sanskrit terminology, but most others are brief. Less forbidding articles address English-language concepts like "Anatomy," "Classical Yoga," "Cosmos" and "Sexuality." A few persons such as Aurobindo Ghose, Caitanya and Shankara are noted. There is no bibliography anywhere. Practitioners of yoga will relish the depiction of schools and practices (with photographs of positions), but beginners may prefer the author's *Yoga: The Technology of Ecstasy* (Los Angeles: Tarcher, 1989).

□ *Summary* In this GLOSSARY nearly all entries are too technical for any but experts.

228 (1991) Ivor Lewis, *Sahibs, Nabobs and Boxwallahs: A Dictionary of the Words of Anglo-India* (Bombay: Oxford University Press, 1991); x & 266 pages; no index; general bibliography, pp. 255-66.

□ *Critique* This jaunty historical GLOS-SARY of about four thousand terms updates a MENIPPEAN masterwork, Henry Jule and A. C. Burnell, *Hobson Jobson: A Glossary of Colloquial Anglo-Indian Words and Phrases* (1886; 2d ed., 1902; reprint, Delhi: Munshiram Manoharlal, 1968). Both books fashion DICTIONARIES of Anglo-Indian usage in such a way as to cross-illuminate Indian and British culture. Lewis supplies etymologies and a splendid bibliography. His "Historical Introduction" canvasses three centuries of fiction and scholarship (pp. 1-44). Browsers will feast.

□ *Summary* Witty explanations of about four thousand terms elucidate ins and outs of British India.

228 (1991) M. L. Varadpande, *A Dictionary of Indian Culture* (New Delhi: Arnold; Edinburgh: Aspect, 1991); 149 pages; no index; no bibliography; line drawings throughout.

□ *Critique* This INTRODUCTORY GLOSSARY of about six hundred practices, places, deities and concepts (but scarcely any persons) defines issues in down-to-earth, occasionally quaint language. All catchwords come in Indian languages. The author of a five-volume *History of Theater in India,* Varadpande excels both as a popularizer and as a mediator between India and the West. This ranks among the handiest INTRODUCTIONS to Indian culture.

□ *Summary* This INTRODUCTORY GLOSSARY explains the basics of Indian culture in plain language. Beginners will delight.

230 (1992-) Ganga Ram Garg, ed., *Encyclopaedia of the Hindu World,* announced in 100 vols. (New Delhi: Concept Publishing, 1992-); 9 vols. to date; vol. 3 (to *AZ*) reaches p. 872; general bibliography (devoid of dates), 1:xiii-xiv.

□ *Critique* Written almost entirely by the editor, this MEGA-ENCYCLOPEDIA explicates places, persons, practices, tribes, deities and texts from all periods, languages and religions. Having written an *International Encyclopedia of Indian Literature,* 8 vols. (1987-91), the editor embarked on one of the colossal one-author endeavors of our time. Only a few entries come from outside experts. Averaging two to four pages, articles recount history soberly but without bibliography. A WHO'S WHO embraces Western scholars (e.g., Edwin Arnold) as well as mythical figures (e.g., Arjuna). The introduction (1:1-90) unfurls a conspectus of South Asian history as well as of literatures written in thirteen languages. This one-author MEGA-ENCYCLOPEDIA cannot

proceed quickly enough. It will render earlier works, not least **219** Walker, *The Hindu World* (1968) obsolete, but a REALLEXIKON of comparable scope by Western scholars is badly needed.

□ *Summary* This feast will delight polymaths and specialists alike. It illuminates literature, modern history and history of scholarship.

231 (1992-) Harbans Singh, ed., *The Encyclopaedia of Sikhism,* planned in 5 or 6 vols. (Patiala: Punjabi University, 1992-); vol. 1 *(A* through *D):* xviii & 607 pages.

□ *Critique* This ENCYCLOPEDIA recruits over 150 (mostly Indian) scholars to recount Sikh and Punjabi history since 1500. Each signed entry supplies bibliography. In volume 1 *(A* through *D)* two-thirds of the articles make up a WHO'S WHO of about 750 leaders, both Punjabi and British. The other third delineate religious observances (e.g., "Bhog"), movements (e.g., "Akali") and individual books of the *Adi Granth.* Apart from "Ahmadiyah," other religions get scant attention. Historians of India will find the WHO'S WHO invaluable, but historians of religion will regret neglect of non-Sikh traditions. A WHO'S WHO and GLOSSARY of self-definition is more lucid but less thorough: Ramesh Chander Dogra and Gobind Singh Mansukhani, *Encyclopaedia of Sikh Religion and Culture* (New Delhi: Vikas, 1995).

□ *Summary* This WHO'S WHO of Sikh leaders and British administrators examines religious practices and movements but omits comparisons to other religions.

232 (1992) Vijaya Ghose, ed., *Tirtha: The Treasury of Indian Expressions* (New Delhi: CMC, 1992); index, pp. 304-21; general bibliography, p. 303; color photographs throughout.

□ *Critique* This winsome GLOSSARY of India (but not Pakistan or Sri Lanka) arrays over thirty-five hundred terms under twenty-one headings. Chapter 18 on "Religion" runs thirty-five pages and chapter 19 on "Sages and Saints" another twenty. Thirty-four pages on "Performing Arts," twenty on "Archaeology/ Architecture," twelve on "Adornment" and ten on "Food" have no parallel elsewhere. Jaunty definitions linger in the memory, but one wishes for individual bibliographies. One hundred fifty color photographs evoke a vast panorama. This is one of the most alluring self-teachers about India.

□ *Summary* This GLOSSARY introduces customs of India with verve. It makes an ideal travel companion.

233 (1994) Karel Werner, *A Popular Dictionary of Hinduism* (Richmond, U.K.: Curzon, 1994); 185 pages; no index; no bibliography (except p. 17); also in paperback.

□ *Critique* This handy GLOSSARY introduces about one thousand terms, places and persons in simple entries devoid of bibliography. Catchwords alternate between Sanskrit and English, and at least half the entries run four lines or less. An introduction sketches periodization and major concepts (pp. 5-18). Clarity prevails, and subtlety peeks through now and then.

□ *Summary* This briefest of GLOSSARIES excels as a self-teacher.

4.2.2 MYTHOLOGY

OVERVIEW: WESTERN EXPERTISE
Although some would argue that mythology so pervades Indian culture as to be inseparable from it, a number of reference works elevate mythology above literature, art, history or folklore. Among the most convenient is **235** Stutley and Stutley.

LIST OF WORKS ANALYZED
234 (1964, 1975) Vettam Mani, *Puranic Encyclopaedia: A Comprehensive Dictionary with Special Reference to the Epic and Puranic Literature*, 4th ed., rev., in English (Delhi: Motilal Banarsidass, 1975); published in Malayalam, 1964.
235 (1977) Margaret Stutley and James Stutley, *A Dictionary of Hinduism: Its Mythology, Folklore and Development, 1500 B.C.—A.D. 1500* (London: Routledge and Kegan Paul, 1977); published in the United States as *Harper's Dictionary of Hinduism: Its Mythology, Folklore, Philosophy, Literature and History* (New York: Harper & Row, 1977)
259 (1981, 1991) Yves Bonnefoy

and Wendy Doniger, eds., *Mythologies*, 2 vols. (Chicago: University of Chicago Press, 1991)
256 (1984) Hans Wilhelm Haussig, ed., *Wörterbuch der Mythologie*, vol. 5, *Götter und Mythen des indischen Subkontinents* (Stuttgart: Klett-Cotta, 1984)
236 (1991) Jan Knappert, *Indian Mythology: An Encyclopedia of Myth and Legend* (London: Aquarian, 1991)

ANALYSIS OF WORKS
234 (1964, 1975) Vettam Mani, *Puranic Encyclopaedia: A Comprehensive Dictionary with Special Reference to the Epic and Puranic Literature*, 4th ed., rev., in English (Delhi: Motilal Banarsidass, 1975); published in Malayalam, 1964; viii & 922 pages; no index; Puranic genealogies, pp. 901-22.

□ *Critique* This WHO'S WHO embraces several thousand deities, characters and places mentioned in epics and the puranas. Although secondary bibliographies are lacking, all locations in the epics and puranas get noted. No entries treat scholars or other moderns. Indispensable for specialists, this magnum opus is too recondite for most others. The same can be said of its chief rival, Sadashiv A. Dange, *Encyclopaedia of Puranic Beliefs and Practices*, 4 vols. (New Delhi: Navrang, 1986), which references objects as well as deities.

□ *Summary* Extracted from an "ocean" of story, this WHO'S WHO serves experts only.

235 (1977) Margaret Stutley and James Stutley, *A Dictionary of Hinduism: Its Mythology, Folklore and Development, 1500 B.C.—A.D. 1500* (London: Routledge and Kegan Paul, 1977); published in the United States as *Harper's Dictionary of Hinduism: Its Mythology, Folklore, Philosophy, Literature and History* (New York: Harper & Row, 1977); xviii & 372 pages; general bibliography, pp. 353-68; list of English subjects with Sanskrit equivalents, pp. 369-72; map, p. xviii; also in paperback.

□ *Critique* This historical GLOSSARY distills reading in English, French and German (but not Hindi), as well as in English translations of ancient texts. A British husband and wife labored more than twenty years compiling twenty-five hundred entries on texts, religious practices, holy places and above all mythic figures but not art. All catchwords are in Sanskrit, but an index states English equivalents. Jain and Buddhist topics get skeletal attention, but since coverage stops at 1500 C.E., Sikhs and Parsis are omitted. A multilingual bibliography numbers nine hundred titles, and footnotes pinpoint their relevance to individual entries. Articles define Sanskrit terms meticulously, whether in religion, science or philosophy. They cite ancient texts abundantly but scant the social sciences. This labor of love invites endless browsing. Margaret Stutley digested the lore into a WHO'S WHO and GLOSSARY: *The Illustrated Dictionary of Hindu Iconography* (London: Routledge and Kegan Paul, 1985). The two works all but supplant a staple, John Dowson, *A Classical Dictionary of Hindu Mythology and Religion, Geography, History and Literature* (London, 1879; at least eleven reprints).

□ *Summary* This DICTIONARY compresses an entire library into a historical GLOSSARY. No other work functions so efficiently as a self-teacher of Hindu mythology.

259 (1981, 1991) Yves Bonnefoy and Wendy Doniger, eds., *Mythologies,* 2 vols. (Chicago: University of Chicago Press, 1991); 2:797-877 on India. Analyzed further under 5.1.1 "Mythology: General." Madeleine Biardeau wrote twenty-three of twenty-six essays on Indian mythology, enlarging her *L'Hindouisme: Anthropologie d'une civilisation* (Paris: Flammarion, 1981). Her articles constitute a tidy book embracing all periods. Essays on "Puranic Cosmology" and "Popular Hinduism" are not to be missed.

256 (1984) Hans Wilhelm Haussig, ed., *Wörterbuch der Mythologie,* **vol. 5,** *Götter und Mythen des indischen Subkontinents* (Stuttgart: Klett-Cotta, 1984); xv & 1040 pages; index, pp. 951-1040; general bibliography (mainly of English-language works), pp. 13-17; 63 black-and-white plates; maps and line drawings throughout. Other volumes are analyzed under 5.1.1 "Mythology: General."

□ *Critique* This exhaustive COMPENDIUM divides into seven GLOSSARIES of mythic figures and events, classified by religion (or culture). A leading German authority has compiled each GLOSSARY, supplying introduction, multilingual bibliographies and illustrations. Two hundred pages on Vedism/Hinduism and 220 on Indian Buddhism expound familiar topics in depth. Seventy-five pages on Jainism and 125 on Dravidian myths are unusual, while chapters on Singhalese folk religion and on religions of seventy-five tribal peoples are almost unheard-of. Hermann Berger's fifty pages on Gypsy myths span Eurasia. Although marred here and there by MENIPPEAN outbursts, the style is lucid, and cross-references abound. Bibliographies are beyond compare, citing chiefly English-language works. If this volume existed in English translation, every Indologist would swear by it.

□ *Summary* This COMPENDIUM supplies exceptionally learned GLOSSARIES of myths in seven South Asian cultures. Everyone will relish the bibliographies.

236 (1991) Jan Knappert, *Indian Mythology: An Encyclopedia of Myth and Legend* (London: Aquarian, 1991); 288 pages; no index; general bibliography, pp. 25-26; also in paperback.

□ *Critique* Using a format that evolved in volumes on **278** African, **284** Pacific and **12** Near Eastern mythology, Knappert combines a WHO'S WHO of deities with a GLOSSARY of places and concepts. About half the entries run just two lines, and all lack bibliographies. Longer entries retell tales and specify symbolism, reporting, for example, that the Buddha's saffron robe indicates "the sunlight of his wisdom" (p. 60). The introduction provides a virtuosic overview (pp. 9-27), but otherwise the insights impress less than in the author's **12** *The Encyclopaedia of Middle Eastern Mythology and Religion* (1993).

□ *Summary* Deft retelling of myths accompanies a telegraphic GLOSSARY. Both serve beginners better than experts.

4.2.3 PHILOSOPHY

OVERVIEW: ELEGANT SELF-

TEACHERS English-language exposi- tions of Indian philosophy and its history excel. They range from the elementary (**240** Pahdi) to the daunting (**237** Potter).

LIST OF WORKS ANALYZED
237 (1970-90) Karl H. Potter, ed., *Encyclopedia of Indian Philosophies,* 5 vols. (Delhi: Motilal Banarsidass; Prince- ton: Princeton University Press, 1970-90)

238 (1984) Ruth Reyna (1904-), *Dictionary of Oriental Philosophy,* 2 vols. (New Delhi: Munshoram Manoharlal, 1984)

239 (1989) John A. Grimes, *A Con- cise Dictionary of Indian Philosophy* (Al- bany: SUNY Press, 1989)

240 (1990) Bibhu Padhi and Minak- shi Padhi, *Indian Philosophy and Relig- ion: A Reader's Guide* (Jefferson, N.C., and London: McFarland, 1990)

ANALYSIS OF WORKS
237 (1970-90) Karl H. Potter, ed., *Encyclopedia of Indian Philosophies,* 5 vols. (Delhi: Motilal Banarsidass; Prince- ton: Princeton University Press, 1970-90); 811; 744; 635; 672; 609 pages; index in each volume. The bibliography in vol. 1 (1970) underwent a second edition (1984).

□ *Critique* This historical LEXICON of Indian philosophies began as a bibliog- raphy of 9222 items in volume 1 (1970; 2d ed., 1984). Each volume delivers signed articles that retrace history of In- dian schools in mind-boggling depth (with massive bibliographies). Religion is not emphasized, but major religious thinkers get exhaustive coverage (e.g., Shankara in vol. 3). Volume 2 (1977) covers Nyaya-Vaisesika, volume 3 (1981) Advaita Vedanta, volume 4 (1987) Samkha (edited by Gerald James Larson and Shankar Bhattacharya), volume 5 (1990) the philosophy of the Grammari- ans (edited by Harold G. Coward and K. Kunjunini Raja). Offering a highly so- phisticated treatment of Indian philoso- phy, this magnum opus will not help beginners.

□ *Summary* Indispensable for historians

of Indian thought, this up-to-date LEXI- CON is too intricate for anyone else.

238 (1984) Ruth Reyna (1904-), *Dictionary of Oriental Philosophy,* 2 vols. (New Delhi: Munshoram Manoharlal, 1984); xx & 419 pages; no index; general bibliography, pp. 217-20, 273-74, 373, 418-49; a few line drawings and photo- graphs.

□ *Critique* Divided into four sections, this GLOSSARY and WHO'S WHO introduces con- cepts and sages in language that is more "reportorial" than "interpretive" (1:xvi). Written as a labor of love by an American- born devotee of Vedanta, the first section anatomizes Hinduism, Buddhism and Jainism but not Sikhism (1:1-220). An entry on the author (p. 159) sketches her career in California and at the British Com- monwealth University of Poona (from 1959). Overviews of "Mathematics," "Medicine" and "Symbolism" vie in pun- gency with a critique of "Psychoanalysis." A second section on Judaism and Islam (1:223-74) and a third on Japan (2:377- 419) are skeletal, but a fourth on China (2:277-373) has no competitor except St. Elmo Nauman, *A Dictionary of Asian Phi- losophies* (New York: Philosophical Library, 1978, and London: Routledge, 1979). Love of the subject pulsates amid cross-ref- erences. The same virtues pervade Reyna's *Introduction to Indian Philosophy: A Sim- plified Text* (Bombay and New Delhi: Tata McGraw-Hill, 1971).

□ *Summary* This enthusiast's GLOSSARY and WHO'S WHO addresses nonphiloso- phers. Ever zestful, the author writes as an outsider turned insider.

239 (1989) John A. Grimes, *A Con- cise Dictionary of Indian Philosophy* (Al- bany: SUNY Press, 1989); viii & 440 pages; brief index, pp. 437-40; no bibliog- raphy; fourteen charts, pp. 413-36.

□ *Critique* This GLOSSARY of Sanskrit terms differentiates denotations among Buddhist, Jain and no fewer than eleven Hindu schools of philosophy. Focus is on denotations rather than on the views they transmit. Pivotal terms like "karma," "dharma" and "moksha" elicit thirteen, fourteen and fifteen denotations respectively. Fourteen charts deploy lineages and typologies (e.g., of chakras). Crisp writing aims at the philosophically trained, but there are no bibliographies. Users of **237** Potter, *Encyclopedia of Indian Philosophies* (1970-90) will find this a boon.

□ *Summary* This GLOSSARY will help philosophers who take up Indian studies, but it demands commitment.

240 (1990) Bibhu Padhi and Minakshi Padhi, *Indian Philosophy and Religion: A Reader's Guide* (Jefferson, N.C., and London: McFarland, 1990); 413 pages; index, pp. 403-13; glossary, pp. 391-402.

□ *Critique* This INTRODUCTION by two American enthusiasts of Indian philosophy supplies nine chapters, each with bibliography, on religions (Vedas/Upanishads, Jainism, Buddhism) and schools of philosophy (Vaiseska-Nyaya and Vedanta). Chapter 9 on "Hindu Gods and Goddesses" excels as a self-teacher.

□ *Summary* Written with verve, this INTRODUCTION packages Indian philosophy and religion for beginners.

4.3 BUDDHISM

4.3.1 GENERAL

OVERVIEW: WESTERN AND ASIAN ENCYCLOPEDISM IN BALANCE
The recent flowering of Buddhism in Europe and the United States has inspired a spate of reference books. American and British works jostle with Asian ones like the Japanese GLOSSARIES and the Sri Lankan **242** *Encyclopaedia of Buddhism* (1961-). The former are grouped under 4.3.2 "Glossaries (Japanese)." In addition, Buddhist philosophy blossoms in a LEXICON, **216** Schuhmacher and Woerner, eds., *The Encyclopedia of Eastern Philosophy and Religion* (1986, 1989). French works stand out. Text and photograph beguile in **241** René de Berval's *Présence du bouddhisme* (1959, 1987). **243** Durix, *Cent Clés pour comprendre le zen* (1976, 1991) captivates as a PHILOSOPHICAL DICTIONARY. An older Japanese bibliography lists no fewer than 15,073 Western titles published through 1960: Shinsho Hanayama, *Bibliography on*

Buddhism (Tokyo: Hokuseido, 1961).

LIST OF WORKS ANALYZED
241 (1959, 1987) René de Berval, ed., *Présence du bouddhisme* (Saigon: France-Asie, 1959); 2d ed., rev. (Paris: Gallimard, 1987)

242 (1961-) G. P. Malalasekera [founding ed.], [then] Jotiya Dhirasekers, [now] W. G. Weeraratne, eds., *Encyclopaedia of Buddhism,* planned in 11 vols. (Colombo, Sri Lanka: Government of Sri Lanka, 1961-)

243 (1976, 1991) Claude Durix, *Cent Clés pour comprendre le zen* (Paris: Courrier du livre, 1976; 2d ed., rev., 1991)

244 (1984) Heinz Bechert and Richard Gombrich, eds., *The World of Buddhism: Buddhist Monks and Nuns in Society and Culture* (London: Thames & Hudson [paperback, 1991]; New York: Facts on File, 1984)

245 (1986) William H. Nienhauser Jr., ed., *The Indiana Companion to Traditional Chinese Literature* (Bloomington, Ind.: Indiana University Press, 1986)

246 (1987) John Snelling [1943-92], *The Buddhist Handbook: A Complete Guide to Buddhist Teaching and Practice* (London: Rider, 1987)

247 (1987, 1989) Joseph M. Kitagawa and Mark D. Cummings, eds., *Buddhism and Asian History* (New York: Macmillan, 1989)

248 (1988) Don Morreale, ed., *Buddhist America: Centers, Retreats, Practices* (Santa Fe, N.M.: John Muir, 1988)

249 (1992, 1995) Louis Frédéric, *Buddhism: Flammarion Iconographic Guides* (New York: Flammarion, 1995)

250 (1993) Charles S. Prebish, *Historical Dictionary of Buddhism* (Metuchen, N.J., and London: Scarecrow, 1993)

251 (1993, 1994) Graham Coleman, ed., *Handbook of Tibetan Culture* (London: Rider, 1993; Boston: Shambhala, 1994)

ANALYSIS OF WORKS
241 (1959, 1987) René de Berval [d.

1987], ed., *Présence du bouddhisme* (Saigon: France-Asie, 1959); 2d ed., rev. (Paris: Gallimard, 1987); 816 pages; glossary, pp. 703-26; bibliography, pp. 727-94; 151 black-and-white photographs. Analyzed on the basis of the 1987 edition.

□ *Scope* This COMPENDIUM of thirty-three articles by French and Asian authorities appeared in the periodical *France-Asie* of Saigon in 1959 to mark the twenty-five hundredth anniversary of the death of the Buddha. This handsome revision drops some articles, slightly revises others (e.g., on the spread of Buddhism), and enlarges the bibliography from eight hundred to fourteen hundred titles (chiefly in English and French, along with a few in German). Written for Europeans who wish to confront Buddhism as "one of the great facts of civilization," this COMPENDIUM dates from a tranquil moment between the defeat of France in Indochina (1954) and the entry of the United States into the Vietnam War (1962). The serenity suggests how differently study of Buddhism might have developed if the Vietnam War had not intruded during the 1960s. Thirty-three articles divide between twenty on early Buddhism (pp. 49-417) and thirteen on its spread throughout Asia (pp. 421-702). The writing is lucid and sometimes poetic, as in Berval, Mus and Tucci (pp. 35-83). Divided into twenty-six headings, a general bibliography favors French and English monographs, while individual articles carry no bibliography of their own. Reprinted from the 1959 edition, 150 photographs furnish rare glimpses of art and architecture. Their poignancy recalls André Malraux's vision of a "museum without walls," making the volume estimable for its illustrations alone.

□ *Strengths* Essays by twenty-one Europeans alternate with those by eleven Asians to delineate both primordial Buddhism and subsequent history (to the late 1950s). Among historical accounts, Paul Lévy's ninety pages on "Chinese Pilgrims in India" is the meatiest. Place by place he retraces itineraries of fourth-century Fa-Hien (pp. 301-17) and seventh-century Hiuan-Tsang (pp. 321-63). André Bareau

enumerates what is known about twenty monks, four nuns and ten laypersons who were disciples of the Buddha (pp. 245-66). Denise Delannoy depicts practices and daily rhythms of monastic life in Tibet of the mid-1950s (pp. 223-41). René de Berval constructs a "Chronology of Buddhist Expansion" into a dozen countries (pp. 424-33). Individual articles on India, Sri Lanka, Burma, Thailand, Laos and Cambodia pertain to Theravada. A second series on China, Korea, Japan, Tibet, Indonesia and Vietnam recounts development of Mahayana in each region. Articles on India, Sri Lanka, Cambodia, Vietnam and Korea are by natives.

Rather more poetic are a half dozen testimonies *(témoignages)* by distinguished European and Asian scholars. Paul Mus urges a new approach to Buddhism; Giuseppe Tucci evokes his discoveries in Tibet; two Sri Lankans (Walpola Rahula and Mahathera Narada) summarize basic teachings. A German convert, Mahathera Nyantiloka (born A. W. F. Güth), likewise sketches fundamentals. Comparison between Hinduism and Buddhism springs from an Indian untouchable, Bhimrao Ramji Ambedkar (1891-1956), who had relaunched Buddhism in India by converting just before he died. All articles boast black-and-white photographs of sculpture and architecture, some of them shot from unusual angles and all with poignant captions. A multilingual bibliography, divided into twenty-six headings across sixty-five pages, delivers nine pages on texts, five on philosophy, eight on art and twenty-five on a dozen regions. Even the best-versed will find novelties in this cornucopia, which appends five pages of other bibliographies.

□ *Weaknesses* This COMPENDIUM celebrates an era. Only the bibliography and pages here and there have been updated beyond the late 1950s. The editor invited French scholars to pioneer postcolonial discourse following the collapse of three generations of involvement in Indo-China. Although no Chinese participate, their absence is redressed by having Rhi Ki-Yong write on Korea, Pang Khat on Cambodia and Mai-Tho-Truyen on Vietnam. The only Japanese contribution is D. T. Suzuki's two pages on "Buddha-Nature." This book charms by evoking a privileged moment in Buddhist studies before the Vietnam War dissolved an early stage of postcolonial rethinking. Charm cannot, however, conceal the aging of certain articles (e.g., on art, Japan, Alexandra David-Neel on Tibet). It is a pity that no one wrote an essay during the 1950s on European converts to Buddhism. An index is sorely missed.

□ *Competitors* This COMPENDIUM on the rise and spread of Buddhism exalts India and Southeast Asia. It must now compete with **250** Prebisch, *Historical Dictionary of Buddhism* (1993), which deploys an even more extensive bibliography, albeit with fewer entries in French. **246** Snelling, *The Buddhist Handbook* (1987) surveys the same material more briefly while stressing Western Buddhism. Articles from **5** Eliade, ed., *The Encyclopedia of Religion* (1987) collected in **247** Kitagawa and Cummings, eds., *Buddhism and Asian History* (1989) include André Bareau on "Hinayana Buddhism" but otherwise recruit scholars who emerged after 1960. Their research is more sober, their demeanor less awestruck. Admiring to a fault, *Présence du bouddhisme* exudes a love of Asia and of Buddhism that now seems innocent.

□ *Summary* A book of beauty that renders homage to Buddhism as a molder of civilization, this COMPENDIUM evokes a bygone era. Photographs, testimonies and regional surveys recall how much has perished of confidence and innocence since the 1950s. A bibliography of French works stands unrivaled.

242 (1961-) G. P. Malalasekera [founding ed.], [then] Jotiya Dhirasekers, [now] W. G. Weeraratne, eds., *Encyclopaedia of Buddhism,* planned in 11 vols. (Colombo, Sri Lanka: Government of Sri Lanka, 1961-); vol. 5 (1993) through "Japan"; 640 pages and 60 to 120 black-and-white plates per volume.

□ *Scope* This ambitious ENCYCLOPEDIA was begun in 1955 to mark the twenty-five hundredth anniversary of the Buddhist era.

Subsidized by UNESCO and edited by Theravadins in Sri Lanka, it examines Buddhism worldwide, emphasizing reception in Europe and North America. Volume 4 (1979-89) inaugurated a policy of omitting Western scholars as well as persons and places that are "merely legendary." Signed articles by Asian and Western scholars describe persons, places, shrines, rites, concepts and movements, most without bibliography. In volume 4 and after, emphasis falls on concepts and on diffusion of Buddhism. Entries reference both Pali and European words. A WHO'S WHO includes teachers, rulers and (through vol. 3) Western scholars. The writing varies from limpid (e.g., Helmuth von Glasenapp) to convoluted (e.g., Bandula Jayawardhana on "Determinism"). Photographs are well selected but poorly printed.

□ *Strengths* Brief articles on places and technical terms are sprinkled among magisterial ones comparing Buddhist and Western philosophies. These offer some of the deepest discussion of comparative philosophy in any reference work on Asia (e.g., "Causality," "Free Will," "Determinism and Indeterminism"). Two entries tackle "God" and "Gods," differentiating a gamut of Western opinions about Buddhist nontheism. R. D. Gunaratne's twelve pages on "Dialectics" contrasts positions of Plato, Aristotle, Kant, Hegel, Marx and Kierkegaard with those of Jain and Buddhist logic, appending a page of bibliography. All regions of Asia elicit lengthy entries, as do major Western countries (e.g., Britain, France, Germany, Italy). Guido Auster's four pages on "Germany, Buddhism in" survey the twentieth century, while a virtuosic essay by Helmuth von Glasenapp recounts medieval European legends and Schopenhauer's praise of Buddhism. Colorful articles depict customs such as "Birth Control," "Charity" and "Commemorative Feasts."

□ *Weaknesses* This work addresses specialists, particularly in philosophy. Some entries are idiosyncratic, as in E. Hector Perera's comparison of Freudian and Buddhist "Depth Psychology." Although the pace of publication has speeded up since

1989, seven volumes are yet to appear. Because the focus narrowed with volume 4, the completed work will be uneven, volumes 1-3 canvassing far more persons and places.

□ *Competitors* This fullest ENCYCLOPEDIA on Buddhism compares Buddhist and Western thought expertly. **250** Prebish, *Historical Dictionary of Buddhism* (1993) is more concise and assembles superb bibliography but shuns comparisons. **241** Berval, ed., *Présence du bouddhisme* (1959, 1987) is more French than Asian in approach and underplays philosophy. **246** Snelling, *The Buddhist Handbook* (1987) sketches 250 Buddhists active in the twentieth century and likewise avoids philosophy. **216** Schuhmacher and Woerner, eds., *The Encyclopedia of Eastern Philosophy and Religion* (1986, 1989) cuts a wider swath (including Hinduism and Taoism) but in much shorter entries. It complements this Asian *Encyclopaedia of Buddhism*. No other reference work compares Buddhism with Western thought so pungently.

□ *Summary* Surveys of Buddhism worldwide and of comparative philosophy distinguish this Sri Lankan ENCYCLOPEDIA. It exhales an aura of Asia.

243 (1976, 1991) Claude Durix (1922-), *Cent Clés pour comprendre le zen* (Paris: Courrier du Livre, 1976; 2d ed., rev., 1991); 367 pages; no index; general bibliography, pp. 200-202; black-and-white photographs and line drawings throughout.

□ *Critique* This crafty PHILOSOPHICAL DICTIONARY delivers one hundred essays in reverse alphabetical order, about one-third of them bearing Asian catchwords. A physician and master of no less than four martial arts, the author practiced Zen in 1956 with a Soto master, Sengoku (d. 1971), whom he evokes (pp. 14-18, 73). Unfolding like origami, the essays deliver aperçus, jolts and inversions, seasoned by hundreds of quotations from Japanese teachers, above all Dogen. Three examples suffice: the piece on "Religion(s)" argues, as Thomas Merton did, that without being a religion Zen enhances practice of any and all religions. An essay on "Flowers" trans-

mits with diagrams a master's precepts for "sweetness" in arrangements. An entry on "Posture" makes human well-being pivot on the fifth lumbar vertebra, the keystone of the spine (p. 116). The author sets anecdotes from his own experience like rocks in a monastery garden that converse across centuries. Zen quotations jostle with Western ones from the likes of St. Benedict, Tauler, Jung and Fromm (misspelled as Frömm). To heighten surprise, parting advice tells us to discard the book (p. 358). Unexpected entries examine "Ego," "Hippies" and "Averroes." Embedding Zen incongruity in a Western mold, reverse alphabetical order never ceases to astonish. No PHILOSOPHICAL DICTIONARY is more original or more unsettling.

□ *Summary* This PHILOSOPHICAL DICTIONARY in reverse alphabetical order illuminates, entertains and unnerves. It wields anecdote like a sword.

244 (1984) Heinz Bechert and Richard Gombrich, eds., *The World of Buddhism: Buddhist Monks and Nuns in Society and Culture* (London: Thames & Hudson [paperback, 1991]; New York: Facts on File, 1984); 308 pages; glossary (by Gombrich), pp. 289-92; bibliography (by Bechert), pp. 293-96; index, pp. 302-7.

□ *Scope* This COMPENDIUM presents eleven signed articles by mainly European authorities on history and customs of Buddhist monastic communities *(sanghas)*. Etienne Lamotte's sixteen pages on the historical Buddha precede chapters on Theravadin monasticism in regions as diverse as India, Afghanistan, Central Asia, Nepal, Sri Lanka, Burma, Thailand, Laos and Cambodia. These are more detailed than chapters on China, Vietnam, Korea or Japan. Eighteen pages on Tibet and Heinz Bechert's overview of "Buddhist Revival in East and West" round out the volume. Each chapter recounts the history and present status of the sangha, while dipping into philosophy and political activity.

□ *Strengths* A stunning feature is sixty-four pages of color and black-and-white photographs that deploy about two hundred images of architecture, sculpture and life of the sangha in thirteen countries. Attaching meaty captions to striking images, four portfolios on the Buddha, Indian Tradition, Buddhism in East Asia, and Tibetan Buddhism fit the text admirably. Authors from Britain, Germany, Switzerland, Belgium, the Netherlands and Scandinavia bring an academic perspective that ignores directives about how to meditate. Michael B. Carrithers and Heinz Bechert recount how monks function in twentieth-century Sri Lanka and Burma, but Per Kvaerne's richly historical chapter on Tibet devotes only one page to destruction since 1950. Heinz Bechert's chapter on revival since 1900 surveys India, Indonesia, Germany, Great Britain and the United States. The same author constructs the volume's bibliography astutely, distributing several hundred titles (in English, French and German) under seven regions, each with six or eight subheads. Richard Gombrich's glossary of terms in seven Asian languages is a model.

□ *Weaknesses* Intended for amateurs rather than scholars, this COMPENDIUM depicts the sangha without adducing other religions. Comparisons among regional variants of Buddhism compensate for a monographic focus. Readers in quest of Buddhist philosophy will find little to gratify them.

□ *Competitors* This is the most searching INTRODUCTION to the sangha in any reference work. More ruminative and admiring, **241** Berval, ed., *Présence du bouddhisme* (1959, 1987) pays less heed to monasticism. Its black-and-white photographs are more artistic but less wide-ranging and deemphasize monasteries. **250** Prebisch's *Historical Dictionary of Buddhism* (1993) covers more individuals and updates bibliography but lacks vivacity. Articles in **5** Eliade, ed., *The Encyclopedia of Religion* (1987) execute comparisons to other religions but do not explore the sangha so lovingly. The absence of a WHO'S WHO necessitates recourse to **246** Snelling's *The Buddhist Handbook* (1987) or **9** Hinnells, ed., *Who's Who of World Religions* (1991).

□ *Summary* Interplay between text and photographs make this a vivid INTRODUC-

TION to history of the sangha in thirteen countries. The bibliography exudes clarity.

245 (1986) William H. Nienhauser Jr., ed., *The Indiana Companion to Traditional Chinese Literature* (Bloomington, Ind.: Indiana University Press, 1986); xlii & 1050 pages; three indexes (names, titles, subjects); general bibliography, pp. xxix-xxxix.

□ *Critique* This masterful HANDBOOK combines a LEXICON of five hundred entries on "writers, works, genres, styles, movements, various influences" in China with a COMPENDIUM of ten essays on schools and genres, chiefly Buddhist. Over two hundred Western scholars scrutinize Buddhist, Confucian, Taoist and other texts. Because the entries feature Chinese titles, resort to the indexes is essential. One wishes that Western scholars would prepare a similar HANDBOOK on Islamic traditional literature, particularly the hadith.

□ *Summary* Written by and for readers of Chinese, this HANDBOOK exceeds the needs of all but experts.

246 (1987) John Snelling (1943-92), *The Buddhist Handbook: A Complete Guide to Buddhist Teaching, Practice, History and Schools* (London: Rider, 1987); ix & 373 pages; index, pp. 366-73; general bibliography, pp. 358-63; WHO'S WHO, pp. 309-54; line drawings throughout.

□ *Critique* An English Buddhist wrote this HANDBOOK to elucidate the various transmissions from antiquity to the present. Written for fellow Buddhists in a style at once jaunty and concise, chapters 3-5 describe the historical Buddha and chapters 6-7 his teaching, while chapters 8-17 differentiate the "Southern Transmission" from seven branches of the "Northern Transmission." Chapters 18-22 trace the spread of Buddhism in the West, while chapter 20 (pp. 271-84) lists European addresses. The WHO'S WHO sketches over 250 twentieth-century Buddhist teachers, classified into clusters of fifty Western, ninety-three Tibetan, sixty-six Zen, seventeen Pure Land, thirteen Nichiren and fifteen miscellaneous. Although non-Buddhists are scanted, Snelling shares with Irving Hexham an admiration for Edward Conze (pp. 241-42). A six-page bibliography is almost entirely in English, and there is no glossary. Historians of Buddhism in the West will find this volume a gold mine. Snelling published a narrative sequel: *Buddhism in Russia* (Rockport/London: Element, 1993).

□ *Summary* In recounting the spread of Buddhism, this lively HANDBOOK dispenses rare biographical information.

247 (1987, 1989) Joseph M. Kitagawa and Mark D. Cummings, eds., *Buddhism and Asian History* (New York: Macmillan, 1989); xi & 414 pages; no index; synoptic outline, pp. 412-14.

□ *Critique* Twenty-nine articles reprinted from 5 Eliade, ed., *The Encyclopedia of Religion* (1987) survey "Foundations," "The Pan-Asian Buddhist World" [seven regions], "Buddhist Schools and Sects," "Dimensions of Religious Practice" [including "Iconography" and "Folk Buddhism"] and "The Path to Enlightenment." Virtuosic performances include Luis O. Gómez's fifty-five pages on "Buddhism in India," André Bareau's twenty pages on "Hinayana Buddhism," Nakamura Hajime's twenty-five pages on "Mahayana Buddhism" and Alex Wayman's fifteen pages on "Esoteric Buddhism." These are among the most intricate analyses of Buddhist thought anywhere.

□ *Summary* This grouping of major articles from 5 *The Encyclopedia of Religion* addresses specialists rather than beginners.

248 (1988) Don Morreale, ed., *Buddhist America: Centers, Retreats, Practices* (Santa Fe, N.M.: John Muir, 1988); xxxix & 350 pages; no index; no bibliography.

□ *Critique* This COMPENDIUM on Buddhism in North America purveys four to seven signed articles on each of four schools (Theravada, Mahayana, Vajrayana, New Directions). It then lists retreat centers of each school throughout North America, totaling over five hundred, more than one-fifth of them in California. Thirty articles assess the various schools and their impact in North America. Tourists, practitioners of Buddhism, and scholars of

American religion will find the treatment more substantive than the title may suggest.

□ *Summary* This GUIDEBOOK becomes a COMPENDIUM on Buddhist life in North America, but without bibliography.

249 (1992, 1995) Louis Frédéric, *Buddhism: Flammarion Iconographic Guides* (New York: Flammarion, 1995); tr. from *Les Dieux du bouddhisme: Guide iconographique* (Paris: Flammarion, 1992); 360 pages; index, pp. 351-59; general bibliography, pp. 344-50; 600 black-and-white photographs and woodcuts; 32 color plates. Analyzed on the basis of the French edition.

□ *Critique* This lavish DICTIONARY classifies images of Buddhas and ancillary deities throughout Asia. Chapter 1 traces transmission of images from India and Burma through Tibet, China and Mongolia to Korea and above all Japan, while chapter 2 deploys eighty line drawings from a Japanese classic to classify gestures, postures and attributes. In chapters 3-11 a WHO'S WHO inventories about three thousand figures ranging from Buddhas (pp. 74-148) and bodhisattvas (pp. 150-98) through female deities (pp. 218-32) and guardians (pp. 234-50) to groups of deities and protectors (pp. 252-82) and a few divinized humans (e.g., Padmasambhava). No other reference book differentiates Buddhist figures so precisely or traces origins so minutely except an overly intricate WHO'S WHO of images: Frederick W. Bunce, *An Encyclopedia of Buddhist Deities*, 2 vols. (New Delhi: D.K. Printworld, 1994). The color plates glow, while seventeenth-century Japanese woodcuts (from Butsuzo-zu-i) supply hundreds of insets. A master lexicon-maker has mapped the unmappable.

□ *Summary* A model DICTIONARY of iconography cuts through thickets of Buddhist lore. The illustrations have no peer.

250 (1993) Charles S. Prebish, *Historical Dictionary of Buddhism* (Metuchen, N.J., and London: Scarecrow, 1993); xxxv & 387 pages; no index; general bibliography, pp. 289-386.

□ *Critique* This historical GLOSSARY and

WHO'S WHO introduces persons, concepts and practices of Buddhism worldwide. The GLOSSARY references concepts (in English, Pali and Japanese), texts, schools of thought and a few cities ("Nara"). The WHO'S WHO embraces Buddhist masters ("Nichiren"), rulers ("Asoka") and Western scholars ("André Bareau"). Entries vary in length from four lines to a full page, eschewing both technical terms and bibliography. Although entries canvass India, China, Japan and the modern West evenly, they do not compare Buddhism with other religions. An introduction sketches the life of the Buddha, the spread of Buddhism (pp. 5-25), and doctrine (pp. 25-34). The marvel of the volume is ninety-two pages of multilingual bibliography, classified into nine headings such as "Text," "Soteriology" and "Sacred Places." This is the handiest bibliography on Buddhism worldwide, almost matching in depth that in **241** Berval, ed., *Présence du bouddhisme* (1959, 1987). Other tools include a "Pronunciation Guide" (pp. xv-xix) and a list of "The Buddhist Scriptures" (pp. xxi-xxvii). Lucid writing and superb bibliography make this INTRODUCTION shine.

□ *Summary* This GLOSSARY and WHO'S WHO serves mainly novices, but the bibliography will astonish even experts.

251 (1993, 1994) Graham Coleman, ed., *Handbook of Tibetan Culture* (London: Rider, 1993; Boston: Shambhala, 1994); 430 pages; two indexes (resources, biographies), pp. 421-30; no bibliographies; maps and line drawings throughout.

□ *Critique* This three-in-one GUIDE prints information from the "Tibetan Cultural Resources Database" that is operated by the Orient Foundation in Bath, England. Part 1 (pp. 37-204) describes Tibetan Buddhist centers throughout the world, arrayed by country. Part 2 (pp. 205-74) furnishes a WHO'S WHO of living teachers (devoid of bibliography). Part 3 (pp. 277-420) offers a GLOSSARY of terms in both Sanskrit and English. Its several hundred entries are unusually direct. The introduction surveys each of the five principal traditions of Tibetan Bud-

dhism. Every student of Tibet will want this book.

□ *Summary* This GUIDE to Tibetan Buddhism inventories contemporary centers and teachers worldwide. The GLOSSARY is a gem.

4.3.2 GLOSSARIES (JAPANESE)

OVERVIEW: USING TERMINOLOGY TO BRIDGE CULTURES Japanese scholars of Buddhism have issued a number of GLOSSARIES, ranging from intermediate to daunting. A fastidious GLOSSARY of the entire culure is Setsuko Kojima and Gene A. Crane, *Dictionary of Japanese Culture* [1987] (Union City, Calif.: Heian, 1991). Painstaking to a fault, these works dispense a perspective of rare delicacy. They are more refined than an Indian competitor: K. Krishna Murthy, *A Dictionary of Buddhist Terms and Terminology* (Delhi: Sundeep Prakashan, 1991).

LIST OF WORKS ANALYZED

252 (1929-30, 1974-) Sylvain Lévi, [later] Paul Demiéville, [then] Jacques May, eds., *Hobogirin: Dictionnaire encyclopédique du bouddhisme d'après les sources chinoises et japonaises* (Paris: Maisonneuve, 1929-30; resumed 1974-)

253 (1965) Iwano Shinyu, ed., *Japanese-English Buddhist Dictionary* (Tokyo: Daito-Shuppansha, 1965)

254 (1983) *A Dictionary of Buddhist Terms and Concepts* (Tokyo: Nichiren Shoshu International Center, 1983)

255 (1984, 1989) Hisao Inagaki with P. G. O'Neill, *A Dictionary of Japanese Buddhist Terms* (Kyoto: Nagata Bunshodo, 1984; Union City, Calif.: Heian, 1989)

ANALYSIS OF WORKS

253 (1929-30, 1974-) Sylvain Lévi, [later] Paul Demiéville, [then] Jacques May, eds., *Hobogirin: Dictionnaire encyclopédique du bouddhisme d'après les sources chinoises et japonaises* (Paris: Maisonneuve, 1929-30; resumed 1974-); also published in Tokyo; fascicules 1-2 (1929-30); fascicule 3 (1974); fascicule 6

(1983) through "Daijizaitan."

□ *Critique* This fabulously learned historical ENCYCLOPEDIA compiles Chinese and Japanese reworkings of ancient Buddhist material. It collates hundreds of sources in Chinese, Japanese and Pali concerning Japanese terminology, particularly of Zen. Conceived by Lévy and Demiéville and edited in French at the Hobogirin Institute in Kyoto, the entries are too technical for a nonspecialist to evaluate. Their density mirrors the prolixity of Chinese and Japanese texts. **249** Frédéric, *Buddhism: Flammarion Iconographic Guides* (1992, 1995) maps Buddhist imagery more accessibly. See "In Memoriam Paul Demiéville (1895-1979)," in *Numen,* 27 (1980): 1-8.

□ *Summary* This ENCYCLOPEDIA of textual niceties offers a ne plus ultra of Buddhist learning. Historical scholarship has nothing more punctilious to show than this.

253 (1965) Iwano Shinyu, ed., *Japanese-English Buddhist Dictionary* (Tokyo: Daito-Shuppansha, 1965); 383 pages; three indexes (of Japanese, Chinese and Sanskrit terms), pp. 341-83; no bibliography.

□ *Critique* This DICTIONARY identifies persons, places, concepts and practices transmitted by Japanese Buddhism. Entries run alphabetically in Japanese (with Japanese characters and Pali equivalents adjacent). Written in dignified English, entries recount basic information on lives, writings and categories in ancient India, China and Japan. Temples in Japan (but not in China) elicit entries. This volume remains more readable than **255** Inagaki and O'Neill, *A Dictionary of Japanese Buddhist Terms* (1984, 1989) but lacks bibliography. Provided one knows Japanese equivalents for Pali terms, this DICTIONARY illuminates Buddhist persons, places and concepts.

□ *Summary* This Japanese-made DICTIONARY offers a refreshing alternative to Western prose about East Asian religion.

254 (1983) *A Dictionary of Buddhist Terms and Concepts* (Tokyo: Nichiren Shoshu International Center, 1983); xvii & 579 pages; three indexes (key words,

Japanese equivalents, Sanskrit and Pali equivalents); maps, pp. 533-44; no bibliography. In 1991 Editions du Rocher published a French translation by René de Berval.

□ *Critique* This Japanese REALLEXIKON furnishes a meticulous GLOSSARY of about fourteen hundred items, including schools, concepts, texts and persons (chiefly Japanese). Definitions are phrased with unusual care, and the WHO'S WHO differentiates lineages and schools diligently. Articles on "Shakyamuni" and "Nichiren Daishonin" are the longest (four and six pages respectively). In deference to numerology, no fewer than ten articles address topics beginning "Eight [types] . . ." and twenty-five begin "Ten [types] . . ." Scholars of religion will find this the soundest of the Japanese GLOSSARIES. It renders Japanese phraseology into elegant English, a feat matched by René de Berval in the French edition. Both transmit tradition with precision.

□ *Summary* This exacting REALLEXIKON encapsulates Japanese Buddhism, particularly of the Nichiren school. The definitions are among the most quotable Buddhist utterances anywhere.

255 (1984, 1989) Hisao Inagaki with P. G. O'Neill, *A Dictionary of Japanese Buddhist Terms* (Kyoto: Nagata Bunshodo, 1984; reprint, Union City, Calif.: Heian, 1989); 535 pages; five indexes, pp. 375-534; bibliography, pp. xiv-xvi.

□ *Critique* This GLOSSARY of Japanese terms supplies both literal and figurative translations. Cross-references abound, and five indexes (of Chinese-Japanese words and characters, Japanese, Chinese, Sanskrit, Pali) will suit linguists. Others will find **253** Shinyu, ed., *Japanese-English Buddhist Dictionary* (1965) more discursive. Unlike the latter, this is a tool, not an amenity.

□ *Summary* This GLOSSARY renders Japanese terms into scrupulous English.

5 ALTERNATIVE APPROACHES

5.1 MYTHOLOGY

5.1.1 GENERAL

OVERVIEW: RESISTING MENIP-PEAN BRAVURA The study of mythology attracts scholars from a range of fields: anthropology, depth psychology, religious studies and literature (both ancient and modern). Reference works itemized here examine myths that are non-European as well as European (particularly ancient Greek, Roman, Norse and Celtic), while invoking a range of disciplines. The only reference books that keep disparate methodologies in play are **257** Ranke, ed., *Enzyklopädie der Märchens* (1977-), **259** Bonnefoy/Doniger, *Mythologies* (1981, 1991) and **215** Akoun, ed., *Mythes et croyances du monde entier* (1985, 1991). Because hardly anyone cherishes every region's myths, need persists for INTRODUCTIONS of all sizes. Toward that end, study of mythology has inspired WHO'S WHOS, several of which break records for exhaustiveness attained by a single author, as in **270** Leach and **268** Mercatante. A superb annotated bibliography of over three hundred English-language works adorns the latter (pp. 699-715). Because classical mythology of ancient Greece and Rome belongs more to literary than to religious studies, books on it do not feature here. Postmoderns can salute, however, an ANATOMY of Greek myth by Roberto Calasso: *The Marriage of Cadmus and Harmony* [1988] (New York: Knopf, 1993).

A HANDBOOK, Michael Croden and Martin Kreiswirth, eds., *The Johns Hopkins Guide to Literary Theory and Criticism* (Baltimore and London: Johns Hopkins University Press, 1993), maps recent methodologies elegantly. In a class by itself is the gigantic HANDBOOK, **257** Ranke, ed., *Enzyklopädie der Märchens* (1977-). Planned in twelve volumes, it rigorously rethinks techniques and traditions of storytelling worldwide. It also differentiates folktales from myth, an issue that religious studies has neglected. Also helpful on this crux is G. S. Kirk, *Myth: Its Meaning and Function in Ancient and Other Cultures* (Berkeley: University of California Press; Cambridge: Cambridge University Press, 1970), especially pages 31-41.

Few fields so incite MENIPPEAN bravado

as does study of mythology. Some of the works analyzed here teeter on the edge of MENIPPEAN overkill, and some authors (e.g., Robert Graves and Barbara Walker) tip over it. Their thesis that women transmit among themselves lore that men have repressed seems to invite excess.

Most of these reference works are better suited to anthropologists and scholars of literature than to scholars of religion. Study of myth fuses with study of religion above all in **5** Eliade, ed., *The Encyclopedia of Religion* (1987), notably in articles by Kees Bolle on "Cosmology" and "Myth." Indeed, **5** *The Encyclopedia of Religion* urges coupling study of myth with study of religion. Of works analyzed in this section, certain chapters in **262** Larrington, ed., *The Feminist Companion to Mythology* (1992) alone pursue that endeavor.

LIST OF WORKS ANALYZED

256 (1965-) Hans Wilhelm Haussig, ed., *Wörterbuch der Mythologie,* vols. 1-2, 4-6 of series "Die alten Kulturvölker" to date (Stuttgart: Klett, 1965-)

257 (1977-) Kurt Ranke, ed., *Enzyklopädie des Märchens: Handwörterbuch zur historischen und vergleichenden Erzählforschung,* planned in 12 vols. (Berlin and New York: de Gruyter, 1977-)

258 (1980) Richard Cavendish, ed. [with Trevor O. Ling], *Mythology: An Illustrated Encyclopedia* (London: Orbis; New York: Rizzoli, 1980)

259 (1981, 1991) Yves Bonnefoy, ed., *Dictionnaire des mythologies et des religions, des sociétés traditionelles et du monde antique,* 2 vols. (Paris: Flammarion, 1981). A "restructured translation" appeared as Wendy Doniger, ed., *Mythologies,* 2 vols. (Chicago: University of Chicago Press, 1991).

260 (1983) Barbara G. Walker, *The Woman's Encyclopedia of Myths and Secrets* (New York: Harper, 1983); also in paperback (San Francisco: Harper, 1986)

215 (1985, 1991) André Akoun, ed., *Mythes et croyances du monde entier,* 5 vols. (Paris: Lidis-Brepols, 1985, 1991). Analyzed under 4.1 "Asian Religions: General."

261 (1988, 1992) Pierre Brunel, ed., *Companion to Literary Myths, Heroes and Archetypes* (London and New York: Routledge, 1992)

312 (1991) Beverly Moon, ed., *An Encyclopedia of Archetypal Symbolism* (Boston and London: Shambhala, 1991). Analyzed under 5.3.3 "Social Sciences of Religion: Psychology."

262 (1992) Carolyne Larrington, ed., *The Feminist Companion to Mythology* (London: Pandora, 1992); also in paperback (San Francisco: Thorsons, 1992)

263 (1993) Roy Willis, ed., *World Mythology* (New York: Henry Holt, 1993)

ANALYSIS OF WORKS

256 (1965-) Hans Wilhelm Haussig, ed., *Wörterbuch der Mythologie,* vols. 1-2, 4-6 of series "Die alten Kulturvölker" (Stuttgart: Klett, 1965-); about 4000 pages; index in each volume; no general bibliography. Volume 5, *Götter und Mythen des indischen Subkontinents* (1984) is evaluated also under 4.2.2 "South Asia: Mythology."

□ *Critique* This HANDBOOK of world mythology assembles monographs published over a period of thirty years. Written by major authorities, articles range in length from fifty to three hundred pages. Volume 1 (1965) covers Egypt and Arabia, volume 2 (1973) Europe, volume 4 (1986) the Caucasus, Armenia, Zoroastrianism and the Beluchis, volume 5 (1984) South Asia and volume 6 (1988) Japan, Taiwan, Korea and Buddhism in China. Volume 3 has yet to appear. The coverage of lesser cultures knows no parallel: volume 2 on Europe encompasses Celts, Hungarians, Finns, Balts, Albanians, Basques and Berbers. Volume 4 offers three hundred pages by Carsten Colpe on Zoroastrianism (4:161-486). This is the longest article on that religion in any reference book, including **199** the *Encyclopaedia Iranica.* Volume 5 covers Hinduism (pp. 1-204), Jainism (pp. 205-84) and Buddhism (pp. 285-507) as well as Gypsies (pp. 773-824) and Tamils (pp. 825-952). Volume 6 expounds indigenous religions in Taiwan and Korea. Each monograph delivers a historical over-

view and a WHO'S WHO of deities, with massive multilingual bibliographies. Written by and for specialists, this HANDBOOK abounds in information found nowhere else. Its only rival is **259** Bonnefoy and Doniger, eds., *Mythologies* (1981, 1991), which is more accessible and imaginative but less all-encompassing.

□ *Summary* This HANDBOOK remains indispensable for mythology of exotic peoples and for monographs on the religions. It deserves to be better known.

257 (1977-) Kurt Ranke, ed., *Enzyklopädie des Märchens: Handwörterbuch zur historischen und vergleichenden Erzählforschung,* planned in 12 vols. (Berlin and New York: de Gruyter, 1977-); seven volumes to 1993 (through "Kleines Volk"); 740 pages each; more than 5000 pages to date.

□ *Scope* This REVISIONIST MEGA-HANDBOOK furnishes signed articles by authorities worldwide on themes, sources, contents and scholars of folktales everywhere. Longer articles feature numbered subsections, and bibliographies overflow. Religious scriptures receive their due, while imaginative articles dissect methodology (e.g., "Folklore," "Computertechnik," "Genre-Theory," "Hermeneutics") as well as scholars (e.g., Ernst Bloch, Dagobert Elias, C. G. Jung). The concept of "Narrative Stock" *(Erzählgut)* underlies the enterprise, which examines a "corpus of tales" in more than a hundred cultures that range from China, India and Germany to Canada, Yemen and Ecuador. Few other multivolume works sustain such a high level of originality or pithiness.

□ *Strengths* This cross-disciplinary MEGA-HANDBOOK animates so many fields that it invites a new genre-label. Articles on "Hagiography" and "Saints" *[Heilige]* rethink how to study saints, while a few of the latter have their folktales expounded (e.g., Francis, Gennaro, George, Helen, Jerome). One or two biblical figures (e.g., Jacob, Joseph the patriarch) receive like treatment. An entry on "Jewish Narrative Stock" elicits nearly thirty pages (7:688-743), while one on "Arabic-Islamic" gets seventeen (1:685-718) and one on

"Celtic" twelve (7:1147-71). A cluster of fifteen entries on "Women" runs sixty pages (5:100-220) with eleven of bibliography, not to mention five pages of bibliography on "Witch" (6:981-992). Other articles delineate periods ("Baroque," "Counter-Reformation"), schools ("Jesuit Narrative Literature") and genres ("Film," "Horror Stories"), while novel insights burst from essays on themes ("Eternal Jew," "Golem"), animals ("Fox," "Hedgehog"), objects ("Foot," "Gallows") and doctrines ("Eschatology," "Hell"). Authors who recast folktales are probed, above all Germans like Gellert, Grass, Hesse and E. T. A. Hoffmann, not to mention Arabs like Hanna Diyab and Americans like Washington Irving and Walt Disney. Few other reference books unleash so many surprises.

□ *Weaknesses* This REVISIONIST masterpiece stretches the assumptions of all who use it. Until the entry on "Myth" appears (in vol. 8), readers will wonder how the editors conceive its relationship to folktales *(Märchen)*. Indeed, one wishes that the planners would issue a separate volume to explain their ambitions. The originality daunts, and a one-volume epitome would be a boon. Until then G. S. Kirk, *Myth: Its Meaning and Function in Ancient and Other Cultures* (1970) makes a useful companion.

□ *Competitors* It is a pity that this pathbreaking work does not coordinate entries with **259** Bonnefoy/Doniger, eds., *Mythologies* (1981, 1991) or with **256** Haussig, ed., *Wörterbuch der Mythologie* (1965-), both of which emphasize myth rather than storytelling. Systematic comparison of the three enterprises would reap rewards. Less systematically, French anthropologists use myth for cultural diagnosis in volume 5 of **215** Akoun, ed., *Mythes et croyances du monde entier* (1985). In contrast to a volume like **260** Walker, *The Woman's Encyclopedia of Myths and Secrets* (1983), no MENIPPEAN excess taints the *Enzyklopädie des Märchens*. Yet scholars of literature, mythology, folklore and religion continue to overlook this masterpiece. No other work revolutionizes stereotypes so stunningly.

□ *Summary* One of the most versatile of contemporary reference books, this MEGA-HANDBOOK is almost too imaginative for its own good. In making everything from the Bhagavid Gita to Walt Disney look fresh, it carries innovativeness to new heights.

258 (1980) Richard Cavendish, ed. [with Trevor O. Ling], *Mythology: An Illustrated Encyclopedia* (London: Orbis; New York: Rizzoli, 1980); 303 pages; index, pp. 298-303; bibliography, pp. 293-95; many color and black-and-white photographs.

□ *Critique* Arranged according to region and religion, this COMPENDIUM dispenses intelligent texts by mostly British authorities. Superbly illustrated, articles vary greatly in length and approach. Three pages on Germany stress Nazi revival of the swastika, while twenty pages on India enumerate deities and tell their stories. Theories of myth, whether Jungian or Eliadian, are avoided. More conventional and thorough than **263** Willis, ed., *World Mythology* (1993), this volume retains its sprightliness.

□ *Summary* This COMPENDIUM retells myths worldwide.

259 (1981) Yves Bonnefoy, ed., *Dictionnaire des mythologies et des religions, des sociétés traditionelles et du monde antique,* 2 vols. (Paris: Flammarion, 1981); xxiv & 618; 585 pages; index, 2:555-85; no general bibliography. The "restructured translation" edited by Wendy Doniger as *Mythologies* (1991) is analyzed in the next entry.

□ *Critique* This LEXICON of mythology and world religions recruited 112 (almost entirely French) specialists to write signed articles on a bewildering array of topics. Most entries are staggeringly erudite and include multilingual bibliography, sometimes with footnotes. At least sixteen types of entry may be distinguished: (1) regions ("Armenia," "Mesopotamia," "Oceania," "Siberia"), (2) cities ("Rome" [in thirty pages]), (3) peoples ("Etruscans," "Eskimos," "Turks and Mongols," "Yoruba"), (4) religions ("Buddhism," "Hinduism," "Christianity and Mythology"), (5) practices ("Hunting," "Shamanism," "Divination"), (6) genres ("Fables", "Myths," "Cosmogonic Myths"), (7) deities and heroes ("Krishna," "Eros," "Orpheus," "Oedipus"), (8) esoteric traditions ("Hermetism," "Kabbala," "Portal Guardians"), (9) insoluble problems ("Death," "Evil," "Origins,"), (10) natural phenomena ("Fire," "Earth," "Mountains") and (11) historical persons ("Augustus," "Cicero," "Plato," "Napoleon as Myth"). Additional types that command just one or two entries include (12) numerals ("five," "seven"), (13) individual epics ("Mahabharata," "Ramayana"), (14) languages ("Ugaritic"), (15) literary movements ("Romanticism") and (16) topographical features ("Ganges"). Although at least a third of the entries concern regions and peoples, none is canvassed fully. Ancient Greece and Rome receive the most attention. Entries on practices or concepts examine just two or three cultures to the exclusion of others. The article on "Festivals," for example, treats ancient Rome, Indonesia and Japan, while that on "Ritual Theater" handles Java and Bali. The French version adopted alphabetical arrangement so as to avoid arbitrary classifications (1:v), but juxtapositions make a browser giddy. A schema that classifies entries into fifty-four cultures and religions (1:xxi-xxiv) provided the basis for Wendy Doniger's restructuring (*see* **259** following).

259 (1981, 1991) Yves Bonnefoy and Wendy Doniger, eds., *Mythologies,* 2 vols. (Chicago: University of Chicago Press, 1991; paperback in 4 vols., 1992); xxx & 646; viii & 622 pages; index, 2:1237-67; no general bibliography; black-and-white photographs throughout. Analyzed also under 4.2.2 "South Asia: Mythology."

□ *Scope* This most learned of English-language ENCYCLOPEDIAS on myth profits from French scholarship and American editing. Four hundred articles probe an astonishing range of topics and are signed with the initials of both author and translator.

□ *Strengths* The restructured edition is easier to browse in than the French origi-

nal. Titles of the four volumes in paperback indicate the rearrangement: *American, African, and Old European Mythologies, Asian Mythologies, Greek and Egyptian Mythologies, Roman and European Mythologies.* Chapters on Asia investigate religion as fully as mythology.

□ *Weaknesses* The table of contents must be read with care in order to grasp Wendy Doniger's restructuring, and the index should always be used. Too few bibliographies are updated beyond 1980.

□ *Competitors* No other work except **256** Haussig, ed., *Wörterbuch der Mythologie* (1965-) tackles the unfolding of mythology among both European and non-Western peoples in such exhaustive and exhausting depth. *Mythologies* makes nearly all other English-language reference works on mythology seem primers. On remote cultures such as "Ossetians," "Maghreb" and "Meroitic Religions" (of the Sudan), this remains the only convenient source, particularly since **256** *Wörterbuch der Mythologie* is found in few American libraries. The two complement one another superbly. Albeit more Eurocentric, **261** Brunel, ed., *Companion to Literary Myths* (1988, 1992) is no less provocative and even less predictable.

□ *Summary* This idiosyncratic COMPENDIUM is a work of infinite resource. Beginners should start elsewhere, since even experts can scarcely exhaust it.

260 (1983) Barbara G. Walker, *The Woman's Encyclopedia of Myths and Secrets* (New York: Harper, 1983); also in paperback (San Francisco: Harper, 1986); x & 1121 pages; no index; general bibliography, pp. 1105-18; black-and white photographs at the head of each letter of the alphabet.

□ *Scope* This MENIPPEAN DICTIONARY unleashes torrents of lore in 1,350 entries about alleged patriarchal distortions in Western and Asian history. The introduction expounds Walker's view that "patriarchal religion declared war on pagan societies where motherhood was once the only important parental relationship" (pp. viii-ix). Walker identifies countless instances of how women's secret lore allegedly redresses patriarchal distortions. Entries vary from a few lines on several hundred mythic figures to fourteen pages on "Motherhood," twelve on "Inquisition" and ten on "Marriage," "Mary," "Menstrual Blood" and "Witchcraft." The WHO'S WHO embraces biblical women, female Christian saints, innumerable goddesses, but just two historical figures (Galileo and Joan of Arc). Christian, Indian and Greek figures abound. Many of the entries propound "aetiologies," (i.e., causal explanations) based on female lore that males allegedly repressed. Ideology reigns.

□ *Strengths* Such a cornucopia of the unconventional cannot fail to instruct. Enticing entries concern objects, whether parts of the body ("Entrails," "Fingers," "Hair"), animals ("Boar," "Cat," "Lion"), techniques ("Birth Control," "Midwifery," "Necromancy"), agricultural products ("Henna," "Honey") or artistic motifs ("Horseshoe Arch," "Furrow," "Mandorla," "Mask," "Swastika"). MENIPPEAN displays abound. In "Cave," "Castration," "Earth" and "Kingship," material from ten or more cultures cascades down the page. Much attention is paid to derivation of names, as in "Lady Godiva" (from goddess), "Mahdi" (from the moon-goddess Mah) and "Magog" (mother of Gog). A phantasmagoria of secrets pours from entries like "Gypsies," "Kali Ma" and "Name." Unfortunately, nearly all the lore cries out to be verified elsewhere. Footnotes abound but hardly ever evaluate a source. One grows weary from wondering how much, if anything, can be believed.

□ *Weaknesses* Like its successor, Walker's *The Woman's Dictionary of Symbols and Sacred Objects* (San Francisco: Harper, 1988), this DICTIONARY of myth and legend purveys an essentialist ideology. Diane Purkiss dissects its assumptions in **262** Larrington, ed., *The Feminist Companion to Mythology* (1992), pages 443-44. Nearly every page exudes the view, advanced also by Robert Graves, that women carry "dark, secret, always unconscious truths that fathers have struggled to repress" (ibid., p. 444). One ceases to believe that women

alone could have transmitted all that Walker discloses. At times, her ideology seems a rhetorical device rather than a scholarly position. Certain longer entries (e.g., "Matrilineal Inheritance," "Sophia") dispense contradictory tales without attempting to coordinate them. This results in MENIPPEAN nightmare. Worst of all, Walker makes no effort to evaluate sources, relegating bibliography to footnotes and a fourteen-page general bibliography. Anti-Christian sarcasm explodes in entries like "Mary," "Inquisition," "Saint Paul" and "Pope Joan." Entries on "Buddhism," "Jainism" and "Asceticism" are hardly more sympathetic and overstate crosscultural borrowing. Yet for all its excesses, this MENIPPEAN DICTIONARY captivates. As with "Ripley's Believe It or Not," one wishes in vain that alleged explanations could be verified. The flaw lies in Walker's conviction that legends handed down by women ring truer than "facts" attested by men.

□ *Competitors* This ideological DICTIONARY is alluring but dangerous. MENIPPEAN self-indulgence precludes self-discipline. To consult **259** Bonnefoy/Doniger, eds., *Mythologies* (1981, 1991) is to enter a different realm, one that is nuanced and documented, even when the material is no less bizarre. The surest corrective is **262** Larrington, ed., *The Feminist Companion to Mythology* (1992), which rebuts Walker's assumptions while examining a wider gamut of cultures. That work persuades as well as astonishes. Even the Jungian insights of **312** Moon, ed., *An Encyclopedia of Archetypal Symbolism* (1992) seem tepid in comparison. A reliable REALLEXIKON with a vaster horizon is **318** Jones, *Larousse Dictionary of World Folklore* (1995). Walker has pressed matriarchal self-definition to the point of MENIPPEAN extravagance. However thrilling to browse in, her book is not only quirky but unreliable. It should never be consulted in isolation.

□ *Summary* This MENIPPEAN DICTIONARY both fascinates and exasperates. Walker's obsessions enhance readability but dispel trust.

261 (1988, 1992) Pierre Brunel, ed., *Companion to Literary Myths, Heroes,*

and Archetypes (London and New York: Routledge, 1992); translated from *Dictionnaire des mythes littéraires* (Paris: Editions du Rocher, 1988); xvi & 1223 pages; index, pp. 1211-23; general bibliography, pp. 1187-210; also in paperback.

□ *Scope* This idiosyncratic LEXICON on literary reception of myth comes from a research team at the University of Paris IV. More than one hundred contributors wrote 123 signed essays (usually of six to ten pages each) on literary myths from Europe, India, China, Japan and Africa (but not Scandinavia or Latin America). As defined in Pierre Brunel's preface, a "literary myth" is a theme that generations of retellers have reworked. Such an "archetype" may originate in storytelling about mythic figures (e.g., "Odysseus" "Sisyphus," "Ishtar") or historical ones (e.g., Emperor "Julian," "Louis XIV," "Nietzsche"). About one-third of the entries come from ancient Greece, a dozen concern the Bible, four or five address African myths (of the Yoruba, Zulu and Dogon peoples), and a number analyze crosscultural themes like "Spinners," "Ogre" and "Manlike Woman." Although occasionally opaque, most of the writing is straightforward. There are no individual bibliographies, but twenty-five pages of general bibliography stand unmatched.

□ *Strengths* This LEXICON digests perhaps two thousand literary texts that retell "literary myths." Greek mythology and the Bible together supply almost half of the core material. Essays on "Cronos," "Daedalus," "Dionysus," "Hermes," "Prometheus" and "Psyche" trace refashionings of their stories throughout European literature. The rise and fall of themes is recounted as rare sources accompany familiar ones. From the Bible come essays on "Abraham," "Cain," "David," "Jacob," "Job" and "Moses." Surprisingly, no entry addresses Thomas Mann's Joseph novels. Female figures from the Bible include "Judith," "Lilith" and "Salome." Themes like "Eden," "Apocalypse" and "Wandering Jew" elicit accounts, and there are nine pages on "Jesus Christ in Literature." Only two saints figure: "Temptation of St. Anthony" and "Joan of Arc." From the ancient Near East come "Ishtar," "Isis" and "Zoroaster," the latter entry examining myriad eighteenth-century texts leading up to Sarastro in *The Magic Flute*. Inevitable entries concern "Tristan" and "Faust." Synoptic articles canvass "Cosmogonic Myths," "Labyrinth" and "Discoveries" (of foreign lands).

Methodology is discussed in Bernadette Bricout's piece on "Tales and Myths" and Colette Astier's on "Literary and Mythological Narratives." Discussions of "Utopia and Myth," "Heroism" and "Historical Figures and Mythical Figures" address issues at the heart of the enterprise. The longest entry comprises forty pages by Françoise Graziani on "Doubles and Counterparts." Throughout, essays inventory familiar and recondite texts, classify themes and propose hypotheses to illuminate reception. Theorists who inspired these pages include Roland Barthes and Mircea Eliade but not Georges Dumézil or Carl Jung. Insistence upon analyzing and not just citing texts avoids MENIPPEAN outbursts.

□ *Weaknesses* This LEXICON betrays its origin by favoring topics from French literature and history. The very notion of "literary myth" reflects French methodology by merging religious and tribal myths with literary retellings, as happens also in **259** Bonnefoy, ed., *Dictionnaire des mythologies* (1981). More damaging, the preface fails to vindicate inclusions and exclusions. An astonishing omission is that of Scandinavia. Inclusion of myths from Mali and Senegal cries out to be justified. Moreover, the roster of historical figures is skewed. We find "Louis XIV" but not Napoleon, Emperor "Julian" but not Augustus, "Joan of Arc" but not Queen Elizabeth I. Although selection of entries (other than on Greece) seems arbitrary, most essays achieve a high degree of coherence. The format occasions two quibbles: a list of contributors is missing, and the index omits names of theorists. This volume calls for a successor that will tackle other themes and spell out criteria of selection.

□ *Competitors* This LEXICON boasts of being experimental. In transmitting research from the University of Paris IV, it breaks ground on how myths are reworked. Many of the essays amplify ones in **259** Bonnefoy/Doniger, eds., *Mythologies* (1981, 1991). The latter's part 6, "Western Civilization in the Christian Era," deploys forty-four entries that complement those here. Bonnefoy's themes range from "Justin the Gnostic," "Pan Among Cabalists and Alchemists of the Renaissance" and "Orpheus in the Renaissance" to "The Androgyne," "The Isis of Romanticism," "Hölderlin's Dionysus" and "Napoleon as Myth." These two French LEXICONS belong together. Volume 5 of **215** Akoun, ed., *Mythes et croyances du monde entier* (1985) is more popular than either. Jeffrey, ed., *A Dictionary of Biblical Tradition in English Literature* (1992) canvasses vastly more material (all inspired by the Bible) but does not pursue methodology so resolutely. **276** Simek, *Dictionary of Northern Mythology* (1984, 1993) traces literary reception of some of the very myths that this work omits. Scholars in the humanities will relish essays in this COMPANION on Greek, Near Eastern and biblical figures. No other work except **257** Ranke, ed., *Enzyklopädie des Märchens* (1977-) deploys so many retellings of so many themes from such diverse cultures.

□ *Summary* This path-breaking LEXICON compiles a couple of thousand retellings of a couple of hundred themes that have been selected rather arbitrarily. Scholars of literature will feast on the bounty, while scholars of religion will marvel to see how ancient materials get transformed.

262 (1992) Carolyne Larrington, ed., *The Feminist Companion to Mythology (London: Pandora, 1992); also in paperback (San Francisco: Thorsons, 1992); 480 pages; two indexes (names, themes), pp. 463-80; no general bibliography; forty black-and-white photographs.

□ *Scope* This REVISIONIST COMPENDIUM rethinks world mythology with the charm of an INTRODUCTION and the rigor of a HANDBOOK. Nineteen authorities (twelve of them from Britain) analyze sources and debates concerning women in world mythology. Sixteen regional chapters cover the Near East, Europe, Asia, Oceania and America (but not Africa), climaxed by three chapters on contemporary issues. Most of the essays inventory female figures in myth, dissect recent debates and propose new perspectives. Pursuing interplay between "constants and variables," the volume explores how study of myth "introduces us to new ways of looking at social structure . . . in particular . . . women's roles across different cultures and historical periods" (p. ix). In seeking to recover originating cultures' interpretations of their own myths, the authors warn against the "hijacking" of myth by any group of interpreters, whether Freudian, Nazi or feminist. In particular, the book repudiates the practice of blurring "differences about the goddesses of different cultures in order to assimilate them to a single supreme figure" (p. x). As the one goddess exfoliates into many, vigor of argument, breadth of perspective and depth of research surge.

□ *Strengths* Few COMPENDIA boast so many highly original chapters that function also as INTRODUCTIONS. In essays by Julia Vytkovskaya on "Slav Mythology," Birgitte Sonne on "Mythology of the Eskimos," Susanna Rostas on "Mexican Mythology" and Elizabeth Diab on "Hawaii," unlikelihood of the topic guarantees freshness. These chapters delineate entire cultures. On "Greece," Barbara Smith inventories four goddesses, nine maidens, five wives, five mothers and one "magical woman" (Medeia), as well as twenty-one "lesser female figures," before classifying roles of women in ritual. In "Celtic Goddesses," Juliette Wood recounts sources and identifies types like "the Sovereignty Figure" as a device for chiding Matthew Arnold and W. B. Yeats for backing "into the twilight." In a bracing chapter on "Scandinavia," the editor differentiates seven types that range from "Wooing the Reluctant Girl" through "Abduction and Betrayal" to "The Warrior Destroyed and the Heroine Who Survives." In writing on "The Hebrew God and His Female Companions," Athalya Brenner vents disillusionment with "one-gender representation of the divine." As regards South Asia, Emily Kearns inventories women's roles in "Indian Myth" before confronting "two simultaneous patterns of apprehension, whereby goddesses both are and are not differentiated" (p. 222). A culture such as India's that devalues differentiation readily assimilates goddesses to a single prototype, for femaleness itself (i.e., the goddess) is said to engender "multiplicity, or its illusion" (p. 223).

Isobel White and Helen Payne isolate "Australian Aboriginal Myth" from that of other cultures on the grounds that aborigines' "mythic beings . . . are human beings with supernatural powers rather than supernatural beings, and they are neither worshipped nor propitiated" (p. 251). Surprisingly, this is the only article to invoke at length Joan Bamberger's seminal paper "The Myth of Matriarchy" (1974). Bamberger argued that myths about loss of the "Rule of Women" recycle a boy's initiation, for that custom tends to impose a "severe and sudden separation from the rule of women to the rule of men . . ." (p. 261). As Bamberger put it, "The myth of the Rule of Women . . . [is] a replay of these crucial transitional stages in the life cycle of an individual male" (p. 261). Three of the most original chapters come at the end. In "Witchcraft as Goddess Worship," Rosemary Ellen Guiley deplores the name "witchcraft" chosen by Gerald B. Gardner for a neopaganism that "presents itself as the antithesis of witchcraft as sorcery" (p. 422). Jane Caputi surveys contemporary women's "quest to reclaim that symbolizing/naming power . . . to discover, revitalize, and create a female oral and visual mythic tradition and use it, ultimately to change the world" (p. 425). Having chided Mary Daly for "Dreaming in Female" and Barbara Walker for rehabilitating the crone, she praises instead Caroline Merchant and ecofeminists like Carol Lee Sanchez. Caputi lauds Sanchez for envisioning "a non-Indian Tribal community" that will recognize "all things in the known universe to be equally sacred" (p. 435).

No less exhilarating is Diane Purkiss's critique of "masculinists" like Robert Graves. They deny women power to poetize but expect them "to regulate male poetic output" (p. 443). Purkiss urges liberation from such "masculine discourse of myths," decrying Graves's obsession with "truths *about* femininity *for* men" in writers as diverse as Mary Renault, Monica Sjöö and Barbara Walker. The latter "adopt the Jungians' essentialist propositions" in order to fancy themselves to be "bearers of secret feminine knowledge actually unavailable to male writers" (p. 444). The volume climaxes by urging a fresh start in telling women's stories. This COMPENDIUM furthers that endeavor. It cuts a wide swath through world mythology without sinking into MENIPPEAN lists.

□ *Weaknesses* Such a book cannot help causing offense, for it challenges single-factor interpretations of every sort. Jungians in particular get scolded as "essentialists" who would lock women into what Purkiss calls "bodily femininity." Indeed, some may object to the word "feminist" in the title because the book criticizes so many varieties of feminism. In such a sweeping book, omission of Africa and of new religious movements in Japan (particularly Tenrikyo) is regrettable. Adding up to thirty-two pages, individual bibliographies cite works almost entirely in English, and they vary enormously in length. There is only one-fourth of a page of titles on the ancient Near East and one-half page on the Maori, compared to three pages each on South America and Australia, and five on Southwest Native Americans. An annotated general bibliography would have strengthened the introduction.

□ *Competitors* All scholars will find this REVISIONIST COMPENDIUM a fountain of information and insight. In assailing ideology, it advances debate on issues great and small. Among positions it rejects is that of **260** Barbara G. Walker, *The Woman's Encyclopedia of Myths and Secrets* (1983), which for all its lore persists in construing women as the "dark continent" of myth. Masculinist ANATOMIES like Robert Graves, *The White Goddess: A Historical Grammar of Poetic Myth* (New York: Farrar, Straus & Cudahy, 1948), or Monica Sjöö, *The Great*

Cosmic Mother: Rediscovering the Religion of the Earth (San Francisco: Harper, 1987) are scolded for restricting women to the task of transmitting among themselves what men have disdained. **272** Ann and Imel, *Goddesses in World Mythology* (1993) assembles data on about six thousand female deities and their attributes, while hailing them now and then as carriers of what males repress. A REVISIONIST LEXICON on adjacent topics is Elizabeth Wright, ed., *Feminism and Psychoanalysis: A Critical Dictionary* (Oxford and Cambridge, Mass.: Blackwell Reference, 1992). It repulses one-sidedness with equal verve. On issues about women, *The Feminist Companion* cuts deeper than **5** Eliade, ed., *The Encyclopedia of Religion* (1987), which offers no articles comparable to these. *The Feminist Companion* ranges wider than **64** Newsom and Ringe, eds., *The Women's Bible Commentary* (1992), whose genre obliges it to exalt biblical texts. Together with Kees Bolle's articles in **5** *The Encyclopedia of Religion,* both books help to bridge the gulf that separates study of myth from study of religion. *The Feminist Companion* belongs in the library of every scholar of myth or world religions. It corrects extravagance of every sort.

□ *Summary* This model HANDBOOK illuminates cultures, dissects controversies and opens vistas. Every humanist should own it.

263 (1993) Roy Willis, ed., *World Mythology* (New York: Henry Holt, 1993); 320 pages; index, pp. 311-20; general bibliography, pp. 308-9; about 300 color photographs in the text; cross-references only in the introduction, pp. 19-34.

□ *Scope* In nineteen chapters arranged geographically, this lavish COMPENDIUM introduces high points of world mythology. By devoting at least ten pages to regions as diverse as the Celtic world, Northern Europe, Mesoamerica, Australia and Oceania, this "World Mythography" invites a reader to construct comparisons. Various chapters narrate major myths (particularly of creation) or analyze topics like "Taoist Myth" (pp. 98-100), "Mongolian Shamanism" (pp. 108-9) or "Early and

Lost Gods" (pp. 192). Other chapters offer ahistorical accounts of such matters as "The Flood" in Sumer and Babylon, "Buddhist Myths" in India, China and Japan, and "Myths and Gods of Ireland." Color illustrations depict artifacts, manuscript illuminations and sculpture as well as a map in each chapter. Notwithstanding sponsorship by the Joseph Campbell Foundation, no school of interpretation prevails, least of all Jungian or Eliadean. Arranged by region, the bibliography cites advanced works (entirely in English). The index references proper names and themes such as "demons," "moon deities" and "tricksters."

□ *Strengths* Juxtaposition of text and image is unmatched, making this the most photogenic INTRODUCTION to world mythology. A typical page deploys a survey of a region's myths, a retelling of one myth, and one or two color illustrations. Concise writing by twenty experts (most of them not well known) highlights a region's tales, emphasizing, for example, malevolent spirits in Eastern Europe, creation myths in China and five principal deities in India (with their "Incarnations"). Forty pages on Greece deliver compact retellings of deities, consorts, heroes and monsters as well as of the Trojan War. Twenty pages on Egypt, twenty on India and forty on ancient Greece constitute the longest chapters, while one or two pages recount basics of Jain, Inuit, Siberian, Mayan and Hawaiian tales. As if to compensate for neglecting history, there is no trace of New Age effusion or anti-European bias. Lack of technical and foreign words makes a glossary superfluous.

□ *Weaknesses* This is a primer, not a LEXICON or historical survey. Offering breadth rather than depth, it ignores religious studies. Roy Willis's introduction, "Great Themes of Myth," classifies themes in an inoffensive Campbellian manner. Only the introduction formulates comparisons among regions, and no entry mentions controversies about method or sources. Scholars of Sumerian, Indo-European or Siberian diffusion will be scandalized at refusal to trace filiations from one culture to another. Inevitably, the more one knows about a region, the less satisfying its chapter becomes.

□ *Competitors* Devoid of pretension, *World Mythology* helps to ease the rigors of **259** Bonnefoy/Doniger, eds., *Mythologies* (1981, 1991) or the selectivity of **312** Moon, ed., *An Encyclopedia of Archetypal Symbolism* (1991). **258** Cavendish, ed., *Mythology: An Introduction* (1980) covers similar ground in a less captivating format. Limpid retelling and luxuriant photographs enhance Veronica Ions, *The World's Mythology in Color* [1974] (Edison, N.J.: Chartwell Books, 1987). As distance between study of myth and study of religion continues to widen, none of these books does anything to bridge the gap. On the functions of myth in religious studies, **2** Crim, ed., *The Perennial Dictionary of World Religions* (1981, 1989) remains useful, and **262** Larrington, ed., *The Feminist Companion to Mythology* (1992) uncommonly stimulating. **7** Cancik, ed., *Handbuch religionswissenschaftlicher Grundbegriffe* (1988-) carries discussion of method to a higher plane. Methodological naiveté notwithstanding, *World Mythology* assists first encounters.

□ *Summary* Visually stunning but methodologically inert, this COMPENDIUM introduces deities, heroes and tales worldwide.

5.1.2 WHO'S WHOS

OVERVIEW: THE NEED FOR A NEW GENRE WHO'S WHOS of deities have multiplied during the past decade. Postmodernism in academia and questers' longing for lost traditions have combined to foster curiosity about deities and mythical heroes. These WHO'S WHOS enable an inquirer to locate a deity by name and often by region. At least one LEXICON is a masterpiece: **275** van der Toorn, Becking and van der Horst, eds., *Dictionary of Deities and Demons in the Bible (DDD)* (1995). Apart from it and **265** Cotterell (1979, 1986), **268** Mercatante (1988) and **269** Allardyce (1991), the others minimize cultural context. **268** Mercatante, *The*

Facts on File Encyclopedia of World Mythology and Legend (1988) is the most comprehensive. Among shorter WHO'S WHOS not analyzed here, a French one that treats two hundred figures excels: Fernand Comte, *The Wordsworth Dictionary of Mythology* (Edinburgh: Chambers, 1988, 1991).

LIST OF WORKS ANALYZED

264 (1931) Bessie G. Redfield, *Gods: A Dictionary of the Deities of All Lands* (New York: Putnam's, 1931)

265 (1979, 1986) Arthur Cotterell, *A Dictionary of World Mythology* (Oxford and New York: Oxford University Press, 1986)

266 (1981) Richard Carlyon, *A Guide to the Gods* (New York: Morrow, 1981)

267 (1984, 1987) Manfred Lurker, *Dictionary of Gods and Goddesses, Devils and Demons* (London: Routledge, 1987; New York: Routledge, 1988); translated from *Lexikon der Götter und Dämonen* (Stuttgart: A. Krämer, 1984)

268 (1988) Anthony S. Mercatante, *The Facts on File Encyclopedia of World Mythology and Legend* (New York: Facts on File, 1988)

269 (1991) Pamela Allardice, *Myths, Gods and Fantasy* (Santa Barbara, Calif.: ABC-CLIO, 1991)

270 (1992) Marjorie Leach, *Guide to the Gods* (Santa Barbara, Calif.: ABC-CLIO, 1992)

271 (1993) Michael Jordan, *Myths of the World: A Thematic Encyclopedia* (London: Kyle Cathie, 1993)

272 (1993) Martha Ann and Dorothy Myers Imel, *Goddesses in World Mythology* (Santa Barbara, Calif.: ABC-CLIO, 1993); also in paperback (New York and Oxford: Oxford University Press, 1995)

273 (1994) Guida M. Jackson, *Encyclopedia of Traditional Epics* (Santa Barbara, Calif.: ABC-CLIO, 1994)

274 (1994) David Adams Leeming and Margaret Adams Leeming, *Encyclopedia of Creation Myths* (Santa Barbara, Calif.: ABC-CLIO, 1994); also in paperback (New York: Oxford University Press, 1996)

275 (1995) Karel van der Toorn, Bob Becking and Pieter W. van der Horst, eds., *Dictionary of Deities and Demons in the Bible (DDD)* (Leiden, New York and Köln: Brill, 1995)

ANALYSIS OF WORKS

264 (1931) Bessie G. Redfield, *Gods: A Dictionary of the Deities of All Lands* (New York: Putnam's, 1931); 347 pages; index (by cultures), pp. 317-47.

□ *Critique* This pioneering WHO'S WHO supplies entries of one to eight lines on deities, heroes and sacred books of world religions. There are no bibliographies. It retains interest as an early attempt to meet a need that has mushroomed.

□ *Summary* This work exudes innocence as a precursor of today's WHO'S WHOS of deities.

265 (1979, 1986) Arthur Cotterell, *A Dictionary of World Mythology* (Oxford and New York: Oxford University Press, 1986); 314 pages; index, pp. 303-14; general bibliography, pp. 297-302; seven maps; 12 black-and-white photographs; also in paperback.

□ *Critique* This one-author WHO'S WHO of deities, heroes and legendary figures is amazingly comprehensive. Entries unfold alphabetically under each of seven regions (West Asia, South and Central Asia, East Asia, Europe, America, Africa, Oceania). Headnotes of about ten pages outline historical developments within each region. Entries narrate tales, sketch context, and outline influence. The section on Europe intermingles Greek, Roman, Celtic and Norse entries and touches on "Bestiaries," "Coronation," "Purgatory" and "Witches." Arranged by regions, the bibliography cites only English-language works, some as old as Sir George Grey's classic on New Zealand, *Polynesian Mythology* (1855).

□ *Summary* This is the fullest brief WHO'S WHO of world mythology available in English.

266 (1981) Richard Carlyon, *A Guide to the Gods* (New York: Morrow, 1981); 404 pages; index, pp. 389-404; no bibliography.

□ *Critique* This one-author WHO'S WHO retells without commentary tales of deities and founders (including the Buddha). Entries are arrayed by regions within continents, so that the Middle East is divided into "Egyptian," "General" and "Gnostic," and then alphabetically within a unit. Length varies from two lines to two pages. Highly unusual are eight pages on gnostic figures such as Cain and John the Baptist (among Mandeans).

□ *Summary* This WHO'S WHO deftly retells the stories.

267 (1984, 1987) Manfred Lurker, *Lexikon der Götter und Dämonen* (Stuttgart: A. Krämer, 1984); English translation, *Dictionary of Gods and Goddesses, Devils and Demons* (London: Routledge, 1987; New York: Routledge, 1988); 451 pages; no index; bibliography, pp. 447-51; some line drawings; also in paperback.

□ *Critique* This DICTIONARY of deities worldwide comes from a German expert on ancient Egyptian religion. Entries state attributes, emblems and genealogy without retelling the tales. There being no individual bibliographies, a master bibliography overflows with French and German titles. Entries are fewer than in Jordan, ed., *Encyclopedia of Gods* (1992) and shorter than in **268** Mercatante, *The Facts on File Encyclopedia of World Mythology and Legend* (1988).

□ *Summary* This DICTIONARY identifies figures from mythology worldwide.

268 (1988) Anthony S. Mercatante, *The Facts on File Encyclopedia of World Mythology and Legend* (New York: Facts on File, 1988); xviii & 807 pages; two indexes (cultural and ethnic, general), pp. 723-807; classified bibliography, pp. 699-715; line drawings throughout.

□ *Critique* This monumental one-author WHO'S WHO of deities, heroes and other figures contains 3,227 entries from world mythology. An annotated bibliography of over three hundred English-language works discloses the depth of research that underpins this tour de force. Varying greatly in length, entries quote tales, state crosscultural equivalences, and list alternative names but lack bibliographies. The introduction (pp. xiii-xviii) outlines schools of interpretation, carefully differentiating among "myth," "legend," "folktale," "fairy tale" and "fable." This most comprehensive one-volume WHO'S WHO of deities and heroes is also one of the most reliable. It marks a heroic achievement by a single author.

□ *Summary* This monumental WHO'S WHO canvasses world mythology with rigor. The classified bibliography is a gem.

269 (1991) Pamela Allardice, *Myths, Gods and Fantasy* (Santa Barbara, Calif.: ABC-CLIO, 1991); 232 pages; no index; bibliography, pp. 230-32.

□ *Critique* This concise one-author DICTIONARY dispenses about five hundred witty articles on deities, heroes and exotic creatures. Figures are described, context elucidated, and comparisons suggested (with cross-references), but tales are not retold. A lively mind has selected oddities as well as standard fare, creating a book to delight the browser.

□ *Summary* This is the most enjoyable WHO'S WHO of deities and creatures.

270 (1992) Marjorie Leach, *Guide to the Gods* (Santa Barbara, Calif.: ABC-CLIO, 1992); xii & 995 pages; index, pp. 923-95; bibliography, pp. 881-922.

□ *Critique* This massive WHO'S WHO compiles about twelve thousand names of deities, each with at least one bibliographical citation. A foreword by Michael Owen Jones of the UCLA Center for the Study of Comparative Folklore and Mythology tells how for twenty-five years the author and her husband combed anthropological literature. Their innovation consists in assigning world deities to fifty-three categories that range from "Weather Gods" and "Fertility" through "Fishing" and "Roads and Locations" to "Justice" and "Gods of Wine." No other WHO'S WHO manipulates such a huge database or devises such intricate classifications. Entries average four to five lines and do not specify alternative spellings, as does **268** Mercatante (1988).

□ *Summary* This work coordinates an exhaustive WHO'S WHO of deities with bibliography of fieldwork on the world's religions.

271 (1993) Michael Jordan, *Myths of the World: A Thematic Encyclopedia* (London: Kyle Cathie, 1993); xvii & 302 pages; index (by culture), pp. 298-302; no general bibliography; chronology, pp. xvi-xvii.

□ *Critique* Written by a self-taught anthropologist, this DICTIONARY groups about three hundred myths worldwide into seventeen chapters such as "Myths of Birth," "Myths of Confrontation" and "Myths of the Otherworld." Each entry states culture of origin and retraces literary provenance before retelling a story. Tight narration and deft juxtapositions make browsing a pleasure. This is one of the better compilations of myths retold. In a previous volume, *Encyclopedia of Gods* (London: Kyle Cathie, 1992), Jordan characterizes twenty-five hundred deities too briefly.

□ *Summary* This DICTIONARY situates three hundred myths provocatively.

272 (1993) Martha Ann and Dorothy Myers Imel, *Goddesses in World Mythology* (Santa Barbara, Calif.: ABC-CLIO, 1993); also in paperback (New York: Oxford University Press, 1995); xx & 655 pages; two indexes (name and attribute), pp. 543-655; general bibliography, pp. 531-42. The Oxford University Press edition has 100 illustrations.

□ *Critique* Compiled by two anthropologists, this WHO'S WHO of goddesses and their attributes distributes about six thousand entries through fifteen geographical sections. Goddesses are held to include those that were "demonized" into "monsters, evil spirits, and witches," as well as "fairies or nymphs" who were "trivialized" (p. ix). Averaging two to five lines in length, entries list attributes and cite one or two sources. Major deities or clusters command entries of one-eighth to one-half a page. They sketch genealogy, retell tales, trace diffusion, specify transformations and cite bibliography. A roster of variant names sketches a web of interlocking cults (concerning, for example, "Artemis," "Isis," and "Amaterasu").

Perhaps five hundred in number, longer

entries sometimes view goddesses as personifying traits that males have shunned. Except in the introduction, emphasis on men's dismissal of women's deities obtrudes less than in **260** Barbara G. Walker, *The Woman's Encyclopedia of Myths and Secrets* (1983). Regional sections vary enormously in length. Eighty pages on India, seventy-five on Greek and Roman empires and fifty on Oceania constitute the longest. Egypt commands twenty-five pages, Africa only twenty. Eastern Europe elicits thirty-five pages, Western Europe (mainly Celtic) only thirty. Forty pages on the Far East canvass China and Japan in loving detail. The shortest sections offer seventeen pages on the Himalayas and six on South America. Each of fifteen regional sections would have benefited from a headnote characterizing that region's deities. A bibliography cites over six hundred English-language works, but without classification. An "Index of Goddesses by Attribute" is a tour de force: under eighty-five imaginative headings like "Hunting," "Insects," "Minerals" and "Selflessness" deities are listed by region. This tool sets *Goddesses in World Mythology* apart. Consistency of terminology and dignity of style further distinguish it.

□ *Summary* This pioneering WHO'S WHO classifies about six thousand female deities by region and attribute. Longer entries are exhilarating.

273 (1994) Guida M. Jackson, *Encyclopedia of Traditional Epics* (Santa Barbara, Calif.: ABC-CLIO, 1994); xviii & 732 pages; index, pp. 675-732; general bibliography, pp. 655-70; 45 black-and-white photographs.

□ *Critique* This DICTIONARY compiles about two thousand entries on figures and titles from oral and written epic worldwide. Plot summaries and cross references abound, but not literary criticism. Entries range in length from three lines to ten pages.

□ *Summary* This fact-crammed DICTIONARY excels at plot summary but avoids theory.

274 (1994) David Adams Leeming and Margaret Adams Leeming, *Encyclo-*

pedia of Creation Myths (Santa Barbara, Calif.: ABC-CLIO, 1994); also in paperback (New York: Oxford University Press, 1996); 330 pages; index, pp. 317-30; general bibliography, pp. 311-13.

□ *Critique* This DICTIONARY retells about one hundred creation myths, nearly half from North America. The retellings are cross-referenced in thematic entries like "Incest in Creation Myths" or "Collision Creation Theory." The writing is vivid and the coverage worldwide.

□ *Summary* Astute retellings and ingenious interpretations buttress this DICTIONARY.

275 (1995) Karel van der Toorn, Bob Becking and Pieter W. van der Horst, eds., *Dictionary of Deities and Demons in the Bible (DDD)* (Leiden, New York and Köln: Brill, 1995); xxxvi & 887 pages; index (of names and concepts) unpaginated at the end; general bibliography (i.e., list of abbreviations), pp. xxii-xxx.

□ *Critique* Edited in Utrecht, this meticulous LEXICON recruited 102 mostly European authorities to scrutinize four hundred names that the Bible assigns to deities, demons and heroes, either explicitly or as part of place names. About a quarter of the names crop up in liturgy (e.g., "Cherubim," "Melchizedek," "Day Star"). Whether dealing with Hebrew or Greek, the writing is exceptionally clear. Heavily cross-referenced to emphasize borrowings, most articles deploy four sections, of which the third runs longest: (1) the name as it emerges in the Bible with a count of the passages; (2) the figure in its culture(s) of origin; (3) the figure's role in the Old Testament, including the Septuagint, and/or the New Testament; (4) multilingual bibliography, running as long as a page (e.g., on "Jesus," "Kurios" and "Logos"). Pivotal terms like "Angel," "God" and "Mediator" command separate entries on usage in the Hebrew Bible and the New Testament. Choice of entries is electrifying: alongside at least twenty Greek deities (e.g., "Aphrodite," "Apollo," "Artemis," "Nike") come Babylonian ones ("Ishtar," "Marduk," "Tiamat"), not to mention Egyptian ("Apis," "Horus," "Isis,"

"Osiris"), Canaanite ("Mot") and Philistine ("Dagon"). Seventeen names incorporating "Baal" fill twenty-four pages, but Latin entries are sparse (e.g., "Fortuna," "Legio"). Phrases that occur only once get their due ("Father of the Lights," "Fear of Isaac"), as do terms pertaining to the deceased (the "Dead," "Rephaim," "Sheol"). Two virtuosic articles debate dozens of hypotheses concerning "Yahweh." Other articles probe mythic parallels to "Joseph" and "Moses" as well as to honorifics like "Dominion," "Saints" and "Most High" ("Hypsistos").

Historians of religion accord similar treatment to "Holy Spirit," "Torah" and "Son of Man." Place names such as "Tigris," "Jordan," "Yehud" and "Zion" likewise get explicated. Several dozen deified objects elicit crosscultural analysis, as in "Fire," "Moon," "Mother," "Oak," "Sea" and "Stars." Heroes like "Aeneas," "Enoch," "Jason" and "Menelaos" also crop up, not to mention personifications like "Wisdom" and "Wrath." Better than any BIBLE DICTIONARY, this LEXICON explains abstract nouns such as "Glory" and "Dynamis." By contextualizing the familiar, this WHO'S WHO springs surprises on every page, not least in the bibliographies.

□ *Summary* This exhilarating LEXICON traces origin and diffusion of all names of deities or heroes mentioned in the Bible. Authority rings out.

5.1.3 REGIONAL

OVERVIEW: MYTH AS INVITATION TO CULTURAL HISTORY

These works expound mythology of a specific region while also sketching a culture. Although they treat religion in some depth, rarely do they implement methodology from religious studies. However informative, these works do not center on religious issues. 276 Simek, *Dictionary of Northern Mythology* is a model of the genre.

LIST OF WORKS ANALYZED

276 (1984, 1993) Rudolf Simek, *Dictionary of Northern Mythology* (Cambridge, U.K.: D. S. Brewer, 1993)

277 (1989) Robert D. Craig, *Dictionary of Polynesian Mythology* (New York: Greenwood, 1989)

278 (1990) Jan Knappert, *The Aquarian Guide to African Mythology* (Wellingborough: Aquarian, 1990)

279 (1991) Margaret Bunson, *The Encyclopedia of Ancient Egypt* (New York: Facts on File, 1991)

280 (1991) Gwendolyn Leick, *A Dictionary of Ancient Near Eastern Mythology* (London and New York: Routledge, 1991)

281 (1992) Jeremy Black and Anthony Green, *Gods, Demons, and Symbols of Ancient Mesopotamia: An Illustrated Dictionary* (London: British Museum; Austin, Tex.: University of Texas Press, 1992)

282 (1992) Sam D. Gill and Irene F. Sullivan, eds., *Dictionary of Native American Mythology* (Santa Barbara, Calif.: ABC-CLIO, 1992)

283 (1992) Peter Berresford Ellis, *Dictionary of Celtic Mythology* (New York: Oxford University Press, 1992; paperback, 1994)

284 (1992) Jan Knappert, *Pacific Mythology: An Encyclopedia of Myth and Legend* (London: Aquarian, 1992); also in paperback (San Francisco: Thorsons, 1992)

ANALYSIS OF WORKS

276 (1984, 1993) Rudolf Simek, *Dictionary of Northern Mythology* (Cambridge, U.K.: D. S. Brewer, 1993); xiv & 424 pages; no index; general bibliography, pp. 381-424.

□ *Scope* This REALLEXIKON of Germanic mythology debuted as *Lexikon der germanischen Mythologie* (Stuttgart: Kröner, 1984). The translation incorporates revisions derived from no fewer than two hundred reviews of the original. The term "Northern" designates Scandinavians, Goths, Angles, and Saxons, but not Celts. Each entry on a mythical figure supplies linguistic facts, brief characterization, deeper information and bibliography, before outlining reception by artists and writers. Besides a WHO'S WHO of mythical beings, articles treat concepts ("Soul," "Fate"), days of the week ("Thursday," "Friday"), lesser figures ("Dwarves," "Berserks") and above all customs ("Burial Mound," "Death Penalty," "Exposure of Children," "Yule"). A riveting entry considers whether Scandinavians built "Temples." Scholars like Jakob Grimm, Sophus Bugge and Georges Dumézil as well as artists like Richard Wagner win entries. Bibliographies overflow with works in Scandinavian languages.

□ *Strengths* The heart of this REALLEXIKON lies in articles on mythic figures. Odin commands six entries, Thor and Baldr four each, totaling twenty-five pages among them. Each article recounts how functions and tales developed, differentiating sources and refuting later misconceptions. An entry on "Loki," for example, reports that he is a "god without a function" (p. 195). Subsections on "Reception" list writers, painters and musicians who depicted or transformed a given theme, particularly after 1750. Thus reinterpretations by Richard Wagner, who actually learned Old Norse, are ascribed to him, as in "Valkyries." Objects and places like the "world tree" (Yggdrasill) or the "center of the earth" (Midgard) are explicated. Articles on methodology define concepts like "Euhemerism" and "Magic" but not "Religion" or "Hermeneutics." Pains are taken to differentiate *interpretatio germanica* (i.e., Germans' renaming of Roman deities) from *interpretatio romana* (i.e., Romans' renaming of Germanic gods). Both differ from *interpretatio christiana,* which demoted heathen gods into devils and dwarves into demons. A number of entries, including two pages on "History of Research," recount the field's struggle to recuperate from Nazi hijacking of it. Few reference books balance critique of sources, narration of myths and catalogs of reception so adeptly.

□ *Weaknesses* As befits a REALLEXIKON, there is no discussion of literary theory or schools of interpretation. Whether by Jung, Lévi-Strauss or feminists, theories of myth are neither expounded nor exemplified. Likewise, countries, peoples and cities

elicit no entries. Nor are the social sciences invoked to illuminate religious practices. Although history of the field emerges in a WHO'S WHO of interpreters, one misses influential ones like Johann Gottfried Herder or Alfred Rosenberg. Forty-four pages of general bibliography list over sixteen hundred titles but without subheadings.

□ *Competitors* Cultural historians of both medieval and modern Europe will relish this REALLEXIKON. It revolutionizes study of Northern mythology by assembling sources, tracing evolution of deities, and explicating customs. Attention to reception since 1800 has no parallel. No other reference work comes close to presenting Germanic mythology so clearly or exhaustively. Volume 2 of **256** Haussig, ed., *Wörterbuch der Mythologie* (1972) is sketchy by comparison, and **259** Bonnefoy/Doniger, eds., *Mythologies* (1981, 1991) offers just sixteen pages on the same material. Carolyne Larrington's chapter "Scandinavia" in her **262** *The Feminist Companion to Mythology* (1992) introduces this heritage. Simek's volume will not soon be replaced.

□ *Summary* This magisterial REALLEXIKON expounds myths and their literary sources, explains customs, and traces reception.

277 (1989) Robert D. Craig, *Dictionary of Polynesian Mythology* (New York: Greenwood, 1989); xlvii & 409 pages; index, pp. 339-409; general bibliography, pp. xxix-xlvii.

□ *Critique* This WHO'S WHO of deities spans the Pacific from New Zealand to Hawaii. About a thousand entries scrutinize individual deities (with bibliography). The author reports that before 1500 seagoing canoes made the Polynesians the world's most widely spread people. Not surprisingly, their mythology ranks among the world's most diverse. Newcomers may prefer the less demanding **284** Knappert, *Pacific Mythology* (1992).

□ *Summary* This WHO'S WHO differentiates hundreds of deities in a degree of detail that specialists will savor.

278 (1990) Jan Knappert, *The Aquarian Guide to African Mythology*

(Wellingborough: Aquarian, 1990); 272 pages; no index; general (English-language) bibliography, pp. 270-72.

□ *Critique* Harvesting thirty years of fieldwork throughout Africa, this DICTIONARY introduces peoples, deities and concepts. In order to highlight divergences among regions, Islam is largely excluded (except for "Mahdi"). Stories concerning animals receive priority, as do categories like "magic," "possession" and "talisman." The writing is less assured than in the author's other INTRODUCTORY DICTIONARIES. Distinctions among regions tend to blur, and lack of individual bibliographies disappoints. The author may have known this material too intimately to knead it into a DICTIONARY.

□ *Summary* This DICTIONARY canvasses indigenous peoples and myths throughout Africa, while largely ignoring Islam and Christianity.

279 (1991) Margaret Bunson, *The Encyclopedia of Ancient Egypt* (New York: Facts on File, 1991); xvi & 291 pages; bibliography, pp. 284-86; index, pp. 287-91; line drawings, charts and maps throughout.

□ *Critique* This GLOSSARY and WHO'S WHO of ancient Egypt covers from 3200 to 1070 B.C.E. Deities, rulers, places, customs and key terms provide a brief REALLEXIKON as well. Religious concepts get explained at length, including a page on Akhenaton and half a page on ma'ah. An entry on "Art and Architecture" runs ten pages. There are no individual bibliographies, but genealogical charts and diagrams abound. Unfortunately, the author omits developments after 1000 B.C.E., not to mention history of Egyptology. The writing is lucid, and illustrations perspicuous. Unbeatable competition comes from a MEGA-ENCYCLOPEDIA, Wolfgang Helck and Wolfhart Westendorf, eds., *Lexikon der Ägyptologie,* 8 vols. (Wiesbaden: Harrassowitz, 1975-87).

□ *Summary* This up-to-date INTRODUCTION excels as a self-teacher.

280 (1991) Gwendolyn Leick, *A Dictionary of Ancient Near Eastern Mythology* (London and New York: Routledge, 1991); xiii & 199 pages; 26 black-and-white plates; no index; general bibliography, pp. 176-78; glossary (of places), pp. 168-75.

□ *Critique* In short entries this GLOSSARY and WHO'S WHO introduces Mesopotamian deities and texts, sometimes with bibliography. It omits Canaan and Egypt. Texts are referenced by opening lines. The longest entry delivers five pages on the "Gilgamesh Epic," while Inanna commands four pages and Marduk two. Synopses of "Cosmogonies," "Flood-myths," "Underworld" and "Demons" integrate the material, as do overviews of "Sumerian Mythology," "Sumerian Kings" and "Hittite Mythology." The work's retellings amplify both **281** Black and Green, *Gods, Demons and Symbols of Ancient Mesopotamia: An Illustrated Dictionary* (1992) and **12** Knappert, *The Encyclopaedia of Middle Eastern Mythology and Religion* (1993).

□ *Summary* This handy WHO'S WHO introduces Sumerian and Babylonian mythology but scants comparisons to other cultures.

281 (1992) Jeremy Black and Anthony Green, *Gods, Demons, and Symbols of Ancient Mesopotamia: An Illustrated Dictionary* (London: British Museum; Austin: University of Texas Press, 1992); 192 pages; no index; general bibliography, pp. 191-92; photographs and line drawings throughout; also in paperback.

□ *Critique* This taut DICTIONARY surveys religion and myth in the successive cultures of Mesopotamia from 3400 B.C.E. to the start of the Common Era. A WHO'S WHO of deities accompanies entries of one to three pages on texts ("Gilgamesh") and religious practices ("Sacred Marriage," "Magic and Sorcery"). The longest entry, on "Death and Funerary Practices," runs four pages. Sharp writing and splendid illustrations make browsing a pleasure. The time span is longer and coverage of religion deeper than in **280** Leick, *A Dictionary of Ancient Near Eastern Mythology* (1991).

□ *Summary* This DICTIONARY introduces Sumerian and Babylonian religion authoritatively.

282 (1992) Sam D. Gill and Irene F. Sullivan, eds., *Dictionary of Native*

American Mythology (Santa Barbara, Calif.: ABC-CLIO, 1992; New York: Oxford University Press, 1994); xxx & 425 pages; index (by tribe), pp. 411-25; general bibliography, pp. 363-410; maps, pp. xx-xxx; black-and-white photographs and drawings throughout.

□ *Critique* This DICTIONARY of myth and ritual retells stories with reverence. Myths crop up under Native American names, while rituals appear in English, as in "Sun Dance," "Sweat Lodge" and "Tobacco Society." Skeletal bibliography accompanies each entry. Crosscultural concepts like "Amulets" and "Names and Naming" elicit long articles. Nearly fifty pages of bibliography should have been classified by topic.

□ *Summary* This INTRODUCTORY DICTIONARY retells myths and expounds rituals in plain language.

283 (1992) Peter Berresford Ellis, *Dictionary of Celtic Mythology* (New York: Oxford University Press, 1992; paperback, 1994); 232 pages; general bibliography, pp. 225-32. Analyzed on the basis of the paperback edition.

□ *Critique* This lively DICTIONARY by an adept of modern Druidism canvasses Celtic mythology throughout the British Isles and Brittany, while briefly mentioning ancient Gaul, Galatia and Iberia. Entries on regions stand out (e.g., Britain, Brittany, Cornwall, Gallia Cisalpina and Ireland), as do surveys of "Celt," "Celtic Church" and "Gaul." Major languages elicit entries as in "Breton," "Gaulish," "Scottish Gaelic" and "Welsh Language." The WHO'S WHO retells tales about hundreds of deities, heroes, beasts and other entities but omits all saints except Brendan. All this proceeds with a twinkle of "mischievous fun" (p. 15). A very few articles treat methodology (e.g., "Oral Tradition," "Head, Cult of," "Invasion Myths") but not archeology or psychology. Even without psychologizing, choice lore abounds, such as the likelihood that Jonathan Swift knew the figure of Iubdan, who in myth visited a diminutive people (p. 137). The introduction (pp. 1-15) differentiates among six surviving Celtic cultures (Irish, Manx, Scots, Welsh, Cornish, Breton) and sketches history of

the study of their literatures, particularly Irish and Welsh. The volume recalls **100** Farmer, *The Oxford Dictionary of Saints* (1978, 1992), which likewise emphasizes Great Britain. Building on an earlier work by Ellis, *A Dictionary of Irish Mythology* (London: Constable, 1987; Santa Barbara: ABC-CLIO, 1989), this DICTIONARY probes literature but not archeology to characterize "one of the great founding cultures of Europe" (p. 58). It complements a REALLEXIKON of archeology, Miranda J. Green, *Dictionary of Celtic Myth and Legend* (London: Thames & Hudson, 1992), which references figures, objects, sites and methods (with 243 photographs). Green redresses Ellis's neglect of material culture.

□ *Summary* This jaunty DICTIONARY delineates history, literature and mythology of six surviving Celtic peoples.

284 (1992) Jan Knappert, *Pacific Mythology: An Encyclopedia of Myth and Legend* (London: Aquarian, 1992); also in paperback (San Francisco: Thorsons, 1992); 334 pages; no index; general bibliography, pp. 333-34.

□ *Critique* In his patented format of WHO'S WHO and DICTIONARY, Knappert retells myths and identifies deities across hundreds of islands, from New Zealand and Australia to Hawaii and Easter Island. Crosscultural comparisons abound. This is one of the most useful of Knappert's four regional DICTIONARIES of mythology. It is more cohesive than **277** Craig, *Dictionary of Polynesian Mythology* (1989), which supplies individual bibliographies. Greater profundity marks Jean Guiart, "General Study of Oceanic Thought" ("Etude générale de la pensée océanienne"), in **289** Jacob, ed., *Encyclopédie universelle philosophique*, 1 (1989): 1532-48.

□ *Summary* Knappert's virtuosity as a lexicon-maker imparts coherence to a swath of cultures and religions.

5.2 PHILOSOPHY OF RELIGION AND ETHICS

OVERVIEW: PHILOSOPHY EXPLICATES RELIGION Philosophy invites

epitomizing, whether in GLOSSARIES, LEXI-
CONS, HANDBOOKS or ENCYCLOPEDIAS.
This section of the directory does not pre-
tend to canvass reference works on philosophy. Instead it calls attention to recent
works that emphasize history of thought,
in English and even more in French. Evaluations are briefer than elsewhere in the
directory. The intent is to identify works
that expound ethics, cultural history and
above all philosophy of religion, a subfield
that boasts no reference book. Works that
combine philosophy with theology are
analyzed under 2.4.1 "Theology: Nonconfessional." A useful introduction to
the literature is Hans E. Bynagle, *Philosophy: A Guide to the Reference Literature*
(Littleton, Colo.: Libraries Unlimited,
1986), which evaluates almost ninety reference books (pp. 15-48). Amid such
profusion, a MEGA-ENCYCLOPEDIA, **289**
Jacob, ed., *Encyclopédie philosophique
universelle,* 5 vols. (1989-92) towers. Its
general bibliography (1:1739-908) unfurls five pages on reference works in
philosophy (1:1752-56) and three on
philosophy of religion (1:1883-86), not
to mention a list of 634 periodicals
(1:1897-908).

A major INTRODUCTION appeared too
late to include: Ted Honderich, ed., *The
Oxford Companion to Philosophy* (Oxford
and New York: Oxford University Press,
1995).

LIST OF WORKS ANALYZED

285 (1967) Paul Edwards, ed., *The
Encyclopedia of Philosophy,* 8 vols. (New
York: Macmillan, 1967)

**115 (1967, 1986) John Macquarrie,
ed.,** *Dictionary of Christian Ethics* (London: SCM; Philadelphia: Westminster,
1967); second edition, James F. Childress
and John Macquarrie, eds., *The Westminster Dictionary of Christian Ethics* (Philadelphia: Westminster, 1986). Analyzed
under 2.8 "The Westminster/SCM Dictionaries."

**286 (1971-) Joachim Ritter [d.
1974] and Karlfried Gründer [since
1974], eds.,** *Historisches Wörterbuch der
Philosophie,* planned in 10 vols. (Basel:

Schwabe, 1971-)

287 (1985) Gordon Stein, ed., *The
Encyclopedia of Unbelief,* 2 vols. (Buffalo:
Prometheus Books, 1985)

**288 (1988) G[eorge] H[enry] R[ad-
cliffe] Parkinson, ed.,** *The Handbook of
Western Philosophy* (New York: Macmillan, 1988)

8 (1989, 1991) Geddes MacGregor,
Dictionary of Religion and Philosophy
(New York: Paragon, 1989; paperback,
1991). Analyzed under 1.1 "The World's
Religions: Alphabetical Reference Books."

289 (1989-92) André Jacob, ed.,
Encyclopédie philosophique universelle, 5
vols. (Paris: Presses Universitaires de
France, 1989-92)

290 (1989-) Richard Goulet, ed.,
Dictionnaire des philosophes antiques,
planned in at least 10 vols. (Paris: CNRS,
1989-)

**291 (1990) Étienne Souriau and
Anne Souriau, eds.,** *Vocabulaire d'es-
thétique* (Paris: Presses Universitaires de
France, 1990)

**292 (1991) Hans Burkhardt and
Barry Smith, eds.,** *Handbook of Meta-
physics and Ontology,* 2 vols. (Munich:
Philosophia Verlag, 1991)

293 (1991) John Yolton, ed., *The
Blackwell Companion to the Enlightenment* (Oxford: Blackwell Reference, 1991;
New York: Blackwell, 1992; paperback,
1995)

**294 (1992) Lawrence C. Becker and
Charlotte B. Becker, eds.,** *Encyclopedia
of Ethics,* 2 vols. (New York and London:
Garland Publishing, 1992)

295 (1992) Peter A. Angeles, *The
HarperCollins Dictionary of Philosophy,*
2d ed., rev. (New York: HarperPerennial,
1992)

296 (1992) Ian P. McGreal, ed.,
Great Thinkers of the Western World (New
York and London: HarperCollins, 1992)

297 (1994) Simon Blackburn, *The
Oxford Dictionary of Philosophy* (New
York: Oxford University Press, 1994)

**81 (1995) David J. Atkinson and
David H. Field, eds.,** *New Dictionary of
Christian Ethics and Pastoral Theology*
(Downers Grove, Ill., and Leicester, U.K.:

InterVarsity Press, 1995). Analyzed under 2.4.2 "Theology: Protestant."

ANALYSIS OF WORKS

285 (1967) Paul Edwards, ed., *The Encyclopedia of Philosophy,* 8 vols. (New York: Macmillan, 1967); about 5000 pages; index, 8:387-544; no general bibliography.

□ *Critique* This historical ENCYCLOPEDIA covers all periods, regions and schools with signed articles and massive bibliographies. Ninian Smart's entries on Asian philosophies retain their luster. The WHO'S WHO of philosophers is one of the most complete ever published. An unsurpassable rival is **289** Jacob, ed., *Encyclopédie philosophique universelle* (1989-92).

□ *Summary* This ENCYCLOPEDIA expounds doctrines and historical comparisons, the bibliographies having become out of date.

286 (1971-) Joachim Ritter [d. 1974] and Karlfried Gründer [since 1974], eds., *Historisches Wörterbuch der Philosophie* (Basel: Schwabe, 1971-); planned in 10 vols.; eight vols. to date (through *SC*); about 6000 pages to date; index volume planned.

□ *Critique* This heroic MEGA-ENCYCLOPEDIA expounds historical usage in philosophy and the humanities generally in cultures East and West from antiquity to the present. The aim is to map *history of usage,* not to dissect issues. Written by more than twelve hundred contributors, thousands of articles locate origins of terms and changes in usage throughout major European and Asian languages from the dawn of writing to the present. Edited by founder Joachim Ritter (d. 1974), the first three volumes are more concise than later ones. Citations and paraphrases abound. A cluster of entries on "Religion" and its compounds is well nigh inexhaustible, not to say MENIPPEAN (8:632-780). Entries on "Mythos/Mythologie" (6:281-318) and "Säkularisierung" (8:1133-61) are equally rich. Each volume begins with its own *Vorbemerkung.* Taken together, these prefaces elucidate methodology in the "history of concepts" *(Begriffsgeschichte).* Fixating

on history, too many entries display MENIPPEAN overinclusiveness. Many readers will prefer **289** Jacob, ed., *Encyclopédie philosophique universelle* because it debates substance and not just usage. Its volume 2, *Les Notions philosophiques: Dictionnaire,* explores vastly more terms, but seldom in equal depth. The *Historisches Wörterbuch* serves devotees not of philosophy but of history of terminology.

□ *Summary* This MEGA-ENCYCLOPEDIA traces history of terms and their usage in major European and Asian languages. MENIPPEAN zeal will exhaust all but the hardiest.

287 (1985) Gordon Stein, ed., *The Encyclopedia of Unbelief,* 2 vols. (Buffalo: Prometheus Books, 1985); xvi & 819 pages; index, pp. 801-19; general bibliography, pp. 754-56; five appendices (on meetings, organizations, publishers, periodicals), pp. 753-99.

□ *Scope* For this vigorously antireligious LEXICON the editor recruited one hundred specialists to write 203 signed articles with bibliography. More than half the articles make up a WHO'S WHO of freethinkers in Europe and North America since 1600. Synoptic articles survey "Unbelief" in European countries, including the Netherlands and Scandinavia, and in their literatures. Each major world religion elicits an entry like "Islam, Unbelief in," as do Asian countries such as India, China, Japan and Australia, not to mention "the Ancient World." These entries apart, the work is unabashedly Eurocentric, ignoring tribal religion, colonialism and field study of religion. The writing is clear (albeit sometimes shrill), and cross-references abound.

□ *Strengths* This historical LEXICON celebrates classical European free thought in articles lauding its protagonists, positions and aversions. As a work of self-definition, *The Encyclopedia of Unbelief* espouses the ideology it describes, occasionally even ridiculing antagonists. A WHO'S WHO of more than one hundred thinkers ranges from the obligatory (P. B. Shelley, G. B. Shaw, H. G. Wells) to the obscure (Joseph McCabe, William Kingdon Clifford, Sylvain Maréchal). Each biography chronicles antireligious writings, campaigns and causes célèbres, sometimes citing out-of-the-way sources. Historical syntheses canvass "Agnosticism," "Humanism," "Skepticism" and "Universalism." Solid historical research underpins these overviews, as it does a long article by H. James Birx on "Evolution and Unbelief." Dialectics distinguishes Kai Nielsen's entry on "Reason" and Antony Flew's on "Miracles, Unbelief in." Lively panoramas unfold in Ralph McCoy's "Freedom of the Press and Unbelief" and Hugh McLean's "Russian Literature, Unbelief in." By way of exception, George V. Tomashevich's entry on "Devil, Unbelief in the Concept of the" extols mythopoeic power in Zoroastrianism. Most of the authors, however, have no truck with myth. To his credit, the editor displays more modesty and imagination than some of his contributors, notably in an entry "Deathbeds of Unbelievers," which refutes legends about Voltaire, Thomas Paine, Robert Ingersoll and Charles Bradlaugh. Even while lamenting this volume's militancy, historians of thought can exploit its WHO'S WHO and historical overviews.

□ *Weaknesses* Advocating philosophical rationalism, this LEXICON ignores recent advances in religious studies. Neither social science nor literary theory is allowed to modify religious issues. No entry singles out "Anticlericalism" as heroes of the Enlightenment and of Victorian free thought hold sway. Nor do mythology or psychoanalysis command entries (apart from ones on Freud and Reich). Some entries, such as that on Ludwig Feuerbach, rely on secondary authorities and venture no conclusions. A sprinkling of humor would have lightened the solemnity. As a work of self-definition for freethinkers, it ignores a wider public. Most scholars will value the WHO'S WHO and the bibliographies more than the ideology.

□ *Competitors* Viewed as a historical LEXICON of one strand within European and American thought, *The Encyclopedia of Unbelief* holds its own among reference works in history of philosophy. Paul Edwards,

editor of **285** *The Encyclopedia of Philosophy* (1967), contributes an aciduslous preface. He seems not to have noticed that articles in the earlier work are more distinguished and more fair-minded than in this. Issues of free thought versus Christian orthodoxy elicit more subtle analysis in 77 McGrath, ed., *The Blackwell Encyclopedia of Modern Christian Thought* (1993). However copious the documentation, ideology can no longer sustain a reference book. Postmoderns will deem this endeavor regressive.

□ *Summary* Historians of European and American thought since 1600 will welcome the WHO'S WHO and the bibliographies but deplore the stridency.

288 (1988) G[eorge] H[enry] R[adcliffe] Parkinson, ed., *The Handbook of Western Philosophy* (London and New York: Macmillan, 1988); 935 pages; two indexes (names, subjects), pp. 921-35; no general bibliography.

□ *Critique* This COMPENDIUM presents thirty-seven articles by mostly British scholars on major themes, problems and schools of European and American philosophy. Ronald W. Hepburn's entry on "The Philosophy of Religion" (pp. 857-77) introduces that field, adding a bibliography of thirty items. Although the format coincides with that of **21** Sutherland et al., eds., *The World's Religions* (1988), articles here are less REVISIONIST. Parkinson also edits the substantial *Routledge History of Philosophy*. Its volume 6, *The Age of German Idealism* (1993), and volume 8, *Twentieth-Century Continental Philosophy* (1994), are not to be missed.

□ *Summary* This COMPENDIUM serves beginners and experts alike.

289 (1989-92) André Jacob, ed., *Encyclopédie philosophique universelle*, 5 vols. in 3 (Paris: Presses Universitaires de France, 1989-92). Volume 1, *L'Univers philosophique* (1989), ed. André Jacob, has a general bibliography (1:1743-1908) and five indexes (1:1911-97). This volume underwent a second edition in 1991. Volume 2 in two parts, *Les Notions philosophiques: Dictionnaire* (1990), edited by Sylvain Auroux, has eleven indexes, 2:3231-97.

Volume 3 in two parts, *Les Oeuvres philoso-phiques* (1992), ed. Jean-François Mattéi, has four indexes, 3:4495-614. These volumes total nearly 10,000 pages. Analyzed further under 3.2.1 "Islam: Religion and Culture," 4.1 "Asian Religions" and 5.3.1 "Social Sciences of Religion, General."

□ *Critique* More than ten years in preparation, this MEGA-ENCYCLOPEDIA of history and issues of philosophy worldwide stands without peer. Volume 1, *L'Univers philoso-phique,* delivers 284 signed articles (each with multilingual bibliography) arranged in seventeen sections. Some twenty-five articles in section 16 on "Traditions and Writings" engage religion directly. Unexpected among these are Jean-Jacques Glassner on "Mesopotamian Philosophy" (1:1637-42), Jean Laclant on "The Thought of Pharaonic Egypt" (1:1642-46) and Gerhard Wehr on "Esotericism and Theosophy Today" (1:1676-80). A general bibliography (1:1743-908) divides into sixty sections. Volumes 2.1 and 2.2, *Les Notions philosophiques: Dictionnaire,* analyze concepts in signed articles of one to two pages (many with bibliography), canvassing Western philosophy in twenty-eight hundred pages and Asian in another 250. Articles on Islamic thought shine. Eleven indexes locate articles grouped by issue, field, religion or region.

Even more mind-boggling, signed articles in volumes 3.1 and 3.2, *Les Oeuvres philosophiques,* summarize the argument of no fewer than 8,178 Western treatises (or articles) and over five hundred Asian ones, with elaborate bibliography on each. Volume 3.2 alone digests no fewer than 3,738 works published between 1889 and 1990, arranged alphabetically by author. A caveat is in order: in each volume one needs to absorb the *Avant-Propos* before plunging in. Jean-François Mattéi's *Avant-Propos* (3:vii-xxii) explains the structure best. Imaginative sweep, precision of analysis, worldwide coverage, unstinting originality and boundless ambition make this one of the most impressive MEGA-ENCYCLOPEDIAS ever undertaken. Denis Huisman, ed., *Dictionnaire des philosophes* [1984], 2d ed., 2 vols. (Paris: Presses Universitaires de France, 1993) adds a WHO'S WHO of three thousand pages. The two projects comprise one of the masterworks of the twentieth century. They inspire awe.

□ *Summary* This MEGA-ENCYCLOPEDIA investigates thought worldwide in astounding depth, diversity and piquancy. Articles in the historical GLOSSARY (vol. 2) on Islam and Asian thought are nonpareil. Volume 3 expounding individual titles is the only work of its kind. More than ten thousand individual bibliographies dazzle the beholder. Such bulk may discourage browser and beginner alike, but experts will marvel.

290 (1989-) Richard Goulet, ed., *Dictionnaire des philosophes antiques,* planned in at least 10 vols. (Paris: CNRS, 1989-); 841 pages in vol. 1 (to "Axiothéa"); index of persons and works in each volume; four black-and-white plates, one color plate per volume.

□ *Critique* This HANDBOOK sorts out writings by and about ancient Greek and Roman philosophers stretching more than a thousand years from pre-Socratics through Augustine. Volume 1 (to "Axiothéa") presents signed entries (with multilingual bibliography) on ancient sources by and about 517 thinkers. With titles and phrases in Greek abounding, triage of sources displaces philosophical analysis. So many secondary works get cited as to require individual numbering within each article. The article on Aristotle comprises thirteen subentries running 170 pages, citing over five hundred items of bibliography. Christian theologians and heretics figure only insofar as they wrote philosophy. Thus Augustine commands ten pages (by Goulven Madec), Ambrose five and Arius none. A remarkable appendix retraces topography and archeology at Plato's Academy (1:693-789). No other period of thought has inspired anything like this MEGA-ENCYCLOPEDIA of texts by and about philosophers. It helps one to comprehend articles in **151** Klauser, ed., *Reallexikon für Antike und Christentum* (1950-) as well as in **67** Haase and Temporini, eds., *Aufstieg und Niedergang der römischen Welt* (1972-), especially volumes 36.1—36.7.

□ *Summary* No historian of ancient thought can afford to neglect this most exhaustive of WHO'S WHOS. Classifying of ancient texts and modern bibliography is unmatched.

291 (1990) Étienne Souriau and Anne Souriau, eds., *Vocabulaire d'esthétique* (Paris: Presses Universitaires de France, 1990); vii & 1415 pages; no index; no bibliography.

□ *Critique* This historical GLOSSARY enlisted thirty-six contributors to write eighteen hundred entries on technical terms in aesthetics. Begun as a labor of love as early as 1931, this gold mine sorts definitions from all periods and schools of thought, but without bibliographies. A briefer competitor, David E. Cooper, ed., *A Companion to Aesthetics* (Oxford and Cambridge, Mass.: Blackwell Reference, 1992), surveys persons and concepts in signed articles with bibliography.

□ *Summary* One of the bulkiest of GLOSSARIES, this work clarifies usage to a nicety.

292 (1991) Hans Burkhardt and Barry Smith, eds., *Handbook of Metaphysics and Ontology,* 2 vols. (Munich: Philosophia Verlag, 1991); 1015 pages; index, pp. 957-1015; no general bibliography.

□ *Critique* This meticulous LEXICON recruited 320 contributors to write on persons, schools, methods and concepts in Western metaphysics from the beginning. Multilingual bibliographies and exacting analysis distinguish the 450 entries. The editors declare an intent "to document the most important traditional and contemporary streams in the two overlapping fields of metaphysics and ontology." Six articles on metaphysics and seven on logic bristle with technicalities. Arresting historical entries include "Arabic School," "Pythagoras, Pythagoreanism" and "Parmenides." Trained philosophers will relish the stringency, but beginners may well prefer Jaegwon Kim and Ernest Sosa, eds., *A Companion to Metaphysics* (Oxford and Cambridge, Mass.: Blackwell Reference, 1995), which handles persons and concepts more accessibly. It is piquant to compare both works with **87** Beinert and Fiorenza, eds.,

Handbook of Catholic Theology (1987, 1995), which airs similar terminology.

□ *Summary* This demanding LEXICON sets a standard for disentangling intricacies.

293 (1991) John Yolton, ed., *The Blackwell Companion to the Enlightenment* (Oxford: Blackwell Reference, 1991; New York: Blackwell, 1992; paperback, Cambridge, Mass.: Blackwell, 1995); 581 pages; index, pp. 561-81; general bibliography, pp. 9-10; black-and-white plates.

□ *Critique* This historical LEXICON scrutinizes the European and to a lesser extent the American Enlightenment (1720-80) in long signed articles and shorter unsigned ones. About half the one hundred contributors are British. A WHO'S WHO identifies over a thousand persons in ten to fifteen lines without bibliography, while topical articles canvass themes, countries and controversies (with English-language bibliography). Entries on religion include "Catholicism," "Protestantism" and "Orientalism" but not "Deism" or "Theology." A sparkling five pages on "Religion" comes from Alister McGrath.

□ *Summary* A thorough WHO'S WHO and imaginative essays distinguish this INTRODUCTION to European and American thought and culture of the eighteenth century.

294 (1992) Lawrence C. Becker and Charlotte B. Becker, eds., *Encyclopedia of Ethics,* 2 vols. (New York and London: Garland Publishing, 1992); 1462 pages; two indexes (to articles and bibliographies), pp. 1341-1462.

□ *Critique* This historical LEXICON dispenses four hundred entries on ethics by 275 contributors. Articles on thinkers, doctrines and controversies average five to eight pages and furnish multilingual bibliographies. A WHO'S WHO embraces major Eastern and Western thinkers of all periods, including Ramanuja, Pascal and G. E. Moore. Each of the world religions elicits a synoptic article such as "Jewish Ethics," "Taoist Ethics" and "Buddhist Ethics." An article entitled "Middle East, Ethical Traditions in Ancient" encompasses Egypt, Sumeria and Iran. Particularly imposing is a ninety-page survey in twelve parts, "History of Western Ethics." The entry "Women Moral Philosophers" inventories more than fifty thinkers. This LEXICON offers richer detail than do forty-seven synoptic chapters in Peter Singer, ed., *A Companion to Ethics* (Oxford and Cambridge, Mass.: Blackwell Reference, 1991). Likewise 115 Childress and Macquarrie, eds., *The Westminster Dictionary of Christian Ethics* (1986) proves less thorough. In this LEXICON writing is lucid, scholarship up-to-date and indexing superb.

□ *Summary* Retracing intellectual history of all periods and regions, this conspectus of ethical thought characterizes thinkers and pinpoints issues. Ethical thinking commands no fuller LEXICON.

295 (1992) Peter A. Angeles, *The HarperCollins Dictionary of Philosophy,* 2d ed., rev. (New York: HarperPerennial, 1992); vii & 343 pages; no index; no bibliography; also in paperback.

□ *Critique* This lively GLOSSARY delivers five- to ten-line definitions of technical terms. A WHO'S WHO describes more than a hundred major philosophers in entries ranging from three lines to twenty (for Hegel). Definitions are among the clearest anywhere, but there is no bibliography. Skill at taxonomy multiplies denotations, supplying thirteen for "Law, scientific" and six for "Animism." Similarly, "Mind, types of theories of" states ten positions, and "Stoics" numbers sixteen doctrines. As a companion to the author's 74 *Dictionary of Christian Theology* (1985), this volume displays even greater precocity. Anyone fond of enumerations will delight.

□ *Summary* Concise definitions, painstakingly coordinated, distinguish this GLOSSARY. No pocket dictionary is handier on terminology and schools.

296 (1992) Ian P. McGreal, ed., *Great Thinkers of the Western World* (New York and London: HarperCollins, 1992); xiii & 572 pages; no index; general bibliography, pp. 561-70.

□ *Critique* This INTRODUCTORY WHO'S WHO arrays signed articles on 116 thinkers in chronological order of birth. It functions well as a self-teacher and complements a DICTIONARY like 8 MacGregor,

Dictionary of Religion and Philosophy (1989, 1991). A companion volume, McGreal, ed., *Great Thinkers of the Eastern World* (New York and London: HarperCollins, 1995), fills a gap.

□ *Summary* Anyone seeking an INTRODUCTION to Western philosophers will enjoy this WHO'S WHO.

297 (1994) Simon Blackburn, *The Oxford Dictionary of Philosophy* (New York: Oxford University Press, 1994); vii & 408 pages; no index; no secondary bibliography.

□ *Critique* This vigorous GLOSSARY and WHO'S WHO offers meticulous definitions and biographies ranging from two lines to two columns. The author canvasses all periods and schools, including Asian ones. He disentangles issues in formal logic as well as controversies in contemporary philosophy. A WHO'S WHO identifies contributions and cites major works by perhaps two hundred thinkers. This "playground for browsers" sprouts formulations that cry out to be quoted but scants religion and omits secondary bibliography.

□ *Summary* This scrupulous GLOSSARY and WHO'S WHO unravels issues both classical and contemporary.

5.3 SOCIAL SCIENCES OF RELIGION

OVERVIEW: UNEVEN COVERAGE

The virtuosity demonstrated by scholars of religion in composing reference books does not extend to the social sciences. Although social scientists have tackled religion for a century and a half, intensively since the 1960s, no major reference works are devoted exclusively to sociology of religion or anthropology of religion. Only recently did psychology of religion begin to command volumes of its own. To be sure, 5 Eliade, ed., *The Encyclopedia of Religion* (1987) filled this gap through articles on the history and methodology of these fields, but inevitably contributions are uneven. A German masterpiece, 7 Cancik et al., eds., *Handbuch religionswissenschaftlicher Grundbegriffe* (1988-), probes concepts, and volume 1 surveys the major fields. General reference works on the social sciences scant religion, although one classic, Edwin R. A. Seligman, ed., *Encyclopedia of the Social Sciences*, 15 vols. (New York: Macmillan, 1930-37), does not. Only two COMPENDIA on the world's religions exalt the social sciences: **307** Clévenot, ed., *L'État des religions dans le monde* (1987) and **22** Baladier, ed., *Le Grand Atlas des religions* (1990). Two contemporary Roman Catholic works exploit the social sciences with cross-disciplinary flair: **137** Jacquemet, ed., *Catholicisme* (1948-) and **110** Sartore and Triacca, eds., *Dictionnaire encyclopédique de la liturgie* (1984, 1992-). The same can be said of a breezy German LEXIKON: Ulrich Ruh, David Seeber and Rudolf Walter, eds., *Handwörterbuch religiöser Gegenwartsfragen* (Freiburg, Basel and Vienna: Herder, 1986). Embodying the "blurring of genres," its hundred articles make soul-searching seem almost easy. More such works are needed.

5.3.1 GENERAL

OVERVIEW: EXPOSITIONS OF METHODOLOGY These general reference works expound methods of the various social sciences. Overviews scrutinize study of religion but do not always advertise that fact. Among the pioneers, **300** Châtelet et al., eds., *Dictionnaire des oeuvres politiques* (1986, 1989) bursts with novelty. No one writing for Christians has assessed how to confront social science better than Richard H. Roberts, "Social Science and Christian Thought" in **77** McGrath, ed., *The Blackwell Encyclopedia of Modern Christian Thought* (1993), pp. 608-16.

LIST OF WORKS ANALYZED

298 (1968, 1990) Claude Grégory, ed., *Encyclopaedia Universalis*, 30 vols. (Paris: Encyclopaedia Universalis, 1968; 2d ed., 1984; 3rd ed., 1990)

299 (1983-85) Frank Whaling, ed., *Contemporary Approaches to the Study of Religion in 2 Volumes*, 2 vols. (Berlin, New York, Amsterdam: Mouton Publishers, 1983-85)

300 (1986, 1989) François Châtelet, Olivier Duhamel and Evelyne Pisier, eds., *Dictionnaire des oeuvres politiques* (Paris: Presses Universitaires de France, 1986; 2d ed., rev., 1989)

301 (1989) Robert Kastenbaum and Beatrice Kastenbaum, eds., *Encyclopedia of Death* (Phoenix: Oryx, 1989); also in paperback (New York: Avon Books, 1993)

302 (1989-91) Helen Tierney, ed., *Women's Studies Encyclopedia*, 3 vols. (New York and London: Greenwood, 1989-91)

289 (1989-92) André Jacob, ed., *Encyclopédie philosophique universelle*, 5 vols in 3 (Paris: Presses Universitaires de France, 1989-92)

303 (1993) Jennifer Bothamley, ed., *Dictionary of Theories* (London and Detroit: Gale, 1993)

304 (1994-) S[igfried] J. De Laet, ed., *History of Humanity*, planned in 7 vols. (Paris: UNESCO; New York: Routledge, 1994-)

ANALYSIS OF WORKS

298 (1968, 1990) [Claude Grégory, ed.] *Encyclopaedia Universalis* (Paris: Encyclopaedia Universalis, 1968-75; 2d ed., 1984; 3rd ed., 1990); first edition in 20 vols.; third edition in 30 vols. (about 30,000 pages): corpus, vols. 1-23; thesaurus index, vols. 24-27; symposia, vols. 28-30.

□ *Critique* During the late 1960s this unrivaled ENCYCLOPEDIA of natural and social sciences commissioned some of France's leading scholars to outline their field in three to six pages. Most articles published in 1968 survive into the 1990 edition, with occasional retouching from the 1970s and bibliography updated through the 1980s. Clarity and comprehensiveness distinguish these INTRODUCTIONS. Anthropology of religion inspires brilliance from Roger Bastide, who writes on "Religious Anthropology," "Initiation" and "Magic." Six articles on "Religion" include François-André Isambert on "Secularisation" and Jacques Maître on "Popular Religion." Four articles on "Myth" deploy Paul Ricoeur on "Philosophical Interpretation" and Marcel Detienne on "Epistemology of Myths." Dario Sabbatucci contributes one of the acutest pieces anywhere on "Syncretism." Separate entries tackle "Animism," "Shamanism" and "Totem and Totemism." Entries tend to cut deeper than their equivalents in 4 Poupard, ed., *Dictionnaire des religions* (1984, 1993). Anyone interested in European approaches to anthropology, sociology, or psychology of religion should frequent these pages, in which entire disciplines elicit model synopses. One wishes that more authors in 5 Eliade, ed., *The Encyclopedia of Religion* (1987) had matched the French at encapsulating methodology.

□ *Summary* Classic overviews of the social sciences of religion are reprinted from 1968. No general English-language reference work comes close to the *Encyclopaedia Universalis* at explicating method.

299 (1983-85) Frank Whaling, ed., *Contemporary Approaches to the Study of Religion in 2 Volumes*, 2 vols. (Berlin, New York, Amsterdam: Mouton Publishers, 1983-85); x & 492 and ix & 302 pages; three indexes (scholars, names, topics), 1:455-92 and 2:283-302; no general bibliography.

□ *Scope* This COMPENDIUM commissioned ten leading scholars to retrace how history of methodology in the humanities and social sciences affects religion. Volume 1 on general approaches presents Ursula King on "Historical and Phenomenological Approaches," Frank Whaling on "Comparative Approaches" and "The Study of Religion in a Global Context," Kees Bolle on "Myths and other Religious Texts" and Ninian Smart on "The Scientific Study of Religion in Its Plurality." Volume 2 on social sciences deploys David Wulff on "Psychological Approaches," Michael Hill on "Sociological Approaches I" (empirical) and Günter Kehrer and Bert Hardin on "Sociological Approaches II" (systematic), Tony Jackson on "Social Anthropological Approaches" and Jarich Osten on "Cultural Anthropological Approaches." Each chapter furnishes massive multilingual bibliography. Indexes of names and concepts are exemplary.

□ *Strengths* Frank Whaling of the University of Edinburgh recruited chiefly British and American colleagues to reconstruct history and debates in major fields of religious studies. These chapters deliver the fullest accounts anywhere, and the bibliographies remain unexcelled. In volume 1 Ursula King's 130-page article on history and phenomenology is a book in itself, with twelve pages of bibliography. With acumen and wit Kees Bolle sums up half a lifetime's reflection on myth. Frank Whaling's 230 pages synthesize a phenomenal amount of material on comparative methods and formulate novel contrasts among six non-Western masters: Ananda Coomaraswamy, Sarvepalli Radhakrishnan, D. T. Suzuki, Seyyed Hossein Nasr, John Mbiti and Wing-Tsit Chan (1:391-443). Volume 2 dispenses the only adequate histories in English of the social sciences of religion. David Wulff's seventy pages anticipate his **311** *Psychology of Religion* (1991), which is even more readable. Michael Hill expounds and criticizes a spectrum of empirical sociologists, while Kehrer and Hardin explore structural functionalism and system theory. Tony Jackson and Jarich Osten divide anthropology between social and cultural. Each chapter defines religion, circumscribes methods of study, and traces lineages from grand masters like Durkheim, Weber, Freud and Malinowski down to the 1970s. Bibliographies are magnificent but need to be updated.

□ *Weaknesses* Ten authors writing thirteen chapters (including four by the editor) cannot achieve cohesion. To move from chapter to chapter disorients, particularly in volume 2. If volume 1 achieves better syntheses, volume 2 proposes richer veins for research. Contributors sketch divergences both across and within fields, attesting to an explosion in approaches. Many readers will wish that all chapters had achieved the cogency of Kees Bolle's on myth.

□ *Competitors Contemporary Approaches* still holds its own. The chief rival in English remains 5 Eliade, ed., *The Encyclopedia of Religion* (1987). Its individual articles probe anthropology, sociology and (less adequately) psychology. Overviews there accompany biographies of 150 scholars as well as entries on concepts like animism, taboo and dynamism. While certain articles in *The Encyclopedia of Religion* excel (not least those by Gregory Alles, Kees Bolle and Roland Robertson), taken together they attain less coherence than those in *Contemporary Approaches*. A German masterpiece, 7 Cancik et al., eds., *Lexikon religionswissenschaftlicher Grundbegriffe* (1988-), synthesizes material more compellingly, adducing an array of German-language works that seldom crop up in English. That HANDBOOK reconfigures the field for the 1990s.

□ *Summary* Indispensable to historians of methodology, *Contemporary Approaches* summarizes debates up to 1980 without achieving synthesis. Contributors view the field as mushrooming beyond the power of summary to corral it.

300 (1986, 1989) François Châtelet, Olivier Duhamel and Evelyne Pisier, eds., *Dictionnaire des oeuvres politiques* (Paris: Presses Universitaires de France, 1986; 2d ed., rev., 1989); viii & 1154 pages; index of persons, pp. 1133-45; no general bibliography.

□ *Critique* This REVISIONIST LEXICON recruited 108 (almost entirely French) authorities to expound and evaluate 163 seminal texts (including seventy French ones) in both political and social theory. Entries of two to fifteen pages deliver often startling analyses of texts ranging from the Pentateuch, Paul's Letters and Maimonides to key works by Sartre, Maritain, Gramsci and Adorno. Scholars of Christian thought will garner a wealth of insights concerning Augustine's *City of God,* Aquinas's *Summa theologica,* Hus's *De ecclesia,* Loyola's *Constitutions of the Company of Jesus* and Calvin's *Institutes.* Bruno Étienne's five pages on the Qur'an bristle with suggestions for reconceptualizing a book that he sees as being not so much a book as a "visual support for recitation." If Islam were to seek another name, Étienne proposes "Qur'anism." For reconstructing chronology of the surahs he recommends a translation by Régis Blachère, *Le Coran,* 3 vols. (Paris: Maisonneuve et Larose, 1947-51).

No less refreshing is Christine Buci-Gluckmann's analysis of Walter Benjamin's poignant *Angelus Novus* (1939-40), not to mention an eye-opening entry on Pierre Clastres's *La Société contre l'état* (1974). The latter's iconoclasm concerning politics in primal societies deserves acclaim. Comte, Durkheim, Weber and Freud receive their due as well as Pascal, Lamennais, Leroux and Renan but not Charles Péguy, Simone Weil or Ernst Bloch. These omissions are redeemed by unexpected inclusions such as Seneca's *Letters to Lucilius* and Suarez's *Defensio fidei* (1611). Few REVISIONIST LEXICONS shed so much light on familiar topics or tackle so many neglected masterpieces. Fueled by the "blurring of genres" within social sciences, searching analysis and choice bibliographies make this a treasure for historians of thought. As a bonus, religion seasons about half the entries.

□ *Summary* This REVISIONIST LEXICON scours texts from all periods and cultures for contributions to social and political theory. Originality abounds, not least regarding religion.

301 (1989) Robert Kastenbaum and Beatrice Kastenbaum, eds., *Encyclopedia of Death* (Phoenix: Oryx, 1989); also in paperback (New York: Avon Books, 1993); xix & 295 pages; index, pp. 287-95; black-and-white photographs throughout.

□ *Critique* For this imaginative LEXICON a seasoned editor recruited sixty contributors to outline information from the social sciences about death and dying. About two hundred practices, concepts, images and beliefs are presented. Bibliography abounds, but there is no WHO'S WHO. Articles on "Deathbed Scenes," "Death Fears and Anxiety" and "Memento Mori" assemble lore from a range of cultures. Cultural history enriches eighteen pages on "Survival Beliefs and Practices" in five Christian denominations and five world religions. Art historians will savor entries on "Cemeteries" and "Tombs." There is much discussion of suicide and of strategies for counseling the dying. A sympathetic article on "Zombie" characterizes voodoo as a means of inducing rejuvenation. Surprisingly readable, the book demystifies the macabre by presenting research from psychology and sociology. The tone is calm, often pastoral, and there is nothing of the gruesome or bizarre. This versatile LEXICON offers something for everyone.

□ *Summary* This dignified LEXICON applies social science to an astonishing array of topics about death today and in the past. Cultural historians will relish the bibliographies.

302 (1989-91) Helen Tierney, ed., *Women's Studies Encyclopedia,* 3 vols. (New York and London: Greenwood, 1989-91); 381,417 & 531 pages; index in each volume; general bibliography, 3:495-97.

□ *Critique* In order to summarize information about the status of women worldwide, this ENCYCLOPEDIA distributes signed articles (with bibliography) among three topical volumes. Volume 1 addresses "Views from the Sciences," volume 2 "Literature, Arts and Learning" and volume 3 "History, Philosophy and Religion." Volume 3 furnishes authoritative statements on such matters as "Arab Women," "Ascetics of India," "Hinduism" and "Purdah." At least fifty countries and regions elicit individual entries. Writing is succinct and bibliographies imaginative.

□ *Summary* Pithy entries about women's roles worldwide enrich this three-part ENCYCLOPEDIA.

289 (1989-92) André Jacob, ed., *Encyclopédie philosophique universelle,* 5 vols. in 3 (Paris: Presses Universitaires de France, 1989-92); 1:1437-569 on "Ethnologique" and 3:4129-489 on "Oral Cultures." Analyzed further under 3.2.1 "Islam," 4.1 "Asian Religions" and 5.2 "Philosophy of Religion and Ethics."

□ *Summary* Part one of this MEGA-ENCYCLOPEDIA delivers twenty-six path-breaking articles on ethnology (1:1437-569). Africa, the Americas and Oceania star (with massive bibliographies). With equal rigor, part three expounds major works of social science, both Western and indigenous (3:4129-489). These pages constitute an ENCYCLOPEDIA of method in ethnology.

303 (1993) Jennifer Bothamley, ed., *Dictionary of Theories* (London and De-troit: Gale, 1993); ix & 637 pages; index of persons, pp. 573-615; classified bibliography, pp. 565-71.

□ *Critique* This GLOSSARY defines over thirty-five hundred hypotheses or theorems from thirteen areas of the natural and social sciences. Twenty-three British contributors define concepts in ten to twenty lines, supplying one bibliographical item per entry. Although mathematics, physics and chemistry predominate, social sciences receive their share. Many entries bear the name of an investigator like Heisenberg or Max Weber. An "Index of People" furnishes birth and death dates of over two thousand thinkers.

□ *Summary* This GLOSSARY will help orient beginners to the natural and social sciences.

304 (1994-) S[igfried] J. De Laet, ed., *History of Humanity,* planned in 7 vols. (Paris: UNESCO; New York: Routledge, 1994-); vol. 1, *Prehistory and Beginnings of Civilization;* xxi & 716 pages; index, pp. 649-716; 140 black-and-white photographs; 70 maps.

□ *Critique* Meticulously planned, this COMPENDIUM aims to interpret global history from perspectives that are global in scope. Volume 1 delivers fifty-nine chapters by fifty authorities, mostly on regions, each with superb multilingual bibliography. Each volume employs an intercontinental team of editors, and coverage grows denser through time. Volume 5 will span the sixteenth to eighteenth centuries, volume 6 the nineteenth century and volume 7 the twentieth. A foreword by Charles Morazé (1:ix-xiv) and introduction by Georges-Henri Dumont (1:xv-xvi) explain the parameters. Billed as a "radical recasting" of a fifteen-volume UNESCO *History of Mankind: Cultural and Scientific Development* (1963-76), the *History of Humanity* promises to interpret global history from an unprecedented range of perspectives. It should become more authoritative with each volume.

□ *Summary* This gigantic COMPENDIUM of world history aspires to become the most global yet attempted. Articles, bibliographies and maps break new ground.

5.3.2 SOCIOLOGY

OVERVIEW: A FIELD IN NEED OF REFERENCE BOOKS No other field so cries out for a LEXICON as this one. There exists no adequate DICTIONARY of the sociology of religion. The closest thing to one is **307** Clévenot, ed., *L'État des religions dans le monde* (1987). A LEXICON of world history, Peter N. Stearns, ed., *Encyclopedia of Social History* (New York and London: Garland, 1994), probes topics like "Festivals," "Mariology" and "Pilgrimage."

LIST OF WORKS ANALYZED

305 (1969) Henri Desroche et al., *Dieux d'hommes: Dictionnaire des messianismes et millénarismes de l'Ère chrétienne* (Paris and the Hague: Mouton, 1969)

306 (1984, 1987) Bryan Wilson and Daisaku Ikeda, *Human Values in a Changing World: A Dialogue on the Social Role of Religion* (London: Macdonald, 1984; Secaucus, N.J.: Lyle Stewart, 1987)

307 (1987) Michel Clévenot, ed., *L'État des religions dans le monde* (Paris: La Découverte/Le Cerf, 1987)

308 (1989) Stuart Mews, ed., *Religion in Politics: A World Guide* (Chicago and London: World Guide, 1989)

309 (1992) Edgar F. Borgatta and Marie L. Borgatta, eds., *Encyclopedia of Sociology*, 4 vols. (New York: Macmillan, 1992)

ANALYSIS OF WORKS

305 (1969) Henri Desroche et al., *Dieux d'hommes: Dictionnaire des messianismes et millénarismes de l'Ère chrétienne* (Paris and the Hague: Mouton, 1969); 281 pages; no index; general bibliography, p. 266; two appendices (listing entries by century and region), pp. 267-81.

□ *Scope* A distinguished French sociologist of religion assembled during the 1960s this WHO'S WHO of founders and announcers of future salvation. The introduction (pp. 1-41) expounds Desroche's model of what we now call new religious movements. Be-

cause that label was not yet current, he coined the term "messialogy" to designate study both of aspirant messiahs and of the followers who await them. Desroche differentiated messianism (belief in a future savior) from millenarianism (the ideology of a socioreligious group led by a self-appointed messiah). A dictionary of messiahs (pp. 45-265) delivers more than a thousand entries, nearly all with multilingual bibliography. The majority of entries make up a WHO'S WHO of (1) founders, (2) proclaimers of second comings and (3) chroniclers of such movements. Regions encompass Europe, the Near East, North America, Brazil, Africa, the Near East and Japan but not India or China. Entries also treat new religious movements (e.g., Kimbangism, Tenrikyo, Fifth Monarchy Men), Islamic sects (e.g., Shi'ism, Babism) and one or two apocryphal gospels (e.g., *Barnabas*). By inviting readers to submit addenda, Desroche hoped to launch a database, but no sequel appeared.

□ *Strengths* A stylish epitomizer has distilled careers and beliefs of nearly a thousand founders and writers. Figures from twenty centuries, five continents and dozens of languages parade side by side. Classifying entries by century and region, an appendix collates the data (pp. 267-79). It shows that almost half the figures come from Europe since the seventeenth century. Not surprisingly, eccentric Frenchmen abound, including some little known like Ernest Hello, Pierre Pradié, Pierre Vintras and Dom Pernety. They accompany warhorses like Saint-Simon, Enfantin and Fourier. Not a few New Englanders crop up, among them Cotton Mather, John Eliot, Samuel Hopkins, Benjamin Gorton and Joseph Emerson. Articles on illuminists like Swedenborg, Jung-Stilling and Hoené-Wronski are models of their kind, although the concept of "illuminist" dangles undefined. From antiquity, the Gnostic Cerinthus (c. 100 C.E.) is celebrated as one of the earliest millenarians, Eusebius is instanced as a collator of second comings, and Lactantius (c. 260-330) is expounded on the Sybilline prophecies. Islam wins ample coverage on topics like "Islam," "Ismaéliens," "Chiisme" and "Mahdi, Mahdisme." A full page explains "Bab-Babisme." African founders of new religious movements number Isaiah Shembe, Simon Kimbangu and William Wade Harris. Cargo cults elicit at least a dozen entries. The book will delight browsers, for few other reference books sketch so many eccentrics or juxtapose such disparate cultures. One browses among movements and leaders, astounded by their audacity and diversity. Guilelessly, *Dieux d'hommes* celebrates messianic hopes of the 1960s.

□ *Weaknesses* Historians will welcome this database, even if sociologists may not. The capsule biographies remain among the most pungent ever written, but the conceptualization has dated. A typology of messiahs (pp. 11-22) is brilliant but quaint. Bibliographies rely too heavily on compilers like Le Roy Edwin Froom (on Americans), Alfred Félix Vaucher (on the Chilean Jesuit, Manuel Lacunza), Auguste Viatte (on European romantics) and Vittorio Lanternari (on European social movements). Certain omissions defy explanation: Nostradamus, Eliphas Lévi and Cao Dai. They seemed to lack appeal during the 1960s.

□ *Competitors* Assembled thirty years ago, this WHO'S WHO subjects piquant information to outdated categories. The latter perpetuate ones used in Seligman, ed., *The Encyclopedia of the Social Sciences* (1930-37), particularly in Hans Kohn's article, "Messianism" (10:356-64). Historians of Europe since 1500 will revel, for entries on several hundred eccentrics have no rival. These entries amplify articles by Jean Séguy on "Religious Non-conformisms" and Antoine Faivre on "Christian Esotericism" in **16** Puech, ed., *Histoire des religions,* 2 (1972): 1229-362. Desroche's entries on Asians and Africans can be updated from **5** Eliade, ed., *The Encyclopedia of Religion* (1987) and **9** Hinnells, ed., *Who's Who of World Religions* (1991). Articles on Islam need to be checked against **202** Glassé, *The Concise Encyclopedia of Islam* (1989). Reliable rethinking of recent European material pervades **77** McGrath, ed., *The Blackwell Encyclopedia of Modern Christian*

Thought (1993) and volume 5 of **215** Akoun, ed., *Mythes et croyances du monde entier* (1985).

□ *Summary* An incomparable epitomizer packed a mind-boggling array of new religious movements and their founders into a somewhat outdated database. No other WHO'S WHO features so many eccentrics.

306 (1984, 1987) Bryan Wilson and Daisaku Ikeda, *Human Values in a Changing World: A Dialogue on the Social Role of Religion* (London: Macdonald, 1984; Secaucus, N.J.: Lyle Stewart, 1987); 364 pages; index, pp. 353-64.

□ *Critique* This PHILOSOPHICAL DICTIONARY developed from conversations between Britain's preeminent sociologist of religion and the third president of the Sokka Gakkai Buddhist organization in Japan. Between 1979 and 1983 they exchanged written comments on "religion as a social phenomenon." These reflections coalesce into eighty-six headings arranged around six themes: (1) "Homo religiosus," (2) "Reason and Responsibility," (3) "The Problems of Organization," (4) "Some Historical Perspectives," (5) "Matters of Mind and Body" and (6) "The Wider Ethical Perspective." A splendid index facilitates access to persons and issues. Making up about two-thirds of the whole, Wilson's essays constitute the nearest thing to a PHILOSOPHICAL DICTIONARY on the sociology of religion that we are likely to see. Ikeda presents Buddhist reflections forthrightly and prods Wilson to compare Asia and Europe. Who among social scientists excels him at spicing rigor with subtlety?

□ *Summary* Few recent essays in sociology of religion generate such pungent insights. Dialectic between East and West flourishes.

307 (1987) Michel Clévenot, ed., *L'État des religions dans le monde* (Paris: La Découverte/Le Cerf, 1987); 640 pages; index, pp. 629-36; chronology, pp. 58-71; no general bibliography; maps and line drawings throughout.

□ *Scope* This virtuosic COMPENDIUM scans the horizon of the world's religions in 140 signed articles, each with French-language bibliography. Authors are nearly all French. Part 1 diagnoses seven contemporary situations (e.g., in Poland, Iran, Israel). Part 2 surveys eight great religions, omitting Sikhism and Zoroastrianism but including three syncretisms (Haitian voodoo, Baha'i, Umbanda). Part 3, "Religions in the World," collates statistics on religious adherence worldwide, segmented into thirty-three regions. Part 4, "Problematics," debates methodology in twenty-three essays. Part 5, "Religion and Society," implements sociology of religion in fifty case studies, many of them highly original. Throughout, the standpoint is nonconfessional and the argumentation refreshing, not least as regards Christianity (pp. 84-144, 437-56, 502-47).

□ *Strengths* This COMPENDIUM abounds in syntheses. Part 3 on religious demography deploys charts, maps and bibliography on thirty-three regions, among them former Indo-China and Central America. Although categories are less nuanced than in **32** Barrett, ed., *World Christian Encyclopedia* (1982), the data are more diverse. Parts 4 and 5 canvass the social sciences of religion, weighing methods and pursuing applications, above all in Europe and the Third World. Model syntheses come from Mohammed Allal Sinaceur on "Islam and Rationality" (pp. 456-62) and Christian Miquel on Hinduism (pp. 254-60, 469-73). Claude Geffré's argument that theology has entered the "hermeneutical age" (p. 451) sets a high standard, while Michel Meslin summarizes a life's work on development of the study of history of religion (pp. 431-36). Case studies in part 5 extend from catechesis in France (pp. 543-47) and Marian apparitions worldwide (pp. 553-57) through the cult of ancestors in Japan (pp. 550-53) to religious publishers (pp. 602-5). Fresh insights flow.

□ *Weaknesses* In part 3 on georeligious statistics, not everyone will favor an arrangement that divides Africa and the Americas into seven sectors each, and Asia into six. Nor are some categories, such as animism and syncretic cults, suitably precise. Certain pivotal topics like new religions (particularly in Japan) get short shrift. Bibliographies are overwhelmingly in French and omit reference books.

□ *Competitors* This brilliant COMPENDIUM folds three or four books into one. No English-language work digests demographic statistics so compactly or compares methods so deftly. **14** Harris et al., eds., *Longman Guide to Living Religions* (1994) classifies some of the same material (devoid of statistics) but with less flair. On demography, the standard work, **32** Barrett, ed., *World Christian Encyclopedia* (1982), is five times longer and far more fastidious, but until a new edition appears in 1997, it can be updated from here. Two other French COMPENDIA, **22** Baladier, *Le Grand atlas des religions* (1990) and **28** Delumeau, ed., *Le Fait religieux* (1993), expand certain approaches that *L'État des religions dans le monde* merely sketches. The three works exemplify French talent for scanning horizons.

□ *Summary* This sophisticated COMPENDIUM digests methodology, demography and case studies in sociology of religion worldwide. Few other volumes of the same size pack such a wallop.

308 (1989) Stuart Mews, ed., *Religion in Politics: A World Guide* (Chicago and London: World Guide, 1989); x & 332 pages; no index; no general bibliography.

□ *Critique* This DICTIONARY by and for political scientists treats about two hundred countries in signed articles (without bibliography). Although most entries run less than half a page, others report religious demography, parties and controversies in individual countries. Mark Juergensmeyer on India (ten pages) and Paul Morris on Israel (fifteen pages) write two of the richest articles. Political scientists will relish the information, but demography unfolds more fully in **32** Barrett, ed., *World Christian Encyclopedia* (1982).

□ *Summary* This DICTIONARY summarizes information about religious parties, debates and conflicts in two hundred nations.

309 (1992) Edgar F. Borgatta and Marie L. Borgatta, eds., *Encyclopedia of Sociology*, 4 vols. (New York: Macmillan, 1992); 2359 pages; index, 4:2283-359; no general bibliography.

□ *Critique* Less than ten out of nearly four

hundred articles in this ENCYCLOPEDIA of methods concern religion. All supply rich English-language bibliography. Rodney Stark writes on "Sociology of Religion" (4:2029-37), while Jeffrey K. Hadden analyzes "Religious Fundamentalism" and "Religious Movements" (3:1637-46). Larry Shinn's twelve pages on "World Religions" (4:2267-79) summarize insights of Black Elk, William James, Paul Ricoeur and Clifford Geertz. Begrudging coverage all but ghettoizes religious studies. The contrast to Seligman, ed., *Encyclopedia of the Social Sciences* (1930-37) could not be sharper, for the latter expounds religions, particularly Islam, in loving detail.

□ *Summary* This ENCYCLOPEDIA of methodology deemphasizes religion.

5.3.3 PSYCHOLOGY

OVERVIEW: A GAP FILLED In the past ten years the psychology of religion has inspired a shelfful of reference works. Many excel as self-teachers, and at least one, **311** Wulff, *Psychology of Religion* (1991), ranks as a masterpiece. No other branch of the social sciences of religion is so well served.

LIST OF WORKS ANALYZED
310 (1985) David G. Benner, ed., *Baker Encyclopedia of Psychology* (Grand Rapids, Mich.: Baker Book House, 1985)
114 (1990) Iris V. Cully and Kendig Brubaker Cully, eds., *Harper's Encyclopedia of Religious Education* (San Francisco: Harper, 1990)
311 (1991) David M. Wulff, *Psychology of Religion: Classic and Contemporary Views* (New York: Wiley, 1991)
312 (1991) Beverly Moon, ed., *An Encyclopedia of Archetypal Symbolism* (Boston and London: Shambhala, 1991)
313 (1991) Rosemary Ellen Guiley, *Harper's Encyclopedia of Mystical and Paranormal Experience* (San Francisco: Harper, 1991)
314 (1991) Arthur S. Berger and Joyce Berger, *The Encyclopedia of Parapsychology and Psychical Research* (New York: Paragon House, 1991)

ANALYSIS OF WORKS
310 (1985) David G. Benner, ed., *Baker Encyclopedia of Psychology* (Grand Rapids, Mich.: Baker Book House, 1985); xxiii & 1223 pages; no index; category index, pp. xiii-xxiii; no general bibliography.

□ *Scope* This masterful LEXICON condenses schools, methods, issues and thinkers in psychology for counselors and laypeople. One hundred seventy mostly American authorities contribute more than one thousand entries, many with bibliography. A "category index" classifies entries under twenty-five headings, marshaling one hundred entries on persons, forty on "Systems and Theories," sixty-two on "Human Development" and several hundred on "Psychopathology" and "Treatment Approaches and Issues." The center of gravity lies in counseling, not psychology of religion or religion as such. Division of labor limits the WHO'S WHO to sketching careers, while synopses of therapies expound thought. Shorter entries constitute a GLOSSARY, defining behaviors like "Confabulation" and "Malingering" as well as countless disorders. Nearly all the writers explain technical matters lucidly and append detailed bibliographies. Judiciousness reigns.

□ *Strengths* Although intended primarily for pastoral counselors, this LEXICON doubles as a self-teacher. It canvasses the field of psychology with astonishing thoroughness, differentiating classical therapies from at least a hundred that emerged since the 1950s. Certain luminaries delineate fields that they helped to shape, such as John G. Finch on "Existential Psychology and Psychotherapy" and Kirk Farnsworth in a glowing article on "Phenemonological Psychology." Classical topics are expounded rigorously (e.g., "Intelligence," "Mental Retardation," "Mind-Brain Relationship," "Brain and Human Behavior"). Historical surveys deliver five to seven packed pages on "Abnormal Psychology" and "Psychology, History of." Insider lore abounds in "Forensic Psychiatry," "Therapeutic Community" and "Resistance in Psychotherapy." Michael Roe classifies six models of life stages in "Life Span Development," while Stephen Evans welcomes return of the concept of the "Self."

Philosophy crops up occasionally as in "Determinism and Free Will" or "Reductionism," but philosophy of language and of dialogue does not. Far commoner are discussions of how to handle, both in oneself and in others, experiences like "Loss and Separation," "Grief," "Jealousy" and "Forgiveness." How-to entries address "Cancer Counseling," "Workaholism" and "Assertiveness Training." On religious matters synopses explore "Spiritual and Religious Issues in Therapy," "Psychological Roots of Religion," "Religion and Personality" and "Demonic Influence and Psychopathology." Practicality pervades "Personnel Selection in Religious Organizations" and "Religious Concept Development." Paul Vitz scintillates on "Psychology as Religion," explicating dozens of typologies, including a stunning one by Christopher Lasch. In 1976 Lasch interpreted Freudianism as Catholic in its insistence on orthodoxy and "sacred texts," Adler and Rogers as "Protestantizing" through catering to the individual, and Jung as combining the two poles in an "Episcopalian" synthesis (p. 933).

The WHO'S WHO ranges from Franz Anton Mesmer and Gustav Fechner through John Dewey and Havelock Ellis to Andras Angyal and Kurt Lewin. The longest biography delivers four pages on the Swiss Calvinist therapist Paul Tournier. The bulk of articles, however, feature North American therapies of the past forty years. Almost unwittingly, this book celebrates North American breakthroughs. Throughout the tone is inviting, even cordial: advice gets dispensed, obscurities named and the human condition illumined. Few reference works so exude hopefulness.

□ *Weaknesses* Although claiming to address conservative Christians, this LEXICON hardly ever lapses into confessional self-definition. Longer articles often climax in a biblical standpoint, but almost never disparagingly. Indeed, many articles on psychoanalytical topics celebrate parallels to Christianity (e.g., "Object Relations Therapy") or minimize differences (e.g., "Gestalt Therapy"). Randie Timpe's entry on

"Christian Psychology" probes pros and cons of integrating psychology with evangelical theology. Throughout, zeal to inform supplants desire to evangelize. Certain issues get short shrift. Gender is discussed chiefly in "Women, Psychology of," and comparison to Asian or African approaches is minimal (apart from Edwin R. Wallace's ingenious piece on "Psychopathology in Primitive Cultures"). Although "Psychology of Religion" is surveyed, one of its leading practitioners, Paul Pruyser, is not. Surveys of "Jungian Analysis" and "Analytical Psychology" avoid naming even one of Jung's followers. A very few articles wallow in jargon (e.g., "Religious Orientation"). Inevitably, bibliographies are becoming dated. An index of persons would have facilitated access to the thousands of names, particularly since this volume features few cross-references.

□ *Competitors* This captivating LEXICON condenses a field for nonprofessionals as ably as any reference book in the social sciences. For counseling the counselors, the obvious rival is Rodney J. Hunter, ed., *Dictionary of Pastoral Care and Counseling* (Nashville: Abingdon, 1990). Addressed to clergy, its articles on psychology are less technical and less historical, encompassing a wider range of life situations (e.g., "Premature Birth," "Rich Persons"). More focused on ethics than on psychology, **81** Atkinson and Field, eds., *New Dictionary of Christian Ethics and Pastoral Theology* (1995) injects Bible-centered theology nearly everywhere.

A COMPENDIUM for counselors is Robert J. Wicks et al., eds., *Clinical Handbook of Pastoral Counseling* (New York: Paulist, 1984; 2d ed., 1992). Its thirty-one chapters are organized by age groups, by method ("Christotherapy," "Crisis Intervention") and by setting (parish, hospital, prison, school). It supplies splendid bibliographies, but the *Baker Encyclopedia* delves more deeply into psychology. The latter makes a marvelous companion to **311** David M. Wulff, *Psychology of Religion* (1991), who unaccountably fails to cite it. Although Wulff envisions psychology of religion more sweepingly, he does not explore clinical issues in adequate depth. One wishes that there existed a comparable pair of volumes to introduce sociology of religion and anthropology of religion. The *Baker Encyclopedia* overlaps with entries on cognitive development in **114** Cully and Cully, eds., *Harper's Encyclopedia of Religious Education* (1990), which favors practice. The *Baker Encyclopedia* excels all these works as a self-teacher. Few if any reference books articulate such profound and versatile understanding of the human condition. Emphasis on North America and its innovations since 1950 makes this an ideal gift for any American enamored of depth psychology.

□ *Summary* This compassionate LEXICON surveys a field, stimulates self-help and articulates human dilemmas. An ethos of mutual helpfulness blooms.

114 (1990) Iris V. Cully and Kendig Brubaker Cully, eds., *Harper's Encyclopedia of Religious Education* (San Francisco: Harper, 1990); xxiii & 716 pages; no index; no general bibliography.

□ *Critique* This updating of the earliest volume (1963) in the Westminster/SCM series recruited 275 American scholars to address a wide range of topics in religious education. Historical articles favor the United States (e.g., "Chautauqua," "Boy Scouts"), while the WHO'S WHO features educators like Comenius and psychologists like Erikson. A GLOSSARY explicates terms in sociology and above all psychology ("Cognitive Dissonance," "Clowning"). Essays of five to ten pages tackle issues like "Art in Religious Education," "Child Development" and "Adult Development." Countries and denominations elicit individual entries. By demonstrating to what extent psychology has permeated the field, this DICTIONARY helps readers to expand horizons.

□ *Summary* This DICTIONARY introduces persons, issues and cultural traditions pertinent to religious education. Psychology wins out.

311 (1991) David M. Wulff, *Psychology of Religion: Classic and Contemporary Views* (New York: Wiley, 1991); xxvi & 640 pages plus 32 pages of glossary,

68 pages of bibliography, and 28 pages of indexes;charts,photosandstatisticaltables in the text.

□ *Scope* Disguised as a TEXTBOOK, this magnificent HANDBOOK encompasses the field in twelve chapters of forty to sixty pages. Exposition and insight flourish at every turn. Chapter 1 outlines history of the field; chapter 2 examines biological approaches to bodily states (G. Stanley Hall); chapter 3 presents behavioral theory and comparative studies of ritual behavior (in dogs and apes). Chapter 4 outlines laboratory experimentation, while chapter 5 probes statistical studies. Chapter 6 on Freud leads to chapter 7 on object-relations theory and narcissism (Suttie, Pruyser, Kohut) and thence to chapter 8 on Erikson. All are gems of synthesis and discernment. Chapter 9 on Jung and chapter 10 on William James offer masterpieces of exposition and critique. Chapter 11 on the German descriptive tradition explores authors neglected in North America (Otto, Spranger, Girgensohn). Chapter 12 on the American humanistic synthesis expounds Allport, Fromm and Maslow, as well as transpersonal psychology. Case studies from major religions (particularly Jewish, Christian, Buddhist and Hindu) dot the text. An epilogue assesses the field in light of both the humanities and the social sciences. Sixty-eight pages of bibliography include a few items in French and German. Indexes of persons and concepts are superb.

□ *Strengths* David Wulff has written the closest thing to a German-style HANDBOOK that North Americans are likely to see. Exhaustiveness, clarity in both organization and explication, and common sense combine to produce a nearly ideal INTRODUCTION to a field. History of the discipline shines. Chapter 1 traces development of the field, differentiating among Anglo-American, German and French traditions. The author highlights major practitioners, devoting no less than four chapters to single figures (their careers, contributions, associates and controversies). These bravura pieces on Freud, Erikson, Jung and James are among the best anyone has written on the masters. The same can be said of the chapter on "Object Relations The-ory and Religion." Nearly every chapter climaxes with several pages of "Evalu-ation," in which the author weighs pros and cons. The style is lucid and nuanced but never boring. Until this volume ap-peared, few would have thought such a HANDBOOK to lie within the capacity of a single author. For a single scholar to syn-thesize literature of the past 125 years while exuding poise, common sense and uncommon insight exceeds all expecta-tions. This work sets a standard for HAND-BOOKS in the social sciences.

□ *Weaknesses* As befits a HANDBOOK, few will read *Psychology of Religion* from cover to cover. Since chapters may be read in any sequence, this advantage could have been advertised by partitioning the book into a part 1 (chaps. 1-4 on empirical approaches), part 2 (chaps. 5-9 on psychoanalytical ap-proaches) and part 3 (chaps. 10-12 on de-scriptive approaches). Naturally, a book that discusses research done by others cannot hope to plug gaps left by them. Thus there is no discussion of gender issues or of Gestalt psy-chologists. One or two figures who emerged in the 1980s are omitted (e.g., Mihaly Csik-szentmihalyi on flow experience).

□ *Competitors* This magisterial HAND-BOOK stands alone. Its only rivals are not books but articles, such as Wulff's seventy-page piece on recent research in **299** Frank Whaling, ed., *Contemporary Approaches* (1983-85). Articles on individual psy-chologists in **5** Eliade, ed., *The Encyclope-dia of Religion* (1987) lack the pulse of a single author, although Peter Homans on "Psychology and Religion Movement" (12:66-75) traverses ground mapped no-where else. Donald Capps's essay, "The Psychology of Religious Experience," in **166** Lippy and Williams, eds., *Encyclopedia of American Religious Experience* (1988) examines six American schools as succes-sors to William James. Hartmut Zinser's chapter on "Religionspsychologie" in **7** Cancik et al., eds., *Handbuch religionswis-senschaftlicher Grundbegriffe* (1988-), 1:87-107, cites authors overlooked by Wulff. **310** Benner, ed., *Baker Encyclope-dia of Psychology* (1985) supplies a WHO'S

WHO and canvasses issues in ways that com-plement Wulff. None of these works, how-ever, comes close to matching his grasp.

□ *Summary* This masterpiece accom-plishes something that cries out to be done for sociology of religion and anthropology of religion. Dispensing exposition, critique and hints for further research, Wulff makes the field accessible and attractive. Mastery resounds.

312 (1991) Beverly Moon, ed., *An Encyclopedia of Archetypal Symbolism* (Boston and London: Shambhala, 1991); xvi & 510 pages; index, pp. 483-508; no general bibliography; 120 color plates.

□ *Scope* This COMPENDIUM of unsigned articles on 120 images from world mythol-ogy expounds Jungian archetypal psychol-ogy in flat prose. Stored and interpreted at the New York Archive for Research in Ar-chetypal Symbolism (ARAS), which grew out of the Ascona conferences of the 1930s, images unfurl under fifteen rubrics familiar to Jungians, such as "Center of the World," "Sacred Animals," "The Divine Child" and "Duality and Reconciliation." Each entry consists of a color plate, a page of "Cultural Context" and another of "Ar-chetypal Commentary," followed by bibli-ography and glossary (of mythic figures). Thus a panorama of the world's religions is sampled. Since this book includes no overviews, readers should frequent the twenty-five-page index, which lists motifs and mythic figures but not persons.

□ *Strengths* Stunning plates constellate the volume. No other COMPENDIUM of my-thology so highlights the visual or so allows symbolic content to structure sequence. Each entry divides into a synopsis of a particular tradition ("Cultural Context") and an unabashedly Jungian explication of an image ("Archetypal Commentary"). Al-though the former is nearly always clearer than the latter, Buddhist images suit the latter approach stunningly (pp. 250-61, 302-16, 330-37). Images are also drawn from several living religions, including the biblical tradition (seventeen), Jewish (five), Christian (twenty-five), South Asian (in-cluding thirteen Hindu and three Jain), East Asian (including six Japanese and five

Chinese), African (ten) and Native American (twelve). Islam wins only two entries and Zoroastrianism none. Among extinct religions, Egypt elicits ten entries, Greece nine, Scandinavia six, and Iran one. Articles on Greece succeed more convincingly than ones on Egypt. A typical entry interprets Bernini's image of "St. Teresa in Ecstasy" as combining "the story of Psyche and Eros—and Renaissance Christian mysticism" (p. 220). Absent a general bibliography, citations appended to entries supply more than five hundred titles, many of them exotic (as on snakes, p. 81, dogs p. 101 and the Navajo, p. 205).

□ *Weaknesses* This visual COMPENDIUM will disquiet beginners, not least because no author dominates. Chapters lack headnotes, and wooden prose discourages browsing. Jungians may savor the juxtapositions, but few others will. Exalting individual images, commentaries sketch no transition from one to the next, so that none of the fifteen rubrics coalesce. To move from Egypt to Africa to Jewish Poland to Fra Angelico (as in "Sacred Kingship," pp. 275-87) or from Japan to Chartres to Nigeria to Egypt (as in "Duality and Reconciliation," pp. 367-79) upsets everyday notions of coherence without advancing Jungian ones. A basic task of lexicography, arrangement, has collapsed.

□ *Competitors* As a reference work by and for Jungians, this visual extravaganza instructs the convinced better than it woos the uninitiated. **259** Bonnefoy/Doniger, eds., *Mythologies* (1981, 1991) delivers more approaches to more material but is no less daunting for beginners. Since DICTIONARIES of mythology tend to eschew psychology, no reference work offers a royal road into Jung except chapters on him in **311** Wulff, *Psychology of Religion* (1991), pages 411-66 and in **215** Akoun, ed., *Mythes et croyances du monde entier* 5(1985): 433-52. Joseph Campbell's various popularizations of Jung (such as the lavishly illustrated *Historical Atlas of World Mythology,* 5 vols. in 2 [New York: Harper, 1983; reprint, San Francisco: Harper, 1988-89]) lack clinical expertise. Subtle explication of Jung and many others un-

folds in a HANDBOOK OF INTERPRETATION: Jean Chevalier and Alain Gheerbrant, eds., *A Dictionary of Symbols* [French ed., 1969; 2d ed., 1982] (Oxford and Cambridge, Mass.: Blackwell Reference, 1994). As an alternative, non-Jungian accounts of fifteen hundred symbols enliven Udo Becker, *The Continuum Encyclopedia of Symbols* [1992] (New York: Continuum, 1994). Even more captivating are seventy historical sketches in Abbé Pierre Miquel, *Dictionnaire symbolique des animaux: Zoologie mystique* (Paris: Léopard D'or, 1991). A superb INTRODUCTION to 780 books by and about Jung is Donald R. Dyer, *Cross-Currents of Jungian Thought: An Annotated Bibliography* (Boston: Shambhala, 1991). For better or worse, Jung probably would have rejoiced that (unlike Freud's) his life's work resists miniaturizing.

□ *Summary* This COMPENDIUM works better as a refresher for Jungians than as an INTRODUCTION for outsiders. Illustrations are sumptuous and bibliographies startling, but commentaries lack continuity.

313 (1991) Rosemary Ellen Guiley, *Harper's Encyclopedia of Mystical and Paranormal Experience* (San Francisco: Harper, 1991); xv & 666 pages; no index; no general bibliography.

□ *Critique* This DICTIONARY assembles reportage concerning three hundred psychic phenomena, divinatory techniques and mystical encounters. Each entry supplies English-language bibliography drawn from some eleven hundred sources (p. xi). A GLOSSARY addresses practices ("Channeling"), movements ("Theosophy") and places ("Findhorn"). A WHO'S WHO encompasses classic figures (e.g., Pythagoras, Paracelsus, Cagliostro) and several dozen twentieth-century psychics (e.g., Edgar Cayce, Aleister Crowley, Ruth Montgomery). Intended for nonspecialists, each entry assembles what other researchers have chronicled, with little or no comment. Psychological experiments are recounted in detail. Some phenomena are declared to be unverified (e.g., "akashic records"), others are left unexplained (e.g., "Crop Circles"), and still others are deemed irrefutable (e.g., "Animal psi").

Accounts of traditional practices like Santería, Hawaiian Huna and Chinese Feng shui are precise, as are those of certain Christian experiences (e.g., "Stigmata"). Some entries describe uncritically what sounds like quackery (e.g., "Hermetic Order of the Golden Dawn"), while others gather doctrines from a mind-boggling array of sources (e.g., "Reincarnation"). Because entries recite but do not challenge, each report must be weighed. Nevertheless, this DICTIONARY musters reportage collected nowhere else. Clear writing and subheadings prevent MENIPPEAN gushing. Anyone seeking English-language bibliography about shamanism, spiritual teachers or "alternate realities" should consult this volume. Few works juxtapose the authentic and the suspect so beguilingly.

□ *Summary* This DICTIONARY reports psychic phenomena and experiments involving them but does not sift evidence.

314 (1991) Arthur S. Berger and Joyce Berger, *The Encyclopedia of Parapsychology and Psychical Research* (New York: Paragon House, 1991); xi & 553 pages; country index, pp. 500-513; bibliography, pp. 514-54.

□ *Critique* This LEXICON analyzes research into paranormal behavior discerningly. More than half of fourteen hundred entries constitute a WHO'S WHO of researchers, mediums and ninety "noted witnesses," including writers such as John Knox and Charles Dickens who recorded paranormal occurrences. Graphic accounts evoke stigmatics, mystics, mediums, faith healers and clairvoyants. In order to further research, the authors decline either to endorse or to reject thousands of reports. The tone is more sober than in Leslie Shepard, ed., *Encyclopedia of Occultism and Parapsychology,* 3d ed., 2 vols. (Detroit: Gale, 1991), which suffers from overinclusiveness. *The Encyclopedia of Parapsychology* provides a reliable point of departure, whether for researchers or curiosity-seekers.

□ *Summary* This LEXICON summarizes reports of the paranormal without gushing or carping.

5.3.4 FOLKLORE

OVERVIEW: FOLKLORISTS AND HAGIOGRAPHERS Folklorists study nonnormative oral traditions, particularly those that survive in literate cultures. In this section two calendars inventory holidays worldwide, while a REALLEXIKON, **318** Jones, *Larousse Dictionary of World Folklore* (1995) canvasses the field. Scholars of Christianity should note that folklorists enlarge HAGIOGRAPHY by examining legends that the church impugns. If hagiographers study saints' lives in order to gratify Christians, folklorists study legends in order to gratify comparatists. A full-fledged dictionary of crosscultural comparisons to saints' lives and cults would be revelatory. Although Christian folklore has yet to inspire such a book, two Catholic ones propose comparisons within Christianity: **95** Walsh, *Dictionary of Catholic Devotions* (1994) and **108** Kelly and Rogers, *Saints Preserve Us!* (1995). In a similar vein an idiosyncratic French volume, **208** Chebel, *Dictionnaire des symboles musulmans* (1995), classifies Islamic folklore. On practices of folk religion worldwide a series by French ethnographers, **215** *Mythes et croyances du monde entier,* 5 vols. (1985) delivers twenty-five hundred pages and fifteen hundred color photographs. It is a browser's paradise.

LIST OF WORKS ANALYZED

257 (1977-) Kurt Ranke, ed., *Enzyklopädie des Märchens: Handwörterbuch zur historischen und vergleichenden Erzählforschung,* planned in 12 vols. (Berlin and New York: de Gruyter, 1977-). Analyzed under 5.1.1 "Mythology: General."

315 (1985, 1990) Jennifer Mossman, ed., *Holidays and Anniversaries of the World,* 2d ed. (Detroit: Gale, 1990)

316 (1989) Iona Opie and Moira Tatem, *A Dictionary of Superstitions* (Oxford and New York: Oxford University Press, 1989)

317 (1992) Margaret Read MacDonald, ed., *The Folklore of World Holidays* (Detroit: Gale, 1992)

318 (1995) Alison Jones, *Larousse Dictionary of World Folklore* (Edinburgh and New York: Larousse, 1995)

ANALYSIS OF WORKS

315 (1985, 1990) Jennifer Moss-man, ed., *Holidays and Anniversaries of the World*, 2d ed. (Detroit: Gale, 1990), xxix & 1080 pages; index, pp. 955-1080; glossary, pp. xix-xxv.

□ *Critique* This calendar allocates two or three pages to each day of the year, listing Christian saints and blesseds, birthdays (mainly since 1700), and historical events in Europe and the United States since about 1200. Each month elicits two pages listing "State, National, and International Holidays." An introduction narrates development of the Western calendar (pp. x-xiii). An index of names, terms and events cites over twenty thousand items. Emphasis falls on Europe and the United States. Confronted by so many facts arrayed arbitrarily, browsers will flag.

□ *Summary* This calendar collates a profusion of anniversaries in Europe and the United States.

316 (1989) Iona Opie and Moira Tatem, *A Dictionary of Superstitions* (Oxford and New York: Oxford University Press, 1989); xv & 494 pages; index, pp. 463-94; general bibliography, pp. 455-62.

□ *Critique* This DICTIONARY gathers from ten centuries British quotations concerning folk beliefs about hundreds of objects. Arranged chronologically, quotations carry no commentary, so that the volume functions as a sourcebook, not a GLOSSARY. The quaint takes over.

□ *Summary* This compilation of British quotations reads like an anthology.

317 (1992) Margaret Read MacDonald, ed., *The Folklore of World Holidays* (Detroit: Gale, 1992); xxix & 739 pages; index, pp. 659-739.

□ *Critique* This calendar describes how almost four hundred holidays are celebrated in 150 countries. Entries (complete with bibliography) range from a few lines to twenty-five pages on the Chinese New Year and thirty on Christmas (canvassing no fewer than sixty-four cultures). Major Christian saints get assigned to countries where their cult occasions a national holiday, as with St. Joseph in Spain. This calendar describes holiday practices more

completely than any other volume.

□ *Summary* This calendar recounts an astonishing array of religious observances.

318 (1995) Alison Jones, *Larousse Dictionary of World Folklore* (Edinburgh and New York: Larousse, 1995); ix & 493 pages; no index; classified bibliography, pp. 469-74; calendar of folkloric events, pp. 481-87; 200 line drawings throughout.

□ *Critique* This crisp REALLEXIKON delineates and interconnects objects and images from oral cultures worldwide. About fifteen hundred entries range from three lines to two pages (e.g., "dance") but lack individual bibliographies. Articles on themes encompass plants ("Fern"), animals ("Eagle") and parts of the body ("Hair"). Enlarging on the author's *Saints* (Edinburgh and New York: Chambers, 1992), the WHO'S WHO favors Western figures, among them major saints like Joseph, Mary Magdalene and Jerome, not to mention colossi of legend like Brendan the Navigator, Julian the Hospitaller and Prester John. Fascination with legend contrasts with wariness of it in critical HAGIOGRAPHIES. Western sagas like the Arthur cycle and the Mabinogion get aligned with Gilgamesh, the Mahabharata and the Arabian Nights. In contrast, non-Western topics tend to get tucked into surveys such as "South Asian Folklore" or "Micronesian Folklore." Entries on methodology, such as devolutionary theory and psychological theory, amplify a section of "Biographical Notes on [thirty-seven] Prominent Folklorists" (pp. 475-80). Religionists can only wish that the author had differentiated normative oral traditions (as in tribal religions) from nonnormative ones (as in folklore). A superb English-language bibliography subdivides into thirty sections. Jones shares with **260** Barbara G. Walker skill in sketching interconnections but exercises far sounder judgment.

□ *Summary* This pithy REALLEXIKON characterizes objects, images and persons in the world's oral traditions. A majority of entries concern Europe and North America, not least Christian saints.

Appendix 1

Favorite Reference Books

The abundance of reference books now on the market impels a winnowing of the titles analyzed in the directory. All lists run in chronological order of first publication.

1.1 A HOME LIBRARY OF REFERENCE BOOKS IN ENGLISH

OVERVIEW Emphasis falls on single-volume works published since 1980. Inexpensive editions are marked with an asterisk. Evaluations state comparisons to other reference books, not to secondary works of other kinds. Works notable chiefly for illustrations are treated in appendix 1.4, "Illustrated Reference Books."

180 (1965, 1986) R. J. Zwi Werblowsky and Geoffrey Wigoder, eds., *The Encyclopedia of the Jewish Religion* (New York: Holt, Rinehart & Winston, 1966); reprinted with very minor revisions (New York: Adama, 1986).

This LEXICON remains one of few Judaic reference works to treat religion without intermingling secular culture.

*2 (1981, 1989) Keith Crim, ed., *The Abingdon Dictionary of Living Religions* (Nashville: Abingdon, 1981); reprinted without alteration as *The Perennial Dictionary of World Religions* (San Francisco: Harper & Row, 1989).

This richest one-volume LEXICON in English on the world's religions is gradually becoming out of date.

32 (1982) David B. Barrett, ed., *World Christian Encyclopedia: A Comparative Study of Churches and Religions in the Modern World, AD 1900-2000* (Nairobi, Oxford and New York: Oxford University Press, 1982).

This incomparable compilation dissects religious demography worldwide. A new edition in three volumes (1997) will sweep the field.

152 (1983, 1992) Angelo di Berardino, ed., *Encyclopedia of the Early Church,* 2 vols. (New York: Oxford University Press, 1992).

This updated translation of an Italian masterwork examines the early church in awe-inspiring depth.

*89 (1983) Gordon S. Wakefield, ed., *The Westminster Dictionary of Christian Spirituality* (London: SCM; Philadelphia: Westminster, 1983).

This most winsome of the Westminster/SCM dictionaries reappraises persons and themes from spirituality worldwide.

*142 (1984) Nicon D. Patrinacos, *A Dictionary of Greek Orthodoxy* (Pleasantville, N.Y.: Hellenic Heritage Publications, 1984).

This little-known gem explicates Eastern and particularly Greek Orthodoxy from within.

181 (1987) Arthur A. Cohen and Paul Mendes-Flohr, eds., *Contemporary Jewish Religious Thought: Original Essays on Critical Concepts, Movements and Beliefs* (New York: Scribner's, 1987).

This model REVISIONIST LEXICON rethinks fundamentals fearlessly.

*80 (1988) Sinclair B. Ferguson and David F. Wright, eds., *New Dictionary of Theology* (Downers Grove, Ill., and Leicester, U.K.: InterVarsity Press, 1988).

This lucid INTRODUCTION untangles Christian theology with utmost fairness.

*62 (1988) James L. Mays, ed., *Harper's Bible Commentary* (San Francisco: Harper, 1988).

Almost alone in the field, this BIBLE COMMENTARY dissects controversies nonconfessionally.

168 (1988) Charles H. Lippy and Peter N. Williams, eds., *Encyclopedia of American Religious Experience*, 3 vols. (New York: Scribner's, 1988).

This huge COMPENDIUM stimulates research on all aspects of religion in North America.

21 (1988) Stewart Sutherland, Leslie Houlden, Peter Clarke and Friedhelm Hardy, eds., *The World's Religions* (London: Routledge, 1988; Boston: G. K. Hall, 1988).

This imaginative and wide-ranging COMPENDIUM rethinks ways to describe living religions.

217 (1988) Ainslee T. Embree, ed., *Encyclopedia of Asian History*, 4 vols. (New York: Scribner's, 1988).

This historical ENCYCLOPEDIA introduces countries, religions and persons from Iran to the Philippines.

*8 (1989, 1991) Geddes MacGregor, *Dictionary of Religion and Philosophy* (New York: Paragon House, 1989; paperback, 1991).

This elegant INTRODUCTION to Christianity and Western thought, indeed to cultural literacy, overflows with tart judgments and quirky bibliography.

183 (1989) Glenda Abramson, ed., *The Blackwell Companion to Jewish Culture: From the Eighteenth Century to the Present* (Oxford and Cambridge, Mass.: Blackwell Reference, 1989).

This British DICTIONARY recapitulates two hundred years of European (Ashkenazi) Jewish culture, particularly in literature, music, film and scholarship.

*202 (1989) Cyril Glassé, *The Concise Encyclopedia of Islam* (San Francisco: Harper, 1989; paperback, 1991).

Virtuosic rethinking of Islamic history, doctrine and mysticism by an American Muslim will gratify beginners and specialists alike.

*58 (1990) Watson E. Mills, ed., *Mercer Dictionary of the Bible* (Macon, Ga.: Mercer University Press, 1990).

This comprehensive REALLEXIKON of the Bible and of extracanonical writings delineates tangibles and downplays theology.

112 (1990) Peter E. Fink, S.J., ed., *The New Dictionary of Sacramental Worship* (Collegeville, Minn.: Michael Glazier/Liturgical, 1990).

American scholars boldly rethink history and doctrine concerning Catholic liturgy.

*169 (1990) Daniel G. Reid, ed., *Dictionary of Christianity in America* (Downers Grove, Ill.: InterVarsity Press, 1990).

This historical LEXICON of American Christianity excels at narrative, analysis and graphics. It belongs in every American's library.

68 (1990) R[ichard] J. Coggins and J. L[eslie] Houlden, eds., *A Dictionary of Biblical Interpretation* (London: SCM; New York: Trinity Press International, 1990).

This British LEXICON on methods of biblical interpretation and their history is both exhaustive and provocative.

9 (1991) John R. Hinnells, ed., *Who's Who of World Religions* (London: Macmillan, 1991; New York: Simon & Schuster, 1992).

Biographies of thirteen hundred figures from the world's religions cut deep, with amazing bibliographies.

60 (1992) David Noel Freedman, ed., *The Anchor Bible Dictionary*, 6 vols. (New York: Doubleday, 1992).

The premier English-language MEGA-ENCYCLOPEDIA of the Bible excels on archeology, social history, and historicity of individual books but not on theology or hermeneutics.

*70 (1992) Joel B. Green, Scot

McKnight and I. Howard Marshall, eds., *Dictionary of Jesus and the Gospels* (Downers Grove, Ill., and Leicester, U.K.: InterVarsity Press, 1992).

This HANDBOOK OF INTERPRETATION fearlessly untangles current scholarship on the Gospels, as evangelicals discriminate the knowable from the unfathomable.

*76 (1992) Donald W. Musser and Joseph L. Price, eds., *A New Handbook of Christian Theology* (Nashville: Abingdon, 1992).

Nearly 150 signed articles (mostly by Americans) reappraise issues old and new with unflagging verve.

93 (1992-) Bernard McGinn, *The Presence of God: A History of Western Christian Mysticism,* planned in 4 vols. (New York: Crossroad, 1992-).

A magisterial history of Western Christian mystics appends an essay on "Theoretical Foundations: The Modern Study of Mysticism." The latter dissects methodology incomparably.

*77 (1993) Alister E. McGrath, ed., *The Blackwell Encyclopedia of Modern Christian Thought* (Oxford and Cambridge, Mass.: Blackwell Reference, 1993; paperback, 1995).

Brilliant alike in planning and execution, this work reconfigures Christian thought of the past two hundred years. Everyone should own this REVISIONIST masterpiece.

*72 (1993) Bruce M. Metzger and Michael D. Coogan, eds., *The Oxford Companion to the Bible* (New York and Oxford: Oxford University Press, 1993).

This blend of a BIBLE DICTIONARY with a HANDBOOK OF INTERPRETATION addresses scholars outside religious studies.

*25 (1993) Arvind Sharma, ed., *Our Religions* (San Francisco: Harper, 1993).

With originality and passion, seven preeminent teacher-scholars expound their own religion and in the process reenvision Hinduism, Buddhism, Confucianism, Taoism, Judaism, Christianity and Islam.

48 ([1990] 1994) René Latourelle, S.J., and Rino Fisichella, eds., *Dictionary of Fundamental Theology* (New York: Crossroad, 1994).

Adapted from an Italian-French masterpiece, this REVISIONIST LEXICON redirects theology toward cultural diagnosis. No volume in English presents twentieth-century Catholic thinking more brilliantly.

*131 (1995) Richard P. McBrien, ed., *The HarperCollins Encyclopedia of Catholicism* (San Francisco: Harper, 1995).

This historical LEXICON canvasses Roman Catholicism effortlessly. Thoroughness and evenhandedness (except in one or two "feature articles") will please all camps.

109 (1995) Clemens Jöckle, *Encyclopedia of Saints* (London: Alpine Fine Arts Collections, 1995).

This REALLEXIKON inventories life, legends, cult sites and artistic depictions of three hundred saints. No other WHO'S WHO disentangles life from legend so rigorously or scans iconography so methodically.

207 (1995) John L. Esposito, ed., *The Oxford Encyclopedia of the Modern Islamic World,* 4 vols. (New York: Oxford University Press, 1995).

Badly needed, this ENCYCLOPEDIA of Islam since 1789 alternates Muslim and non-Muslim perspectives. Evaluative annotations in the bibliographies deserve emulation.

275 (1995) Karel van der Toorn, Bob Becking and Pieter W. van der Horst, eds., *Dictionary of Deities and Demons in the Bible (DDD)* (Leiden, New York and Köln: Brill, 1995)

This crosscultural LEXICON unleashes historians to investigate all deities and heroes mentioned in the Bible. Surprises abound.

1.2 PREEMINENT REFERENCE BOOKS IN FRENCH AND GERMAN

OVERVIEW Emphasis falls on works that have no rival in English. None has been translated, and nearly all outdo any English-language counterpart in both acumen and bibliography.

1.2.1 FRENCH
49 (1928-) Louis Pirot [1881-

1939], ed., *Dictionnaire de la Bible: Supplément* (Paris: Letouzey et Ané, 1928-); 12 volumes to 1994 ("Sexualité").

In recent volumes, this grandest of BIBLE DICTIONARIES plumbs incomparable depth, not least on methodology and on history of controversies.

88 ([1932] 1937-1994) Marcel Viller, S.J. [founding editor; many successors], *Dictionnaire de spiritualité, ascétique et mystique* (Paris: Beauchesne, 1937-1994).

This magnificent MEGA-ENCYCLOPEDIA reinterprets persons and issues with precision and imagination.

137 ([1941] 1948-) G. Jacquemet, ed., *Catholicisme: Hier—aujourd'hui—demain,* about 15 vols. planned (Paris: Letouzey et Ané, 1948-).

This is the richest contemporary MEGA-ENCYCLOPEDIA of Christian thought. From volume 7 (1972) on, coverage of methodology and of European (above all French) persons and places is superlative.

*243 (1976, 1991) Claude Durix [1922-], *Cent Clés pour comprendre le zen* (Paris: Courrier du livre, 1976; 2d ed., rev., 1991).

No more jolting PHILOSOPHICAL DICTIONARY exists than these meditations on Zen by a master of martial arts. He interweaves anecdotes uncannily.

4 (1984, 1993) Paul Poupard, ed., *Dictionnaire des religions* (Paris: Presses Universitaires de France, 1984; 3d ed. in 2 vols., 1993).

This remains the most thorough and virtuosic LEXICON on the world's religions.

110 (1984, 1992-) Domenico Sartore and Achille M. Triacca, eds., *Dictionnaire encyclopédique de la liturgie,* planned in 2 vols. (Turnhout: Brepols, 1992-); adapted from the Italian.

This REVISIONIST ENCYCLOPEDIA infuses cultural anthropology into study of liturgy, thereby transforming "theory of liturgy" into "meta-liturgics." Italian and French creativity dazzles.

*224 (1987) Louis Frédéric, *Dictionnaire de la civilisation indienne* (Paris: Laffont, 1987).

This DICTIONARY condenses lore of South Asia more efficiently than any other.

*307 (1987) Michel Clévenot, ed., *L'État des religions dans le monde* (Paris: La Découverte/Le Cerf, 1987).

This COMPENDIUM unleashes the social sciences on demography, controversies and case studies in religion worldwide. Originality resonates.

289 (1989-92) André Jacob, ed., *Encyclopédie philosophique universelle,* 5 vols. (Paris: Presses Universitaires de France, 1989-92).

Among the astounding achievements of French culture, this masterpiece commands greater respect with each use. It stands in a class by itself for rigor, imaginativeness and comprehensiveness as to region, topic and thinker.

22 (1990) Charles Baladier, ed., *Le Grand atlas des religions* (Paris: Encyclopaedia universalis, 1990).

Astute texts, three thousand items of bibliography and five hundred color photographs make this a premier volume on the world's religions.

*28 (1993) Jean Delumeau, ed., *Le Fait religieux* (Paris: Fayard, 1993).

French authorities contribute incisive chapters on the world's religions, enriched by choice information.

150 (1994) Philippe Levillain, ed., *Dictionnaire historique de la papauté* (Paris: Fayard, 1994).

This nonconfessional REALLEXIKON applies unheard-of acumen and depth to papal history and institutions.

125 (1995) Pierre Gisel, ed., *Encyclopédie du protestantisme* (Paris: Cerf; Geneva: Labor et Fides, 1995).

This exuberantly REVISIONIST LEXICON rethinks history and issues of Protestantism in Europe. Novelty matches cogency.

*208 (1995) Malek Chebel, *Dictionnaire de symboles musulmans: Rites, mystique et civilisation* (Paris: Albin Michel, 1995).

This unpredictable DICTIONARY expounds Islamic folklore with panache. Cross-references and bibliography are second to none.

1.2.2 GERMAN
151 ([1941] 1950-) Theodor Klauser [d. 1984] and [since 1984] Ernst Dassmann, eds., *Reallexikon für Antike und Christentum: Sachwörterbuch zur Auseinandersetzung des Christentums mit der antiken Welt,* 16 and 1/2 vols. to date (Stuttgart: Hiersemann, 1941-).

This staggeringly rich evocation of classical antiquity and early Christianity is one of the monuments of our time.

140 (1971, 1990-93) Endre von Ivánka, Julius Tyciak and Paul Wiertz, eds., *Handbuch der Ostkirchenkunde* (Düsseldorf: Patmos, 1971; 2d ed. in 3 vols., 1990-93).

This COMPENDIUM on the Eastern churches is the fullest in a Western language.

31 (1976-) Gerhard Müller, ed., *Theologische Realenzyklopädie,* 24 vols. to date (Berlin: de Gruyter, 1976-).

This MEGA-ENCYCLOPEDIA dispenses the longest articles and biggest bibliographies on major persons, places and issues concerning Christianity and its relations to other religions.

44 (1983) Hanfried Krüger, Werner Löser and Walter Müller-Römheld, eds., *Ökumene Lexikon: Kirchen, Religionen, Bewegungen* (Frankfurt am Main: Verlag Otto Lembeck and Verlag Josef Knecht, 1983).

This superbly edited LEXICON scrutinizes ecumenical bodies, leaders and activities.

45 (1986-) Erwin Fahlbusch et al., eds., *Evangelisches Kirchenlexikon: Internationale theologische Enzyklopädie,* 3d ed., planned in 4 vols. (Göttingen: Vandenhoeck & Ruprecht, 1986-).

The most penetrating contemporary ENCYCLOPEDIA of Christianity worldwide canvasses countries and concepts but omits persons.

85 (1987-89) Emerich Coreth, Walter M. Neidl and Georg Pfligersdorfer, eds., *Christliche Philosophie im katholischen Denken des 19. und 20. Jahrhunderts,* 3 vols.(Graz, Vienna and Cologne: Styria Verlag, 1987-89).

This HANDBOOK reinterprets Catholic philosophy and theology since 1800. If translated into English, its panorama of French, German and Italian theologians would transform attitudes.

7 (1988-) Hubert Cancik, Burkhard Gladigow and Matthias Laubscher, eds., *Handbuch religionswissenschaftlicher Grundbegriffe,* planned in 5 vols. (Stuttgart: Kohlhammer, 1988-).

This HANDBOOK on methodology of religious studies dissects hundreds of concepts. It is the fullest resource anywhere on history and methodology of the field.

128 (1993-) Walter Kasper, ed., *Lexikon für Theologie und Kirche,* 3d ed., planned in 10 vols. (Freiburg: Herder, 1993-). The first two volumes indicate that this will be an exceptionally rich and up-to-date LEXIKON, not just of Catholicism but of Christianity and indeed of world religions.

1.3 REFERENCE BOOKS SUITABLE FOR BROWSING

OVERVIEW This select list features English-language works of one volume whose verve and incisiveness induce the unwary to read on, intrepidly exploring previously unheeded topics. Quality of writing is what triumphs, given that only one or two of the works furnish illustrations (apart from **220** Schwartzberg, ed., *A Historical Atlas of South Asia*). These books cry out to be savored.

*73 (1963, 1988) John Macquarrie, *Twentieth Century Religious Thought* (London: SCM; Philadelphia: Trinity Press International, 1988).

This spirited TEXTBOOK expounds over two hundred thinkers arrayed across 121 sections. Seldom do the past hundred years of philosophy and theology cohere so ingeniously.

220 (1978, 1992) Joseph E. Schwartzberg, ed., *A Historical Atlas of South Asia* (Chicago: University of Chicago Press, 1978); second impression with additional material (New York: Oxford University Press, 1992).

This model HISTORICAL ATLAS analyzes

all aspects of South Asian history through 150 pages of plates and a like expanse of captions. The latter read beguilingly, and graphics delight the eye. Few other AT-LASES transform a subject so decisively.

61 (1981) W. Gunther Plaut, ed., The Torah: A Modern Commentary (New York: Union of American Hebrew Congregations, 1981).

This Reform Jewish COMMENTARY on the Pentateuch digests thousands of interpretations. One hundred fifty clusters of "Gleanings" from previous interpreters demand rereading.

*306 (1984, 1987) Bryan Wilson and Daisaku Ikeda, Human Values in a Changing World (London: Macdonald, 1984; Secaucus, N.J.: Lyle Stuart, 1987).

Dialogues between Europe's leading sociologist of religion and Japan's foremost organizer of Buddhism make up a PHILOSOPHICAL DICTIONARY. Miniessays cut deep on eighty-six topics concerning social sciences of religion.

223 (1985, 1987) Parshotam Mehra, A Dictionary of Modern Indian History, 1707-1947 (Delhi: Oxford University Press, 1985; reprinted with corrections, 1987).

Four hundred essays on persons, events and movements from two and one-half centuries display the pungency of a good curry. Rarely does historical learning get expounded so spicily.

*148 (1986) J. N. D. Kelly, The Oxford Dictionary of Popes (New York: Oxford University Press, 1986; paperback, 1988).

Unflagging acumen carries the reader through 270 papal biographies, recounted at equal length no matter what the period. No one else has chronicled papal history so winningly.

*35 (1988) Jaroslav Pelikan, The Melody of Theology: A Philosophical Dictionary (Cambridge: Harvard University Press, 1988); also in paperback.

Eighty-eight ruminations on persons, places and issues pivotal to the history of Christianity repay endless rereading.

8 (1989, 1991) Geddes MacGregor, Dictionary of Religion and Philosophy (New York: Paragon House, 1989; paperback, 1991).

This sprightliest of DICTIONARIES brings to life persons, concepts and practices from Western philosophy and religion. Few reference works so disarmingly combine accuracy with insouciance.

183 (1989) Glenda Abramson, ed., The Blackwell Companion to Jewish Culture: From the Eighteenth Century to the Present (Oxford and Cambridge, Mass.: Blackwell Reference, 1989).

Teased from entry to entry, a reader traverses 250 years of Jewish creativity.

*111 (1989) Edward N. West, Outward Signs: The Language of Christian Symbolism (New York: Walker, 1989).

Written for believer and nonbeliever alike, this witty GLOSSARY explicates symbolism inherent in Christian architecture, liturgy and vestments. Hundreds of line drawings and anecdotes pack punch.

*156 (1990) Everett Ferguson, ed., Encyclopedia of Early Christianity (New York and London: Garland Publishing, 1990).

Designed to entice the beginner as well as to enrich the expert, this LEXICON makes the first six hundred years of Christianity pulsate. Few multiauthor works read so irresistibly.

*58 (1990) Watson E. Mills, ed., Mercer Dictionary of the Bible (Macon, Ga.: Mercer University Press, 1990).

Few BIBLE DICTIONARIES ingratiate themselves, but this one does. Emphasizing tangibles, most of the articles move imperceptibly from the pivotal toward the arcane.

76 (1992) Donald W. Musser and Joseph L. Price, eds., A New Handbook of Christian Theology (Nashville: Abingdon, 1992).

One hundred forty-seven entries canvass contemporary Christian thought with startling originality. Few English-language books in any field juggle so many contemporary issues so compellingly.

106 (1992) Enzo Lodi, Saints of the Roman Calendar (New York: Alba House, 1992). Translated from the Italian by Jordan Aumann.

With lightness of touch this calendar of 204 feasts in the Roman liturgy retells saints' stories and pinpoints relevance for today. Liturgical in intent, this HAGIOGRAPHY makes most others seem either skeletal or labored.

192 (1992) Lewis Glinert, *The Joys of Hebrew* (New York and Oxford: Oxford University Press, 1992).

This wittiest of GLOSSARIES insinuates about six hundred Hebrew words and phrases into a reader's unconscious. The anecdotes are among the drollest anywhere.

206 (1994) Annemarie Schimmel, *Deciphering the Signs of God: A Phenomenological Approach to Islam* (Albany: SUNY Press, 1994).

Seldom have wisdom, learning and organizing skill combined so masterfully as in this PHENOMENOLOGY. Awestruck, the reader absorbs the fruits of a lifetime spent pondering Muslim encounters with God.

1.4 ILLUSTRATED REFERENCE BOOKS

OVERVIEW These reference books feature photographs, some sumptuous and others elegiac, of practices in the world's religions. Images of worship, initiation, pilgrimage and mourning predominate, while fine arts recede. Whether read singly or together, these volumes delight the eye and move the spirit. There is no better way to enlarge one's acquaintanceship with religious behavior. Almost invariably, Asian and tribal religions prove photogenic, while Judaism and Baha'i less often do. Images from tribal religions proliferate in **32** Barrett, ed., *World Christian Encyclopedia* (1982) and **19** *Eerdmans' Handbook to World Religions* (1982).

(1954) Henry James Forman and Roland Gammon, *Truth Is One: The Story of the World's Great Living Religions in Pictures and Text* (New York: Harper & Brothers, 1954).

More than two hundred black-and-white photographs feature worshipers in ten religions. The images occur nowhere else and in many cases evoke a lost world.

The text, however, is better disregarded. A classic from the same period is Pierre Verger, *Dieux d'Afrique* (Paris: Hartmann, 1954), whose 159 photos of West Africa and Bahia, Brazil, cast a spell.

241 (1959, 1987) René de Berval, ed., *Présence du bouddhisme* (Saigon: France-Asie, 1959); second edition, revised (Paris: Gallimard, 1987).

Assembled in 1959, 150 black-and-white photographs distinguish this "museum without walls." Buddhist sites have seldom looked so poignant.

17 (1974) Isma'il Ragi al Faruqi and David Sopher, eds., *Historical Atlas of the Religions of the World* (New York: Macmillan, 1974).

Historical maps and occasional black-and-white photographs adorn twenty chapters on major religions. The maps have yet to be bettered.

126 (1979-80) Gabriel Le Bras, ed., *Les Ordres religieux: La Vie et l'art*, 2 vols. (Paris: Flammarion, 1979-80).

Over fourteen hundred photographs per volume, half in color, depict buildings and other works of art created by contemplative and military orders (vol. 1), as well as by active ones (vol. 2). No other work documents visual achievements of European Catholicism so profusely.

32 (1982) David B. Barrett, ed., *World Christian Encyclopedia: A Comparative Study of Churches and Religions in the Modern World*, A.D. 1900-2000 (Oxford and New York: Oxford University Press, 1982).

Hundreds of small black-and-white photographs evoke religious practices worldwide, not least in Oceania and Africa (particularly on pp. 39-111). Few of the photos appear anywhere else.

19 (1982) *Eerdmans' Handbook to the World's Religions* (Grand Rapids, Mich.: Eerdmans, 1982); published in Britain as *The Lion Handbook to the World's Religions* (Tring: Lion Publishing, 1982).

The text features small photographs, notably of tribal rituals.

244 (1984) Heinz Bechert and Richard Gombrich, eds., *The World of Buddhism: Buddhist Monks and Nuns in*

Society and Culture (London: Thames & Hudson; New York: Facts on File, 1984). Also in paperback (London: Thames & Hudson, 1991).

Sixty-four pages of portfolios in both color and black-and-white furnish about two hundred images of Buddhist monasticism in thirteen countries. The captions probe.

215 (1985, 1991) André Akoun, ed., *Mythes et croyances du monde entier,* 5 vols. (Paris: Lidis-Brepols, 1985, 1991).

About three hundred color photographs per volume enrich trenchant texts and apt bibliography, making this the most opulent survey of myth and religion worldwide. Volume 5, *Le Monde occidental moderne,* excels at cultural diagnosis.

200 (1986) Isma'il R. al Faruqi and Lois Lamya al Faruqi, *The Cultural Atlas of Islam* (New York: Macmillan, 1986).

Hundreds of black-and-white photographs, seventy-seven maps and subtle texts fathom Islamic arts.

55 (1986) Geoffrey Wigoder, ed., *Illustrated Dictionary and Concordance of the Bible* (New York: Macmillan, 1986).

Hundreds of color photographs of Near Eastern places and objects enliven this BIBLE DICTIONARY.

20 (1987) Peter Bishop and Michael Darton, eds., *The Encyclopedia of World Faiths: An Illustrated Survey of the World's Living Religions* (New York: Facts on File, 1987).

Eight portfolios devote eight pages each to color photographs of major themes. Captions cut deep.

22 (1990) Charles Baladier, ed., *Le Grand Atlas des religions* (Paris: Encyclopaedia Universalis, 1990).

More than five hundred color photographs evoke religious practices around the world. Images from antiquity and today, from Asia and Europe, are juxtaposed cunningly.

312 (1991) Beverly Moon, ed., *An Encyclopedia of Archetypal Symbolism* (Boston and London: Shambhala, 1991).

Taken from several dozen cultures, each of 120 color plates elicits two or three pages of Jungian commentary with

choice bibliography.

232 (1992) Vijaya Ghose, ed., *Tirtha: The Treasury of Indian Expressions* (New Delhi: CMC, 1992).

Winsome color photographs of all aspects of South Asian life embellish an introductory GLOSSARY.

27 (1993) Peter B. Clarke, ed., *The World's Religions: Understanding the Living Faiths* (Pleasantville, N.Y.: Reader's Digest; London: Marshall Editions, 1993).

Four hundred color photographs and forty-three maps aid visualization of ten religions.

263 (1993) Roy Willis, ed., *World Mythology* (New York: Henry Holt, 1993).

Over four hundred small color photographs and distinctive maps adorn retelling of the world's myths.

1.5 REFERENCE BOOKS ON WOMEN AND RELIGION

OVERVIEW Since the early 1980s women have compiled reference works on feminist issues in religion and above all on female deities. By far the best are **262** Larrington, ed., *The Feminist Companion to Mythology* (1992) and **64** Newsom and Ringe, eds., *The Women's Bible Commentary* (1992).

260 (1983) Barbara G. Walker, *The Woman's Encyclopedia of Myths and Secrets* (New York: Harper, 1983); also in paperback (San Francisco: Harper, 1986).

(1988) Barbara G. Walker, *The Woman's Dictionary of Symbols and Sacred Objects* (San Francisco: Harper, 1988).

The thesis that women transmit what men repress is hammered out with MENIPPEAN overkill.

(1989-91) Helen Tierney, ed., *Women's Studies Encyclopedia,* 3 vols. (New York and London: Greenwood, 1989-91).

Volume 3 on "History, Philosophy and Religion" examines women's status in over fifty countries and in major religions. Articles are pithy and often imaginative.

262 (1992) Carolyne Larrington, ed., *The Feminist Companion to Mythology* (London: Pandora, 1992); also in paperback (San Francisco: Thorsons, 1992).

Fastidious analysis, outspoken critique and unfailing originality distinguish this masterpiece.

64 (1992) Carol A. Newsom and Sharon H. Ringe, eds., *The Women's Bible Commentary* (Louisville: Westminster/John Knox, 1992).

Sixty-four chapters by women reappraise the Hebrew Bible and the New Testament with vigor and brilliance.

(1992) Elizabeth Wright, ed., *Feminism and Psychoanalysis: A Critical Dictionary* (Oxford and Cambridge, Mass.: Blackwell Reference, 1992).

An imaginative LEXICON reassesses psychoanalytic schools, particularly those of Jung and of Lacan, from the standpoint of women's issues.

272 (1993) Martha Ann and Dorothy Myers Imel, *Goddesses in World Mythology* (Santa Barbara, Calif.: ABC-CLIO, 1993); also in paperback (New York: Oxford University Press, 1995).

Ingenious interweaving among goddesses, cultures and themes enriches this WHO'S WHO.

Appendix 2

Reference Books
That Cry Out
to Be Written

OVERVIEW The directory of reference books in religious studies has called attention to gaps in the literature. The following eight projects cry out to be undertaken in the near future.

2.1 CONCERNING A PARTICULAR RELIGION OR REGION

2.1.1 CHRISTIAN MONASTICISM WORLDWIDE

Although Christian monasticism continues to attract thousands of scholars, no one recently has compiled either a survey of the historical sweep or a LEXICON of orders, places and persons. An Italian MEGA-REALLEXIKON, Guerrino Pelliccia and Giancarlo Rocca, eds., *Dizionario degli istituti di perfezione*, 8 vols. to date [through *SPIRITUALI*] (Rome: Edizioni Paoline, 1973-), purveys massive detail (in 7000 pages) on orders, founders, countries and practices but scants both methodology and spirituality. A German DICTIONARY of almost five hundred pages, Georg Schwaiger, ed., *Mönchtum, Orden, Klöster: Von den Anfänge bis zur Gegenwart* (Munich:

Beck, 1993), canvasses orders and practices (but not persons or places) and lacks bibliographies. A worthy overview, **129** Duchet-Suchaux and Duchet-Suchaux, *Les Ordres religieux: Guide historique* (1993) lacks an adequate WHO'S WHO, as does **126** Le Bras, ed., *Les Ordres religieux: La Vie et l'art* (1979-80). A magisterial HANDBOOK, compiled in three editions between 1896 and 1933, remains unusually readable, although out of date: Max Heimbucher, *Die Orden und Kongregationen der katholischen Kirche* [1896/1933], 2 vols. (reprint, Paderborn: Schöningh, 1980). Ivan Gobry's *Les Moines en Occident*, 3 vols. (Paris: Fayard, 1985-87) synthesizes history to about 750 C.E.

What is needed is a LEXICON to canvass orders, persons and places from the beginnings to the present, with attention to methodology and current bibliography. Format could emulate **156** Ferguson, ed., *Encyclopedia of Early Christianity* (1990) or **169** Reid, ed., *Dictionary of Christianity in America* (1990). As it is, one must consult up to a dozen reference works covering different periods and regions. The fullest coverage on Europe in a single volume remains **29** Cross, ed., *The Oxford Dictionary of the Christian Church* (1957, 1974), whose bibliographies badly need updating. As years go by, **128** Kasper, ed., *Lexikon für Theologie und Kirche,* 10 vols. (1993-) promises to become a preferred tool.

2.1.2 THE QUR'AN AND HADITH

Anyone familiar with BIBLE DICTIONARIES, COMMENTARIES and HANDBOOKS OF INTERPRETATION cannot but lament the lack of comparable tools concerning the Qur'an and hadith. Jewish and Christian biblical scholars have sponsored hundreds of reference works prepared by thousands of scholars for use by millions of readers. Surely some of the expertise expended on biblical scholarship could be mobilized to produce a critical dictionary of the Qur'an. Such a work would temper the audacity of **209** Bell, *A Commentary on the Qur'an* (1991). It would expound the latest information and controversies concerning figures, places and themes. By its very existence, such a volume would highlight differences between Qur'anic studies and biblical studies. In contrast to the Bible, the Qur'an exemplifies (1) the primacy of a single language, Arabic, (2) the absence of a "synoptic problem" (i.e., nonexistence of other canonical narratives concerning the Prophet), (3) the lack of extracanonical books and (4) the prohibition on pursuing archeology in Saudi Arabia. All these conditions divide study of earliest Islam from biblical studies.

The hadith lend themselves equally to a LEXICON. Portrayal of traditionists (i.e., discriminators of authentic oral traditions), characterization of collections and their contents, and assessment of Western versus Islamic scholarship would disseminate this material to a wider public. Highly technical discussions in **198** Gibb et al., eds., *The Encyclopaedia of Islam* (1960-) need to be reworked for a broader audience.

2.1.3 RELIGIONS OF SOUTH ASIA

A LEXICON of religions in South Asia by Western scholars (particularly social scientists) would digest the flood of publications of the last thirty years. It could be as compact and REVISIONIST as **202** Glassé, *The Concise Encyclopedia of Islam* (1989) or as monumental and fact-oriented as **199** Yarshater, ed., *Encyclopaedia Iranica* (1985-). As it is, encyclopedias by Indian scholars like **230** Garg, *Encyclopaedia of the Hindu World* (1992-) or **231** Singh, ed., *The Encyclopaedia of Sikhism* exalt exhaustiveness above insight and scant the social sciences. **216** Schuhmacher and Woerner, eds., *The Encyclopedia of Eastern Philosophy and Religion* (1986, 1989) devotes only 150 pages to Indian ideas and persons, while **235** Stutley and Stutley, *A Dictionary of Hinduism* (1977) extends only to 1500 C.E. The fullest single volume remains **224** Frédéric, *Dictionnaire de la civilisation indienne* (1987). A multivolume LEXICON on Hinduism, Jainism, Sikhism, Indian Buddhism, yoga and perhaps tribal religions would benefit everyone.

2.1.4 NEW RELIGIONS OF ASIA

A LEXICON of new religious movements throughout Asia would feature Taiwan, Korea, Vietnam, Indonesia, India and above all Japan. Such a work should trace worldwide dissemination (diasporas) of the new religions as well as reassess the category "new religious movement." Social scientists and area specialists could expound research from three decades, emphasizing comparisons among regions. As it is, one must forage among assorted tools. **214** *Kodansha Encyclopedia of Japan,* 9 vols. (Tokyo: Kodansha, 1983) canvasses major movements in Japan. To expand coverage into all of Asia would entail a massive LEXICON. A worldwide survey by Françoise Champion in **28** Delumeau, ed., *Le Fait religieux* (1993), pages 741-72, offers a refreshing start. A GLOSSARY by Benjamin Beit-Hallahmi, *The Illustrated Encyclopedia of Active New Religions, Sects and Cults* (New York: Rosen, 1993) concerns mainly North America.

2.1.5 RELIGION IN AFRICA

A LEXICON or COMPENDIUM on religions of Africa would encompass indigenous ones, Christianity, Judaism and Islam as well as independent ("institutional") churches and other hybrid forms. Such a work might also canvass African diasporas in the Americas (particularly Brazil and the Caribbean). At present, **32** Barrett, ed., *World Christian Encyclopedia* (1982) remains indispensable on individual countries, as will its second edition expected in 1997. Barrett's *Schism and Renewal in Africa* (Nairobi: Oxford University Press, 1968) surveyed six thousand independent churches. A reference book on independent churches remains a lacuna. Meanwhile, twenty chapters in Thomas Blakely et al., eds., *Religion in Africa: Experience and Expression* (London: Curry, 1994) provide a point of departure. Also crucial are three chapters in **23** Ries, ed., *Traité d'anthropologie du sacré*, vol. 1 (Paris: Desclée, 1992), pages 255-329. An exhilarating synthesis unfolds in Robert Farris Thompson, *Face of the Gods: Art and Altars of Africa and the African Americas* (Munich: Prestel, 1993). No less magisterial is Adrian Hastings, *The Church in Africa, 1450-1950* (Oxford: Clarendon, 1994), while Elizabeth Isichei, *A History of Christianity in Africa: From Antiquity to the Present* (London: SPCK, 1995) tackles an even longer period. All these works need to be kneaded into a LEXICON.

2.2 ACADEMIC DISCIPLINES

2.2.1 SOCIOLOGY OF RELIGION

Although psychology of religion has inspired outstanding reference books, sociology of religion has not. American and British scholars have reshaped the field, but they have yet to create a reference work. A textbook comparable to **311** Wulff, *Psychology of Religion* (1991) would transform access to the discipline. So would a LEXICON comparable to **310** Benner, ed., *Baker Encyclopedia of Psychology* (1985). An alternative would be to couple sociology and anthropology with psychology in *A Dictionary of the Social Sciences of Religion*.

Besides discussing methods, national schools, concepts and case studies, such a work should offer a WHO'S WHO of scholars.

2.2.2 ANTHROPOLOGY OF RELIGION

Few fields of the social sciences so urgently need a LEXICON as anthropology of religion. French-speaking schools and English-speaking schools cry out to be co-ordinated with one another. On the French side scholars have delineated in treatises (but not yet in COMPENDIA) a field that they call *anthropologie religieuse*. With partisan zeal **23** Ries, ed., *Traité d'anthropologie du sacré*, planned in 7 vols. (Paris: Desclée, 1992-) amplifies Eliade's concept of *Homo religiosus*. Articles in **298** *Encyclopaedia universalis* dating from 1968, notably those by Roger Bastide, dissect major concepts for a general audience, as do entries by Alphonse Dupront in **4** Poupard, ed., *Dictionnaire des religions*, (1984, 1993). Michel Meslin assesses all this in *L'Expérience humaine du divin: Fondements d'une anthropologie religieuse* (Paris: Cerf, 1988). Italians also excel at cultural anthropology of religion, as demonstrated by **110** Sartore and Triacca, eds., *Dictionnaire encyclopédique de la liturgie* (1984, 1992-). The Italian school may need publicizing in Britain and America even more than does the French.

On the English-speaking side, at least thirty anthropologists win entries in **5** Eliade, ed., *The Encyclopedia of Religion* (1987). A TEXTBOOK by Brian Morris, *Anthropological Studies of Religion: An Introductory Text* (Cambridge: Cambridge University Press, 1987) sketches the history of the field. Robert H. Winthrop, *Dictionary of Concepts in Cultural Anthropology* (New York and London: Greenwood Press, 1991) elucidates concepts like "Magic," "Ritual" and "Totemism," supplying English-language bibliography. A startlingly original essay, Francis Huxley, *The Way of the Sacred* (London: Aldus, 1974), falls just short of constituting a PHILOSOPHICAL DICTIONARY. Whether French, Italian, British or American, all these approaches need to be integrated into a LEXICON.

2.2.3 HISTORY OF SCHOLARSHIP IN RELIGIOUS STUDIES

There is no biographical handbook that analyzes pivotal figures in the development of religious studies. Biographies in **5** Eliade, ed., *Encyclopedia of Religion* (1987) make a start, as do those in **7** Cancik et al., eds., *Handbuch religionswissenschaftlicher Grundbegriffe,* vol. 1 (1988) and **4** Poupard, ed., *Dictionnaire des religions* (1984, 1993). A model could be Ward W. Briggs and William M. Calder III, eds., *Classical Scholarship: A Biographical Encyclopedia* (New York: Garland, 1990). In addition to exhaustive bibliographies, fifty REVISIONIST essays on seminal figures since 1770 rethink the history of classical studies. A comparable work on path-breaking humanists and social scientists of religion could revolutionize history-writing about religious studies since 1850.

Indexes

Note on Foreign-Language Works: Except in the Index of Titles, references to French works carry an *f* after the page number (e.g., 27f), German works carry a *g* (e.g., 28g), and Italian works an *i* (e.g., 29i). Where no *f*, *g* or *i* appears, the work is in English.

Index of Titles

Inclusions. Titles that elicit an entry in the Directory are indexed to that entry only, and *not* to mentions within other entries. Mentions of such titles outside of entries are, however, indexed (i.e., in the introductions, the glossary, overviews and appendices). Titles of works that elicit an entry in the Directory carry the serial number in the index. Titles of works that elicit no entry are indexed wherever mentions occur.

Exclusions. Mentions of a title under WEAKNESSES and COMPETITORS are *not* indexed, except when this is the only mention. Titles that occur solely in the glossary are *not* indexed. These are the only titles not indexed at all.

Index of Authors

Inclusions. Authors and editors of *books* are indexed both to entries concerning their books and to mentions of such books within other entries under the headings SCOPE and STRENGTHS. Authors of an *article* in a reference book are indexed if and only if at least one of the following conditions pertains:

1. if the individual also wrote or edited a reference book
2. if he/she wrote two or more articles that are cited
3. if he/she wrote just one article that is analyzed in depth
4. if he/she is highly renowned

Exclusions. Unlike titles, authors are not indexed from mentions of their works in the two introductions, the glossary or the appendices. Nor are authors indexed to mentions of reference books under the headings WEAKNESSES or COMPETITORS, except when these are the only mentions.

Index of Topics

Inclusions. This index locates reference books and articles on the topics listed. A citation here means that an article or a reference book treats the topic. Mythical figures and deities appear here, not in the Index of Persons.

Exclusions. Catchwords from the glossary and table of definitions are not indexed. Individual books of the Bible are not indexed. Lesser topics in disciplines like psychology of religion are not indexed.

Index of Persons

Inclusions. This index locates reference books and articles *about* the persons indexed. A citation here means that an article or in a few cases an entire reference book treats that person.

Exclusions. Authors of reference books or of articles in them appear not here but rather in the Index of Authors. Deities and mythical figures appear in the Index of Topics. Among biblical figures only major ones like Abraham, Moses and Paul figure here.

Index of Places

Inclusions. This index locates reference books and articles that mention the places indexed. Places (i.e., empires, countries, regions, cities) and peoples or religions named for them (e.g., Tibetans) are indexed here.

Exclusions. Minor biblical places are not indexed. Peoples whose name is not regional (e.g., Celts) are indexed in the Index of Topics. Likewise, members of religions whose name is not regional (e.g., Hindus) are indexed in the Index of Topics.

Addendum

Works Published
During 1996 and 1997

This addendum evaluates forty-five works published during 1996 and 1997 as well as late 1995. All but one are published in English. The works are numbered sequentially and arranged according to the headings in the Directory of Reference Works. Updated editions of works analyzed in the Directory of Reference Works are discussed only when the revisions are extensive. These are identified by the letter a after the original sequence number. If asked to single out the very best dozen of these books, I would name **319, 321, 29a, 328, 329, 333, 337, 180a, 344, 350, 354** and **358.**

1 THE WORLD'S RELIGIONS

1.1 ALPHABETICAL REFERENCE BOOKS

3a (1995) John Hinnells, ed., *A New Dictionary of Religions* (Oxford and Cambridge, Mass.: Blackwell, 1995); xxxvii & 760 pages; index, pp. 677-760; bibliography, pp. 577-676.

□ *Critique* This DICTIONARY offers fourteen hundred unsigned articles on leaders, movements, concepts and practices. Updated and expanded from **3** Hinnells, ed., *The Penguin Dictionary of Religions* (1984), this work is less subtle than **321** Bowker, ed., *The Oxford Dictionary of World Religions* (1997) but offers an incomparable English-language bibliography, not least on methodology.

□ *Summary* Convenient entries accom-

pany an exceptional bibliography.

319 1996) Jane Shoaf Turner, ed., *The Dictionary of Art*, 34 vols. (London: Macmillan; New York: Grove's Dictionaries, 1996); 32,600 pages; index in vol. 34; 15,000 illustrations.

□ *Critique* Besides scrutinizing every aspect of the world's art, this titanic ENCYCLOPEDIA provides substantive articles on the world's major religions. Buddhism, Hinduism, Confucianism and even Sikhism, not to mention Christianity and Islam, receive lengthy entries. Such entries stand separate from book-length articles on art produced by these religions. Bibliographies are magnificent. No other general reference work on the world's art treats religion so authoritatively.

□ *Summary* Meaty articles on the world's religions and on their art will help every sort of reader.

320 Diane Apostolos-Cappadona, *Encyclopedia of Women in Religious Art* (New York: Continuum, 1996); xvii & 442 pages; 101 black-and-white plates; general bibliography, pp. 401-4.

□ *Critique* This DICTIONARY and WHO'S WHO presents more than two thousand short entries on the iconography of women in the world's religions. Entries of ten to twenty lines examine deities, heroines, saints, places, animals and parts of the body, but without bibliography. Entries on the major religions discuss their images of women.

□ *Summary* Beginners will profit from this DICTIONARY, but experts will crave something deeper.

321 (1997) John Bowker, ed., *The Oxford Dictionary of World Religions* (Oxford and New York: Oxford University Press, 1997); xxiv & 1111 pages; topic index, pp. 1075-102; no general bibliography.

□ *Critique* This magnificent LEXICON and GLOSSARY all but eclipses any predecessor. Eighty-two hundred unsigned entries, about half of them less than ten lines in length, exceed in range those of any previous single volume. Astute articles on persons, concepts, scriptures and methods only occasionally contain bibliography, but it is choice. The definitions are unusually quotable. Bearing the stamp of the editor, articles on scholars (e.g., Evans-Wentz, Zaehner) and method (e.g., "Sociology of Religion," "Symbol, Symbolism") exude wisdom.

□ *Summary* Every scholar of religion will want to own this most quotable of masterpieces.

1.2 COMPENDIA

322 (1995) Gérard Chaliand and Jean-Pierre Rageau, *The Penguin Atlas of Diasporas* (London and New York: Viking Penguin, 1995; paperback 1997); xxii & 182 pages; no index; no bibliography; 65 color maps; 30 charts; 30 black-and-white photographs.

□ *Critique* This French-originated ATLAS charts emigrations by eleven ethnic groups. Receiving by far the most coverage, Jews command 70 of the 180 pages and 30 of the 64 maps. Armenians elicit twenty pages and Gypsies seventeen. Others attracting shorter coverage include Blacks, Chinese, Indians, Irish, Greeks, Lebanese, Palestinians, Vietnamese and Koreans. The maps alternate between schematic and detailed, and there is no bibliography anywhere. Historians of Judaism will marvel at the visual aids.

□ *Summary* Maps and photographs evoke Jewish, Armenian and Gypsy emigrations in colorful detail, and those of other groups more sketchily.

2 CHRISTIANITY

2.1 GENERAL

323 (1996) Charles Panati, *Sacred Origins of Profound Things* (London and New York: Penguin Arkana, 1996); xi & 594 pages; index, pp. 577-94; bibliography, pp. 571-75; small black-and-white images throughout.

□ *Critique* Thirty-six chapters arranged in twelve parts present about a thousand entries digesting Christian (predominantly Catholic) lore, interspersed with some Jewish and Islamic material (particularly in chapters 14 and 15 on saints). Entries range in length from five lines to two pages, most running half a page. Chapters 4 and 5 on angels, 9 on vestments, 12 on Christian feasts, 13 on Jewish feasts and 29-32 on realms after death abound in choice information. None of the entries has its own bibliography.

□ *Summary* Information, much of it otherwise inaccessible, is packaged concisely, even jauntily. Beginning students will adore this book.

324 (1996) Peter and Linda Murray, *The Oxford Companion to Christian Art and Architecture* (Oxford and New York: Oxford University Press, 1996); xii & 596 pages; no index; bibliography, pp. 585-93; glossary of architectural terms, pp. 577-83; about 200 black-and-white photographs; 12 color plates.

□ *Critique* This historical DICTIONARY serves seekers of cultural literacy. Its seventeen hundred entries thoroughly treat Christian art of East and West to about 1500 and selectively thereafter. Persons (artists, saints, popes, reformers), genres, cities, iconographic themes and religious orders of major importance are described, but lesser ones go unmentioned. Three surveys of "Byzantine . . . ," "Gothic . . ." and "Romanesque Art and Architecture" scintillate. Entries lack individual bibliographies, and the general bibliography emphasizes art history rather than church history.

□ *Summary* Newcomers either to art history or to Christian history will rejoice, but experts will recoil at the omissions.

29a (1997) F. L. Cross, succeeded by E. A. Livingstone, ed., *The Oxford Dictionary of the Christian Church,* 3d ed. (Oxford and New York: Oxford University

Press, 1997); xxxvii & 1786 pages; no index; list of abbreviations, pp. xxiii-xxxiii.

☐ *Critique* This heavily revised third edition of a classic LEXICON retains its luster. Interpretations and bibliographies have been masterfully updated. To be sure, entries remain unsigned and North America gets somewhat scantily treated, but the writing is as lucid as ever, and twentieth-century topics abound. No finer one-volume reference work on a major religion exists in English.

☐ *Summary* This historical LEXICON has no English-language peer in any field of religious studies.

2.2 ECUMENISM

2.3 BIBLICAL STUDIES

2.3.1 BIBLE DICTIONARIES
325 (1995) John J. Rousseau and Rami Arav, *Jesus and His World: An Archaeological and Cultural Dictionary* (Minneapolis: Fortress, 1995; London: SCM, 1996); xxiii & 392 pages; three indexes, pp. 369-92; bibliography, pp. 365-67; 72 illustrations; 23 tables.

☐ *Critique* A product of the Jesus Seminar, this DICTIONARY examines 108 "locations, artifacts, and customs . . . in the light of archaeology." Each entry comprises six sections: Importance, Scripture References, General Information, Archaeological Information, Implications for Jesus Research, and Bibliography. Reflecting the down-to-earth detail favored by the Jesus Seminar, this work digests archaeology compactly and explores hypotheses about places and activities frequented by Jesus (but not his postresurrection followers). Maps, illustrations and bibliographies are first-rate.

☐ *Summary* Astringent in dismissing "pious Franciscan archaeology" (p. xiii), this DICTIONARY disseminates the methods and findings of the Jesus Seminar. It makes a provocative guidebook to Israel.

2.3.2 BIBLE COMMENTARIES
326 (1997) John H. Walton and Victor H. Matthews, *The IVP Bible Background Commentary: Genesis—*

Deuteronomy (Downers Grove, Ill.: InterVarsity Press, 1997); 284 pages; no index; four maps, pp. 281-84; bibliography, pp. 9-11.

☐ *Critique* This seductive COMMENTARY (based on the New International Version) elucidates the Near Eastern context of Israelite religion in verse-by-verse entries and sidebars (e.g., "The Date of the Exodus"). Archaeological, geographical and ethnographic data abound, but issues of authorship, dating and midrash are omitted. Lists of "Major Tablets . . ." and "Major Inscriptions of Old Testament Significance" assemble references scattered throughout the text. This is a worthy sequel to Craig S. Keener, *The IVP Bible Background Commentary: New Testament* (1993).

☐ *Summary* This masterpiece of popularization marshals archaeological and ethnographic findings with clarity and charm.

327 (1997) Howard Clark Kee, Eric M. Meyers, John Rogerson and Anthony J. Saldarini, *The Cambridge Companion to the Bible* (Cambridge and New York: Cambridge University Press, 1997); vi & 616 pages; two indexes, pp. 584-616; bibliography, pp. 281-87, 434-40, 576-83; 125 black-and-white photos and maps; 16 color plates.

☐ *Critique* This attractive beginner's COMMENTARY introduces biblical books and their cultural contexts. Twenty-three chapters are arranged into three parts: "The Old Testament World," "Jewish Responses to Greco-Roman Culture" and "The Formation of the Christian Community" (up to about 200 C.E.). Continuous narrative dotted with sidebars expounds the kind of topics expected in a biblical INTRODUCTION. Focusing on entire books rather than individual passages, the authors expound recent findings with flair. Three bibliographical essays assess works in English but ignore methodology.

☐ *Summary* Limpidity of writing and of layout makes this introductory COMMENTARY a gem.

2.3.3 HANDBOOKS OF INTERPRETATION
328 (1997) Ralph P. Martin and Pe-

ter H. Davids, eds., *Dictionary of the Later New Testament and Its Developments* (Downers Grove, Ill., and Leicester, U.K.: InterVarsity Press, 1997); xxx & 1289 pages; three indexes (Scripture, subject, articles), pp. 1243-89; no general bibliography.

☐ *Critique* This HANDBOOK OF INTERPRETATION applies to Acts, Hebrews, the General Epistles and Revelation the kind of evangelical acumen demonstrated in **70** Joel B. Green and Scot McKnight, eds., *Dictionary of Jesus and the Gospels* (1992) and **71** Gerald Hawthorne and Ralph P. Martin, eds., *Dictionary of Paul and His Letters* (1993). The Christian community from its beginnings to about 150 C.E. is scrutinized in more than 240 articles by a hundred scholars. This work constitutes that rarity, a patrology of the apostolic fathers by evangelical scholars. Fairmindedness, lucidity and comprehensiveness make this a must.

☐ *Summary* Imaginative in scope and cogent in analysis, this HANDBOOK OF INTERPRETATION encompasses the apostolic period.

2.4 THEOLOGY

2.4.1 NONCONFESSIONAL

329 (1995) Leslie Houlden and Peter Byrne, eds., *The Companion Encyclopedia of Theology* (London and New York: Routledge, 1995); xxiv & 1092 pages; index, pp. 1036-92; no general bibliography.

☐ *Critique* This REVISIONIST COMPENDIUM rethinks issues in theology and cultural criticism. The genre of "Companion Encyclopedia" exemplifies what might be called a "Handbook of Contemporary Issues." Forty-eight essays, many of them innovative, not to say path-breaking, are distributed among six sections: "Bible," "Tradition," "Philosophy," "Spirituality," "Practical Theology," and "Scene and Prospect." Grace Jantzen pioneers a new field in "Feminism in the Philosophy of Religion," and masterful integrations of past and present come from Keith Ward, Terry Tastard, Frank Burch Brown and

Walter Hollenweger. John Kent writes searchingly on "The Character and Possibility of Christian Theology Today." Entries are much longer than those in **356** Clarke and Linzey, eds., *Dictionary of Ethics, Theology and Society* (1996).

☐ *Summary* In this "Handbook of Contemporary Issues," Anglo-American theologians have fashioned a masterpiece of cultural diagnosis.

330 (1996) Letty M. Russell and J. Shannon Clarkson, eds., *Dictionary of Feminist Theologies* (Louisville: Westminster John Knox; London: Mowbray, 1996); xxix & 351 pages; no index; bibliography, pp. 327-51.

☐ *Critique* This REVISIONIST DICTIONARY enlists 185 women to write almost three hundred signed articles on concepts, but not on persons or events. Articles on "Feminist Theologies" divide regionally into "Asian," "European," "Jewish" and "North American" (pp. 100-116). Often radical, the entries can be trendy as well. No school, denomination or ideology predominates.

☐ *Summary* This outspoken DICTIONARY canvasses issues raised by women theologians, both Christian and Jewish, from all camps.

331 (1996) John Templeton Foundation, *Who's Who in Theology and Science* (New York: Continuum, 1996); xviii & 713 pages; five indexes, pp. 619-705.

☐ *Critique* This WHO'S WHO delineates hundreds of scholars who publish works on the interactions between science and religion; it also lists organizations and journals in the field. Although issues are not discussed, this volume facilitates every sort of symbiosis between religious thought and natural science.

☐ *Summary* Anyone interested in the relationship between religion and science will benefit from this WHO'S WHO.

2.4.2 PROTESTANT

2.4.3 ROMAN CATHOLIC

2.5 SPIRITUALITY

2.6 HAGIOGRAPHY (LIVES OF SAINTS)

332 (1996) Annette Sandoval, *The Directory of Saints: A Concise Guide to Patron Saints* (New York: Dutton, 1996); 309 pages; index, pp. 299-309; bibliography, pp. 295-97; calendar of saints, pp. 264-75.

☐ *Critique* This DICTIONARY offers almost a thousand brief entries on places, professions, ailments and menaces. Roman Catholic patrons of each are sketched in winsome prose. The range astonishes, as does the ingenuity that connects individual saints with human needs. Browsing is a delight.

☐ *Summary* This jaunty DICTIONARY surveys an unheard-of variety of places and activities that have attracted patron saints.

2.7 LITURGY

333 (1996) James-Charles Noonan Jr., *The Church Visible: The Ceremonial Life and Protocol of the Roman Catholic Church* (New York and London: Viking Penguin, 1996); xiv & 553 pages; two indexes (names, subjects), pp. 542-53; bibliography, pp. 539-41; glossary, pp. 394-418; 123 color photographs.

☐ *Critique* This sumptuous HANDBOOK retraces with loving care minutiae of the papal court. Niceties of diplomacy, liturgy and protocol are explained, diagrammed and photographed. No other volume provides remotely comparable precision or vividness.

☐ *Summary* This lavish HANDBOOK delineates the functioning of the Vatican with sure-handedness and affection.

2.8 THE WESTMINSTER/SCM DICTIONARIES

2.9 CHURCHES AND DENOMINATIONS

2.9.1 PROTESTANTISM

2.9.2 ROMAN CATHOLICISM

2.9.2.1 DICTIONARIES

334 (1997) William J. Collinge, *His-torical Dictionary of Catholicism* (Lanham, Md.: Scarecrow, 1997); xx & 551 pages; index, pp. 547-51; bibliography, pp. 471-545; chronology, pp. 25-32.

☐ *Critique* This DICTIONARY of cities, movements, doctrines, concepts and some persons introduces a wide array of material, with bibliographies. The thousand-odd entries omit most popes (who are listed, pp. 439-48) and saints. This volume provides a useful introduction but does not match in range or depth **29a** *The Oxford Dictionary of the Christian Church*, 3d ed. (1997).

☐ *Summary* This DICTIONARY offers ample English-language bibliography and lucid exposition of the basics. The WHO'S WHO is highly selective.

2.9.2.2 FRENCH MEGA-ENCYCLOPEDIAS

2.9.3 EASTERN CHRISTIANITY

335 (1995) David Coomler, *The Icon Handbook: A Guide to Understanding Icons and the Liturgy, Symbols and Practices of the Russian Orthodox Church* (Springfield, Ill.: Templegate, 1995); 319 pages; no index; 174 black-and-white plates; 8 color plates; general bibliography, pp. 313-14.

☐ *Critique* This DICTIONARY of Russian (but not Greek) icons describes some two hundred images, most of them illustrated in drawings. Iconography is delineated, but not lives of saints.

☐ *Summary* This DICTIONARY interprets Russian icons. Beginners will quail at the wealth of detail.

336 (1996) Michael Prokurat, Alexander Golitzin and Michael D. Peterson, *Historical Dictionary of the Orthodox Church* (Lanham, Md.: Scarecrow, 1996); xvii & 440 pages; no index; bibliography, pp. 349-440; chronology, pp. 11-18.

☐ *Critique* This historical DICTIONARY and WHO'S WHO fills a gap. Almost a thousand learned articles cover Greece, the Near East, Russia, eastern Europe and North America. Doctrine, politics and expansion elicit generous coverage, but liturgy less so. The multilingual bibliography is unequaled.

□ *Summary* Deft summaries of careers, disputes and doctrines fill this well-crafted DICTIONARY.

2.10 PERIODS OF CHURCH HISTORY

2.10.1 SURVEYS OF THE PAPACY AND NATIONAL CHURCHES

2.10.2 EARLY CHURCH (TO 600/800)

328 (1997) Ralph P. Martin and Peter H. Davids, eds., *Dictionary of the Later New Testament and Its Developments* (Downers Grove, Ill.: InterVarsity, 1997). See above.

337 (1996) Simon Hornblower and Anthony Spawforth, eds., *The Oxford Classical Dictionary*, 3d ed. (Oxford and New York: Oxford University Press, 1996); liv & 1640 pages; no index; general bibliography, pp. xxix-liv; no illustrations.

□ *Critique* This historical LEXICON and WHO'S WHO updates a classic. Coverage of Christianity is expanded to incorporate church fathers and their cultural contexts in what amounts to a minipatrology. Most entries carry skeletal bibliography. Philip Rousseau's article "Christianity" poses REVISIONIST questions about the spread of that religion.

□ *Summary* No scholar of classical antiquity can afford to ignore this masterpiece of condensation.

2.10.3 MEDIEVAL CHURCH (313-1400)

2.10.4 EARLY MODERN CHURCH (1400-1700)

2.10.5 MODERNITY (SINCE 1700)

338 (1995) J. D. Douglas, ed., *Twentieth-Century Dictionary of Christian Biography* (Grand Rapids, Mich.: Baker Book House; Carlisle, Cumbria, U.K.: Paternoster, 1995); 439 pages; no index; no bibliography.

□ *Critique* This WHO'S WHO of Christian leaders worldwide is uncannily comprehensive. About eight hundred signed entries average half a page but lack bibliography. Laconic writing evokes career, authorship and controversies of the famous and not so famous. Full-scale biographies are noted where available.

□ *Summary* A master editor balances range with pithiness.

2.10.6 NORTH AMERICA

339 (1996) Edward L. Queen II, Stephen R. Prothero and Gardiner H. Shattuck, *Encyclopedia of American Religious History*, 2 vols. (New York: Facts on File, 1996); x & 800 pages; two indexes, pp. 757-800; no general bibliography; 120 illustrations.

□ *Critique* This fact-crammed LEXICON recounts American (but not Canadian) religious history in seven hundred articles on persons, events and movements, but not methodology. The three authors divide the task between them. The WHO'S WHO includes some rabbis, and Asian religions each elicit one or two entries. Entries on "Native American Religions" fill fourteen pages. No other A-to-Z work covers such a wide swath of American religions, but bibliographies are skeletal.

□ *Summary* This LEXICON digests an unprecedented range of information but lacks methodological acumen.

340 (1997) Michael Glazier and Thomas J. Shelley, eds., *The Encyclopedia of American Catholic History* (Collegeville, Minn.: Michael Glazier/Liturgical, 1997); 1632 pages; no index; 300 black-and-white photographs.

□ *Critique* This massive REALLEXIKION and WHO'S WHO explores the history of Roman Catholicism in the United States, but not in Canada. More than twelve hundred signed articles, each with bibliography, treat persons, dioceses, religious communities and events, but theology and interdenominational comparisons get slighted.

□ *Summary* This attractive REALLEXIKON of American Roman Catholic history surpasses all others in range of coverage, but lacks subtlety.

3 OTHER PROPHETIC RELIGIONS

3.1 JUDAISM

3.1.1 GENERAL
180a (1997) R. J. Zwi Werblowsky and Geoffrey Wigoder, eds., *The Oxford Dictionary of the Jewish Religion* (Oxford and New York: Oxford University Press, 1997); xviii & 764 pages; no index; no general bibliography.

□ *Critique* This rigorous LEXICON scrutinizes all aspects of Jewish religion while downplaying secular culture and issues of methodology. More than half the entries are newly commissioned and signed. The others are rewritten by the editors from 180 Werblowsky and Wigoder, *The Encyclopedia of the Jewish Religion* (1965). Nearly all entries carry bibliographies but of widely varying length. Biblical scholarship, rabbinic literature and Jewish law preponderate. Specialists will revel, but non-Jews will probably prefer the vivacity of Louis Jacobs, *The Jewish Religion: A Companion* (New York: Oxford University Press, 1995).

□ *Summary* A model of erudition, this LEXICON combines precision with austerity. Love of the subject is presupposed rather than courted.

3.2.2 INTRODUCTORY GLOSSARIES

3.2 ISLAM

3.2.1 RELIGION AND CULTURE
341 (1995) Howard M. Federspiel, *A Dictionary of Indonesian Islam* (Athens: Ohio University Press, 1995); xxx & 297 pages; no index; bibliography, pp. xxvii-xxx.

□ *Critique* This WHO'S WHO and GLOSSARY describes Indonesian Muslims and their practices in about two thousand brief entries. Interpretation is minimal.

□ *Summary* Regional specialists will profit from this WHO'S WHO.

342 (1996) Janine and Dominique Sourdel, *Dictionnaire historique de l'Islam* (Paris: Presses Universitaires de France, 1996); xii & 1010 pages; index, pp. 957-1010; bibliography, pp. 873-907; genealogies and maps, pp. 911-56.

□ *Critique* This REALLEXIKON excels at expounding history of all periods and regions and at defining Arabic terms. The authors describe rulers, movements, cities, regions, legal issues and divine titles diligently. No other Western single volume explicates so many Arabic terms (particularly concerning places, doctrines and laws). Western scholars receive no coverage, and theology is treated more fully in 202 Glassé, *The Concise Encyclopaedia of Islam.*

□ *Summary* This elegant REALLEXIKON explains Arabic terms cogently and recounts history incisively. Nonreaders of Arabic will feast.

343 (1996) Azim A. Nanji, ed., *The Muslim Almanac: A Reference Work on the History, Faith, Culture and Peoples of Islam* (Detroit: Gale, 1996); xxxv & 581 pages; index, pp. 521-81; bibliography, pp. 507-17; glossary, pp. 493-505; about 150 black-and-white photographs.

□ *Critique* This fact-centered COMPENDIUM arranges thirty-nine chapters into twelve sections. Chapters 3-12 survey regions, 17-19 spirituality, 20-21 law, 22-23 visual art, 24-27 literature and 28 folklore. Avoiding issues of methodology, straightforward articles introduce cultural history. The English-language bibliographies are excellent.

□ *Summary* This introductory COMPENDIUM serves nonspecialists.

3.2.2 THE QUR'AN

4 ASIAN RELIGIONS

4.1 GENERAL
344 (1997) Brian Carr and Indira Mahalingam, eds., *Companion Encyclopedia of Asian Philosophy* (London and New York: Routledge, 1997); xxiii & 1136 pages; index, pp. 1085-136; no general bibliography; glossary, pp. 1043-84.

□ *Critique* This path-breaking COMPENDIUM arranges forty-eight signed articles into six sections: Persian (i.e., Zoroastrian), Indian, Buddhist, Chinese, Japanese and

Islamic philosophy. A two-page introduction accompanies each section, and every article carries detailed bibliography. Articles of the highest acumen treat major thinkers (e.g., Nagarjuna, Avicenna) and schools (e.g., "Later Vedanta," "Daoism in Chinese Philosophy"). Issues in "Morals and Society" receive a chapter in each of the six sections. Renowned contributors include Karl H. Potter, Ninian Smart on the Buddha, Hajime Nakamura on knowledge and reality in Buddhism, and Masao Abe on Buddhism in Japan. The analyses are up-to-date and often path-breaking, but presuppose training in philosophy.

□ *Summary* This magisterial COMPENDIUM fills a gap for advanced students. The bibliographies are superb.

345 (1997) Eliot Deutsch and Ron Bontekoe, eds., *A Companion to World Philosophies* (Oxford and Malden, Mass.: Blackwell, 1997); xviii & 587 pages; index, pp. 581-87; no general bibliography.

□ *Critique* This historical COMPENDIUM treats non-Western (i.e., Asian, African and Islamic) philosophy in forty-five signed chapters, arranged into six sections. Historical overviews, Chinese philosophy, Indian philosophy, Buddhism (edited by Ninian Smart), Islam and contemporary trends average seven chapters each. More introductory than the **344** *Companion Encyclopedia of Asian Philosophy* (1997), this work supplies convenient surveys with bibliography.

□ *Summary* This COMPENDIUM introduces non-Western philosophies through authoritative overviews.

4.2 SOUTH ASIA

4.2.1 GENERAL

346 (1995) *Reference Encyclopedia: India 2001* (Bangalore: South Asia, 1995); about 600 pages; thousands of line drawings.

□ *Critique* This captivating COMPENDIUM recounts details of twenty-six "dimensions" of South Asian culture in chapters ranging in length from eight pages to forty-eight (on religions). Each chapter is paginated separately. Treatment of architecture, art, music and above all dance is thorough and ingeniously illustrated. Tourists will profit from this panorama of Indian culture.

□ *Summary* Accounts of places, persons, art forms and religions exude enthusiasm and local flavor.

347 (1996) Surjit Mansingh, *Historical Dictionary of India* (Lanham, Md.: Scarecrow, 1996); xl & 512 pages; no index; glossary, pp. xiii-xxi; chronology, pp. xxiii-xxxiv; maps, pp. xxxv-xl; bibliography, pp. 449-505.

□ *Critique* Fact-filled entries explain dynasties, regions, leaders and religions. This may be the most convenient single-volume reference book in English on South Asian history. The English-language bibliography is stunning.

□ *Summary* Lucid entries expound a wealth of detail on all aspects of South Asian history.

348 (1996) Gavin Flood, *An Introduction to Hinduism* (Cambridge and New York: Cambridge University Press, 1996; paperback 1997); xviii & 341 pages; bibliography, pp. 305-28; twenty black-and-white photographs.

□ *Critique* This TEXTBOOK combines the rigor of a HANDBOOK with the originality of an essay. No better introduction to the history of Hinduism exists.

□ *Summary* This TEXTBOOK rethinks fundamentals.

349 (1997) Bruce M. Sullivan, *Historical Dictionary of Hinduism* (Lanham, Md.: Scarecrow, 1997); xvii & 345 pages; no index; bibliography, pp. 265-344; chronology, pp. xiii-xvii.

□ *Critique* This historical DICTIONARY examines places, deities, concepts, arts and scholars in about a thousand entries. There are no individual bibliographies, but the general bibliography is one of the best anywhere. The article on Indology lists about twenty-five scholars who receive individual entries. This work functions as a GLOSSARY and WHO'S WHO for those who lack access to larger works. Explanations are lucid, but scholarly controversies get scanted.

□ *Summary* This concise DICTIONARY introduces the basics. Cross-references abound, and the bibliography is a must.

4.2.2 MYTHOLOGY

4.2.3 PHILOSOPHY

4.3 BUDDHISM

4.3.1 GENERAL

4.3.2 GLOSSARIES (JAPANESE)

5 ALTERNATIVE APPROACHES

5.1 MYTHOLOGY

5.1.1 GENERAL

5.1.2 WHO'S WHO

350 (1996) Kenneth McLeish, *Myths and Legends of the World Explored* (London: Bloomsbury; New York: Facts on File, 1996); xxxi & 736 pages; index, pp. 687-736; no bibliography; 26 black-and-white illustrations.

□ *Critique* This WHO'S WHO digests myths worldwide in more than twelve hundred entries. They are classified into seventeen regions, each with a survey article. Myth is, McLeish suggests, "concerned not with tidiness but with the gaps, chinks, hinges, holes, awkwardnesses, uncertainties and epiphanies of life" (p. vi). Retellings incorporate variants, and about a fifth of the entries survey later literary uses. Cross-references abound, but bibliography is absent. A few entries examine elusive topics like "immortality" and "prophecy," while some sixty others collate cross-references to matters like "lightning" and "shape-changers." Myths about the Buddha and Mahavira figure, but not about prophets like Abraham or Zoroaster. Comparatists will revel, but they will crave bibliography.

□ *Summary* Lucid retellings, ingenious cross-references and splendid layout make this WHO'S WHO one of the most acute in any field. Every comparatist should own it.

5.1.3 REGIONAL

5.2 PHILOSOPHY OF RELIGION AND ETHICS

351 (1995) Robert Audi, ed., *The Cambridge Dictionary of Philosophy* (Cambridge and New York: Cambridge University Press, 1995); xxxviii & 882 pages; index of select names, pp. 873-82; no bibliography.

□ *Critique* With more than four thousand entries, this DICTIONARY purveys definitions and reflective essays, both often strikingly original. The contributors are overwhelmigly North American, and no living person receives an entry. Absence of bibliographies is balanced by the innovativeness of many entries.

□ *Summary* This DICTIONARY abounds in arresting definitions and novel observations.

352 (1996) Stuart Brown, Diana Collinson and Robert Wilkinson, eds., *Biographical Dictionary of Twentieth-Century Philosophers* (London and New York: Routledge, 1996); xxi & 947 pages; three indexes, pp. 903-47; "Guide to Schools and Movements," pp. 876-902.

□ *Critique* This WHO'S WHO characterizes more than a thousand twentieth-century philosophers and theologians in signed articles, each with bibliography by and about that thinker. Major Asian thinkers (e.g., Nishitani) are included. Acute analysis and choice judgments make this a superb tool for beginners and experts alike.

□ *Summary* Unparalleled breadth of coverage joins pungent judgments to make this WHO'S WHO indispensable.

353 (1996) Michael Payne, ed., *A Dictionary of Cultural and Critical Theory* (Oxford and Cambridge, Mass.: Blackwell, 1996; paperback 1997); 644 pages; index, pp. 638-44; bibliography, pp. 580-637.

□ *Critique* This DICTIONARY and WHO'S WHO expounds movements in twentieth-century cultural studies (particularly French and German), with choice bibliographies. The editor's entry on biblical studies (pp. 58-64) is almost painfully judicious.

□ *Summary* Newcomers to contemporary methodologies will welcome this guide to the complexities.

354 (1997) Philip L. Quinn and Charles Taliaferro, eds., *A Companion to*

Philosophy of Religion (Oxford and Cambridge, Mass.: Blackwell, 1997); xvi & 639 pages; index, pp. 623-39; no general bibliography.

□ *Critique* This REVISIONIST COMPENDIUM compiles seventy-eight articles on backgrounds, issues, subfields and movements in philosophy of religion. Chapters on Wittgensteinianism and Thomism are the only ones to center on individuals. Chapters 1-7 survey non-Christian religions, while chapters 8-13 examine historical backgrounds of Western philosophy of religion. Chapters 24-65 concern issues of theism, and chapters 66-75 offer "Philosophical Reflection on Christian Faith." Written chiefly by analytical philosophers who are receptive to theism, the articles will thrill professionals but may daunt beginners.

□ *Summary* This fastidious COMPENDIUM explores its field with rigor and imagination.

5.3 SOCIAL SCIENCES OF RELIGION

5.3.1 GENERAL

355 (1996) David Levinson, *Religion: A Cross-Cultural Encyclopedia* (Santa Barbara, Calif.: ABC-CLIO, 1996); xx & 288 pages; index, pp. 279-88; general bibliography, pp. 265-75; some black-and-white photographs throughout.

□ *Critique* This introductory LEXICON of the social sciences of religion presents forty-one articles on concepts and sixteen on major religions, each with English-language bibliography. Lucid exposition of notions like "Mana," "Asceticism" and "Revitalization Movements" expound history, applications and controversies.

□ *Summary* This one-author LEXICON introduces methods and concepts of social science deftly. Every college library should own it.

356 (1996) Paul Barry Clarke and Andrew Linzey, eds., *Dictionary of Ethics, Theology and Society* (London and New York: Routledge, 1996); xxx & 926 pages; index, pp. 905-26; no general bibliography.

□ *Critique* This adventurous LEXICON promotes interactions among social science, ethics and theology in order to diagnose contemporary culture. Exploring recent "breaches with tradition," more than 250 signed entries show "how deeply that tradition [of Western thought] has been written into our society, how each apparent crisis or revolution is in some ways only a palimpsest on what precedes it, and how that tradition has written and re-written itelf over such palimpsests as it has developed" (p. vii). The contributors are almost all British. Predictable entries include Eileen Barker on "New Religious Movements," but unforeseeable ones like John Wilson on "Political Correctness" or Paul Barry Clarke on "Noise" predominate. Interdisciplinary inquirers will revel.

□ *Summary* This path-breaking LEXICON synthesizes social science with theology and ethics. Cultural criticism abounds.

357 (1997) Robert Banks and R. Paul Stevens, eds., *The Complete Book of Everyday Christianity: An A-to-Z Guide to Following Christ in Every Aspect of Life* (Downers Grove, Ill.: InterVarsity Press, 1997); xiv & 1166 pages; three indexes, pp. 1149-66; no general bibliography.

□ *Critique* This one-of-a-kind DICTIONARY on dilemmas of contemporary American life integrates social science research with evangelical wisdom. Eminently practical, over three hundred essays (almost half of them by the two editors) on "life activities, interests and concerns" explore Christian ethics in the light of recent sociology, psychology and economics. Biblical references nestle next to the latest social science research. Entries range from "Automobile" and "Credit Card" to "Death" and "Soul." No matter of daily life is too mundane or too lofty for inclusion, but intellectual pursuits like "dialogue"and "ecumenism" are missing. This work complements the more theoretical 356 Clarke and Linzey, eds., *Dictionary of Ethics, Theology and Society* (1996).

□ *Summary* With ingenuity and rigor, this down-to-earth DICTIONARY focuses biblical insight and social science lore onto everyday concerns. Few recent works reward browsing so richly.

5.3.2 SOCIOLOGY

5.3.3 PSYCHOLOGY

312a (1996) George R. Elder, *An Encyclopedia of Archetypal Symbolism*, vol. 2: *The Body* (Boston: Shambhala, 1996); xvi & 452 pages; index, pp. 425-50; no general bibliography; 100 color plates.

□ *Critique* This REVISIONIST COMPENDIUM elucidates one hundred artistic images of the human body chosen from thirteen thousand at the Archive for Research in Archetypal Symbolism in New York City. A Jungian scholar of comparative religion, George Elder excels at formulating in novel ways both cultural context and archetypal symbolism. Asserting the "universal interiorization" of these expressions of "sacred energy" (p. ix), he presents Jungian thought with authority and wit. More than a dozen cultures get illuminated, and each entry has a bibliography of five or six items, often choice. This second volume of **312** *An Encyclopedia of Archetypal Symbolism* is clearer and bolder than the first one.

□ *Summary* This refreshing COMPENDIUM rethinks one hundred images of the body, directing Jungian vision across cultures and controversies.

5.3.4 FOLKLORE

358 (1996) Jan Harold Brunvand, ed., *American Folklore: An Encyclopedia* (New York: Garland, 1996); xvii & 794 pages; index, pp. 777-94; no general bibliography; about 100 black-and-white photographs.

□ *Critique* This magnificent LEXICON revolutionizes access to the field. Signed articles on folklorists, methods, peoples, regions, customs and holidays preempt the literature. The development of the methodology of folklore and of its major findings emerges unforgettably. Every historian of North America should own this book.

□ *Summary* This landmark work opens the field of American folklore to nonspecialists. Lucidity and comprehensiveness prevail.

5.3.5 ANTHROPOLOGY

359 (1997) Stephen D. Glazier, ed., *Anthropology of Religion: A Handbook* (Westport, Conn.: Greenwood, 1997); viii & 542 pages; index, pp. 523-38; general bibliography, pp. 517-22.

□ *Critique* This COMPENDIUM digests recent English-language anthropology of religion. Nineteen chapters by American specialists include six on ritual and five on "Shamanism and Religious Consciousness." Designed to help professionals initiate field research, individual chapters include English-language bibliographies that run five to ten pages. Todd T. Lewis writes thirty-five pages on "Buddhist Community: Historical Precedents and Ethnographic Paradigms," plus fourteen pages of bibliography. Jim Birckhead adds seventy pages on "Reading 'Snake Handling': Critical Reflections." Regrettably, Continental European visions of the field are ignored.

□ *Summary* This COMPENDIUM reexamines American methodologies in anthropology of religion. The bibliographies are magnificent.